PROBATION AND PAROLE

THEORY AND PRACTICE

Howard Abadinsky

Prentice Hall
Upper Saddle River, New Jersey 07458

Library of Congress Cataloging-in-Publication Data

Abadinsky, Howard, (date)
    Probation and parole : theory and practice / Howard Abadinsky. —
    6th ed.
        p.   cm.
    Includes bibliographical references and index.
    ISBN 0–13–233388–0
    1. Probation—United States.   2. Parole—United States..
    I. Title.
    HV9278.A2   1997
    364.6'3'0973—dc20   96–409
                                                        CIP

Acquisitions editor: Neil Marquardt
Editorial assistant: Rosemary Florio
Editorial/production supervision and
    interior design: Linda Pawelchak
Copy editor: Andrea Hammer
Cover design: Jayne Conte
Manufacturing buyer: Ed O'Dougherty
Managing editor: Mary Carnis

© 1997, 1994, 1991, 1987, 1982, 1977 by Prentice-Hall, Inc.
Simon & Schuster /A Viacom Company
Upper Saddle River, New Jersey 07458

Printed in the United States of America
10 9 8 7 6 5 4 3

ISBN 0-13-233388-0

Prentice-Hall International (UK) Limited, *London*
Prentice-Hall of Australia Pty. Limited, *Sydney*
Prentice-Hall Canada Inc., *Toronto*
Prentice-Hall Hispanoamericana, S.A., *Mexico*
Prentice-Hall of India Private Limited, *New Delhi*
Prentice-Hall of Japan, Inc., *Tokyo*
Simon & Schuster Asia Pte. Ltd., *Singapore*
Editora Prentice-Hall do Brasil, Ltda., *Rio de Janeiro*

*To dedicated probation and parole officers
and the American Probation and Parole Association*

CONTENTS

PART
I

PROBATION

CHAPTER 2   PROBATION AND THE COURTS:
HISTORY AND ADMINISTRATION   24

CHAPTER 3   THE JUVENILE COURTS, JUVENILE
JUSTICE, AND YOUNG OFFENDERS   43

CHAPTER 4   **PRESENTENCE INVESTIGATION   105**

CHAPTER 5   **SUPERVISION OF PROBATIONERS   147**

PART II	PAROLE

PART
III

TREATMENT AND SUPERVISION IN PROBATION AND PAROLE

CHAPTER 9   TREATMENT THEORY   **285**

PART IV

SPECIAL PROGRAMS AND RESEARCH

CHAPTER 12 **INTERMEDIATE PUNISHMENTS 411**

PREFACE

The first edition of this book was written while I was a senior parole officer with the New York State Division of Parole. Since that time, new concepts (or sometimes simply buzzwords) have impacted the field. Some, such as *community-based corrections*, the *justice model, determinate sentencing*, and more recently *intermediate punishments* and *range of sanctions*, have impacted both the theory and practice of probation and parole. As sentiments toward crime and criminals hardened, political changes generated by (often pandering) politicians produced such incongruities as *mandatory sentences* with *sanctioning flexibility*. The results of "tough-on-crime" statutes and the "war on drugs" have clogged our correctional facilities. Sound-bite polemics have replaced careful and thoughtful policy development. These swirling waters of criminal justice serve as a backdrop for the discussion of probation and parole in this book.

Instead of merely depending on the scholarly literature, often written by outstanding researchers with little or no experience as probation and parole officers, this book continues to make use of materials from probation and parole agencies throughout the country. I have made some changes in structure. A new chapter on probation and parole officers has been added; the descriptive material on special programs and intermediate punishments is now integrated with research and discussions on their effectiveness. A final chapter—In Conclusion—has been added to tie the book together. As in previous editions, review questions appear at the end of each chapter.

The instructor's resource guide available for this book provides a model curriculum, summaries of each chapter highlighting the most important information, and test questions.

The author would like to thank his editors at Prentice Hall Robin Baliszewski and Neil Marquardt and production editor Linda B. Pawelchak, as well as the following reviewers of this edition: Diane Dwyer, SUNY—Brockport; Joann K. Snyder, Western Michigan University; and James Stinchcomb, Miami-Dade Community College.

ACKNOWLEDGMENTS

Note: Names with an asterisk are new to the sixth edition.

Bryn Armstrong
(Nevada Parole Board)

Eldon H. Audsley*
(Kansas City, MO, Probation Services)

Robert Bayer
(Nevada Department of Probation and
  Parole)

Jeffrey Bercovitz*
(Indiana Judicial Center Probation and
  Juvenile Services)

Barbara Broderick
(New York State Division of Parole)

Paul W. Brown
(United States Probation)

Jeanette Bucklew*
(Iowa Department of Corrections)

John W. Byrd
(United States Pretrial Services, San
  Antonio)

Barbara Carter*
(Florida Department of Corrections)

Gary Cesarz
(New Mexico Corrections Department)

Donald Cochran*
(Massachusetts Commissioner of
  Probation)

C. Gerald Connor*
(Rockland County Probation Department)

Olivia Craven
(Idaho Commission of Pardons and
Parole)

E. Robert Czaplicki*
(Onondaga County, New York, Probation
Department)

Joy Davidoff*
(New York State Division of Parole)

Victor D'Ilio*
(New Jersey Bureau of Parole)

Harry T. Dodd*
(Florida Probation and Parole Services)

Paul J. Dodd
(Connecticut Adult Probation)

Robert Dougherty
(St. Leonard's House/Chicago)

Susan Dunn*
(Ohio Department of Rehabilitation and
Correction)

Debbie Eng
(Minnesota Department of Corrections)

Duane A. Erickson*
(Minnesota Department of Corrections)

Rudy J. Evenson
(Idaho Department of Corrections/
Community Services)

Larry A. Fields*
(Oklahoma Department of Corrections)

Todd N. Fisk
(Connecticut Department of Corrections/
Community Services)

Tracy D. Fisk*
(Nevada Division of Parole and
Probation)

Gene Forrest
(Arkansas Board of Parole and
Community Rehabilitation)

Charles E. Fowler*
(New Jersey Bureau of Parole)

Virginia M. Gibbons*
(Texas Department of Criminal Justice—
Pardons and Parole Division)

Elizabeth Gillespie
(Kansas Department of Corrections/
Community Services)

Gail Goldman
(San Francisco County Adult
Probation)

Barbara Glass*
(State of Washington Juvenile
Rehabilitation Administration)

Dave Gould*
(Oregon Office of Juvenile
Corrections)

James R. Grundel*
(Illinois Probation Services Division)

Natalie R. Hardy*
(Massachusetts Parole Board)

Norman L. Helber*
(Maricopa County, AZ, Adult Probation
Department)

Vincent J. Iaria*
(Suffolk County, NY, Department of
Probation)

Doug Irwin*
(Kansas Office of Judicial
Administration)

Charles R. Jeffords*
(Texas Youth Commission)

Frank Jenson
(Nebraska Administrative Office of the
    Courts/Probation)

Larry Johnson*
(Colorado Division of Youth Services)

Ken Jones
(Mississippi Department of Corrections)

Robert Kaplan
(New York State Division of Parole)

Jo Kautz
(Texas Youth Commission)

Jacqueline Klosak
(Cook County, IL, Adult Probation)

Samuel A. Lewis*
(Arizona Department of Corrections)

Sheila Logue
(Florida Department of Corrections/
    Probation and Parole)

Mark Mandler*
(Colorado Juvenile Parole Board)

Melvin Maxwell*
(Oklahoma Department of Corrections)

Julia Magruder-Mosby
(Maryland Division of Parole and Probation)

Mark Mandler
(Colorado Juvenile Parole Board)

*Bonita McKay
(Colorado Division of Adult Parole
    Supervision)

Andrew Molloy Jr.
(Virginia Department of Corrections)

John S. Nettles*
(Alabama Board of Pardons and Paroles)

Leslie Pair
(Georgia Community Corrections Division)

John K. Parmenter
(Colorado Department of
    Corrections/Adult Parole)

Ronald W. Parrett*
(17th Judicial Circuit, Illinois)

Dimitria D. Pope*
(Texas Department of Criminal Justice)

William D. Ridgely
(Wisconsin Department of
    Corrections/Probation and Parole)

Rich Rose
(California Youth Authority/Parole)

Arlene M. Sauser*
(San Francisco Adult Probation)

Dave Savage*
(Oregon Division of Community Corrections)

Darlene C. Schimmel
(Michigan Department of
    Corrections/Field Operations)

Ruth Smith
(Indiana Department of Correction)

Robert C. Steinman*
(Michigan Department of
    Corrections/Field Operations)

*Michael W. Sweet
(California Youthful Offender Parole
    Board)

Donald R. Taylor*
(Mississippi Division of Youth Services)

Joe Thergood
(New Mexico Corrections
    Department/Probation and Parole)

George Torodash*
(New York State Division of Parole)

C. William Van Scoy*
(Administrative Office of United States
    Courts)

Paul J. Werrell*
(Lehigh County, PA, Juvenile Probation
    Department)

Richard R. Wilson*
(Pima County, AZ, Juvenile Court)

Chuck Wolk
(California Department of Corrections
Parole and Community Services)

Edmund B. Wutzer
(New York State Division of Probation
and Correctional Alternatives)

John K. Zachariah
(Cuyahoga County, Cleveland, Juvenile
    Court Probation)

Timothy Z. Zadai
(Massachusetts Parole Board)

Walter Zaharevitz*
(Hawaii Paroling Authority)

Darlene E. Zelazny
(Pennsylvania Board of Probation and
    Parole)

ABOUT THE AUTHOR

Howard Abadinsky was a parole officer and senior parole officer for the state of New York for almost 15 years, and a deputy sheriff/inspector for Cook County, Illinois, for eight years. He is currently professor and associate director of criminal justice at Saint Xavier University in Chicago. The author is a graduate of Queens College of the City University of New York and holds an M.S.W. from Fordham University and a Ph.D. in sociology from New York University. He is the author of numerous books on crime and justice. Dr. Abadinsky welcomes comments on his work and can be reached at Saint Xavier University, 3700 W. 103rd Street, Chicago, IL 60655.

PROBATION AND PAROLE IN CRIMINAL JUSTICE

Probation and parole are linked to particular segments of the criminal justice system, and criminal justice is tied to a system of laws most frequently invoked against a distinct type of offender. Law reflects the need to protect the person, the property, and the norms of those who have the power to enact laws—*the criminal law reflects power relations in society*. Thus, the harmful activities of those with power are often not even defined as criminal (such as certain antitrust violations) but may instead constitute only a civil wrong. For example, the Eleventh U.S. Circuit Court of Appeals overturned the fraud convictions of five Texas oilmen involved in a Florida fuel-oil pricing conspiracy that occurred in the mid-1970s. As a result of the scheme, customers of the Florida Power Corporation paid as much as $7.5 million in overcharges. The court ruled that although the actions may have been "against the public interest," they were not illegal (*Chicago Tribune*, December 17, 1981: sec. 2: 3).

Marshall Clinard and his associates (1979) note that when the criminal law is invoked, the results may represent distinctions in power; burglary prosecutions, for example, routinely invoke more significant penalties than do business crimes. They noted that

a single case of corporate law violation may involve millions and even billions of dollars of losses. The injuries caused by product defects or impure or dangerous drugs can involve thousands of persons in a single case. For example, in the electrical price-fixing conspiracy of the 1960s [see R. A. Smith, 1961a,b], losses amounted to over $2 billion, a sum far greater than the total losses from the 3 million burglaries in any given year. At the same time, the average loss from a larceny-theft is $165 and from a burglary $422, and the persons who commit these offenses may receive sentences of as much as five to ten years, or even longer. For the crime committed by large corporations the sole punishment often consists of warnings, consent orders, or comparatively small fines. (1979: xix)

In 1980, for example, 37 manufacturers were accused of being part of an 18-year nationwide conspiracy to fix the prices of corrugated containers and sheets, a multibillion-dollar scheme that defrauded American consumers. Thirty-four manufacturers merely settled "out of court," an option not available to most persons who become the clients of probation and parole agencies (*New York Times*, June 17, 1980: D1). In 1985, General Electric pleaded guilty to defrauding the U.S. Air Force by filing 108 false claims for payment, and E. F. Hutton pleaded guilty to 2000 counts of wire and mail fraud. Ralph Nader states that these incidents constitute "crime without criminals" because not a single person was imprisoned (1985: 3F). In that same year, Eli Lilly and Company pleaded guilty to failing to report the dangers of the arthritis drug Oraflex, which had been linked to at least 26 deaths—the company was fined $25,000 (*New York Times*, September 1, 1985: 6E). A similar situation involved the SmithKline Beecham Corporation, a drug company whose product was tied to the deaths of 36 persons—the firm was fined $100,000 (Shenon, 1985a,b). In 1993, despite evidence of criminal wrongdoing, the nation's largest manufacturer of wood-fiber construction panels was subjected to civil fines for underreporting environmental pollution. The $11.1 million fine was a small price to pay for being able to avoid the expense of installing pollution control equipment that was required of its competitors, providing the law-violating company with a significant market advantage (Schneider, 1993). Then there is the savings-and-loan scandal, costing an estimated $100 billion.

Robert Lefcourt argues:

The myth of "equality under law" would have us believe that everyone is subject to society's laws and those who violate laws are subject to prosecution. Yet in criminal courts across the country it can be easily observed that law enforcement affects most exclusively the workingman and the poor. . . . The other criminals, the extremely wealthy, the corporations, the landlords, and the middle-class white-collar workers are rarely prosecuted and almost never suffer the criminal court process as defendants. (1971: 22)

Or, as the title of a book by Jeffrey Reiman (1995) points out: *The Rich Get Richer and the Poor Get Prison.*

RICH MAN, POOR MAN, CRIMINAL MAN

The United States is the most economically stratified of industrial nations. "The wealthiest 1 percent of American households—with net worth of at least $2.3 million each—owns nearly 40 percent of the nation's wealth. . . . Further down the scale, the top 20 percent of Americans—households worth $180,000 or more—have more than 80 percent of the country's worth, a figure higher than in other industrial nations" (Bradsher 1995: C4). Indeed, the United States has the widest income gap between rich and poor in the industrialized world (Bradsher, 1995c); it also has the highest rate of crime, drug abuse, and births to unwed mothers.

What Is a Crime? Who Is a Criminal?

Quite simply, a *crime* is any violation of the criminal law, and a *criminal* is a person convicted of a crime. These definitions raise an important question: Is a person who violates the criminal law a "criminal" if he or she is not apprehended or convicted? Consider that most reported crimes do not result in an arrest and conviction. Furthermore, National Crime Survey reports indicate that most crimes simply are not reported to the police. Thus, have probationers or parolees who are not arrested again been rehabilitated, or have they become more successful at avoiding detection? (Or have the police become less adept or corrupt?)

Index Crimes

Crime statistics are regularly compiled by the Federal Bureau of Investigation and divided into eight categories indicated in the *Uniform Crime Report*. The eight categories, or "index crimes," are those most likely to be reported by victims, that occur frequently, and that are serious by nature or as a result of their frequency of occurrence. They are divided into crimes against persons and crimes against property.

Crimes Against the Person

1. *Homicide*: causing the death of another person without legal justification or excuse
2. *Rape*: unlawful sexual intercourse by force or without legal or factual consent
3. *Robbery*: unlawful taking or attempted taking of property that is in the immediate possession of another, by force or threat of force
4. *Assault*: unlawful intentional inflicting or attempted inflicting of injury on the person of another

Crimes Against Property

5. *Burglary*: unlawful entry of any fixed structure, vehicle, or vessel used for regular residence, industry, or business with or without force with the intent to commit a felony or larceny

6. *Larceny-theft*: unlawful taking or attempted taking of property other than a motor vehicle from the possession of another, by stealth, without force and without deceit, with intent to deprive the owner of the property permanently

7. *Motor vehicle theft*: unlawful taking or attempted taking of a self-propelled road vehicle owned by another, with the intent of depriving him or her of it, permanently or temporarily

8. *Arson*: intentional damaging or destruction or attempted damaging or destruction by means of fire or explosion of property without the consent of the owner, or of one's own property with or without the intent to defraud

Other relatively frequent (nonindex) crimes include those that are *victimless*, referring to violations of the law unlikely to be reported by their victims, particularly drug offenses, prostitution, and gambling; *fraud*: using deceit or intentional misrepresentation of fact with the intent of unlawfully depriving a person of property; *driving under the influence*: operating any motor vehicle while drunk or under the influence of liquor or psychoactive substances; and *public order offenses*: violations of the peace or order of the community, or threats to public health through unacceptable public conduct; interfering with governmental authority; violating civil rights or liberties; weapons offenses; bribery; and tax law violations. There are also corporate crimes that include restraint of trade, securities violations, environmental pollution, and toxic waste-related offenses. [Crime statistics are also compiled by the National Crime Survey (NCS) based on information from a random survey of the population conducted by the Census Bureau. The NCS has revealed a high level of nonreporting of crimes by victims.]

It is important for the study of probation and parole to consider who actually becomes identified as a criminal. Remember that there are corporate offenders who *do not* usually become identified as criminals. A composite sketch of the "average" offender convicted of a crime would reveal that he (more than 90 percent are male) is usually young (more than 40 percent are younger than age 20; more than 70 percent are younger than age 30), poor, and often from a minority group. Such persons tend to be clustered in particular sections of urban America—ones that are heavily policed—a fact that increases the likelihood of arrest and conviction. Persons who have already been arrested become part of the official records of law enforcement agencies. This increases their susceptibility to further arrests, a fact of life with which all probation and parole personnel must deal. However, on average, only about one crime in four is cleared by an arrest. (The result is prisons populated by the least skillful criminals with multiple convictions.)

Some offenders are given an opportunity to avoid being put through the criminal justice process. Later, this chapter examines the use of programs that seek to "divert" offenders out of the criminal justice system and into some other method of being handled. Such programs can easily become another method for providing differential treatment whereby the middle class can avoid the stigma and severity of the criminal process, whereas the poor are made to face the full force and fury of criminal sanctions.

In response to the question of who is a criminal, some observers see the offender as a *victim* of poverty, discrimination, unequal and unjust laws, and law enforcement. In 1902, Clarence Darrow, the famed trial lawyer, noted that "the people who go to jail are almost always poor people" (1975: 29), and most persons on probation and parole come from an underclass. Almost a century later, persons convicted of corporate crimes are still able to avoid the stiff sanctions that typically befall the perpetrators of more conventional crime—those most likely to be committed by persons from deprived economic circumstances.

RESPONDING TO CRIME

Early responses to deviant behavior ranged from the payment of fines to trial by combat, banishment, and death by torture. *Lex talionis*—an eye for an eye—a primitive system of vengeance, emerged and was passed down from generation to generation as each family, tribe, or society sought to preserve its own existence without recourse to a written code of laws. About 4000 years ago, Hammurabi, King of Babylonia, set down a code of laws. Although in written form, his laws continued the harsh tradition of *lex talionis*—many crimes, including theft and harboring a runaway slave, were punishable by death (Harper, 1904).

Later, the Hebrews adopted the concept of an eye for an eye, but under biblical law this meant financial compensation for the victim of crime or negligence (there was no compensation for murder, which carried the death penalty), except for the "false witness," in which case "ye shall do unto him, as he had purposed to do unto his brother" (*Deuteronomy* 19: 19). A perpetrator who was unable to pay compensation was placed in involuntary servitude, a precursor to the concept of probation. The servitude could not last more than six years—release had to occur with the sabbatical year—and masters had rehabilitative obligations and responsibilities toward their charges. [Under the Code of Hammurabi, "If the thief has nothing wherewith to pay he shall be put to death" (Harper, 1904: 13)].

The Romans derided the use of fines for criminal offenses and used the death penalty extensively in ways that have become etched in history. The fall of the Roman Empire resulted in there being little "rule of law" throughout Europe. When law was gradually restored, fines and restitution became an important form of punishment as those in power sought to increase their wealth. Offenders who were unable to pay, however, were often enslaved or subjected to mutilation or death. A parallel issue in contemporary criminal justice, the extensive use of restitution, is discussed in Chapters 11 and 12.

Trial by combat also flourished, in part because of the difficulty of proving criminal allegations. With the spread of Christianity, trial by combat was reserved for private accusations, whereas crimes prosecuted by the crown called for trial by ordeal, an appeal to divine power. A defendant who survived the ordeal—passing through fire, for example—was ruled innocent. The unsuccessful defendant often received verdict and punishment simultaneously.

Trial by ordeal was eventually replaced with *compurgation* ("wager of law"): The accused was required to gather twelve reputable persons who would swear to the defendant's innocence. Reputable persons, it was believed, would not swear falsely for fear of divine retribution. Compurgation eventually evolved into testimony under oath and trial by jury (Vold and Bernard, 1986). Throughout the Middle Ages in Europe, there was a continuation of the extensive use of torture to gain confessions, and public executions were often accompanied by torture, flaying, or the rack.

Despite biblical admonitions—"You shall not respect persons in judgment; ye shall hear the small and the great alike" (*Deuteronomy* 1: 17)—for many centuries disparity existed in the manner in which punishment was meted out, with the rich and influential receiving little or no punishment for offenses that resulted in torture and death for the less fortunate. This practice was challenged forcefully in the 18th century with the advent of *classical theory.*

CLASSICAL THEORY

Classical theory is an outgrowth of the European *Enlightenment* period of the 18th century (sometimes referred to as the "Age of Reason") whose adherents rejected spiritualism and religious explanations for criminal behavior. During this era, philosophers—such as Charles-Louis de Secondat; Baron de La Brede et de Montesquieu (1689–1755), usually referred to simply as Montesquieu; and Francois-Marie Arouet Voltaire (1694–1778)—spoke out against the French penal code and punishments that were both inhumane and inequitable. Jean Jacques Rousseau (1712–1778) and Cesare Bonesana, Marchese di Beccaria, usually referred to as Cesare Beccaria (1738–1794), argued for a radical concept of justice based on *equality.* At a time when laws and law enforcement were unjust and disparate, and punishment often brutal, they demanded justice based on equality and punishment that was humane and proportionate to the offense. This revolutionary doctrine—*equality*—influenced the American Revolution with the declaration that "all men are created equal," and the French Revolution whose National Assembly enacted a "Declaration of the Rights of Man and Citizen" (1789), which emphasized the equality of all citizens. The roots of this legal and political philosophy can be found in the concepts of natural law and contract theory.

Natural law is expressed in the classical concept of a *social contract*: a mythical state of affairs wherein each person agrees to a pact—a social contract—the basic stipulation of which is that, all men being created equal, conditions of law are the same for all: "The social contract establishes among the citizens an equality of such character that each binds himself on the same terms as all the others, and is *thus* entitled to enjoy the same rights as all the others" [Rousseau (1762) 1954: 45, emphasis in original]. According to classical thought, by nature man is free and endowed with natural rights, a philosophical basis for the first ten amendments to the U.S. Constitution, the "Bill of Rights." The natural law concepts of John Locke (1632–1704), according to which all men are by nature free, equal, and independent, and no one can be subjected to the political power of another without his own consent, were incorporated in the U.S. Declaration of Independence as "all men are created equal" whose "governments are instituted among men, deriving their just powers from the consent of the governed." Locke referred to the natural law right of "life, liberty, and property," whereas Thomas Jefferson enumerated the inalienable right to "life, liberty, and the pursuit of happiness."

The classical notion of the *social contract* stipulates that all men being created equal, conditions of law are the same for all. Thus Rousseau asserts, "One consents to die—if and when one becomes a murderer oneself—in order not to become a murderer's victim" (1954: 48). To be safe from crime, all people have consented to punishment if they resort to crime. This constitutes the greatest good for the greatest number; the social contract is rational and motivated by selfishness (Roshier, 1989).

Contrary to the manner in which law was being enforced, the classical school argued that the law should respect neither rank nor station—all men are created equal—and punishment is to be meted out with a perfect uniformity. This premise was given impetus by Cesare Beccaria who in *An Essay on Crimes and Punishments* (1764; English edition, 1867) states that laws should be drawn precisely and matched to punishment intended to be applied equally to all classes of men. The law, he argued, should stipulate a particular penalty for each specific crime, and judges should mete out identical sentences for each occurrence of the same offense (1963). This makes the administration of justice rational, whereas law is taken, uncritically, as given. Punishment has as its purpose deterrence and must be "the minimum possible in the given circumstances, proportionate to the crime, dictated by the laws" (Maestro, 1973: 33). The prosecution of defendants must be accomplished without resort to torture, which was common during this period. Not only is torture inhumane but is a highly unreliable method of determining guilt. Unlike the position of Rousseau stated earlier, Beccaria opposed capital punishment. Thus, "humane" must be added to "rational" and "legalistic" as descripters of classicalism [although Bob Roshier (1989) disputes this point].

According to the classical position, punishment is justified because the offender who violates the social contract is rational and endowed with *free will.* This concept, which has biblical origins (*Deuteronomy* 30: 15), holds that every person has the ability to distinguish and choose between right and wrong, and between being law abiding or criminal. In other words, behavior that violates the law is a *rational choice* made by a person with free will—in legal terms, *mens rea.* The classical school argues, however, that because human beings tend toward *hedonism*—that is, they seek pleasure and avoid pain—they must be restrained, by fear of punishment, from pleasurable acts that are unlawful. Accordingly, the purpose of the criminal law is not simply *retribution* but also *deterrence.* In sum, the "individual is responsible for his actions and is equal, no matter what his rank, in the eyes of the law" (Taylor, Walton, and Young, 1973: 2). This approach has an economic perspective in *utilitarianism*—the cost-benefit analysis of behavior. According to Gary Becker (1968: 176): "A person commits an offense if the expected utility to him exceeds the utility he could get by using his time and resources at other activities." Becker argues that "a useful [utilitarian] theory of criminal behavior can dispense with special theories of anomie, psychological inadequacies, or inheritance of special traits [all discussed in Chapter 9] and simply extend the economist's usual analysis of choice" (1968: 40). This approach parallels that of classical economics—capitalism—in which free persons are motivated by rational self-interest, based on the principles of the free market and (purportedly) beneficial to the entire society.

Two additional requirements—*certainty* and *promptness*—round out the classical position. If law is to serve its deterrent purpose, the would-be violator must be in fear of the consequences. This element of fear requires certainty, whereas promptness, seemingly based on a primitive form of behaviorism (discussed in Chapter 9), is necessary to make a more lasting impression—connecting the deed to the punishment.

The classical approach supported the interests of a rising 18th-century middle class that was demanding legal equality with the privileged noble class, as well as protection from the economic-driven predations of the lower class. A contradiction remains between the defense of equality and the emphasis on maintaining an unequal distribution of wealth and property. Crime could, indeed, be a rational response to severe differentiations in wealth and opportunity. Free will is an oversimplification, because one's position in society determines the degree of choice with respect to committing crimes: "A system of classical justice of this order could only operate in a society where property was distributed equally," where each person has an equal stake in the system (Taylor, Walton, and Young, 1973: 6). It is irrational for a society, which in too many instances does not offer a feasible alternative to crime, to insist that criminal behavior is simply a matter of free will; the nature of our prison population for more than 200 years belies this claim. Nevertheless, as noted by Anatole France (1927: 91), "the law [based on classicalism], in its majestic equality, forbids both the poor man and the rich man to sleep under bridges, to beg in the streets, and to steal bread."

In sum, there are eight basic tenets of classicalism (Taylor, Walton, and Young, 1973):

1. Human beings are rational.
2. All persons are created equal.
3. All persons have an equal stake in society and, thus, an equal stake in preventing crime.
4. Free will endows each person with the power to be law abiding or criminal.
5. People tend toward hedonism.
6. The purpose of punishment is deterrence.
7. Punishment must be meted out fairly, with absolute equality, and in proportion to the offense.
8. Punishment must to be prompt and certain.

The pictorial representation of classical theory appears on many courthouses and documents in the form of a woman—"Justice"—carrying scales and wearing a blindfold. The classical view provides the basis for *definite/determinate sentences,* which are discussed in Chapter 7.

NEOCLASSICISM

According to the classical position, punishment is justified because the offender who violates the social contract is rational, endowed with free will, and, therefore, responsible for his or her actions no matter what the person's rank. The focus is on laws and the legal system, not the nature of criminal motivation. In fact, under the U.S. system of justice, an explanation is not a justification unless it reaches the level of a (legal) compulsion, at which point the law does not blame the perpetrator—no *mens rea*. Classicalism provides the basis for a rational legal system that is relatively easy to administer, except for one annoying problem: Implementing a criminal code with perfect equality proved elusive. This problem became apparent when the French Code of 1791 attempted to implement Beccaria's reforms. Equality and proportionality proved more difficult in practice than in theory, and the French increasingly added to the discretionary powers of judges in the form of neoclassicism (Roshier, 1989).

Neoclassicism maintains the basic belief in free will, while paving the way for the entry of mitigation (and subsequently aggravation) into criminal justice by considering

1. Past criminal record
2. Insanity and retardation
3. Infancy

Punishment can be justified only if crime is freely chosen, intentional, and rational—that is, reasoned behavior. "The neoclassicist revisions created an entrée for the nonlegal expert—particularly the psychiatrists, and later, the social workers—into the courts" (Taylor, Walton, and Young, 1973: 8). These experts determine the presence of mitigation, and the system is able to continue to maintain a belief in free will. Allowing for the possibility of differences between offenders raises the specter of *determinism*—that is, to varying degrees, the offender's choices are limited, which is the basic premise of positivism.

POSITIVE THEORY

Positivism, as formulated by Auguste Comte (1798–1857), refers to a method for examining and understanding social behavior. Comte argued that the methods and logical form of the natural sciences—the scientific method—are applicable to the study of man as a social being, producing the field of *social sciences*. Social phenomena, Comte stated, must be studied and understood by observation, hypothesis, and experimentation in a new discipline that he called *sociology*. Classical theory is based on philosophy and law, whereas positive theory is based on *empiricism* in an effort to determine the *cause* of crime.

The positive approach to the study of crime became known as *criminology*, a discipline whose early efforts are identified with Cesare Lombroso

(1835–1909), a Venetian physician. In his *L'uomo delinquente* (*The Criminal Man*), first published in 1876, Lombroso argued that the criminal is a "primitive throwback" to earlier developmental stages through which noncriminal man had already passed—the influence of *social Darwinism* is obvious (Degler, 1991). Lombroso's research centered on physiological characteristics believed indicative of criminality, although his later work (published in 1911) noted the importance of environmental factors in causing crime (Lombroso, 1968). Instead of the classical emphasis on criminal behavior as rational, positivists tended to see it as a symptom of some form of pathology: biological, psychological, or social. (Positive theories of crime are reviewed in Chapter 9.)

SOCIAL DARWINISM

The move toward using science to explain criminality received a major impetus from the work of Charles Darwin (1809–1882). Although his first book (*Origin of Species*, published in 1859) was concerned exclusively with nonhuman organisms, his second (*Descent of Man*, published in 1871) included the idea that humanity was shaped by the forces of natural selection. Darwin's thesis was advanced by the English philosopher Herbert Spencer (1820–1903), who coined the phrase "survival of the fittest," the credo for social Darwinism. Spencer (1961: 305) argued that "there can be no rational apprehension for the truths of Sociology until there has been reached a rational apprehension of the truths of Biology." And, according to Spencer (1961: 2), biology did not support help for the downtrodden: "As fast as they increase the provision for those who live without labor, so fast do they increase the number who live without labor; and that with an ever-increasing distribution of alms, there comes an ever-increasing outcry for more alms."

Darwin's theory of natural selection supplied the conceptual ammunition for an ideology (later labeled as social Darwinism), which allayed the qualms of the rich about not helping the poor by telling them that the latter's sufferings were an inevitable price that could occur only through the struggle for existence ending in the survival of the fittest and the elimination of the unfit (Andreski 1971: 26). "If the unworthy are helped to increase, by shielding them from that mortality which their unworthiness would naturally entail, the effect is to produce, generation after generation, a greater unworthiness" (Spencer 1961: 313). "Fostering the good-for nothing at the expense of the good is an extreme cruelty. It is a deliberate storing-up of miseries for future generations. There is no greater curse to posterity than that of bequeathing them an increasing population of imbeciles and idlers and criminals" (1961: 314).

Darwin and Spencer were concerned with a general construct of human evolution and its effect on society. Criminal anthropology, initiated by the work of Lombroso, employed evolution to explain criminals. Lombroso contributed to the study of crime by using, albeit in a rather imperfect way, the tools of science and shifting the field of inquiry from law and philosophy to empiricism. Positive theory places emphasis not on the crime but on the criminal. It contradicts the theory of free will for which positivists have substituted *a chain of interrelated causes* and, at its most extreme, a *deterministic* basis for criminal behavior: The criminal could not do otherwise. Because criminal behavior is the result of social and psychological, if not physiological, conditions over which the offender has little or no control, he or she is not culpable (in legal parlance, lacks *mens rea*) and thus punishment is inappropriate. However, because criminals do represent a threat to society, they must be "treated," "corrected," "rehabilitated" (or according to early Lombrosians, separated from society, perhaps castrated or executed). In practice, the change in emphasis from punishment to correction did not necessarily result in a less severe response to criminal offenders. Some modern critics contend that rehabilitation opened the door to a host of questionable schemes for dealing with offenders under the guise of "treatment" and "for their own good." The American Friends Service Committee notes: "Retribution and revenge necessarily imply punishment, but it does not necessarily follow that punishment is eliminated under rehabilitative regimes" (1971: 20). The positive view provides a basis for the juvenile court discussed in Chapter 3 and the *indeterminate sentence* discussed in Chapter 7.

The views of the classical and positive schools are important because they transcend their own time and continue to influence contemporary issues in criminal justice. The question remains: *Do we judge the crime or the criminal?* This is a central question in the continuing debate over sentencing—definite versus indeterminate—that is discussed in Chapters 7 and 8. Probation and parole, it is often argued, emanate from a positivistic response to criminal behavior, a view that is disputed in this book.

Classical Theory		**Positive Theory**
Free Will		Determinism
Choice		Cause
Punishment/Deterrence		Treatment/Incapacitation

If, as the classical view argues, a person has free will and is rational, he or she will weigh the costs of committing (or not committing) a crime. The threat of sanctions is seen as an effort to tilt the weighing process away from crime. The classical approach would view enhancing education and job skills as increasing choice away from crime. Positive theory would view this response as a treatment dealing with the causes of crime.

Probation and parole are part of criminal justice. The next section locates these two services within that system.

AMERICAN CRIMINAL JUSTICE

American criminal justice is characterized by competing expectations. Americans have wanted

> a criminal justice system that apprehends and visits harm upon the guilty (*punishment*); makes offenders more virtuous, or at least more law abiding (*rehabilitation*); dissuades would-be offenders from criminal pursuits (*deterrence*); protects innocent citizens from being victimized by convicted criminals (*incapacitation*); and enables most criminals to return as productive citizens to the bosom of the free community (*reintegration*). [We] have wanted the system to achieve these contradictory public goals without violating the public conscience (*humane treatment*), jeopardizing the public law (*constitutional rights*), emptying the public purse (*cost containment*), or weakening the tradition of State and local public administration (*federalism*). (DiIulio, 1993: 6, emphasis in original)

American criminal justice is also unique, the outgrowth of a fundamental distrust of government. Authority is divided between central (federal) and state governments, and at each level power is diffused further, shared by three branches—executive, legislative, judicial—in a system referred to as the "separation of powers." Furthermore, in each state authority is shared by governments at the municipal, county, and state levels. Thus, policing is primarily a function of municipal government, whereas jails are usually run by the county (often by the sheriff) and prison and parole systems by the state—and there is a separate federal system of criminal justice (Figures 1.1 and 1.2). (Probation may be administered in a variety of ways, discussed in Chapter 2.) As those who work in criminal justice recognize, there is a lack of joint planning and budgeting, or even systematic consultation, between the various agencies responsible for criminal justice. The result is *a system that is not systematic.*

Levels of Government	Branches of Government
Federal	Executive
State	Legislative
County	Judicial
Municipal	

Although criminal justice agencies, whose members range from police to parole officers, are interdependent, they do not, *in toto*, constitute a system arranged with parts so as to form a unity. Although the operations of criminal justice agencies lack any significant level of coordination, each affects the others. A disproportionate share of the criminal justice budget (about 42 percent) goes to that agency having

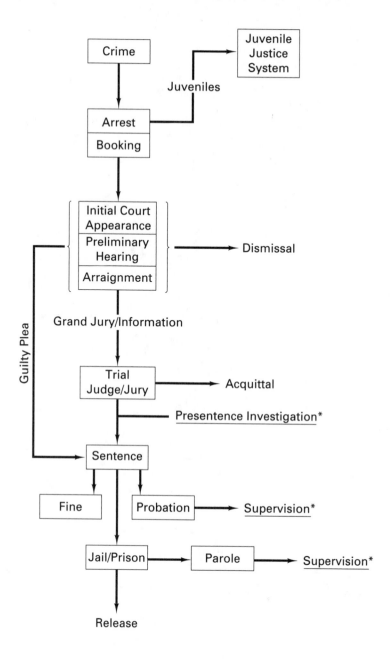

*Points at which probation and parole officers typically enter the system.

FIGURE 1.1   Probation and parole in a state criminal justice system.

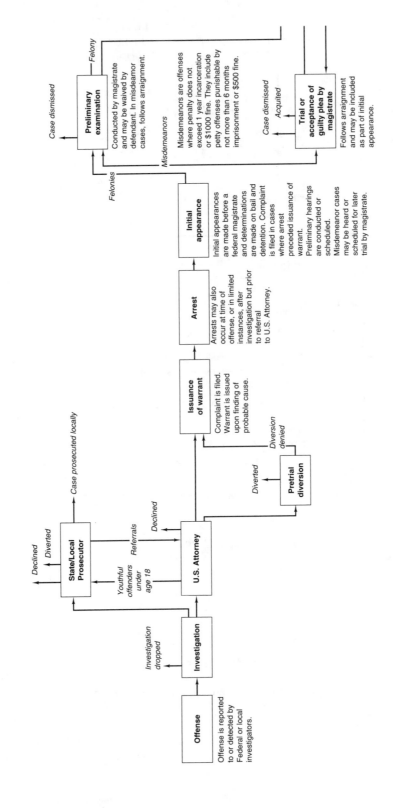

FIGURE 1.2   Federal criminal justice case processing system. Note: The figure continues from the top right to bottom left. (*Source:* U.S. Bureau of Justice Statistics, 1983.)

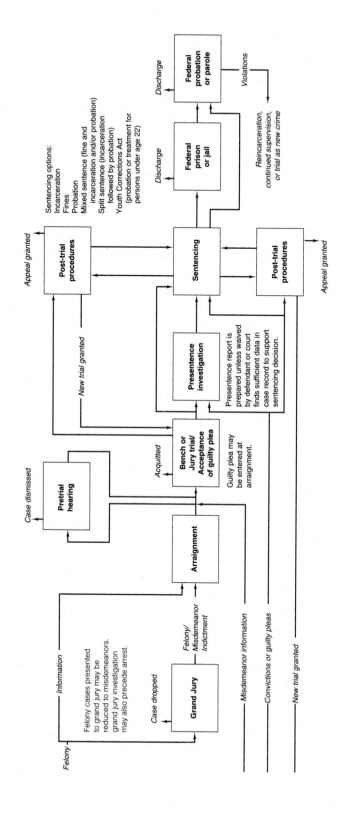

Sentencing options:
Incarceration
Fines
Probation
Mixed sentence (fine and incarceration and/or probation)
Split sentence (incarceration followed by probation)
Youth Corrections Act (probation or treatment for persons under age 22)

FIGURE 1.2 (continued)

15

the most public visibility, the police (plus 6 percent for federal law enforcement). The courts, prosecutors, and public defenders receive about 22 percent; corrections receives about 29 percent (U.S. Department of Justice Statistics). (An additional 1 percent goes for miscellaneous functions.) As a result, more persons are brought into the system by the police than the rest of the system can handle adequately.

Because they are overburdened, judges and prosecutors tend to concentrate on the speedy processing of cases. This, in turn, encourages "bargain justice," which is frequently neither a bargain nor just. When a probation agency is understaffed, judges tend to send marginal cases to prison instead of using probation. Because prisons are underfunded and overcrowded, there is pressure on the parole board to accelerate the release of inmates, overburdening parole supervision, which is also usually understaffed. In recent years some states have abolished their parole systems; although this may have made political sense, it does not respond to the problem of prison overcrowding. As pressure builds on prisons, usually the result of judicial scrutiny and financial considerations, prison officials are forced to release inmates without benefit of the type of analyses usually provided by a parole board. Prison overcrowding also places pressure on the judicial system, and more persons are placed on probation as the revolving door of criminal justice continues to spin.

SPINNING WHEELS OF JUSTICE

Prisons and jails continue to be overcrowded and community corrections, probation and parole, particularly probation, continue to be underfunded. People who formerly were sentenced to State prison often end up on probation caseloads because of the overcrowding; most of our caseloads are high, resources are lacking, and there is a great deal of recidivism.

Source: Annual Report of the San Francisco Adult Probation Department (1991: 5).

ENTERING THE SYSTEM

Most crime is not responded to by the criminal justice system because it has not been discovered or reported to the police; when reported, most crimes are never solved. For the police to arrest a suspect, they must have a level of evidence known as *probable cause*. The Ohio Adult Parole Authority offers the following definition: "Reasonable grounds for suspicion supported by facts and circumstances sufficiently strong in themselves to lead a reasonably cautious person to believe that a person is guilty of a particular crime." Probable cause is also the level of evidence required to initiate a probation or parole violation, and it is significantly less than that necessary to convict a defendant in a criminal trial.

Beyond a Reasonable Doubt

Guilt in a criminal trial

Finding of delinquency in juvenile court

Clear and Convincing Evidence

Used in extraordinary civil cases, such as commitment and child custody

Preponderance of the Evidence

Most civil cases

Status offense cases in juvenile court

Probation and parole violation

Probable Cause

Search warrants

Arrest warrants

Warrantless arrests

When the police effect an arrest, the subject is transported to a holding facility, usually a police station equipped with cells—a "lockup." As opposed to a jail, a lockup is used on a temporary basis, for 24 to 48 hours. During this time, the suspect will be booked, photographed, and fingerprinted, and the police will request that formal charges be instituted by the prosecutor's office. A fingerprint check reveals if the suspect has a previous arrest record, is wanted for other charges, or is on probation or parole.

PRETRIAL COURT APPEARANCES

Depending on what time of the day the arrest occurred and whether it happened on a weekday, weekend, or court holiday, the suspect may have to spend 24 hours or longer in the lockup before being transported to court. At the first appearance, the primary question concerns bail, and the initial appearance may actually be a bond hearing at which bail is the only issue. If a defendant is under probation or parole supervision, the bail decision is affected; for example, in some jurisdictions, a probation or parole warrant will be filed to preclude release on bail. In some jurisdictions, probation officers or other specialized court personnel will interview defendants with a view toward assisting the judge in making a bail decision. If the subject is unable to provide bail, or a probation/parole warrant is filed as a detainer, he or she will be kept in jail pending further court action.

PRETRIAL SERVICES AND DIVERSION

Contemporary bail reform efforts can be traced back to a Vera Foundation project in New York City in 1961. In response to a jail overcrowding problem, in a three-year experiment, the Vera Foundation proved the feasibility and efficacy of a system of bail, based not on personal assets, but on verified social criteria. Programs based on these findings are usually referred to as *pretrial services.*

A few years later, the President's Commission on Law Enforcement and Administration of Justice (1972) pointed out that prosecutors often deal with offenders who need treatment or supervision but for whom criminal sanctions would be excessive. Programs implementing this theory are referred to by many names, including *pretrial diversion* and *deferred prosecution.* These programs use the fact that an arrest has occurred as a means of identifying defendants in need of treatment or, at least, not in need of criminal prosecution. They generally incorporate specific eligibility criteria, a service program, and the opportunity to monitor and control the decision not to prosecute. In eligible cases, the prosecutor agrees not to prosecute for periods ranging from 3 to 12 months, contingent on satisfactory performance during the pretrial period, often under the supervision of a probation officer or similar worker. At the end of a successful pretrial supervision period, the charges are dismissed. This type of diversion helps to remove minimal-risk cases from crowded court calendars while providing services to those who are in need of such help.

Onondaga County, New York, has had a program in place for more than 30 years whose goal is to ensure that no person arrested for a crime remains in jail solely because of an inability to post bail. The unit is staffed by a probation officer and four probation assistants who screen all detained defendants and, when appropriate, recommend persons for pretrial release (PTR) and community supervision. Seven days a week, a probation assistant screens those defendants who have been arrested in the past 24 hours. The defendant's prior record is reviewed, and those individuals who are selected as possible candidates for PTR are then individually interviewed. Eligibility is determined by using a risk assessment instrument. Referral and acceptance of appropriate services is often a condition of these individuals' release. Alcohol and drug abuse are the most frequent problems of defendants being considered for PTR. If it is determined that there is an appropriate community treatment program in which the defendant will not present a threat to the community and will likely reappear in court, the defendant is recommended to the court for PTR.

As with probation cases, PTR clients are required to abide by individual conditions that may include weekly contact with a probation assistant, referrals to community agencies, and continuance in school or employment. The PTR unit also provides a liaison function for the probation department and the courts. PTR staff appear at calendar calls to make PTR recommendations, dispense information on people placed on probation, and gather requests for presentence investigations.

The Florida Department of Corrections operates a pretrial intervention program that diverts first-time defendants who are accused of third-degree felonies or misdemeanors from prosecution; they must volunteer for the program and agree to abide by deferred prosecution conditions of supervision that include restitution and payment of supervision costs. Consent must also be given by the victim, prosecutor, and judge. The subject is placed under the supervision of a correctional probation officer for a period that generally lasts from 90 days to 6 months. Those who complete the program successfully have their charges dismissed; those who fail are subject to prosecution for their original offense.

At pretrial hearings (sometimes referred to as an initial appearance, preliminary hearing, or arraignment), the official charges are read, the need for counsel considered, and bail set or reviewed (if it has already been set at a bond hearing). Typically, these hearings last only a few minutes. If the case is a misdemeanor, it may be adjudicated at this time, often by a plea of guilty or dismissal of the charges on a motion by the prosecutor. If the charge(s) constitutes a felony, a *probable cause* hearing is held to determine if the arresting officer had sufficient evidence, *probable cause*, to justify an arrest. This hearing takes the form of a short minitrial, at which the prosecutor calls witnesses and the defense may cross-examine and call its own witnesses.

If the judge finds probable cause—evidence sufficient to cause a reasonable person to believe that the suspect committed a crime—the prosecutor files an *information* (presents details of the charges), which has the effect of bringing the case to trial. In some states the prosecutor may avoid a probable cause hearing by presenting evidence directly to a *grand jury*—generally, 23 citizens who hear charges in secret. If they vote a *true bill*, the defendant stands *indicted,* and the case proceeds to trial.

TRIAL OR GUILTY PLEA

Few cases entering the criminal justice system actually result in a jury trial, an expensive and time-consuming luxury that most participants attempt to keep to a minimum; about 85 to 95 percent of all criminal convictions are the result of a guilty plea, and most guilty pleas are the result of *plea bargaining*. This widely condemned practice for disposing of cases involves an *exchange*: The defendant agrees to waive his or her constitutional right to a jury trial, providing the prosecutor with a "win," and saving the court a great deal of time and effort; the defendant is rewarded for this behavior by receiving some form of sentencing leniency (the impact of plea bargaining on probation services is discussed in Chapter 4). If plea negotiations fail to result in an agreement, or if one or the other side refuses to bargain, the case is scheduled for trial. [For an extensive discussion of plea bargaining, see Abadinsky (1995).]

The trial is an adversary proceeding in which both sides are represented by legal counsel and whose rules are enforced by a judge. To sustain a criminal charge, the prosecutor must prove the *actus reus* and *mens rea*. *Actus reus* means a wrongful act or deed; it refers to the need to prove that a violation of the criminal law—a crime—actually occurred. The *actus reus* consists of a description of the criminal behavior and evidence that the accused acted accordingly. *Mens rea*, or "guilty mind," is a legal standard and refers to the question of *intent*. The prosecutor must be able to show that the defendant had a wrongful purpose—willfulness—in carrying out the *actus reus*. The defendant is presumed innocent; therefore, defense counsel does not need to prove anything but will typically attempt to raise doubts about the evidence or other aspects of the prosecution's case.

Each side can subpoena witnesses to present testimony and can cross-examine adverse witnesses. The defendant can take the stand on his or her own behalf, or, if the defendant prefers not to testify, can maintain the Fifth Amendment privilege against self-incrimination. Defendants who are on probation or parole often decline to testify because this would subject them to cross-examination and result in a disclosure of their criminal record to the jury. After lawyers for each side have introduced all of their evidence, the judge instructs the jury on the principles of law applicable to the case. Every jury is told (charged by the judge) that the facts pointing to the guilt of the defendant must be established *beyond a reasonable doubt*, as opposed to the *preponderance* (greater weight) *of the evidence,* which is the standard in civil and some juvenile cases and probation and parole violation hearings.

The jury now retires to deliberate in private; in most jurisdictions, the jury's decision for guilt or acquittal must be unanimous, or the result is a *hung jury*. If the jury cannot reach a unanimous verdict, the jurors are discharged; if the prosecutor decides to proceed, the case must be tried a second time before a different jury. Except in some relatively rare instances when there are violations of both federal and state law, the defendant who is acquitted cannot be tried again for the same charges because this would constitute *double jeopardy* (which is prohibited by the Fifth Amendment). If the jury finds the defendant guilty of one or more of the charges, the case moves to the sentencing stage, and the probation officer enters the case, usually for the first time. (In some jurisdictions, the probation officer is involved in gathering information—the *pre-plea investigation*—for the judge during plea bargaining.)

SENTENCING

After a verdict or plea of guilty, the judge decides on the sentence, although in some states the sentence is decided by the jury, particularly in cases of murder (Zawitz, 1988). The sentencing function reflects societal goals, which may be in conflict:

1. *Retribution*: punishment dimension (*lex talionis*, an eye for an eye, or just deserts), which expresses society's disapproval of criminal behavior
2. *Incapacitation*: reducing the opportunity for further criminal behavior by imprisonment

3. *Deterrence*: a belief that punishment will reduce the likelihood of future criminal behavior by the particular offender (*individual/specific deterrence*), or by others in society who fear similar punishment (*general deterrence*)

4. *Rehabilitation*: a belief that by providing services—social, psychological, educational, or vocational—an offender will be less likely to commit future crimes

5. *Restitution*: having an offender repay the victim or society in money or service for the harm committed

Sentencing can be further complicated by concern for

- *Proportionality*: that punishment be commensurate with the seriousness of the crime
- *Equity*: that similar crimes receive similar punishment
- *Social debt*: that the severity of punishment should consider the offender's prior criminal record (Zawitz, 1988)

These issues are discussed in subsequent chapters.

The trial judge sets a date for a sentencing hearing and in many jurisdictions will order a presentence investigation to be conducted by the probation department. A probation officer will search court records; examine other reports (such as psychiatric and school records); and interview the defendant, spouse, employer, arresting officer, and, sometimes, the victim. Information from the presentence investigation will be presented in the form of a written presentence or probation report, which frequently contains the probation officer's sentencing recommendation. After reviewing the report, the judge conducts a sentencing hearing at which both defense and prosecution are allowed to make statements. The judge then imposes a sentence: fine, suspended sentence, probation, incarceration, or any combination thereof. A prison sentence may be definite (classical) or indeterminate (positive), depending on state law.

A sentence of probation places the defendant, now a "convict," under the supervision of a probation officer. A sentence of incarceration results in the defendant being sent to jail (if convicted of a misdemeanor) for not more than one year, or to a state (or federal) prison if convicted of a felony. In most jurisdictions, a parole board can release the defendant (now an "inmate") before the expiration of his or her sentence. In other states and the federal system, the inmate can be released early as the result of accumulating time off for "good behavior." Parolees, and, in many states, persons released for good behavior, come under the supervision of a parole officer (the actual title varies from state to state).

APPEALS

Although the prosecutor cannot appeal a verdict of acquittal, the defendant is free to appeal a guilty verdict in hopes of obtaining a reversal. The defendant can ask an appellate court to review the proceedings that culminated in his or her conviction. In fact, American criminal justice is rather unique for the extensive postconviction review procedures to which a defendant is entitled. A prison inmate may petition the trial court for a new trial or take an appeal to the state's intermediate appellate court, and, if unsuccessful there, can still appeal to the state court of last resort. If unsuccessful in state court, he or she can petition the Supreme Court. The prisoner can also attack the conviction "collaterally," that is, using indirect means, by way of a writ of *habeas corpus*, claiming that his or her constitutional rights were violated in some way by the state court conviction. Having exhausted direct and indirect appeals in state courts, the inmate can move over to the federal courts, claiming again that the conviction was unconstitutional, usually on grounds of lack of due process.

The appellate court cannot act as a trial court, that is, receive new evidence concerning the facts already established at the original trial. It is limited to addressing new theories or legal arguments regarding the law applicable to these facts. The appellate court can uphold the verdict, overturn it, or order it reversed and remanded to the trial court for a new trial. The appellate court can also render decisions that affect other cases by setting a precedent or handing down a ruling that governs the actions of criminal justice officials; for example, in *Morrissey v. Brewer* the Supreme Court ruled that parolees are entitled to some basic forms of due process before they can be returned to prison for violation of parole. [For a discussion of the appellate role of the courts, see Abadinsky (1995).]

PROBATION AND PAROLE: WHY BOTHER?

Why be concerned with probation or parole? Some simply say, "If you do the crime, do the time." Although later chapters elaborate on this issue, consider the following. The average yearly cost of supervising a person on probation is estimated at about $1000; the annual cost of supervising a person on parole is estimated at $1200. The annual average cost of housing an inmate in prison is about $12,000 (in Arkansas, it is $7500), although in some states, for example, Illinois (more than $17,000), New York (about $25,000) or Minnesota ($30,000), it is considerably higher. However, the cost of imprisonment is typically underestimated because it leaves out many actual expenses, such as fringe benefits for employees, which average more than 25 percent of salaries. Accurate cost estimates for probation and parole simply do not exist (McDonald, 1989). The cost of building a maximum security prison averages more than $70,000 per cell. Although a state can float bonds to underwrite the cost of prison building, thereby absorbing the cost (which includes substantial interest) over a long period, operating costs and staff salaries, for example, must be paid immediately out of the state's operating budget—it may be politically easier to build a prison than to staff and operate one. Adding to these costs are the problems of acquired immunodeficiency syndrome (AIDS) and tuberculosis, and the increasing number of geriatric offenders, often the result of "get-tough" and "three-strikes-and-you're-out" (actually in for life) legislation. The cost of housing an inmate over the age of fifty with health problems is more than $60,000 a year. There are about 1 million persons in America's prisons, and jails house about an additional 500,000 inmates. Factors of cost, mediated by overcrowded prisons, have led to a dramatic expansion in the use of probation and parole. In 1979, for example, there were 1,086,535 persons on probation; in 1987, there were 2,242,053, an increase of more than 100 percent. By 1990, the number had risen to 2,671,000, with the current figure at more than 3 million. In 1979, 218,690 persons were on parole from American prisons; in 1987, 362,192, an increase of more than 65 percent. By 1990, that number had risen to 531,000, with the current figure at about 700,000 (U.S. Bureau of Justice Statistics).

In 1994, Congress passed the Violent Crime Control and Law Enforcement Act, which provides prison construction grants. To qualify, however, states must have laws requiring persons convicted of a violent offense to serve at least 85% of their prison sentence—few states have the necessary resources to do so.

Now that this overview of criminal justice is complete, Chapter 2 focuses on the courts and probation administration.

REVIEW QUESTIONS

1. In what way does criminal law reflect power relations in society?
2. How does the definition of crime determine who is subjected to probation and parole?
3. How is the enforcement of criminal law a factor in determining who is subjected to probation and parole?
4. What are the eight index crimes?
5. What is the classical theory of law and justice?
6. How does neoclassicalism differ from classicalism?
7. What distinguishes positive theory from classical theory with respect to crime and criminal behavior?
8. Under a strictly positivistic view of criminal behavior, why is there an absence of culpability or *mens rea?*
9. Why is the system of criminal justice in the United States not systematic?
10. What are the effects of providing the police with an inordinate percentage of the allocations for criminal justice?
11. What are the five societal goals of sentencing?
12. What concerns can complicate sentencing?
13. What is the importance of probation and parole in criminal justice?

PROBATION AND THE COURTS: HISTORY AND ADMINISTRATION

A probation agency provides three basic services to the courts:

1. Juvenile services
2. Presentence investigation
3. Supervision of offenders

The administration of these services may be under the auspices of the judiciary or an agency in the executive branch of government; in either event, a probation agency provides services to the judicial branch of government.[1] Before examining these services and their administration, it is necessary to look first at federal and state court systems.

COURT SYSTEMS: FEDERAL AND STATE

In only one case is the jurisdiction of a court established by the U.S. Constitution: Article III, Section 2, states that "the judicial power of the United States shall be vested in one supreme Court, and in such inferior Courts as the Congress may from time to time ordain and establish." Similarly, state courts derive their authority from state constitutions and legislative enactments.

---

[1]There are some exceptions. For example, in New York State, probation officers supervise offenders conditionally released from county jails. Before 1989, this had been the responsibility of the New York State Division of Parole.

JURISDICTION

Jurisdiction is basic to understanding the organization of a court system; it is the geographic area, subject matter, or persons over which a court can exercise authority. The area of geographic jurisdiction is referred to as *venue*, and it can be limited to a particular district, city, or county. Venue in criminal cases is relatively simple—it is where the crime is alleged to have occurred. The jurisdiction of a state court never extends beyond that state's borders. Although there are systems of trial and appellate courts in each state, most are not at all systematic. The history that shaped our judicial systems has mitigated against uniformity.

In both federal and state justice systems, there are four levels of courts stratified by their jurisdiction:

1. *Lower court:* limited jurisdiction
2. *Superior court:* general trial jurisdiction
3. *Intermediate appeals court:* appellate jurisdiction
4. *Supreme court:* final appellate jurisdiction

THE FEDERAL COURTS

There is a *U.S. District Court* in each of the 94 federal judicial districts (89 within the 50 states, and 5 for the U.S. territories and the District of Columbia) (Figure 2.1). Each state has at least 1 (only one district crosses a state line), and heavily

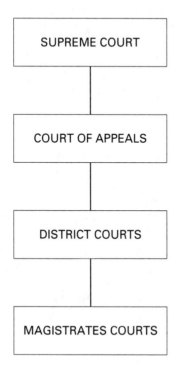

FIGURE 2.1 Organization of federal courts for criminal cases.

populated states, such as California, New York, and Texas, have as many as 4. There are about 600 district court judges and several retired—or senior—judges who assist as trial judges. The number of judges assigned to each district varies with the size of the population, the largest being the Southern District of New York, located in Manhattan, which has 27. Each judicial district has a U.S. attorney (federal prosecutor), a U.S. marshal, and a chief probation officer; they are assisted by hundreds of employees: assistant U.S. attorneys, deputy U.S. marshals, and U.S. probation officers. As opposed to most state judges, all federal judges are appointed to lifetime terms by the president (with the "advice and consent" of the Senate); lifetime tenure helps to insulate judges from both political pressures and popular sentiment.

In dealing with criminal cases, district courts employ *U.S. magistrates,* attorneys who are appointed by the district court judges for terms of eight years (or four years in the case of those who serve only part-time). The magistrate, sometimes called "commissioner," is authorized to issue warrants and to conduct preliminary hearings and nonfelony trials held without a jury. A U.S. magistrate is usually the first judicial officer before whom a federal criminal defendant appears. Decisions of a magistrate can be appealed to a district court judge. District courts have *general jurisdiction* (meaning that they can hold trials in any type of case) involving the violation of federal statutes. However, they actually have *exclusive jurisdiction* in only a relatively few types of criminal cases—most crimes involve violations of state law—and often their jurisdiction is shared with state courts. For example, drug trafficking and bank robbery are both federal *and* state crimes. As a result of efforts to deal with organized crime, many state crimes, if committed in a certain pattern, also violate the (federal) Racketeer Influenced and Corrupt Organizations (RICO) statute; for example, bribing a *state* judge [see Abadinsky (1994) for more information].

The *U.S. Court of Appeals* (sometimes referred to as *circuit court*) has jurisdiction over cases already decided in a federal district court—it does not act as a trial court. The country is divided into eleven circuits, each of which embraces several states, and a twelfth circuit, which serves the District of Columbia. The Second Circuit, for example, serves New York, New Jersey, and Connecticut. Each circuit court has at least four judges, and a circuit with a great deal of litigation, such as the Second Circuit, will have more than twenty appellate judges. The chief judge (the most senior judge in terms of service in the circuit who has not reached 70 years of age) has supervisory responsibilities for the circuit. Court of appeals cases are usually considered in panels of three judges, although, occasionally, important cases will be heard by the full court of the circuit (referred to as *en banc*). Judges of a court of appeals (appellate courts have no juries) review issues of law that have been applied by the district courts in their circuit, and the rulings of a court of appeals are binding on only the district courts in their circuit, although they may influence other circuits and even the Supreme Court. Each circuit has a Supreme Court justice assigned to it who is empowered to act in emergencies when the Supreme Court is not in session; this most often involves cases of capital punishment, and the justice can order a stay until the High Court convenes.

The *U.S. Supreme Court*, the only court established by the Constitution, is unique—it is the least democratic U.S. governmental institution. The president (executive branch) and the Congress (legislative branch) must, more or less, be responsive to the concerns of the voting public, whereas the judicial branch remains aloof. Although the other branches of government reflect popular sentiment, the Supreme Court can render the decisions of elected executives and legislators null and void—that is, *unconstitutional.* The Supreme Court can protect the rights and interests of persons who, in a democratic society, are weak, who do not represent a significant block of votes or source of funds, and who may be unpopular, such as accused criminal offenders. The Supreme Court decisions that this book examines, for example, have provided important rights to juveniles, prison inmates, probationers, and parolees—persons whose rights are not likely to be championed by elected officials.

As the highest court in the federal system, the Supreme Court is *the* court of last resort. The eight associate justices and the chief justice, who presides over the deliberations of the Supreme Court, are appointed for life by the president. Unlike the court of appeals, since 1914 (except in certain rather rare circumstances) the Supreme Court has had the power to decide which cases it will consider. Before the Court will consider an appeal, a *writ of certiorari* is required—a minimum of four justices must agree to place the case on the Court's calendar—and *certiorari* is granted in less than 4 percent of the cases appealed to the Supreme Court. The decisions of a state court of last resort are appealed directly to the Supreme Court. In the federal system, there are also specialized courts, such as the court of claims, but only the court of military appeals handles criminal matters.

THE STATE COURTS

State court systems are characterized by decentralization based on territorial jurisdiction or on the nature of the case, and sometimes both. This system resulted from the need to bring the courts closer to litigants in an expanding nation where transportation was primitive. Each court played an important political and social role in the life of its community. When court convened in the county seat, often only once a month, it was a major event. Many people came to town, conducted business, discussed politics, and socialized with one another (Walker, 1980). Those were the days before radio, motion pictures, and television, and people flocked to the courtrooms to hear the oratory of noted attorneys. Courtroom oratory and successful advocacy gained an attorney a following and clients (Friedman, 1973). Following the Revolutionary War, there was a trend throughout the states toward establishment of a separate appellate branch. The lower courts were neglected and became unwieldy, inefficient, and in many areas tied to corrupt political machines—a link that would remain a problem in many urban areas well into the 20th century.

Although there is one unitary federal court system, there are 50 state court systems. Even though the system of each state resembles that of the others (Figure 2.2), each has a distinct history, and no two court systems are exactly alike.

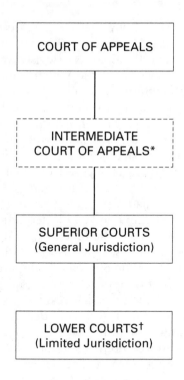

Note: Whereas there is only one federal system, each state has its own court structure. This diagram, although approximating all, does not necessarily reflect any single court system.

*Some states have an intermediate court of appeals between the superior court and the court of last resort.

†These would include county courts, magistrates courts, traffic courts, justices of the peace, and juvenile courts.

FIGURE 2.2   Organization of state courts for criminal cases.

States present a confusing array of court systems with names that only add to the confusion. For example, in states with a *unified court system,* such as Illinois, there is no "lower court" (equivalent to the magistrate's court in the federal system). Thus, all preliminary hearings and misdemeanors will be heard in superior court (called the circuit court in Illinois and the supreme court in New York). In most states, however, there is a lower court that has limited jurisdiction. Sometimes referred to as magistrate's court, city or county court, police court, and, in some rural areas, justice of the peace court, a lower court has authority to try misdemeanors (crimes for which, in most states, the maximum penalty is one year of imprisonment), traffic offenses, and sometimes juvenile cases; it is also the entry level for felony cases. This court will receive a defendant shortly (usually within 24 hours) after an arrest for an initial appearance that involves the formal reading of charges and setting of bail. In felony cases, the lower court may arrange for counsel and conduct a preliminary (probable cause) hearing. Because this is a court of limited jurisdiction, if the charge(s) constitutes a felony, the case will be moved to the grand jury (in states that use this body for charging offenders) or directly to superior court (on the basis of a prosecutor's information).

The lower courts typically dispense what many observers refer to as *rough justice* (Feeley, 1979; Robertson, 1974). That is, they are characterized by heavy caseloads—about 90 percent of all criminal cases are disposed of at this level—and speed: Justice dispensed rapidly, often in a minute or less. Anything that tends to delay case processing is avoided. Under such circumstances, little attention may be paid to the niceties of individualized justice and due process, which serve to slow down the pace of case processing. The defendant who insists on his or her "rights" may be viewed as disruptive, and this can entail costs. The defendant is likely to receive higher bail or a severer sentence than is the norm. Conversely, the typical case adjudicated in a lower court receives rather lenient treatment, a force for gaining the acquiescence of defendants. Persons on probation or parole are in a particularly disadvantageous position during this stage of criminal justice. A plea of guilty, although it may result in leniency from the lower court, can cause the defendant's probation or parole to be revoked.

A *superior court* has general jurisdiction, meaning that it can try any type of case: violations (e.g., traffic offenses), misdemeanors, and felonies, although this court usually handles only felony cases. Most cases entering superior court have been transferred from a lower court (directly via a prosecutor's information or by way of the grand jury). Because the superior court receives only a small percentage of the cases that enter the criminal justice system, the hectic pace encountered in the lower court is absent. Because of the seriousness of felony charges, there is usually scrupulous concern for due process. There is also a lack of jury trials, most cases being adjudicated by a judge (in a "bench trial") or negotiations that end in a plea of guilty.

An *intermediate court of appeals* exists in about half the states; the courts are called "intermediate" because on the judicial organization chart they are situated between the superior court and the state's highest court. As is the case with all appellate courts, the intermediate court of appeals does not try cases; it receives cases on appeal from the superior court. An appeal from the decision of an intermediate court of appeals goes to the court of appeals. In states without an intermediate court of appeals, an appeal from superior court goes directly to the *court of appeals*, the state *court of last resort*. Decisions of the court of appeals are binding on all of the courts in the state, unless overturned by the U.S. Supreme Court.

From the Revolution until 1832, most states provided for both elected and appointed (by the legislature or governor) judges. In that year, Mississippi initiated the popular election of all judges; in 1846, New York did the same. Within 10 years, 15 of the 29 states that then made up the Union had followed suit, and every state that entered the Union after 1846 stipulated the popular election of all or most of its judges (Hurst, 1950). Several other states experimented with both electoral and appointment systems, sometimes, as Texas did, going back and forth (Friedman, 1973).

Currently, most state court judges and justices (appeals court judges) are elected on a partisan (identified by political party—Republican or Democrat) or nonpartisan basis. In a single state, some judges may be elected (on a partisan or nonpartisan basis), whereas others are appointed, usually by the governor. In some states, there is a so-called merit system for filling judicial vacancies: A gubernatorial commission nominates several persons for each judicial vacancy, and the governor must pick one of them. The judge serves for one year, and his or her name is submitted to the voters for confirmation—or removal. [For the advantages and disadvantages of each of these systems, see Abadinsky (1995).]

JUVENILE COURTS

The juvenile court system differs from state to state and even within states. Jurisdiction over juveniles may be located in a separate juvenile court, in a specialized branch of the superior court, or in various types of courts of limited jurisdiction. It is possible that within one state, jurisdiction may be located in two or more different types of courts. Because the juvenile court differs so dramatically from the adult criminal court, it is treated separately in Chapter 3.

PROBATION HISTORY

Although probation has antecedents that reach back to biblical times, its American history dates back to the 19th century.

EARLY PROBATION AND JOHN AUGUSTUS

The concept of probation evolved out of the practice of *judicial reprieve*, used in English courts to serve as a temporary suspension of sentence to allow a defendant to appeal to the crown for a pardon. Although originally intended to be only a temporary postponement of punishment, it eventually developed into a *suspended sentence* whereby punishment was never actually imposed. In the United States, the suspended sentence was used as early as 1830 in Boston and became widespread in U.S. courts, although there was no statutory authorization for such practice. At first, judges used "release on recognizance" or bail and simply failed to take further action. By the mid-19th century, however, many courts were using a judicial reprieve to suspend sentences, and this posed a legal question.

"A judge had always had the power to suspend a sentence, if he felt for some reason that the trial had miscarried. But could judges suspend sentences wholesale, after trials that were scrupulously fair, simply to give the defendant a second chance?" (Friedman, 1973: 518). In 1894, this question was litigated in New York, and the court determined that the power to suspend sentence was inherent in criminal courts only when this right had been granted by the legislature. In 1916, the U.S. Supreme Court, in a case that affected only federal courts, ruled that judges did not have the discretionary authority to suspend a sentence. In its decision, however, the Court stated that Congress could authorize the temporary or indefinite suspension of sentences—a predecessor to probation statutes (Cromwell et al., 1985).

The term *probation* was applied by John Augustus to the practice of bailing offenders out of court followed by a period of supervised living in the community. This pioneer of modern probation was born in Woburn, Massachusetts, and became a successful shoemaker in Boston. In 1852, a *Report of the Labors of John Augustus* was published at the request of his friends, and in it Augustus wrote: "I was in court one morning . . . in which the man was charged with being a common drunkard. He told me that if he could be saved from the House of Correction, he never again would taste intoxicating liquors: I bailed him, by permission of the Court" (1972: 4–5). Thus began the work of the nation's first probation officer, a volunteer who worked without pay.

Augustus's first experience with a drunkard led to an interest in helping others charged with the same offense. Augustus would appear in court and offer to bail a defendant. If the judge agreed, which usually happened, the defendant would become Augustus's charge. The shoemaker would assist the offender in finding work or a residence; Augustus's own house was filled with people he had bailed. When the defendant returned to court, Augustus would report on his progress toward rehabilitation and recommend a disposition of the case. These recommendations were usually accepted. During the first year of his efforts, Augustus assisted ten drunkards who, because of his work, received small fines instead of imprisonment. He later helped other types of offenders, young and old, men and women, and was able to report only ten absconders (persons who jumped bail or probation) out of 2000 cases.

Augustus continued his work for 18 years and generally received support from judges and newspapers that reported on his efforts. Prosecutors, however, viewed him as an interloper who kept court calendars crowded by preventing cases from being disposed of quickly. Policemen and court clerks opposed his work because they received a fee for each case disposed of by a commitment to the House of Correction. As a result of his probation work, Augustus neglected his business and eventually experienced financial ruin; he required the help of friends for his support.

Several aspects of the system used by Augustus remain a basic part of modern probation. Augustus thoroughly investigated each person he considered helping, considering "the previous character of the person, his age and the influences by which in the future he would likely be surrounded" (1972: 34). Augustus not only supervised each defendant but kept a careful case record that he submitted to the court. Augustus died in 1859, and until 1878, probation in Massachusetts continued to be the work of volunteers.

EARLY PROBATION STATUTES

In 1878, the Massachusetts legislature enacted the first probation statute, authorizing the mayor of Boston to hire a probation officer who would be supervised by the superintendent of police. For the first time, the position of probation officer was given official recognition as an arm of the court. The law authorized a probation officer to investigate cases and recommend probation for "such persons as may reasonably be expected to be reformed without punishment." Probation was made available in Boston to young and old, men and women, felons as well as misdemeanants. In 1880, the legislature granted to all municipalities the authority to employ probation officers, but few towns and villages did so. In 1891, the power to appoint probation officers was transferred to the lower courts, and each was required to employ a probation officer. In 1898, this requirement was extended to the superior courts as well. The second state to adopt a probation statute was Vermont, 20 years later—the lapse in time is attributable to the poor communications of that period. In 1898, Vermont authorized the appointment of a probation officer by the courts in each county, each officer serving all the courts in a particular county.

Another New England state, Rhode Island, soon followed Vermont with a probation law that was novel—it placed restrictions on who could be granted probation, excluding persons convicted of treason, murder, robbery, arson, rape, and burglary. This practice violated a basic tenet of positive theory: Judge the offender, not just the offense. The restrictive aspects of Rhode Island's probation law, however, were copied by many other states. The Rhode Island probation law, which applied to children and adults, also introduced the concept of a state-administered probation system. A state agency, the Board of Charities and Correction, appointed a state probation officer and deputies, "at least one of whom should be a woman" (Glueck, 1933: 231).

In 1894, Maryland authorized its courts to suspend a sentence generally or for a specific time, and judges could "make such order to enforce terms as to costs, recognizance for appearance, or matters relating to the residence or conduct of the convicts as may be deemed proper." The courts of Baltimore began using agents of the Prisoner's Aid Society and later appointed salaried probation officers. In 1897, Missouri enacted a "bench parole law," which authorized courts to suspend sentence under certain conditions. The courts also appointed probation officers, misnamed "parole officers," to carry out this probation ("bench parole") work (Glueck, 1933).

PROBATION AT THE TURN OF THE CENTURY

The spread of probation was accelerated by the juvenile court movement, which started in the Midwest and developed rapidly (discussed in Chapter 3). In 1899, Minnesota enacted a law that authorized the appointment of county probation officers, but the granting of probation was limited to those under 18 years of age. Four years later, this was changed to 21 years of age. In 1899, Illinois enacted the historic Juvenile Court Act, which authorized the world's first juvenile court. The law also provided for the hiring of probation officers to investigate cases referred by the courts, but it made no provision for payment of the probation officers.

Charitable organizations and private philanthropists provided the funds for the Cook County Juvenile Court to hire probation officers. At the end of the first year, there were six probation officers, supported by the Juvenile Court Committee of the Chicago Women's Club. In addition, in each police district a police officer spent part of his time out of uniform performing the duties of a probation officer. On July 1, 1899, Illinois's first juvenile court judge addressed the captains of Chicago's police districts: "You are so situated that you, even more than the justices, can get at the underlying facts in each particular case brought before you by the officers of your command. I shall want you to select some good reliable officers from each district for the work of investigating juvenile cases" (Schultz, 1973: 465). In 1899, Colorado enacted a compulsory education law that enabled the development of a juvenile court using truant officers as probation officers. By 1925, probation was available for juveniles in every state (Glueck, 1933).

It was not until 1901 in New York that legislation authorizing the appointment of probation officers was enacted—until that year they were volunteers (Linder and Savarese, 1984). In 1908, Suffolk County on Long Island appointed its first probation officer: "At the time, there was little appreciation of the value of probation, and the appointment was more in the nature of an experiment. As a part-time position, the probation officer had no office, and the probationers reported to him at his home, or by mail." The county appointed a full-time probation officer in 1919, and he was given a small office. Probation for juveniles was authorized in Pennsylvania in 1903 and extended to adults in 1909: Except for the offenses of murder, administering poison, kidnapping, incest, sodomy, rape, assault with intent to rape, and arson or burglary of an inhabited dwelling, a judge could suspend the sentence and place the offender on probation. Although Texas enacted the Suspended Sentence Act in 1913 to provide an alternative to incarceration, probation supervision of the convicted offender was not required until 1947. Probation for adults in Alabama did not begin until 1939, when the governor approved an enabling act giving the legislature power to authorize adult probation. Before that, it had been held that courts did not have the inherent power to suspend sentences because it was deemed to be an encroachment on the executive power to pardon, commute, and reprieve. By 1956, probation was available for adults in every state (Task Force on Corrections, 1966).

The first directory of probation officers in the United States, published in 1907, identified 795 probation officers working mainly in the juvenile courts. Like the first probation officer in Illinois, Alzina Stevens, many were volunteers, and some who were paid worked only part-time. Training for probation officers was either limited or nonexistent; appointments were often based on considerations of political patronage and salaries were typically low even when compared with those of unskilled laborers.

ADMINISTRATION OF PROBATION

Probation in the United States is administered by more than 2000 separate agencies. In about three-quarters of the states, adult probation is located in the executive branch of state government (where it is typically combined with parole). For example, adult probation in Georgia is a division of the State Department of Offender Rehabilitation (Figure 2.3), which also includes the state prison system and parole board (Board of Offender Rehabilitation); or in Pennsylvania where probation is combined with parole as an independent agency under the Board of Probation and Parole (Figure 2.4). More than one-half of the agencies providing juvenile probation services, however, are administered on the local level. Juvenile probation may be provided by a separate juvenile agency or a (juvenile or family) division of the same agency that administers adult probation as in Nassau County, New York (Figure 2.5). Fortunately, the administration of parole, which is discussed in Chapter 7, is much less complex: one agency per state and always in the executive branch. Even with parole, however, there is a slight variation: In some states (e.g., Pennsylvania), persons paroled from a local jail come under the supervision of a *county* probation and parole department.

The administration of probation systems can be separated into six categories, and a state may have more than one system in operation:

- *Juvenile.* Separate probation services for juveniles are administered on a county or municipal level, or on a statewide basis.
- *Municipal.* Independent probation units are administered by the lower courts or the municipality under state laws and guidelines.
- *County.* Under laws and guidelines established by the state, a county operates its own probation agency.
- *State.* One agency administers a central probation system providing services throughout the state.
- *State combined.* Probation and parole services are administered on a statewide basis by one agency.
- *Federal.* Probation is administered nationally as an arm of the courts. Federal probation officers also supervise parolees.

The state of Iowa is divided into eight judicial districts, each with a local correctional department operating under a board of directors. The board appoints a director who administers probation, parole, and related services that are funded and monitored by the Iowa Department of Corrections. In Texas, probation services are located in 120 Community Supervision and Corrections Departments (CSCD), organized by the judges of each judicial district and funded by supervision fees and state aid.

Two basic issues arise in the administration of probation services.

1. *Should probation be part of the judicial or executive branch of government?*
2. *Should probation be under county or state jurisdiction?*

Those who support placement of probation services into the judicial branch (Nelson, Ohmart, and Harlow, 1978) contend that:

- Probation is more responsive to the courts, to whom it provides services, when administered by the judiciary.
- The relationship of probation staff to the courts creates an automatic feedback mechanism on the effectiveness of various dispositions.
- Courts will have greater awareness of the resources needed by the probation agency.

- Judges will have greater confidence in an agency for which they are responsible, allowing probation staff more discretion than they would allow members of an outside agency.
- If probation is administered on a statewide basis, it is usually incorporated into a department of corrections. Under such circumstances, probation services might be assigned a lower priority than they would have as part of the judicial branch.

Those who oppose the placement of probation in the judiciary note the following disadvantages:

- Judges, trained in law, not administration, are not equipped to administer probation services.
- Under judicial control, services to persons on probation may receive a lower priority than services to the judge, for example, presentence investigations.
- Probation staff may be assigned duties unrelated to probation.
- The courts are adjudicatory and regulative; they are not service-oriented bodies.

Placement in the *executive branch* (which means as part of the same agency that administers state parole) has these features to recommend it:

- All other human service agencies are within the executive branch.
- All other corrections subsystems are located in the executive branch.
- With executive branch placement, program budgeting can be better coordinated, and an increased ability to negotiate fully in the resource allocation process becomes possible.
- A coordinated continuum of services to offenders and better use of probation personnel are facilitated.

E. Kim Nelson and her colleagues (1978: 92) conclude:

When compared, these arguments tend to support placing probation in the executive branch. The potential for increased coordination in planning, better utilization of personnel and improved services to offenders cannot be dismissed.

A state administered probation system has decided advantages over local administration. A total system planning approach to probation as a subsystem of corrections is needed. Such planning requires state leadership. Furthermore, implementation of planning strategies requires uniformity of standards, reporting, and evaluation as well as resource allocation.

Mitchell Silverman (1993: 89) points out, however, that

State control typically means probation agencies administered by the state executive branch with centralized administrators who are frequently far removed, both physically and intellectually, from the probation officer in

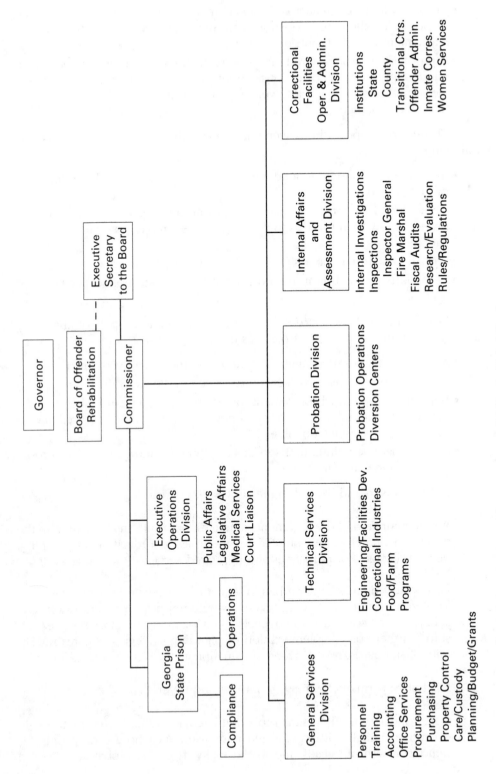

FIGURE 2.3 Organizational chart for Georgia's Department of Offender Rehabilitation.

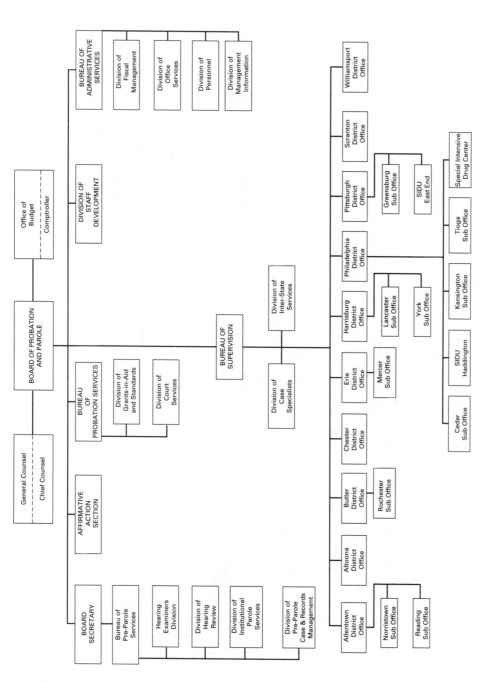

FIGURE 2.4   Organizational chart for Pennyslvania's Board of Probation and Parole.

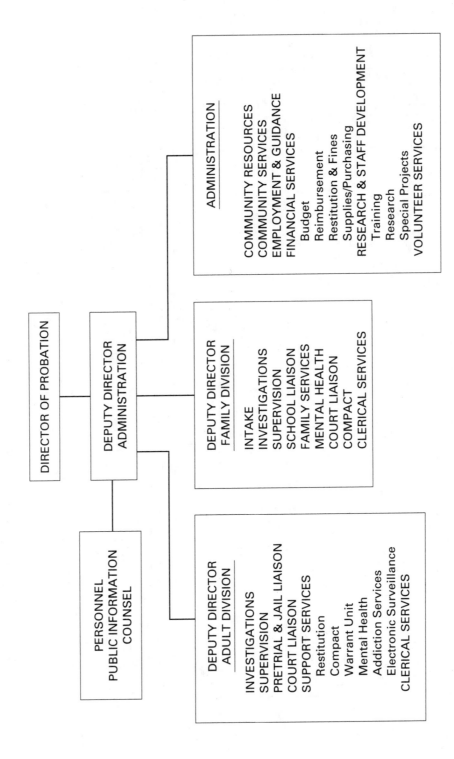

DIRECTOR OF PROBATION

PERSONNEL
PUBLIC INFORMATION
COUNSEL

DEPUTY DIRECTOR
ADMINISTRATION

DEPUTY DIRECTOR
ADULT DIVISION

INVESTIGATIONS
SUPERVISION
PRETRIAL & JAIL LIAISON
COURT LIAISON
SUPPORT SERVICES
  Restitution
  Compact
  Warrant Unit
  Mental Health
  Addiction Services
  Electronic Surveillance
CLERICAL SERVICES

DEPUTY DIRECTOR
FAMILY DIVISION

INTAKE
INVESTIGATIONS
SUPERVISION
SCHOOL LIAISON
FAMILY SERVICES
MENTAL HEALTH
COURT LIAISON
COMPACT
CLERICAL SERVICES

ADMINISTRATION

COMMUNITY RESOURCES
COMMUNITY SERVICES
EMPLOYMENT & GUIDANCE
FINANCIAL SERVICES
  Budget
  Reimbursement
  Restitution & Fines
  Supplies/Purchasing
RESEARCH & STAFF DEVELOPMENT
  Training
  Research
  Special Projects
VOLUNTEER SERVICES

FIGURE 2.5   Organizational chart for Nassau County, New York's Department of Probation.

the field. Often the central administrators have little knowledge and understanding of the important factors that are operating in the local community where the individual probation officer works. The distance has the potential of creating conflicts of interest when the state level policy-makers demand from the field worker one approach to clients while, at the same time, the local community, in which the probation officer and client live, demands another.

Probation services as part of the executive branch involves the state government under the office of the governor. Probation services may be part of a larger department of corrections, as in Georgia, or part of an independent probation and parole agency, as in Alabama. Probation services as part of the judicial branch of government usually places these services under the judges of the county. For example, in New Jersey:

> The judges of the County Court in each county, or a majority of them, acting jointly may appoint a *chief probation officer, [and] such men and women probation officers* as may be necessary. Probation officers and *volunteers in probation* shall be appointed with standards fixed by the Supreme Court. All *probation officers* and *volunteers in probation* shall be responsible to and under the supervision of the *Chief Probation Officer* of the county who shall be responsible to and under the supervision of the judge of the county court or, in counties having more than one judge of the county court, the county court judge designated by the Assistant Judge to be responsible for the administration of the *probation department* in the county in accordance with the applicable statutes, rules of the Supreme Court, and directives of the Chief Justice, the Administrative Director of the Courts, and the Assignment Judge of the county. (Emphasis in original)

Probation administered by the judiciary (usually) on a *county level* promotes diversity. Innovative programming can be implemented more easily in a county agency because it has a shorter line of bureaucratic control than a statewide agency. A county agency can more easily adapt to change, and the successful programs of one agency can more easily be adopted and unsuccessful programs avoided by probation departments in other counties. Those most familiar with the local community, its resources, attitudes, and politics will be responsible for providing probation services; this can increase public confidence in the services provided by the agency. Although the judiciary is nominally responsible for the administration of probation, the day-to-day operations are in the hands of a professional administrator—the chief probation officer.

Conversely, county-level administration results in a great deal of undesirable variance between agencies. For example, the ratio of probation officers to clients may differ dramatically from one county to the other—this would not happen with a statewide agency. Because each county sets its own budget, probation staff cannot be shifted from a low-ratio county to a high-ratio county to equalize the services provided. In New Jersey, for example, the State Advisory Board for Probation in its 1985 report noted that whereas juvenile supervision caseloads statewide averaged about 80 per officer, in individual counties the range was between 35 and 145. For adult probation caseloads, the state average of 160 ranged from 71 to 284, amounting to a fourfold difference between the extremes.

The New Jersey board found variance with respect to the amount each county expended on probation services and "a great deal of variation in the way work is processed. Thus, the sequence of probation work from county to county is far from uniform" and the board noted:

> There is no accepted definition of what comprises quality probation services. Probation supervision, for example, suffers from a lack of definition and structure, making it difficult to determine what is high quality supervision. Finally, there is great variance from county to county in the environment which produces the need for probation services, creating large differences among counties in the work probation services must perform. The extent and seriousness of criminal, social, and economic problems has important implications for staffing, procedures, and resource requirements from county to county.

The latter finding, of course, can serve as an argument for county control of probation services. The board, however, raises a question: Does the lack of uniformity in administering probation make justice less equitable statewide?

This issue has led states with county-based probation systems to create statewide oversight agencies for better coordination and uniformity of probation services—only Indiana and California operate probation locally without a state oversight agency (Parent et al., 1994). In Illinois, for example, the Probation Division of the Administrative Office of the Illinois Courts works to "improve the quality and quantity of probation and related court services throughout Illinois, provide more uniformity of organization, structure, and services, and increase the use of probation as a meaningful alternative punishment for nonviolent offenders. As part of these efforts, for example, the division promulgates regulations for the hiring and promotion of all probation personnel throughout the state."

The Texas Community Justice Assistance Division (formerly the Texas Adult Probation Commission) is responsible for establishing statewide standards and providing state aid to those local adult probation departments that choose to participate and are in compliance with the standards. As part of these efforts, the division has supported research and experimental probation programs throughout Texas. The commission has promulgated a "Code of Ethics for Texas Adult Probation Officers" and published standards for all phases of adult probation in Texas. For example, caseload size: "A caseload average within a department should be calculated by dividing the number of cases under direct supervision by the number of officers within the department devoting 80 percent or more of their time to direct case supervision. The average caseload of a probation officer in a department should not exceed 100 cases." Although commission standards are not mandatory, the failure of a probation department to maintain them can result in a loss of the considerable funding provided by the commission. For example, the commission provides $100 for each presentence investigation report completed by a probation department.

The New York State Division of Probation and Correctional Alternatives sets extensive statewide guidelines and standards for probation agencies that even include office design. For example, according to the "Requirements for Training in Fundamentals for New Probation Officers and Probation Officer Trainees":

(a) All probation officers and probation officer trainees shall successfully complete, within the first four months of service, a basic program in the fundamentals of probation practice, which conforms to the guidelines as adapted by the State Director of Probation [who heads the Division of Probation].

(b) This program shall consist of a minimum of 70 hours of training.

(c) The training shall:
   1. aid the probation officer and PO trainee in understanding the underlying philosophies and legal basis of the probation process;
   2. provide him with an understanding of his role in the community and in the criminal justice system; and
   3. introduce various principles, methods and techniques that will enable him to acquire knowledge and skills, and to develop attitudes which may be employed to accomplish the functions of the probation process.

(d) A basic program in the fundamentals of probation practice conducted by a local department shall be certified, in advance, by the State Director of Probation.

(e) A written examination shall be given at the conclusion of the basic program.

(f) Probation officers and PO trainees who fail the examination of the basic program, shall be required to pass a second examination within three months. Failure to pass the second examination shall require the officer to retake and complete the next available basic program. This subdivision shall not in any way impair, abridge or limit the exercise of any rights possessed by an employer of such an officer in accordance with applicable law governing his employment [read: his or her employment may be terminated].

(g) All new probation officers shall also comply with the peace officer training provisions of state law. The division also requires continuing in-service training (a minimum of 21 hours) for all probation officers, managers, and supervisors on an annual basis.

Now that this chapter has examined the history of probation and administration of probation agencies, Chapter 3 turns to probation in the juvenile court.

REVIEW QUESTIONS

1. What are the three basic services provided by a probation agency?
2. What are the responsibilities of a U.S. magistrate?
3. Why do the federal courts have exclusive jurisdiction in relatively few criminal cases?
4. What is meant by a "court of limited jurisdiction"?
5. What category of courts do not try cases?
6. What is meant by a "court of general jurisdiction"?
7. What is the jurisdiction of a U.S. district court?
8. Why is the U.S. Supreme Court the least democratic part of the U.S. tripartite form of government?
9. Why do the lower courts often dispense what has been referred to as "rough justice"?
10. What is a "court of last resort"?
11. What is the difference between a suspended sentence and probation?
12. What activities of John Augustus are part of the services of a modern probation agency?
13. What led to the dramatic increase in the use of probation officers in the United States?
14. What are the six categories into which the administration of probation services can be placed?
15. What are the advantages and disadvantages of placing probation services in the judicial branch of government?
16. What are the advantages of placing probation services in the executive branch of government?
17. How can uniformity be encouraged in states where probation services are administered on a county level?

THE JUVENILE COURT, JUVENILE JUSTICE, AND YOUNG OFFENDERS

The system of justice used for juveniles in the United States is based on a philosophy radically different from the one on which the adult criminal justice system rests. Before we examine the services provided by a probation agency to the juvenile court, it is necessary to understand the history and philosophy of this unique institution.

THE HISTORY OF THE JUVENILE COURT

In Europe, from Roman times to the late 18th century, children were routinely abandoned by their parents; the classical philosopher Rousseau, for example, abandoned five of his children to foundling homes. Most children were subsequently subjected to extreme levels of deprivation and exploitation (Boswell, 1989). A rather indifferent attitude toward children became a characteristic of America, where children became creatures of exploitation, with child labor remaining an important part of economic life into the 20th century. Children of the poor labored in mines (where their size was an advantage), mills, and factories under unsanitary and unsafe conditions. Laws prohibiting children younger than 12 years of age from employment and limiting the workday of those older than 12 years of age to 10 hours were routinely disregarded. Increased industrialization and urbanization and the resulting 10- and 12-hour workdays left many children without parental supervision, and family disorganization became widespread. Many children took to living in the streets, where they became part of the rampant vice and disorder that permeated large parts of the urban environment.

In the early days of colonial America, the family remained the mainstay of social control, "although by 1700 the family's inability to accommodate and discipline its young was becoming more apparent" (Mennel, 1973: xxii). Numerous laws began to appear threatening parents for failing to discipline their children properly. Furthermore, the British practice of transporting wayward young to America for indenture—which often involved neglect, cruelty, and immorality—left many youngsters without supervision as they fled from these onerous circumstances. By the end of the 18th century, it became obvious that a "system of social control would have to be developed apart from the family which would discipline homeless, vagrant, and destitute children—the offspring of the poor" (Mennel, 1973: xxvii). This need led to the rise of houses of refuge.

HOUSE OF REFUGE

In 1817, the Society for the Prevention of Pauperism was established in response to the problem of troubled and troublesome children: In 1824, it was renamed the Society for the Reformation of Juvenile Delinquency. The society conducted campaigns against the "corrupting" influence of taverns and theaters and opposed the use of jails to house children. Their efforts led to the establishment of houses of refuge (Krisberg, 1988).

The first house of refuge opened in New York in 1825 and was quickly followed by one in Boston (1826) and another in Philadelphia (1828). These institutions provided housing and care for troublesome children who might otherwise be left in the streets or, if their behavior brought them into serious conflict with the law, sent to jail or prison. The house of refuge was used "not only for the less serious juvenile criminal, but for runaways, disobedient children or vagrants" (Empey, 1979: 25–26). Orphan asylums were used for abandoned or orphaned children, for the children of women without husbands, or for children whose parents were deemed unfit. Robert Mennel points out that these institutions "were established to inculcate children with the values of hard work, orderliness, and subordination and thereby ensure their future good behavior" (1973: 8). To achieve these ends, however, discipline and punishments were often brutal, and the house of refuge in New York experienced group escapes and inmate uprisings.

Although these institutions were operated by private charities, their public charters included the first statutory definitions of juvenile delinquency and provided the basis for the state to intervene in the lives of children who were neglected or in need of supervision, in addition to those youngsters who had committed crimes (Walker, 1980). In these charters was embodied a "medieval English doctrine of nebulous origin and meaning" (Schlossman, 1977: 8) known as *parens patriae*, originally referring to the feudal duties of the overlord to his vassals and later the legal duties of the monarch toward his or her subjects who were in need of care, particularly children and the mentally incompetent. In its original form, *parens patriae* provided the Crown with authority to administer the estates of landed orphans (Sutton, 1988).

"With the independence of the American colonies and the transplanting of the English common-law system, the state in this country has taken the place of the crown as the *parens patriae* of all minors" (Lou, 1972: 4). This concept gave almost complete authority over children to the state—the Bill of Rights simply did not apply to children (*Ex parte Crouse*, 4 Wharton 9, 1838)—and *parens patriae* became the legal basis for the juvenile court. Although this concept has become identified with the rehabilitation of juvenile delinquents, it originally applied only to dependent children.

THE CHILD SAVERS

As immigration, industrialization, and urbanization continued, the fearful image of masses of undisciplined and uneducated children gave rise to the *child-saving movement*. Led by upper-class women of earlier American ancestry, the child savers were influenced by the nativist prejudices of their day, as well as *social Darwinism*: Natural selection resulted in an inferior underclass in need of control but not of aid in the sense of the modern social welfare state. Something had to be done to save these children from an environment that would lead them into only vice and crime and cause them to be the progenitors of the same. Reforming juvenile justice, notes Anthony Platt, became the task of women who "were generally well-educated, widely-traveled, and had access to political and financial resources" (1974: 77). The juvenile court was the result of their efforts, although controversy surrounds the interests and motivations of the child savers.

Platt argues that these women, although they "viewed themselves as altruists and humanitarians dedicated to rescuing those who were less fortunately placed in the social order," were actually motivated by boredom and middle- and upper-class social, economic, and political interests (1974: 3). "The child-savers were concerned not with championing the rights of the poor against exploitation by the ruling class but rather integrating the poor into the established social order and protecting 'respectable' citizens from the 'dangerous classes' " of people, who might otherwise be drawn into social revolution if not criminality (Platt quoted in Empey, 1979: 31). According to Platt, the juvenile court would serve to protect propertied and commercial interests from the predations of lower-class youngsters while ensuring an adequate supply of disciplined and vocationally trained labor. In fact, however, many states had already separated juvenile cases from those of adults without establishing a distinct juvenile court. David Rothman (in Empey, 1979: 37) places the issue in perspective: The juvenile court movement "satisfied [both] the most humanitarian of impulses and the most crudely self-interested considerations."

THE JUVENILE COURT

Although a juvenile might be sent to a house of refuge, an orphan asylum, or a reformatory—there was confusion over which children should be relegated to which institution—they could be arrested, detained, and tried as would any adult accused of a crime. Although some modifications of the trial process with respect to juveniles occurred as early as 1869, it was the *Illinois Juvenile Court Act of 1899* that established the first law creating a special comprehensive court for juveniles. Consistent with the concept of *parens patriae*, in addition to children who were delinquent—persons younger than 16 years of age who had violated the law—the juvenile court was given jurisdiction over neglected and dependent children:

> For the purposes of this act the words dependent child and neglected child shall mean any child who for any reason is destitute or homeless or abandoned; or has not proper parental care or guardianship; or who habitually begs or receives alms; or who is found living in any house of ill fame or with any vicious or disreputable person; or whose home, by reason of neglect, cruelty or depravity on the part of its parents, guardian or other person in whose care it may be, is an unfit place for such a child.

Nondelinquents in whom the court was interested became known as *status offenders*. Within 25 years of the Illinois Juvenile Court Act, every state but one had adopted legislation providing for one or all of the features of a juvenile court organization (Lenroot and Lundberg, 1925). In Cuyahoga County (Cleveland), the first session of the juvenile court occurred on June 4, 1902, with 20 boys younger than 16 years of age appearing; the initial case involved a 14-year-old boy charged with delinquency for stealing a pair of shoes—he was placed in "care and custody" of one of the three dozen volunteers who served as probation officers. A juvenile court was established in the Territory of Arizona on March 21, 1907; later that year, a probation officer was appointed in Pima County "to make such investigation as may be required by the Court, to be present if practicable when juvenile cases are heard, to furnish such information and assistance as the judge may require, and to take charge of any child, before trial and after trial, as may be directed by the Court."

A book originally published in 1927 provides insight into the prevailing concepts of the juvenile court (Lou, 1972: 2):

> These principles upon which the juvenile court acts are radically different from those of the criminal courts. In place of judicial tribunals, restrained by antiquated procedure, saturated in an atmosphere of hostility, trying cases for determining guilt and inflicting punishment according to inflexible rules of law, we have now juvenile courts, in which the relations of the child to his parents or other adults and to the state or society are defined and are adjusted summarily according to the scientific findings about the child and his environments. In place of magistrates, limited by the outgrown custom and compelled to walk in the paths fixed by the law of the realm, we have now socially-minded judges, who hear and adjust cases according not to rigid rules of law but

to what the interests of society and the interests of the child or good conscience demand. In the place of juries, prosecutors, and lawyers, trained in the old conception of law and staging dramatically, but often amusingly, legal battles, as the necessary paraphernalia of a criminal court, we have now probation officers, physicians, psychologists, and psychiatrists, who search for the social, physiological, psychological, and mental backgrounds of the child in order to arrive at reasonable and just solutions of individual cases.

Lou's statement clearly embodies the position of the positive theory—or, critics might say, positivism run amok, with the child being denied the most basic due process rights. The unstructured and informal system of juvenile justice used in Illinois quickly became the standard as juvenile courts were established throughout the United States. The differences between the adult criminal court and the juvenile court even extended to the terminology used.

Adult Criminal Court	Juvenile Court
Defendant	Respondent
Charges/indictment	Petition
Arraignment	Hearing
Prosecution/trial	Adjudication
Verdict	Finding
Sentence	Disposition
Imprisonment	Commitment
Inmate/prisoner	Resident
Parole	Aftercare

The terminology, consistent with the concept of *parens patriae*, reflects a nonpunitive approach to dealing with troubled and troublesome children (Figure 3.1). Critics often decry the lack of sufficient punishment inflicted in the juvenile court. Such comments indicate a complete misunderstanding of this court, which *should not punish*. Although the concept of *parens patriae* is paternalistic and not inconsistent with the concept of punishment (Weisheit and Alexander, 1988), the use of a punitive approach in juvenile court would make it simply a *criminal court for children* and, therefore, without grounding as a separate system of justice. Thus, although one could logically argue for abolishing the juvenile court, a juvenile court that imposes punishment has no basis in American history or in logic.

Because of the noncriminal approach, though, the usual safeguards of *due process* that were applicable in criminal courts were absent in juvenile court proceedings: rights to counsel, to confront and cross-examine adverse wit-

Adoptions: custody hearings, which grant custody to the prospective adoptive parents, and adoption hearings, which grant final adoption

Adjudication: (1) hearing at which the minor enters a plea to one or more allegations of the petition and at which the judge pronounces the child a delinquent minor; (2) contested hearing (trial) at which witnesses testify and evidence is presented at the conclusion of which the judge determines whether or not the child has been found to be a delinquent minor

Advisory: hearing for youth paper-referred to court at which the petition detailing the delinquent allegations is presented, a determination is made whether the minor qualifies for appointed counsel, and a trial review date is selected

Detention: hearing held within 24 hours of the filing of a petition for a detained youth at which counsel is appointed and the court considers whether the minor should be detained or released from custody

Disposition: hearing, analogous to the adult court sentencing, for which the probation officer prepares a comprehensive report of the adjudicated child's background and at which the judge determines what action(s) the court will take

Restitution: hearing at which the judge determines what restitution to a victim the child must pay to satisfy the conditions of probation

Review: review of the child's adherence to probation conditions to consider revising these conditions or terminating the minor from probation

Revocation: hearing to determine if the minor has violated probation by failure to adhere to the conditions of probation or by committing a delinquent act

Transfer: hearing to determine if the juvenile court should retain jurisdiction for the allegations set forth in the petition or whether the matter should be transferred for prosecution to the adult court

Trial review: hearing at which the child requests that the charges be set for a contested adjudication (trial) or at which he/she admits one or more allegations of the pending petition

FIGURE 3.1   Guide to the most common hearings held at the juvenile court. (*Source:* Pima County, Arizona, Juvenile Court.)

nesses, and to avoid self-incrimination. Because the focus of the juvenile court was on providing help, procedures were often informal, if not vague, and the judge, with the assistance of the probation officer, was given broad powers over young persons. Platt argues:

> Granted the benign motives of the child savers, the programs they enthusiastically supported diminished the civil liberties and privacy of youth. Adolescents were treated as though they were naturally dependent, requiring constant and pervasive supervision. Although the child savers were rhetorically concerned with protecting children from the physical and moral dangers of an increasingly industrialized and urban society, their remedies seemed to aggravate the problem. (1974: 4).

The increasing concern about the operation of the juvenile court is reflected in the *Gault* decision (details in Chapter 5), a 1967 case in which the U.S. Supreme Court ruled in favor of basic due process rights for persons adjudicated in juvenile court.

PROCEDURES IN THE JUVENILE COURT

The legal age of a juvenile varies from state to state from 15 to 18 years of age. The *parens patriae* philosophy is apparent in most jurisdictions where a juvenile is not routinely fingerprinted or photographed by the police, and a juvenile's name is not usually printed in the newspapers. The juvenile court is often closed to the public, and its records are kept confidential. In many states, there are provisions for having a juvenile record sealed—not subject to examination except by special court order, and in some jurisdictions expunged (Figure 3.2). Until 1992, the Federal Bureau of Investigation (FBI) collected records only of juveniles tried as adults. In that year, however, new regulations gave the FBI's National Crime Information Center (NCIC) authority to receive juvenile court information. Although states do not have to submit juvenile court records to the FBI, the NCIC can instantly transmit to law enforcement agencies and within days to some employers juvenile court records formerly kept confidential.

The juvenile court typically handles four types of cases:

1. *Delinquency*: behavior that, if engaged in by an adult, would constitute a crime
2. *Status offense*: behavior that, if engaged in by an adult, would not constitute a crime but (in accord with *parens patriae*) provides the basis for governmental intervention: for example, demonstrating chronic truancy, being beyond the control of parents or guardians, or running away
3. *Neglect or abuse*: children who are subjected to neglect or abuse by parents or guardians
4. *Dependency*: children who do not have parents or guardians available to provide proper care

As part of status offense, or separately under a special *addicted* category, juveniles may be subjected to juvenile court jurisdiction as a result of addiction to alcohol or drugs.

Instances of delinquency, status offense, neglect or abuse, or dependency that come to the attention of the authorities are often handled in a manner that does not involve the formal justice apparatus. School officials or the police, for example, may refer such cases directly to public or private social welfare or child protective agencies (Figure 3.3). Alternatively, the police may make a *station adjustment*, so that the child is allowed to return home with parents or guardians without further action. Those situations that come to the attention of the juvenile court enter by way of the intake section, which is usually staffed by (juvenile) probation officers.

STATE OF KANSAS
COURT SERVICES
INFORMATION PERTAINING TO
EXPUNGEMENT OF JUVENILE RECORDS
K. S. A. 38-1610

Any records or files specified in this code concerning a juvenile offender may be expunged upon application to a judge of the court of the county in which the records or files are maintained. The application for expungement may be made by the person who is the juvenile offender or, if a minor, by the person's parent or next friend.

There shall be no expungement of records or files concerning acts committed by a juvenile which, if committed by an adult would constitute: (1) indecent liberties with a child, (2) aggravated indecent liberties with a child, (3) aggravated criminal sodomy, (4) enticement of a child, (5) indecent solicitation of a child, (6) aggravated indecent solicitation of a child, (7) sexual exploitation of a child, (8) aggravated incest, (9) endangering a child, or (10) abuse of a child, or acts which would constitute an attempt to commit a violation of any of the offenses specified in this paragraph.

After a hearing, the court shall order the expungement of the records and files if the court finds that: (A) the person has reached 21 years of age or that two years have elapsed since the final discharge of the person; (B) since the final discharge of the person, the person has not been convicted of a felony or of a misdemeanor other than a traffic offense or adjudicated a delinquent or miscreant under the Kansas juvenile code or a juvenile offender under the Kansas juvenile offenders code and no proceedings are pending seeking such a conviction or adjudication; and (C) the circumstances and behavior of the petitioner warrant expungement.

Upon entry of an order expunging records or files, the offense shall be treated as if it never occurred, except that the offense may be considered if: (1) the petitioner is a person 16 years of age or over who is charged with a felony or with more than one offense of which one or more is a felony after having been adjudicated in two separate prior juvenile proceedings as having committed an act which would constitute a felony if committed by an adult and the adjudications occurred prior to the date of the commission of the new act charged, (2) upon conviction of a crime or adjudication in a subsequent action under this code the offense may be considered in determining the sentence to be imposed or disposition to be made.

The expungement of a felony adjudication does not relieve a person of complying with any state or federal law relating to the use or possession of firearms.

I have been provided a copy of the above juvenile offenders code.

Consult your attorney for any questions regarding expungement of juvenile records.

_____
Offender

_____
Court Services Officer

_____
Date

FIGURE 3.2   Expungement of Juvenile Records (Kansas).

INTAKE

Children are referred to the juvenile court by the police, parents, school officials, or other public or private agency personnel. In some jurisdictions, all cases are received by a probation officer (PO) assigned to the intake or complaint unit. In others, cases that involve criminal complaints are first sent to the prosecutor's office. Intake in the juvenile court is unique; it permits the court to screen cases not only on jurisdictional and legal grounds, but on social dimensions as well. The PO interviews the presenting agent, the young person, and the child's par-

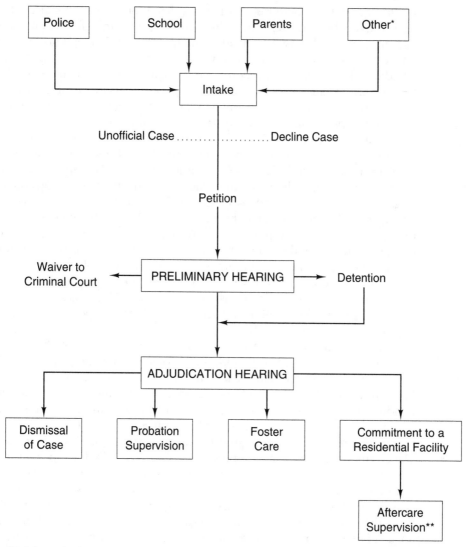

FIGURE 3.3   Juvenile court process.

ents or guardians. The officer then reviews court files for previous records concerning the child and, if the case involves a serious crime or child abuse and has not already been screened by the prosecutor, consults with that office. At this stage, the probation officer has a dual function: legal and social service.

The *legal function* requires that the PO determine if the juvenile court has jurisdiction and also requires that the child and parents be advised of the right to counsel and the right to remain silent during the intake conference. H. Ted

Rubin argues that "defense attorney participation at a[n intake] conference is rare, waivers of rights tend to finessed, and the norm is for parents to encourage the child to discuss his or her participation in the alleged offense with the intake officer" (1980: 304). In many states, fewer than one-half of the juveniles adjudicated as delinquent receive the assistance of legal counsel (Feld, 1988). When defense attorneys are present in juvenile court, tension is inherent in their responsibilities to the client: "a choice between the traditional adversary role (or the procedural model that regulates professional behavior in the criminal court) and the historic treatment or rehabilitative concerns of the family [juvenile] court" (Fabricant, 1983: 41). Barry Feld reports that even when juveniles are represented by counsel, "attorneys may not be capable of or committed to representing their juvenile clients in an effective adversarial manner. Organizational pressures to cooperate, judicial hostility toward adversarial litigants, role ambiguity created by the dual goals of rehabilitation and punishment, reluctance to help juveniles 'beat a case,' or an internalization of a court's treatment philosophy may compromise the role of counsel in juvenile court" (1988: 395). Indeed, he notes that the presence of counsel may actually be disadvantageous to the juvenile—those represented by attorneys tending to receive more severe dispositions. Nevertheless, Feld, a law professor, advocates legislation that mandates counsel and does not permit a waiver of this important constitutional right.

The *social service function* involves an assessment of the child's situation—home, school, physical, and psychological—and can provide the basis for *adjusting* the case, handling it informally without the filing of a petition. This happens in about one-half of the cases reaching the juvenile court, when the situation is not serious, when the matter can best be handled by the family, and when neither the child nor the public is in any danger (Zawitz, 1988). If the young person and parents agree to informal processing, the juvenile can be placed under supervision of a probation officer, usually for a period of 90 days (Figure 3.4). Although this may save the young person and his or her parents from the trauma of court action, unofficial handling has its critics. Informal processing requires an explicit or tacit admission of guilt. The substantial advantages that accrue from this admission (the avoidance of court action) also act as an incentive to confess. This approach casts doubt on the voluntariness and truthfulness of admissions of guilt.

JUVENILE INTAKE IN GRANT COUNTY (MARION), INDIANA

Most cases received by the probation department are referred by school officials and law enforcement officers after receiving and investigating complaints from private citizens. Referring agents complete an intake information form and on receipt, the probation department orders the child and his or her parent(s)/guardian(s) to report to the probation department for a preliminary inquiry.

The preliminary inquiry is conducted by the intake PO for the purpose of determining whether the child committed a delinquent act and the interests of society or the child require further action. The PO advises the child and parents of the nature of the inquiry, the alleged offense, and their constitutional rights. If the child and parents choose to discuss the alleged offense, and if there is a determination of delinquency, the PO recommends to the court and to the prosecutor's office either that a formal petition alleging delinquency be filed or that the matter be adjusted informally.

If the PO decides during the preliminary inquiry that an informal adjustment should be entered into, parent(s) and child must complete a preliminary investigation form that provides information about the child and the child's family: offense, education, siblings, employment, hobbies, and recreation. An agreement is negotiated, and the child and parent(s) sign an informal agreement form describing the disposition agreed on and the terms of that disposition—for example, driver's license restriction, curfew, sessions with a PO, or referral to a community treatment—drug or alcohol—program or for psychological treatment. An informal adjustment agreement cannot extend beyond six months. If at the end of that time the terms have not been followed, or if the child commits another offense, the original charges can be filed with the court as a petition. Should the PO recommend a petition instead of an informal adjustment, the prosecutor will file same with the court alleging delinquency.

The period of informal probation can be a crucial time in the life of a young person. If successful, the youngster may avoid further juvenile court processing; if unsuccessful, the child will face the labyrinth that is the juvenile court process and the serious consequences that can result. No one is more aware of this than the probation officer who, using all the skills and resources at the officer's command, attempts to assist the youngster and the youngster's parent(s) through the crisis. Counseling, group therapy, tutoring, vocational guidance, psychiatric and psychological treatment, and recreational services, if they are available, will be put to use to help the young person. If informal efforts are unsuccessful, the PO can file a petition that will make the case an official one. The filing of a petition is made through the prosecutor or directly via the clerk of the court, who sets a date for the first of three types of juvenile court hearing.

FIGURE 3.4   Informal probation agreement.

IN THE EIGHTH JUDICIAL DISTRICT COURT OF THE STATE OF NEVADA
IN AND FOR THE
COUNTY OF CLARK JUVENILE DIVISION

INFORMAL SUPERVISION AGREEMENT
In the matter of Michael Nelson
DATE OF BIRTH: July 12, 1980
COMPLAINT: School Vandalism
    The minor admits the alleged offense as stated above.

The minor understands that an Informal Supervision period is an attempt by Clark County Juvenile Court Services, the minor, and his parents to resolve the alleged problems without formal judicial action.

The minor does hereby waive the right to a speedy trial and understands that he has the right to legal counsel and the right to remain silent throughout these proceedings and hereby waives these rights.

The minor understands that any information obtained during the supervision period will be admissible in evidence at any adjudicatory hearing and that the minor may withdraw from the Informal Supervision process at any time and demand an adjudicatory hearing.

The minor understands that the Clark County Juvenile Court Services or the District Attorney reserves the right to proceed on any petition heretofore filed against the undersigned and/or to proceed on other petitions for any new offense and may proceed to seek an adjudication on the pending matter in the event the minor fails to cooperate in the attempt at adjustment.

The minor and his parents further understand that the terms of this Informal Supervision Agreement are as follows:

1. That the minor will report in person to Probation Officer John Kerwin at the Clark County Juvenile Court Services, 3401 East Bonanza Road, Las Vegas, Nevada every Monday, on a weekly basis, until May 30, 1994.

2. That the minor will obey all laws of the city, county, state, and federal governments.

3. That the minor will attend school, unless legally excused, and make every effort to maintain good conduct and an acceptable scholastic record.

4. That the minor will obey the reasonable and proper orders of his parents.

5. That the parents agree to make restitution for the damage caused by the minor to school property.

We agree to the terms and conditions of this Informal Supervision Agreement and waive the rights as stated above.

Signed *Doris Nelson*   Date_____
    (Parent)

Signed *Kevin Nelson*   Date_____
    (Parent)

Signed **Michael Nelson**   Date_____
    (Minor)

ORDER

Good cause appearing, therefore, the minor is placed under Supervision for a period of 90 days, reviewable (if a petition was filed) on the 30th Day of May, 1994 at the hour of 10:00 A.M.
    Dated this February 28, 1994

Michael Harrison
(Judge or Referee)

FIGURE 3.4   (continued)

Preliminary Hearing

Preliminary hearings consider those matters that must be dealt with before the case can proceed further. At the first hearing, the judge (or in some jurisdictions a referee) informs the parties involved of the charges in the petition and of their rights in the proceeding. If the case involves an abused, neglected, or dependent child, a *guardian ad litem* is usually appointed to act as an advocate for the child. Depending on the jurisdiction, this person may be an attorney or trained lay advocate and is often a volunteer. If appropriate, the hearing may be used to determine whether an alleged delinquent should remain in detention or shelter. If the judge determines, usually with the help of the probation officer, that the respondent's behavior makes him or her a danger to himself or herself or to the safety of others, or that he or she will probably not return to court voluntarily, the judge can order that the child remain in or be remanded to custody.

Kent County (Grand Rapids), Michigan, Juvenile Detention

The facility, which was opened in 1963, provides secure custodial care for a maximum of 45 youngsters, 12 to 16 years of age, in three living units: two for boys and one coeducational. Forty-seven staff members are responsible for programmed activities in which the emphasis is on group living through a behavioral management program. A token economy (discussed in Chapter 9) is used, permitting residents to earn points for engaging in positive behavior. These points are necessary for the youth to participate in various recreational activities and to purchase special snacks. Detention facility activities are designed to provide the staff with opportunities to understand the youngsters better and, at the same time, offer outlets for active, healthy adolescents who are living under controlled conditions.

Individualized instruction is provided at each resident's actual functioning level, and volunteer tutors are available for additional help in reading and math. Students earn credits toward a diploma, and these are transferred to an appropriate school program when the resident leaves the facility. Daily use is made of the gymnasium and outdoor athletic fields. In addition, teams from other local juvenile facilities are invited to compete at the facility in various athletic events. Many college, civic, and other community groups provide special activities and seasonal parties for the residents. A day room within each living unit provides an area for a variety of leisure-time activities, such as ping-pong and other table games, and television. A video cassette recorder is used for educational and entertaining movies. Adjoining the day rooms are quiet rooms that provide private space for letter writing and reading. A shop stocked with snacks, games, cards, and magazines provides an opportunity for youngsters to spend some of the points they have earned for good behavior. A separate game room with unique activities is also available on a privilege basis. Medical, dental, psychological, and religious services are available for each resident.

Detention facilities for juveniles have generally been inadequate. In some jurisdictions, they are merely separate sections of an adult jail. Federal statutes require that states receiving funds under the 1974 Juvenile Justice and Delinquency Prevention Act eliminate the jailing of juveniles by 1988; in that year, 22 of 52 states and territories receiving the funds were notified that they were not in compliance with this mandate (Schwartz, Harris, and Levi, 1988). Meda Chesney-Lind (1988) found that girls are often detained in jails for shoplifting and running away from home. California outlawed the practice of jailing of juveniles in 1986, and Utah makes the practice a misdemeanor. In New York City, the primary detention facility for juveniles, Spoffard, has been plagued with violence and other problems characteristic of adult jails. The Cook (Chicago) County Juvenile Temporary Detention center (Audy Home) has been beset with problems including the assault and gang rape of residents. This overcrowded facility houses youngsters 10 to 17 years of age.

IN-HOME DETENTION

In Dauphin County (Harrisburg), Pennsylvania, the Juvenile Probation Department uses *in-home detention*, which provides supervision for juveniles who otherwise would be held in a detention facility. The program has two probation officers who share a caseload that does not exceed 14 youngsters. The clients are visited once or twice a day at home, school, or place of employment. A rigidly enforced curfew is set in cooperation with the youngster's parents. In-home detention is limited to 60 continuous days.

Candidates for the program are referred by the juvenile intake probation officer or juvenile "line" probation officer for juveniles who are awaiting a disposition based on allegations of delinquency. If the In-Home Detention Unit has already screened the case, admittance occurs immediately after the detention hearing. Otherwise, admission occurs at the earliest possible time after a   determination to accept. The criteria for a referral to the program include:

1. *Age.* The youngster must be between 10 and 17 years of age.
2. *Home.* The juvenile must have a home, real or surrogate, in which he or she may be placed, and its location must not offer a geographic impediment to daily supervision.
3. *Parents.* The youngster's parents, at the very least, must not be resistive to daily supervision of their child.
4. *Client.* The juvenile must not present a distinct, serious threat to the community and must exhibit a cooperative attitude concerning the basic elements of the program, including

    a. Daily contacts by a probation officer

    b. Daily school attendance/employment

    c. A curfew

    d. Compliance with other individualized guidelines as set forth by the PO

Youngsters who become involved in delinquent activity, persistent evasion of supervision, or exhibit persistent uncooperative and belligerent behavior may be removed from the program by probation administrators. A youngster is terminated from the program when the court makes a disposition of the case. The day before a juvenile in the program is scheduled to appear in court, a written report on his or her attitude and adjustment while in the program is given to the judge, district attorney, and defense counsel. This report can influence the court's disposition.

In Cuyahoga County (Cleveland), Ohio, the Home Detention Project has been in existence since 1981 and was established as an alternative to the "warehousing" of juveniles in the detention center. Youngsters referred to the juvenile court as delinquents or status offenders may be assigned to the program at intake, or at any time before disposition. To provide the program's staff with the legal authority to send a youth to the detention home if his or her behavior subsequently requires it, each juvenile is technically admitted to the detention center. Afterward, youngsters and their parents or guardians meet with the program supervisor to discuss and sign a contract delineating the rules of home arrest, a violation of which can cause a referral to the detention center.

In-home detention usually lasts 17 days, and each youth is assigned to a caseworker who ensures that all court dates are met. The caseworker also works to keep the youngster out of any further trouble by counseling and spending time with him or her, having lunch together, attending sports events, and similar activities. Every day, unscheduled face-to-face contacts with the youth occur, and the caseworker also contacts the parents daily. The caseworker maintains a log that documents compliance (or lack of it) with the program requirements. Teachers are asked to complete a daily school report form that verifies attendance and behavior. Before the court hearing, the caseworker provides the judge/referee with a report summarizing the youngster's history in the program (Ball, Huff, and Lilly, 1988).

Dependent, neglected, or abused children and status offenders may be placed in foster care or a residential shelter. Under such circumstances, the judge will often appoint a temporary guardian for the child, a *guardian ad litem*, usually a representative of a child welfare agency, but sometimes a relative or friend of the family or lay volunteer.[1] The judge may also issue an order of protection containing specific restrictions on a potential abuser or assailant, a violation of which allows the penalties for contempt of court—summary imprisonment. Noting that most state prison inmates in California were physically or sexually abused as children, and, furthermore, that most adult offenders at one time passed through the juvenile justice system, the Santa Clara County Probation Department screens each juvenile at intake to find out if they are or were the victims of physical or sexual abuse.

[1]The national Court Appointed Special Advocate (CASA) program originated in Seattle in 1977 and now has more than 30,000 volunteers nationwide. The CASA volunteer is trained and appointed to act as a *guardian ad litem* and thereby speak in juvenile court on behalf of children who are victims of abuse or neglect.

ADJUDICATORY HEARING

The adjudicatory hearing—"trial"—is for the purpose of deciding ("adjudge") whether the child should be made a ward of the juvenile court because he or she is delinquent, a status offender, abused, neglected, or dependent. If appropriate, the child (respondent) makes a plea, either an admission or denial of the allegations contained in the petition. The plea process has been the subject of criticism because "much of the country either has not addressed it at all or has not fully developed standards regarding the guilty plea process in juvenile court" (Sanborn, 1992: 142). Thus, pleas are being rendered by juveniles who are either incapable of fully understanding the process or to whom the process has not been adequately explained, bringing into question intelligence, voluntariness, and accuracy. This is particularly troubling in view of the move toward a more punitive response in juvenile court (discussed later in this chapter).

If a denial is made, evidence must be presented to prove "beyond a reasonable doubt" that a delinquent act occurred or, in the case of a status offender, with a simple "preponderance of evidence" that the child is in need of court supervision. If the allegations are sustained, the judge makes a *finding of fact* (that the child is delinquent, abused, neglected, or otherwise in need of supervision), sets a date for a dispositional hearing, and orders a social investigation or predisposition report.

PREDISPOSITION REPORT

The goal of the juvenile court is to provide services. To do so on the basis of the best available information, the judge orders a predispositional investigation. The probation officer who conducts the investigation will present his or her findings in a report that includes the sociocultural and psychodynamic factors that influenced the juvenile's behavior, providing a social history that is used by the judge to determine a disposition for the case. Because the judge's decision will often be influenced by the contents of the report, it must be factual and objective—a professional statement about the child's family, social and educational history, and any previous involvement with public or private agencies. It also indicates the physical and mental health of the child, as reported by a court psychologist or psychiatrist. The report will typically include the following:

1. Review of court records
2. Review of school records
3. Review of police records
4. Interviews with the respondent
5. Interviews with family members
6. Interviews with teachers and school officials
7. Interviews with employers, youth workers, and clergy whenever deemed appropriate

The Juvenile Division of the Circuit Court
The City of St. Louis
Presiding Judge: Honourable Gary M. Gaertner

In the interest of: *Date of Report:*
   Timothy Wells   June 17, 1994

Birthdate: Case No.: 50550
   July 22, 1980 (verified)
                                Juvenile Officer:
                                   William Russell

Previous Police and / or Court History

5-26-92 Unauthorized Use of Fire Hydrant. Worker Russell. Timothy Wells was taken into custody at 12:30 P.M. at 3124 Hoffman on 5-18-92 by Officer Purcell. The arrest occurred after the officer observed Timothy with a fire hydrant wrench in his hand, turning on the fire hydrant at 3124 Hoffman. The officer turned off the above hydrant and the one on the next corner east at Lake and 15th Avenues. Case serviced and closed on 7-29-92.

5-10-94 Trespassing and Peace Disturbance. Worker Russell. Timothy Wells was taken into custody at his home, 3201 Octavia, at 8:30 A.M., on 4-17-94 by Officers Moore and Keller. The arrest occurred following a complaint filed on 4-15-94 by Bruce Kelly, Assistant Principal at Hawthorne School. Mr. Kelly reported that an ex-student at Hawthorne, Timothy Wells, came into the school yard and created a disturbance. When asked to leave, Timothy used profanity and threatened Mr. Kelly with bodily harm. Insufficient evidence, warrant refused; case referred to probation department for informal adjustment. The worker closed the case of 5-12-94 by referring the family to the St. Louis Speech and Hearing Center.

5-24-94 Common Assault. Worker Russell. Timothy Wells was taken into custody at 3038 Douglass at 6:45 P.M., on 5-21-94 by Officers Flynn and Burger. The arrest occurred following a complaint by one John Bullen of 3827 Broadway (on official court supervision on a suspended commitment to MSTS). Bullen reported that he was struck on the head with a baseball bat by Timothy Wells during a fight with Timothy and his brothers, Earl and William, and a sister Dolores.

Following an investigation, Timothy Wells, Earl Wells, and John Bullen were all conveyed to the Juvenile Court and booked for common assault. All warrants were refused for insufficient evidence, and the matter was referred to the probation department for an informal adjustment. The case was closed on 5-27-94 after enrolling Timothy (Earl and William) in the Work Restitution program for four weeks and referring Timothy to the St. Louis Speech and Hearing Center. On the following day, the worker learned of the petition for the present offense.

FIGURE 3.5   Sample socal investigation report.

Reason for Hearing

On 5-10-94, Timothy allegedly attempted to steal three pairs of sunglasses from the Kresge's Store, 7800 Kingston Road in St. Louis, Missouri.

Timothy has remained in the home since the alleged offense on 5-10-94. He has since received one subsequent referral for common assault. He has also been present and worked well on three Saturday mornings of the Work Program for Probationers.

Collateral Contacts

Informants. The child's parents, Florence and Marvin Wells, were interviewed in their home on 6-5-94. Numerous other contacts have been made with them since two other children, Earl and William, were assigned to the supervision of this worker on 2-20-94. Both parents seem interested and have been cooperative with this court representative.

Contacts with Other Agencies

St. Louis Speech and Hearing Center. The Center was contacted by telephone on 6-8-94 to verify Timothy's appointment for a hearing evaluation. Timothy has such an appointment scheduled for 2:30 on 6-26-94. The Center is capable of providing diagnostic and treatment services for an apparent hearing and speech disorder.

Family History

Home. Timothy resides with both parents, four sisters, two brothers, and a nephew at 3201 Octavia. The residence is a one-story brick home which includes three bedrooms, living room, kitchen, and an ample basement which has been partially converted for additional living quarters for Timothy, Earl, and William. A home visit made on 6-5-94 revealed that the residence is nicely furnished and was neat and orderly. Mr. and Mrs. Wells are purchasing the residence and make monthly installment payments of $912.00. The family moved to their present location in 1984.

Father. Marvin Wells was born in St. Louis on 12-1-54. He was the youngest of eight children. Mr. Wells reports that he finished high school and two years of business college before beginning employment as a machinist at Weiss Welding Works. He was employed there between 1978 and 1989. With the promise of a higher salary, he worked for the Kramer Tool Co., from 1989 to 1992 but returned to his former employer. He currently works from 3:30 P.M. to midnight Monday through Friday and grosses approximately $2,700 per month.

Mother. Florence Wells was born in St. Louis on 2-21-56. She was the fourth of eight children. She reports that she has completed high school and began work about three years ago when her youngest child, Christine, started school. Mrs. Wells has been working as a nurse's aid at the Laurel Heights Nursing Home. She works from 6:30 A.M. to 3:00 P.M. Sunday through Friday and earns approximately $1,600 per month. Mrs. Wells has stated that she has been suffering from hypertension for the past sixteen years.

Parents' Attitude. Marvin and Florence Wells blame Timothy for the present offense. He has admitted that he tried to steal the sunglasses. His parents feel that they are capable of discipline supervision and care for Timothy but they also admit that he has problems for which they need assistance. They feel that Timothy is angry and depressed because of an apparent hearing handicap. They are willing to seek help with this problem.

FIGURE 3.5 *(continued)*

Other Family Information

The other children are Andrea (BD: 9-2-75), Alicia (BD: 12-11-77), Dolores (BD: 1-14-78), Earl (BD: 8-15-80), William (BD: 12-1-83), and Christine (BD: 5-16-88). Dolores, Earl, and William are also known to the Court. Dolores received a referral on 9-6-93 for peace disturbance and loitering (a group demonstration at Westside High School), serviced and closed on 1-27-94. Dolores is a student at Westside High School, and has a preschool-age son, Michael, who also lives with the family. Earl has three referrals and William has one referral. At a hearing held on 1-21-94, Earl and William were found to have committed a common assault and were both placed on official court supervision on a suspended commitment to Missouri Hills. They have been cooperative in keeping weekly appointments with the worker and following my instructions. There seem to be no special problems between Timothy and his siblings. However Timothy is most argumentative with William.

Personal History

Early Development. Timothy was a full-term baby born without complications. Mrs. Wells stated that Timothy was unusually prone to illness in his childhood. He seemed to catch everything. She went so far as to state that the family moved to their present home in 1982 because the family physician recommended gas heat for Timothy over the coal-burning furnace, which they had in their last residence.

Health. Timothy is a black male who is 5 feet 4 inches tall and weighs 150 pounds. He is of medium complexion with brown eyes and black hair. Mrs. Wells reports that Timothy gets sick when he becomes overly excited.

Timothy has an apparent hearing and speech disorder. The problem reportedly was initially diagnosed by the school doctor at Northridge School who stated that Timothy would be totally deaf in his left ear by 17 years of age.

School. No direct school contact can be made during the summer vacation. However, Mr. and Mrs. Wells stated that Timothy was suspended from Hawthorne School in 1993 for behavior problems. He began school at Northridge School in September 1993 and continued there until around January 1994. Mrs. Wells reported that Timothy enjoyed school there and did well because he liked his teacher, Sister Frances. However when Sister Frances left the school, Timothy's school problems resumed. Mrs. Wells stated that she then stopped sending Timothy to the school because they could no longer afford it. She attempted to enroll Timothy in the public schools but could not make the arrangements. Thus Timothy did not attend any school for the second semester of the past school year.

Employment. None.

Leisure-Time Activities. Timothy enjoys boxing, basketball, and football. However, his parents won't permit him to participate because of health reasons. Timothy and his parents report that he has no close friends.

Religion. Timothy is Baptist but is inactive in church.

General Personality. When asked, Timothy said he didn't think about himself. He said he has no problems and gets along with people. However, he also said that he has no friends, nor does he need them.

FIGURE 3.5 (*continued*)

Child's Attitude. Timothy admits and accepts responsibility for his behavior. He stated that he doesn't know why he tried to steal the sunglasses. He said he had $6 in his pocket at the time. Timothy has a very negative attitude. He appears sullen and angry and his verbal responses are generally short and gruff, especially if you must ask him to repeat himself. He also has a short temper.

Psychological or Psychiatric Evaluation

Timothy was given a psychological evaluation on 7-12-93 by the Rev. Raymond A. Hampe, Ph.D., associate director, Department of Special Education, Archdiocese of St. Louis. A battery of three tests was administered. Timothy was referred by Malcolm Bliss Health Center for placement in special class because of behavior problems at school (Hawthorne).

Timothy was seen as functioning in the borderline to slow range of mental ability with probable higher potential which is unavailable due to emotional factors and major weakness in his grasp of language concepts. "Timothy is an immature, willful, anxious, sensitive boy who has strong achievement motivation and desires to be accepted. He does not see himself as being successful and accepted and therefore is greatly frustrated." Timothy projected hostility toward the examiner but cooperated. No obvious sensory or motor impairments were noted.

In summary, Timothy was seen as being anxious for success but expecting failure. Recommendations were for the parents to offer additional responsibilities and privileges marked by confidence in his ability to succeed. A special school placement was offered to eliminate the normal school's constant source of negative self-evaluation.

Summary and Evaluation

This is the matter of Timothy Wells, who will be fourteen years old on 7-22-94. Timothy is before the court for stealing three pairs of sunglasses from the Kresge's Store in St. Louis, Missouri, on 5-10-94. He admits doing so but offers no explanation. Timothy has a total of four referrals to the court, three of which occurred in May of this year.

Timothy's home situation is satisfactory. The parents are responsible working people who are purchasing a home. They express interest in their children and have demonstrated cooperation with this worker in connection with Earl and William, who are currently under supervision. The parents acknowledge that Timothy is a "problem child," and Mrs. Wells brought Timothy to my attention even before he officially came to the attention of the court.

Timothy is seen as an angry and frustrated youth. He has a low tolerance for frustration and a short temper which displays it. Timothy is sensitive to failure and has come to expect it of himself. He professes no problems which require correction but seems incapable of following advice and instructions.

Timothy apparently has some form of hearing and speech disorder. Mrs. Wells feels that his hearing is poor and speculates that Timothy has learned to compensate somewhat by learning to read lips. His speech is characterized by brief, to-the-point statements, which are rather unclear. Timothy is scheduled for a thorough hearing evaluation on 6-26-94.

Timothy is seen as an appropriate candidate for rehabilitation within the community. His three referrals in May 1994 seem to indicate that his need to act out has reached a peak level. Although angry and frustrated at the world around him, Timothy's referrals are not of a serious nature. He is therefore not regarded as a serious threat to persons or property although his unstable emotional characteristics might

FIGURE 3.5 (*continued*)

indicate some further form of striking back. However, a strong incentive can be offered to curb recidivism.

The plan for Timothy involves a thorough hearing and speech evaluation and follow-up on recommendations made for therapy. Timothy should also undergo psychiatric therapy, most realistically at the Child Guidance Center. Further, Timothy should be enrolled in a special school setting where teaching is individualized and tutorial in nature and where the program is stimulating and rewarding for appropriate behavior. Such programs are offered at Providence School and Project Door. No firm recommendation can be made in regard to a specific school, as the referral procedure is still under way. Furthermore, Timothy should have a regular weekly appointment with his Deputy Juvenile Officer for further counseling and to coordinate plans.

Alternative Plans

Placement in either a community group home or at Missouri Hills. Placement outside the home has been ruled out because Timothy's problems do not include poor parental supervision. Rather, his problem involves insecurity, which can best be treated in his home.

Restitution

The Victim Assistance Program report states that there was no loss suffered by the Kresge's Store, as the three pairs of sunglasses involved were recovered. Furthermore, Timothy has worked well the past three Saturdays in the Work Program for Probationers. He has one more Saturday left in the original enrollment from the informal adjustment, so it is felt that he has made ample service restitution to the community.

Plan

It is therefore recommended that Timothy Wells be committed to the Division of Children's Services for placement at Missouri Hills. Further that the commitment be held in abeyance and said minor remain in the home of his parents on Official Court Supervision and subject to the following special rules. That said minor cooperate in prescribed hearing and speech therapy. To cooperate in prescribed psychiatric therapy. To keep a weekly appointment with the Deputy Juvenile Officer through September 1994. And further that the Deputy Juvenile Officer investigate an appropriate school setting for said minor for the fall term of 1994.

Respectfully submitted,

William Russell
_____
William Russell
Deputy Juvenile Officer

Approved by:

Susan Davidson
_____
Susan Davidson
Supervisor

FIGURE 3.5 (*continued*)

8. Interviews with complainant, police officer, or witnesses
9. Results of any psychological or psychiatric examinations
10. Recommendation, which should include the treatment alternatives available in the case

Probation officers must present their findings with supportive statements as to the actual situation found in the investigation. Other than a recommendation, suppositions or opinions are to be avoided. Sometimes the recommendation of the PO is not included in the report but is transmitted orally to the judge. The completed report should enable the judge to make the best disposition available based on the individual merits of the case and the service *needs* of the young person (Figure 3.5). One problem encountered at the disposition stage is the paucity of available alternatives for helping a youngster. This can be exacerbated by an (inexperienced) probation officer who recommends treatment that is simply not available. A youngster will often be placed on probation because of a lack of feasible alternatives.

DISPOSITION HEARING

William Price and his mother sat uneasily before the judge. The allegations of the amended petition had been sustained on the basis of a full admission. The judge was looking through the probation officer's report for information on which to base his disposition. His eye was drawn to the psychologist's report attached to the court report. The courtroom was silent, all eyes on the judge.

In the report William was described as "fairly handsome" and "athletically built." The judge glanced up and looked directly at the boy. William turned his eyes away. The judge decided that the boy might be called handsome despite his "waterfall" haircut and a slight case of acne, but he was certainly not sufficiently robust to be dubbed "athletic."

The psychologist's report indicated that William might or might not be aggressive to girls in the future. "That's not much help," the judge thought, "it could apply to most young men. Chances are the boy feels worse about the situation than the girl. At least he *looks* remorseful."

"William, do you realize you could have seriously injured that girl?"

"I didn't mean to hurt her. I thought it was what she wanted."

"That was a dangerous supposition, young man. I hope you realize by now that any use of violence in any circumstances can have the most serious consequences. Society doesn't regard such things lightly."

"Yes, sir."

"Besides the offense with the girl, you also ran away from the officer who was trying to arrest you."

"I'm sorry about that. I guess I lost my head."

"Are you in the habit of losing your head?"

"No, sir. I just wasn't thinking."

"William," the judge said sternly, "I have serious doubts about allowing you to remain in the community. How do I know you won't lose your head again and really hurt someone the next time?"

"I promise, Judge. I won't do anything foolish again."

The judge turned to Mrs. Price and said sympathetically, "I know it has been very difficult for you to raise William by yourself. It would be a pity for all that effort to go to waste."

Tears welled up in Mrs. Price's eyes. "Yes, Your Honor. Please let William come home. I know he'll be good. And I've changed my job now so I can be with him more," she said in a trembling voice.

William's eyes were focused on his mother while she talked. The judge noted that concern for her was mirrored in his face.

"How has Bill been doing since he came home from Juvenile Hall, Mrs. Price?"

"Just like always, Judge. He's a good boy."

"William," the judge said, "what would you do with yourself if I allowed you to remain in your home?"

"Go to school."

"I see you are one year behind in your school grade. Do you plan to finish high school?"

"Yes, sir." William's face noticeably brightened.

"And then what do you plan to do?"

"I guess I'll go in the service."

The judge looked at the probation officer. "Mr. Clarke, I'm going to follow your recommendation and make William a ward of the court and place him on probation. If he stays out of trouble during the next year, I want him brought back to court so we can terminate his case. By my calculation he could be off probation about nine or ten months before he graduates. This should be long enough so that his record will not hinder him from entering the service."

The judge turned back to William. "I hope you've learned a lesson from this, son. You stay out of trouble and you should have a good opportunity to make something of yourself. The burden is on you. Don't spoil your chances for a career and for a decent life for yourself and your mother."

"Thank you, Judge," Mrs. Price said. "William is a good boy. I don't think he'll make any more trouble for anyone."

She and her son left the room, the boy with his arm around her shoulders.

Source: Lawrence E. Cohen, *New Directions in Processing of Juvenile Offenders: The Denver Model* (Washington D.C.: U.S. Government Printing Office, 1975).

DISPOSITION HEARING

Traditionally, the disposition stage of the juvenile court process has been based on the concept of *parens patriae*. Distinctions between dispositions were based on the *needs* of children and not necessarily the behavior that brought a case to the attention of the juvenile court; dispositions were based not on *justice* but on *rehabilitation*. Although the Supreme Court ruled that the juvenile court must adhere to due process, its *raison d'être* as a separate court continued to be as a vehicle for providing social services to children in need. In some jurisdictions, however, the line between the adult criminal court and the juvenile court has become blurred as the latter moves toward a *justice model*—what the youngster *deserves*—rather than a *social service model*—what the youngster *needs*. (The *justice model* for adults is discussed in Chapter 6.) The state of Washington provides an example of this trend.

The state of Washington abrogated the doctrine of *parens patriae* in 1977 and in its place adopted a new philosophy based on a *justice model* (Schram et al., 1981: 65):

- Make juvenile offenders accountable for their criminal behavior.

- Provide for punishment commensurate with age, crime, and criminal history. Nowhere is the rehabilitation of the juvenile offender mentioned as a purpose or intent [in the law].

As part of this approach the Washington Division of Juvenile Rehabilitation promulgated "Juvenile Disposition Sentencing Standards" to guide juvenile court judges in making uniform dispositions based not on the needs of the child but on the delinquent behavior—a classical approach. This, of course, reduces the role of the probation officer in juvenile court. Colorado, Idaho, and New York have mandatory minimum periods of incarceration for juveniles—a clear distortion of the purposes of the juvenile court. In Washington, and other states that have adopted a "hard line" on juvenile offenders, statutes enable reconsideration of severe sentences for a variety of mitigating circumstances, including "manifest injustice." In fact, write Patricia Harris and Lisa Graff (1988), the "hard line against juveniles" is often less than meets the eye: Few of the harsher statutory provisions are mandatory. The state of Washington also relinquished juvenile court jurisdiction over status offenders. Barry Feld (1992: 59) refers to jurisdictional modifications that have narrowed "the scope of juvenile courts at the 'hard' end through the removal of serious juvenile offenders and at the 'soft' end through the removal of noncriminal status offenders."

CONTRACTION OF JUVENILE COURT JURISDICTION

| *Serious juvenile offenders* ◀─────────────▶ *Status offenders* |
| (to criminal court) | (to private programs) |

STATUS OFFENDERS

As the juvenile court has moved closer to the adult criminal court in both the application of legal principles and use of punishment, there has been a corresponding shift away from exercising jurisdiction over status offenders. Official intervention by the legal system into the lives of children who have not been accused of criminal behavior—status offenders—has long been a center of controversy. Back in 1976 this writer argued:

The juvenile court's continued use of coercion and the stigma it creates are grounds for serious concern. The "bottom line" of juvenile court authority is the policeman, ready to use his revolver, club and handcuffs to carry out the court's orders. A society that considers preventive detention repulsive has, in some strange way, learned to tolerate the threat or the actual use of force against persons who have not been found guilty of a crime. (p. 458)

Those who support continued jurisdiction of the juvenile court over status offenders (sometimes referred to as "minors in need of supervision," MINS; "children in need of supervision," CHINS; or "persons in need of supervision," PINS) argue that status offenders are not essentially different from those youngsters committing delinquent acts—they are children in need of services; without the intervention of the juvenile court, these services would not be forthcoming. Opponents argue that juvenile court intervention does not help youngsters because the services are often inadequate, and intervention intensifies existing problems by stigmatizing children. In other words, a juvenile may not be able to discern the subtle differences between the juvenile court and the criminal court—differences that are becoming vague (as in the *justice model*). Thus, the child, as well as the child's parents, friends, and community, may react to juvenile court intervention as if the child were facing charges in criminal court.

Edwin Schur warns that the "labeling" that results can set in motion "a complex process of response and counter-response with an initial act of rule-violation and developing into elaborated delinquent self-conceptions and a full-fledged delinquent career" (1973: 30). However, one research effort found that "the majority of those whose first referral was a status offense did not become more serious delinquents. If anything, they became something considerably less than serious delinquents" (Sheldon, Horvath, and Tracy, 1989: 214). A study by Waln Brown and his colleagues (1991) contradicted the labeling argument: Youngsters adjudicated in juvenile court on their first referral were less likely to have criminal records as adults than those whose referrals were delayed until further misbehavior.

Status offense (MINS, CHINS, PINS) petitions are most often filed on behalf of the children's parents, ostensibly because the youngsters are beyond their control. The child's behavior often is merely a symptom of a wider problem. Children frequently become status offenders by running away from pathological family situations or alcoholic or abusing parents. Girls are often subjected to juvenile court for sexual behavior that goes unnoticed when committed by boys. Children who are found to be status offenders are usually warned or placed on probation in their initial encounter with the court. Probation can include placement in a shelter, group home, or foster care. If a youngster fails to cooperate with the treatment program, he or she can be returned to court for further disposition, which can lead to placement in a secure facility, such as a training school. The Juvenile Justice and Delinquency Prevention Act of 1974 requires the deinstitutionalization of status offenders. Harry Swanger reported that it sometimes required litigation to accomplish, but "by 1986 all states seemingly met this laudable goal." He notes, "slippage has occurred and researchers have documented wholesale replacement of juvenile court institutionalization of status offenders with 'voluntary' mental health commitments in some states" (1988: 211).

CHINS in Clark County (Las Vegas), Nevada

The most common status offenses involve those youngsters who are unmanageable, runaways, or truants. Clark County responds by using community-based shelter care, counseling, and a network of community resources.

CRISIS INTERVENTION

Families in need of immediate assistance may come to the Admissions/Intake Division at Juvenile Court, which operates on a 24-hour basis, and meet with an intake officer who is experienced in crisis management. The officer will conduct an intake interview to

- Evaluate and assess the family situation and needs
- Determine if alternative counseling or short-term emergency shelter care services are appropriate without further juvenile court intervention
- Determine, if applicable, what services may be directly provided by the juvenile court—for example, information/referral, extended evaluation, psychological consultation, or 90-day probation supervision

DIAGNOSTIC INTERVIEWS

The intake officer will consult with law enforcement and school officials and gather as much information as possible to assess thoroughly the family's situation. After completing the assessment, the officer develops a plan of action that requires continued parental involvement; the intent is to promote family unity. The officer will also explore parental rights and responsibilities regarding CHINS. Clark County Juvenile Services recognizes that CHINS' behaviors are difficult for everyone to deal with, and that at times parents become extremely frustrated with their children and look to the court for quick and easy solutions, which are not available. To help CHINS to grow up and behave better takes time, work, and patience. Court programs can be effective only if the parents and concerned others agree to address the problem.

COMMUNITY SERVICE REFERRALS

The community offers many excellent resources for families in need, and intake officers are aware of the various services of both public and private agencies. When a family's needs can best be met through a referral to one of them, such a plan of action is preferable. These agencies may divert CHINS from the court and into the most appropriate setting available within the community. Through such brokering, families may access the services they need.

EMERGENCY SHELTER CARE

Some children are temporarily out of control. When the parent-child relationship has deteriorated to a point at which temporary separation is necessary, the intake officer can arrange for the child to be placed in an emergency shelter care facility and refer the family to the probation division for continued supervision under a Family Services Agreement. The county has contracts with five emergency shelter care homes, and CHINS are referred to these facilities rather than being confined in the court's secure detention center for delinquents.

FAMILY SERVICES AGREEMENT

Some children continue to exhibit severer and more chronic CHINS behavior despite previous service attempts. For these CHINS, the probation department has an ongoing supervision program. The Family Services Agreement is an informal voluntary contract between the family and the juvenile court that spells out mutual responsibilities and service expectations. Basically, it provides for three months of supervision by a probation officer and outlines what can be expected of the child, parents, and the court. Participation in individual or family counseling is usually indicated, and if the child is temporarily removed from the home and placed in shelter care, the agreement specifies the conditions for length of stay, reunification efforts, and financial obligations. Children are expected to obey reasonable and proper orders of their parents, attend school regularly, and participate in a treatment plan tailored to their individual needs. The PO monitors these expectations, coordinates interagency efforts, and participates in direct counseling with the child.

MENTAL HEALTH SERVICES

Psychological screenings and referrals for psychiatric services can be made in those instances in which a severely emotionally disturbed child comes to the court's attention as a CHINS referral.

JUVENILES IN CRIMINAL COURT

At the other end of the juvenile justice spectrum are youngsters who can be tried as adults in criminal court (Figures 3.6 and 3.7); this action must be in accord with the *Breed* decision discussed in Chapter 4. About 25,000 juvenile cases a year are transferred to criminal court, with juvenile court judges accounting for about 12,000. Most, but not all, states require transfer hearings before a waiver of jurisdiction to adult/criminal court. Every jurisdiction in the United States has one or more methods for transferring juvenile cases to the adult criminal court; three basic mechanisms are available to accomplish this transfer:

1. *Statutory exclusion.* Statutory provisions exclude certain crimes from the jurisdiction of the juvenile court. Some states exclude only the most serious offenses against *persons*, such as murder, rape, or robbery with a firearm. In addition to the most serious crimes against persons, some states exclude traffic, boating, fish and game, and other minor violations, which typically do not involve incarceration. This approach is a purely classical one.

WAIVER OF JURISDICTION, MARYLAND

(a) The Juvenile Court may waive the exclusive jurisdiction conferred by state law with respect to a petition alleging delinquency for:

1. A child who is fifteen years old or older, or
2. A child who has not reached his/her fifteenth birthday, but who is charged with committing an act which if committed by an adult, would be punishable by death or life imprisonment.

(b) The court may not waive its jurisdiction until after it has conducted a waiver hearing, held prior to an adjudicatory hearing and after notice has been given to all parties as prescribed by the Maryland Rules. The waiver hearing is solely to determine whether the court should waive its jurisdiction.

(c) The court may not waive its jurisdiction unless it determines, based on the preponderance of the evidence presented at the hearing, that the child is an unfit subject for juvenile rehabilitative measures. For the purpose of determining whether to waive its jurisdiction, the court shall assume that the child committed the delinquent act alleged.

(d) In making its determination the court shall consider the following criteria individually and in relation to each other on the record:

1. Age of the child
2. Mental and physical condition of the child
3. The child's amenability to treatment in any institution, facility, or program available to delinquents
4. The nature of the offense and the child's alleged participation in it
5. The public safety

FIGURE 3.6 Juvenile court waiver to adult court.

2. *Judicial waiver.* Virtually all states permit juvenile court judges to "waive" (transfer) their jurisdiction over certain juvenile offenders, usually on a motion by the prosecutor. This discretion is limited by statutory criteria regarding such factors as age, type of offense, prior record, amenability to treatment, and dangerousness: "[L]egislative exclusion uses the seriousness of the offense to control decisions about adult status, whereas judicial waiver relies upon clinical assessments of amenability to treatment or dangerousness to decide child versus adult status" (Feld, 1992: 66).

3. *Prosecutorial discretion.* In a few states, prosecutors can charge juveniles in either juvenile or adult courts. This discretionary power may be limited by statutory criteria regarding age and type of offense.

THE CHANGING JUVENILE OFFENDER

In Massachusetts, the percentage of juvenile court cases resulting from offenses against persons increased from 1989 to 1993 by more than 200 percent. In Pima County (Tucson), Arizona, during the same period, the increase was 193 percent. In Texas, from 1980 to 1990, juvenile arrests for violent crimes increased more than 190 percent. In Washington, over the past six years, an increase of about 30 percent in the number of violent offenders in the state's juvenile institutions has occurred. The "proportion of violent crimes committed by juveniles is disproportionately high compared with their share of the U.S. population, and the number of these crimes is growing" (Snyder and Sickmund, 1995: iv).

The state of Florida, in a dramatic move toward a justice model, enacted legislation in 1981 that provides prosecutors with almost unlimited discretion—

FIGURE 3.7 Waiver of jurisdiction, Indiana.

STATE OF INDIANA
COUNTY OF GRANT JUVENILE DIVISION

IN THE MATTER OF
Michael Silver; DOB: 8/14/79
A CHILD ALLEGED TO BE DELINQUENT
PROSECUTOR'S MOTION FOR WAIVER OF JUVENILE JURISDICTION
The State of Indiana, by the undersigned Deputy Prosecuting Attorney, hereby alleges and represents to the Court as follows:

1. That said child, Michael Silver, was born on the 14th day of August in the year 1979, and was fourteen (14) years of age or older, and under eighteen (18) years of age, at the time of the charged offense.

2. That said child is subject to the jurisdiction of the Juvenile Court herein by virtue of a Petition Alleging Delinquency having been filed on the 4th day of March in the year 1994.

3. That the act charged would be an offense if committed by an adult, to wit: ATTEMPTED MURDER.

4. That said offense charged is:

   (x) heinous or of an aggravated character;

   (x) an act against person;

   (x) part of a repetitive pattern of offenses (even though less serious in nature) in that the child has heretofore been arrested and/or adjudicated for: UNLAWFUL POSSESSION OF A FIREARM.

5. That there is probable cause to believe that said child committed the offense charged herein, and that said child is beyond rehabilitation under the juvenile justice system, and that it is in the best interest of the safety and welfare of the community that said child be required to stand trial as an adult, and that a waiver of juvenile jurisdiction is sought under the provisions of I.C. 31-6-2-4(b).

WHEREFORE, your petitioner requests that a hearing be set by the Court to determine whether juvenile jurisdiction should be waived herein, and that after said hearing that the Court waive juvenile jurisdiction over the offense charged herein to the Criminal Court of Grant County, a Court that would have jurisdiction over the offense charged if that act were committed by an adult, and said waiver to be for the offense charged, and any lesser included offenses.
   Dated this 6th day of April, 1994.

John L. Jamisen
John L. Jamisen
Deputy Prosecuting Attorney

"when the public interest requires it"—to transfer 16 and 17 year olds to criminal court. A study of transfer practices in Florida revealed that the direct transfer provisions have seldom been used for the serious and chronic offenders for whom transfer is arguably justified. In fact, the study found that relatively few cases are subjected to the direct transfer provisions and that "many of those who are transferred seem inappropriate" (Bishop, Frazier, and Henretta, 1989: 195).

A youth tried in adult criminal court, depending on the state, may be sent to an institution operated by the same agency with responsibility for adults—a department of correction—or to a specialized agency that provides institutionalization for juveniles and young adults. For example, the Illinois Department of Corrections has a Juvenile Division that receives delinquents and juvenile offenders who have not reached their 21st birthday—at which time they may be transferred to an adult facility. In California, a judge has the option to sentence offenders 16 to 20 years of age to state prison but order them housed in a California Youth Authority (discussed subsequently in this chapter) facility until their 25th birthday or expiration of their sentence, whichever occurs first. Offenders under 16 years of age in New York are sent to a facility operated by the Division for Youth (discussed later in this chapter), whereas those who have reached their 16th birthday are sent to a reformatory operated by the Department of Correctional Services.

Both conventional wisdom and research in corrections have revealed that juvenile offenders in adult facilities present a significant management problem for institutional officials. A study by Marilyn McShane and Frank Williams, for example, found that compared with other young inmates, "imprisoned juvenile offenders exhibited significant adjustment problems in the institutional environment" (1989: 266).

Inger Sagatun, Loretta McCollum, and Michael Edwards (1985) report a lack of significant difference in sentence outcome for youngsters adjudicated in juvenile court and those tried in criminal court, controlling for the severity of the offense. They note that the juvenile court is not as lenient as its critics would have it, and furthermore:

> minors are likely to be looked upon as special persons by prosecutors, probation officers, and judges in the criminal courts. They are younger than the main population of defendants before the criminal courts. Even jurors may view the young person in criminal court differently. In the cases examined, there were more findings of "not guilty" in the criminal court than in the juvenile court. The labeling process may be different in the two courts. While a minor may be looked upon as a hardened criminal in the juvenile court, (s)he may be viewed as a mere innocent youngster in criminal court. (1985: 87)

In another study, more than 90 percent of the judicial waiver or prosecutorial discretion cases tried in adult court resulted in guilty verdicts, with fines or probation imposed on one-half of the convicted juveniles. Those juveniles convicted of serious violent offenses, however, were likely to receive terms of incarceration: 14 percent to jail; 63 percent to prison with an average sentence of 6.8 years (Hamparian et al., 1982). Carole Barnes and Randal Franz found that in the jurisdiction they studied, "Property offenders with a long history of property offenses tend to receive a substantially lighter sentence in adult court than they would have received when moving up the ladder in juvenile court. Conversely, personal and aggravated personal offenders with few prior offenses received significantly more punitive treatment in adult court than did comparable offenders in juvenile court" (1989: 133).

Despite an increasing number of juvenile arrests for serious crimes, relatively few facilities exist for the most violent adolescents. As a result, youths are often released after less than a year of confinement (Treaster, 1994b).

JUVENILE COURT JUDGES

Central to implementing the helping philosophy of the juvenile court is the juvenile court judge. However, the position presents an anomaly—although most judicial posts require only a knowledge of law and legal procedure, the juvenile court judge, in addition, needs a working knowledge of several disciplines: sociology, psychology, and social work. Were persons with such backgrounds readily available, the relatively low prestige of the juvenile court would make their recruitment difficult. In most states, the juvenile court is located at the bottom of the judicial organizational chart, and the position of juvenile court judge is often seen as the entry level for a future appointment to a more prestigious court. (Exceptions would include Illinois and Arizona, where the juvenile court is part of the superior court.)

In response to these difficulties, some states have mandated training for juvenile court judges, often provided by, or in conjunction with, the National Council of Juvenile Court Judges. The council sponsors a national college located on the campus of the University of Nevada at Reno. The college trains judges and holds periodic sessions throughout the year on topics designed to help juvenile court judges keep abreast of the laws and behavior approaches related to the problems of delinquency, neglect, and child abuse. Other topics include drug and alcohol abuse, juvenile institutions and their alternatives, and waiver of cases to the criminal court. Some jurisdictions use *referees* or *masters*, specialized attorneys who represent the judge and who are empowered to hold certain juvenile court hearings.

JUVENILE COURT DISPOSITIONS

A wide variety of juvenile court dispositions exists:

- Reprimand with unsupervised probation
- Probation with supervision
- Foster care with or without probation
- Private school or residential treatment

- Training school
- Mental hospital
- Group home
- Community-based day treatment
- Community-based secure facility

Juveniles are sometimes released in the custody of their parents for placement in private boarding schools, military academies, sanitoria, and so on. This disposition is most often limited to children from at least middle-income status, and Dale Mann notes: "One obvious effect is to guarantee that public institutions for juvenile offenders serve an underclass population" (1976: 12). Jerome Miller (1992: 5) states:

> A two-tiered system of residential care has grown up across the country with a dramatic surge in short-term hospitalization in private psychiatric hospitals for recalcitrant, disobedient, or drug-abusing suburban adolescents. Whether or not this approach works, the effect is to spare these youngsters the correctional diagnosis and the labels which undermine hope—"psychopath," "sociopath," "unsocialized aggressive." Such terms apply only to the children of the poor and the racial minorities who populate our youth correctional institutions.

Female offenders often receive harsher treatment in juvenile court because of the lack of alternative programs for them: "Although a sentencing judge may be willing to consider a variety of dispositional alternatives, he or she is often faced with only one program possibility—the state training school or reformatory" (Female Offender Resource Center, 1979: 13). In addition,

> once institutionalized, girls are afforded fewer services and program opportunities than boys. Boys, on the other hand, suffer from disadvantages which result from confinement in larger institutions which are filled to capacity.
>
> We can only speculate as to the reasons for these discrepancies. Some people in the juvenile justice system justify the differences in programs and services available in girls' institutions by arguing that it is cost effective to spend the limited funds which do exist on boys who commit more serious crimes and who outnumber girls in the system nearly four to one. (Female Resource Center, 1979: 13)

JUVENILE DISPOSITIONS

Basic to dispositions in the juvenile court is the concept of *least restrictive alternative*, meaning that a disposition should not be more restrictive than that which will adequately serve the needs of the child. The following review of dispositions generally follows this principle, progressing from the less to the more restrictive.

Low to High

Probation supervision

Day treatment

Group home

Residential treatment center

Training school

ADMINISTRATION OF JUVENILE SERVICES

The administration of juvenile services is complex, with different levels and branches of government sharing responsibility. Juvenile probation is administered by the juvenile court in most states, although a few states have a statewide executive branch agency administering juvenile probation. State institutions for delinquent juveniles are always in the executive branch:

> However, the states vary in the type of executive department they choose to place the responsibility for juvenile corrections: the social service department, the corrections department, or separate departments for either family and children's services or youth services. The trend is to remove the responsibility for juvenile corrections from adult departments and place it either in a youth services or a family and children's services department. The majority of states still place responsibility for the administration of juvenile corrections within social service departments. (Hurst and Torbet, 1993: 11)

PROBATION SUPERVISION

Probation supervision is used in about one-half the adjudicated delinquency cases. Probation supervision is appropriate for children who are not seriously delinquent or in obvious need of intensive services available only in a residential setting (Figure 3.8). However, youngsters with severe behavior problems may be placed on probation, not because it is necessarily the most appropriate response, but because probation is the only response available.

As a condition of probation, juveniles are usually required to obey their parents or guardians, attend school regularly, be home at an early hour in the evening, and avoid disreputable companions and places. The PO supervising the youngster works toward modifying some of the juvenile's attitudes to help the child relate to society in a law-abiding, prosocial manner. At the root of antisocial behavior in many juveniles is a difficulty in relating to authority and

SUPERIOR COURT OF THE STATE OF CALIFORNIA
IN AND FOR THE COUNTY OF SANTA CLARA
JUVENILE COURT

MINOR

No.
ORDER OF PROBATION

At a regular Hearing before the above-entitled Court on
the Court ordered that you were:

.... 1. Declared a Ward of the Court and permitted to return to your home on Probation
and your care, custody, control and conduct to be under the supervision of the
Probation Officer.
.... 2. Returned to your home on Probation under the supervision of the Probation Officer
for a period not to exceed six months.

It is further ordered by the Court that you are required to:

1. Obey your parents or guardian.
2. Obey all laws of the community, including curfew, traffic and school laws.
3. Follow the school or work program approved by the Probation Officer.
4. Follow the instructions of the Probation Officer relating to your conduct at home, at school and in the community.
5. Report in person to the Probation Officer or the Court at such time and place as may be designated by the Probation Officer.
6. Comply with any special conditions of Probation and, if restitution has been ordered, you must make payment as promptly as possible and as directed by your Probation Officer.
7. Notify the Probation Officer of any anticipated change of address or other important changes.
8. Consult with the Probation Officer without hesitation when you are in need of further advice.

In addition to the above, the Court orders the following special conditions of your Probation:

....
....
....
....
....

This Order will remain in effect until further Order of the Court. Your case may be reviewed by the Court
and your program modified, depending on the progress you made.

Failure to comply with any of the above instructions will be a violation of this Order and may result in a
further Hearing before the Court.

_____
Judge of the Juvenile Court

The foregoing Order has been read by me or read to me and I fully accept it and understand its contents.

_____
Signature of Ward or Probationer

_____
Signature of Parent or Guardian

FIGURE 3.8 Juvenile court order of probation, California Superior Court.

authority figures. Parents, school officials, and others who have represented
authority to the young person have caused him or her to develop a negative,
even hostile, attitude toward authority in general. This leads to rebellion at
home and at school, or against society in general. The probation officer must

help the young person revise his or her ideas about people in authority by providing a role model as a healthy authority figure or by helping the young person develop healthy attitudes toward others who can provide a desirable role model. These persons may be teachers, athletic coaches, or perhaps a recreation leader in the community.

LEHIGH COUNTY, PENNSYLVANIA, SCHOOL-BASED PROBATION PROGRAM

In the central Pennsylvania county of Lehigh, juvenile probation officers are stationed in the high schools where, in addition to monitoring probationers attending school, they visit classrooms to talk to students and faculty about the juvenile justice system. The program seeks to improve attendance and grades, avoid suspensions, and decrease the need for institutional placement. The POs are available to deal with clients involved in school violations. The officers also make home visits and involve family members in the student's program. The POs coordinate re-entry conferences for students returning to school after suspension to help increase their chances of a positive reintegration.

The probation officer must be able to accept the young person and be able to demonstrate an attitude of respect and concern. At the same time, the PO must be honest and firm with the youngster, setting realistic limits for him or her—something parents are often unable (or unwilling) to do. Misbehavior or antisocial activities cannot be accepted, but the client must be.

In the course of the helping process, the probation officer will involve the family and meet with the young person on a regular basis. The PO will work with school officials, sometimes acting as an advocate for the child to secure for the client a public school placement, which is often a difficult task. The youngster has often exhibited disruptive behavior at school and officials are, understandably, resistant to his or her return. If necessary, the officer will seek placement in a foster home for the client (and in some circumstances, adoption).

DAUPHIN COUNTY, PENNSYLVANIA, ADOLESCENT FOSTER HOME CARE PROGRAM

Established in 1980, the Adolescent Foster Home Care Program (AFHC), in cooperation with the County Social Services and Youth Agency, recruits, screens, and trains foster parents and provides specialized services to both dependent and delinquent youth. One of the long-established, paramount contributing factors to juvenile delinquency is a dysfunctional home environment. Institutional placement for juveniles who need to be removed from their natural homes is not always in the best interest of a particular child.

Therefore, the Dauphin County Probation Office views foster home care as a feasible alternative living situation for certain adjudicated delinquent juveniles—those who have committed minor offenses, usually stemming from inadequate parental supervision or conflict in the natural home. The purpose of the AFHC program is to provide carefully screened delinquent youth experiences in family living that are essential to positive and constructive growth and development.

The foster home care specialist is an experienced probation officer who works with the youth, his or her natural family, and the foster family toward the ultimate goal of re-establishing the youth in the natural home. If returning to the natural home is not deemed to be in the best interest of the youth, an alternative placement goal is established and worked toward (e.g., independent living, armed services, or job corps).

THE REFERRAL PROCESS

1. A delinquent youth is referred to the Adolescent Foster Home Care Program by the active probation officer, either an intake officer or line officer.

2. The foster home care specialist reviews all available information concerning the youth and the natural family. He or she interviews the youth and the natural family to explain the program and to determine the appropriateness of the referral.

3. If the foster home care specialist deems the child to be amenable to treatment in foster home care (rather than in some other modality of treatment), he or she schedules a placement planning conference with the child and youth agency to identify a prospective foster family.

4. A weekend preplacement visit for the prospective foster family and foster youth is arranged and implemented by the foster home care specialist. In this way, both the adolescent and the foster family have the opportunity to express any concerns they may have regarding the proposed placement. If foster family members do not feel that they can meet the needs of a particular youth, they may disapprove the placement in their home.

5. After a successful preplacement visit with the foster family, the youth is scheduled for a juvenile court dispositional hearing. The assigned probation officer recommends to the juvenile court judge that the youth be placed in the custody of the Dauphin County Social Services for Children and Youth Agency for placement in the AFHC Program. The youngster is also placed on strict probation under the supervision of the Juvenile Probation Office. The foster home specialist supervises all delinquent youth in foster home care. In most cases, the youth is also placed on suspended commitment to an appropriate juvenile facility where the youth would go should he or she fail to comply with the terms of the AFHC program. Only the juvenile court judge can commit juveniles to the program.

PROGRAM DESCRIPTION

Each youth in the AFHC program is placed on strict probation supervision under the foster home care specialist, who serves as both a probation officer and a caseworker for the foster youth and foster family. Probation rules include a curfew and mandatory school attendance or employment.

The foster parents serve as important members of the treatment team; along with the foster care specialist and any other professional involved with the youth, they participate in defining the needs of the youth and his or her family and assist in implementing goals established for the youth during placement.

Within 30 days of a youth's placement, a Family and Placement Service Plan is developed based on the individualized needs and interests of the foster youth. It includes goals and objectives to be accomplished by the youth and natural family, as well as specific actions to be taken by all parties to reach the stated objectives. The anticipated length of foster home care placement is also included in the plan. The plan is reviewed and updated every six months by means of a six-month review hearing held at the Juvenile Probation Office. The review is conducted by a juvenile master who is appointed by the juvenile court judge. The youth, foster parents, natural parents, and foster home care specialist are present at each six-month hearing. The juvenile court master ensures that the objectives of the Family and Placement Service Plan are being achieved and makes written recommendations to the court.

Initially, the foster home care specialist will have at least one personal contact each week with the youth and foster family to monitor the placement, to provide support services to foster parents, to assure the youth's compliance with the probation rules, and to assist the youth in the development and implementation of the placement objectives. As the needs of the client allow, supervision may be reduced to a minimum of two personal counseling contacts per month. The specialist will also meet with the natural family at least once per month for counseling and information sharing about the youth's progress and will supervise all home visits made by the youth. The specialist maintains regular contact with school personnel and/or employer while the youth is in care.

When the goals of the Family and Placement Service Plan have been achieved and the foster home care specialist believes that the child can be successfully reunited with the natural family (or alternative placement goal), he or she will recommend to the juvenile court judge that the youth be released from the program. If the youth returns to the natural or surrogate home, he or she remains under probation supervision for approximately three months to assure continued successful community adjustment and to allow the foster home care specialist to provide continued support services to the reunited family unit.

Many orders of probation require restitution or community service (Figures 3.9, p. 81, and 3.10, p. 82). *Restitution* refers to the compensation provided by an offender to his or her victim; it can involve financial payments or a service alternative. An increasing interest in restitution as a condition of probation has been spurred by an increasing concern for the victims of crime. The *service* alternative is often imposed on youngsters who are unable to provide financial restitution, although it rarely means direct service to the victim. Instead, the juvenile usually is involved in unpaid work for a nonprofit community agency, such as the Salvation Army or the Red Cross.

If the youngster violates any of the conditions of probation, the PO prepares a violation of probation report and the youngster can then be subjected to a motion to revoke probation in favor of a more restrictive setting such as an institutional placement (Figure 3.11, p. 83).

DAY TREATMENT

Community-based day treatment programs are cost-effective because they avoid the need to provide the total care environment of residential programs.

PROJECT RISE

Pima County, Arizona, which includes the city of Tucson, provides an example of a community-based noncustodial response to troubled youth. Over the years, the Pima County Juvenile Court has found that there is a strong correlation between a child's school problems and delinquent behavior. All too often, school officials and the juvenile court would work in isolation. In 1982, a project at Howenstine School was begun to combine the treatments of the dual problems of delinquency and school failure. This program was a joint venture between the Tucson Unified School District and the Pima County Juvenile Court. Teachers, teacher aides, probation officers, and probation aides worked side by side with a few juveniles to provide maximum supervision and a favorable environment for learning. The success of the Howenstine program was responsible for the Sunnyside School District inaugurating a similar program in 1983. Both programs are now known as Project RISE (Reentry into Successful Education).

Juvenile Court Services
BLACK HAWK COUNTY – BUCHANAN COUNTY – GRUNDY COUNTY
P.O. Box 1468
312 East 6th Street
WATERLOO, IOWA 50704
Phone (319) 291–2506

RE: Restitution

This letter is in regard to restitution for damages brought about in the

which occured on

If the offense is provable, our office will recommend reimbursement in your behalf. What we need is sufficient evidence of damages. Please fill out the enclosed restitution report. When the form has been completed, it should be signed and notarized on the back side. You may bring the form to Juvenile Court Services to get it notarized at no cost to you. Attach all supporting documentation to the report and return the information to Juvenile Court Services. If no restitution is involved, please write "none" on the form and return the form with any additional comments.

This information is needed immediatiely. If we do not receive it before

without an explanation of delay, our office cannot act in your behalf. You will have to take up the matter in Small Claims Court for reimbursement of your loss.

Please cooperate with us in this matter. We think it is important that juveniles be made responsible for their actions. Also, we feel victims should be reimbursed for their misfortunes.

Sincerely,

Kathy L. Thompson
Restitution Assistant

Enclosure

FIGURE 3.9 Letter to a victim, Waterloo, Iowa.

Project RISE is a full-time day program for about 40 youngsters, combining the best of the educational and juvenile justice systems from which the project receives its clients. The goals of the program are to reduce serious delinquent activity, improve school attendance, decrease school behavioral problems, raise the child's reading level by two years, and inculcate positive social values and survival skills in the youth. To accomplish these goals, Project RISE is housed in facilities separate from the mainstream high schools. Students are either transported to school or issued city bus passes. The staff-to-child ratio is extremely low, assuring intensive daily supervision in an innovative learning environment.

As children progress, their success is rewarded within the context of a behavior modification system (behavior modification is discussed in Chapter

Superior Court of the District of Columbia

Social Services Division   Family Branch

Restitution Agreement
Juvenile Community Service Program

Superior Court of the District of Columbia
Social Services Division – Family Branch

I, _____ , agree to participate in the Juvenile Restitution Program.
I agree to all the requirements listed below under the checked paragraphs:

DIRECT SERVICE TO VICTIM. _____ was a victim of this offense.
I will work directly for   him   her   for a total of _____ hours in the following
manner:

MONEY RESTITUTION. As a result of my offense _____ suffered
monetary damages. I agree to repay   him   her   for the total sum of
$ _____ , to be paid in the following manner:

COMMUNITY SERVICE. I agree to pay the community for my offense by performing
_____ hours of community service. I will perform this service in the following
manner:

_____

_____

_____

_____

_____

_____

_____

I agree that this agreement will become a condition of my probation and I further recognize
that if I break this agreement, the Social Services Division may request that the Court revoke
my probation and commit me to the Department of Human Services. I also recognize that I
must fulfill other conditions in order to participate on probation in the Restitution Program.
These conditon are:

_____

_____

_____

_____

PROBATIONER'S SIGNATURE: DATE:

ATTORNEY FOR DEFENDANT: DIVISION OF SOCIAL SERVICES:

COMMUNITY WORKER: VICTIM:

CORPORATION COUNSEL: MEDIATOR:

FIGURE 3.10   Restitution agreement, Washington, D.C.

```
                          IN THE CIRCUIT COURT OF
                          JACKSON COUNTY, MISSOURI
                              JUVENILE DIVISION

IN THE INTEREST OF
James Matthews
M/DOB: 7/12/76
PETITION NO. JV87-10010
LIFE NO. 11326


MOTION TO REVOKE PROBATION

COMES NOW the Juvenile Probation Officer and moves the Court to enter an order revoking the
above-named juvenile's probation and, in support thereof, states to the Court:

1. On the 2nd day of November, 1993, the Court committed the above-named juvenile to the
   custody of the Juvenile Officer at McCune and suspended execution of said commitment and
   placed the juvenile in the custody of his mother, subject to rules of probation.

2. The juvenile has violated the following term of his probation: To obey all law and ordinances.

3. The juvenile violated the aforesaid term of probation in that:
   On or about November 22, 1994, in Jackson County, Missouri, the juvenile knowingly altered
   and defaced a motor vehicle, a 1994 Nissan 300ZX automobile, without the consent of the
   owner thereof, in violation of Section 569.080 (Tampering, First Degree - Class C Felony), for
   which the juvenile would be criminally responsible if tried as an adult,

   WHEREFORE, the Juvenile Officer prays the Court revoke the juvenile's probation and enter
a dispositional order in the best interests of the juvenile.
                                      Forestal Lawton
                                      Forestal Lawton
                                      Juvenile Officer
```

FIGURE 3.11   Motion to revoke probation.

9). In this manner, undesirable activities and habits are eliminated, and healthy, socially acceptable behaviors are reinforced. The child's self-image is bolstered by repeated successes in interpersonal as well as academic tasks. Emphasis is placed on frequent organized outings to broaden the child's growing socialization.

DAY TREATMENT IN KENTUCKY

To reduce the number of youth who are institutionalized in costly mental health and correctional facilities, the Kentucky Division of Children's Residential Services operates 17 community-based day treatment centers for youth 12 to 17 years of age, most of whom are males. Some of the centers are operated by the state, whereas most are contracted out to private nonprofit groups. The average cost is $30 a day per student. Students are troubled youth referred by schools, parents, or juvenile court. On admission, the youth is evaluated by a treatment team comprising a juvenile counselor, treatment aide, and teacher. Based on the assessment, a treatment plan is designed that includes educational, vocational, and behavioral goals. The programs operate five days a week and follow the school year, although there is extended programming for the summer months (Hobbs and Kennedy, 1992).

FIRESTONE COMMUNITY DAY CENTER

Located in the Watts section of Los Angeles, California, this school serves youngsters on probation who have failed in the public school system. They have below-average academic skills and a history of behavioral and disciplinary problems. The individualized learning program is designed to develop the youth's self-esteem through improved academic performance; it is believed that this will translate into greater educational and vocational pursuits. There is a maximum enrollment of 35, and the students are in the classroom four hours each day, five days a week. Classes are year-round. The youngsters stay in the program from one semester to two years. When they complete the program, students return to the public schools, start employment, or continue their education. After a short follow-up period, they are dismissed from probation if they have successfully completed other conditions of probation (Krisberg et al., 1994).

THE GROUP HOME

Residential treatment can be classified according to the degree of custodial care provided. At the lower end of this scale is the group home. The group home may be privately operated under contract with the state (or other level of government), or it can be operated by the state. Generally, anywhere from six to fifteen youngsters live in the home at any one time. The typical home has several bedrooms and baths, as well as a large living room, dining area, and basement recreation area. The interior of the home approximates that of a large single-family dwelling. Group homes are usually located in residential areas that are in proximity to public transportation, public schools, and recreation facilities.

The group home is for youngsters who

- Are in unresolvable conflict with their parents but are not seriously disturbed or psychotic
- Have inadequate homes and need to develop skills for independent living
- Need to deal with community social adjustment problems in a therapeutic family environment
- Need to deal with individual adjustment problems and to learn about themselves in relation to others
- Need to develop self-confidence through successful experiences

Each resident has daily chores, such as doing dishes, making the bed, or mowing the lawn. Houseparents, usually a married couple with graduate degrees in a therapeutic discipline, such as social work or psychology, perform surrogate parent roles by preparing or overseeing the preparation of meals, enforcing a curfew, and helping with homework, as well as other tasks usually handled by parents in healthy families. Youngsters attend local schools on a full-time basis, or they have a schedule that incorporates both school and employment.

There are group counseling sessions conducted by group workers geared to help the residents understand and overcome problems that have led to the placement and to define goals consistent with their individual ability. Individual counseling programs are provided for those youngsters who need help in preparing for independent living and improving their family relationships. Day-by-day counseling and conflict resolution are handled by the houseparents.

The most difficult aspects of the group home are relationships with the surrounding community—typically, vigorous neighborhood resistance exists to placing such a facility in most areas. Although both professionals and laypersons generally agree that the group home concept is an excellent one for many youngsters coming to the attention of the juvenile court, this has not been translated into widespread acceptance of the reality. Group homes, not only for troubled youngsters but also for the retarded and other handicapped persons, have been vigorously and all too often successfully resisted by local residents (Holloway, 1995). This problem has become so severe that in 1989 the U.S. Department of Justice brought suit against a Chicago suburb (Chicago Heights) because the municipality refused to permit the building of a group home for fifteen retarded adults (Johnson, 1989a). A similar suit was brought by United Cerebral Palsy against a group of Southeast Dade County (Florida) homeowners who were attempting to thwart the opening of group homes for disabled persons (Hartman, 1994). The 1988 Federal Fair Housing Act, which bars discrimination against disabled persons, has been interpreted by the courts as outlawing local zoning laws that deny housing to retarded persons, the mentally ill, and drug addicts. In 1995, the Supreme Court ruled that this statute prohibits municipalities from using single-family zoning to bar group homes. In this case, the city of Edmonds, Washington, had attempted to prevent a national organization, Oxford House, from operating a group home for recovering substance abusers (*City of Edmonds v. Oxford House*, No. 94-23). Although we may accept the moral imperative and recognize the value of helping the unfortunate, it is too often a concern for real estate values that prevails. *L'hypocrisie est un hommage que le vice rend à la vertu.*

RESIDENTIAL TREATMENT CENTER

The term *residential treatment center* (RTC) is being used to identify private and public institutions that provide residential care for youngsters, with or without intervention of the juvenile court and devoid of coercive elements associated with correctional facilities—locks, bars, and barbed fences. Generally, the RTC provides a wide variety of enriched services, and the private RTC receives a great deal of public funding. Despite the fact that almost all receive tax-levy money, the private RTC retains the privilege of screening its residents, a luxury not afforded public institutions. One study found, however, that in southern California considerable competition exists for residents between private facilities, and juveniles admitted to private institutions do not significantly differ from those sent to public facilities (Shichor and Bartollas, 1990). Private centers can also mix adjudicated delinquents, status offenders, and voluntary clients in a manner that would not be permissible in a public institution, although the mixing of delinquent and nondelinquent children runs contrary to the prevailing wisdom in the field (Curran, 1988).

LOG CABIN RANCH

The San Francisco Juvenile Court operates a county rehabilitation facility offering residential care for boys ranging in age from 15 to 18 years. The Log Cabin Ranch has a total capacity of 86, and one-third of the overall school program is devoted to the appropriate vocational instruction. The ranch offers four vocational programs: auto mechanics, electronics, building maintenance, and culinary arts. After four weeks of orientation and testing, qualified students are assigned to one of the programs. Successful graduates are assigned to job developers who are responsible for the placement of these youths in apprenticeship programs or part- or full-time employment, depending on the age, skills, and needs of the particular youth.

Log Cabin provides a full range of counseling services to its students. Both individual and group counseling are prescribed, and reports detailing each student's progress are submitted every six weeks. Case conferences involving the student, his probation officer, the head teacher, and the assistant director are held at regular intervals and provide each student with individualized attention and feedback. The Forensic Health Services of the Department of Mental Health provides psychological services, crisis intervention, individual counseling, and consultation.

The School Department offers the necessary individualized remedial instruction in basic skill areas, and a learning specialist from the Court School provides individual assessments of each youth's learning abilities. Computer-assisted instruction is available to the students on an individual basis. Log Cabin Ranch is an active member of the Central Coast Ranch League, fielding competitive teams in basketball, softball, volleyball, and cross-country.

HIGHFIELDS

On the former estate of Charles A. Lindbergh, near Hopewell, New Jersey, Highfields was established in 1950 under private auspices. Although it was taken over by the state of New Jersey in 1952, Highfields provides a prototype for many private juvenile facilities throughout the United States.

The treatment objective at Highfields is to give delinquent boys an opportunity for self-rehabilitation by achieving a series of preliminary and prerequisite goals. Few formal rules exist because the purpose is to enable the youngster to develop a nondelinquent orientation through *guided group interaction* (GGI).

Grant Grissom and William Dubnov (1989) provide the distinguishing characteristics of GGI:

- GGI is a group process involving five to twelve group members and a trained adult group leader. Attendance is mandatory.
- The objective is the alteration of delinquent behavior. This is achieved by channeling group pressures toward prosocial goals. Behaviors and values are considered to reflect adaptations to the peer social group rather than immutable personality characteristics.

- The peer group wields genuine power in the treatment process. It may set its own agenda, place one of its members on the "hot seat" (i.e., subject his behavior to extensive scrutiny by the group), or prescribe negative sanctions (e.g., work detail or withdrawal of privileges) to alter a member's deviant behavior.
- Each member is required to explain how he got into trouble. On the basis of his response and the ensuing discussion, he is assigned problems or "roadblocks" that he must overcome. Acceptance by the group comes with evidence of the member's efforts to overcome these group-assigned problems. Status is accorded for assisting others and making the effort to understand the "why" of one's own and others' behavior.

The leader channels group pressures and molds norms so that prosocial behavior and the expression of prosocial attitudes are reinforced, and delinquent norms or attitudes are challenged. He manages the formal process by seeing to it that every boy "tells his story." He reminds the group that negative sanctions must be applied constructively and not be strictly punitive.

Youngsters work or attend school during the day and in the evening meet in groups of about ten for a daily therapy session lasting 90 minutes. The purpose is to assist residents to develop an understanding of their problems through unstructured interaction with others in similar circumstances (Finckenauer, 1984: 198):

> The subjects discussed in GGI revolve around the current problems of group members and the group itself. These problems emerge as a result of interaction with significant others, primarily peers, in a group setting. . . . The major emphasis in this technique is on the group and its development, rather than upon an exhaustive analysis of each individual group member. . . . Guided group interaction is considered to be most effective with adolescents because they seem to be more responsive to peer influences than any other age group.

Highfields has no guards or locked doors, and authoritarian leadership is deliberately absent. The 20 residents, who have been adjudicated as delinquents and placed on probation, remain at Highfields for four months. Family and friends are encouraged to visit, and residents are given passes to visit nearby areas and sometimes go home on furlough. These privileges can be lost for misbehavior—the entire group is punished for the actions of any of its members. Several studies exist on the effectiveness of Highfields; claims and counterclaims abound.

GLEN MILLS

Located in Delaware County, Pennsylvania, Glen Mills covers 800 acres that include athletic fields—football, baseball, and track, a 100-year-old administration building, red-brick Victorian-era cottages, academic buildings, and a chapel. This facility is an open institution—always referred to as a school and residents as students—devoid of any coercive elements, which were once part of Glen Mills (e.g., locks, bars, gates, and fences), with a population of about 600, many of whom have committed serious felonies. Each cottage houses 40 to 50 students, subdivided into four living areas of 10 to 15 students. Each cottage has a staff that includes a senior counselor, two counselor-teachers, and a counselor-specialist.

Like Highfields, Glen Mills is based on GGI; there is an absence of formal rules:

> Reliance upon rules to maintain control in institutions for delinquents suffers from several weaknesses. . . . [T]he delinquent has been socialized in a subculture which places high value on the ability to manipulate or "con" others, especially authority figures. Since many have little respect for authority and a strong incentive (i.e., peer group status) to disobey them, the imposition of rules confirms the delinquents' view of authority as oppressive and provides them with an opportunity to earn their stripes by "getting over on" (subverting) those in authority. Rules are rarely presented (never convincingly) as in the best interests of the boy. They are seen as instruments of control established by and for the convenience of institutional authorities; staff spend an inordinate amount of time enforcing them. They represent a challenge which the boys readily accept as part of a game that the institution finds difficult to win without abandoning all pretense at rehabilitation. (Grissom and Dubnov, 1989: 15)

Instead, unwritten group norms (e.g., respect each other, take care of property, confront norm violations) are closely monitored, with transgressors being confronted in a nonthreatening manner to avoid humiliation; positive behavior is rewarded. Escapes are not an issue because all a student has to do is request to leave, and transportation is provided—he will be sent back to juvenile court. Disagreements about confrontations and other matters are the subject for cottage group meetings. Chronic misbehavior results in expulsion and a return to juvenile court. The school screens out youngsters who like to intimidate others or who are quick to respond aggressively when challenged.

Glen Mills is essentially a school, and the program centers on vocational and academic education. Classes typically have between 10 to 16 students and provide individualized instruction; counselor-teachers conduct classes in the cottage. Research concludes that "Glen Mills' reincarceration rate is at least 10 percent (and possibly as much as 35 percent) lower than would be expected on the basis of national averages" (Grissom and Dubnov, 1989: 166).

A persistent problem for the juvenile court in providing alternative institutional care for youngsters is the ability of private treatment institutions to refuse to accept children who do not "fit in." Probation officers can be frustrated in their attempt to find suitable placement for certain youngsters because of this problem. The PO makes an evaluation based on professional judgment; this is transmitted to the judge in the form of a recommendation. However, in the final stage, the private institution can decide that the youngster is "incompatible" with its program (read: "too delinquent" or "too disturbed"); the RTC often accepts only youngsters who are referred to by probation officers as "boy scouts." The court is then faced with the alternative of probation or a training school.

OREGON JUVENILE CORRECTIONS ASSESSMENT CENTER

The Juvenile Corrections Assessment Center (JCAC) is the central receiving point for juveniles committed to the training schools by the courts. The JCAC is a time-limited program designed to produce consistent assessments and appropriate placements for committed youth in the community and close custody treatment programs.

Male youth who are committed to the training schools are transported to the JCAC located at MacLaren School in Woodburn, Oregon. Female youth are transported to Hillcrest School in Salem, Oregon. Within a two-week period, the youth undergo educational testing, drug/alcohol self-assessments and sex offender screening. Private providers interview and assess youth who may be diverted to their community programs.

The Close Custody Review Board reviews each case and places the youth in a program that addresses community protection issues and meets the youth's treatment needs. Youth who are not diverted to the community are placed within the close custody system, which is made up of four camps and the two training schools: Hillcrest and MacLaren.

TRAINING SCHOOL

The training school is a public institution that accepts all youngsters committed by the courts. Each training school is usually set up to handle particular categories of juveniles, who may be assigned on the basis of age, aggressiveness, or delinquent history. This is done to avoid mixing older children with younger ones, adjudicated delinquents with status offenders, or more disturbed youngsters with those having less serious problems. The training school usually provides a level of security not available in other types of juvenile institutions (although less than that offered in a correctional facility). Juveniles are committed to training schools based on the following criteria:

- A *finding of fact* occurs, indicating that the child has committed an offense that would be punishable by imprisonment if committed by an adult.
- The parents are unable to control their child or provide for his or her social, emotional, and educational needs.
- No other child welfare service is sufficient.
- The child needs the services available at the training school.

Los Angeles County Probation Department
Residential Treatment Program

The Los Angeles County Probation Department Residential Treatment Program is divided into two age groupings: senior, 16 to 18 years of age, and junior, 13 to 15 years of age. One junior camp and two senior camps are secure (fenced); the remainder are open (not fenced) camps. The security camps are used to maintain those minors who represent a significant escape risk—essentially impulsive youngsters with a low degree of self-control. In these camps, emphasis is placed on developing self-control.

The system is composed of 15 institutions; 14 are located in mountain settings. An intake facility with 60 beds is maintained at San Fernando Valley Juvenile Hall. Almost all boys ordered to camp are screened here for medical or psychiatric problems, and academic levels are established before the minor is assigned to a camp. Girls are processed directly from the juvenile hall in which they are detained. Deputy probation officers in all camps provide ongoing individual and group counseling to all camp wards. Treatment programs are individual—the length of stay for each minor is dependent on the minor's individual progress in the camp setting.

The principal objective of junior camps is to evaluate academic skills and achievement. These youngsters spend the bulk of the program day in school. Work is limited to in-camp maintenance and culinary assistance. The focus in senior camps is oriented more toward instilling work ethic disciplines. Senior youngsters ordinarily spend one-half of each day in school and one-half in parks and recreation work crews. A juvenile alternative work services program has been implemented whereby work crews are provided to public agencies on a contract basis. Extensive vocational training in such areas as welding, foundry work, and automobile repair is available at one of the camps.

The establishment of the Lyman School for Boys in Massachusetts, which opened in 1847 for 400 boys, began an era of providing separate facilities for juvenile offenders. These prejuvenile court facilities—training or reform schools—were patterned after adult prisons. They were regimented with large impersonal dormitories. Each provided some basic medical and dental treatment and limited educational and vocational training. Although the juvenile court "forced a breach in the wall of the criminal justice system," notes Jerome Miller (1992: 8), it did not fully resolve the question of whether to treat or punish, and this dilemma "was complicated by the existence of reform schools, which had been around for most of the century before the juvenile court was invented. Their presence ensured that juvenile offenders would receive the worst the system could offer—punishment labeled as treatment."

JUVENILES IN MASSACHUSETTS

Under the leadership of Jerome Miller, Massachusetts closed most of its training/reform schools in favor of contracting with private providers—Lyman, under this program, was the last to close in 1972 (Miller, 1992). By 1975, however, the Department of Youth Services (DYS) was coming under increasing criticism because, it was alleged, deinstitutionalization did not provide enough public accountability or security—fewer than 50 secure beds were available in the state. This number has increased dramatically as has the commitment of youngsters deemed dangerous; although the typical juvenile delinquent sent to the DYS is discharged after his or her 18th birthday, particularly dangerous youngsters may, with permission of the court, be held until 21 years of age. Those younger than 17 years of age who are convicted of murder in adult court are committed to DYS and subsequently transferred to prison as adults.

Over the years, there has been an increased emphasis on vocational training, remedial education, and rehabilitation through the use of social workers, teachers, psychiatrists, psychologists, and recreation workers. Like a prison or hospital, a training school operates 168 hours per week; this fact, combined with the level of security and services provided, makes the training school an expensive institution in which annual costs can easily run in excess of $30,000 per resident. One training school, the Warwick School for Boys, is located 55 miles from New York City. It is one of the training schools operated by the New York State Division for Youth (DFY). The school is a pleasant-looking institution with 700 acres of lawns and trees; it houses about 170 residents in several dormitories. Some individual rooms are also assigned on a "merit" basis. The residents are adjudicated delinquents who have committed offenses ranging from petty larceny to serious felonies, all before their 16th birthday.

The school has about 180 staff members, and no walls or gates are around the school—security is maintained through the use of supervised activities and a high staff-to-resident ratio. The daily schedule calls for two hours of compulsory academic instruction and two hours of physical education, with additional services for those who require more help. Both individual and group counseling are provided, as is vocational training in such areas as mechanical drawing, woodworking, electricity, and painting.

The Giddings State School of the Texas Youth Commission is a maximum security facility for more than 300 juveniles, mostly boys (96 percent); more than 25 percent have committed murder. Located in a rural community about 50 miles northeast of Austin, a high fence surrounds the grounds, which are like those of a college campus, with low, one-story buildings. Only the lock-up rooms—for rule violators—provide a prison-like aura. An accredited high school and extensive vocational training—for automobile repair, welding, and building trades—a gym, indoor pool, game room, and television rooms in the dorms are also available. Sports teams, and arts and crafts instruction are some of the other extracurricular activities. Residents sleep in large open rooms arranged barracks style. The training school provides specialized treatment for violent sex offenders, those chemically dependent, and "capital offender treatment." Treatment includes guided group interaction. The members live, eat, and attend class together; problems are dealt with in a group process. Medical, psychiatric, and psychological services are all provided at the facility. The recidivism (reincarceration) rate for Giddings releasees after three years is slightly more than 30 percent.

THE YOUTH AUTHORITY

Some states, for example, California, Ohio, and New York, have a state agency responsible for receiving cases from both juvenile and criminal courts. Typically, youngsters adjudicated delinquents in juvenile court, persons prosecuted and convicted under youthful or young offender statutes in criminal court, and juveniles prosecuted in criminal court under mandatory or optional waiver provisions are remanded to the youth authority for a period of confinement and aftercare (parole) supervision.

CALIFORNIA YOUTH AUTHORITY

The California Youth Authority (CYA) operates varied and specialized programs to provide care and custody for wards in institutions and on parole. After a ward is committed by the court and accepted by the authority, he or she is transferred to a reception center and clinic for about four weeks for evaluation and testing before making an appearance before the seven-member Youthful Offender Parole Board. Community assessment reports are generated by CYA parole agents after visiting the ward's family and contacting appropriate local agencies. These reports add information about the ward's family and community relationships to information gathered by the clinic staff from the ward, probation reports, and any psychological or educational testing done at the clinic. All of this information is compiled into a document called a clinic study and presented to the Youthful Offender Parole Board. The board uses this report in making decisions about the ward. Once the ward appears before the board and decisions about length of stay and program are made, the ward is transferred to his or her institution to begin a program.

The CYA has eleven institutions and six forestry camps located throughout the state. A youth is assigned to one based on age, maturity, delinquent sophistication, educational/vocational needs, security needs, and behavior. Although in most cases wards are placed in an institution or conservation camp for a period and then released on parole, a few are placed on parole immediately after diagnostic studies. Under certain circumstances, a ward committed from a criminal court may be assigned to an institution of the Department of Corrections. Commitments from both criminal and juvenile courts may also be assigned to an institution of the Department of Mental Health.

While in a CYA institution, younger wards attend school all day, whereas older ones might be in school part-time and in vocational training part-time. Many are assigned jobs within the institution, for example, working on the grounds or in food preparation. All wards are assigned a counselor, and some are placed in psychiatric or psychological treatment. The CYA has special programs for drug and alcohol abusers, sex offenders, and the seriously mentally ill. Because of limited resources, not everyone needing specialized treatment can be assigned to these programs.

When the ward is considered ready for parole by the Youthful Offender Parole Board, the parole agent makes all the necessary arrangements for his or her return to the community. The agent contacts family members, law enforcement, and other agencies and assesses the need for special conditions of parole that the ward must follow. The agent then completes the re-entry report, which includes a preliminary parole plan describing employment, training, and school and establishes goals to be achieved during the first 30 to 90 days. For the first 90 days on parole, intensive re-entry services are provided. The parole agent has frequent contact with the ward and his or her family and provides needed brokerage with community agencies. The level and intensity of supervision gradually diminish as the ward becomes increasingly self-sufficient. The decision to reduce the level of supervision uses a classification system that determines the level of control necessary based on the ward's potential risk score and his or her need for supportive services.

OHIO DEPARTMENT OF YOUTH SERVICES

The Ohio Department of Youth Services (DYS) is the state agency that provides a safe, secure environment, education, vocational guidance, and other developmental programs for young people 12 to 18 years of age who have been charged with felony-level offenses and committed to the department by one of the state's 88 county juvenile courts. The department's philosophy emphasizes care that is aimed at ultimate reintegration of troubled youth into the community. Planning for this reintegration begins at the time of commitment to DYS. A team consisting of DYS staff and the youth and his or her family establishes a plan of development when the youth is committed to DYS. Obtainable goals, including educational goals, are established to help the youth develop self-control and discipline. The DYS Youth Recovery Program focuses on helping youth become free from chemical dependency, developing skills to avoid further contact with the juvenile justice system, and eliminating vocational handicaps as a result of being chemically dependent.

Five institutions, two institutional complexes, and eight regional offices are within the jurisdiction of the Department of Youth Services. These regional offices are located in every major metropolitan center in the state. Youth assignments to DYS institutions are made on the basis of age, felony level of offense committed, and the proximity of the DYS institution to the youth's home. About 1600 youngsters are in DYS facilities and 1800 in the aftercare program.

Each institution has a fully accredited school that all youth are required to attend. Educational opportunities are available for all residents, including those with learning disabilities and special needs. Vocational programs in several of the DYS institutional high schools offer youth a variety of possible career paths to choose from once they are reintegrated into their communities. These programs include automobile mechanics, graphic arts, building maintenance, small engine repair, cosmetology, and barbering. A variety of recreational activities and extracurricular activities are available at each institution. At one location, youth have the chance to be on the award-winning DYS drill team or in the break-dancing group, which gives public performances throughout the year at schools and community events. Youth at DYS make positive contributions to the community through the volunteer work they do in litter control programs and by working with elderly citizens.

NEW YORK STATE DIVISION FOR YOUTH

Established in 1945, the New York State Division for Youth (DFY) is the oldest comprehensive agency serving youth in the United States. The agency operates the state training schools and secure facilities for juveniles tried as adults and regulates juvenile detention facilities. Youngsters are classified according to the level of security they require and are assigned to the most appropriate DFY facility or program of the three described in the following sections.

SECURE CENTERS

Ranging in size from 10 to 100 beds, these facilities are characterized by physically restricting construction, hardware, and procedures, including security fencing and screens. The facility is either a single building or a small cluster of buildings in close proximity, surrounded by a security fence. Most centers have single rooms that are locked at night. They are located in nonurban areas and virtually all services are provided on the grounds—a "total institution." The secure center admits juvenile offenders tried in adult courts and serious delinquents adjudicated in family (juvenile) court. They typically have an extensive history of delinquent behavior and involvement with the juvenile justice system, including prior institutional commitments. Many exhibit serious psychological and emotional problems. Certain residents may be given the privilege of temporary release from facility grounds for carefully regulated periods for special reasons—for example, a death in the family, medical or dental treatment, community services program, industrial training, education, or work release.

One of these centers is located at Goshen, about 75 miles from New York City, and houses 60 residents who are serving criminal sentences for felonies committed before 16 years of age, and several for murder. Residents 18 to 20 years old can be transferred to an adult facility, and at 21 years of age, all unexpired terms must be completed at an adult institution. At Goshen, residents receive vocational education, academic tutoring, counseling, and recreational services, all under strict discipline—the superintendent is a former marine sergeant with a master's degree in social work. This facility is expensive: in excess of $75,000 per year for each resident.

LIMITED SECURE CENTERS

Ranging in size from 36-bed centers to 120-bed training schools, limited secure centers are located in rural areas and characterized by highly structured programs with virtually all services provided on the grounds. Residents are frequently transferred to less secure settings before returning to their home community. These facilities are also used for certain youth previously placed in secure centers as a first step in their transition back to the community.

NONCOMMUNITY-BASED FACILITIES

Moderately structured and varied noncommunity-based facilities are for youth who need to be removed from the community but are not high security risks. Limited trips for community activities, under close staff supervision, are an integral component of these programs. The facilities are most often located in rural areas and may admit only certain serious delinquents. Some of the residents have previously been placed in secure and limited secure facilities and are transferred as part of the transition back to their own communities. In other cases, youth who have been initially placed in community-based programs and have been unable to function there are transferred to these residential centers— they are in the middle of the DFY's continuum of residential services. These centers may admit all categories of delinquents, status offenders, and youths placed as a condition of probation, as well as cases placed through a bureau of child welfare (i.e., without court intervention).

YOUTH DEVELOPMENT CENTERS

Specialized community-based youth development centers are configured and staffed to provide an entire array of services to youths within their community-based structure. These centers may admit delinquents, status offenders, youth placed as a condition of probation, and adolescents placed through a bureau of child welfare.

GROUP HOMES/CENTERS

Group homes are small residential units with seven to ten beds located in residential neighborhoods that use community resources to provide for many of the needs of the residents: education, medical/dental services, recreation, and so on. Residents are allowed frequent and unescorted access to the community. These centers may admit delinquents, status offenders, youths placed as a condition of probation, or those placed through a bureau of child welfare.

FOSTER HOMES/ALTERNATIVE PROGRAMS

Foster home and alternative programs serve youths who have been placed with the DFY but who can function in an alternative home situation rather than in an institutional setting: delinquents, status offenders, and those placed as a condition of probation or through a bureau of child welfare. Many of the (nonsecure) facilities used by the DFY are the result of contracts with private residential child care agencies.

AFTERCARE

Once a youth is in placement at either a DFY or private child care agency, a Youth Service Team counselor monitors his or her progress and serves as a liaison between the facility, the family, and the community. The counselor assists facility staff efforts to meet a youth's service needs as defined in the service plans and to modify such plans to meet developing needs. Aftercare services include a variety of counseling and brokering services for youth who have been released from facilities and are living at home. Individual advocacy is provided by aftercare staff to help youth obtain services for which they are eligible, such as schooling or medical help, and to help them take advantage of opportunities for which they must apply, such as jobs or scholarships. This frequently involves intervening directly on a youth's behalf to try to reduce the reluctance of some agencies to accept or serve youth with delinquent backgrounds.

States without a specialized youth authority/commission typically have their juvenile facilities under the auspices of the same department responsible for incarcerating adults. In Illinois, for example, the Juvenile Division of the Department of Corrections receives delinquents adjudicated in juvenile court and those youngsters tried as adults in criminal court. (From 1954 to 1970, these were responsibilities of the Illinois Youth Commission, which was subsequently abolished.) The Juvenile Division provides secure custody and rehabilitation programs to about 1500 youths 13 to 21 years of age in six centers statewide that range from minimum to maximum security. Per resident, annual cost is between $25,000 and $40,000. (By way of comparison, average annual costs in the state of Washington are above $45,000.)

ADULT CRIME, ADULT TIME

The Juvenile Medium Security Facility at Bordentown, New Jersey, is an unimposing two-story brick building that opened in 1983. It houses about 100 youngsters—mostly 16 to 18 years of age. Each inmate has a cell in which his or her movements can be watched, "schooling is minimal, therapeutic counseling has all but been abandoned, and solitary confinement for up to 30 days is the principal means of trying to change behavior" (Treaster, 1994a: 1). The cost is more than $60,000 per inmate per year. Illinois operates a maximum security facility at Joliet for juveniles at a more modest cost: a little over $34,000; however, the facility is understaffed and overcrowded.

AFTERCARE AND PAROLE

Aftercare is the planned release of a juvenile from a residential placement (group home, residential treatment center, training school, correctional institution) to supportive services in the community. The juvenile may be supervised by the juvenile probation agency (as is the case with Glen Mills) or other aftercare (parole) worker. Aftercare services are usually provided by the same state agency that administers the juvenile training schools (Hurst and Torbet, 1993). For example, I worked for the New York State Department of Social Welfare, which used to operate the state training schools. My job title was "youth parole worker," and I was responsible for supervising juveniles released from the boys' training schools. In 1978, New York enacted the Juvenile Offender Law, which mandates that youngsters 13 to 19 years of age who commit certain felonies be subjected to prosecution in adult criminal court. If convicted, the youngster can serve a term in a secure facility of the DFY. During that term, the juvenile becomes subject to the jurisdiction of the New York State Board of Parole for a release decision—parole—and eventual community supervision by a parole officer. Thus, the same agency that supervises adult felons in New York, the Division of Parole, also supervises juveniles convicted of certain violent felonies. In the state of Washington, parole counselors from the Juvenile Rehabilitation Administration (JRA) supervise those released from JRA institutions for a period of no more than 24 weeks (except for certain sex offenders).

Similarly, in Minnesota, parole agents of the Department of Corrections supervise juveniles who have been sentenced to a correctional facility. The release of a juvenile from a correctional institution in Minnesota is the responsibility of a juvenile hearing officer, who uses a scale that incorporates the severity of the offense and the delinquent history (Figure 3.12). For example, a juvenile who committed burglary second degree would have a *severity level* of II; if his or her *delinquent history factors* equaled 2, the inmate would normally be paroled sometime between the fifth and eighth month. The scale makes no reference to rehabilitation or prognosis—it is a "justice model."

In Michigan, youngsters 12 to 19 years of age who have been adjudicated delinquent or found to be in need of supervision (status offenders) by the juvenile division of a probate court can be committed to the Department of Social Services for placement in their own home, a foster home, group home, youth camp, diagnostic center, halfway house, residential treatment center, or state training school. In Michigan, status offenders are often committed to the Department of Social Services when the particular juvenile court has insufficient resources available for the youngster. The department offers secure juvenile res-

JACKSON COUNTY JUVENILE COURT SERVICES
McCUNE SCHOOL FOR BOYS

REQUEST FOR CONDITIONAL RELEASE/AFTERCARE
NAME: Michael DeWitt
BIRTH DATE: July 12, 1978
ADDRESS: 1900 West Briar Place
ENROLLMENT: June 6, 1994
DATE OF REPORT: November 28, 1994

I. REASON FOR PLACEMENT

Michael was committed to the McCune School for Boys on June 6, 1994, by Judge Harrison for Sexual Abuse.

II. ADDITIONAL REFERRALS

There have been no additional referrals.

III. ADJUSTMENT DURING PRESENT PERIOD OF SUPERVISION

While at McCune, Michael has made substantial advancement. Upon entrance into the program he was unable to work with his peers. Michael was often the target of harassment from other residents. He had told a story about his being offered chili to eat from resident Timothy Mordell working in the cafeteria. Michael asked if the meat in it was human flesh, and the incident became the source of ridicule during the remainder of his stay at McCune.

Over the past six months, Michael learned how to deal more appropriately with the harassment. He was also able to overcome racial problems that he had experienced since entering McCune. He has learned to deal with his prejudice in a fashion that permitted friendships to be established interracially.

He did so well in the McCune School that he was selected for Resident of the Week on three occasions. His grades reflect this:

English	B+
Science	A
Physical Ed	A
Vocational Preparation	A
Math	A
Social Studies	A
Citizenship	A

There were no problems in the community, and Michael spent almost all of his furlough time with his parents. On one occasion, his mother brought Michael back to McCune early because they saw and spoke with an individual who was associated with the victim. The resident and his mother were fearful that this individual would accuse Michael of some indiscretion, so he wanted to check back in at McCune. No complaints were received.

The only medical problem was the result of Michael striking a glass hallway window and putting his hand through it on the weekend of June 26, 1994, following a verbal altercation with another resident. Michael was taken to the hospital where he received both stitches and a medical furlough.

IV. FAMILY SITUATION AND RELATIONSHIPS

Michael is an only child and lives at the above address with his parents, Charles and Barbara DeWitt; his relationship with his parents has improved significantly while being at McCune. Barbara DeWitt has attended virtually every Family Group Therapy session. As a result, mother and child have moderated their interactions; previously, they were characterized by emotional exaggeration. Michael earned all but two possible home visits.

V. DIAGNOSIS AND PLAN OF TREATMENT

Michael has completed all four of the four phases of the program. He has made great strides in the areas of authority, peer interaction, school and family relationships. Possible problems in the future will involve his reputation for sexual acting out, although this has not yet been the case. He has been on furlough and attended Newtown High School.

VI. SPECIFIC RECOMMENDATION

Michael has successfully completed his three-week furlough period. McCune staff, as well as his family, feel Michael is ready to return home. It is, therefore, recommended that Michael DeWitt be placed on Conditional Release and receive the services of an Aftercare Worker.

Carol Spalding
Carol Spalding
Social Worker

idential treatment facilities, which may be used as the "last resort" for the most seriously delinquent youth. Delinquent wards remain under state authority until discharged by the Youth Parole and Review Board (YPRB) or attainment of 19 years of age. The YPRB is a three-member board within the Department of Social Services that conducts parole release, violation of parole, and discharge hearings for state delinquency wards. The Colorado Juvenile Parole Board is responsible for release decisions concerning juvenile delinquents who have been committed to the Department of Institutions. It grants, denies, revokes, suspends, or modifies conditions of parole to youth offenders who have been adjudicated as delinquent. The board is comprised of seven members—four from various state executive departments, two citizen members, and a local elected official—appointed by the governor and confirmed by the senate. Most hearings are conducted by panels comprised of two board members; in cases of offenders committed as violent juveniles, the entire board must consider release (Figure 3.13).

Aftercare supervision is similar, if not identical, to probation supervision and, as noted earlier, is sometimes provided by a juvenile probation agency. The first responsibility of the aftercare worker is to plan for the release and place-ment of the young person. Placement plans include where the juvenile will live, whether he or she is to work or attend school or a training program, or both, and arrangements for any supportive services that may be needed by the client that are available in the community. The young person released/paroled from a train-ing school may be returned to his or her own home, if this is desirable, or be placed in an alternative setting such as foster care, a group home, or halfway house. (Halfway houses are discussed in Chapter 11.) The aftercare worker usu-ally investigates placement alternatives and finalizes a program plan that is sub-mitted to training school officials and those responsible for the release decision.

Once back in the community, the young person will be supervised by an aftercare worker, probation officer, or parole officer. The youngster will be required to abide by a set of rules and regulations, the violation of which can cause a return to a "secure setting" (Figure 3.14). The worker will make regular visits to the youngster's residence, school, or place of employment. The worker

Juvenile Commitment to the Minnesota Department of Corrections

		Projected Institution Length of Stay in Months			
Severity Level	Most Serious Current Offense	Delinquent History Factors			
		0	1	2	3
I	Violation of Probation Contempt of Court Prostitution Assault – 4th & 5th Degree Drivers Under Influence of Alcohol Negligent Fires Burglary – 3rd & 4th Degree Damage to Property – $2,500 or less Forgery – $2,500 or less Possession of Controlled Substance Receiving Stolen Goods – $2,500 or less Theft – $2,500 or less Unauthorized Use of Motor Vehicle Dangerous Weapons (not including firearms) Trespass All Other Misdemeanors and Gross Misdemeanors	4 – 3	5 – 3	6 – 4	7 – 5
II	Assault – 2nd & 3rd Degree Burglary – 2nd Degree Damage to Property – Over $2,500 Forgery – Over $2,500 False Imprisonment Receiving Stolen Goods – $2,500 Felony Possession/Sale of Controlled Substance Theft From Person Theft – Over $2,500 Arson – 3rd Degree Criminal Sexual Conduct – 3rd & 4th Degree Simple Robbery Terroristic Threats Criminal Vehicular Homicide Dangerous Weapons – Firearms	6 – 3	7 – 4	8 – 5	9 – 6
III	Burglary – 1st Degree Criminal Negligence Resulting in Death Aggravated Robbery Arson – 1st and 2nd Degree Criminal Sexual Conduct – 1st & 2nd Degree Kidnapping Manslaughter Assault – 1st Degree	10 – 6	11 – 7	12 – 8	13 – 9
IV	Murder (all degrees)	**	**	**	**

* Commitment offenses not specifically listed shall be placed on the grid at the discretion of the hearing officer at the time of the initial institution review.
** Murder shall be dealt with on an individual basis.

FIGURE 3.12 Projected institution length of stay, in months.

COLORADO JUVENILE PAROLE BOARD

SUBJECT: Conditions of Parole

POLICY: 119

EFFECTIVE DATE: October 11, 1989

APPROVED BY: Sandra D. Burns, Chairperson

_____ is placed on parole, effective
_____ subject to the following terms and conditions:

1. You are paroled to live with _____
    at _____
    you may not move from this address, or any other approved placement without first
    obtaining the approval of your parole counselor.
2. You must obey all laws (federal, state, and local) while on parole, and all court orders
    regarding payment of restitution
3. You must actively participate in a full-time, supervised program. Examples are school, work
    or vocational training.
4. You must contact your parole counselor when, where and how he/she tells you.
5. You must not possess or use drugs or alcohol.
6. You must report any contacts with law enforcement agencies to your parole counselor
    immediately.
7. You must not carry any deadly weapon.
8. You must not leave the State of Colorado or the State of _____
    without first obtaining the approval of your parole counselor.
9. If you violate the law or the terms and conditions of your parole, your parole may be
    modified, suspended, or revoked and you may be returned to a Division of Youth Services
    program.
10. You must comply with this/these additional condition(s) while on parole.

    A. _____

    B. _____

    C. _____

11. You will be on parole until _____. Your parole, however, will be extended
    for each day you are on Escape status while on parole.

I hereby acknowledge that the terms and conditions of parole have been explained to me, that I
understand them, that I agree to obey them, and that I have been informed of the possible
consequences if I do not obey the terms and conditions of my parole.

_____

Parolee

The above terms and condition were approved by the hearing panel and explained to the
parolee on the _____ day of _____ , 19 ____.

_____   _____
Board Member   Board Member

FIGURE 3.13   Conditions of parole.

COLORADO DIVISION OF YOUTH SERVICES
Central Region

Name: Willis, Carol   Risk Score: 2
DOB: 2-22-76   Region/Client Manager: Central/Sims
Comm. Date: 4-10-91   Parole Counselor: Sims
Hrg. panel Date: 4-7-92   Date of Report: 3–19–92
Com. County: Jefferson   Sentence: Minimum months 0
Current Placement: Pine Street   Maximum months 24

Parole Adjustment Report

Original Placement and Plan:
Carol was paroled on April 7, 1992 to live with her parents Jill and Tim Willis at 440 Hampton Place, Arvada. Carol had no other authorized placements. She left her parents' home on June 23, 1992 without the permission of her parents or parole officer.

Level of Supervision:
Carol was on maximum supervision. That included weekly contacts with her parole officer and twice weekly contacts with her tracker.

Employment/Vocational/Education:
Upon parole, Carol was placed in the Excelsior Youth Center Day Treatment Program. She was transported to and picked up from Excelsior five days per week from April 7, 1992 through June 5, 1992. This was done to enable Carol to finish her school semester and for her and her parents to continue in therapy.
Carol was enrolled in the Jefferson County Youth Summer Employment Program and began working on June 15, 1992. This was to last until July 31, 1992. Carol was registered to begin school at Arvada West High School on August 17, 1992.

Arrests and Dispositions:
Carol had no arrests prior to her runaway on June 23, 1992. When she was contacted by the Arvada Police on July 17, 1992 she was charged with Giving False Information. There is a hearing set for September 14, 1992 at 9:30 am in the Arvada Municipal Court.

Restitution:
There was no court-ordered restitution.

Parole Violation:
Carol went to work on June 23, 1992. She left work without permission that same day and did not return. The parole officer received a call from Mr. Willis on June 23, 1992 stating that Carol had left. I asked Mr. Willis to call me on June 24, 1992 if Carol did not show up. Mr Willis called on June 24, 1992 to tell me that Carol had not shown up. At that time the parole officer placed a warrant for Carol's arrest.

At this time, both Carol and Mr. and Mrs. Willis feel that returning home is not an alternative, The parole officer feels that emancipating Carol at 16 years of age is unrealistic. The parole officer has been unable to find an appropriate placement for Carol in order to continue her parole.

Therefore, I am recommending Carol's parole be violated.

FIGURE 3.14   Violation of parole.

will involve family and school officials in an effort to facilitate the young person's reintegration and rehabilitation.

AFTERCARE IN DAUPHIN COUNTY, PENNSYLVANIA

Aftercare is the responsibility of juvenile aftercare workers who have caseloads of not more than 25 youngsters who are in placement or are receiving postplacement services. All delinquent and most dependent youths placed in a group home or institutional care by the juvenile court become clients of the program. The goals of aftercare are to reduce the amount of time that a youth spends in placement and to reduce the rate of recidivism experienced by youths returning from institutional care. The aftercare workers serve as case managers bridging the gap between the community and the placement resource and as counselors, helping the youth to improve decision-making ability. Each aftercare worker is assigned to specific placement resources so that all county youth at a particular placement have the same aftercare worker.

The aftercare worker begins involvement with the case during placement discussions before the dispositional hearing. The worker acts as an advisor during the placement planning process and, when possible, accompanies the intake worker and the client to the preplacement interview at the placement resource. Whenever possible, the worker attends the court hearings for a client who is being recommended for a placement resource to which he or she is assigned.

The worker assists in the transportation of the client to the placement resource and ensures that the child, parents, and institutional staff understand the role that the aftercare worker will play during and after placement. Within 30 days of the youth's placement, the worker prepares a written family service plan stating the short- and long-term service objectives, the services to be provided, and the anticipated length of the placement. At least once each month, the aftercare worker visits the youth and the staff at the placement resource, attends institutional meetings, and assists in the development of the treatment plan and monitors its implementation.

During placement, the aftercare worker meets at least once a month with the youth's family for counseling and information sharing about the youth's progress and supervises all home visits made by the youth. In the fifth month of the youth's continuous placement, the worker prepares a written review of the placement and family services plan in preparation for the six-month review-of-placement hearing before the juvenile court master. Before the youth's release, the aftercare worker coordinates the development of an aftercare plan that will be followed during postplacement supervision. To implement these aftercare plans effectively, the worker must develop cooperative relationships with schools, employers, and local social service agencies.

After release from the placement resource, the aftercare worker supervises the client for three to six months. Initially, at least one personal contact is made each week to provide counseling and monitor the aftercare plan goals. As the needs of the client allow, supervision may subsequently be reduced to a minimum of two personal counseling contacts per month. Cases are reviewed with the aftercare supervisor at least once each month. On completion of the aftercare plan goals, the aftercare worker recommends to the juvenile court judge that supervision be terminated and the case closed.

REVIEW QUESTIONS

1. What is the traditional philosophy of the system of justice used for juveniles in the United States?
2. What led to the establishment of the juvenile court?
3. What is the "justice model" in juvenile court?
4. Why does the juvenile court represent a manifestation of positive theory?
5. How does the concept of *parens patriae* conflict with due process?
6. What are the different types of cases that may come under the jurisdiction of a juvenile court?
7. What are the responsibilities of a juvenile court intake officer?
8. What are the basic types of hearings in juvenile court?
9. What is a "waiver" of juvenile court jurisdiction?
10. Why is it particularly difficult to be a judge in juvenile court?
11. Why are the juvenile services provided to girls usually inferior to those provided to boys?
12. What is "the least restrictive alternative" concept?
13. What is the difference between a training school and a residential treatment center?
14. What are the purposes of juvenile aftercare?
15. What agencies provide juvenile aftercare services?

PRESENTENCE INVESTIGATION

4

Chapter 3 examined the variety of juvenile services provided by a probation agency. The second basic service provided by a probation agency is the presentence investigation (PSI), which is the basis for a presentence report (sometimes referred to as a "probation" report, or simply a PSI). After the conviction of a defendant and before a sentencing hearing, a judge may (depending on the circumstances and the statutes of the jurisdiction) order a PSI, which reflects positive theory interest in the offender (not just the offense).

PRESENTENCE INVESTIGATION REPORT

The PSI has five basic purposes:

1. The primary purpose is to help the court make an appropriate disposition of the case. The report should help in deciding for or against probation and determining the conditions of probation, or in deciding among available institutions and determining the appropriate length of sentence. The American Bar Association (ABA) states that "the primary purpose of the presentence report is to provide the sentencing court with succinct and precise information upon which to base a rational sentencing decision" (1970: 11).

2. The PSI serves as the basis for a plan of probation or parole supervision and treatment. The report indicates problem areas in the defendant's life, his or her capacity for using help, and the opportunities available in the environment and community. During the investigation, the defendant usually begins to relate to the probation department, learning how probation officers work and getting some understanding of the nature of the agency.

3. The PSI assists jail and prison personnel in their classification and treatment programs. Institutions are often dependent on the report when the inmate is first received, a time when little is known other than what is contained in commitment documents: conviction and sentence data. The PSI helps institutional staff to understand and classify the offender; it can provide valuable information that will help in planning for the care, custody, and rehabilitation of the inmate. This includes everything from the type of custody required and the care of physical needs to the planning of the various phases of the institutional program. Many institutions will have little, if any, background or social, medical, and psychological information other than that provided by the PSI report. This means that the report will have an effect on the way in which an inmate is viewed and approached by institutional personnel because they will take the word of the probation officer over that of the offender. The ideal report can give focus and initial direction to institutional authorities for treatment and training as well as care and management.

4. If the defendant is sentenced to a correctional institution, the report will eventually serve to furnish parole authorities with information pertinent to release planning and consideration for parole, as well as determination of any special conditions of supervision.

5. The report can serve as a source of information for research in criminal justice. Unfortunately, because of a lack of uniformity in form and content, not to mention quality, the usefulness of many or most presentence reports may be limited for research purposes.

In recent years, an additional dimension—determining the financial condition of defendants—has become important in preparing a presentence report. In the 1984 Criminal Fine Enforcement Act, Congress cited the need to determine a defendant's ability to pay fines. Financial information is also necessary to assess the defendant's ability to make restitution and to pay any probation supervision fees, which have become rather common in many jurisdictions. Some states include a separate *victim impact statement* (VIS) that is attached to the PSI and usually includes a "description of the harm in terms of financial, social, psychological, and physical consequences of the crime. The VIS also includes a statement concerning the victim's feelings about the crime, the offender, and the proposed sentence" (Erez, 1990: 26).

Victim Impact Statement, Maryland

- Identify the victim of the offense. (Should the victim be deceased, information will be gathered from the surviving spouse, adult children, or closest blood relative.)
- Itemize economic losses suffered by the victim as a result of the offense.
- Identify any physical injury suffered by the victim as a result of the offense along with its seriousness and permanence.
- Describe any change in the victim's personal welfare or familial relationships as a result of the offense.
- Identify any request for psychological services initiated by the victim or the victim's family as a result of the offense.

The PO attempts in the report to "focus light on the character and personality of the defendant, and to offer insight into his problems and needs, to help understand the world in which he lives, to learn about his relationships with people, and to discover salient factors that underlie the specific offense and conduct in general" and to "suggest alternatives in the rehabilitation process" (Division of Probation, 1974: 48). The report is not expected to show guilt or innocence, only to relate the facts that the PO has been able to gather during the course of the PSI (Figure 4.1).

Content of Presentence Investigation Report

Presentence reports should be flexible in format, reflecting a difference in the background of different offenders and making the best use of available resources and probation department capabilities. A full report should normally contain the following items:

1. A complete description of the offense and circumstances surrounding it, not limited to the aspects developed for the record as part of the determination of guilt.
2. A statement from the victim and a description of the victim's status, the impact on the victim, losses suffered by the victim, and restitution due the victim.
3. A full description of any prior criminal record of the offender.
4. A description of the educational background of the offender, present employment status, financial status, and capabilities.
5. A description of any military record.
6. The social history of the offender, including family relationships, marital status, dependents, interests and activities, residence history, and religious affiliations.
7. The offender's medical history and, if desirable, a psychological or psychiatric report.

THOMAS S. GULOTTA
COUNTY EXECUTIVE

ROBERT J. BENNETT
DIRECTOR OF PROBATION

PROBATION DEPARTMENT
SOCIAL SERVICES BUILDING
COUNTY SEAT DRIVE & ELEVENTH STREET
P.O. BOX 189
MINEOLA, NEW YORK 11501

URGENT: Reply Needed By ——————
Sentence Date:
Re:
Defendant:
Case #   Docket #

Dear

This Department is conducting a court-ordered investigation of the defendant in the above-captioned offense. You may have suffered a loss, or otherwise be eligible to receive restitution. If this is the case, the court may order full or partial reimbursement of your losses.

In addition to specific losses or damages, you also may claim repayment for time lost from work due to injuries or court appearances, as well as materials used cleaning up premises or making repairs.

A Probation Officer may already have contacted you regarding your description of the crime, the impact it had on you, and any recommendation you may have regarding sentence. Please be advised that your Victim Impact Statement will be communicated to the court and that the District Attorney of the County of Nassau will make available to you a copy of that statement in the courtroom on the above-captioned sentence date.

It is important that you call the undersigned Restitution Investigator immediately. Your prompt return of the enclosed Statement of Losses, with copies of bills, receipts, appraisals, estimates, etc. will expedite our efforts on your behalf. We must hear from you by the reply date above or we will not be able to include your Statement of Losses in our report to the court. Please respond even if no restitution is desired, so that we may avoid inconveniencing you with any further contact.

Very truly yours,

————————————————   ————————————————
Restitution Investigator   Tel. No.

Encl.

FIGURE 4.1   Letter from the Nassau County Probation Department.

8. Information about environments to which the offender might return or to which the defendant could be sent should probation be granted.

9. Supplementary reports from clinics, institutions, and other social agencies with which the offender has been involved.

10. Information about special resources that might be available to assist the offender, such as treatment centers, residential facilities, vocational training services, special educational facilities, rehabilitation programs of various institutions to which the offender might be committed, special programs in the probation department, and other similar programs that are particularly relevant to the offender's situation.

11. A summary and analysis of the most significant aspects of the report, including specific recommendations as to the sentence. A special effort should be made in the preparation of PSI reports not to burden the court with irrelevant and unconnected details.

Source: American Probation and Parole Association.

In recent years, some jurisdictions have been including prediction scales in their PSI reports. These instruments rate the defendant according to criminal history, education and employment record, family and marital history, companions, alcohol and drug problems, emotional and personal attributes, and attitude or orientation—supportive of crime and unfavorable toward convention. A total score recommends for or against probation and level of supervision. The state of Colorado has been a pioneer in these efforts.

INTERVIEWS

In probation and parole, much of the necessary information is received directly from people. Thus, report quality is often dependent on the interview skills of probation and parole personnel. In the PSI, a great deal of information is gained by interviewing the defendant: "Interviews shall be directed toward obtaining and clarifying relevant information and making observations of the defendant's/respondent's behavior, attitudes and character" (*N.Y. State Code of Criminal Procedure*, 350.6–3ii). These interviews are conducted in all types of surroundings: from hot and noisy detention pens, where dozens of people may be awaiting a court hearing, to the relative quiet of the probation office.

A quiet, comfortable setting with a maximum of privacy is the best environment for an interview. A place that lacks privacy or has numerous distractions will adversely affect the productivity of the interview. Sometimes interviews are conducted in the defendant's home. This provides an opportunity to observe the offender's home situation and adds an additional and sometimes vital dimension to the report. In New York, statutes advise:"Whenever possible, interviews with the defendant/respondent shall be at the probation office; however, visits to the defendant's/respondent's residence may be made when there is an indication that additional information will be obtained that is likely to influence the recommendation or court disposition."

The interview is an anxiety-producing situation for the defendant. Previous experiences in similar situations, such as questioning by the police, may have been unpleasant. The PO tries to lower the anxiety level by cordially introducing himself or herself and explaining the purpose of the interview and the PSI report. This approach is especially important for the defendant who is not familiar with the criminal justice system in general and the court process in particular.

The PO may try to deal with matters of concern to the defendant. A married male defendant may be engaged in a discussion of how his wife and children can secure public assistance in the event that he is imprisoned. The PO might offer to write a letter of referral for his wife to take with her to the welfare department or other social agency that can provide assistance. Female offenders with children will need help in planning for their care in the event of a sentence of imprisonment. In some way, the officer must show genuine concern and interest in the defendant, while at the same time being realistic enough to expect many answers and statements that will be self-serving. Because the probation officer's contact with the defendant is limited, the officer cannot expect to probe deeply into the defendant's personality.

Some defendants will be overtly hostile; others will mask their hostility or anxiety with "wisecrack" answers. The PO must control both temper and temperament. He or she is the professional and must never lose sight of that fact during an interview. In questioning, generalized queries (e.g., "What have you been doing?") should be avoided (lest the interviewer be told: "Nothin' much"). Questions should be specific but require an explanation rather than a simple yes or no answer. The PO must avoid putting answers into the defendant's mouth— for example, by asking "Did you quit that job because it was too difficult?"

When the PSI is complete, the defendant should be reinterviewed to give him or her an opportunity to refute certain information or clarify any aspect of the report that may be in conflict with other parts of the report. In addition to the defendant, the PO may interview the arresting officer, the victim, employers, and significant others in the defendant's environment, such as spouse, parents, siblings, teachers, and clergy.

REVIEW OF RECORDS AND REPORTS

The probation officer will be reviewing records and reports in the course of the presentence investigation. The first is the arrest record of the defendant, referred to as a "rap sheet." This record will take the form of an arrest sheet(s) of a law enforcement agency, such as the state police. Each rap sheet entry is usually the result of the subject being fingerprinted. The sheet typically contains numerous abbreviations that must be deciphered by the PO if the record is to be useful—for example, *Att Burg* (attempted burglary) or *DUI* (driving under the influence). The arrest sheet does not describe the offense and may not even indicate if it is a felony or misdemeanor; it simply contains the official charge, for example, *Burg 2*. There is usually no mention of the premises that were burgled or what, if anything, was taken. In addition, the sheet often omits the disposition of the arrest. The officer may not be able to determine from the arrest report what happened to a particular case. Therefore, it is often necessary to check court records or to contact out-of-state agencies to determine the disposition of a case.

The nature of the defendant's prior record is important. The law usually provides for a harsher sentence if the defendant has a prior felony conviction(s). In addition, the defendant's eligibility for probation and a variety of treatment programs, such as drug rehabilitation, may be affected by a prior criminal record. The probation officer is especially interested in any information that may influence the sentence that was omitted during the trial, particularly any mitigating or aggravating circumstances, and information that can provide a different perspective on the case. The officer will review any previous PSI reports, as well as reports of other correctional agencies that have had contact with the defendant. These might include training schools or residential treatment centers and prison and parole agencies. The PO may also be interested in reviewing the educational records of the defendant. With the increasing number of substance-abusing defendants coming into the criminal justice system, probation officers must review this dimension of each defendant and explore the appropriateness of a recommendation for chemical abuse treatment.

If any psychiatric or psychological reports are available, the PO will review and analyze them. To do this review, he or she must understand the nomenclature and the meaning of any tests used by mental health professionals. The PO should make a judgment as to whether a psychiatric or psychological referral should be made during the PSI. Indiscriminate referrals to mental health or court-based clinics waste resources—a crime may be rational, and criminal behavior is not generally symptomatic of an internalized conflict. In cases in which symptoms of mental disorder are apparent, and in those situations in which the offender may benefit from an exploration of his or her problems, a referral should be made. If no referral is made, and a lack of psychiatric and psychological information exists, the PO should present his or her own observations concerning the defendant's intellectual capacity and personality—for example, level of social functioning and contact with reality. If the probation officer has received conflicting information about the defendant and is unable to reconcile the discrepancies, this difficulty should be pointed out in the report and not left up to the reader to discover (or, more likely, not discover).

Of crucial importance in any presentence report are the sections entitled "Evaluative Summary and Recommendation" (although in some jurisdictions a recommendation is not provided). In Nevada, statutes require the PSI to contain "a recommendation of a definite term of confinement or an amount of fine or both." Nothing should appear in either of these sections that is not supported by the rest of the report. The summary contains the highlights of the total report and should serve as a reminder to the reader of the information that has already been presented. The recommendation is a carefully thought-out statement, based on the officer's best professional judgment. It contains the alternatives that are available in the case and reflects the individualized attention that each case received (Carter, 1966).

PSI Process in Nevada

The defendant pleads guilty, *nolo contendere* (no contest), or is found guilty after trial. A date is scheduled for sentencing, usually 30 days away. The district attorney refers the case file to the Division of Parole and Probation, at which time an officer is assigned to the case, and he or she begins to research the offender's criminal history and records. Eventually, the defendant completes a preliminary questionnaire and is interviewed by the investigating officer.

During the interview and from the questionnaire, the officer obtains information regarding the offender's social and environmental background, employment history, education, mental health and substance abuse problems, residential stability, support systems, finances, military experience, future goals, and his or her feelings regarding the offense. The investigator must strive to be a perceptive listener and skilled interviewer who lends a keen ear toward attitudes, remorse, candor, and a cooperative spirit. It is important to remember that officers interview all types of people, including juveniles, first-time offenders, career criminals, members of organized crime, the mentally disturbed, substance abusers, and white-collar criminals. As one might assume, these people can be hostile, manipulative, and con-wise; or they may be pleasant—their crime(s) notwithstanding.

The investigator must then begin to verify as much information as possible by contacting the victim, the police, and any other relevant persons/agencies. He or she then begins to formulate the report. Using sentencing guidelines, the officer determines the probation success probability and length of sentence by responding to the applicable factors. The report is dictated, typed, proofread, approved, and distributed. The officer's recommendation addresses the risk and needs of the offender, the community, and the victim. The report may recommend special conditions of probation appropriate for the offender and his or her criminal activity.

Officers attend sentencing hearings and are called upon to answer questions by the judge, district attorney, and defense counsel. Recommendations, however, are disclosed only to the judge.

Robert Carter (1966: 41) notes that the probation officer is in a unique position with respect to making a recommendation to the judge: "The officer has had an opportunity to observe the defendant in the community, not only from a legal-judicial, investigative perspective, but also from the viewpoint of a general life style." To present a meaningful recommendation, the PO must have knowledge of the resources and programs that are available. An inexperienced probation officer may submit a recommendation for a treatment program that is not available either in the community or at a correctional institution.

One issue that the PO must decide is the recommendation for or against a sentence of probation. In many jurisdictions, a conviction for certain crimes, or a previous felony conviction, precludes a sentence of probation—the PO must know the statutes of the jurisdiction. The officer must also weigh the potential danger the defendant poses to the community, must evaluate the defendant's rehabilitative potential and ability to conform to probation regulations, and must consider whether probation will be construed by the community as too lenient in view of the offense, or by the defendant as "getting away with it."

Carter (1978: 15) recommends that the PSI report be tailored to meet the needs of the criminal justice system and be relatively short. He quotes John Hogarth:

> There is considerable research evidence suggesting that in human decision-making the capacity of individuals to use information effectively is limited to the use of not more than five or six items of information. In many cases, depending on the kind of information used, the purposes to which it is put, and the capacity of the individual concerned, the limit is much less. Despite this evidence there is a noticeable tendency for presentence reports to become longer. One of the most unfortunate myths in the folklore concerning sentencing, is the notion that the courts should know "all about the offender." Quite apart from whether much of the information is likely to be reliable, valid or even relevant to the decision possibilities open to the court, the burden of a mass of data can only result in information overload and the impairment of the efficiency in which relevant information is handled. This suggests that if probation officers wish to improve the effectiveness of their communications to magistrates they would be advised to shorten their reports.

This advice, and the overburdened nature of most probation agencies, has led to the popularity of the short-form PSI report.

SHORT- AND LONG-FORM PRESENTENCE INVESTIGATION REPORTS

There are two basic types (some might argue three—the third type is discussed under sentencing guidelines later) of PSI reports; the short form is usually less exhaustive and less time consuming. The *N.Y. State Code of Criminal Procedure* (350.6–2) states:

> The abbreviated investigation for short-form reports shall consist of the defendant's legal history and primarily current information with respect to: the circumstances attending the commission of the offense, family and social situation, employment and economic status, education and, when available, physical and mental conditions. Such investigation may also include any other matter which the probation department conducting the

investigation deems relevant to the recommendation or court disposition and must include any matter directed by the court.

Figure 4.2 is an example of the short form, and Figure 4.3 is an example of the long form.

FIGURE 4.2 Short-form presentence investigation report.

ONONDAGA COUNTY PROBATION DEPARTMENT

PRESENTENCE REPORT

COURT: __ONONDAGA COUNTY__

JUDGE: HON. J. KEVIN MULROY

PROSECUTOR: __JOANNE NAGLE__

LEGAL COUNSEL: DONALD D'AMICO

CASE NUMBER: __93-4641__
NAME: __JAMISON, RALPH__
AKA/MAIDEN: __N/A__
AGE/DOB: __11/27/69__
ADDRESS: __173 Briar Place__
__Tully, New York 13159__
PHONE: __315-779-4653__

INDICTMENT#: __91-3-19__
DOCKET#: __4763__
DR#: __N/A__
COURT CONT.#: _____
NYSID#: __86543210__
FBI#: __428-930-64__

OFFENSE DATE: ____9/9/93____ ARREST DATE: ____12/13/93____ CONVICTION DATE: ____6/24/94____
ORIGINAL CHARGES __SEXUAL ABUSE 1ST__ FINAL CONVICTION: _____SEXUAL ABUSE 1ST_____

CHARGE CODE: _____130.65 NYS PENAL LAW_____
A CLASS "D VIOLENT" FELONY

BY: PLEA: ____X____ VERDICT: _____

	NAME	DOB	NAME	DOB
CODEFENDANT/CORRESPONDENT:	N/A			

RESTITUTION: N RELATIONSHIP TO VICTIM: ACQUAINTANCE VICTIM IMPACT: Sent: X Received: _ NA: _
DISPOSITION DATE: ____8/5/94____ PLEA BARGAIN: _____UNKNOWN_____

FAMILY COURT HISTORY: N CRIMINAL HISTORY: N PROBATION/PAROLE/PRETRIAL RELEASE HISTORY N
INCARCERATIONS/PLACEMENTS: __N__ PENDING CHARGES: __N__
SOURCE OF SUPPORT: K. TIRES/FT/200/WK RESIDES WITH/RELATIONSHIP: ERNEST & SHIRLEY PARENTS
EDUCATION: 12TH CHILDREN: 0 HEALTH/DISABILITY: N MENTAL HEALTH: Y SUBSTANCE ABUSE: Y

DISPOSITION: DATE:

CIRCUMSTANCES OF THE OFFENSE

On September 9, 1993, the defendant forced an 8-year-old female, the daughter of his employer's paramour, to touch his penis, then rubbed her vagina with his hand, followed by lying on top of the victim while clothed and "humping her."

DEFENDANT'S STATEMENT

Defendant states that he and the victim were sleeping on her living room floor when he began touching her. He wants to make it clear that he and the child were at least partially clothed. He expressed little remorse, minimizes the serious nature of the offense, and claims that his behavior was an isolated event brought on by depression over problems at home, particularly with his father.

VICTIM IMPACT

The victim's mother states that there is no financial restitution to be made but wants it known that they feel very betrayed by the defendant whom they trusted and considered to be a friend. She says that the child has attended counseling but remains fearful that the defendant will hurt her again. The family wishes to have the defendant receive maximum incarceration for his crime.

MENTAL HEALTH

Defendant has been referred to Child and Family Services for treatment in an adult male sexual perpetrator's group.

SUBSTANCE ABUSE

Defendant admits to drinking a few beers twice a week and says he had consumed three beers on the night of the present offense, although he does not see his use as problematic and does not believe it caused him to commit the crime. Although there is no evidence that the defendant uses illegal drugs, military records show that his association with a civilian drug user led to narcotics and stolen property being found in the defendant's car.

COMMENTARY

This immature and egocentric defendant is lacking in insight and a sense of personal responsibility, making him unlikely to understand and admit the serious nature of his crime unless initially faced with a period of incarceration.

RECOMMENDATION

	Incarceration	State _____
_____	Incarceration	State _____
_____	Probation	Local _____
x	Shock Probation	
_____	Conditional Discharge	
_____	Alternative Program	
_____	YO Eligible _____	
	Required _____	
_____	Certificate of Relief	
	Eligible _____	
_____	Restitution	
x	Other (i.e., Fine, Community Service) Order of Protection for Victim and Family	

ATTACHMENT(S)

_____	Prior Presentence Investigation
_____	Juvenile History
x	NYSID
_____	Motor Vehicle Abstract
_____	Substance Abuse Evaluation
_____	Psychiatric, Psychological, or Mental Health Information
_____	Victim Impact
x	Conditions of Probation
_____	Other _____

FIGURE 4.2 (*continued*)

DATE/AUTHOR

_____

Linda W. Limpert
Probation Officer

_____

Gayle A. Anderson
Probation Supervisor

FIGURE 4.2   (*continued*)

FIGURE 4.3   Long-form presentence investigation report.

DEPARTMENT OF PUBLIC SAFETY AND CORRECTIONAL SERVICES

DIVISION OF PAROLE AND PROBATION
PRESENTENCE INVESTIGATION

Name: BLEACH, Charlotte Marie
Alias: None
Telephone Number: 222-7777
Address: 8515 Carver Beach Road
　　　　　Apt. B
　　　　　Odessa, Md 21601
Date of Birth: 5/6/70   *Age:* 24
Place of Birth: Odessa, MD
Sex: Female　　　*Race:* White
Height: 5'4"　　　*Weight:* 140
Marital Status: Separated
Occupation: Checker (Part time)
Education: 11th Grade
Social Security Number: 212-21-2111
Driver's LicenseNumber: B-220-195-887-076
SID Number: 02001G2
FBI Number: 444-277-L3
Defense Attorney: John S.Hawkins
State's Attorney: John Anders
Sentencing Judge:
Date of Disposition:

Date Referral Recieved: 1/3/95
Date Completed: 2/3/95
Investigator: Alexandria Decker
Investigator's Phone Number: 222-1234

Court: Odessa Co. District Court
Indictment Number: 001100612
Offense: Assault & Battery

Trial Judge: Charles L. Brooks
Trial Date: 1/3/95
Plea: Not Guilty
Trial: Court
Detainers: None

Bond: $10,000 Unsecured
Custody: Not Applicable
Codefendants & Status: None

Disposition:

Description of Present Offense:

On May 6, 1994, Charlotte Marie Bleach assaulted Ms. Carol Morgan at Adam's Bar and Grill in Odessa, Maryland. The offense occurred at 12:30 A.M. The defendant and Ms. Morgan had been seated at a bar drinking beer for several hours and an argument ensued when Ms. Morgan accused Mrs. Bleach of "running with her husband." Mrs. Bleach denied the accusation, but the argument escalated to the point that Mrs. Bleach struck Ms. Morgan in the face with her fist. Ms. Morgan fell to the floor striking her head on a barstool. The Odessa Police Department was called and Mrs. Bleach was arrested and charged.

Ms. Morgan was taken to the Odessa Hospital for treatment. The extent of her injuries have not been determined. According to the police report, the defendant appeared to have been intoxicated when arrested; in fact, she passed out in the police car on the way to jail.

Statement of Defendant:
Mrs. Bleach could not recall any of the details of the offense thus the police report was reviewed. The subject stated that she went to the bar with Ms. Morgan around 7:30 P.M. The two women are friends, though they have not seen each other since. While at the bar, Mrs. Bleach drank two beers over an approximate five-hour period. She does recall the argument about Ms. Morgan's accusation of Mrs. Bleach running with her husband. In regards to the assault, Mrs. Bleach cannot remember it but said, "If I really did that, I'm sorry."

Criminal Record:

Juvenile
A check with the local office of the Juvenile Services Administration revealed no juvenile record.

Adult

Date/Place of Offense	Offense	Date/ Disposition	Source	Representation
8/13/90 Odessa, MD	Disorderly Conduct	9/20/90 Fined $10	Odessa Police Dept.	Waived

According to the Police Department's report, the subject was acting in a disorderly matter on Main Street, Odessa, Maryland on 8/13/87. When asked to leave the area, she refused and was subsequently placed under arrest.

Date/Place of Offense	Offense	Date/ Disposition	Source	Representation
4/17/93 Odessa, MD	Disorderly Conduct	6/20/93 Fined $60 & $15 costs	Odessa Police Dept.	Waived

The subject was arrested for causing a disturbance in the Memco Department Store, Odessa, Maryland. Mrs. Bleach was engaged in a heated argument with the manager and refused to leave the store.

Date/Place of Offense	Offense	Date Disposition	Source	Representation
5/10/94 Odessa, MD	Shoplifting	Case settled on 6/20/94 at request of State	Odessa Co. Dist. Court	Waived

FIGURE 4.3 *(continued)*

The subject was accused of taking a sweater out of the AMES Department Store without paying for it. On the trial date, however, the prosecuting witness failed to appear and the State settled the charge.

Motor Vehicle Record:
A check with the Maryland Department of Transportation revealed the defendant has a valid class D license which is due to expire on May 6, 1997. She currently has three points against her license (7/4/94 - Reckless Driving).

Institutional / Parole & Probation History:
A review of the defendant's prior record indicates no periods of incarceration for any convictions nor any periods of probation supervision.

Personal History:
Charlotte Marie Bleach (nee Wright) was born in Odessa, Maryland on May 6, 1970. She is the youngest of four children borne to the union of Oliver and Edith Wright. The defendant's parents were lifetime residents of Odessa County. When the defendant was 11 years old, her mother died. This investigator spoke to the father, Oliver Wright and her older sister, Melissa Nelson, at Mr. Wright's home. Mr. Wright had little information to offer concerning his daughter. He appeared embarrassed about Mrs. Bleach's legal problems. He did say he always did the best he could for the family. Ms. Nelson is eight years older than the defendant. She thinks the subject was greatly effected by her mother's death. Also, Ms. Nelson offered that the subject married too young and was not ready for the responsibility and financial pressure of raising two sons. Ms. Nelson states she is concerned about the subject and suspects she drinks too much. In addition, Ms. Nelson commented that her sister has a negative attitude toward men. As far as Ms. Nelson knows, the subject has not had a "serious relationship" since her husband left.

The defendant was reluctant to discuss her mother's death. She said she missed her mother, but the family has never discussed the effects of the death among themselves. Mrs. Bleach did state that an older brother, who lives in Frederick, had been arrested for assault while drinking.

Mrs. Bleach married George Allen Bleach on March 4, 1989 in Odessa, Maryland. A set of twins (Jim and John) was born to this union in June, 1989. In December of that year, the couple separated. Mrs. Bleach stated that her husband left after he had been running around. The defendant also said her husband has not contributed to the support of the children.

At the present time, Mrs. Bleach lives in a two-bedroom apartment with her two children. She has been residing there for about one year and indicates that she has no intentions of moving in the near future. The offender's apartment is moderately furnished and appears well kept. Although the apartment is located in a moderate income area, the subject only pays $300 per month rent because the apartment is federally subsidized.

Education:
Mrs. Bleach attended the Odessa County High School, withdrawing at the completion of grade 11. School records indicate that she had an average intelligence when tested in 1988. Her grades were average. School records indicate that she did not cause any discipline problems.

FIGURE 4.3 (continued)

Employment:

Name /Address of Employer	Dates	Positions	Salary	Termination
A&P Tea Company Main Street Odessa, Md	2/15/93 Present	Checker	$400 per wk.	N/A

Mr. Paul Jones, manager, stated that the defendant was dependable. He will continue employment even though she has been convicted on this charge.

| Acme Packing Co. Odessa, MD | 4/2/89 1/3/93 | Packer | $235 | Quit to go to the A&P |

The Acme Packing Company was sold to a new owner in 1993 and former personnel records indicate the subject was a good worker, but began missing work at the end of employment.

Health:

Mrs. Bleach's only physical ailment is high blood pressure which she has been taking medication for since March, 1991. This investigator spoke to Dr. Lester Brown, and he confirms the subject's condition and treatment. He did offer that lately, Mrs. Bleach has missed appointments.

The defendant denied any problem with alcohol. She was introduced to alcohol by her family when she was 10 years old. When 18, she began to drink with her friends. Mrs. Bleach said she drinks to relax and it usually takes four beers to feel relaxed. Sometimes, she does drink five or six beers. In addition to this incident, there was another occasion when she suffered a memory lapse while drinking.

Mrs. Bleach started smoking marijuana at 14. In the past, she has used the drug more than once per week, but has not used it for approximately two years.

Financial:

Assets	Obligations
Salary - $450 per week	Rent - $400 per month
Automobile - 1975 Volkswagon	Utilities - $58 per month
Child support - $75 per week	

Her husband is under court order to pay $75 per week child support, but has made no payments in the last two years and a warrant is currently outstanding for his arrest.

Other Significant Factors:

None.

Alexandria Decker   Date
Senior Agent
Odessa Office
222-1234

FIGURE 4.3   (continued)

Approved:

_____
Robert Blake   Date
Field Supervisor I

AD/smf
D/T: 2/3/95

Evaluation:

Charlotte Marie Bleach is appearing before the Court to be sentenced on a charge of Assault and Battery. This writer believes that her involvement in this offense may have had its beginnings in two tragic, earlier circumstances in Charlotte's life; the death of her mother and the desertion of her husband. The defendant seems to have failed to adjust to the death of her mother even though 13 years have elapsed. She has avoided entering into any serious male relationships in the entire seven years of separation from her husband and it is to be noted that Mrs. Bleach's criminal history begins only eight months after her husband's departure.

There seems to be a pattern of difficulty in controlling anger as seen in the defendant's two prior convictions for Disorderly Conduct. The present offense also documents an inability to control anger. It also appears that Mrs. Bleach might be developing a problem with alcohol. This is the second time the defendant has drank to a point of a memory lapse.

On the positive side, the subject has a good work record and has done her best to meet her obligations to her children without the aid of a husband. Her employer is willing to continue her employment even though she has been convicted on this charge.

Recommendation:

The defendant appears to be an individual who could best be treated in the community rather than in an institution. She does not appear to be a threat to society. Therefore, this investigator recommends probation with the following conditions: 1) that she pay restitution, 2) that she be evaluated at the Odessa County Mental Health Department to determine if mental health and/or alcohol counseling is indicated.

_____
Alexandria Decker   Date
Senior Agent
Odessa Office
222-1234

FIGURE 4.3 *(continued)*

Approved:

_____
Robert Blake   Date
Field Supervisor I

AD/smf
D/T: 2/3/95

FIGURE 4.3   *(continued)*

REQUIRING A PRESENTENCE INVESTIGATION REPORT

In some states, the law requires a PSI report for crimes punishable by more than one year of imprisonment; in others, the judge retains the discretion to order a report. In New York and Michigan, for example, a long-form report is required in all felony cases; in misdemeanor cases, the report is discretionary and, when done, is usually in the short form. In Missouri and Nevada, a PSI is mandatory in all felony cases unless the defendant waives the requirement—in which case, at the judge's discretion, a PSI may still be compiled. In Texas, no legal requirement exists that a PSI be prepared in each felony case; the trial judge has discretion to order a report or to sentence without one. In Illinois (Chapter 38, 1005-3-1), "A defendant shall not be sentenced for a felony before a written presentence report of investigation is presented to and considered by the court," although this right is frequently waived by the defense counsel because a plea agreement has already been arranged.

PLEA BARGAINING

Most court cases in the United States, criminal and civil, are settled not by trial but by negotiation (or dropping of the action). In the criminal justice system, negotiated settlements are referred to as *plea bargaining*—an ad hoc exchange between a defendant who agrees to plead guilty to a criminal charge and a prosecutor who, explicitly or implicitly, offers leniency in return. Plea bargaining is criticized for providing criminals with excessive leniency and coercing defendants to waive their constitutional rights to a trial. Its extensive use can be explained by the time it saves the prosecutor and defense, and the certainty of outcome it offers to both. (For a more detailed discussion of plea bargaining, see Abadinsky [1995].)

PLEA BARGAINING AND THE PRE-PLEA INVESTIGATION

In many jurisdictions, the extensive use of plea bargaining has reduced the need for a PSI. A plea bargain requires that the defendant enter a plea of guilty in return for some form of sentence leniency. In many jurisdictions, the plea agreement actually specifies the sentence that the defendant will receive. Under such conditions, a presentence report would not serve any useful purpose at a sentencing hearing. Plea bargaining, however, has resulted in the use of a pretrial/plea investigation report in many, if not most, jurisdictions (Figure 4.4).

If prosecutor and defense counsel negotiate a plea agreement and the judge retains a great deal of discretion over the sentence to be imposed (which is the case in many states), the judge may request a pretrial investigation before agreeing to the negotiated plea. In Illinois, for example, for a simple burglary as a first offense, the judge has the discretion to sentence an offender to a term of three, four, or five years, all the way up to fourteen years. In Cook County, which includes the city of Chicago, judges often require a pretrial/plea investigation report before confirming a plea agreement; in fact, short-form pretrial reports are more frequent than PSI reports.

The practice of using a pre-plea investigation report (PPI) requires that the defendant agree to the investigation; in New York (*Code of Criminal Procedure*, 350.10),

> The probation department shall conduct a pre-plea investigation only upon a court order and written authorization by the defendant, his attorney, the prosecuting attorney and the judge ordering the investigation. Such written authorization shall include statements that no probation department personnel will be called to testify regarding information acquired by the probation department, that information obtained by the probation department may not be used in a subsequent trial, and that this exemption does not apply to defense or prosecution material which may be included in the plea report.

Probation officers in Georgia are instructed: "If the defendant or his/her attorney refuses to sign the authorization, discontinue the investigation and report this fact to the court." In Ohio, a PSI cannot be conducted prior to a finding of guilty

> unless the defendant, on advice of counsel, has consented to allow the investigation to proceed before adjudication, and adequate precautions are taken to ensure that information disclosed during the presentence investigation does not come to the attention of the prosecution, the court or the jury prior to adjudication.

As in Georgia, "refusal of the defendant, his attorney or both to sign the waiver shall constitute an end to the investigation."

STATE OF FLORIDA
DEPARTMENT OF CORRECTIONS
PROBATION AND PAROLE SERVICES
PRE-PLEA RELEASE FORM

Defendant _____Circuit _____County _____

Docket No. _____

DEFENDANT'S APPROVAL TO CONDUCT A PRESENTENCE
INVESTIGATION BEFORE CONVICTION OR PLEA

I, _____ defendant, hereby consent to a Presentence investigation by the Department of Corrections, Probation and Parole Serivces Office, for the purpose of obtaining information useful to the Court in the event I should hereafter plead guilty, or *nolo contendere*, or be found guilty.

By this consent, I do not admit any guilt or waive any rights and I understand that any report prepared can be shown to the Court before I have been found guilty only if I so agree in writing. Otherwise, I understand that any report prepared will not be shown to anyone unless and until I have been found guilty or entered a plea of guilty or *nolo contendere*.

I have read, or had read to me, the aforegoing consent and fully understand it. No promise has been made to me as to what final disposition will be made of my case.

_____   _____
(Date)   (Signature of Defendant)

_____   _____
(Date)   (Defense Attorney)

DEFENDANT'S CONSENT TO THE COURT'S INSPECTION OF THE PRESENTENCE
INVESTIGATION PRIOR TO PLEA OR FINDING OF GUILT

I, _____ defendant, hereby consent to review of my presentence investigation report by a Circuit Judge at any time, including the time prior to entry of a plea of guilty or *nolo contendere* or a finding of guilt.

I have read, or had read to me, the aforegoing consent and fully understand it. No promise has been made to me as to what final disposition of my case will be.

_____   _____
(Date)   (Signature of Defendant)

_____   _____
(Date)   (Defense Attorney)

_____   _____
(Date)   (Prosecuting Attorney)

FIGURE 4.4   Florida Pre-Plea Release Form.

Sentencing Guidelines

Sentencing guidelines have reduced, and in some cases obviated, the need for a PSI. Several states and the federal government use sentencing guidelines in an attempt to limit judicial discretion and reduce sentence disparity—a turn toward classicalism. In Minnesota, for example, sentencing guidelines were instituted in 1980 and are changed periodically (Figure 4.5). A judge is provided with a sentencing grid that considers only the severity of the instant offense and the offender's prior criminal history. Departures from mandatory sentences derived from the grid are permitted only under limited circumstances. Probation officers (actually, state parole and probation agents) are responsible for completing the sentencing guidelines worksheet and calculating the presumed sentence; they no longer write PSI reports (Doom, Roerich, and Zoey, 1988).

The Federal Sentencing Reform Act of 1984, which became effective in 1987, was designed to reduce sentence disparity and phase out parole release by 1992. The statute also generated a great deal of confusion and litigation—many judges opposed the legislation's sentencing guidelines that removed much judicial discretion. On January 18, 1989, however, the Supreme Court ruled that the 1987 sentencing rules, established by a commission created under the 1984 statute, were constitutional (*Mistretta v. United States*, 488 U.S. 361). This ruling did not end the controversy: Appeals over guidelines interpretation have burdened appellate courts, and judges have been concerned about the lack of consideration given to such factors as age, education, and family ties for rendering sentencing decisions.

The commission established 43 offense levels and assigned each federal offense to one of the levels: murder, for example, scores 43; blackmail, 9. Judges must impose sentences according to these levels, adding to or subtracting from them based on factors such as the offender's age, prior record, use of a firearm, or cooperation with the prosecution. Any deviation from the guidelines requires a written explanation. The guidelines manual is thicker than this book, and hundreds of amendments have been added. Inmates can earn a maximum of 54 days off their sentence per year for good behavior (instead of the more typical one day for each day served).

The 1984 law resulted in radical changes in the content and format of the PSI and significantly changed the role of federal probation officers. Instead of preparing presentence investigations based on a positivistic approach to the offender, the PO must now focus on the details of the offense and prior criminal history (Figure 4.6). Franklin Marshall, a federal PO in Philadelphia, points out that it has become imperative "that every detail about offense and offenders be included when these reports are prepared. Otherwise, minor point fluctuations on either offense level or criminal history can make a significant difference of several years in time to be served by convicted offenders" (1989: 10).

David Adair and Toby Slawsky (1991: 60) state that in preparing the presentence report, "the probation officer sets out the details of the offense and the

Italicized numbers within the grid denote the range within which a judge may sentence without the sentence being deemed a departure.

Offenders with nonimprisonment felony sentences are subject to jail time according to law.

CRIMINAL HISTORY SCORE

SEVERITY LEVELS OF CONVICTION OFFENSE		0	1	2	3	4	5	6 or more
Sale of a Simulated Controlled Substance	I	12*	12*	12*	13	15	17	19 18-20
Theft-Related Crimes ($2500 or less) Check Forgery ($200-$2500)	II	12*	12*	13	15	17	19	21 20-22
Theft Crimes ($2500 or less)	III	12*	13	15	17	19 18-20	22 21-23	25 24-26
Nonresidential Burglary Theft Crimes (more than $2500)	IV	12*	15	18	21	25 24-26	32 30-34	41 37-45
Residential Burglary Simple Robbery	V	18	23	27	30 29-31	38 36-40	46 43-49	54 50-58
Criminal Sexual Conduct Second Degree (a) & (b)	VI	21	26	30	34 33-35	44 42-46	54 50-58	65 60-70
Aggravated Robbery	VII	48 44-52	58 54-62	68 64-72	78 74-82	88 84-92	98 94-102	108 104-112
Criminal Sexual Conduct, First Degree Assault, First Degree	VIII	86 81-91	98 93-103	110 105-115	122 117-127	134 129-139	146 141-151	158 153-163
Murder, Third Degree Murder, Second Degree (felony murder)	IX	150 144-156	165 159-171	180 174-186	195 189-201	210 204-216	225 219-231	240 234-246
Murder, Second Degree (with intent)	X	306 299-313	326 319-333	346 339-353	366 359-373	386 379-393	406 399-413	426 419-433

First-degree murder is excluded from the guidelines by law and continues to have a mandatory life sentence.
At the discretion of the judge, up to a year in jail or other nonjail sanctions can be imposed as conditions of probation.

FIGURE 4.5   Minnesota sentencing guidelines grid.

defendant's criminal history. The probation officer then applies the sentencing guidelines to those facts."

> The presentence report has become more a legal document than a diagnostic tool, citing facts, statutes, and guidelines, justifying and supporting positions the guidelines treat as relevant in arriving at a sentencing range. The format and presentation of information is dominated by facts related to the offender's offense behavior and criminal history, the two primary factors establishing a defendant's sentencing range. Social and personal history information is reported, however, primarily to aid the court in choosing a point within the range, imposing conditions of release, and/or departures. (Denzlinger and Miller, 1991: 51)

IN UNITED STATES DISTRICT COURT
FOR THE WESTERN DISTRICT OF OREGON

UNITED STATES OF AMERICA	)	
	)	
vs.	)	**PRESENTENCE INVESTIGATION REPORT**
	)	
Michael Mali	)	**Docket No.** CR 94-010-01-KGG

Prepared for: The Honorable Kelly G. O'Grady
U.S. District Judge

Prepared by: Craig T. Finkle
U.S. Probation Officer
Breaker Bay, OR 97010
(503) 111-4281

Assistant U.S. Attorney	**Defense Counsel**
Mr. Robert Nelson	Mr. Arthur Birg
United States Courthouse	737 North 7th Street
Breaker Bay, OR 97010	Breaker Bay, OR 97045
(503) 111-1219	(503) 112-2763

Sentence Date: June 5, 1995

Offense: <u>Count one</u>: Conspiracy to Violate Federal Narcotics Laws
(21 U.S.C. § 846)—10 years to Life/$4,000,000 fine

Release Status: Detained without bail since 6/19/93

Detainers: None

Codefendants:
Sammy Maples—CR 94-011-02	Authur Kent—CR 94-011-04
John Smith—CR 94-011-03	Leon Williams—CR 94-011-05

Related Cases: None

Date Report Prepared: 5/15/95   **Date Report Revised:** 5/26/95

Identifying Data:

Date of Birth:	3/19/62
Age:	32
Race:	White
Sex:	Male
S.S. #:	292-09-3156
FBI #:	422-22-67B
USM#:	73621-679
Other ID #:	Not Applicable
Education:	11th grade
Dependents:	Two
Citizenship:	U.S.

FIGURE 4.6   Presentence investigation report focusing on details of offense and prior criminal history.

Legal Address: 1430 Bird Avenue
                       Breaker Bay, OR 97001

Aliases: None

Optional Photograph

PART A. THE OFFENSE

Charges and Convictions

1. Michael Mali, Sammy Maples, Arthur Kent, John Smith, and Leon Williams were named in a two-count indictment returned by a Western District of Oregon grand jury on November 1, 1994. Count one charges that from December 1991 until June 19, 1994, the defendants conspired to violate the federal narcotics laws, in violation of 21 U.S.C.§ 846. Count two charges that on June 19, 1944, the defendants possessed with intent to distribute 500 grams or more of heroin, in violation of 21 U.S.C. §§ 812, 841(a)(1), 841(b)(1)(B) and 18 U.S.C. § 2.

2. On December 1, 1994, Michael Mali and Sammy Maples both pled guilty to count one and are scheduled to be sentenced on June 9, 1995. On December 12, 1994, Leon Williams pled guilty to count one, and he is scheduled to be sentenced on June 13, 1995. On December 13, 1994, Arthur Kent pled guilty to count one and is scheduled to be sentenced on June 15, 1995. All of the above defendants have pled guilty in accordance with the terms of a written plea agreements which require a plea of guilty to count one in return for the dismissal of count two in the original indictment. On December 14, 1994, John Smith was found guilty on count two after a jury trial, and he is scheduled to be sentenced on June 15, 1995.

3. The assistant U.S. attorney has filed a motion pursuant to 18 U.S.C. § 3553(e) and U.S.S.G. § 5K1.1, advising that the defendant has provided substantial assistance to the government. Accordingly, the government will recommend a sentence below the mandatory minimum sentence and applicable guideline range.

FIGURE 4.6   (*continued*)

The Offense Conduct

4. This case was initiated by the Drug Enforcement Administration in December 1992, upon the receipt of information from a confidential informant that Michael Mali and Sammy Maples were involved in the distribution of multiple-ounce quantities of heroin from an apartment located in the Breaker Bay housing project. Subsequent investigation revealed that Mali and Maples were regularly distributing heroin to Arthur Kent. After several months of investigation and surveillance, drug enforcement agents learned that Kent regularly purchased heroin from Mali and Maples, and sold the heroin to Leon Williams, who would travel to the Breaker Bay area each month from Bodega Bay, Oregon, a small community approximately 200 miles south of Breaker Bay. Williams gave Kent the money to purchase the heroin, but generally waited in a parked car near the housing project while Kent conducted the heroin transaction inside apartment 4J in the housing project. Mali and Maples relied on a number of heroin sources, including two unidentified Asian males, and on at least two occasions, John Smith.

5. According to information provided by a confidential informant and testimony presented at John Smith's trial, sometime in August 1992, Mali met Smith while they were being held by local police authorities on unrelated drug charges. While in custody, Mali told Smith that he sold small quantities of heroin in Breaker Bay and relied on various suppliers. Mali complained that his suppliers were unreliable and frequently provided him with heroin of poor quality. Smith, although cautious and somewhat suspicious of Mali, revealed that he might be aware of other suppliers whom Mali might use once he was released from custody and ready to resume his drug distribution operation. The two exchanged telephone numbers and agreed to discuss the use of Smith's suppliers in the future. Several days later, Mali was released from custody and shortly thereafter resumed his heroin distribution operation with his partner Maples.

6. In late December 1992, Mali contacted Smith by telephone and discussed the possibility of obtaining 10 ounces of heroin. After several weeks of negotiations, Smith agreed to meet with Mali at Mali's apartment in the housing project. On February 14, 1993, Smith was observed by federal agents outside the housing project near Mali's apartment, accompanied by an unidentified Hispanic male. Prior to entering the apartment building, Smith was observed handing a package, which investigators later learned contained 300 grams of heroin, to the Hispanic male. Once inside the apartment, Mali tested a small sample of the heroin, and agreed to purchase the package of heroin for $70,000. Mali gave Smith the $70,000 in cash, and, in turn, Smith directed the Hispanic male to give Mali the package of heroin. A short time later, Smith and his companion were observed leaving Mali's apartment.

7. Later that afternoon, federal agents observed Arthur Kent and Leon Williams driving a 1993 Porsche in the vicinity of the housing project. Williams parked the vehicle nearby and Kent was observed carrying a brown duffle bag as he entered the housing project where he proceeded to Mali's apartment. According to the confidential informant, once inside the apartment, Kent briefiy spoke to Mali and the two proceeded to a back bedroom where Mali was known to weigh and package drugs. A few moments later, Kent and Mali returned to the living room of the apartment and Mali was carrying the brown duffle bag that Kent brought to the apartment. Mali then emptied the duffle bag that contained a large sum of U.S. currency, bound in $50, $20, and $10 denominations. Mali assured Kent that he would find the heroin to be of high quality and agreed to provide additional quantities of heroin to Kent whenever his out-of-town buyer needed them. A short time later, Kent left the apartment and returned to the vehicle in which Williams was waiting.

8. For several months, agents maintained surveillance on Mali's apartment, and on several occasions, the agents monitored Smith's arrival at Mali's apartment, followed by the arrival of Kent and Williams. On each occasion, Williams would remain outside, sitting in the 1993 Porsche, while Kent entered Mali's apartment. Kent would deliver a large duffle bag to the

FIGURE 4.6 (continued)

apartment and return a short time later carrying a small package under his arm. On June 14, 1993, an undercover agent of the Drug Enforcement Administration, posing as a drug purchaser, met with Mali in the vicinity of the housing project to negotiate the purchase of 10 grams of heroin. Mali told the undercover agent that he expected to receive a shipment of heroin the following day and that, while he anticipated transacting a large heroin deal with another out-of-town customer, he would be able to sell the undercover agent 10 grams of heroin from the shipment for $7,000.

9. For the next two days, federal agents maintained 24-hour surveillance of the housing project, and on June 19, 1993, the agents observed Smith when he arrived at Mali's residence carrying a shopping bag. Smith arrived at the apartment with the shopping bag and had a gun, which was visible in his waist band. Smith remained in Mali's apartment and a short time later, Williams and Kent arrived. As on previous occasions, Williams remained in the car parked nearby while Kent went to Mali's apartment, carrying a blue gym bag. Shortly thereafter, the agents entered the apartment, and the defendants scattered. The agents observed Maples, Kent, and Smith seated in the back bedroom of the apartment, and they were all placed under arrest without incident. Other federal agents, who were positioned outside of the apartment building, observed Mali as he jumped out of the apartment's kitchen window and landed in a patch of bushes on the ground below, where he was placed under arrest. At the time of his arrest, a loaded .38-caliber revolver was found in the bushes near the spot where Mali landed. In addition, other agents proceeded to the parked Porsche where Williams was waiting. At the time of Williams's arrest, agents recovered a .357 magnum from his waist band. Williams told the agents that he had driven to Breaker Bay from Bodega Bay and had driven Kent to the vicinity to visit some friends.

10. The agents searched Mali's apartment and recovered a large quantity of suspected heroin from the toilet that the defendants had attempted to destroy. The agents safeguarded the seized narcotics using plastic bags. The following day, the bags were reopened and the water/heroin solution was drained into plastic bottles for laboratory submission. According to the results of a later laboratory report, the agents recovered a total of 725.12 grams of 20 percent pure heroin. In addition, the agents recovered an additional 55.4 grams of 20 percent heroin from the top of the refrigerator in the kitchen, and heroin residue from a table in the bedroom, along with an Ohaus triple beam scale, a strainer, and other drug-related paraphernalia. Moreover, the agents seized $103,160 in cash bundles of U.S. currency from the blue gym bag that the agents had previously observed being carried by Kent, and $16,870 from Kent's jacket pocket.

11. The agents then proceeded to apartment 6J, where, according to confidential informant information, Mali was believed to store narcotics proceeds and other property. The apartment was occupied by Michael Mali's mother, Carol Mali, who consented to a search of the apartment. Agents recovered an additional $13,000 in cash and jewelry, later appraised to be valued at $50,000.

12. All of the participants in this offense shared equally important functions in this loosely organized heroin distribution operation. Defendant John Smith was the supplier of the heroin for the February 14, 1993 and June 19, 1993 transactions. Michael Mali and Sammy Maples were the brokers, while Arthur Kent was the middleman (and Williams's courier). Williams was a buyer, who authorities believe operated a street-level heroin distribution operation in Bodega Bay, Oregon, and he frequently traveled to Breaker Bay to purchase heroin. A total of 1090.52 grams (or slightly more than one kilogram) of heroin were distributed during the course of this offense, with an estimated wholesale value of $350,000.

Victim Impact

13. There are no victims in this offense.

FIGURE 4.6   (*continued*)

Adjustment for Obstruction of Justice

14. Although the defendant attempted to flee prior to his arrest, he was apprehended almost immediately. The probation officer has no other information to suggest that the defendant impeded or obstructed justice.

Adjustment for Acceptance of Responsibility

15. During an interview with drug enforcement officials shortly after his arrest, and later during an interview with the probation officer, Mali readily admitted his involvement in this offense. In substance, Mali acknowledged that he participated in this conspiracy to distribute heroin and takes full responsibility for his conduct.

Offense Level Computation

16. The 1990 edition of the *Guidelines Manual* has been used in this case.

17. **Base Offense Level:** The guideline for a 21 U.S.C. § 846 offense is found in U.S.S.G. § 2D1.4. That section provides that the base offense level for a narcotics conspiracy shall be the same as if the object of the conspiracy or attempt had been completed. In this case, the defendant conspired to distribute 1090.52 grams of heroin. In accordance with the provisions found in U.S.S.G. § 2D1.1(a)(3)(c)(6), the base offense level is 32.   32

18. **Specific Offense Characteristic:** Pursuant to the provision found in U.S.S.G. § 2D1.1(b)(1) because the agents retrieved a loaded .38-caliber revolver in the bushes where the defendant was arrested, the offense level is increased by two levels.   +2

19. **Victim Related Adjustments:** None   0

20. **Adjustment for Role in the Offense:** None   0

21. **Adjustment for Obstruction of Justice:** None   0

22. **Adjustment for Acceptance of Responsibility:** The defendant has shown recognition of responsibility for the offense and a reduction of two levels for Acceptance of Responsibility is applicable under U.S.S.G. § 3E1.1.   -2

23. **Total Offense Level:**   32

Chapter Four Enhancements

24. **Career Criminal Provision:** In accordance with the provisions found in U.S.S.G. § 4B1.1, because the defendant was at least 18 years old at the time of the instant offense, the instant offense is a felony controlled substance offense, and the defendant has at least two prior felony controlled substance convictions as detailed below, Mali is a career criminal and the adjusted offense level is 37.   37

25. **Adjustment for Acceptance of Responsibility:** The defendant has shown recognition of responsibility for the offense and a reduction of two levels for Acceptance of Responsibility is applicable under U.S.S.G. § 3E1.1.   -2

26. **Total Offense Level:**   35

PART B. THE DEFENDANT'S CRIMINAL HISTORY

Juvenile Adjudication(s)

FIGURE 4.6   (*continued*)

27. None

Adult Criminal Conviction(s)

Date of Arrest	Conviction/ Court	Date Sentence Imposed/Dispo.	Guideline/ Points	
28. 3/2/84 (age 22)	Criminal Sale of Controlled Substance, Class D Felony, Breaker Bay Superior Court, Breaker Bay, Oregon Dkt. #86541	9/23/84, 5 years probation	4A1.1(c)	1

The defendant was represented by counsel. Mali was arrested, along with Sidney Reynolds, after Breaker Bay police officers observed them selling a quantity of heroin to a third individual not arrested. At the time of arrest, the police recovered 20 glassine envelopes of heroin, which, according to a later laboratory report, had a total net weight of 3 grams. Mali was represented by counsel and subsequently pled guilty as noted above, although during his interview with the Breaker Bay county probation officer, he denied his guilt in the offense, stating that he pled guilty in return for the assurance that he would be placed on probation supervision. According to local county probation records, Mali successfully completed probation supervision and was given an early discharge from that supervision on September 27, 1986.

29. 4/4/88 (age 26)	Criminal Sale of Controlled Substance, Class C Felony, Breaker Bay Superior Court, Breaker Bay, Oregon Dkt. # 86926	10/24/88, 2 to 4 years imprisonment, paroled 8/4/90 parole revoked 2/27/91, returned to custody.	4A1.1(a)	3

The defendant was represented by counsel. Police officers observed the defendant passing glassine envelopes to others in exchange for money. At the time of his arrest, police officers recovered 55 glassine envelopes containing 2.5 grams of heroin and 16 glassine envelopes containing 26 grains of cocaine, marked "Freeze," wrapped to Mali's arm. Mali failed to return to court as scheduled, and on July 26, 1988, a bench warrant was issued for his arrest. The defendant was subsequently returned to court when he was arrested on a new unrelated charge. During his interview with the probation officer, Mali freely acknowledged possession of the narcotics, although he explained that the drugs were for his own personal use. Mali was arrested on the below-listed charges shortly after his release on parole. According to state parole officials, the defendant's parole was violated, and he was returned to state custody. His sentence ran to expiration.

30. 4/14/88 (age 26)	Criminal Possession of Marijuana, 5th degree, Class B Misd., Breaker Bay Criminal Court, Breaker Bay, Oregon Dkt. #89541	4/19/88, 7 days imprisonment	4A1.1(c)	1

FIGURE 4.6 (continued)

The defendant was represented by counsel. Mali was arrested and originally charged with assault, resisting arrest and criminal possession of marijuana, while at liberty on bail in connection with the above-mentioned offense.

31.	8/19/90 (age 28)	Robbery 3rd degree, Class E Felony, Breaker Bay Superior Court, Breaker Bay, Oregon	2/27/91 18 months to 3 years imprisonment, paroled 8/4/92 discharged maximum expiration on 8/4/93	4A1.1(a) 3

The defendant was represented by counsel. Mali was arrested by Breaker Bay Transit police officers after he snatched a gold chain from a victim's neck. According to the victim, who sustained minor injuries, the defendant approached him at gun point and demanded that he remove the gold chain. When the victim resisted, Mali snatched the chain and fled, but was apprehended when he ran into two transit officers who were standing nearby. The term of imprisonment ran concurrently with his parole revocation of February 27, 1991.

According to information provided by the Oregon State Department of Corrections and a review of his parole supervision file, while incarcerated, Mali received five disciplinary reports, which specifically included threats and disturbing the order of the facility, failure to abide by posted rules, and refusing direct orders. The defendant lost his privileges, and on two occasions he was placed in solitary confinement for short periods of time.

The defendant was released to parole supervision on August 4, 1992 to reside with his grandmother, Claudia Mali in Breaker Bay, and worked as a messenger and a waiter while under supervision. While the defendant's overall adjustment to parole supervision was satisfactory, he was arrested in the instant offense prior to his maximum expiration of parole supervision supervision of August 4, 1993. The Oregon State parole officials have declined to file parole violation charges and have advised that Mali's parole supervision was allowed to expire.

Criminal History Computation

32. The criminal convictions above result in a subtotal criminal history score of 8.

33. At the time of that the instant offense was committed, Mali was on parole supervision for his August 19, 1990, offense. In accordance with the provisions of U.S.S.G. § 4A1.1(d), two points are added.

34. The instant offense was committed less than two years following Mali's release from custody on August 4, 1992, for the sentence imposed regarding the offense of August 19, 1990 As such, pursuant to U.S.S.G. § 4A1.1(d), one point is added.

35. The total criminal history score is 11, and according to the sentencing table found in chapter 5, part A, 10 to 12 criminal history points establish a criminal history category of V; however, the defendant's criminal history category is enhanced to VI because he is considered a career criminal.

36. As detailed above, the defendant has three prior felony convictions involving controlled substances and a crime of violence, and as such pursuant to the provisions found in U.S.S.G. § 4B1.1, Mali is a career criminal and his criminal history category must be VI.

FIGURE 4.6   (*continued*)

Personal and Famly Data

37. Michael Mali was born on March 19, 1962, in Breaker Bay, Oregon, to the union of Carl and Carol Mali, nee Hewson. His parents were never married and seldom lived together, making it necessary for his mother to obtain public assistance for financial support. According to the defendant, his father died in 1990 following a massive heart attack. Prior to his death, the father collected public assistance for financial support and had difficulty maintaining employment. Michael has one brother, David Mali, age 33, who was reared by his maternal grandmother in Washington, D.C. David was previously convicted of narcotics charges in the District of Columbia in May 1991 and sentenced to 30 months' imprisonment. At the present time, David is serving a three-year term of supervised release in this district and is living with his mother, age 67, at the Breaker Bay public housing development in the apartment where the defendant was arrested in the instant offense.

38. The defendant was reared by his paternal grandmother, Claudia Mali, now age 75, who has resided at the Breaker Bay housing project at 1430 Bird Avenue, for the past 30 years. According to the defendant, he has a good relationship with his mother and brother David, although he acknowledged that he has not seen them in several months primarily because his mother abuses alcohol and is difficult to talk to when she is intoxicated.

39. According to the defendant's grandmother, she assumed responsibility for Michael when he was approximately 12 years old because of the frequent fights and discord in the mother's residence, which is located in a nearby building within the same housing project. Michael was a quiet child and was frequently neglected by his mother, who never provided a positive living environment for Michael and frequently allowed him to miss school. The defendant's mother has a reported history of narcotics abuse and was frequently hospitalized and treated for alcohol and narcotics abuse. The grandmother explained that she was employed as a laundry worker prior to her retirement eight years ago and now collects social security insurance and retirement benefits for financial support. She explained that she has always felt that Michael had the potential for positive contributions to the community but was frequently "'sidetracked" by his friends.

40. The defendant has never been married, but from 1986 until 1990 maintained a long-term relationship with his former girlfriend Jackie Smith, now age 27. This union produced one child, Chanel Mali, now age five, who currently resides with Smith's mother in an apartment at the Breaker Bay housing project. Several attempts to contact Ms. Smith have been unsuccessful.

41. Simultaneously, from 1980 until the present, Mali has maintained an ongoing relationship with Sandra Dee, now age 26. This union has produced one child, Cynthia Mali, who was born on October 1, 1992. Mali states that for approximately four months prior to his arrest, he was residing in a third-floor apartment in a three-family house in Bodega Bay, Oregon, which he shared with Ms. Dee that rented for $600 per month. Mali states that after his arrest, Ms. Dee lost the apartment because she was unable to pay the rent and now resides with her mother in an apartment on the lower west side of Breaker Bay. Attempts to contact Ms. Dee have proven negative in that she has failed to appear at the probation office for several scheduled interviews. Although the defendant describes his relationship with Ms. Dee in positive terms, he has elected to reside with his grandmother upon his release from custody.

Physical Condition

42. Michael Mali is 5'7" tall and weighs 170 pounds. He has brown eyes and brown hair and, at the time of our interview, he wore a mustache and goatee. The defendant states that he is in

FIGURE 4.6   (continued)

good general health but noted that he was hospitalized in April 1992 and treated for a gunshot wound to the arm, which he states he received from a stray 9-mm hollow point round fired by his codefendant, Leon Williams, at someone else in a dispute. The defendant states that the bullet broke his arm, and he still has bullet fragments in his arm. Medical records have been requested and are awaited. In addition, Mali noted that he was hospitalized in 1988 after he received a stab wound on his left arm during an argument with his then girlfriend, Jackie Smith.

Mental and Emotional Health

43. The defendant states that he has never been seen by a psychiatrist and describes his overall mental and emotional health as good. We have no documented evidence to suggest otherwise. During our interview, the defendant communicated effectively, but his demeanor is streetwise and tough.

Substance Abuse

44. The defendant states that prior to his arrest he drank alcohol almost every day; however, he does not believe that he is in need of alcohol treatment. The defendant revealed that he has smoked marijuana regularly since 1985 and from 1987 until 1988, he inhaled cocaine and smoked crack cocaine. According to Mali, prior to his state incarceration, he spent approximately $200 a day to support his cocaine addiction but has been relatively drug-free since his release from state custody, although he will occasionally inhale small quantities of cocaine at parties. While in state custody, Mali completed the Network Substance Abuse Program. He attended an outpatient drug treatment program for a brief period after he tested positive for cocaine in January 1993 while under parole supervision. At the time of his arrest in this offense, a urine specimen collected from the defendant by a pretrial services officer tested positive for marijuana and opiates.

Educational and Vocational Skills

45. Mali attended Breaker Bay High School from September 1980 until October 6, 1983, when he was discharged in the first semester of the 12th grade at age 19. According to school officials, the defendant had a poor scholastic record but had an average attendance record and attitude. According to state corrections records, the defendant was administered the BETA IQ test in November 1988 and scored 93. The defendant was enrolled in adult education programming and a pre-GED course in July 1989 until December 1989, while in custody but was removed from the program due to disciplinary action. While in the program he was characterized as an average student, according to available academic reports. Prior to his removal, Mali was characterized as an average student. While incarcerated, the defendant participated in a vocational training building-maintenance program from December 1989 until May 5, 1990 and took office machine repair courses from September 23, 1989, until May 5, 1990. Mali received average to excellent evaluations and was awarded a certificate in plumbing and basic electronics.

Employment Record

46. Mali states that he was briefly employed by messenger services prior to his state prison sentences. While under parole supervision, Mali was gainfully employed for a messenger service, was a waiter, and later a cook until approximately February 1993. Mali was also employed as a porter and dishwasher, earning $7.00 per hour, with Caroline's at the Breaker Bay Sea Port from October 2, 1992 until he resigned in February 1993 According to a representative from Caroline's, Mali was reliable and a good worker and would be considered for rehire.

47. Mali candidly admitted that during significant periods of employment, he sold marijuana, cocaine, and heroin to support himself. Mali asserts that he has earned as much as $18,000 a

FIGURE 4.6   (continued)

day from his narcotics activities. Such claims cannot be directly verified, but the government seized approximately $13,000 in cash and $5,500 in jewelry from the apartment of the defendant's mother on the day of the defendant's arrest. Mali states that he used the money to enjoy the ""fast life," which included the purchase of a 1991 Audi 5000, also recently seized by the government.

Financial Condition: Ability to Pay

48. The defendant prepared a signed financial statement, wherein he reported no assets or liabilities. His counsel has been appointed by the court, and a recent credit bureau inquiry reveals that the defendant has never established credit. Mali has no known sources of income and upon his release he will be financially dependent on others.

PART D. SENTENCING OPTIONS

Custody

49. **Statutory Provisions:** The minimum term of imprisonment for this offense, a Class A felony, is ten years, and the maximum term of imprisonment is life, pursuant to 21 U.S.C. § 846 and 841(b)(1)(A).

50. **Guideline Provisions:** Based on an offense level of 35 and a criminal history category of VI, the guideline range of imprisonment is 292 to 365 months.

Impact of Plea Agreement

51. Under the plea agreement, Mali has entered a guilty plea to count one, the conspiracy count, in return for the dismissal of all other counts. Pursuant to U.S.S.G. § 3D1.2(d), counts involving the same transaction are grouped together into a single group. All of the substantive counts in this offense pertain to the same transactions. Accordingly, a conviction on the additional counts would not affect the offense level or any other guideline calculation.

Supervised Release

52. **Statutory Provisions:** If a term of imprisonment is imposed, a term of supervised release of five years must also be imposed, pursuant to 21 U.S.C. § 846 and 841(b)(1)(A).

53. **Guideline Provisions:** The guideline range for a term of supervised release is at least five years, pursuant to U.S.S.G. § 5D1.2(a).

Probation

54. **Statutory Provisions:** The defendant is ineligible for probation pursuant to 21 U.S.C. § 846 and 841(b)(1)(A).

55. **Guideline Provisions:** The defendant is ineligible for probation, pursuant to U.S.S.G. § 5B1.1(b)(1).

Fines

56. **Statutory Provisions:** The maximum fine for this offense is $4,000,000, pursuant to 21 U.S.C. § 846 and 841(b)(1)(A).

57. A special assessment of $50 is mandatory, pursuant to 18 U.S.C. § 3013.

58. **Guideline Provisions:** Pursuant to U.S.S.G. § 5E1.2(c)(3) the minimum fine in this offense is $20,000, and the maximum fine is $4,000,000.

FIGURE 4.6 (*continued*)

59. Subject to the defendant's ability to pay, the court shall impose an additional fine amount that is at least sufficient to pay the costs to the government of any imprisonment, probation, or supervised release, pursuant to U.S.S.G. § 5E1.2(i). The most recent advisory from the Administrative Office of the U.S. Court suggests that a monthly cost of $1,210.05 be used for imprisonment, a monthly cost of $91.66 for supervision, and a monthly cost of $938.44 for community confinement.

Restitution

60. Restitution is not an issue in this case.

Denial of Federal Benefits

61. **Statutory Provisions:** Pursuant to 21 U.S.C. § 862, upon a second conviction for possession of a controlled substance a defendant may be declared ineligible for any or all federal benefits for up to five years as determined by the court.

62. **Guideline Provisions:** Pursuant to U.S.S.G. § 5F1.6, the court may deny eligibility for certain federal benefits of any individual convicted of distribution or possession of a controlled substance.

PART E. FACTORS THAT MAY WARRANT DEPARTURE

63. The assistant U.S. attorney has filed a motion pursuant to 18 U.S.C. § 3553(e) and U.S.S.G. § 5K1.1, advising that the defendant has provided substantial assistance to the Government. Accordingly, the Government will recommend a sentence below the mandatory minimum sentence and applicable guideline range.

Respectfully submitted,

Chief U.S. Probation Officer

by _____
Craig T. Finkel
U.S. Probation Officer

Approved:

_____
Mark T. Clark   Date 5/30/95
Supervising U.S. Probation Officer

FIGURE 4.6   (*continued*)

SENTENCING RECOMMENDATION

UNITED STATES DISTRICT COURT FOR THE WESTERN DISTRICT OF OREGON
UNITED STATES V. MICHAEL MALI DKT. # CR 91-010-01-KGG

TOTAL OFFENSE LEVEL: 35
CRIMINAL HISTORY CATEGORY: VI

	Statutory Provisions	**Guideline Provisions**	**Recommended Sentence**
CUSTODY:	10 years to life	292 to 365 months	180 months
PROBATION:	Ineligible	Ineligible	Not applicable
SUPERVISED RELEASE:	5 years	At least 5 years	5 years
FINE:	$4,000,000	$20,000 to $4,000,000	$0
RESTITUTION:	Not applicable	Not applicable	Not applicable
SPECIAL ASSESSMENT:	$50	$50	$50

Justification

We have been advised by the assistant U.S. attorney, who has filed a motion for downward departure in this case, that Mali entered into a cooperation agreement shortly after his arrest. In addition to his testimony at the trial of his codefendant, John Smith, Mali has reportedly provided substantial and extraordinary cooperation relative to organized crime figures, over and beyond the scope of this offense. Although the government has filed a motion for downward departure, the conduct in this offense, coupled with the defendant's prior criminal record, would have otherwise supported a sentence near the higher end of the guideline range. Mali has an extensive criminal record, which includes two prior drug-related convictions. At the age of 32, Mali has a limited employment record and, by his own admission, has primarily supported himself through lucrative narcotics trafficking. He has a history of violence and appears to be extremely streetwise and tough. As such, his overall prognosis for rehabilitation is extremely poor, he poses a risk for recidivism, and a sentence of 15 years imprisonment appears appropriate for the protection of the community.

The mandatory five-year statutory term of supervised release is recommended in this case with a special condition requiring drug testing and treatment in view of the defendant's history of drug and alcohol abuse. Although the defendant is subject to the provision of federal benefit denial, in view of his expected jail sentence, these provisions will expire prior to his release from custody. The defendant does not have the ability to pay a fine at this time. No fine is recommended, and, therefore, the fine payment should be waived by the court. Although the court may deny federal benefits to the defendant for up to five years, denial of such benefits is not recommended. Unless the defendant were to receive less than a five-year sentence in this case, the period of ineligibility would expire while he is incarcerated.

Voluntary Surrender

The defendant has been detained without bail since his arrest. In light of his conviction and expected lengthy jail sentence, Mali is not eligible for voluntary surrender in accordance with the provisions found in 18 U.S.C. § 3143(a)(2).

FIGURE 4.6 (*continued*)

Recommendation

It is respectfully recommended that sentence in this case be imposed as follows:

Pursuant to the Sentencing Reform Act of 1984, it is the judgment of the court that the defendant, Michael Mali, is hereby committed to the custody of the Bureau of Prisons to be imprisoned for a term of 180 months.

Upon release from imprisonment, the defendant shall be placed on supervised release for a term of five years. Within 72 hours of release from the custody of the Bureau of Prisons, the defendant shall report in person to the probation office in the district to which the defendant is released.

While on supervised release, the defendant shall not commit another federal, state, or local crime. The defendant shall be prohibited from possessing a firearm or other dangerous device, and he shall not possess a controlled substance. In addition, the defendant shall comply with the standard conditions of supervised release as recommended by the United States Sentencing Commission. The defendant shall also comply with the following special conditions of supervised release: The defendant shall participate in a program of testing and treatment for drug and alcohol abuse, as directed by the probation officer, until such time as the defendant is released from the program by the probation officer.

THE COURT FINDS that the defendant does not have the ability to pay a fine.

IT IS ORDERED that the defendant pay a special assessment in the amount of $50 for count one which shall be due immediately.

Respectfully submitted,

Chief U.S. Probation Officer

by   _____
Craig T. Finkel
U.S. Probation Officer

Aproved:

_____
Mark T. Clark   Date 6/2/95
Supervising U.S. Probation Officer

FIGURE 4.6   (*continued*)

Confidentiality of the Presentence Investigation Report

Some controversy exists concerning whether the contents of the PSI report should be disclosed to the defendant or his or her attorney. The basic argument against disclosure is that sources of information must be protected or they will hesitate to provide information. Family members or employers may fear retribution from the defendant if they provide negative information. In addition, law enforcement agencies may be reluctant to provide confidential information if the defendant or the defendant's attorney will be privy to it.

The basic argument in favor of disclosure is to enable the defendant to contest information that he or she considers unfair and to be protected from the effects of unfounded information. Norm Larkins (1972: 59) states: "Disclosure of information has led probation officers [in Alberta, Canada] to develop techniques whereby the information obtained by them and presented in the report is more objective and accurate (with less reliance on hearsay information)." Before the initial interview with the defendant is conducted, "it is explained that a copy of the report will be made available to the offender or his legal counselor prior to sentencing. It is the duty of the offender to bring to the judge's attention any mistakes or omissions which he feels would be important in influencing the sentencing."

The ABA recommends that all information that adversely affects the defendant be discussed with the defendant or his or her attorney. The President's Commission on Law Enforcement and Administration of Justice stated that "in the absence of compelling reasons for non-disclosure of specific information, the defendant and his counsel should be permitted to examine the entire presentence report" (1972: 356). The National Advisory Commission on Justice Standards and Goals recommended that the PSI be made available to the defense and the prosecution. The commission rejected the argument that sources of information will dry up: "(1) those jurisdictions which have required disclosure have not experienced this phenomenon; and (2) more importantly, if the same evidence were given as testimony at trial, there would be no protection or confidentiality" (1973: 189).

The U.S. Supreme Court has consistently upheld the confidentiality of the presentence investigation report. This has been based on the (presumed) neutrality/objectivity of the probation officer—he or she has no interest in punishment; by disposition and training the PO is a helping, not a prosecutorial, agent. Thus, in the 1949 case of *Williams v. New York* (337 U.S. 241), the judge imposed a sentence of death based on information contained in the PSI report. The defendant had been convicted of murder, but the jury recommended life imprisonment. The PSI—to which the jury was not privy—revealed that Williams was a suspect in 30 burglaries. Although he had not been convicted of these crimes, the report indicated that he had confessed to some and had been identified as the perpetrator of others. The judge had referred to parts of the report indicating that the defendant was a "menace to society."

Williams appealed the death sentence, arguing that the procedure violated due process of law "in that the sentence of death was based upon information supplied by witnesses with whom the accused had not been confronted and as to whom he had no opportunity for cross examination or rebuttal." The Supreme Court rejected this argument, stating:

> Under the practice of individualizing punishments, investigational techniques have been given an important role. Probation workers making reports of their investigations have not been trained to prosecute but to aid offenders. Their reports have been given high value by conscientious judges who want to sentence persons on the best available information rather than on guesswork and inadequate information. To deprive sentencing judges of this kind of information would undermine modern procedural policies that have been cautiously adopted throughout the nation after careful consideration and experimentation. We must recognize that most of the information now relied upon by judges to guide them in the intelligent imposition of sentences would be unavailable if information were restricted to that given in open court by witnesses subject to cross-examination. And the modern probation report draws on information concerning every aspect of a defendant's life. The types and extent of this information make totally impractical if not impossible open court testimony with cross-examination. Such procedure could endlessly delay criminal administration in a re-trial of collateral issues.

Williams was executed.

In the federal system, the contents of the PSI, pursuant to *Rule 32 F.R. Crim.P.*, have been disclosed to the defendant, his or her counsel, and the attorney for the government since 1983, and the 1984 Sentencing Reform Act "largely rejected the sentencing philosophy expressed in Williams" (Adair and Slawsky, 1991: 58). Under the federal system of sentencing guidelines, the contents of the report determine the parameters for imposing a sentence. As a result, the sentencing hearing has become increasingly hostile. In response to defense attorney objections, the probation officer "is obligated to review the objections, reinvestigate if necessary, reevaluate decisions made, and discuss the findings with counsel. Any unresolved objections must be summarized for the court in an addendum to the report. On occasion this process consumes more time than the preparation of the presentence report" (Denzlinger and Miller, 1991: 51).

In some jurisdictions, law or custom allows the defendant access to the report, whereas some states give the judge the option of disclosing the contents of the report. In Texas, the statutes require that the entire contents of the report be revealed to the defendant. However, a trend exists toward adopting the position previously used in the federal system: The PSI can be revealed to the defendant or counsel, but the *Rules of Criminal Procedure* exclude the probation officer's recommendation and any "diagnostic opinion [such as a psychiatric report] which might seriously disrupt a program of rehabilitation, sources of information obtained upon a promise of confidentiality, or any other information which, if disclosed, might result in harm, physical or otherwise, to the defendant or other persons."

In Michigan, although the court must permit the prosecutor, the defendant's attorney, and the defendant an opportunity to review the report prior to sentencing, "the court may exempt from disclosure information or a diagnostic opinion which might seriously disrupt a program of rehabilitation or sources of information obtained on a promise of confidentiality. . . . Any information exempted from disclosure by the court must be specifically noted in the PSI and is subject to appellate review" (*Procedure of the Michigan Department of Corrections* No. OP-BFS-71.01).

CRITICISM OF THE PRESENTENCE INVESTIGATION REPORT

Abraham Blumberg (1970) maintains that some judges do not read the presentence report, whereas others carefully select passages condemning the defendant to read aloud in the courtroom to justify their sentences. He argues that many judges discount the report because of the hearsay nature of the information. Walter Dickey (1979: 33–34) reports on the types of inaccurate or misleading information he found in the PSI reports of one state:

(1) rumors and suspicions that are reported without any factual explanations; (2) incomplete explanations of events that leave a misleading impression; (3) factual errors relating, usually, to the criminal record of the offender.

Rumors and suspicions are often reported in presentence reports and identified as such. The report that the rumor exists may be accurate. What is objectionable is the fact that the subject of the rumor may cause the reader to give more weight to the rumor than it deserves, if any. If the rumor is without foundation, reference to it is particularly troubling.

It is difficult to assess the impact of rumors, although they sometimes seem to directly affect correctional decisions. For example, one sex offender's presentence report contained the statement that the offender "was rumored to have killed his mother." This was referred to in several parole decisions before it was investigated. Upon inquiry, it was determined to the satisfaction of the parole board that the offender had been confined in another state at the time of his mother's death and had no connection to it.

Some reports do not contain complete information and are therefore misleading. One inmate's report contained the statement that he "had been arrested for attempted first degree murder after a barfight. The charges were later dropped." Investigation showed that the reason the charges were dropped was that the inmate was actually the victim of an attack and not the aggressor. The other person involved was later charged with a crime for the attack.

The most frequently recurring factual problem with the reports is related to past offenses. The so-called "FBI Rap Sheet" or "Yellow Sheet" is part of the report. It contains a confounding listing of past offenses that is frequently repetitious (i.e., it reports the same offense more than once). The repetitions are not so identified. Past charges do not always contain their disposition, so the reader is never sure how many offenses there actually were which were dropped and why, what the facts underlying the charges and offenses are, and what the outcome was.

Willard Gaylin (1974) is concerned with the enormous dependence on the PSI that he argues tends to make the probation officer, rather than the judge, the sentencer. Numerous studies have indicated a high correlation between the recommendation of the PO and the judge's sentence. Research by the American Justice Institute (1981), for example, using samples from representative probation departments throughout the United States, found that recommendations for probation were adopted by the sentencing judge between 66 and 95 percent of the time (Figure 4.7). A study of 1994 sentencing recommendations in Nevada revealed a concurrence rate of 97 percent when probation was recommended and 88 percent when the recommendation was imprisonment. A study in one Iowa judicial district revealed much less congruity and in a surprising direction: In many cases, those recommended for incarceration (44 percent) were, instead, sentenced to probation or some lesser sanction, such as diversion or a fine. The researchers concluded that these decisions were probably the result of a plea bargain and prosecutor's recommendation for a nonincarceration sentence (Campbell, McCoy, and Osigweh, 1990).

Rodney Kingsnorth and Louis Rizzo (1979) investigated the relationship between plea bargaining, the probation officer's recommendation, and the final disposition of the case in a large western county. In this county, after the defendant has accepted a "bargain" in exchange for a plea of guilty, the case is sent to the probation department for a PSI report. Kingsnorth and Rizzo found a high correlation (93 percent) between the recommendation and the sentence. However, Robert Dawson (1969) states that the probation officer may write into the PSI the recommendation that the PO believes will be well received by the judge. Eugene Czajkoski (1973) suggests that the prosecutor often finds a way of communicating the plea bargain agreement to the probation department, and the latter responds with a conforming recommendation. Conversely, Dickey (1979: 30) found that in Wisconsin

> The prosecutor is often influenced by the recommendation in the report and the information underlying it. Some prosecutors frequently adopt the report's recommendations as their own recommendation to the court or use it as a benchmark in deciding on their recommendation. Sometimes a plea agreement will include the condition that the prosecutor will adopt the report's recommendation as his own.

Kingsnorth and Rizzo indicate that in the county they studied, the minutes of the plea-bargaining session, including the details of the negotiated agree-

RECOMMENDATION AND SENTENCE	DISTRICT OF COLUMBIA	STATE OF CONNECTICUT	COUNTY OF DELAWARE	COUNTY OF LOS ANGELES	COUNTY OF MULTNOMAH	STATE OF NEW JERSEY	COUNTY OF SANTA CLARA	STATE OF TEXAS
For or against probation	83%	82%	86%	87%	87%	66%	91%	95%
Probation/ incarceration (unspecified)	79	74	78	72	63	63	83	93
Probation/ incarceration (specified)	73	72	78	61	60	62	73	93
Treatment	91	86	NA	95	77	82	88	92
Financial obligation	85	85	NA	95	68	67	95	98
Surveillance	NA	NA	NA	99	92	NA	97	NA

The offender random sample established a high correlation between probation officers' recommendations and judicial sentencing. Levels of agreement between recommendations and sentences were measured in three different ways. The first measure shows the level of agreement between recommendations and sentences "for or against probation." The second measure examined probation/incarceration combinations. The third measure takes into condsideration specified forms of probation/incarceration (e.g., supervised probation with jail on weekends).

Levels of agreement between recommended and court-ordered treatment (alcohol, drug, psychiatric); financial obligation (fine, restitution, community service work); and surveillance (search and seizure, chemical testing); have also been ascertained. Level of agreement is defined narrowly. If, for example, alcohol and drug treatment were recommended, and only alcohol treatment was ordered by the court, the recommendation and court order were not found in agreement.

FIGURE 4.7   Levels of agreement between recommendations and sentences. (*Source:* American Justice Institute, 1981: 165).

ment, are sent to the probation department before the submission of the presentence report. They conclude that "probation officer concurrence with previously negotiated sentence agreements is a consequence, not of case characteristics, but of pressures emanating from the organizational structure of which the probation department is a part, namely the court system itself" (1979: 9). These and other studies serve to remind us that the probation officer is simply one actor in a rather complex setting. How much influence the PO can exert may often depend on procedural or structural variables, or perhaps the officer's force of personality.

In many jurisdictions, the PO is overburdened with presentence investigations and does not have the time to do an adequate investigation and prepare a (potentially) useful report. In courts in which the judge usually pays little or no attention to the contents of the report, the PO will not be inclined to pursue the necessary information and prepare well-written reports. Jonas Robitscher (1980: 35), an attorney and psychiatrist, states that although psychiatric reports and evaluations contained in the PSI often make the difference between probation, a short sentence, or a long sentence, "Many of these reports and evaluations contain dynamic formulations about the cause of behavior based on as little as twenty minutes spent with the subject of the report."

Dickey found a most distressing problem related to the issue of erroneous information in the report:

> Even when an alleged error is challenged at sentencing and a contrary finding made, it does not necessarily follow that the report will be corrected. When a judge makes a finding of fact that is inconsistent with the presentence report, he usually states the finding in the record of the sentencing hearing. Without more, this leaves the report itself uncorrected. The sentencing transcript is not made a part of the report; it is not attached to it. The oral finding does not signal anyone to amend the report or any of the copies of it. Subsequent users of the report, correctional and parole authorities, rely on the uncorrected report. Rarely is the report amended to reflect additional information or findings of fact inconsistent with it at sentencing. (1979: 35)

In Michigan, however, state law requires that "if the court finds that challenged information is inaccurate or irrelevant, that finding will be made part of the court record, and the inaccurate or irrelevant information must be stricken from the report prior to distribution." To improve the reliability of the report, the Massachusetts commissioner of probation provides the following standards:

- The probation officer should identify the sources of information in the report.
- The PO should make personal contact with informants or sources of information, when practicable, who can substantiate information. The PO should clearly state in the report those instances in which information has not been substantiated.

- The PO should obtain pertinent documentation, such as letters, clinical reports, school reports, and certified statements, when practicable. The PO should indicate when information in the report is supported by such documentation.
- Sources of information should be identified in most instances; however, this does not exclude from a report relevant information from unnamed sources or informants with whom the PO has had personal contact. If a probation officer includes such information in an investigative report, the PO shall clearly indicate in the report that the information was obtained from sources or informants not being identified in this report.

Dickey (1979) points out that defendants are often dissatisfied with the role of their attorneys in the sentencing process. Federal District Court Judge Irving Cooper (1977: 101) has stated: "It is particularly distressing that many attorneys for the defense, who have proven themselves competent as to the facts and law in the case at trial . . . display on sentence hardly more than a faint glimmer as to who their clients really are as human beings." Dickey (1979: 36) adds:

> Another source of the sense of injustice is the belief that lawyers do not provide the court with positive information about the offender to supplement the presentence report which, it is frequently asserted, is incomplete. Sophisticated defendants realize that even the most forceful statements, if they are general, are of little value to their case. They recognize the importance of presenting the court with alternatives to confinement (i.e., job or school plan, place to live) if probation is sought or a specific statement of plans after release if a short period of confinement is the goal. These defendants are usually dissatisfied because they feel the court is forced to rely on an incomplete report because their lawyers did not provide the additional information.

In response to this problem, the Legal Aid Society in New York City has used social workers to prepare sentencing memoranda for use by defense counsel at the sentencing hearing. In Buncombe County, North Carolina, I set up a similar effort using senior undergraduate students from Western Carolina University. The students worked for the public defender, providing presentence reports for use by defense counsel. Other profit and nonprofit agencies prepare presentence reports, and privately—for-profit—commissioned PSI reports have proliferated. This trend raises a serious question of equal justice because only those with the necessary financial resources can commission such a report.

REVIEW QUESTIONS

1. Why is the presentence report a manifestation of positive theory?
2. What is the primary purpose of a PSI report?
3 What are the other purposes to which the PSI report can be put?

4. What are the categories of information contained in a PSI report?
5. What are the sources of information for a PSI?
6. Why is the nature of a defendant's prior criminal record important for a probation officer to determine?
7. What variables are considered in making a recommendation for or against a sentence of probation?
8. What is the law and practice with respect to requiring a PSI report?
9. How has plea bargaining affected the PSI report?
10. Why can the federal PSI be considered a classical approach?
11. What are the arguments for and against the contents of a PSI report being disclosed to a defendant or defense counsel?
12. What is the basis of the Supreme Court's determination that a PSI report is confidential?
13. What are the various criticisms of the PSI report?
14. What has led to the use of the privately commissioned PSI report?
15. Why does the privately commissioned PSI report raise a question of equal justice?

SUPERVISION OF PROBATIONERS

The dynamics of probation (and parole) supervision are discussed at length later in Part III. This chapter examines the granting of probation, conditions of probation, length of supervision, violation of probation, and the legal decisions affecting probation (Figure 5.1).

GRANTING PROBATION

Most states have statutory restrictions on who may be granted probation in felony cases. Crimes, such as murder, kidnaping, and rape, often preclude a sentence of probation, as do second or third felony convictions. In Texas, a defendant may elect to be sentenced by a jury but can thereby receive probation only if it is proved that he or she "has never before been convicted of a felony in this or any other State." In any event, no person in the Lone Star state is eligible to receive probation for a felony unless assessed a sentence of 10 years or fewer by a judge or jury. In Georgia, a defendant who pleads guilty (or *nolo contendere*—"no contest") and who has never before been convicted of a felony can be placed on probation without the court entering a judgment of *guilty.* If the person successfully completes the terms of probation, he or she "shall not be considered to have a criminal conviction." In Arizona, only first-time nondangerous offenders are eligible for probation (Kennedy, 1988).

When probation is a statutory alternative, judges (and, in some cases, juries) differ in their approach to granting it. Although the recommendation of the pro-

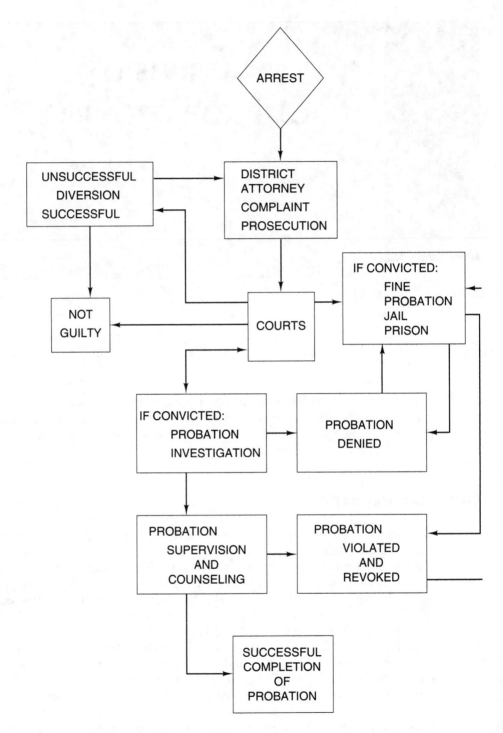

FIGURE 5.1   Organizational chart of the San Francisco adult probation process.

bation department would be important—it is difficult to envision many cases in which a judge would grant probation against the recommendation of the probation officer—judges may also seek advice from the police and prosecutor. The geographic area where the court is situated may also affect the granting of probation. Social and political attitudes in rural and urban jurisdictions can differ and thus affect the process. When court calendars are crowded, as they are in many urban areas, plea bargaining is more likely to result in probation being granted. The pressing problem of jail and prison overcrowding also exerts influence. Dean Champion (1988a) found that in the rural districts he studied, many felons are placed on probation as the result of a plea bargain. In Tennessee, this appears to be directly related to the severe prison overcrowding experienced by that state. The judge's feelings toward the particular offense or the offender may also enter into the sentencing decision. The many factors that determine if a defendant is granted probation contribute to the continuing controversy over "differential punishment," a challenge to the classical approach to criminal justice.

However, some factors, to a greater or lesser extent, are considered in all cases relative to the granting of probation: the age and rehabilitation potential of the defendant; the defendant's criminal record, including indications of professional criminality, organized crime (Abadinsky, 1994), and crimes of violence; the defendant's relationship with his or her family; evidence of any deviant behavior, such as drug abuse or sex offenses; and the attitude of the community toward the particular offense and the particular offender. Other questions also may be considered: Does the defendant's attitude toward the offense indicate genuine remorse? Was probation promised to the defendant to induce him or her to plead guilty? Will being placed on probation enable the defendant to provide the victim with restitution? Will being placed on probation enable the defendant to provide support and care for his or her family?

The sentencing judge must also consider the quality of service provided by a probation agency. Unfortunately, in too many jurisdictions, probation is nothing more than a suspending of sentence because little or no supervision is actually provided. Under such circumstances, a judge who might otherwise be inclined to place an offender on probation may, instead, impose a sentence of imprisonment. The cost to both the offender and the taxpayer is high—according to most estimates imprisonment costs from 10 to 13 times as much as probation. In many jurisdictions, a built-in incentive actually exists for sentences of imprisonment, even when probation is a feasible alternative. If probation services are funded by the county, and the cost of prisons is always borne by the state, each defendant sent to prison instead of being placed on probation represents a savings to county government. This result can be overcome with a *probation subsidy* through which the state reimburses the county for offenders placed on probation instead of being sentenced to a state prison.

The ABA presents the advantages of probation rather than imprisonment (1970: 3–4):

1. The liberty of the individual is maximized by such a sentence; at the same time, the authority of the law is vindicated and the public effectively protected from further violations of the law.

2. The rehabilitation of the offender is promoted affirmatively by continuing normal community contacts.

3. The negative and frequently stultifying effects of confinement are avoided, thus removing a factor that often complicates the reintegration of the offender into the community.

4. The financial costs of crime control to the public treasury are greatly reduced by reliance on probation as an important part of the correctional system.

5. Probation minimizes the impact on innocent dependents of the offender.

The ABA (1970: 3–4) sets forth three conditions for a sentence of imprisonment rather than probation:

1. When confinement is necessary to protect the public from further criminal activity by the defendant.

2. When the offender is in need of correctional treatment that can effectively be provided if he or she is confined.

3. When the seriousness of the offense would be unduly depreciated if a sentence of probation were imposed.

CONDITIONS OF PROBATION

Although the Task Force on Corrections (1966: 34) observed more than three decades ago that "differential treatment requires that the rules [of probation] be tailored to the needs of the case and of the individual offender," this suggestion is often not put into practice. Probation agencies require a defendant to sign a standard form, which usually contains a variety of regulations that may or may not reflect the client's individual needs. There are also special conditions that can be imposed by the judge or the probation department, such as ordering a child molester to avoid places frequented by children.

Edwin Sutherland and Donald Cressey (1966) state that when conditions of probation are too restrictive, the probation officer is inclined to overlook their violation. This can result in the PO losing the respect of the probationer, making the supervision process difficult. The ABA (1970: 9) recommends that the conditions of probation be spelled out by the court at the time of sentencing and emphasizes that they should be appropriate for the offender.

The APPA recommends that the only condition that should be imposed on every person sentenced to probation is that the probationer lead a law-abiding life during the period of probation: "No other conditions should be required by statute, but the probation officer in making recommendations [in the PSI report] should recommend additional conditions to fit the circumstances of each case." In a draft of a position statement, the APPA recommends that conditions "be reasonably related to the avoidance of further criminal behavior and not unduly restrictive of the probationer's liberty or incompatible with his freedom of religion. They should not be so vague or ambiguous as to give no real guidance."

The APPA draft states that conditions may appropriately include, but not be necessarily limited to, matters such as the following:

- Cooperating with the program of supervision
- Meeting family responsibilities
- Maintaining steady employment or engaging or refraining from engaging in a specific employment or occupation (e.g., a drug abuser prohibited from employment in a medical setting)
- Pursuing prescribed educational or vocational training
- Undergoing medical or psychiatric treatment
- Maintaining residence in a prescribed area or in a prescribed facility established for, or available to, persons on probation
- Refraining from consorting with certain types of people or frequenting certain types of places
- Making restitution for the fruits of the crime, or reparation for losses or damages caused thereby
- Paying fines, restitution, reparation, or family support
- Requiring the probationer to submit to search and seizure
- Requiring the probationer to submit to drug tests (e.g., urine tests) for analysis as directed by the probation officer

Probation regulations in different probation agencies tend to be similar (Figures 5.2 and 5.3). They typically exhort the probationer to live a law-abiding life, work, and support dependents. They require that the offender inform the PO of his or her residence, and that permission be secured before leaving the jurisdiction of the court. Some require that the probationer obtain permission before getting married, applying for a motor vehicle license, or contracting any indebtedness. Many probation departments require that the offender pay a supervision fee, restitution, or community service as a condition of probation. In Pennsylvania, for example, probation and parole clients must pay $25 per month unless the fee is waived. In Virginia, clients who are unable to pay the supervision fee may apply for an exemption; they need to prove unreasonable hardship based on insufficient monthly net income. G. Frederick Allen and Harvey Treger (1994: 39) found that fines and restitution, "if used appropriately and judiciously, can be an effective criminal sanction," although they recognized a bias by probation officers against collections efforts: POs viewing themselves more as *helpers* than *collectors*.

OBJECTIVES OF PROBATION SUPERVISION

(a) To provide public protection in keeping with the special duties of a probation officer
(b) To prepare the probationer for independent, law-abiding living

STATE OF NEVADA
DEPARTMENT OF PAROLE AND PROBATION
CARSON CITY, NEVADA 89710

PROBATION AGREEMENT AND RULES

Criminal Case No...............................

THE STATE OF NEVADA,
                    Plaintiff,
          vs.   **ORDER ADMITTING DEFENDANT TO PROBATION**
                    Defendant   **AND FIXING THE TERMS THEREOF**

DEFENDANT is guilty of the Crime of...
.... , a Felony or Gross Misdemeanor.

DEFENDANT is sentenced to a term of imprisonment in the ....
for .... years. Execution of that sentence is suspended and the DEFENDANT is hereby
admitted to probation for .... years under the following conditions:

    1. REPORTING/RELEASE: Upon release by the Court you are to report directly and in person to the Department of Parole and Probation. You are required to submit a true and correct written monthly report to your supervising probation officer each month on forms supplied by the Probation Department. In addition, you shall report as directed by your probation officer.

    2. RESIDENCE: You shall not change your place of residence, employment, nor leave the community without first obtaining permission from your probation officer in each instance.

    3. INTOXICANTS: You shall not drink or partake of any alcoholic beverages whatsoever/to excess (.10 blood alcohol or above, as determined by any medically recognized valid test, shall be sufficient proof of excess).

    4. CONTROLLED SUBSTANCES: You shall not use, purchase, possess, give, sell or administer any controlled substance, nor any dangerous druge, unless first prescibed by a licensed physician. You shall submit to drug testing as required by your probation officer.

    5. WEAPONS: You shall not possess or have under your control any type of weapon.

    6. ASSOCIATES: You will not associate with people who have criminal records.

    7. COOPERATION: You shall at all times cooperate with your probation officer and your behavior and attitude shall justify the opportunity granted to you by this probation.

    8. LAWS and CONDUCT: You shall comply with all municipal, county, state and federal laws, ordinances and orders and conduct yourself as a good citizen. You shall comply with convicted person registration requirements where applicable.

    9. OUT-OF-STATE TRAVEL: You shall not leave the state without first obtaining written permission, in each instance, from your probation officer.

    10. EMPLOYMENT PROGRAM: You shall seek and maintain employment, or maintain a program as approved by the Probation Department.

    11. SPECIAL CONDITIONS OF PROBATION:

....
....
....
....

    The Court reseves the right to modify these terms of Probation at any time and as permitted by law. DATED this ....
day of ...., 19 ...., in the .... Judicial District Court of the State of Nevada, in and for the
County of ....

....
District Judge

AGREEMENT BY PROBATIONER

    I do hereby waive extradition to the State of Nevada from any State in the Union and I also agree that I will not contest any effort to return me to the State of Nevada. I have read, or have had read to me, the foregoing conditons of my probation, and fully understand them and I agree to abide by and strictly follow them and I fully understand the penalties involved should I in any manner violate the foregoing conditions. I have received a copy of this document and NRS 176.225.

....
Probationer   Date

APPROVED..
      Probation Officer   Date

FIGURE 5.2   Probation Agreement and Rules, Nevada.

PROBATION/PAROLE RULES

CLIENT NAME	CASE NUMBER

The following rules are in addition to any court-ordered conditions. Your probation or parole may be revoked if you do not comply with any of your court-ordered conditions or if you violate any of the following rules:

1. You shall avoid all conduct which is in violation of federal or state statutes, municipal or county ordinances or which is not in the best interest of the public welfare or your rehabilitation.
2. You shall report all arrests or police contact to your agent within 72 hours.
3. You shall make every effort to accept the opportunities and counseling offered by supervision.
4. You shall inform your agent of your whereabouts and activities as s/he directs.
5. You shall submit a written monthly report and any other such relevant information as directed by your agent.
6. You shall make yourself available for searches or tests ordered by your agent including but not limited to urinalysis, breathalyzer and blood samples or search of residence or any property under your control.
7. You shall not change residence or employment unless you get approval in advance from your agent, or in the case of emergency, notify your agent of the change within 72 hours.
8. You shall not leave the State of Wisconsin unlesss you get approval and a travel permit in advance from your agent.
9. You shall not purchase, trade, sell or operate a motor vehicle unless you get approval in advance from your agent.
10. You shall not borrow money or purchase on credit unless you get approval in advance from your agent.
11. You shall not purchase, possess, own or carry any firearm or any weapon unless you get approval in advance from your agent. Your agent may not grant permission to carry a firearm if you are prohibited from possessing a firearm under Wis. Stats. 941.29, or federal law.
12. You shall abide by all rules of any detention or correctional facility in which you may be confined.
13. You shall provide true and correct information verbally and in writing, in response to inquiries by the agent.
14. You shall report to your agent as directed for scheduled and unscheduled appointments. Your scheduled appointments are at the following time and place:

15. You shall follow any specific rules that may be issued by an agent to achieve the goals and objectives of your supervision. The rules may be modified at any time, as appropriate. The specific rules imposed at this time are:

I have reviewed and explained these rules to the client.		I have received a copy of these rules.	
SIGNATURE OF AGENT	AREA #	SIGNATURE OF CLIENT	DATE

FIGURE 5.3 Probation agreement and rules, Wisconsin.

(c) To provide an opportunity for full participation of the probationer in planning his or her activities in the community

(d) To identify, use, and create resources in the community to fulfill program needs of probationers

(e) To provide a system of differential supervision based on the classification and program needs of all probationers

(f) To conduct a cost-effective supervision program

(g) To provide restitution or reparation to victims of criminal acts whenever applicable

Source: N.Y. State Code of Criminal Procedure.

PROBATION SUPERVISION IN PHILADELPHIA

Once a person has been sentenced to probation, a probation officer is assigned to conduct an orientation to the rules of supervision and assess the needs and risks of the offender. The PO then works with the offender to ensure that special conditions that have been stipulated by the judge are met. This department has placed a high priority on the collection of restitution, which is a frequent stipulation imposed by judges. A probation plan is then developed that will aid the offender in completing his or her term successfully.

When necessary, referrals are made to community-based agencies to help clients who require intensive and special treatment for severe drug, alcohol, and mental health problems. These clients may have the option of remaining in a treatment facility, if necessary, even when their probation has expired. Offenders who are poly–drug abusers or who have obvious psychiatric problems are evaluated by the department's assessment team, composed of psychologists and a psychiatric social worker. A supervision plan is then developed to assist the PO in supervising the case.

If it is found to be appropriate, some clients are referred to a residential drug treatment program at the Philadelphia State Hospital, which provides group and individual counseling to drug abusers and is administered by a staff person from this department. The department also has a special unit that provides group counseling to clients who cannot or will not take advantage of community mental health services. This unit operates under the supervision of a trained psychologist and serves primarily psychiatric and sex offenders. Offenders charged with driving under the influence are supervised within a special unit called the Alcohol Highway Safety Unit. This unit handles cases that are both within pretrial and post-trial status. The unit monitors the offender's attendance in safe-driving school and in the specified treatment facility.

The Victim Services Unit provides appropriate direct and referral services to victims, helps coordinate victim services among providers so that resources can be provided efficiently and effectively, and increases victim input at sentencing and before an inmate's release on parole.

LENGTH OF SUPERVISION

The length of probation terms vary from state to state. The ABA recommends that the term should be 2 years for a misdemeanor conviction and 5 years for a felony. In Illinois, it is 4 years for the more serious felonies and 30 months for other felonies; for a misdemeanor, it is 1 year. In Texas, "the court may fix the period of probation without regard to the term of punishment assessed, but in no event may the period of probation be greater than 10 years or less than the minimum prescribed for the offense for which the defendant was convicted." In the federal system, termination for a misdemeanor may occur at any time and for a felony after 1 year.

Some states authorize early termination of probation without actually having statutory guidelines as to when it is to be exercised. In most states, however, probation statutes provide for the termination of probation and the discharge of the offender from supervision before the end of the term. This allows the judge some needed flexibility because it is difficult to determine, at the time of sentencing, how long the term should actually be. In Texas, for example: "At any time, after the defendant has satisfactorily completed one-third of the original probationary period or two years of probation, whichever is the lesser, the period of probation may be reduced or terminated by the court." In Illinois, "the court may at any time terminate probation . . . if warranted by the conduct of the offender and the ends of justice." In Oklahoma, probation supervision "shall not normally exceed two years unless it is determined [that] the interests of the public and the probationer would be best be served by an extended period of supervision not to exceed the length of the original sentence." In Virginia, probation may be terminated for cases placed on supervision for two years or more after serving one-half or three years, whichever comes first.

The decision to terminate probation early and discharge the offender from supervision should be based on exemplary conduct. Unfortunately, the termination decision may not have any direct relationship to the merits of the case but is often a reflection of the need to keep caseloads down to a manageable size. This means that probationers may be discharged even though they are in need of further supervision.

VIOLATION OF PROBATION

The *New York State Code of Criminal Procedure* (352.3) states:

> Probation as a sentence or disposition is a means of offering the offender the opportunity for law-abiding adjustment in the community. Although the probationer is not deprived of his liberty, his life situation is circumscribed by the conditions which are intended to ensure protection of the community and adjustment of the probationer through effective supervision. It is the Probation Department's responsibility to see that the condi-

tions of probation are properly enforced and to inform the court of any significant deviation.

There are two types of probation violation:

1. *Technical.* When any of the conditions of probation has been violated, a technical violation of probation exists.
2. *New offense.* When a violation involves a new crime, it is a nontechnical or new offense violation.

The probation response to a violation is a matter of considerable discretion. For example, in Philadelphia, the Adult Probation Department advises its probation officers: "Minor violations of probation/[county]parole do not necessarily need to be brought to the attention of the sentencing Judge, but may be handled between the P.O. and the p/p [probationer/parolee] if such violations are not repeated and do not develop into a pattern."

In many jurisdictions, Allen County, Pennsylvania, and New York, for example, the PO has the authority to "discuss the alleged violation(s) with the probationer and inform him that repeated or more serious violation(s) will be dealt with by the court" (Figure 5.4). If the behavior continues, but a formal violation of probation in not necessary, in New York, "the court shall be informed of the alleged violation(s) and the department's action to date . . . [and] a recommendation may be made to the court requesting that the court require that the probationer appear before it . . . for a judicial reprimand."

Eugene Czajkoski is critical of the discretionary powers exercised by probation departments; he maintains that technical violations, for example, changing residence without immediately notifying the PO, are often ignored until it is believed that the probationer has committed a new crime. "Invoking the technical violation thus becomes the result of the probation officer making the adjudication that a crime has been committed. The probationer has a hearing on the technical violation, but is denied a trial on the suspected crime which triggered the technical violation" (1973: 13). As we shall see, it is easier to find a person "guilty" of a violation of probation than it is to prove criminal charges (Figure 5.5).

The revocation process originates with probation officers who exercise what Czajkoski (1973) refers to as a "quasi-judicial role" in that they decide whether or not to seek revocation. The probation officer's attitude toward the probationer and the violation will influence whether revocation action is initiated. Although the actual procedures differ from jurisdiction to jurisdiction, typically the PO confers with his or her superiors; if a violation is considered serious enough, a notice will be filed with the court. The case will then be placed on the court calendar, and the probationer will be given a copy of the alleged violations and directed to appear for a preliminary or *probable cause hearing.* In some jurisdictions, the preliminary hearing is conducted by an official other than a judge, and in some jurisdictions, for example, Texas: "A probationer is not entitled to a preliminary hearing or examining trial to determine whether there is probable cause to proceed to a revocation hearing." In Texas, in cases

```
ALLEN COUNTY PROBATION DEPARTMENT

                    Violation Notice No:


You are hereby given notice that on or about the _____ day of
_____ , 19_____ , you violated Rule No. _____
of the Allen County Probation Department Rules and Regulations.

By signing/initialing this notice, you are hereby stating that your Probation
Officer, _____ has discussed the violation with you.
Further, you are informed that although no action may be taken at this time,
should further violations occur warranting a Probable Cause Hearing, this
violation may and can be included in same.

Be advised a copy of this notice will be retained in your probation file.




_____
Date Notice Served




_____        _____
Probationer                    Cause




_____
Probation Officer
```

FIGURE 5.4   Probation violation notice.

of violation the case goes directly before a judge for a revocation hearing. (A
probable cause hearing is necessary only if the probationer is to be held in custody pending the revocation hearing.) In any event, if a probationer fails to
respond to a notice or summons (Figure 5.6) to appear for a hearing, the judge
will usually issue a warrant (Figure 5.7). A probationer may also waive the right
to a preliminary hearing (Figure 5.8).

COURT NOTIFICATION OF A TECHNICAL VIOLATION OF PROBATION

STATE OF NEW JERSEY — SUPERIOR COURT OF NEW JERSEY

-VS- — Bergen County

MICHAEL JOHNSON — Indictment No. S-584-91-01

BEFORE THE HONORABLE

Alfred D. Schiaffo

I, RICHARD L. ALBERA, Chief Probation Officer of the County of Bergen, aforesaid, do hereby charge that MICHAEL JOHNSON late of the Borough of Totowa, County of Passaic was on the 28th day of September, 1991, convicted in the above-entitled Court on a charge of Possession of a Controlled Dangerous Substance (Cocaine) with the Intent to Distribute and that upon said conviction the Court rendered the following judgment:

On December 2, 1991;

COUNT 1—$3000.00 fine and three (3) years probation.

July 20, 1992—Violation of probation: Probation continued with added condition of serving sixty (60) days in Bergen County Jail.

That the said MICHAEL JOHNSON did violate the terms and conditions of said probation in the following respects:

1. Violated Rule No. 2 by failing to report on December 6, 1990; December 13, 1992; December 20, 1992; December 27, 1992; January 17, 1993; January 24, 1993; January 31, 1993; February 28, 1993; or any date subsequent to March 4, 1993, although directed to report on a once-per-week basis.
2. Violated Rule No. 1, by being under the influence of Controlled Dangerous Substance, to wit: Cocaine on November 8, 1992; November 29, 1992; January 3, 1993; January 11, 1993; and February 21, 1993, as witnessed by abnormal results of urinalysis submitted on those dates.

Dated: March 21, 1993

Richard L. Albera
Chief Probation Officer

FIGURE 5.5 Court Notification of a Technical Violation of Probation.

STATE OF ILLINOIS
SEVENTEENTH JUDICIAL CIRCUIT
WINNEBAGO COUNTY

NOTIFICATION OF ALLEGED PROBATION VIOLATIONS

NAME: Mario B. Benti   CHARGE: Theft over $300.00
ADDRESS: 3642 Renthrow Street   DATE GRANTED: 4/30/93
              Rockford, IL 61103   TERMINATION DATE: 10/30/95

CASE #:   93CF-507

The above-named probationer has violated the following conditions of his probation in that

1. Defendant failed to pay restitution in the amount of $2085 as ordered.

2. Defendant failed to pay statutory fine and costs as ordered.

3. Defendant failed to pay probation fees of $15 per month as ordered.

4. Defendant failed to report to his probation officer "when and how directed."

5. Defendant was arrested for Violation of an Order of Protection and Criminal Damage to Property on or about 2/1/94.

RECOMMENDED OPTIONS

( ) Extension of probation for payment of costs, fees, restitution, or for completion of counseling.

( ) Recommend petition be filed—probation modified.

(x) Recommend petition be filed—probation vacated.

( ) No petition at this time.

PROBATION OFFICER'S COMMENTS

1. Defendant has been working full time through Corporate Services since 11/30/93, earning $6 per hour.

2. Defendant was on parole for forgery when he was arrested and convicted for theft over $300, for which he is on probation. Parole has since been revoked.

3. Defendant claims he was evaluated by Treatment Alternatives to Street Crime (TASC) for probation back in 1987 but was not accepted for drug treatment. He claims has never been to treatment before. During this term, this PO has attempted to assist the subject in getting into treatment. He was placed on the waiting list at Sojourn House, Freeport, but was taken off said list for failure to call in weekly as directed. (See attached letters.) Therefore, he has had the opportunity to get help for drug problems but failed to comply with what was required. He carries a diagnosis of cocaine and cannabis dependency.

4. Defendant said he has a record for Theft of Firearm in Beloit, WI. He has two (2) prior residential burglary convictions. (Refer to the pretrial services reports in file.)

Gary M. Meyers
Gary M. Meyers
Probation Officer   February 2, 1994

FIGURE 5.5 *(continued)*

CAUSE NO.: _____

NOTICE OF PROBABLE CAUSE HEARING

DATE FILED: _____

TO: ....

ADDRESS: ....

You are hereby given notice of a Probable Cause Probation Violation Hearing to be

conducted _____ , 19 _____ , at _____ A.M.
P.M.

at the _____

It is alleged you have violated your probation in the following manner to-wit:

Violation of any one of the above conditions of probation and suspended sentence could cause you to be returned to the Judge of original jurisdiction and thus result in the revocation of your suspended sentence and probation and commitment to the institution as the Court originally sentenced you to.

You are entitled to have witnesses to present evidence in your behalf and to challenge or question these allegations at the time of the Probable Cause Hearing.

_____
HEARING JUDGE or OFFICER

NOTICE SERVED BY: _____ Date: _____ Time: _____

WITNESS: _____

FIGURE 5.6   Notice of a Probable Cause Hearing.

WARRANT FOR ARREST OF PROBATIONER

STATE OF GEORGIA   } COUNTY OF _____

VS.

_____ NO. _____

TO THE SHERIFF OF THE ABOVE NAMED COUNTY OR
OTHER LAW ENFORCEMENT OFFICER OF THE STATE:

Under authority of the Georgia Statewide Probation Act you are hereby commanded to take the body of

_____

of the following address _____

_____

and safely keep _____ until _____ may be returned to this Court, there to
answer to a charge of violation of the following conditions of probation:

_____

_____

_____

Probationer is charged with violation of said conditions, in willful disregard of a Court Order,
specifically as follows:

_____

_____

_____

Issued this _____ day of _____ 19 _____

Sworn to and subscribed before me

This _____ day of

_____ , 19 _____   Probation/Parole Supervisor

_____   _____
Notary Public   Judge
(SEAL)

FIGURE 5.7   Warrant for Arrest of Probationer, Georgia.

COMMONWEALTH OF PENNSYLVANIA :   IN THE COURT OF COMMON PLEAS
                                    DAUPHIN COUNTY, PENNSYLVANIA
                V.   :
                                    :   NO(S):
                                    :   CHARGE(S):   CD 19_____

Waiver of Prerevocation Preliminary Hearing

I hereby waive (give up) my right to have a prerevocation preliminary hearing in the above captioned case. I understand that I have been accused of committing certain violations of my probation/parole as set forth on the notice of alleged violations dated _____

I understand and it has been explained to me that:

_____ 1. I am not required to waive (give up) my right to have a prerevocation preliminary hearing.

_____ 2. The prerevocation preliminary hearing (sometimes called a "Gagnon 1 hearing") is held for the purpose of having a neutral (impartial) hearing officer determine whether there is probable (reasonable) cause to believe that I have committed acts which would constitute a violation of my probation/parole conditions.

_____ 3. At such prerevocation preliminary hearing I would have an opportunity to speak in person, present witnesses and documentary evidence and confront and cross-examine adverse witnesses (unless the hearing officer specifically finds good cause for not allowing confrontation.)

_____ 4. At such prerevocation hearing, the hearing officer may also make a determination as to probable cause to detain me pending a revocation hearing to be scheduled before the Dauphin County Court of Common Pleas.

_____ 5. At such prerevocation hearing, I would be able to have the evidence against me disclosed and obtain a written summary of the hearing from the hearing officer.

_____ 6. After having all of the above explained to me, and being given a chance to read this document and ask questions, I was further advised that I could have a lawyer represent me at such prerevocation hearing and that if I could not afford to pay for a lawyer for this hearing that the Court would appoint a lawyer free of cost to me.

Understanding all of the above, I still give up my right to have a prerevocation preliminary hearing.

DATE: _____   _____
                                          PROBATIONER/PAROLEE

_____   _____
WITNESS   PROBATION/PAROLE OFFICER

FIGURE 5.8 Waiver of Prerevocation Preliminary Hearing, Pennsylvania.

PRELIMINARY/PROBABLE CAUSE HEARING

The accompanying flowchart (Figure 5.9) indicates the possibilities presented at each stage of the probation revocation process. At the preliminary hearing, the probationer can deny the charges of probation violation or plead guilty to them. If the plea is "guilty," the judge may deal with the case at once. If the probationer denies the charges, the judge will decide if there is sufficient (probable) cause to believe that probation was violated (in order to remand the probationer to custody), and a revocation hearing is scheduled. The judge may remand the probationer to custody pending the hearing or can release him or her on bail or on his or her own recognizance. The probation department will subsequently prepare a violation of probation report (Figure 5.10): "The report shall contain a summary of the probationer's supervision activities to date, and the alleged facts which would be sufficient, if proven, to establish any violation(s) of probation occurred" (*N.Y. State Code of Criminal Procedure*, 352.6).

As opposed to a narrow legal document, the violation of probation report contains information about the probationer's behavior under supervision—for example, employment record—and is presented to the judge prior to the revocation hearing.

FIGURE 5.9   Probation Violation Flowchart.

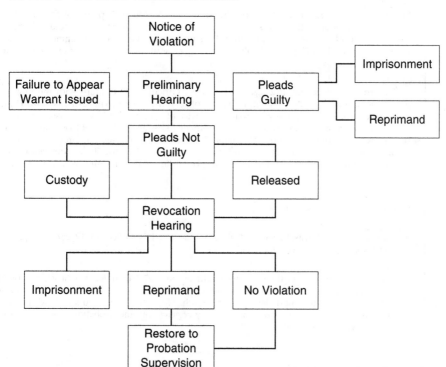

STATE OF ALABAMA

OFFICER'S REPORT ON DELINQUENT PROBATIONER

PROBATIONARY JUDGE: Wm. H. Gordon, Montgomery Circuit Court

PROBATIONER: Louis Merchant

RACE, SEX, AGE: white, male, 30 years old

OFFENSE: Theft of property, first degree

DATE OF CONVICTION: 2/17/94

SENTENCE: two years suspended; two years probation

DATE OF PROBATION: 2/17/94; EXPIRES: 4/10/95

RESTITUTION PAID: $359

SUPERVISION FEE PAID: 3 months in arrears

DELINQUENT CHARGES

CHARGE NO. 1: New Offense—Burglary III

Legal Facts

Subject was arrested on 12/24/94 by the Montgomery Police Department for the offense of burglary, third degree. Bond was set at $2500. A preliminary hearing was held 1/5/95, and the case was bound over to the Grand Jury. Indictment was returned, arraignment held, and the case set for trial 2/17/95. A Probation Officer's Authorization of Arrest was issued on 12/25/94.

Details

Police reports reflect that at 2 A.M. on 12/24/94, Officer Michael Stern with the Montgomery Police Department, while on routine patrol, observed a white male exit Accurate Hardware, 4240 Ames Road, Montgomery, Alabama, by way of a back window in possession of a box. The subject fled on foot but was caught by Officer Akers about 300 feet from the building. The person was identified as Louis Merchant. He had in his possession property identified as having come from Accurate Hardware by the manager, A. L. Pope. It was determined that the hardware store had been entered by forcing open an air conditioning vent at the rear of the store.

CHARGE NO. 2: Failure to Report

Legal Facts

A probation warrant was issued and given to the Sheriff's Office on 12/25/94 to prevent the subject's release pending court action.

Details

According to the records of the supervising officer, on 2/17/94, subject was instructed by Officer Michael Akers regarding probation rules and regulations and especially that he must report to the probation office by the third day of each month. He stated that he understood all rules and regulations. Subject failed to report or have any contact with the probation officer for months of October, November, and December 1994.

FIGURE 5.10   Probation violation report.

On 9/19/94, he reported for the month of September. He stated he forgot to report by the third of the month. He was reprimanded and directed to report in accordance with instructions.

On 10/10/94, I visited his residence. He was not present. His mother, Mae Merchant, said she had not seen him in three days. I asked that she have him report. On 10/15/94, I wrote subject a letter to report and received no response. On 10/25/94, I visited his home, and the subject was not present. His mother said he had received my letter. I requested that she attempt to have her son report and advised her of the consequences if he failed.

On 11/10/94, a letter was sent to the subject reminding him of the need to report. On 11/15/94, I called his residence and spoke with his 17-year-old sister, Susan Merchant, and requested that she tell him to report. On 11/20/04, I visited the residence and spoke to the subject's father, Joseph Merchant, requesting that he ask the subject to report.

On 12/6/94, I visited the subject's residence and spoke to his parents. They stated he had been told to report but refused. On 12/10/94, I wrote a letter instructing him to report within seven (7) days or I would file a report of Violation of Probation, which would cause him to be arrested. He failed to contact the probation office thereafter.

SUPERVISION SUMMARY

The probationer resided with his parents until September 1994. He worked steadily with Biloxi Industries until July 1994. A reduction in the work force caused the subject to be laid off. He reported regularly until September. During this period, he reported, and his attitude was satisfactory. Law enforcement officers suspected he was involved with persons using drugs. No evidence of his using or selling drugs existed.

Recommendation
I recommend revocation.

Signed and dated at Montgomery, Alabama, 5 January 1995

Michael Akers
Michael Akers
Probation and Parole Officer

FIGURE 5.10 (*continued*)

REVOCATION HEARING

At the revocation hearing, the probationer will have an opportunity to testify and present witnesses. In Texas and other jurisdictions, "It is quite common for the defense attorney and the prosecutor to plea bargain in probation revocation proceedings as they do when new criminal charges are filed" (Dawson, 1983: 61). An attorney may be present to represent the probationer (according to the provisions outlined in the *Mempa* and *Gagnon* decisions discussed later in this chapter). If the judge finds no violations, the probationer is restored to supervision. If the judge sustains any of the charges brought by the probation department, the probationer can be reprimanded and restored to supervision, or probation can be revoked and imprisonment ordered. In most cases, the defendant is actually sentenced at the time of conviction, but the imposition of sentence is suspended in favor of probation. Less frequently, the defendant is placed directly on probation without being sentenced. In the latter case, if the violation charge(s) is sustained, the judge can revoke probation and sentence the probationer to a term of imprisonment. The sentence, however, must be in accord with the penalty provided by law for the crime for which the probationer was originally convicted.

Proof of guilt in a criminal trial must be *beyond a reasonable doubt*, but at a probation revocation hearing need not be greater than by a *preponderance of the evidence*, a lower standard used in civil cases. In a criminal trial, the testimony of an accomplice usually has to be corroborated, but no such requirement exists for revocation hearings. Evidence that would not ordinarily be admitted in a criminal trial, such as hearsay testimony, can be entered into evidence at a revocation hearing. When the judge renders a decision on the charges, he or she can consider only the evidence presented at the hearing. When making a decision as to the disposition of a probationer found in violation, the judge can consider many items, such as employment record, relationship to spouse and children, and efforts at drug treatment. The range of options after a finding of "guilty" has been increasing as states seek to avoid the traditional two-dimensional outcomes—prison or continue supervision—that can impact on prison overcrowding or, at the other extreme, undermine the supervision process. Responses can now include short terms in a local jail or halfway house, electronic monitoring, intensive supervision, or some combination thereof (all discussed in Chapter 12).

STREET TIME

A defendant is convicted of burglary and sentenced to three-and-one-half years' imprisonment (written 3-6-0: three years, six months, zero days). His sentence is suspended in favor of probation. The probationer spends one year (1-0-0) under supervision and then violates the conditions of probation in an important respect. After a revocation hearing, the judge revokes probation and orders the probationer to begin serving the 3-6-0 sentence in prison. Must the offender serve a maximum of 3-6-0 in prison, or is the 1-0-0 year of probation supervision ("street") time to be subtracted from the 3-6-0 sentence?

The answer to this question varies from state to state. Some states do not recognize the time spent under supervision as time served against the sentence unless the full probationary term is successfully completed. A minority of states provide street-time credit for probation violations not involving the commission of a new crime; others leave it to the discretion of the judge.

LEGAL DECISIONS AFFECTING PROBATION

As the least democratic of our three branches of government, the judiciary—particularly the federal courts and, especially, the U.S. Supreme Court—can decide cases in a manner that may be politically unpopular. It can champion the legal rights of persons who (1) do not represent a significant block of votes or a source of campaign funding or (2) cannot generate a great deal of media attention, sympathy, or public support. Thus, in 1966, the Supreme Court rendered the famous *Miranda* decision (*Miranda v. Arizona*, 384 U.S. 436), which mandated that police suspects be informed of certain rights (to remain silent, to have counsel) before any questioning. The following year, in another Arizona case, the Supreme Court rendered the *Gault* decision, which gave important rights to juveniles (discussed later in this chapter). In that same year the *Mempa* decision gave probationers the right to counsel in certain instances of probation violation. The Court continued to show an interest in persons with a "disadvantaged status"—juveniles, probationers, welfare recipients, prison inmates, the mentally ill, and parolees—in the many cases that are discussed in this section and later in Chapters 6 and 8.

Legal decisions that affect probation usually affect parole and vice versa. For example, the *Gagnon* decision to be discussed in this section used the *Morrissey* decision (discussed in Chapter 8), which concerned parole violation, as a precedent. However, for purposes of study, the significant decisions in probation and parole have been divided according to the primary thrust of the case.

THE JUVENILE COURT

Chapter 3 noted that the juvenile court operated for many decades without attention or adherence to due process requirements or scrutiny by the judicial branch of government. This era of juvenile court history ended during the latter half of the 1960s, an era marked by the judicial activism of the Supreme Court with respect to issues involving civil liberties. Because of the central role of the probation officer in the court, juvenile cases decided by the Supreme Court affected on probation services.

In 1966, the Supreme Court reviewed the operations of the juvenile court in *Kent v. United States* (383 U.S. 541). While on probation, Morris Kent, 16 years of age, was convicted in (adult) criminal court of raping a woman in her Washington, D.C., apartment and sentenced to a prison term of 30 to 90 years.

In juvenile court, he would have faced a maximum term of incarceration until 21 years of age. In accord with existing federal statutes, the case had first been referred to the juvenile court, where over the objections of defense counsel, jurisdiction was waived to the criminal court. On appeal, in a 5–4 decision, the Supreme Court ruled that before a juvenile can be tried in criminal court, he or she is entitled to a waiver hearing with counsel, and if jurisdiction is waived, the judge must state the reasons.

In *Kent*, the Supreme Court reversed a hands-off policy that had been in existence since the juvenile court was established in 1899. In its decision, the Court expressed concern over the lack of due process in the juvenile court:

> While there can be no doubt of the original laudable purpose of juvenile courts, studies and critiques in recent years raise serious questions as to whether actual performance measures well enough against theoretical purpose to make tolerable the immunity of the process from the reach of constitutional guarantees applicable to adults. There is much evidence that some juvenile courts, including that of the District of Columbia, lack the personnel, facilities and techniques to perform adequately as representatives of the State in a *parens patriae* capacity, at least with respect to children charged with law violation. There is evidence, in fact, that there may be grounds for concern that the child receives the worst of both worlds; that he gets neither the protections accorded to adults nor the solicitous care and regenerative treatment postulated for children.

The following year, 1967, the Supreme Court decided the case of Gerald Gault (*In re Gault*, 387 U.S. 1),[1] age 15, who had been arrested by the police on the complaint of a female neighbor that he and his friend had made lewd and indecent remarks over the telephone. Gerald's parents were not notified of their son's arrest and did not receive a copy of the juvenile court petition charging him with delinquency. Furthermore, Gerald was not advised of his right to remain silent or his right to counsel. The complainant was not present at the hearing, nor did the judge speak with her on any occasion. Instead, Gerald's mother and two probation officers appeared before the juvenile court judge in his chambers. No one was sworn and no transcript was made of the proceeding.

At a second hearing, a conflict occurred concerning what had transpired at the first hearing. For the second time, the complainant was not present; the judge ruled that her presence was not necessary. Gerald was declared to be a juvenile delinquent and committed to a state training school for a maximum of six years—until his 21st birthday. Had Gerald been an adult, older than 18 years of age, the maximum sentence would have been a fine of not more than $50 or imprisonment for not more than 60 days. Because no appeal in juvenile court

---

[1]In states that do not provide an appellate process for juvenile court cases, as in the case of Arizona, they are cited as *In re* (in the matter of) as opposed to the more conventional format of *Gault v. Arizona*.

cases was permitted under Arizona law, Gerald's parents filed a petition of *habeas corpus* (a legal challenge to custody), which, although it was dismissed by the state courts, was granted (*certiorari*) a hearing by the U.S. Supreme Court.

In its decision, the Supreme Court acknowledged the helping—*noncriminal*—philosophy on which the juvenile court is based; but the decision also revealed a sense of outrage over what had transpired in the case of Gerald Gault: "Under our Constitution, the condition of being a boy does not justify a kangaroo court." The justices stated that *even* a child cannot be denied reasonable standards of due process; he or she is entitled to

1. Written notice of the charges
2. Right to counsel
3. Protection against self-incrimination
4. Right to confront and cross-examine witnesses
5. Right to have written transcripts and appellate review

Because of the noncriminal nature of the juvenile court, instead of the *proof beyond a reasonable doubt* standard used in criminal trials, the level of evidence for a finding of delinquency was typically that used in a civil proceeding: *preponderance of the evidence.* In 1970, in the case of *In re Winship* (397 U.S. 358), the Supreme Court noted: "The reasonable-doubt standard plays a vital role in the American scheme of criminal procedure. It is a prime instrument for reducing the risk of conviction resting on factual error." Accordingly, the Court ruled that "the constitutional safeguard of proof beyond a reasonable doubt is as much required during the adjudicatory stage of a delinquency proceeding as are those constitutional safeguards applied in *Gault.*"

The right to an impartial jury in criminal trials is guaranteed by the Sixth Amendment, but the Supreme Court decided against granting this right in juvenile proceedings. In the 1971 decision of *McKeiver v. Pennsylvania* (403 U.S. 528), the Court ruled that a juvenile court proceeding is not a criminal prosecution within the meaning of the Sixth Amendment. Accordingly, the Court held: "The imposition of the jury trial on the juvenile court system would not strengthen greatly, if at all, the factfinding function." Nevertheless, 16 states permit the use of juries in juvenile court (Zawitz, 1988).

In 1975 the Supreme Court was faced with the question of *double jeopardy*—which is prohibited by the Fifth Amendment—with respect to the juvenile court. *Breed v. Jones* (421 U.S. 519) concerned a 17 year old who was the subject of a juvenile court petition alleging armed robbery. After taking testimony from two prosecution witnesses and the respondent, the juvenile court judge sustained the petition. At a subsequent disposition hearing, the judge ruled that the respondent was not "amenable to the care, treatment and training program available through the facilities of the juvenile court" and ordered that Breed be prosecuted as an adult. The youngster was subsequently found guilty of armed robbery in criminal (superior) court, which led the Supreme Court to rule: "We hold that the prosecution of respondent in Superior Court, after an adjudicatory proceeding in Juvenile Court, violated that Double Jeopardy Clause of the Fifth Amendment, as applied to the States through the Fourteenth Amendment."

In 1984, the Supreme Court (*Schall v. Martin*, 467 U.S. 253), in a strong affirmation of the concept of *parens patriae*, upheld the constitutionality of the preventive detention of juveniles. *Schall* involved a New York statute that authorizes the detention of juveniles arrested for an offense when there is "serious risk" that before trial, the juvenile may commit an act that, if committed by an adult, would constitute a crime. In this case Gregory Martin, 14 years of age, with two others, was accused of hitting a youth with a loaded gun and stealing his jacket and sneakers; when arrested, he was in possession of the gun. The Court found that juveniles, unlike adults, "are always in some form of custody." That is, "by definition, [they] are not assumed to have the capacity to take care of themselves" but "are assumed to be subject to the control of their parents, and if parental control falters, the State must play its part as *parens patriae*." The Court stipulated that the detention cannot be for purposes of punishment and must be strictly limited in time; the Court found that the maximum detention under the New York statute, seventeen days for serious crimes and six days for less serious crimes, was proper.

The basis for these decisions has been the constitutional concern for *due process* contained in Amendments Four through Eight. The Fourteenth Amendment, which was adopted in 1868 to protect newly freed slaves, applied these amendments to the states: "No state shall make or enforce any law which shall abridge the privileges or immunities of citizens of the United States; nor shall any State deprive any person of life, liberty, or property, without due process of law." However, the courts did not uniformly apply the Fourteenth Amendment to all constitutional guarantees. In 1961, the Supreme Court decided the case of *Mapp v. Ohio* (367 U.S. 643). In *Mapp*, the Court ruled that evidence (pornographic materials) seized by the police in violation of the Fourth Amendment could not be admitted to evidence in a *state* trial (such evidence was already inadmissible in federal trials since 1914). This decision provided a basis for the so-called *exclusionary rule*, which *does not* apply to probation (or parole) violation proceedings—evidence seized by the police in violation of the Fourth Amendment can generally be used in a probation (or parole) violation hearing.

CONDITIONS OF PROBATION

In general, the courts can impose any conditions of probation that are reasonably related to the rehabilitation of the offender (e.g., to undergo treatment for drug addiction) or the protection of community (e.g., to avoid the possession of any weapons). The state has a compelling interest in setting limits on the behavior of probationers, and the Fourth Amendment notwithstanding, probationers enjoy a diminished expectation of privacy. Thus, an offender with a history of drug addiction can be required to submit to periodic urinalysis; as a condition of probation, a warrantless search by a probation officer is permitted, although the same search by a police officer would constitute a violation of the Fourth

Amendment. Probationers can be required to report in person and to answer all reasonable inquiries by the PO, the Fifth Amendment right to remain silent notwithstanding, although the probationer need not incriminate himself or herself (*Minnesota v. Murphy* 104 S.Ct. 1136 [1984]). Probationers can be required to avoid bars or "notorious" parts of a city (e.g., areas where a great deal of drug trafficking is known to occur).

In 1982, the U.S. Court of Appeals for the Fifth Circuit reviewed a case involving the First Amendment (*Owens v. Kelley*, 681 F.2d 1362). The plaintiff (probationer) claimed that a probation condition requiring him to participate in a program called "Emotional Maturity Instruction" violated his First Amendment freedom of religion because of the religious content of the course. The court stated that a "condition of probation which requires the probationer to adopt religion or to adopt any particular religion would be unconstitutional. . . . It follows that a condition of probation which requires the probationer to submit himself to a course advocating the adoption of religion or a particular religion also transgresses the First Amendment."

Owens also challenged a probation condition that required him to "submit to and cooperate with a lie detector test . . . whenever so directed by the Probation Supervisor [title of probation officers in Georgia] or any other law enforcement officer." The probationer claimed that this condition violated his Fifth Amendment privilege against compelled self-incrimination. The court of appeals rejected this claim: "The condition on its face does not impinge upon Owens' Fifth Amendment rights. The condition does not stipulate that Owens must answer incriminating questions. If any question is asked during [the lie detector] examination which Owens believes requires an incriminating answer he is free to assert his Fifth Amendment privilege, and nothing in the probation condition suggests otherwise."

PROBATION VIOLATION AND THE THREE THEORIES OF PROBATION

Traditionally, a person on probation has not been considered a free person, despite the fact that the probationer is not incarcerated. The basis for imposing restrictions (conditions) on a probationer's liberty—and for punishing violations—is contained in three theories.

1. *Conditional privilege.* Probation is an act of mercy by the judge that has not been earned by the defendant. As such, probation can simply be withdrawn if any condition of the privilege is violated.

2. *Contract theory.* Each probationer is required to sign a *contract*—a stipulation agreeing to certain terms in return for conditional liberty. As in any contractual situation, a breach of contract can result in penalties—in this case, revocation of probation.

3. *Custody theory.* Persons placed on probation in lieu of imprisonment are in the legal custody of the court and, therefore, quasi-prisoners, with their constitutional rights being abridged accordingly. Under such condi-

tions, the court has the authority to move the convict from a community setting to a prison setting in the event of a violation of the conditions of supervision.

Legal decisions discussed in this chapter have challenged these theories.

PROBATION REVOCATION

In 1967, the Supreme Court ruled (*Mempa v. Rhay*, 389 U.S. 128) that under certain conditions a probationer is entitled to be represented by counsel at a revocation hearing. In 1959, Jerry Mempa entered a plea of guilty to the charge of "joyriding" in a stolen car in the state of Washington. Imposition of sentence was deferred, and Mempa was placed on probation for two years on the condition that he spend 30 days in the county jail. About four months later, the Spokane County prosecutor moved to have Mempa's probation revoked on the ground that he had been involved in a burglary while on probation. Mempa, who was 17 years old at the time, was not represented by counsel at his revocation hearing, nor was he asked whether he wished to have counsel appointed for him.

At the, hearing, Mempa was asked if it was true that he had been involved in the alleged burglary, and he answered in the affirmative. A probation officer testified without cross-examination that according to his information Mempa had been involved in the burglary and had previously denied participation in it. Without asking the probationer if he had any evidence to present or any statement to make, Mempa's probation was revoked, and he was sentenced to 10 years' imprisonment. The judge added that he would recommend to the parole board that Mempa be required to serve only one year.

In a companion case considered by the Court, William Earl Walkling was placed on probation (for burglary) with imposition of sentence deferred. At a subsequent revocation hearing, Walkling informed the court that he had retained an attorney. When the attorney did not arrive on time, the court proceeded with the hearing, at which a probation officer presented hearsay testimony to the effect that the probationer had committed 14 separate acts of forgery and grand larceny. The court revoked probation and imposed a sentence of 15 years. No record was kept of the proceeding. The *Walkling* case was consolidated with the *Mempa* case by the Supreme Court.

The Supreme Court noted that previously it had held that the right to counsel is not confined merely to representation during a trial. The Court stated that counsel is required at *every* stage of a criminal proceeding when substantial rights of an accused criminal may be affected, and sentencing is one of these critical stages. In *Mempa*, the Court stated that counsel could aid in marshaling facts; introducing evidence of mitigating circumstances; and, in general, assisting the defendant in presenting his or her case with respect to sentence. The Court ruled that some rights could be lost if counsel were not present at a sentencing hearing, and "we decide here that a lawyer must be afforded at this proceeding whether it is labeled a revocation of probation or a deferred sentencing." The importance of the *Mempa* case goes beyond the limited finding made by the Court—it was the first time that the Supreme Court had ruled in favor of the rights of a person on probation.

In the next important probation/parole case (*Morrissey v. Brewer*, 1972), the Supreme Court stipulated that the amount of due process rights to which a person is constitutionally entitled is directly related to the potential loss that can result. The greatest amount of potential loss is clearly in a criminal case—total liberty and, at times, life itself—may be forfeited. Thus, the criminal process represents the extreme end of the due process continuum: rights to counsel, to remain silent, to a jury trial, and to cross-examine adverse witnesses. Located somewhere at the other extreme would be the due process rights of a student to challenge a course grade. Where are probation and parole located along this due process continuum?

In *Morrissey v. Brewer* (discussed in Chapter 8) the Court ruled that parolees accused of violating the conditions of parole are entitled to certain due process rights, including a preliminary and revocation hearing. In 1973, the Court rendered a similar decision in the case of a probation violation, *Gagnon v. Scarpelli* (411 U.S. 778). In 1965, Gerald Scarpelli pled guilty to a charge of armed robbery and was sentenced to 15 years' imprisonment, but the sentence was suspended and he was placed on probation for 7 years. The probationer was given permission to reside in Illinois (under the Interstate Compact discussed in Chapter 11), where he was placed under the supervision of the Cook County Adult Probation Department. Shortly afterward, Scarpelli was arrested in a Chicago suburb with a codefendant and charged with burglary. The following month, his probation was revoked, and Scarpelli was incarcerated in the Wisconsin Reformatory to begin serving the 15 years to which he had originally been sentenced. At no time was he afforded a hearing; Scarpelli appealed.

Scarpelli was released on parole in Wisconsin, at which time his appeal reached the U.S. Supreme Court. He claimed that revocation of probation without a hearing and counsel was a denial of due process. The Court ruled that, in legal jargon, Scarpelli had a *liberty interest*: "Probation revocation, like parole revocation, is not a stage of a criminal prosecution, but does result in a loss of liberty. Accordingly, we hold that a probationer, like a parolee, is entitled to a preliminary and a final revocation hearing under the conditions specified in *Morrissey v. Brewer*, supra." In other words, as noted in a 1982 state of Texas decision (*Rogers v. State*, 640 S.W.2d 248), liberty on probation, although indeterminate, "includes many of the core values of unqualified liberty, such as freedom to be with family and friends, freedom to form other enduring attachments of normal life, freedom to be gainfully employed, and freedom to function as a responsible and self-reliant person." In *Gagnon*, the Supreme Court held that a probationer is entitled to

1. A notice of the alleged violations.
2. A preliminary hearing to decide if there is sufficient (probable) cause to believe that probation was violated (to remand the probationer to custody).

3. A revocation hearing, which is "a somewhat more comprehensive hearing prior to the making of the final revocation decision." At these hearings, the Court ruled, the probationer will have the opportunity to appear and present witnesses and evidence on his or her own behalf, and a conditional right to confront adverse witnesses.

With respect to the right to counsel, the Court was ambiguous: "We . . . find no justification for a new inflexible constitutional rule with respect to the requirement of counsel. We think, rather, that the decision as to the need for counsel must be made on a case-by-case basis." In practice, however, probationers have been afforded the right to privately engaged or appointed counsel at probation revocation hearings.

Now that we have completed this examination of the courts and probation, the next chapter reviews prisons and parole.

REVIEW QUESTIONS

1. What are the variables that can affect the granting of probation?
2. Why, in some jurisdictions, is there a built-in incentive to sentence a defendant to prison instead of probation?
3. What are the advantages of a sentence of probation?
4. Under what conditions is a sentence of imprisonment to be preferred over a sentence of probation?
5. Why would offenders be discharged from probation when their behavior did not justify early termination of supervision?
6. Why is the judiciary in a better position than the other branches of government to guarantee the rights of probationers and parolees (and others)?
7. What did the Supreme Court rule in the case of *Kent v. United States?*
8. What rights did the *Gault* decision provide respondents accused of delinquency in juvenile court?
9. According to the *Winship* decision, what is the standard of proof required in a delinquency proceeding?
10. What did the *McKeiver* decision rule with respect to jury trials in juvenile court?
11. What was the issue in *Breed v. Jones*, and what did the court rule?
12. What three theories have formed the basis for imposing restrictions on a probationer's liberty?
13. What have the courts ruled with respect to conditions of probation?
14. What was the issue decided in the case of *Mempa v. Rhay?* What was the real significance of the *Mempa* case?
15. What rights were provided to persons accused of violating probation in the case of *Gagnon v. Scarpelli?*

A HISTORY
OF AMERICAN
PRISONS

"The degree of civilization in a society is revealed by entering its prisons."
—Dostoyevsky, *The House of the Dead*

Probation		Parole
Presentence Report		Preparole Report
Court		Board
Probation Supervision		Parole Supervision

Whom will we find upon entering America's prisons? More than 1 million persons: 94 percent are male; more than half are black; about 10 percent are Hispanic; more than 60 percent are younger than 30 years of age, and well over half have not completed high school; and more than 30 percent are incarcerated for drug offenses. About one-half grew up primarily in one-parent households, and many have been victims of child abuse.[1] About one-half were unemployed or employed only part-time at the time of their arrest. In America's prisons are persons who are poorer, darker,[2] younger, and less educated than the rest of the population. It should come as no surprise that America leads the industrial world by a factor of four in the percentage of its citizens that are incarcerated while having the widest gap between rich and poor (Bradsher, 1995b; Myers, 1995; Bureau of Justice Statistics).

What will we find upon entering America's prisons? In one word: *overcrowding*, a system not capable of managing such a large population in a manner that meets constitutional standards. Conditions were so bad for the approximately 4500 inmates in Alabama in 1976 that a federal judge placed that state's entire prison system in a receivership that was not relinquished until the end of 1988. In that year, Alabama had more than 11,000 inmates, and 10 other prison systems were operating under court orders to improve conditions, with at least one major institution in 40 additional jurisdictions, including the District of Columbia, Puerto Rico, and the Virgin Islands, under court orders to alleviate overcrowding or other unconstitutional conditions.

In New York from 1976 to 1991, the prison population almost tripled; in 1991, about 60,000 inmates were housed; in 1995, more than 68,000—135 percent of capacity. A similar problem exists in California, where the prison population rose from 22,000 in 1982 to 102,000 in 1991; by 1995, the figure was more than 125,000. The federal prison system is operating at more than 160 percent capacity. Between 1980 and 1986, New Jersey's prison population increased by 136 percent, and Virginia's[3] by 111 percent. In Illinois in 1989, more than 21,000 inmates inhabited state correctional facilities designed for 16,492; by 1994, the number was above 37,000—60 percent over capacity. In 1993, a federal court judge returned control of Tennessee's prison system to the state—Tennessee prisons had been under federal supervision since 1981 because of overcrowding. In Connecticut, 6 of the state's 15 prisons have been under court orders to reduce overcrowding. Between 1982 and 1991, Connecticut's prison population rose from 4870 to 10,814; by 1995 it was more than 15,000. In 1985, the state of Texas signed an agreement to end overcrowding in its prison system; Texas had been under federal supervision since a judge ruled that conditions in its prisons violated constitutional guarantees against cruel and unusual punishment. To meet constitutional standards, Texas has been granting time off for good behavior at the rate of up to 90 days for every 30 days served. Nevertheless, in 1995, Texas had more than 120,000 inmates.

---

[1] For an examination of research into the issue of child abuse and delinquent/criminal behavior, see Smith and Thornberry (1995).

[2] This point applies even in Hawaii, where the Hawaii Paroling Authority reports that persons of indigenous Hawaiian and part-Hawaiian ancestry are grossly overrepresented in the state's prisons in comparison with the general population.

[3] Virginia abolished parole in 1994.

Except for Texas, none of these jurisdictions is in the "top ten" when it comes to rates of incarceration per 100,000 residents (Bureau of Justice Statistics). That dubious honor goes to

Texas	636
Louisiana	530
Oklahoma	508
South Carolina	494[4]
Nevada	460
Arizona	459
Georgia	456
Alabama	451
Michigan	428
Florida	406

In 1980, 139 people were in America's prisons for every 100,000 residents; today the figure is more than 375.

In Michigan, the legislature had to enact the Prison Overcrowding Powers Act of 1983 to allow for the automatic release of inmates as new commitments were received. Prisoners' minimum parole eligibility dates can also be reduced by 90 days each time the governor declares an "overcrowding emergency." In Oklahoma, whenever the prison population exceeds 95 percent of capacity, inmates who have served at least 15 percent of their sentence and are within 1 year of their parole consideration date can be released. Legislation to accomplish this release was necessary because of the severity of overcrowding—previously the state was simply releasing inmates without benefit of parole supervision. Absconding from this pre-parole conditional supervision is considered an escape from prison. In Florida, if the prison population reaches 98 percent for a period of 7 consecutive days, the Department of Corrections has the authority to release certain inmates that meet established criteria. In Connecticut, a state law mandates the immediate release of 10 percent of the prison population if the number of male prisoners exceeds 110 percent of capacity for 30 consecutive days. Security problems generated by overcrowding are exacerbated by America's antiquated prisons. In Illinois, for example, the "newest" maximum security prison was opened in 1920. Along with a number of other states, Illinois is building a "supermax" prison at a cost of $120,000 per cell.

A tremendous increase in the number of prison facilities and expansion of existing facilities during the last few years—in excess of 30,000 beds—has not had a significant impact. At any one time between 10,000 and 20,000 inmates are being housed in local jails because of a lack of state prison space: "Instead of releasing inmates early when the state system is crowded, some states refuse admissions. Twenty-two states in 1990 had 18,380 state prisoners held in local jails because of prison overcrowding" (Illinois Department of Correction, 1992: 53). Many jails are also under court order to reduce overcrowding. For a

---

[4]South Carolina abolished parole in 1995.

decade, spending on prisons has been the fastest- or second fastest-growing part of state budgets: "The bills have arrived for those tough crime laws" (Hinds, 1993: B16).

The United States has the dubious distinction of being first when it comes to incarcerating citizenry. How did we reach this crisis? The historical review in this chapter and Chapter 7 is designed to help answer this question.

ORIGINS OF THE AMERICAN SYSTEM OF PRISONS

The American colonies inherited an English approach to crime and punishment, and the English system of laws into the 18th century impresses one with the extent to which the death penalty was used, often for seemingly minor offenses. Jerome Hall states: "Thus it is believed that Henry VIII [1491–1547] executed 72,000 thieves and vagabonds during his reign"; under George III (1738–1820), as many as 220 offenses were punishable by death (1952: 116). Robert Lilly and Richard Ball (1987) state that by 1780, 350 capital crimes existed, most of which were for property offenses. [In practice, however, there was extensive use of pardons and the dismissal of indictments for technical reasons (Kelman, 1987).] At the same time, England established institutional approaches to the old and the infirm, vagrants, beggars, homeless children, as well as certain criminals: gaols, bridewells, and houses of correction (Hirsch, 1992). Local jails emerged throughout the American colonies usually under management of a sheriff. These poorly constructed institutions, David Rothman (1971: 56) notes, "were not only unlikely places for intimidating the criminal, but even ill-suited for confining him"—escapes were frequent.

In Massachusetts, under Puritan rule, fines and corporal punishment—stocks, pillory, lashes, and dunking—prevailed. Capital punishment was relatively rare (Hirsch, 1992). Dramatically different conditions in England and the colonies resulted in differing needs, and this affected the response to criminals. In England, land was scarce and an excess labor supply had the potential for political and social unrest. "As a matter of policy," notes Bradley Chapin, "it must have seemed that no great harm was done if the hangman thinned the horde of vagrant Englishmen. In the colonies, the need for labor urged the use of penalties that might bring redemption" (1983: 9). Consequently, beginning with William Penn in 1682, the use of capital punishment in the American colonies was severely restricted and virtually banned for property crimes (Melossi and Pavarini, 1981).

In Pennsylvania, however, the Quakers were in an economic quandary: Because British law was so severe, colonial juries would often find defendants not guilty rather than subject them to the extreme punishments that were in place for property offenses. "In this way, criminals had escaped all discipline, and the community had allowed, even encouraged, them to persist in their ways" (Rothman, 1971: 60). And it was Quaker property that was often at risk in Philadelphia, where their Calvinist urgings—honesty, thrift, and hard work—resulted in economic success as a rising commercial class. [For the relationship between Calvinism and economic success, see Weber (1958).] The use of imprisonment provided a way to mete out punishment in a manner that was proportionate to the severity of the offense, a classical concept. This notion appealed to both the humanitarian and economic concerns of the Quakers, who rejected the Calvinist belief in the immutability of human character in favor of redemption (Hirsch, 1992).

Three intertwined developments led to the establishment of the American system of prisons: Calvinism, the American Revolution, and classical theory. Thorsten Sellin states, "The credit for the gradual substitution of imprisonment for corporal and capital punishments must go to the [classical] philosophers of the 18th century" (1967: 19). After the revolution, a repugnance for things British inspired Americans to discard corporal punishment in favor of imprisonment, a process that was complete at about the time of the Civil War. The type of imprisonment that resulted had its origins in quasi-Calvinist socioreligious doctrine, which can be seen in the life of John Howard (1726–1790), and the work of Quaker reformers in Philadelphia and New York; Howard coined the term *penitentiary* as a place to do penance (Teeters, 1970).[5]

WALNUT STREET AND OTHER EARLY PRISONS

The first prison in the United States was authorized by the Connecticut legislature in 1773, and that same year the colony converted an abandoned copper mine into a prison for serious offenders (Durham, 1989c). Newgate (not to be confused with a New York prison by the same name) consisted of a wooden lodging house for communal habitation built about 20 feet below the surface. The first keeper, a retired military officer, lived across the road, and a lack of security personnel presented a problem. Within three weeks of receiving its first prisoner, the prisoner managed to escape, and escapes continued to plague Newgate. As opposed to early prisons established elsewhere, no reformative or rehabilitative agenda existed, and it was expected that the prison would be self-supporting. In the early days of the prison, miners were hired to provide inmate instruction, but mining failed to achieve a profit. Other trades were initiated, but they also failed to achieve any level of economic success. The revolutionary war and a rash of violent incidents led to the closing of Newgate in 1782; it reopened in 1790 as a Connecticut state prison (Durham, 1989c).

By 1762, Quaker reformers in Philadelphia were successful in having the list of capital offenses limited and substituting fines and imprisonment for torture and execution for many offenses; in 1786, the Pennsylvania legislature enacted penal reform to replace capital punishment for certain crimes. The law called for convicted felons who were lodged in the Walnut Street Jail to be subjected to hard labor "publicly and disgracefully imposed . . . in streets of cities and towns, and upon the highways of the open country and other public works" (Atherton, 1987: 1). With shaved heads, bizarre dress, and wearing

---

[5]While serving as sheriff of Bedfordshire, John Howard was appalled by the conditions he found in English prisons and campaigned for reform, aided by his book *The State of Prisons in England and Wales* (1777).

heavy metal balls and chains riveted to their ankles, the convicts working in the streets drew the ridicule and abuse of passing crowds—the work was both onerous and humiliating. However, Paul Takagi (1975) states that convicts working in the city streets drew large crowds of sympathetic people, including friends and relatives of the prisoners. They made contact, and, at times, liquor and other goods were given to the convicts. In any event, at the urging of Benjamin Rush, the Philadelphia Society for Alleviating the Miseries of the Public Prisons (later renamed the Philadelphia Prison Society and then the Pennsylvania Prison Society) was formed at the home of Benjamin Franklin in 1787. In 1789, the society succeeded in having the 1786 law repealed.

John Howard, the son of a Calvinist merchant, was born in England in 1726. His interest in penal reform led him to publish *The State of the Prisons* a year after the American Declaration of Independence. Working out of a strong religious commitment, Howard influenced other religiously endowed reformers, Quakers of the Philadelphia Society for Alleviating the Miseries of the Public Prisons, with whom he was in contact. As a result, in 1790 a law was enacted creating a penitentiary in a portion of the Walnut Street Jail (Atherton, 1987); the Walnut Street Jail became a state prison based on a Calvinist model of hard labor and religious study. Takagi (1975) argues, however, that it was the Episcopalians of the Philadelphia Society who argued for hard labor, and solitary confinement was stressed by the Quakers.

At Walnut Street, most inmates were confined in separate cells and released to work in a courtyard during the day at a variety of tasks: handicrafts, such as weaving and shoemaking; and routine labor, such as beating hemp and sawing logwood, all in total silence. The "hardened and atrocious offenders," persons who formerly would have been whipped, mutilated, or executed, were confined in isolation and almost total darkness with nothing but a Bible: "The old Quakers, sensitive as they were to the inflicting of bodily pain, seem to have been unable to form in their minds an image of the fearful mental torture of solitude in idleness" (Wines, 1975: 152). These convicts were blindfolded on arrival and remained in their cells until released; they never saw another inmate. Inspectors from the Prison Society provided oversight at Walnut Street and had the authority to hire and fire penitentiary officials.

Solitary confinement was seen as a way of preventing fraternization between prisoners, behavior that would only lead to the spread of evil inclinations among inmates. In 1833, two researchers reported:

> If it is true that in establishments of this nature, all evil originates from the intercourse of the prisoners among themselves, we are obliged to acknowledge that nowhere is this vice avoided with greater safety than at Philadelphia, where the prisoners find themselves utterly unable to communicate with each other; and it is incontestable that this perfect isolation secures the prison from all fatal contamination. (Beaumont and de Tocqueville, 1964: 57).

Michael Ignatieff notes that John Howard and the Quakers shared a common religious lifestyle that led them to favor imprisonment as a form of purgatory, "a forced withdrawal from the distractions of the senses into silent and solitary confrontation with the self." It was out of solitude and silence that the convict "would begin to hear the inner voice of conscience and feel the transforming of God's love" (1978: 58). News of the "success" of Walnut Street attracted many persons from other states and countries. One of these visitors was a Quaker from New York, Thomas Eddy (1758–1827), who had been imprisoned briefly as a Tory during the Revolutionary War.

Eddy was influenced by what he saw in Philadelphia, and as a result of his efforts, New York constructed its first penitentiary in Greenwich Village. Newgate was named after the famous British prison, and Eddy became its first agent. Consistent with the prevailing belief of prison reformers, Eddy maintained that the goal of deterrence required inflicting pain on criminal offenders (Lewis, 1965). However, he discarded the idea that it was necessary to keep inmates in solitary all day; instead, convicts slept in congregate rooms measuring 12 feet by 18 feet and housing eight inmates. Fourteen cells for solitary confinement were used as punishment for violating prison rules. Eddy encouraged religious worship, established a night school, and approved of provisions in the law that prohibited corporal punishment at Newgate. Despite improvements in treatment at the prison, in 1802, a bloody riot and mass-escape attempt required calling in the military. In response to these developments, Eddy recommended that future penitentiaries use single cells for all inmates at night and shops where they could work in strict silence during the day. His suggestions were incorporated into a new prison that was built in Auburn, New York.

Eddy was either removed because of political considerations (Lewis, 1965) or resigned in protest when, in 1803, the state turned the prison industries over to a private contractor (McKelvey, 1972). In either event, difficulties increased at Newgate, and a return to flogging was legislated in 1819 (Lewis, 1965). In 1828, the penitentiary was abandoned in favor of a newly completed prison at Sing Sing. In Philadelphia, overcrowding caused the demise of Walnut Street; industry and isolation became unworkable in the congested prison; discipline lapsed and riots ensued (McKelvey, 1972): "While the original inspectors were still active in the oversight of the prison, thus preventing rampant corruption of guards and overseers, there was little they could do to prevent the decline of the conditions of the jail. The funds needed to create a system of solitary confinement were simply greater than had been anticipated" (Dumm, 1987: 105).

PENNSYLVANIA AFTER WALNUT STREET

The Pennsylvania Prison Society succeeded in having prisons built at Pittsburgh (Western State Penitentiary opened in 1826) and Cherry Hill/Philadelphia (Eastern State Penitentiary opened in 1829). These institutions featured massive stone walls around a building that branched out from a central rotunda like the spokes of a wheel—architecture influenced by the *panopticon* penitentiary, a circular design advanced by the British classical philosopher Jeremy Bentham (1748–1832). The design has a guardhouse at the center and prevented prisoner contact, and inmates remained in their (12- by 7-feet, 16-feet-high) cells and work area except for one hour of exercise in a yard also designed to prevent inmate contact. Prisoners could not see one another even at Sunday religious services because pews were designed as individual cubicles. The Pennsylvania system "isolated each prisoner for the entire period of his confinement. According to its blueprint, convicts were to eat, work, and sleep in individual cells, seeing and talking with only a handful of responsible guards and selected visitors. They were to leave the institution as ignorant of the identity of other convicts as on the day they entered" (Rothman, 1971: 82):

> The guiding principles were punishment and reformation through penitence: The convicted prisoner was to be kept totally separated from other prisoners, but not from human contact. The avenue to reform was through repentance—the true and deep recognition of one's "sins" and acceptance of God's leadership in one's life. It was obvious that prisoners left totally alone would be unable to follow this path; for this, guidance was needed, good examples, people who could help the convict accept responsibility for his/her crimes and embark on the difficult path of repentance and redemption. (Atherton, 1987: 7)

Guidance and role models were provided by four groups of people who visited prisoners: prison staff, chaplains, officials of the Prison Society, and the Board of Inspectors.

The penitentiary reached its apex during the 1830s; facilities proliferated and "visitors traveled great distances to view American prisons in action" (Hirsch, 1992: 112). It was during this period that the French philosopher/politician Alexis de Tocqueville (1805–1859), most noted for his *Democracy in America* (1835), traveled to the United States to study its penitentiary system. Although he came away with a generally favorable view, economics would soon lead to the demise of the penitentiary, which had been adopted by only two other states, New Jersey and Rhode Island. (Stateville, in Illinois, which opened in 1925, has one unit based on the panopticon design—it is the only one currently in operation in the United States.)

The Pennsylvania system proved expensive—the cost of constructing an institution for solitary confinement was staggering, and little profitable exploitation of inmate labor under such conditions could occur (McKelvey, 1972). At the beginning of the 19th century, an increasing need for labor existed: New legislation made slave trading more difficult, new territories were settled, and rapid industrialization with a corresponding increase in wages occurred. Prisons with solitary confinement deprived the market of needed labor (Melossi and Pavarini, 1981). As a result, most states patterned their prisons after the next great milestone in American prison history, an institution suggested by Thomas Eddy, which became the world's most frequently copied prison. Even New Jersey and Rhode Island abandoned the Pennsylvania model. Beginning in the 1860s, the isolation of prisoners at Eastern State Penitentiary was breaking down, and inmates began sharing cells. "In 1913 the system, which had become so diluted as to be unrecognizable, was officially abolished and from then on, it became just another Auburn-type prison" (Teeters, 1970: 11).

Auburn Prison

Auburn Prison opened in 1819 and as designed by its first agent, William Brittin, featured a center that comprised tiers of cell blocks surrounded by a vacant area—the yard—with a high wall encircling the entire institution. Each cell measured 7 by 3.5 feet and was 7 feet high:

> It was designed for separation by night only; the convicts were employed during the day in large workshops, in which, under the superintendency of Elam Lynds [1784–1855], formerly a captain in the army, the rule of absolute silence was enforced with unflinching sternness. Captain Lynds said that he regarded flogging as the most effective, and at the same time the most humane, of all punishments, since it did no injury to the prisoner's health and in no wise impaired his physical strength; he did not believe that a large prison could be governed without it. (Wines, 1975: 154)

Instead of replacing corporal punishment with imprisonment, as was advocated by the religious reformers, the practice of flogging became widespread in the penitentiary system—criminals were punished with imprisonment, and prisoners were punished with flogging and other forms of corporal punishment. No written regulations governed the use of the whip; guards were simply authorized to impose flogging when "absolutely necessary."

Auburn divided its inmates into three classes. The most difficult inmates were placed in solitary; a less dangerous group spent part of the day in solitude and worked the rest of the time in groups; the "least guilty" worked together throughout the day and were separated only at night when they returned to their individual cells. As in Walnut Street, solitary confinement played havoc on the psyche—inmates jumped off tiers, cut their veins, and smashed their heads against walls. Solitary confinement in Auburn was discontinued except as punishment for violations of prison rules (Lewis, 1965).

New Yorkers believed that the complete isolation of prisoners from arrival to release was inhumane, unnatural, and cruel. Far from reforming men, they felt such absolute solitude resulted in insanity and despair. In addition, there was the issue, perhaps more pressing, of expense to the state. Inmates restricted to their cells 24 hours a day contributed nothing to the cost of their own confinement. The state had to provide all food, clothing, supplies, and materials to its prisoners:

> If the prisoners were to learn the advantages and satisfactions of hard work and thrift, New York authorities believed, there could be no better way than to be compelled to work together in harmony. If such a system also offered the potential for inmates to grow and harvest their own vegetables, raise and butcher their own meat, make their own clothes, and manufacture other items for use or sale by the state, such a boon to the state's budget could not be reasonably ignored. (New York State Special Commission on Attica [Attica Commission], 1972: 8)

Under the system developed by Lynds, an army captain in the War of 1812, who became warden when William Brittin died in 1822, prisoners worked in small, strictly supervised units in workshops and out of doors during the day-time and returned to individual cells at night. They dressed in grotesque and ridiculous-looking black-and-white–striped uniforms and caps; they marched in complete silence, worked in complete silence, and ate in complete silence: "A breach of this rule was punished by flogging. Discipline was extremely strict in all other respects. Inmates were required to keep their eyes downcast when walking" (Eriksson, 1976: 50). Auburn developed the infamous lockstep shuffle: Inmates stood in line with the right foot slightly behind the left and the right arm outstretched with the hand on the right shoulder of the man in front of him; they moved together in a shuffle, sliding the left foot forward, then bringing the right foot to its position just behind the left, then the left again, then the right. Citizens were encouraged to visit the prison, where for a small fee they could view the inmates, an act that was designed to cause further degradation. Pris-oners were known only by number and, as in Pennsylvania, their reading mat-ter was limited to a Bible.

Beaumont and de Tocqueville report on their visit to Auburn where

> nothing is heard in the whole prison but the steps of those who march, or the sounds proceeding from the workshops. But when the day is finished, and the prisoners have retired to their cells, the silence within these vast walls, which contain so many prisoners, is like that of death. We have often trod during night those monotonous and dumb galleries, where a lamp is always burning: we felt as if we traversed catacombs; there were a thousand living beings, and yet it was a desert solitude. (1964: 65)

The administrators of Auburn believed that their most important task was the breaking of an inmate's spirit to drive him into a state of submission. Some had differences of opinion about what to do after the "breaking" process. One school of thought stressed deterrence as its goal and was determined to derive as much economic benefit from inmate labor as possible. In fact, in the early years, Auburn actually made a net profit for the state. Another school of thought held that rehabilitation was the ultimate goal, and that, after breaking, inmates should be helped through education and religion so that they could return to society better persons (Lewis, 1965).

The Auburn system consisted of an unrelenting routine of silence, hard labor, moderate meals, and solitary evenings in individual cells six days a week: "Their labor is not interrupted until the hour of taking food. There is not a sin-gle instant given to recreation" (Beaumont and de Tocqueville, 1964: 65). On Sundays, when there was no work, inmates attended church—in silence—where they were addressed by the prison chaplain who stressed the American virtues of simple faith and hard work (Attica Commission, 1972). The Auburn-style prison became the prototype for American prisons; it was cheaper to con-struct than those of Pennsylvania and allowed for a factory system that could make profitable use of inmate labor. The concept of reformation gradually declined; by the end of the 19th century, rehabilitation had virtually disappeared—prisons were viewed simply as places to keep criminals incarcerated as cheaply as possible. This view was reflected even in the name of the warden's first assistant, the "principal keeper" (Attica Commission, 1972). Prisons became bleak and silent factories with labor pools of broken people disciplined with summary floggings.

CONVICT LABOR

Sellin notes that imprisonment has its roots in penal servitude: "The prisons operated on the Auburn plan, in particular, were, most of them, notorious for the maltreatment of prisoners and for the excessive labor required of them in an attempt to meet the demand of legislators that prisons be self-supporting and even show a profit if possible" (1967: 21). The use of convict labor often made American prisons not only self-supporting institutions, but also profit-making enterprises throughout the 19th and well into the 20th century. Auburn Penitentiary balanced its books in 1829 and produced a profit of $1800 in 1831, and Sing Sing netted $29,000 in 1835 (Melossi and Pavarini, 1981). In Alabama, prison labor netted the state profits of almost $1 million annually, and just one prison industry manufacturing shirts in Florida netted that state almost $150,000 annually (Gillin, 1931). Minnesota's Stillwater Prison netted $25,000 annually as late as 1930 and served as a model for other northern prisons (Hagerty, 1934). In 1964, the Arkansas state penitentiary showed a net profit of nearly $500,000; it also gave rise to the scandalous conditions uncovered at the Tucker Prison Farm, which were portrayed in the motion picture *Brubaker*. However, prison industries also prevented the forced idleness that plagues many contemporary correctional institutions and helped maintain discipline.

Three systems were used to exploit convict labor:

1. *Contract system.* Convict labor was sold to private entrepreneurs who provided the necessary machinery; tools; raw materials; and, in some cases, the supervisory staff. In many cases, the prison was built as a factory with walls around it: "As late as 1919 a committee of the American Prison Association reported, after a national survey, that most prisons worked their prisoners in a manner reminiscent of the early forms of penal servitude and that reformation was an empty word" (Sellin, 1967: 21).

2. *Lease system.* Prisoners were leased out to private business interests for a fixed fee. This system was used extensively in agriculture and mining, particularly in the South. In Florida, for example, in 1877, the state "transferred the control and custody of prisoners to private contractors who could now employ them anywhere in the State. Prisoners were leased to individuals and corporations and set to work in phosphate mines and in and in turpentine camps in forests" (Sellin 1967: 22).

3. *State-use system.* Prison inmates produce goods for use or sale by state agencies, for example, office furniture and license plates. Other than that necessary for prison maintenance, this work is the most frequent form of prison labor in use today.

By 1874, the contract system was used in 20 state prisons, the lease system in 6, and a mixed system in 7 (Mohler, 1925). For wardens of the convict labor era, notes Alexis Durham, the ability to turn a profit was the determining factor in whether he kept his job: "The nineteenth century's most famous wardens first gained recognition because of their fiscal success" (1989a: 127). Wardens unable to run self-sufficient institutions were replaced by legislators forced to appropriate funds to maintain the prison.

During the latter part of the 19th and into the 20th century, numerous scandals involved the use of inmate labor. The growing labor union movement in the United States saw inmate labor undermining employee leverage for increased wages and improvements in working conditions. At times, inmate labor was leased out to break strikes. The National Anti-Contract Association, a manufacturers' group whose members suffered from having to compete with goods produced by cheap convict labor, campaigned against the contract system. These activities resulted in laws curbing convict labor in several industrial states: Massachusetts, New York, and Pennsylvania; the federal government enacted legislation in 1887 that forbid the contracting of any federal prisoners (McKelvey, 1977).

In the states of the Confederacy, the lease system continued to be widespread into the 20th century, when southern states slowly began to abolish the practice, the last to do so being Alabama in 1928 (Sellin, 1967). The contract system remained widespread until the Great Depression, and the passage of the Hawes-Cooper Act in 1929 and the Ashurst-Sumners Act in 1935. These federal statutes eventually curtailed the interstate commerce in goods produced with convict labor, and their constitutionality was upheld by the Supreme Court in 1936 (*Whitfield v. Ohio*, 297 U.S. 439).

The curtailing of convict labor had two long-ranging effects:

1. It increased the cost of imprisonment and thus encouraged the development of parole.
2. It forced prison officials to find other ways to deal with prison idleness. As a result, many prisons initiated programs to train and educate their inmates.

MODERN PRISON INDUSTRIES

In 1979, Congress enacted the Percy Amendment, which removed the blanket federal restrictions on the sale of prisoner-made goods in interstate commerce. Instead, the amendment sets forth minimum conditions under which such sales can occur, including consultation with labor unions, the need to avoid any impact on local industries, and a requirement that inmates be paid the prevailing local wage for work of a similar nature. The law also permits the establishment of pilot projects using prison labor by private enterprise. By 1987, 38 such projects employed more than 1000 inmates (Auerbach et al., 1988).

In response to prison overcrowding and prison construction costs, some states now utilize inmate labor to build correctional facilities. These states are typically those in which organized labor is relatively weak, such as South Carolina where inmates have been constructing new correctional facilities and expanding and renovating existing facilities: "With the exception of installing locks and ordering supplies, inmates work in all phases of construction in the field and in the office" (Carter and Humphries, 1987: 3). An audit of inmate construction projects revealed that they took twice as long to build, but labor costs were 50 percent less than private contracting. Inmates also received valuable training and work experience. Inmates are volunteers from medium- and minimum-security institutions; they are paid $0.35 an hour and become eligible for salary increases and bonuses. They also receive additional days off their sentences depending on their level of skill, which serves as an incentive to improve their skills through available training programs. Unsatisfactory performance or rule violations result in being dropped from the program. In other states, inmates are not paid but receive time off their sentences while learning employment skills. Inmate-worker turnover and the need to take counts of inmates several times a day reduce the efficiency of these construction projects.

The state of California uses more than three thousand inmates in its Conservation Camp Program. In 38 conservation camps run by the Department of Corrections in cooperation with the Department of Forestry and Fire Protection, inmates fight fires that periodically threaten the state's forests. They also clear streams, plant trees, and do flood control work and other community service projects. The inmates are carefully screened volunteers; those with histories of violent crimes, sex offenses, arson, or escape are excluded. The inmates receive two weeks of training and are paid $1.45 to $3.90 a day and $1 an hour during firefighting assignments. In North Carolina and about a dozen other states, inmate volunteers staff tourist information services. From behind prison walls and barbed wire, female inmates answer telephone inquiries from people who call the toll-free tourist information number. Inmates are either unsalaried or receive a minimum wage for their work, $1 a day or less. In Arizona and California, however, inmates perform reservation services for hotel chains during peak seasons and are paid minimum wage (McDowell, 1991). In Illinois, prison inmates produce more than 280 products, ranging from desks and other office equipment to cleaning supplies and hot dogs. Inmate workers earn from $0.30 to $1.15 an hour—3 percent is deducted to defer the cost of incarceration—and one-half day off their sentence for each day of work (Marx, 1994b).

THE "BIG HOUSE"

The construction of Auburn-type prisons ceased with the onset of the depression in 1929; in its place emerged what John Irwin (1980) refers to as the "Big House." Architecturally, it is an Auburn-style prison: one- or two-inmate cells clustered in cell blocks on tiers surrounded by a high stone wall with guard towers, often holding in excess of two thousand inmates. Unlike Auburn, however, silence, hard labor, the lockstep shuffle, and official use of corporal punishment were absent. The cells had toilets and sinks, were ventilated and heated, and had more space than the typical Auburn cell. In the Big House inmates were frequently permitted to furnish and decorate their own cells. The better-equipped institutions had recreational facilities, baseball diamonds, and basketball and handball courts. Many prisoners were black, but in most Big Houses outside the South, the inmates were mostly white. A great deal of idleness and an absence of rehabilitative programming were problems.

Scholarly studies of the prison environment, such as the one by Donald Clemmer (1958) during the 1930s, reported a phenomenon that became known as *prisonization* and the existence of an *inmate subculture*. Prisonization refers to the process by which an inmate is socialized into the prison environment. Although they may arrive with varied backgrounds, prisoners share a common suspicion and fear of other inmates and guards. In response, they tend to align themselves into cliques that serve to counter, if not subvert, the power of prison officials. These cliques form the basis of the prison subculture that emerged in the less rigid environment of the Big House. This subculture developed and enforced its own rules. Several contemporary scholars argue, however, that the subculture found in the Big House by earlier researchers did not develop in prison but was actually brought into the Big House by inmates who shared a common subcultural orientation. In either event, the guards faced a terrifying problem.

Big House guards were vastly outnumbered by inmates who were organized into cliques and formed a distinct subculture in opposition to the prison administration. Although prison officials could rely on help from outside forces, such as the state police and National Guard, sufficient coercive force was not immediately available for them to be routinely in effective control of the institution. Corporal punishment was no longer (officially) permitted, and loss of "good time" (time off for "good behavior") or solitary confinement often proved ineffective in controlling behavior in the volatile atmosphere of a prison. As a result, Irwin (1980) states, guards developed effective informal control strategies involving personal agreements and corrupt favoritism:

1. *Personal agreements* between guards and inmates were implicit or tacit exchange relationships in which an inmate would refrain from rule-violative behavior in return for some favor or special consideration from a guard.

2. *Corrupt favoritism* involved guards who granted special privileges to key prisoners who served as inmate leaders, in return for their support in maintaining order.

The Big House inmate leaders helped to maintain order

- By keeping their own violations within acceptable limits, and by supporting the prevailing prison norm, which required inmates to "do your own time"—that is, mind your own business and "don't make no waves" (which encouraged conformity)
- By threatening or actually using violence against prisoners who disrupted the prison routine and thereby endangered the privileged inmates' special arrangements with the guards

We have moved from Walnut Street and the Pennsylvania system to Auburn and the Big House; the next stop is in California, where a new model of penology, based on positive theory, developed.

CORRECTIONS

Toward the end of World War II, a penological revolution occurred in California, where former prosecutor Earl Warren (1891–1974) had been elected governor in the wake of a prison scandal. Under Warren's leadership, California reorganized its prison system according to the positivistic ideal of individual reformation. The system was organized not for punishment, but around rehabilitation. California would apply the methods of the behavioral sciences to *correct* criminal behavior.

To operationalize the new approach to penology, California implemented an extreme version of the *indeterminate sentence.* Judges would remand a criminal with an indefinite sentence to the California Adult (or Youth) Authority, which would determine his or her *treatment* needs through a process of classification and assign the *convict-client* to an appropriate facility—not a prison but a *correctional institution.* A convict would remain "under treatment"—incarcerated—until the Adult Authority determined that the client had been rehabilitated, at which time he or she would be paroled to a community-based treatment program—that is, supervision by a parole agent.

CLASSIFICATION IN CALIFORNIA

A person sentenced to incarceration is first sent to a reception center for two to four weeks. Here, the inmate is examined by physicians, psychologists, and educators. A correctional counselor works with this team to determine which of the sixteen institutions is appropriate for the inmate.

The counselor calculates a sociometric score for each inmate to determine custody classification, based on the following factors:

1. Length of sentence
2. Age
3. Marital status
4. Employment history
5. Social stability
6. Education
7. Warrants from other jurisdictions
8. Escape or attempts
9. Prior commitments
10. Past behavior in prison

Although the score typically determines prison and program, the counselor can make a special placement based on extenuating factors, such as the inmate's physical and mental health, prison space available, and security concerns.

At the receiving prison, a classification committee meets within 14 days to assign the inmate to a primary program. The committee offers the inmate a variety of programs; if all programs are declined, the inmate cannot earn time off the court-imposed sentence ("good time").

Inmates and institutions are classified into four levels reflecting security factors (escape potential, violence potential, and inmate needs) posed by the inmate and the resources of the institution to deal with the risk. The goal of classification in corrections is to place inmates in the lowest custody level consistent with public safety.

> *Level I* consists of open dormitories without a secure perimeter for inmates with less than a 30-month sentence, minor histories of criminality, and some history of social stability. About 35 percent of all inmates are level I.
>
> *Level II* uses open dormitories but with secure perimeter fences and armed coverage. This level is for inmates with sentences of more than 30 months, minor histories of criminality, few escapes, low potential for institutional violence, and few indications of social stability. About 15 percent of inmates are level II.
>
> *Level III* consists of individual cells surrounded by fenced or walled perimeters and armed coverage. These institutions are for inmates with somewhat longer sentences, significant prior criminal histories, prior "walk-away escapes," disciplinary problems during prior incarcerations, and a general lack of social stability. About 25 percent of inmates are level III.
>
> *Level IV* institutions have cells surrounded by fenced or walled perimeters, electronic security, more staff, and armed officers both inside and outside the institution. These inmates have long histories of extensive criminal behavior and serious disciplinary problems during past incarcerations, histories of escapes, or terms of such length that escape is highly probable, and no social stability. About 25 percent are level IV.

Prisons no longer existed in California; they became "correctional institutions." Guards were no longer present; they became "correction officers." Wardens no longer existed; they became "superintendents." New institutions—medium- and minimum-security correctional facilities—were built. Adult Authority clients could be moved from maximum- to medium- to minimum-security facilities, and to parole. Or, if their behavior required they could be moved from parole supervision back into the institution for further "treatment in a secure setting."

Into these correctional institutions came the *treaters*; new superintendents often had extensive education in the behavioral sciences, and their institutions employed teachers, social workers, psychologists, and psychiatrists to implement a rehabilitative regimen. Slowly, but steadily, the California system was copied, at least in part, by all the other states and the federal system—prisons virtually disappeared from the United States. Parole and the indeterminate sentence became intertwined with the idea of corrections and a medical model approach to dealing with criminal behavior, subjects discussed in Chapter 7.

CORRECTIONAL FACILITIES IN ILLINOIS

Illinois has three types of prisons for adult males:

Maximum security. There are two inmates to a cell, and the entire facility is surrounded by walls containing guard towers (four prisons).

Medium security. Two inmates to a cell, and the entire facility is surrounded by fences and guard towers. There is more freedom of movement for inmates than at maximum security institutions (eleven prisons).

Minimum security. These facilities are usually surrounded by a fence and guard towers, but inmates can move more freely around the facility; and they live in dormitory-style rooms divided into cubicles (seven prisons).

Source: Marx, 1995b.

CORRECTIONAL INSTITUTIONS: DIVISIONS, REBELLIONS, AND RIOTS

Despite the corrections revolution, prison officials remained preoccupied with management and security issues; most of the allocations for correctional institutions were for administration and security, leaving about 5 percent for items that could reasonably be labeled "rehabilitative." Providing such services has always been problematic. Correctional salaries are relatively low, and most prisons are located in rural areas not particularly attractive to urban graduates trained in therapeutic disciplines. Inadequate funding results in vocational training that is out of date and often of little use to inmates seeking employment based on skills developed in the correctional institution.

The problems encountered by the corrections approach were compounded by differences between correction officers and the "treaters." Older members of staff, particularly those responsible for prison security, were often resistant to the changes brought in by the treaters. This resistance could be expected from an examination of their differing backgrounds. Correction officers were typically rural, white Protestants, socially and politically conservative with, at best, a high school education; they tended to be poorly trained. The treaters tended to be reform-minded urban college graduates, many of whom were Catholics and Jews—and women.

Furthermore, the rhetoric did not match the reality, and prisoners soured on rehabilitative programs that raised unrealistic expectations (Irwin, 1980: 63):

"After prisoners were convinced that treatment programs did not work (by the appearance of persons who had participated fully in treatment programs streaming back to prison with new crimes or violations of parole), hope shaded to cynicism and then turned to bitterness."

Blake McKelvey points out that during the 1950s prisoners were usually divided to the point of impotence: "The prisonization process, which had aligned the great majority of inmates against their keepers, had also divided them from one another, making effective collaboration extremely difficult. Only a rumor of an excessively brutal incident or a report of revolts elsewhere could arouse a sense of community sufficient to support a riotous outbreak" (1977: 323). McKelvey adds that there were such outbreaks during the 1950s in California, Louisiana, Massachusetts, Michigan, Missouri, New Jersey, Ohio, Pennsylvania, and Washington.

Into this environment came thousands of new black and Hispanic inmates. During the 1950s, the number of blacks and other nonwhites committed annually to adult federal and state prisons increased from 17,200 to 28,500 (McKelvey, 1977), and this figure continued to grow during the 1960s and 1970s. Although the predominantly white inmates of the Big House could relate to their keepers, the young urban black and Hispanic found no such comfort. In 1954, the Supreme Court handed down its decision in *Brown v. Board of Education of Topeka, Kansas* (347 U.S. 483) and set off the civil rights revolution in the United States.

Rising black consciousness occurring in the wider community took on more radical dimensions inside the prison. The Black Muslims emerged as a major separatist organization and confronted prison officials with demands based on religious freedom. The antiwar movement and activities of radical groups, such as the Black Panthers and Students for a Democratic Society (SDS), stirred and politicized inmates, black and white. These inmates confronted correctional officials with demands often couched in Marxist terminology.

The traditional relationship between inmates and correction officers, *rapprochement* based on private agreements or corrupt favoritism, started to come apart. Inmates became increasingly militant in their refusal to cooperate with their keepers. Correctional officials responded in the best tradition of the Big House—with repression that touched off violence in institutions throughout the country, including riots at California's San Quentin in 1967 and Holmesburg Prison in Philadelphia in 1970. Correctional institutions simmered throughout the 1960s and into 1971, when in September the focus of attention shifted to a small upstate New York town where the last of the Auburn-style prisons was built.

ATTICA

The state prison at Attica (a town that in 1971 had a population of fewer than 3000) was completed in 1931 and boasted of being the most secure, escape-proof prison ever built; at the time, it was also the most expensive prison ever built. Attica was a response to an outbreak of prison riots throughout the United

States in the late 1920s. In 1929, Clinton Prison in Dannemora, New York, experienced a riot protesting overcrowded conditions; three inmates were killed. In that year, the prison at Auburn experienced a general riot in which inmates used firearms; the assistant warden was killed, and four inmates escaped before the prison was brought back under control.

Typical of prisons in New York and elsewhere, Attica was placed in a rural area where residents would accept the institution as a basis for employment and other economic benefits. On July 8, 1970, Attica, and the other state prisons in New York, received a name change: On that date the names of all the state's maximum security prisons were changed. There were no more prisons; in their places, instead, stood six maximum security "correctional facilities." The prison wardens became "institutional superintendents"; the former principal keepers became "deputy superintendents"; and the old-line prison guards awakened that morning to find themselves suddenly "correction officers." "No one's job or essential duties changed, only his title" (Attica Commission, 1972: 18).

Fourteen months later, Attica Correctional Facility had more than 2000 inmates who were locked in their cells for 12 to 16 hours a day being "rehabilitated," and who spent the remainder of the day with little to occupy their time. No gymnasium was available, and recreational opportunities were limited. Any meaningful rehabilitation programs were almost totally absent. Showers were available for most inmates—once a week.

Most inmates were black and Hispanic from the downstate New York area or upstate cities, such as Buffalo, Syracuse, and Rochester. All but one (he was Puerto Rican) of the fewer than 400 correction officers were non-Hispanic whites drawn primarily from the communities surrounding Attica. Although the superintendent had a master's degree in correctional administration, correction officers who began their jobs between World War II and the late 1950s received no formal training. Those who started after that were given two weeks of training. They were expected to enforce the dozens of petty rules typical of correctional institutions and to relate in a meaningful way to inmates with whom they had little in common.

Attica had a large number of Black Muslims (members of the Nation of Islam) who had difficulty with a prison diet that was heavy with pork. Muslims also objected to the lack of ministers. Correctional officials would not allow the ministers, many of whom had prison records, into Attica. Black Muslims spent their recreation time in the yard engaging in worship and highly disciplined physical exercise. The correctional staff, which never understood the Black Muslims, was quite fearful of this group, who exhibited military-type discipline and remained aloof from both staff and other inmates.

Typical of large correctional institutions, in Attica "popular conceptions of homosexual advances and assaults in prison were not exaggerated" (Attica Commission, 1972: 78). Correction officers were unable to protect inmates who were forced to resort to forms of self-protection, such as carrying a "shiv" (homemade knife), in violation of prison rules (1972: 79): "The irony was not lost on the inmates. They perceived themselves surrounded by high walls and gates, and tightly regimented by a myriad of written and unwritten rules; but when they needed protection, they often had to resort to the same skills that had brought many of them to Attica in the first place."

The Riot. During the summer of 1971, a number of peaceful protests by inmates over conditions at Attica occurred. Leaders of previously antagonistic inmate groups, such as the Young Lords, a Puerto Rican group, and the Black Panthers and Black Muslims, gained greater political awareness, submerged their differences, and joined with white inmates in a peaceful effort to effect changes at Attica. The new solidarity among inmates frightened officials. The superintendent responded by attempting to transfer the leaders as "troublemakers." He was prevented from doing so by the new Commissioner of the Department of Correctional Services Russell G. Oswald. Oswald, who had been chairman of the New York State Board of Parole, met with inmate representatives at the prison but was called away on a personal emergency—his wife was seriously ill—before any agreement could be arranged.

On September 8, 1971, when a correction officer attempted to discipline two inmates who appeared to be sparring, a confrontation ensued. The incident passed without any action on the part of the outnumbered staff. That evening officers appeared and took the inmates from their cells. A noisy protest ensued during the evening, and it was renewed when inmates gathered for breakfast on the morning of September 9. A melee broke out, correction officers were taken hostage, and a riot quickly developed. Prison officials had no plan, nor had they been trained to deal with such an emergency. As a result, within 20 minutes inmates secured control of the four main cell blocks and seized 40 hostages. Correction officers were beaten and one died later as a result of his wounds. The Black Muslims, who had not taken part in the initial uprising, moved to protect the hostages who were used as a basis for negotiations. An inmate committee for that purpose was formed.

Commissioner Oswald found that when he arrived at Attica the police were not prepared to retake the prison immediately. By the time that sufficient forces had gathered, negotiations were already underway and Oswald chose to continue them in an effort to avoid more bloodshed. At the request of the inmate committee, several outside observers were permitted to enter Attica, including reporters, lawyers, and politicians. Although the negotiations were quite disorganized, Oswald agreed to most of the inmate demands for improved conditions at Attica. The negotiations broke down, however, over the issue of complete amnesty because one of the injured officers had died after the negotiations began.

On the morning of September 13, in a poorly planned and uncoordinated nine-minute assault, heavily armed state police and correction officers retook the prison: Two hostages were seriously injured by the inmates, and ten hostages and twenty-nine inmates were killed by state troopers and correction officers (Wicker, 1975). In 1989, the New York State Court of Claims awarded $1.3 million to seven inmates who, although they had not participated in the uprising, had been injured at Attica by state police gunfire (Kolbert, 1989).

A number of official investigations occurred in the aftermath of the rebellion at Attica. In particular, rehabilitation, the parole board, and indeterminate sentencing came in for severe criticism. Cullen and Gilbert point out that

Americans in the first half of the 1970s were faced with the prospect of an intractable crime rate and confronted with the reality—powerfully symbolized by Attica—that their prisons were both inhumane and grossly ineffective. In this context, a culprit was needed to take the blame, and a candidate was readily found. Rehabilitation would take the rap. (1982: 6)

MODERN CORRECTIONAL INSTITUTIONS

Did the events at Attica result in any lasting changes? At Attica, Islam is now a recognized religion; inmates are allowed to stay in the exercise yard into the evening; and prisoners who can afford them are allowed television sets in their cells (Cohen, 1992). Observers of the current state of our prisons, however, would be hard-pressed to document any positive changes of substance. A distinct political turn to the right has increased the number of prison commitments and lengthened the terms of imprisonment in many states that now have no parole system with which to deal with overcrowding. This has been exacerbated by politicians scrabbling on board the "tough on crime" bandwagon with policies that, while they fail to deal with public protection, pander to constituent emotions. Some have focused on making prison life *more* difficult by prohibiting television, exercise equipment, and other recreational material that aid prison officials in maintaining discipline and control. In some states, legislation bars certain amenities—air conditioning, for example—that inmates do not have.

John Irwin and James Austin (1994: 82, 111) point out:

Now prison administrators and other policy makers have completely abandoned the goal of reducing prisoners' isolation from outside society. They build prisons in the remotest regions of the state with only security in mind and further reduce contact with outside organizations and individuals through their custody-oriented policies. These practices, along with greatly diminished rehabilitative resources, are producing prisoners who have deteriorated in prison and return to the outside much less equipped to live a conventional life than they were when they entered. . . . We should be concerned by the fact that the prison systems are spewing out such damaged human material, most of whom will disappear into our social trash heap, politely labeled the "homeless" or the underclass, or, worse, will violently lash out, perhaps murdering or raping someone, and then be taken back to the dungeon.

During an era when crime has been declining, the prison population increased dramatically. In fact, it is difficult to posit a relationship between increased imprisonment and the rate of crime. Lester Velie and Jerome Miller (1983): 31) point out, for example, that while Texas and Pennsylvania have similar-sized populations, Texas imprisons three times as many offenders as Pennsylvania, yet crime in Texas grew 2 percent from 1983 through 1984; crime in Pennsylvania declined 1.9 percent. The Washington, D.C., incarceration rate is three and one-third that of the country. Yet whereas crime declined nationally 3 percent from 1983 through 1984, in Washington it dropped 0.7 percent.

WOMEN IN PRISON

Many of the life experiences and needs of women offenders differ from those of men offenders; however, criminal justice institutional practices, services, and facilities have largely been fashioned for men. Today few jails and prisons have separate inmate classification and intake procedures for women, even though women have unique needs and evidence different behavior from men in custody. A large percentage of jails and prisons do not provide for the medical and psychological problems of chemically dependent women. While most women offenders have children for whom they are or were responsible, few institutions provide facilities and child care services needed to facilitate visits with children. Even though most women offenders are single mothers who obtain little or no financial help from the children's fathers, vocational training within corrections tends to reinforce traditional low-paying occupations for women. (Wellisch, Anglin, and Prendergast, 1993: 18)

ACQUIRED IMMUNODEFICIENCY SYNDROME (AIDS) AND TUBERCULOSIS

During the 1990s, adding to the numerous safety and health problems endemic to prisons is that presented by AIDS and its precursor immunodeficiency virus (HIV), first identified in the United States in 1981. Intravenous drug users and male homosexuals have been identified as primary groups at risk from the disease, and prisons house many intravenous drug users and inmates who resort to homosexual practices in the absence of available female partners [see Hammett (1989) for a review of this issue]. Inmates frequently sport prison tattoos, and the sharing of the tattoo needles is a source of infection. The disease is the single greatest cause of death in New York prisons (Clines, 1993), and the number of HIV positive cases in correctional institutions increased 66 percent from 1990 to 1993, reaching almost 12,000, 94 percent of whom are male—roughly in proportion with the gender distribution in prisons and jails (Hammett et al., 1994).

Additional dangers arrived at the prison gate with increases in tuberculosis (TB); "TB is not usually a highly contagious disease but, given the right conditions . . . the probability of transmission increases significantly" (Wilcock, Hammett, and Parent, 1995: 2). In a Minneapolis bar, one patron with TB infected 45 persons in 1992 (Altman, 1995).

Tuberculosis presents particularly serious problems, as well as intervention opportunities, for correctional institutions. Prisons and jails, like other congregate facilities, are high-risk settings for the spread of tuberculosis infection. Living conditions are invariably crowded, and many buildings have antiquated systems with poor ventilation and air circulation. Inmates are already more susceptible to TB infection and TB disease because of factors associated with their high-risk lifestyles and inadequate access to health care services, as well as increased prevalence of HIV/AIDS among them. Finally, the appearance of multidrug resistant tuberculosis raises the threat of an often untreatable disease spreading in a closely confined population. (Hammett, Harrold, and Epstein, 1994: xi)

Tuberculosis infection is spread through the air in tiny droplets containing the bacterium exhaled by persons with active TB disease, primarily when they cough or sneeze. TB commonly affects the lungs but may attack other parts of the body (Hammett et al., 1994). Inmates weakened by AIDS are at particular risk for new drug-resistant strains of TB, but all inmates and prison personnel are at risk from this contagious disease, which in 1992 killed a correction officer at New York's Auburn Correctional Facility. Tuberculosis can be contracted by an otherwise healthy individual because the disease is spread by coughing in an environment without adequate ventilation: "Not only do inmate populations contain concentrations of persons at risk for both TB and HIV, but the facilities themselves are high-risk settings for TB transmission because of crowded conditions and poor ventilation" (Crawford, 1994: 31). The Centers for Disease Control have guidelines for isolating persons with active TB; however, in a prison setting, these are expensive to implement, and most prisons are inadequate for dealing with TB.

DRUGS

Prison officials are also acknowledging the difficulties created by the widespread use of drugs in their institutions: "Drug use has become a major problem with a variety of ramifications, including threats to prison order, violence among inmates, and corruption of guards and other employees" (Malcolm, 1989c: 1), and this problem is apparently widespread (Purdy, 1995). In Pennsylvania, for example, during the past 6 years, 11 inmates died of drug overdoses (Associated Press, 1995). The dramatic increase in convicted drug offenders has been a driving force behind prison overcrowding and the smuggling of drugs into correctional institutions.

In Illinois in 1989, for example, the number of convictions for drug offenses increased by 50 percent, driving up the prison population to nearly 32 percent over capacity (Anonymous, 1989). The number of inmates imprisoned in Illinois for drug offenses between 1985 and 1989 increased more than 300 percent. In Illinois, "Drug offenders have been the fastest growing segment of the prison population for several years" (Illinois Department of Corrections, 1992: 19). According to the Department of Corrections, the number of inmates over capacity in Illinois has reached the equivalent of eight new prisons. In

New York, the number of inmates serving time for drug-related offenses has surpassed those imprisoned for any other type of crime.

VIOLENCE

Prison violence is widespread: Assaults on employees increased from fewer than 1700 a year in 1988 to more than 13,000 in 1994 (Porter, 1995). In 1985, dozens of inmates were murdered by other inmates in Texas prisons—until 1980 Texas boasted of having the most orderly and peaceful prison system in the United States. This ended when a federal court held that the entire Texas prison system was unconstitutional, primarily because of overcrowding, and took control away from state officials [*Ruiz v. Estelle*, 503 F.Supp. 1265 (1980); at the end of 1992, the *Ruiz* lawsuit was settled, a federal judge ruling that Texas was in compliance with constitutional requirements]. A particularly grisly prison outbreak occurred at the New Mexico State Penitentiary, which was built in 1957 to house 850 inmates. On February 1, 1980, the prison had nearly 1000 inmates and was badly understaffed; only 18 correction officers were on duty when prisoners took over the institution. Although the prison was quickly retaken by police and National Guard, inmates had systematically slaughtered 33 of their fellow prisoners—many of whom were tortured to death.

SEXUAL VIOLENCE

He was forced to have oral sex with one inmate. A second demanded anal intercourse. When he refused, the inmate tore off his pants, shoved a pillow over his head so he couldn't scream, and raped him. It was quite painful. For the next four hours several dozen inmates dragged him from cell to cell, raping him. The next night, he was gang raped again (Marx, 1995).

Overcrowding was seen as a major reason for the 1989 two-day prison riot at the Correctional Institution at Camp Hill, Pennsylvania, a facility built to house 1826 that had 2607 inmates; more than 118 persons were injured, and one-half of the facility's 31 buildings were destroyed. At the Southern Ohio Correctional Facility at Lucasville, overcrowding was a modest 120 percent of capacity—the lowest for all of the state's prisons. Nevertheless, in 1993, led by a Muslim faction aligned with members of the Aryan Brotherhood, inmates rioted, seized 18 staff members as hostages, killing 1 correction officer and 9 inmates, and injuring 48 inmates and several correction officers—one lost an eye—before surrendering. Prison overcrowding has been exacerbated by a substantial increase in drug prosecutions, and the perennial problem of prison discipline and violence has been exacerbated by court orders limiting the authority of correctional officials and the phenomenon of prison gangs.

PRISONS AND THE COURTS

Throughout most of our history, the courts have been unwilling to intervene in matters pertaining to prisons "out of concern for federalism and separation of powers and a fear that judicial review of administrative decisions would undermine prison security and discipline" (Jacobs, 1980: 433). Once the requirements of due process had been met, leading to conviction and sentencing, the judiciary had taken a "hands-off" policy. Prisons are difficult to manage, and this difficulty made judges reluctant to impose their legal standards in place of the expertise of prison administrators. In 1961, however, the Black Muslims began to litigate their First Amendment claims in New York, California, and the District of Columbia. As Claire Cripe (1977), points out, these cases served to "open the floodgates" of prison litigation. Once the courts became involved in prisons, they had no easy way to withdraw.

In 1968, 14 years after segregation in public schools was declared unconstitutional, the U.S. Supreme Court ruled that the racial segregation of prisoners violated the Fourth Amendment (*Lee v. Washington*, 390 U.S. 333). The following year the Court ruled that prison officials must permit prisoners ("jailhouse lawyers") to assist their fellow inmates with legal questions (*Johnson v. Avery*, 393 U.S. 483). In 1971, the Court expanded this right by requiring prison officials to provide legal materials, law books, legal forms, and so on, for inmates (*Younger v. Gilmore*, 404 U.S. 15). In 1974, the Court extended its previous decisions by requiring correctional officials to provide either adequate law libraries or adequate legal assistance (*Bounds v. Smith*, 430 U.S. 817). That same year, the Court limited the power of prison officials to censor inmate letters (*Procunier v. Martinez*, 417 U.S. 817). In 1989, however, the Court (*Thornburgh v. Abbott*, 104 L.Ed.2d 459) limited the *Procunier* decision to *outgoing* mail and held that incoming items can quickly circulate throughout the institution and be a source of disorder. Accordingly, the Court gave prison officials greater flexibility in censoring publications that inmates may receive: "In the volatile prison environment, it is essential that prison officials be given discretion to prevent such disorder."

In 1974, the Supreme Court ruled that prisoners are entitled to minimal due process protections whenever disciplinary action threatens their "liberty" by imposing solitary confinement and loss of privileges of good time (*Wolff v. McDonnell*, 418 U.S. 817): "[T]hough his rights may be diminished by the needs and exigencies of the institutional environment, a prisoner is not wholly stripped of constitutional protections when he is imprisoned for a crime. There is no iron curtain drawn between the Constitution and the prisons of this country." In 1977, however, the Court apparently decided to draw a line between the prison and the Constitution: It rejected the notion that prisoners had the right under the First Amendment to organize an inmate union (*Jones v. North Carolina Prisoners' Union*, 433 U.S. 119). In 1978, the Court ruled that solitary confinement in a harsh setting for more than 30 days constitutes cruel and unusual punishment (*Hutto v. Finney*, 437 U.S. 678).

A great deal of litigation has arisen over prison conditions, particularly with respect to overcrowding. Federal and state courts in many jurisdictions have ordered prison officials to reduce inmate populations and to take other corrective steps to bring their institutions into line with constitutional requirements. In 1979 (*Bell v. Wolfish*, 441 U.S. 520) and 1981 (*Rhodes v. Chapman*, 452 U.S. 337), however, the Supreme Court overturned lower court decisions that found overcrowding per se to be unconstitutional. The Court ruled that the Constitution does not require inmates to be housed in single cells; double-bunking is permitted even for those prisoners in jail awaiting trial, who are legally still innocent. In *Chapman*, the Court ruled that prison conditions were constitutional as long as the totality of the conditions does not "involve the wanton and unnecessary infliction of pain." The 1994 federal "Crime Bill" prohibits federal judges from finding that prison or jail overcrowding is unconstitutional "in general terms." The statute requires a plaintiff to prove that the overcrowding causes the infliction of cruel and unusual punishment—a violation of the Eighth Amendment—*on that particular inmate.*

In 1983 (*Hudson v. Palmer*, 468 U.S. 517), the Supreme Court ruled that the Fourth Amendment's protection against unreasonable search and seizure does not apply to prison cells. In a 5–4 decision, the Court held: "The recognition of privacy rights for prisoners in their individual cells simply cannot be reconciled with the concept of incarceration and the needs and objectives of penal institutions." In *Hudson*, the Court overturned a U.S. court of appeals decision that had upheld the right of a convicted bank robber in Virginia to sue prison officials for the destruction of his property resulting from a search of his cell by correction officers. In 1994, the Court ruled unanimously that prison officials can be found liable for failing to protect inmates from the violence of other inmates. The successful litigant, an inmate at the federal prison at Terre Haute, Indiana, alleged that the beatings and rapes he suffered were the result of official indifference (*Farmer v. Brennan* No. 92-7247). In a 1995 decision [*Sandin v. Conner* (No. 93-1911)], a 5–4 majority made it substantially more difficult for prisoners to challenge prison officials: only when their actions impose "atypical and significant hardship on the inmate." Prison officials should have, the Court ruled, the flexibility "in fine-tuning of the ordinary incidents of prison life." The case involved an inmate in Hawaii who had not been allowed to call witnesses at a disciplinary hearing that imposed solitary confinement for 30 days—he lacked a "liberty interest" (an issue that was discussed in Chapter 5 and is examined again in Chapter 8).

PRISON GANGS

Some gangs developed in prison, often as mutual-protection groups; others were brought into the institution by convicted gang members. In either case, the contemporary prison has provided fertile soil for the proliferation and growth of these often dangerous entities. In most instances, gangs are organized along racial or ethnic lines. Instead of the politicized groups of the 1960s, an array of gangs with exotic-sounding names has appeared. So extensive is gang membership that a U.S. court of appeals in Illinois concluded that 90 percent of Pontiac Correctional Center's inmates are gang members and that they were running much of prison life (Crawford, 1988). The gangs have increased the potential for violence with members using the power of their gang affiliations for various extortionate practices. Inmates without the protection of the gang are vulnerable and often easy prey for the violence-prone gang members. Attempts by correctional officials to dissipate the power of the gangs by transferring their leadership to other institutions have often served only to spread the phenomenon. The gangs often transcend the prison, with members active inside and outside the institution. The prevalence of gangs has serious implications for parole officers.

Gang members engage in extortion and drug and weapons trafficking: "Many prison gangs have a 'blood-in-blood-out' policy, meaning that an inmate may became a member only after killing or assaulting another prisoner or staffer and that his blood will be spilled before he is allowed to quit the gang. Members released from prison remain in the gang, often providing support and enforcement for the organization outside" [President's Commission on Organized Crime; (PCOC), 1986: 75]. The U.S. Department of Justice has identified 114 different gangs with greatly varying structures, the largest being the Mexican Mafia, Aryan Brotherhood, Black Guerilla Family, Texas Syndicate, and La Nuestra Familia. In all five, either murder or the drawing of blood is a prerequisite for membership.

THE MEXICAN MAFIA

Reputed to be the most powerful of the prison-organized groups (also known as "la M"—pronounced em-a—and *MEXIKANEMI*), the 400-member Mexican Mafia comprises primarily Mexican American convicts and ex-convicts from the barrios of East Los Angeles. Its origins are traced to the Deuel Vocational Institute in Tracy, California, where in 1957, 20 young Mexican Americans from the Maravilla area of East Los Angeles began the Mexican Mafia as a self-protection group. The PCOC notes that they soon "began to control such illicit activities as homosexual prostitution, gambling, and narcotics. They called themselves the Mexican Mafia out of admiration for *La Cosa Nostra*" (1986: 73). Attempts by the Department of Corrections to diminish gang power by transferring members to other institutions only helped to spread their influence. Vigorous recruiting occurs among the most violent Mexican-American inmates, particularly those housed in adjustment centers for the most dangerous and incorrigible. In 1967, Mexican Mafia reliance on wholesale violence increased, and in that year members attacked the first Mexican American outside their group. This attack on an inmate from rural northern California led to the formation of a second Mexican-American gang, *La Nuestra Familia*, with whom the Mexican Mafia has been feuding since 1968.

By the mid-1960s the Mexican Mafia had assumed control over prison heroin trafficking and numerous other inmate activities. In 1966, it started to move its operations outside the prison and is reputedly attempting to organize Hispanic gangs into a confederation to confront black Los Angeles gangs for control of the drug trade (Mydans, 1995). The gang asserts control over drug trafficking by Hispanic street gangs and collects "street taxes" in exchange for the privilege of staying in business and protection against encroachment by other gangs.

COMMUNITY-BASED CORRECTIONS

By the 1960s, the "correctional" expectations of prisons were not being fulfilled: "The spending of years in confined quarters, perhaps as small as eight by ten feet, in a setting dominated by a toilet and a possibly criminally-aggressive cellmate, can hardly be considered conducive to encourage socially acceptable behavior upon release" (Hahn, 1976: 6). The prison is what Erving Goffman (1961: xiii) refers to as a *total institution*: "a place of residence and work where a large number of like-situated individuals, cut off from the wider society for an appreciable period of time, together lead an enclosed, formally administered round of life." As such, these institutions have a tendency to mold persons into compliant and often shapeless forms to maintain discipline and a sound working order, or for less utilitarian reasons. The prison provides a dreary uniformity that leaves little room for self-assertion and decision-making—the requisites for living in the free community.

"Even the most well-developed treatment program," Paul Cromwell points out, "if totally contained within the institution, will lack one ingredient essential to an inmate's success after release. The missing factor is contact with the community and family" (1978: 68) to counter the negative influence of the inmate subculture. Instead of abandoning the rehabilitative ideal, supporters of the corrections approach in the late 1960s and early 1970s argued for a new approach they referred to as *community-based corrections*.

Belinda and Bernard McCarthy trace the concept of community-based corrections "back to the years following World War II, when returning veterans encountered adjustment problems as they attempted to reenter civilian life" (1984: 9). The successful integration of many servicemen was accomplished with assistance ranging from informal outpatient counseling to education; job preparation; and, in some cases, intensive therapy in residential settings. In 1967, the President's Commission on Law Enforcement and Administration of Justice stated: "Institutions tend to isolate offenders from society, both physically and psychologically, cutting them off from schools, jobs, families, and other supportive influences and increasing the probability that the label of criminal will be indelibly impressed upon them. The goal of reintegration is likely to be furthered much more readily by working with offenders in the community than by incarceration" (1972: 398). The commission added that the high cost of incarceration also served to make community-based corrections a more attractive alternative.

In 1965, the Federal Rehabilitative Act authorized programs designed to aid in the rehabilitation of offenders while holding down the number of persons in prison. In 1968, Congress enacted the Omnibus Crime Control and Safe

Streets Act, which led to the establishment of the Law Enforcement Assistance Administration (LEAA). With encouragement and funding from LEAA, state correctional officials began to look outside the prison for ways to rehabilitate offenders. The approach they adopted centered on reintegrating the offender back into the community, and it became known as "community-based corrections." Vernon Fox (1971: 1) states that community-based corrections refers to that part of corrections, other than traditional probation, prison, and parole, which makes use of community resources to assist the more traditional functions. Its purposes include:

1. "Mobilization and management of community resources to assist in the rehabilitation of offenders"
2. "Provision of alternatives to incarceration in a way that is compatible with the public interest and safety"

Several programs are generally offered as part of community-based corrections, including diversion, pretrial release, deferred sentencing, halfway houses, and work release.

1. *Diversion.* The President's Commission on Law Enforcement and Administration of Justice (1972) noted that for many persons who come to the attention of the criminal justice system, criminal sanctions would be excessive; however, these persons are often in need of treatment or supervision. Because the courts are overburdened with cases, programs that provide needed services for nonserious offenders, while easing court congestion, proved attractive. Diversion programs were operated by or in conjunction with police and prosecutor's offices; they dealt with adults and juveniles. Instead of being arrested and/or prosecuted, these offenders were sent for "treatment." Criticism of diversion centered on research indicating that persons who are diverted would often not have been arrested or prosecuted in the first place—diversion programs frequently *increased* ("net widening") the number of persons involved in criminal justice.

2. *Pretrial release.* Persons who lack the funds necessary to be released on bail and are detained pending trial suffer from significant disadvantages. The jail experience itself is punishing, but the person is also separated from the community: family and friends, as well as places of employment. This experience handicaps the defendant and also burdens the criminal justice system, which must provide for the pretrial detention. Pretrial release programs use investigators—sometimes probation officers—to screen persons after they have entered the criminal justice system and before bail has been set. This approach enables the judge to make an informed bail decision, particularly in cases in which the investigator indicates that the defendant is a good candidate for release on his or her own recognizance (ROR). Some programs expanded to include supervision and a variety of services to persons on ROR.

3. *Deferred sentencing.* A program of deferred sentencing usually involves a plea of guilty followed by either restitution or some form of community service instead of a sentence. Satisfactory completion of the conditions of the deferred sentence results in the charges being dropped; conversely, a failure can result in incarceration. Some programs use probation officers to supervise deferred offenders.

4. *Halfway houses.* This type of facility may be operated by a public or private agency. Some provide room and board and help with employment; others provide, in addition, a whole range of social services. Halfway houses may be used to place probationers in lieu of prison (halfway in) or for parolees in need of supportive services when they are released from prison (halfway out).

5. *Work release.* Like the halfway house, work release is designed to prepare inmates for the freedom of community living. Typically, an inmate leaves the institution or work-release center during the day for employment and returns at the end of the work day. Work release may also be granted to secure employment or to attend job training or educational programs.

David Greenberg questions some of the basic assumptions of community-based corrections: "One might ask why, if the community is so therapeutic, the offender got into trouble there in the first place? Indeed, an offender's home community, where he is already known as a delinquent or criminal, might pose more obstacles to the abandonment of criminal activity than some new residential location" (1975: 4). Furthermore, Greenberg argues, to the extent that criminal behavior is a rational response to the lack of lawful employment opportunity, it is beyond the ability of community-based corrections to correct.

The impetus for the expansion of community-based corrections was the availability of federal funding; Andrew Scull notes that "since the creation of the Law Enforcement Assistance Administration, efforts have been under way to manipulate federal funding and support for state and local law enforcement so as to provide sizable financial incentives for the development of community corrections' programs" (1977: 45). During the early 1980s, however, funding through LEAA dried up, and the agency was dismantled. State and local governments, already severely pressed for services while trying to hold the line on taxes, slowly abandoned the often costly programming that adequate community-based corrections required. And the focus on the rehabilitative potential of the prison changed dramatically, *incapacitation* becoming the "principal justification for imprisonment in American criminal justice: offenders are imprisoned in the United States to restrain them from offending again while they are confined" (Zimring and Hawkins, 1995: 3). But how much incapacitation can we afford? In part, the answer to this question has led to the development of privately built and operated prisons.

PRISONS FOR PROFIT

Although prisons have proved to be a costly liability for state governments since the Great Depression, some localities and private entrepreneurs view them as a source of potential income. For example, in 1989 the town of Horton, in northeastern Kansas, population 2100, planned to build a 1000-cell prison, which, for a fee, would house inmates from jurisdictions experiencing prison overcrowding problems (Robbins, 1989). The farming community of Appleton, Minnesota, has a population of about 1500, and in 1992 an empty 472-bed medium-security prison, one that the town built at a cost of $28.5 million. The town issued prison bonds in anticipation of the economics of imprisonment. Although the state has an overcrowded prison system, Minnesota does not have money available to make use of the Appleton facility (Terry, 1993). In 1993, however, after a national search, an agreement was reached with Puerto Rico to house 170 of the commonwealth's inmates at Appleton.

One of the more recent responses to the problem of an increasing prison population has been the "privatization" of corrections. Joan Mullen points out: "Confinement service or facility management contracts are another way of expanding corrections capacity—without imposing any burden for facility construction on the government" (1985: 4). Private firms have been able to establish and operationalize facilities more quickly than public agencies, which are constrained by a variety of political and bureaucratic requirements.

According to Charles Logan (1990: 75), competition between public and private prisons will provide long-needed improvements in incarceration:

> Competition does not just contain costs; it advances other goals as well. When it is possible for a commercial company to take business away from a competitor (including the state) by showing that it can do a better job, then that company becomes a self-motivated watchdog over other companies (and over the state). Such a company will have an interest in critically evaluating the quality of its competitors' services and an interest in improving its own.
>
> In the case of prisons, the existence of competition, even potential competition, will make the public less tolerant of facilities that are crowded, costly, dirty, dangerous, inhumane, ineffective, and prone to lawsuits. Indeed, the fact that these conditions have existed for so long in monopolistic state prisons is a big part of what makes private prisons seem attractive.

The private facility has long been accepted in the area of juvenile care, whereas with adults this facility is more controversial. Several dozen of these facilities exist; most, but not all, are equipped to handle only minimum-security inmates and are thus more closely related to halfway houses (discussed in Chapter 11) than traditional prisons. The largest customer of the private facility has been the U.S. Immigration and Naturalization Service (INS), which has contracted out the detention of illegal aliens to the Corrections Corporation of America, Inc. (CCA) based in Nashville. In 1985, the CCA proposed a takeover of the entire correctional system in Tennessee, but that bid was rejected by the state legislature. Another INS prison contractor, Esmor Correctional Services, was the subject of a scathing report that found poorly trained guards preying on immigrant detainees, a situation that resulted in a violent uprising (Dunn, 1995). The firm has successfully bid on numerous corrections projects by submitting low bids and cutting costs (Sullivan and Purdy, 1995). The Corrections Corporation of America, on the other hand, has received high marks for its running of two prisons in Tennessee (Butterfield, 1995b).

Entry of the private sector into what has traditionally been thought of as a public responsibility is controversial; for example, it has been opposed by the

National Sheriffs' Association, although state correction commissioners have tended to be more supportive. Supporters of the idea contend that private operators can maintain or exceed the level of services provided by public agencies at less cost. They are not bound by the bureaucracy or mandated salaries and retirement benefits of government agencies. Opponents question the propriety of handing over to private entrepreneurs so basic a public responsibility as punishment. Opposition has been vigorous on the part of organized labor, particularly by the American Federation of State, County, and Municipal Employees (AFSCME), which represents many prison workers.

Although minimum-security facilities have generated less concern, the question of turning over medium- and maximum-security prisoners to a private firm has troubled observers who point out that in such institutions the constant threat of the use of force, including deadly physical force, exists. The privately employed security officers are typically trained at the same state academies that train public correction officers and enjoy the same peace officer powers. Whether private employees should be entrusted by government with such authority is an unanswered legal question. In at least one case, a guard for a private prison operating under contract with the INS accidentally discharged a shotgun, killing one inmate and wounding another (*Medina v. O'Neil*, 589 F. Supp. 1028 S. D. Tex. 1984). At the other end of the spectrum of possibilities, in 1990, the leader of a multimillion-dollar drug ring used a .25-caliber handgun to overpower his guards and escape with two other inmates from a jail being run by the Wackenhut Corporation under contract with Bexar County, Texas. Some opponents contend that to keep jail and prison space at a maximum level, private corrections corporations would seek to make Americans even more fearful of crime, through advertising and political campaigns. Other issues include the following: What will happen in the event of a strike by the private employees of a private prison? What if the firm decides to go out of business or enters into bankruptcy?

One of the most basic of many legal issues involves the power of government to delegate its authority to private entrepreneurs to provide as basic a service as imprisonment. "A private entity," notes Ira Robbins, "exercises governmental power when it deprives a person of life, liberty, or property at the behest of government" (1988: 36–37). Because a private prison might have an economic interest in imposing a punishment that denies privileges (thereby decreasing prison costs) or denying good-time credits (which keeps the inmate incarcerated, from which the firm may benefit financially), the prison would not typically be permitted control over such actions. Arguments for contracting out prison services would also appear to justify similar contracting for police services—or, perhaps, probation and parole.

PRIVATE PRISONS: PRO AND CON

Supporters of contracting out of prison responsibilities argue that

1. Public prisons have done a poor job of maintaining inmates in a secure and safe environment.

2. The private sector can more quickly and cheaply build prisons and ease overcrowding by avoiding bureaucratic red tape and the need for voter approval for financing prison construction.

3. The private sector can more quickly implement new ideas and programs to perform correctional functions better.

4. The private sector can perform correctional functions more efficiently and less expensively than the public sector. Private institutions usually pay their staff less and employ fewer security personnel. This reduction is accomplished by designing the prisons in such a way as to control inmates better with fewer staff members.

Opponents argue that

1. The power to deprive people of their liberty should not be delegated to private firms.

2. The power to use coercive force, including deadly force, should not be delegated to private firms.

3. Private employees are free to go on strike—who would staff the prison?

4. Private prisons could refuse to accept certain inmates, for example, those with AIDS.

5. The firm could go bankrupt.

6. The profit motive could delay the release of inmates economically beneficial to the private prison.

7. Security and services could be lowered to increase profits.

Source: Zawitz (1988).

The next chapter examines the development of parole and the indeterminate sentence.

REVIEW QUESTIONS

1. How does the prison population differ from the rest of the population in the United States?

2. Why were colonial juries often unwilling to find defendants guilty?

3. What were the three intertwined developments that led to the establishment of the American system of prisons?

4. What was the Quaker approach to punishment?

5. What led to the demise of the Walnut Street Jail?

6. What are the characteristics of the Pennsylvania system?

7. Why did most states pattern themselves after the Auburn system rather than the Pennsylvania system?

8. What are the characteristics of the Auburn system?

9. What are the three categories of convict labor?

10. What factors led to the demise of most forms of convict labor?

11. What were the long-range effects of the curtailing of convict labor?

12. What is a "Big House" prison?

13. What are prisonization and inmate subcultures?

14. How did guards maintain control of a Big House despite being vastly out-numbered by inmates?

15. What led to the reemergence of positivism in penology after World War II?

16. What are the purposes of classification in prison?

17. What were the factors that led to the prison disturbances of the 1960s and early 1970s?

18. What has made the problem of prison discipline more difficult today than in the period of the Big House?

19. What is "community-based corrections"?

20. What led to the popularity of community-based corrections?

21. What are the programs traditionally included in community-based corrections?

22. What led to the demise of community-based corrections?

23. Why was the corrections approach difficult, if not impossible, to implement in prisons?

24. What are the pros and cons of using private prisons?

PAROLE AND THE INDETERMINATE SENTENCE

Parole, from the French *parol,* referring to "word of honor," was a means of releasing prisoners of war who promised not to resume arms in a current conflict. Modern parole, the conditional release of convicts by a parole board before the expiration of their sentence, has several antecedents.

TRANSPORTATION TO AMERICA

In colonial America early in the 17th century, a shortage of labor led to the transporting of children—the indentured poor and delinquents—as well as the pardoning of criminals from England. In the beginning, no specific conditions were imposed on those who received these pardons. However, after several of those pardoned evaded transportation or returned to England before the expiration of their term, certain restrictions had to be imposed. Around 1655, the form of pardons was amended to include specific conditions and provide for the nullification of the pardon if the recipient failed to abide by the conditions imposed.

During the early days of transportation, the government paid a fee to contractors for each prisoner transported. Subsequently, this arrangement was changed, and the contractor was given "property in service"—custody of the prisoner until the expiration of his full term. Once prisoners were delivered to the contractor, the government took no further interest in their welfare or behavior unless they violated the conditions of the pardon by returning to England prior to the expiration of their sentences.

When the pardoned felons arrived in the colonies, their services were sold to the highest bidder. The contractor then transferred the "property in service" agreement to the new master and the felon was no longer referred to as a criminal but became an *indentured servant*. These indentures bear a similarity to the procedure now followed by parole boards. Like the criminal *qua* indentured servant, a prisoner released on parole agrees in writing to accept certain conditions. A release form is signed by the prisoner and the parole board, and some of the conditions imposed today on parolees are similar to those included on the indenture agreement (New York State Division of Parole, 1953). The termination of the Revolutionary War ended transportation to America, and England then sent her convicts to Australia, until 1879 (Hughes, 1987).

MACONOCHIE AND NORFOLK ISLAND

Torsten Erikkson refers to 1840 as the year in which "one of the most remarkable experiments in the history of penology was initiated" (1976: 81). In that year, Alexander Maconochie (1787–1860) became superintendent of the British penal colony on Norfolk Island, about 930 miles northeast of Sidney, Australia. He set out a philosophy of punishment based on reforming the individual criminal: The convict was to be punished for the past and trained for the future. Because the amount of time needed to instill self-discipline and train a criminal could not be estimated in advance of sentencing, Maconochie advocated sentences that were open-ended, what is known today as an *indeterminate sentence.* He set up a system of *marks* to be earned by each inmate based on good behavior; a sentence could not be terminated until a certain number of marks had been achieved.

Norfolk housed the most dangerous felons, and riots occurred both before Maconochie's arrival and after he left the island. His system, however, brought tranquility to the colony. Convicts passed through three stages on the way to release, each with an increasing amount of personal liberty; misbehavior moved an offender back to an earlier stage. Although Maconochie's experiment at Norfolk was successful from the standpoint of penology, the experiment was opposed by authorities back in Australia who viewed it as "coddling criminals" while incurring extra costs on the government. Maconochie was relieved of his position in 1844 and returned to England, where he campaigned for penal reforms as a writer and speaker. One of those he influenced was Walter Crofton.

CROFTON AND THE IRISH SYSTEM

In 1853, Parliament enacted the Penal Servitude Act, which enabled prisoners to be released—paroled—on a *ticket of leave* and supervised by the police. That same year, Sir Walter Crofton (1815–1897) was commissioned to investigate conditions in Irish prisons and in 1854 became director of the Irish prison system. Crofton was familiar with the work of Alexander Maconochie, and their views on the reformation of criminals were similar. The *Irish system* that Crofton established was based on Maconochie's work at Norfolk Island and consisted of four stages:

1. The *first stage* involved solitary confinement for nine months; during the first three months, the inmate was on reduced rations and was allowed no labor whatsoever. It was reasoned that after three months of forced idleness, even the laziest prisoner would long for something to do. He would then be given full rations, instructed in useful skills, and exposed to religious influences.

2. In the *second stage*, the convict was placed in a special prison to work with other inmates, during which time he could earn marks to qualify for a transfer to the third stage.

3. *Stage three* involved transportation to an open institution where the convict, by evidencing signs of reformation, could earn release on a ticket of leave.

4. In the *fourth stage*, ticket of leave men were conditionally released and, in rural districts, supervised by the police; those residing in Dublin, however, were supervised by a civilian employee who had the title of inspector of released prisoners. He worked cooperatively with the police, but his responsibility was to secure employment for ticket of leave men. He required them to report at stated intervals, visited their homes every two weeks, and verified their employment—he was the forerunner of a modern parole officer.

DEVELOPMENTS IN THE UNITED STATES

A modified version of the Irish system was adopted in England, and Crofton's work was widely publicized in the United States. American supporters of the Irish system, however, did not believe that adoption of the ticket of leave would ever be accepted in the United States. Their attitude was apparently based on the belief that it would be un-American to place any person under the supervision of the police, and they did not believe that any other form of supervision would be effective. A letter written by Crofton in 1874, in reply to an inquiry sent to him by the secretary of the New York Prison Association, stressed that the police of Ireland were permitted to delegate competent persons in the community to act as custodians for ticket of leave men, and he suggested a similar system for the United States (New York State Division of Parole, 1953). These principles were first implemented in the Elmira Reformatory.[1]

ELMIRA REFORMATORY

In 1869, a reformatory was authorized for Elmira, New York, to receive male offenders between the ages of 16 and 30. The following year, the first convention of the American Prison Association met in Cincinnati. A paper based on the Irish system, dealing with the idea of an indeterminate sentence and the possi-

---

[1]Massachusetts enacted a law in 1845 that provided for a corrections agent to assist released prisoners.

bilities of a system of parole, was presented by the noted Michigan penologist Zebulon R. Brockway. The prison reformers meeting in Cincinnati urged New York to adopt Brockway's proposal at Elmira. When the Elmira Reformatory opened in 1876, Brockway was appointed superintendent.

Brockway drafted a statute directing the sending of young first offenders to Elmira under an indeterminate sentence not to exceed the maximum term that was already in place for nonreformatory offenders. The actual release date was set by the board of managers based on institutional behavior: "After the inmate accumulated a certain number of marks based on institutional conduct and progress in academic or vocational training, and if the investigation of his assurance of employment was positive, he could be released" (New York State Division of Parole, 1984: 6). According to Alexander Pisciotta (1994: 7–8), "the Elmira system was designed to instill youthful offenders with the habits of order, discipline, and self-control and to mold obedient citizen-workers." According to Brockway (1926: 111), this was a difficult task because the inmates "constitute a living antisocial human mass not easily resolved and brought into accord with the orderly life of a good community."

Frederick Wines, a colleague of Brockway, described the principles on which the Elmira system was based, a clear manifestation of positive theory:

> Criminals can be reformed; that reformation is the right of the convict and the duty of the State; that every prisoner must be individualized and given special treatment adapted to develop him to the point in which he is weak—physical, intellectual, or moral culture, in combination, but in varying proportions, according to the diagnosis of each case; that time must be given for the reformatory process to take effect, before allowing him to be sent away, uncured; that his cure is always facilitated by his cooperation, and often impossible without it. (1975: 230)

Cooperation was fostered by corporal punishment and the use of inmate classifications, according to which privileges were dispensed. Behavior judged to be "reformative" was rewarded by reclassification, which meant increased privileges, eventually leading to release on parole. On being admitted to Elmira, each inmate was placed in the second grade (of classification). Six months of good conduct meant promotion to the first grade—misbehavior could result in being placed in the third grade, from which the inmate would have to work his way back up. Continued good behavior in the first grade resulted in release—America's first parole system.

Paroled inmates remained under the jurisdiction of reformatory authorities for an additional six months, during which the parolee was required to report on the first day of every month to his appointed guardian (from which parole officers evolved) and provide an account of his situation and conduct. Some believed that a longer period under supervision would be discouraging to the average parolee. "Inmates were released conditionally, subject to return if the Board believed there was actual or potential reversion to criminal behavior" (New York State Division of Parole, 1984: 6). However, no real attention was given to the training of prisoners toward their future adjustment in the community, and both prison administrators and inmates soon accepted the idea that reformed or unreformed, allowance of time for good behavior was automatic, and release at the earliest possible date was a right rather than a privilege. After release, supervision was either nonexistent or totally inadequate. [This deficiency was also the case in other states, for example, Minnesota and Illinois (Pisciotta, 1992)].

ELMIRA REFORMATORY

Brockway believed that his charges "belong to the grade of humanity that is inferior. The whole inmate population may be divided in this connection into two grades of inferiority—those whose defectiveness is apparent and others whose mental and moral defects are concealed under good (and sometimes quite brilliant) capabilities in given directions" (1926: 110). Elmira was

> overcrowded, understaffed, and grossly mismanaged. Key treatment programs did not fulfill their stated goals and objectives. Violence, escapes, smuggling, theft, homosexuality, revolts, arson, and other forms of inmate resistance were serious problems. Inmates suffered extraordinarily harsh punishments—including severe whippings and months of solitary confinement in dark, cold dungeons—and deliberate psychological torture. Elmira was, quite simply, a brutal prison. (Pisciotta, 1994: 33–34)

The Elmira system—which included military-style uniforms, marching, and discipline—was copied by reformatories in other states, such as the Massachusetts Reformatory at Concord, the Minnesota State Reformatory at St. Cloud, and the Illinois State Reformatory at Pontiac, and made applicable to all or part of the prison population in states, such as Pennsylvania, Michigan, and Illinois (Pisciotta, 1992; Wines, 1975). Ohio and California had parole release statutes in place before the turn of the 20th century (Zevitz and Takata, 1988). In 1907, New York extended indeterminate sentencing and parole release to all first offenders except those convicted of murder. In 1913, Massachusetts established the Commonwealth Board of Parole; before that, the commissioner of prisons and many correctional institutions conducted independent discharge or conditional release programs. Margaret Cahalan (1986) reports that by 1922, parole was used in 44 states; Pennsylvania was added in 1923. In 1930, New York established a three-member full-time parole board, transferring release decisions from the Department of Corrections, and by 1939 only three states (Florida, Mississippi, and Virginia) did not have provisions for parole. (According to the South Carolina parole board, however, that state did not begin to use parole until 1941; Virginia established a parole system in 1942.)

The great impetus for the expansion of the use of parole release, however, had to wait until the Great Depression, as these statistics for parole release indicate (Cahalan, 1986):

1923 = 21,632
1926 = 19,917
1930 = 29,509
1936 = 37,794

The depression, which began in 1929 and ended with the onset of World War II, resulted in many unemployed workers and, as noted in Chapter 6, led to legislation that effectively abolished the economic exploitation of convict labor. This abolishment was accompanied by the prohibitive cost of constructing prisons, prison overcrowding, and an outbreak of prison riots. A 1931 report (National Commission on Law Observance and Law Enforcement) described the overcrowding of America's prisons as "incredible"; Michigan, for example, had 78.6 percent more inmates than its original capacity; California, 62.2 percent; Ohio, 54.1 percent; and Oklahoma, 56.7 percent. In 1923, 81,959 inmates were in prison (74 per 100,000 population); in 1930, 120,496 (98 per 100,000 population); and in 1940, the eve of World War II, 165,585 (125 per 100,000 population) (Cahalan, 1986). *Pressing economic conditions, not the press of prison reform, led to the popularity of parole release:* By 1935, more than 60,000 persons were on parole in the United States, although only six states had what was described as "suitable" parole systems (Prison Association of New York, 1936). New York, a pioneer in parole release and supervision, established the Division of Parole in 1930, on the heels of prison riots (Dressler, 1951). Jonathan Simon (1993: 70) reports that before the depression, parole systems stressed employment—"criminals were idlers who needed to be disciplined"—and depended on employers to monitor parolees. This was undermined by widespread unemployment during the depression and, at the same time, pressure to release more persons on parole. With World War II, industrial production increased, unemployment decreased, and parolees became eligible (for the first time since 1833) for military service.

POSITIVISM REEMERGES

Despite its ravaging consequences, war can also provide the impetus for many long-lasting social and scientific advances: With total mobilization, widespread unemployment often ends, and improvements in manufacturing, communication, transportation, and medicine occur. During World War II, the United States experienced such important developments as the jet plane and the rocket, streptomycin, radar, sonar, and atomic energy. The war also provided psychologists with funds and an environment for extensive research and experimentation (Herman, 1995). By the end of the war, the horizons of science appeared to be unlimited, and the influence of positive theory and positivism reemerged in penology.

The great faith in science was occurring during a period of concern over the apparent rise in crime as measured by the *Uniform Crime Report*. The war had kept the wheels of industry spinning; unemployment did not exist. Suddenly, wartime production had ceased, and millions of young men who had been trained to kill and destroy, and who had done little else for several years, were returning from overseas. The vast allocation of societal resources in wartime had proved successful in the area of science; perhaps a corresponding commitment of resources could prove successful in dealing with the problem of crime: a (scientific) "war on crime," introducing the medical model.

THE MEDICAL MODEL

The positivistic approach to crime and criminals seeks to explain and respond to criminal behavior in a manner that is not dependent on issues of law, philosophy, or theology. Instead, criminal behavior is to be examined using the principles and methods of science, much as physical illness is subjected to examination by the physician (Robitscher, 1980: 44): "This new approach to criminal behavior stressed deviance as pathology. The criminal was not seen as 'bad' but as 'mad,' and he was to be given the benefit of the medical approach to madness. He should be helped to understand his unconscious motivation and to go through a process of psychoanalytic change."

"In its simplest (perhaps oversimplified) terms," states Donal MacNamara, "the medical model as applied to corrections assumed the offender to be 'sick' (physically, mentally, and/or socially); his offense to be a manifestation or symptom of his illness, a cry for help" (1977: 439). The medical metaphor extended to the postconviction process:

1. *Examination* = presentence investigation report
2. *Diagnosis* = classification
3. *Treatment* = correctional program

According to the medical model, as applied to corrections, the effects of a treatment program are subjected to review by the parole board, which determines if the offender is sufficiently rehabilitated to be discharged from the correctional institution. A positive response means that treatment will continue on an outpatient basis in the form of parole supervision. The American Friends Service Committee (AFSC) sums up the rationale for this approach: "It rejects inherited concepts of criminal punishment as the payment of a debt owed to society, a debt proportioned to the magnitude of the offender's wrong. Instead it would save the offender through constructive measures of reformation, [and] protect society by keeping the offender locked up until the reformation is accomplished" (1971: 37).

The medical model is based on two questionable assumptions:

- Criminals are "sick" and can thus benefit from treatment/therapy.
- The behavioral sciences can provide the necessary treatment/therapeutic methods.

Although a paucity of systematic research supported this approach to criminal behavior, the medical/corrections model was adopted in most states, in theory, if not practice. William Parker argues that the theory never actually matched the practice: "The theory of rehabilitation has made some changes in the prison: terminology has changed, there are more programs, sweeping floors is now work therapy. . . . The theory of rehabilitation has merely been imposed upon the theories of punishment and control" (1975: 26).

From its inception in California in 1944 under Governor Earl Warren, the corrections approach continued without serious opposition into the 1970s. Any opposition came primarily from the right of the political spectrum, as exemplified by the attacks of John Edgar Hoover; he saw parole as "coddling" criminals, releasing them before they completed their sentence. During the 1970s, however, the attack on the corrections approach shifted to the political left.

In 1971, the Quaker-sponsored AFSC published the first comprehensive attack on the indeterminate sentence and parole. The committee noted that the indeterminate sentence and parole rested on a view of crime as a result of individual pathology that can best be "cured" by treating *individual* criminals. Such an approach, the AFSC noted, downgrades environmental factors, such as poverty, discrimination, and lack of employment opportunities. Furthermore, the committee argued, even if the medical model approach is valid, the achievement level of the behavioral sciences does not offer a scientific basis for treatment.

The work of the AFSC had only limited impact and no practical effect until 1974. In that year, Robert Martinson published a review of correctional treatment efforts—"What Works?" (1974), to which he answered: virtually nothing! "What Works?" was actually a synopsis of the research findings of Martinson, Douglas Lipton, and Judith Wilks; the complete work was published the following year (Lipton, Martinson, and Wilks, 1975). This work surveyed 231 studies of correctional programs up until 1968 about which Martinson (1974: 25) concluded: "With few and isolated exceptions, the rehabilitative efforts that have been reported so far have had no appreciable effect on recidivism." Although the Martinson summary is more critical than the larger report, both lent credence to the arguments of the AFSC. In a review of the Lipton et al. (1975) research, a panel of the National Research Council concluded that it was "reasonably accurate and fair in the appraisal of the rehabilitation literature." In fact, the panel concluded, Lipton et al. "were, if anything, more likely to accept evidence in favor of rehabilitation than was justified" (Sechrest, White, and Brown, 1979: 31).

According to Paul Gendreau and Robert Ross, the research examined by Martinson was dated; furthermore, substantial literature since 1968 (Martinson's cutoff date) demonstrated "that successful rehabilitation of offenders had been accomplished, and continued to be accomplished quite well" (1987: 350). In fact, "between 1973 and 1980 reductions in recidivism, sometimes as substantial as 80 percent, had been achieved in a considerable number of well-controlled studies. Effective programs were conducted in a variety of community and (to a lesser degree) institutional settings, involving predelinquents, hard-core adolescent offenders, and recidivistic adult offenders, including heroin addicts" (1987: 350–51). And these results were not short-lived: "Follow-up periods of at least two years were not uncommon, and several studies reported longer follow-ups"

(1987: 351; see Gendreau and Ross for a review of this literature). The debate over correctional treatment effectiveness continues today (see, e.g., Andrews et al., 1990; Lab and Cullen, 1990), with rigorous analysis indicating positive outcomes in a variety of studies.

Whatever the merits, criticism of the indeterminate sentence, corrections, and parole increased. David Fogel presented a *justice model* in which he criticized the unbridled discretion exercised by correctional officials, particularly parole boards, under the guise of "treatment": "It is evident that correctional administrators have for too long operated with practical immunity in the backwashes of administrative law. They have been unmindful that the process of justice more strictly observed by the visible police and courts in relation to rights due the accused before and through adjudication must not stop when the convicted person is sentenced. The justice perspective demands accountability from all processors, even the 'pure of heart' " (1975: 192).

Instead of the often hidden discretion exercised by parole boards, Fogel recommended:

1. A return to flat time/determinate sentences, with procedural rules in law limiting sentencing discretion
2. The elimination of parole boards and parole agencies

Furthermore, Fogel argued, whatever "treatment" is offered in a prison should be voluntary and should in no way affect the release date of an inmate. Andrew von Hirsch (1976) offered the concept of *just deserts*, according to which the punishment is to be commensurate with the seriousness of the crime—a return to the classical approach: "A specific penalty level must apply in all instances of law-breaking which involves a given degree of harmfulness and culpability" (von Hirsch and Hanrahan, 1978: 4). Indeterminacy and parole are to be replaced with a specific penalty for a specific offense.

The Twentieth Century Fund Task Force on Sentencing offered the *presumptive sentencing system*: Each category of crime would have a presumptive sentence "that should generally be imposed on typical first offenders who have committed the crime in the typical fashion" (1976: 20; italics deleted). For succeeding convictions or other aggravating circumstances, the judge could increase the presumptive sentence by a specific, albeit limited percentage. Mitigating circumstances could, similarly, reduce the presumptive sentence.

In sum, the basic thrust of these criticisms and proposals was to limit judicial discretion, eliminate the indeterminate sentence, and abolish the parole board. Here was an issue on which both the political left and right could agree—but for different reasons. Alfred Blumenstein notes:

In the mid-1970 a striking consensus of the political left and the political right emerged in opposition to the indeterminate sentence. The political left was concerned over the excess of discretion in decisions about individual's liberty and the excessive disparity that appeared in sentences in presumably similar cases. The political right appeared to be far more concerned about "leniency" than about disparity. They viewed the parole boards as excessively ready to release prisoners early, and expressed shock that prisoners were back on the street on parole well before the maximum sentence. (1984: 130, edited).

Franklin Zimring and Gordon Hawkins (1995: 9) point out that this coalescing of otherwise divergent views "is a pretty reliable indication that some of the participants in the policy debate do not have a clear understanding of the practical implications of their stance."

GOOD POLITICS CAN GENERATE BAD POLICY

The parole board is always vulnerable to criticism, and parole release often proves a tempting target for demagogic attack. After all, no one supports the release of a prison inmate who subsequently commits a heinous crime—the value of predictive hindsight. The issue, of course, is not *if* an inmate should be released but what mechanism will be used to make the release decision. Prisons are overcrowded, and virtually all inmates will eventually be released: facts usually overlooked in the focus on a particular crime or parolee. Nevertheless, governors in many states—for example, Virginia, South Carolina, and Michigan—would rather advocate abolishing parole than have to defend such a politically vulnerable system.

As sentiments toward crime and criminals hardened, political changes generated by (often pandering) politicians have led to "tough on crime" statutes that have further clogged our correctional facilities. "Sound-bite policy" replaced careful and thoughtful policy development. In Michigan, for example, Governor John Engler proposed abolishing parole and establishing a determinate sentencing system—"truth in sentencing" he calls it. He also proposed elimination of "good-time" credit "for violent criminals and make the threat of additional punishment the best incentive for inmates to behave in prison." These proposals must be viewed against the realities of Michigan's prison population, which increased 220 percent since 1985, a year when the state was automatically releasing inmates as new commitments were received. Michigan parole supervises about 13,000 offenders a year (probation supervises another 55,000).

In at least nine states, prosecutors were active in leading the fight for abolishing the indeterminate sentence and parole. "Clearly, parole was an easy target for those looking for political opportunities," notes Barbara Krauth, and "the emotional appeal of an attack on the system that released criminals to the streets may have benefitted some political careers more than it actually addressed any of the complex problems of criminal justice" (1987: 52). By 1980, eight states had already adopted some form of determinate sentencing, including the pioneering state of California (in 1977); the federal government and several other states have abolished the indeterminate sentence and parole release since that time, although a few, for example, Colorado and Connecticut, have reintroduced the indeterminate sentence and parole supervision.

The federal Sentencing Reform Act of 1984, which abolished the indeterminate sentence, was designed to reduce sentence disparity and phase out parole release by 1992. However, the discretion lost by judges has been assumed by prosecutors. The result has been longer prison terms and an increasingly overcrowded federal prison system (Margolick, 1992). As the next section indicates, this scenario has often been repeated in state systems.

Indeterminate and Determinate Sentencing

Under the indeterminate sentence, originally established as part of the Elmira system, a judge imposes a prison term that has both a minimum and a maximum length. For example, a defendant convicted of a class 3 felony could receive a sentence with a minimum of three years (written 3–0–0) and a maximum of nine years (written 9–0–0); the actual release of the inmate (between 3–0–0/9–0–0) is determined by a parole board. Except in three states (Benekos, 1992), a provision is also made for *good time*, which is deducted from the maximum sentence because of good institutional behavior, typically one-third. For example, an inmate with a maximum sentence of 9–0–0 could accumulate up to 3–0–0 years of good time, thus being released after 6–0–0 years without the intervention of the parole board.

Under a system of indeterminate sentencing, persons convicted for the same class of offense could receive different sentences. In New York, for example, first-degree robbery carries a minimum sentence that ranges from 2–0–0 to 6–0–0 and a maximum sentence range of 8–4–0 to 25–0–0. Even those who receive the same sentence, for example, 3–0–0/9–0–0, can be released (paroled) at different times: 3–0–0, or 4–0–0, or 5–0–0, or . . . all the way up to 9–0–0 (minus "good time"). Criticism of the indeterminate sentence has involved this differential treatment of persons convicted of similar crimes, which is contrary to the classical approach to criminal behavior:

> [C]ritics of the indeterminate sentence argued that the treatment model has never realized its lofty objectives in practice and that, given the nature of the correctional system, these goals never will be realized. Furthermore, they maintained that the indeterminate sentence has created a situation of gross sentencing disparity that no longer can be justified by referring to treatment goals. (Goodstein and Hepburn, 1985: 17)

In response to criticism of indeterminate sentencing and parole boards, a variety of so-called flat, determinate, or definite sentence schemes have been adopted. Although each requires the setting of a *specific* sentence—no minimum and maximum—they differ according to the amount of discretion left to the judge:

1. *Definite sentence/no discretion.* The legislature provides for a specific sentence for each level of offense. For example, all crimes that constitute a class 2 felony would require the judge to impose a specific sentence—no deviations permitted. If a class 2 felony was punishable by imprisonment for 7 years, all judges would be required to sentence all defendants convicted of a class 2 felony to 7–0–0.

2. *Definite sentence/wide discretion.* The legislature provides for a range of sentences for each level of offense. For example, a class 2 felony would be punishable with a sentence between 3–0–0 to 7–0–0. Under this system the judge retains discretion to sentence a class 2 offender to 3–0–0, or 4–0–0, all the way up to 7–0–0. The sentence imposed is definite—for a specific number of years—but the judge's discretion is wide.

3. *Presumptive/narrow discretion.* The legislature limits discretion to a narrow range of sentences for each level of offense; for each level, a presumed sentence exists from which the judge cannot deviate except if aggravating or mitigating circumstances apply, and then in only a limited manner. In other words, if a defendant is convicted of a class 2 felony, the judge would be required to set a sentence of (for example) 5–0–0. On a showing of *aggravation* by the prosecutor, however, the judge could increase the presumptive sentence to (for example) 6–0–0; on a showing of mitigation by the defense, the judge could decrease the presumptive sentence to (for example) 4–0–0. In some states, such as Minnesota, the presumed sentence is increased by a fixed amount based on the severity of any prior convictions (*see* Figure 4.2).

4. *Presumptive/wide discretion.* As in the presumptive sentence with narrow discretion, the legislature provides three possible terms for each class of felony. However, although each class has a presumptive sentence, the judge may decrease (for mitigation) or increase (for aggravation) by significant amounts: (Figure 7.1). For example, in Arizona, for mitigation, the judge can lower the sentence by a few months or as much as three years (depending on the class of offense); for aggravation, the judge can increase the sentence by as much as 100 percent. A departure from the presumptive sentence, however, requires a "written statement of factual findings and reasons for the departure" (Kennedy, 1988: 8).

Determinate sentencing systems usually include a provision for "good time" to promote prison discipline: Illinois provides one day for every day served—50 percent off the sentence; the state of Washington provides one-third off the sentence for most offenses and 15 percent for certain serious violent crimes. In Illinois, a defendant sentenced to a determinate sentence of 5–0–0 would be released (presuming good behavior) after 2–6–0. In practice, good time is deducted in advance, when the offender is first received at the institution; misbehavior results in time being added. In some states, an inmate may be entitled to additional time off the sentence for exemplary performance: "meritorious good time" or "industrial good time." These grants of additional time off

OFFENSE	RANGE	PRESUMPTIVE SENTENCE (YRS.)	AGGRAVATING FACTORS, ADD UP TO	MITIGATING FACTORS SUBTRACT UP TO (YRS.)	MAXIMUM FINE ($)
Murder	30–60 yrs.	50	10 yrs.	10	10,000
Class A felony	20–50 yrs.	25	20 yrs.	10	10,000
Class B felony	6–20 yrs.	10	10 yrs.	4	10,000
Class C felony	2–8 yrs.	4	4 yrs.	2	10,000
Class D felony	6 mos.–3 yrs.	1.5	1.5 yrs.	1	10,000
Class A misdemeanor	0–1 yrs.	None	NA	NA	5,000
Class B misdemeanor	0–180 days	None	NA	NA	1,000
Class C misdemeanor	0–60 days	None	NA	NA	500

FELONY SENTENCING ENHANCEMENTS

ENHANCEMENT DESCRIPTION	MINIMUM	MAXIMUM
Violent habitual criminal	Life without parole	
Habitual criminal	1x presumptive	3x presumptive; 30-yr. maximum
Use of assault weapon	1x presumptive	2x presumptive; 10-yr. maximum
Habitual controlled substance offender	3 yrs.; (1 yr. if more than 3 yrs. since last prior)	8 yrs.

FIGURE 7.1 Presumptive sentencing, Indiana

are usually the result of prison overcrowding in states without parole release. They may also be used to reduce sentence minimums so that inmates can more quickly qualify for parole release.

In Florida, which abolished the indeterminate sentence and parole release in 1983, one-third is taken off the sentence when the inmate is received at a correctional institution, called Basic Gaintime. On the first day of each month, an inmate can receive an additional 20 days off, Incentive Good time, as a reward for attending classes, satisfactory work performance, and general good behavior. One-shot Meritorious Gaintime gives up to 60 days for exemplary performance. As a result of critical overcrowding, in 1987, the legislature provided for Provisional Release Credit, an additional 60 days per month whenever the prison system is over 97.5 percent of capacity. As a result of these schemes, the average Florida inmate served a little over one-third of his or her sentence (Malcolm, 1989a). In response, the legislature put its "get tough" mode in full gear and—ignoring the pressing problem of prison overcrowding—enacted mandatory minimum sentences for a host of offenses (Bales and Dees, 1992), which, of course, exacerbated overcrowding and required new schemes for early release. The wheels of Florida justice continue to spin: In 1993, Florida became one of the first states to repeal mandatory sentences for several crimes, particularly possession of small amounts of drugs. The following year, as a result of increased prison construction and a reduction in the number of felony cases receiving prison sentences, Florida achieved compliance with court-ordered reductions in prison population. The state's governor ordered a cutback in the amount of good time granted to inmates who had been serving about 45 percent of their sentence.

Florida's experience reveals the often poor fit between theory and practice when it comes to "getting tough on criminals." Although sentencing guidelines impose severer sentences, "inmates may actually serve shorter and shorter sentences and also serve smaller proportions of their sentences than they did prior to the implementation of the guidelines" (Griswold, 1989: 49).

In many states without parole, an inmate released under good time ("mandatory release") provisions is placed under the supervision of a parole officer. In the absence of discretionary release, however, the incentive for adequate funding of offender supervision is often absent—no one (governor or parole board) can be held accountable for the serious misconduct of mandatory releases. In Illinois, for example, a budget crisis in 1987 led to the layoff of 98 of the state's 159 parole agents. Most were reinstated at the beginning of 1989, and 29 new agents added, because of a substantial increase in parole violations and new arrests among releasees against whom no delinquency action was taken because parole agents were not available—violations had dropped from 35 to 20 percent. By 1995, however, the number of agents was down to 69, and they were "supervising" about 30,000 offenders. In the state of Washington, parole release and supervision were abolished in 1984. Subsequently, the public reacted adversely to serious offenders being released without community supervision, and in 1988, supervision was restored.

ABOLISHING PAROLE

When a board has no ability to *select* those who will be granted release, they are forced to supervise a population not of their own choosing. . . . It is impossible to assure cooperation of offenders when they know they must be released regardless of their willingness to agree to certain conditions. And we have seen, in states such as Illinois, that when the parole board loses its discretion over release, it tends to lose its visibility and power in the system. Field supervision tends to be underdeveloped and, eventually, underfunded and understaffed. (American Probation and Parole Association, 1995: 14)

Although in theory the determinate or definite sentence was supposed to reduce unwarranted variation in sentencing and amount of time served in prison, the practice has been otherwise. No state, for example, has adopted a determinate sentence with no discretion, whereas several have adopted schemes with wide discretion. Thus, in Illinois, a defendant convicted of selling narcotics as a first offense can receive a *determinate* sentence of anywhere from 4-0-0 all the way up to 30-0-0; Illinois has no parole board. Herbert Covey and Mary Mande found that in Colorado determinate sentencing did not reduce unwarranted variation, "but it may have enhanced the discretionary powers of prosecutors" (1985: 270).

The issue of discretion presents the most obvious deficiency in the proposals set out by Fogel, von Hirsch, and others. Although they propose to deal with discretion exercised by judges and parole boards, they fail to deal with *prosecutorial discretion*. This discretion is typically exercised privately, outside the scrutiny of official review; prosecutorial discretion affects sentencing more often and more significantly than does judicial discretion. Although a judge, acting under a definite system with narrow discretion or a presumptive system with narrow discretion must apply a specific sentence for a particular class of crime (in the absence of mitigation or aggravation), the prosecutor, using charging powers, determines the particular class of crime and whether to move for aggravation or oppose a motion for mitigation.

In return for cooperation—a plea of guilty—the prosecutor can reduce the class of crime for which the offender will be charged; he or she may also agree not to move for mitigation or to accept mitigation offered by defense counsel. By manipulating the charging decision, the prosecutor, not the judge, can often determine the actual sentence. Thus, determinate sentencing can increase the ability of a prosecutor to engage in plea bargaining. In many instances, determinate sentencing merely shifts discretion away from judges and parole boards and toward the prosecution end of criminal justice. In other words, release decisions are being made at the front end rather than the back end of the system. Because the defendant's primary interest is in how much time he or she must actually serve, new laws limiting "good time" (under so-called truth in sentencing provisions) are now added to the plea bargaining equation.

Furthermore, the abolition of parole boards, a practical accomplishment of determinate sentencing schemes, ignores the role of the board in reducing the sentence disparity that the classicalists decry. Because the parole board reviews the sentences of all state prisoners, it is in a position to act as a panel for mediating disparate sentences for similar criminal behavior. In Nebraska, for example, the board of parole "serves as an 'equalizer.' Within the framework of the law, it attempts to produce equity and uniformity in the sentencing structure caused by the inherent disparity which understandably results from having ninety-three prosecuting offices and multiple judicial districts." The Georgia Board of Pardons and Paroles states that "the board's unique central position and authority allow it to reduce sentencing disparity. Excessive harshness is more readily reduced, but excessive leniency in the form of a too-light confinement sentence may be corrected partially by parole denial." Figure 7.2 provides a hypothetical example of the parole board as sentencing review panel.

A second issue with respect to parole has been given scant attention. Some presume (AFSC, 1971; Fogel, 1975; MacNamara, 1977) that parole is based on a medical model or some humanitarian effort gone astray. However, the history of prisons and parole in the United States underscores the fact that parole release has been used, possibly abused, as a mechanism for maintaining prison discipline and reducing prison overcrowding. The parole board evolved out of the power of governors to issue pardons to selected convicts. Before the creation of parole boards, governors often used their pardoning powers to relieve prison overcrowding.

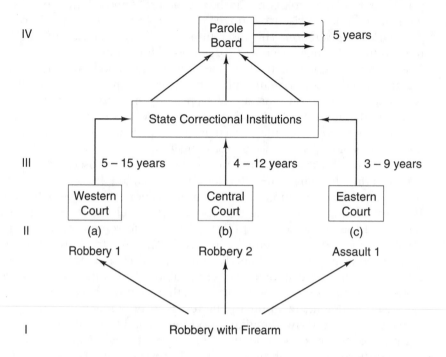

IV   Parole Board → } 5 years

State Correctional Institutions

III

5 – 15 years   4 – 12 years   3 – 9 years

Western Court   Central Court   Eastern Court

II   (a)   (b)   (c)

Robbery 1   Robbery 2   Assault 1

I   Robbery with Firearm

I   Three offenders, (a) (b) (c), each enter stores in different counties within the same state. They each brandish loaded revolvers and rob several hundred dollars.

II   Defendant (a) is processed in Western Court. Attempts at plea bargaining fail, he stands trial and is convicted of First Degree Robbery.
Defendant (b) is processed in Central Court. He is alowed to plead guilty to Second Degree Robbery.
Defendant (c) is processed in Eastern Court. He is allowed to plead guilty to First Degree Assault.

III   Defendant (a) is sentenced to a minimum of 5 years and a maximum of 15 years in state prison.
Defendant (b) is sentenced to a minimum of 4 years and a maximum of 12 years in state prison.
Defendant (c) is sentenced to a minimum of 3 years and a maximum of 9 years in state prison.

IV   The parole board, recognizing that the three defendants have committed the same criminal acts and despite variations in the legal category of conviction (Robbery 1, Robbery 2, Assault 1), requires that each serve 5 years before being paroled.

Under a determinate sentencing scheme devoid of a parole board, the sentences for this hypothetical example would be:

defendant (a) would serve 8 years;
defendant (b) would serve 6 years;
defendant (c) would serve 4 years.

FIGURE 7.2   Probation board as sentencing review panel.

DISPARATE JUSTICE

All parole boards, either implicitly or explicitly, serve the vital function of equalizing justice between judges, courts, and counties. Board members removed from the heat of trial are familiar with case practices in all jurisdictions, and are able to apply a common statewide standard of justice. Left to their own devices, the differences in judges, district attorneys, defense counsel, juries, community temperament and the sophistication of defendants produces some very strange and disparate results. (Holt, 1995: 20)

In the middle of the 19th century, pardons accounted for more than 40 percent of the releases from U.S. prisons (Hibbert, 1968). In Ohio, for example, whenever the state prison exceeded a certain number of inmates, the governor granted pardons to make room for new prisoners. In 1867, Nevada created a pardon board with the power to release inmates through commutation. In 1909, the board's authority was expanded to include the parole of prisoners who were required to report to the governor's private secretary at least once per month. In 1898, Virginia passed an act permitting prisoners who had served one-half of their sentence to file a petition with the governor, who upon the recommendation of the board of penitentiary directors, could grant a conditional pardon. The act was later amended—the word "parole" was substituted for pardon and release authority transferred from the governor to the penitentiary directors. As late as 1938, "parole" was simply a conditional pardon in many states.

In Florida, the pardon board often presided over as many as 200 pardon applications a day until the Parole and Probation Commission was established in 1941. In Utah, the Board of Pardons continues to have parole responsibilities, and the Alabama Board of Pardons and Paroles, established in 1939, has final authority on all pardons. The Vermont Parole Board was created in 1968; until that time, release from prison was by conditional pardon granted by the governor. That parole release is a device for controlling the prison population can be seen by examining statistics from Texas. In 1980, with 15,257 prison admissions, the parole board released 5660 inmates. In 1991, when prison admissions reached more than 37,000, the parole board released more than 31,000 inmates—an increase of more than 400 percent (Bodapati, Marquart, and Cuvelier, 1993). Nationally, increases in the prison population result in even greater increases in the parolee population: In 1983, 437,248 prisoners and 251,708 parolees resulted in a ratio of 58 percent; in 1988, 627,402 prisoners and 407,977 parolees resulted in a ratio of 65 percent (National Institute of Justice).

Blumenstein (1984: 131) points out: "One of the functions the parole agencies carried out during the period of indeterminate sentencing was serving as a 'safety valve' for crowded prisons. As prison populations began to approach or exceed the prison capacity, the parole board could simply lower the threshold of the degree of rehabilitation that warranted release." The clear use of parole as a safety valve for prison population control is highlighted by the Texas experience. Faced with overcrowding during the 1980s, Texas simply increased parole releases: "In 1983, about 40 percent of inmates were released on parole after their first hearing. By the end of the decade, this had increased to nearly 80 percent" (Kelly and Ekland-Olson, 1991: 604). A similar situation occurred in Georgia, where, in 1980, 14,000 inmates were in prison; a decade later, 44,000 were prisoners. County jails were backing up with prisoners sentenced to state prison, and a class-action lawsuit—which state leaders believed they would lose—was initiated. In response, the parole board accelerated the parole release of thousands of inmates (for which the board was labeled "soft on crime").

In many states using determinate sentencing, the same release function is being carried out by prison officials using good-time provisions. However, prison officials lack the information, time, or expertise to make rational release decisions—a reason why parole boards developed. Those who see parole as simply a rehabilitative device have bought the *rhetoric* but not the *reality*—parole is more realistically understood as *risk management.* Corrections officials in several states that have abolished the indeterminate sentence have, by necessity, caused by *overcrowding,* become de facto parole boards. Indeed, in Florida, as the result of overcrowding (and a federal lawsuit) the parole board was reconstituted as the Control Release Authority to act under the state's determinate sentencing laws in essentially the same manner as it had before under indeterminate sentencing.

As schemes for relieving overcrowding in the absence of parole increased, in 1990, Connecticut dumped the determinate sentence, reintroducing indeterminate sentencing and parole release. In Maine, the first state to abandon parole release, along with parole supervision, a clemency board assists the governor in making commutation decisions whose purpose is to relieve prison overcrowding (Burke, 1988). Postrelease supervision was reestablished by Maine's judges in the form of split sentences—"judicial parole"—whereby offenders are sentenced to imprisonment followed by a period of probation supervision (Anspach and Monsen, 1989). Even in New York, which has indeterminate sentencing and parole, the Department of Correctional Services has been using work release to deal with severe overcrowding. Persons placed on work release are often those not eligible for or denied parole release (Navarro, 1994). In 1995, a new governor put an end to this practice but failed to deal with the reality of a prison system at 130 percent of capacity. Indeed, he has promised to prohibit the paroling of violent offenders (while also reducing state spending and taxes).

David Greenberg and Drew Humphries (1980) argue that the forces of the political right co-opted the issue of sentencing reform and abolition of parole and were successful in implementing changes that are increasing the length of time served by offenders, now without the possibility of parole release, in a prison atmosphere devoid of any rehabilitative component. Illinois provides an example: The state went from indeterminate to determinate sentencing in 1978, and since that time "tough on crime" legislation has significantly increased the penalties for criminal behavior without any available modification via the parole board. In a strong defense of the correctional/rehabilitative model (Figure 7.3), Francis Cullen and Karen Gilbert (1982: xxix) state: "Whatever its failings, criminal justice reha-

	CORRECTIONS MODEL (POSITIVISM)	JUSTICE MODEL (CLASSICALISM)
Cause of crime	Psychological/sociological factors over which the offender has little or no control	A rational choice made by the offender operating with free will
Sentence	Indefinite; parole	Definite/determinate
Sentencing goals	Rehabilitation	Punish and deter
Discretion	High	Low; stress on equality of punishment commensurate with the offense

FIGURE 7.3 Corrections model versus justice model.

bilitation has thus persisted as a rationale for caring for offender needs and not for making the wayward suffer. Without its humanizing influence," they argue, "the history of American corrections would be even bleaker than is now the case."

WORKIN' ON A CHAIN GANG

Dressed in white uniforms, shackled at the ankle in 3-pound irons and bound together by 8-foot lengths of chain, 320 prisoners work 12-hour shifts on the roads and fields of Limestone County, Alabama. The Limestone Correctional Facility is the first U.S. prison to revive the chain gang in more than 30 years (Leland and Smith, 1995). Other states have since established chain gangs.

The relevant question is now at issue: Do we entrust the decrease of prison populations, reduction of sentencing disparity, and risk management of criminal offenders to judges, prison officials, or parole boards? A review of the history that led to the establishment of parole in the first instance argues for this discretion to be the responsibility of a professional parole board.

Now that the review of the history of prisons and parole is complete, Chapter 8 examines the services provided by a parole agency.

REVIEW QUESTIONS

1. What is the connection between the system employed by Alexander Maconochie at Norfolk Island and the indeterminate sentence?
2. What was the Irish System established by Walter Crofton?
3. What is meant by the "Elmira system"?

4. What conditions led to the popularity of parole release in the United States?

5. What are the characteristics of the penological revolution that occurred at the end of World War II?

6. What is meant by the medical model approach to criminal behavior?

7. What are the questionable assumptions on which the medical model approach to corrections is based? Why are they questionable?

8. What is the difference between an *indeterminate* and a *determinate* or *definite* sentence?

9. What is the basis of criticism of the indeterminate sentence?

10. How do the four types of determinate, or definite, sentences differ?

11. What is meant by good time, and how does it affect inmates?

12. What is the relationship between determinate sentencing and plea bargaining?

13. What has developed in light of prison overcrowding and the absence of parole release in some states?

14. Why is parole an easy political target?

15. What are the arguments in favor of maintaining parole release?

Parole Administration and Services

Three basic services can be provided by a parole agency: parole release, parole supervision, and executive clemency. In several states that have abolished parole release—California and Illinois, for example—parole officers/agents continue to supervise offenders released (not by a parole board but) on "good time."

The administration of parole is less complex than that of probation because parole services are administered centrally on a statewide basis.

ADMINISTRATION OF PAROLE SERVICES

Parole involves three separate but interdependent components: release, supervision, and (violation) revocation (Runda, Rhine, and Wetter, 1994). There are two basic models for administering parole:

1. *Independent model.* A parole board is responsible for making release and revocation determinations *and* for the supervision of persons released on parole (and good time). It is independent of any other state agency. This model is used in New York.

2. *Consolidated model.* The parole board is an autonomous panel within a department that also administers correctional institutions. The board makes release and revocation decisions, but supervision of persons

released on parole (and good time) is under the direction of the commissioner of corrections. This model is used in Colorado and Rhode Island, and most other states.

In both models, probation services are sometimes combined with parole services in a single statewide agency. For example, in three states—Alabama, Missouri, and South Carolina—the parole board also administers probation. Vermont uses a consolidated model in which probation services are part of the Department of Corrections. In Pennsylvania, the courts have the statutory alternative of referring presentence investigations and the supervision of probationers and (county jail) parolees to the Board of Probation and Parole rather than the county probation department. In Nevada, probation and parole supervision are the responsibility of the Division of Parole and Probation headed by a chief appointed by the governor and are located within the Division of Motor Vehicles and Public Safety. In Alabama, the Board of Pardons and Parole determines which prisoners serving in the jails and prisons of the state shall be paroled, and the Jefferson County Parole Board exercises jurisdiction over jailed inmates in that county.

The Task Force on Corrections (1966) summarized arguments for the independent model:

- The parole board is in the best position to promote the idea of parole and to generate public support and acceptance. Because the board is often held accountable (by the public, news media, public officials) for parole failures, it should be responsible for supervising parolees.
- The parole board in direct control of administering parole services can more effectively evaluate and adjust the system.
- Supervision by the parole board and its officers properly divorces parole release and parolees from the correctional institution.
- An independent parole board in charge of its own services is in the best position to present its own budget request to the legislature.

The Task Force on Corrections (1966) also summarized the arguments for including both parole services and institutions in a single department of corrections:

- The correctional process is a continuum; all staff, institutional and parole, should be under a single administration rather than be divided, with resultant competition for public funds and friction in policies.
- A consolidated correctional department has the advantage of consistent administration, including staff selection and supervision.
- Parole boards are ineffective in performing administrative functions. Their major focus should be on case decisions, not on day-to-day field operations.
- Community-based programs partway between institutions and parole, such as work release, can best be handled by a single centralized administration.

Critics contend that the independent model tends to be indifferent or insensitive to institutional programs; that the parole board, in this model, places undue stress on variables outside the institution. Conversely, critics of the consolidated model argue that the parole board will be under pressure to stress institutional factors in making parole decisions, although these are of dubious value in making a parole prognosis.

CONDITIONAL RELEASE

Conditional release is the term used to describe inmates released on good time. As noted in previous chapters, inmates in most states are eligible for good time; that is, they can accumulate days, months, and years off their maximum sentence by avoiding institutional infractions and participating in prison programs. In addition, some states have meritorious good time for exemplary behavior and emergency good-time provisions to reduce the prison population in cases of severe overcrowding. In states using the indeterminate sentence and parole board, good time can usually be accumulated at the rate of 10 days per month—one-third off the maximum sentence. In some of these states, good time may also be subtracted from the minimum sentence, making the inmate eligible for parole before the minimum sentence has actually been served. In states using determinate sentencing, good time usually amounts to one day off for every day served. In Maryland, which uses indeterminate sentencing, good time is granted at the monthly rate of five days for good behavior; five days for performing industrial, agricultural, and administrative tasks; and an additional five days for making satisfactory progress in vocational and educational training.

Most states in which parole release has been abolished have retained supervision requirements for offenders released on good time—conditional releasees. In California, for example, all persons serving nonlife terms are released to community supervision that cannot exceed three years. In some of these states, decisions regarding good time and revocation of conditional release are the responsibility of a variety of boards: in California, it is the Board of Prison Terms; in Illinois, it is the Prisoner Review Board. In Missouri, the Board of Probation and Parole was placed in the Department of Corrections and Human Services, where it deals with questions of good time and supervision revocation. In Minnesota, where the parole board has been abolished, supervision of conditional releasees is the responsibility of the commissioner of corrections, who delegates this authority to the executive director of adult release.

These (nonparole) boards are also responsible for making parole decisions for persons imprisoned under indeterminate sentencing statutes that have since been repealed and for persons serving "life sentences." Some also serve as a "pardons board," considering requests for the granting of executive clemency.

In California, the board was given the additional responsibility to review "all determinate sentences to state prison and to notify the sentencing court of any case in which the board determines the sentence to be disparate"—lawful and justified, but nevertheless, disparate: "The court then had the opportunity to recall the sentence and resentence the defendant in a more uniform manner." The sentence review function proved to be a failure—few cases were actually sent for resentencing. In 1992, the legislature removed the sentence review requirement (Holt, 1995).

In California, as in most states, the Department of Corrections is responsible "for deducting good time credit from the sentence and for establishing procedures to deny good time credit." If good time is denied to an inmate, the person can appeal through department appeals procedures. A final department appeal, however, can be submitted for review to the Board of Prison Terms, which conducts a hearing on the matter. In Illinois, the Prisoner Review Board has broader responsibilities:

> Through panels of at least 3 members [the board has 10 members] hear and decide cases brought by the Department of Corrections against prisoners in custody of the Department for alleged violation of Department rules with respect to good conduct credits . . . in which the Department seeks to revoke good conduct credits, if the amount of time at issue exceeds 30 days or when, during any 12-month period, the cumulative amount of credit revoked exceeds 30 days. However, the Board is not empowered to review the Department's decision with respect to the loss of 30 days of good conduct credit for any prisoner or to increase any penalty beyond the length requested by the Department; . . . Upon recommendation of the Department the Board restores good conduct credit previously revoked.

THE PAROLE BOARD

In most states, parole board members are appointed by the governor (in Utah, they are appointed by the Board of Corrections), although board membership and terms of office vary.

PAROLE BOARDS

- The Alabama Board of Pardons and Paroles has three members who serve six-year terms.
- The Georgia Board of Pardons and Paroles comprises five members appointed for seven-year terms.
- The Hawaii Paroling Authority consists of a full-time chairperson and two part-time members appointed for four-year terms.
- In Maryland, the Parole Commission consists of seven members who serve terms of six years.
- The Massachusetts Parole Board has seven members appointed for terms of five years.

- The New Jersey State Parole Board consists of seven members who serve staggered terms of six years.
- The New York State Board of Parole has fifteen members who serve six-year terms.
- The Ohio Parole Board consists of seven members who are picked for employment from civil service lists and serve indefinite terms.
- The Pennsylvania Board of Probation and Parole consists of five members who serve terms of six years.
- In South Carolina, the Board of Probation, Parole, and Pardons Services consists of seven members who serve six-year terms.
- The Texas Board of Pardons and Paroles has eighteen members who serve six-year terms.
- The Utah Board of Pardons has three members who serve six-year terms.
- The Vermont Parole Board has five members who serve five-year terms.

Parole boards have been criticized because members may lack relevant background or education. In only a few states, specific professional qualifications are required for board members. William Parker states that "the only real qualification may be the political responsiveness and reliability of the board members to the appointing power" (1975: 30). New York requires that "Each member of the board shall have graduated from an accredited four-year college or university with a degree in the field of criminology, administration of criminal justice, law enforcement, sociology, law, social work, psychology, psychiatry, or medicine and shall have had at least five years of experience in one or more of such fields." Maryland requires "at least a B.A. or B.S. degree in one of the social or behavioral sciences or related fields . . . [and] at least three (3) years experience in a responsible criminal justice or juvenile justice position, or equivalent experience in a relevant profession such as law or clinical practice." In Vermont the governor "shall appoint as members persons who have knowledge of and experience in correctional treatment, crime prevention or related fields, and shall give consideration, as far as practicable, to geographic representation to reduce necessary travel to the various parole interview centers of the state."

The role of patronage politics in the selection of parole board members is similar to that of many other responsible government positions, although the relatively low salary and extensive travel requirements tend to make parole-board membership less attractive to those with other opportunities for political appointments.

PAROLE BOARD PROCEDURES

Parole board members usually hold release hearings in the state's prisons. The members of the board panel will have available a case folder prepared by an institutional parole officer (or correctional staff person) containing information about each inmate: the presentence investigation report; institutional reports relative to education, training, treatment, physical and psychological examinations, and misconduct; and a release plan in the event that parole is granted (Figure 8.1, p. 236). Typically, from one to three members briefly interview an inmate who is eligible for parole.

In some states, this aspect of parole release is handled by hearing examiners, who interview the inmate and report back to the board with a recommendation; some states do not conduct hearings or interviews—decisions are made on the basis of written reports. In New Jersey, a hearing officer considers each inmate for release at an interview session held between four and six months before parole eligibility. If parole is recommended by the hearing officer, the case is reviewed by a panel of parole board members. If they accept the recommendation, a parole release date is set. If the hearing officer recommends against parole, or if the parole panel denies parole, a panel hearing at which the inmate appears is arranged (Figure 8.2, p. 241).

According to David Stanley, the parole hearing is of dubious value. "It is a traumatic experience for the inmate, and parole board members are subjected to the rigors of holding hearings far away from home, with hours spent in travel and in prisons" (1976: 42). Furthermore, Stanley reports that hearings "are of little use in finding out whether the inmate is likely to succeed on parole" and argues that a strong case can be made for abolishing parole hearings:

> In cases where the information in the file and the board's own precedents plainly show that parole must surely be granted or denied, the hearing is a charade. In cases where the outcome is not so obvious it is a proceeding in which the inmate is at a great disadvantage and in which he has reason to say anything that will help his chances for parole. The atmosphere at such a hearing is full of tension and latent hostility. Under these circumstances the hearing is an ineffective way to elicit information, evaluate character traits, and give advice, all of which parole boards try to do. (1976: 43)

One way to deal with some of these issues is to permit the inmate to have representation at the hearing. The National Advisory Commission on Criminal Justice Standards and Goals believes that representation helps promote a feeling of fairness and can enable an inmate to communicate better and thus participate more fully in the hearing. The commission states that "representation can also contribute to opening the correctional system, particularly the parole process, to public scrutiny" (1973: 403). The commission makes note of the fact that representation at parole hearings may be considered "annoying" to parole officials—there is fear that the hearing may take the form of an adversary proceeding—but adds that "these inconveniences seem a small price for the prospective gains." The Hawaii Paroling Authority not only permits representation at its release hearings, but offers inmates the right to appointed counsel if they cannot afford to hire an attorney. However, this is unusual—most jurisdictions do not permit representation at parole hearings. For example:

- Pennsylvania: "As the interview is not an adversarial process, the Board does not permit counsel representation at these interviews."
- Maryland: "Relatives or other interested and responsible individuals may request a conference with the Commission, submit letters, or other pertinent data relative to an inmate's parole consideration at any time prior to the hearing. They may not appear at parole hearings."
- Wisconsin: "Representation by legal counsel during the interview is not allowed." [However,] "A spokesperson for the inmate will be allowed . . . in cases of severe speech impediment or where the inmate suffers a severe physical disability which impedes verbal communication, or in cases where the inmate's primary language is not English and the individual lacks adequate fluency to represent himself or herself."
- South Carolina: While representation by an attorney at a parole hearing is not necessary, "an inmate may retain an attorney, if he so desires."
- Vermont: "[T]he Board in its discretion may hear oral statements or arguments by attorneys or other persons with a valid interest in the case before the Board." Furthermore, "it is the Board's policy to grant the inmate's legal representative access to the inmate's parole packet at a reasonable time in advance of the parole hearing."

In 1979, the U.S. Supreme Court (*Greenholtz v. Inmates*, 442 U.S. 1) ruled that the Constitution does not require that an inmate be given the opportunity to participate in parole board hearings (or to be informed of the reasons for denial of parole). However, Stanley concludes:

> Given the present parole system, hearings are necessary as an expression of our national tradition and culture. A man has his day in court before he is convicted and sentenced. In all sorts of situations we feel outraged if a person is not even confronted with the evidence before something adverse is done to him. In the hearing the prisoner is at least given a chance to state his case, correct erroneous statements, and impress the board with his determination (real or alleged) to reform. (1976: 43)

VICTIM PARTICIPATION

More than 30 states permit victims or their next of kin to appear before the parole board, and about a dozen others permit written statements to be considered at the parole hearing. In Nevada, for example, state law "provides that victims of crimes may attend meetings of the Nevada Board of Parole Commissioners. The Parole Board will provide notice of pending parole hearings if the victim of crime provides the board with a current address and requests such notice." The South Carolina Department of Probation, Parole, and Pardon Services sends a 30-day written notice of parole hearings to crime victims. The notice specifies the date, location, and time of the parole hearing and the victim's right to attend and present testimony. (In addition, "should a parolee be charged with a violation of his/her parole agreement, the victim or witness has

STATE OF NEW YORK—EXECUTIVE DEPARTMENT—DIVISION OF PAROLE
INMATE STATUS REPORT FOR PAROLE BOARD APPEARANCE

10/89 BD. INITIAL

Name: Hughes, Sam   *DOB:* 12/23/62   *NYSID:* 4172822M
                             CR: 12/27/95   *ME:* 12/27/98

Rec'd Date: 7/13/87;

Crime, (felony class), sentence & date p(lea) or v(erdict)

1.) Att. Robbery, 1(c)   2.) Att. Robbery, 1 (c)
    1-6-0/4-6-0   1-6-0/4-6-0 cs.
    7/8/90-p.   7/8/90-p.

Guideline Range: 20-38 months

Mand. SPP: No ; *Citizen:* Yes ; *INS Warrant:* No ; *Other Warrants:* No

Official Statements: Judge: No ; DA: No; Def. Atty.: No ;

Certificate of Relief: E I Y.O.

Codefendants: William, Ruby - no information in computer

Special Conditions Recommended: SOME/Academic program or vocational program; periodic urinalysis; outpatient drug treatment program.

Parole Residence: Sylvia Butler Hughes, wife; 3140 Atlantic Avenue, Brooklyn, NY 718-485-4104, Apt. 3B.

Parole Employment: None submitted. Inmate interested in youth counseling.
Comments: None

Present Offence Offense #1:
On 8/5/89 at 9:15 A.M., Hughes and Williams followed a 10-year-old male complainant and his 10-year-old cousin from a store into the lobby of 668 Howard Avenue. Once inside the building, the subject displayed a knife, twisted the complainant's arm and demanded money from him. The subject cut the complainant's left finger and then took $18.00 from him. Both subjects then fled.

The complainant reported this incident to the police.

On 8/5/89, the complainant identified the defendants in the street at 9:32 A.M. Both defendants were placed under arrest by police officers of the 73rd Precinct.
    The arresting officer recovered a gravity knife from the defendant's pants pocket as well as $18.00.
    After being placed under arrest and advised of his rights, the subject made no statement, but his codefendant, Williams, stated, "I don't know what happened; he grabbed the little boy and the next thing I knew he was running so I ran."

Present Offense #2:
On 12/18/89, a 16-year-old girl who was six months pregnant entered the elevator at 2770 86th Street at about 6:25 P.M. The subject followed her into the elevator, placed his hand inside his jacket as if he had a weapon and announced a holdup. The subject took $105.00 worth of clothing from this complainant and fled.
    On 1/3/90, at 8:45 P.M., the complainant, a 10-year-old boy, entered the elevator at 2770 86th Street where he was confronted by the subject. The subject pointed a knife with a long blade at

FIGURE 8.1   Inmate status report for parole board appearance.

the complainant and demanded money from him. The subject took $1.75 from the complainant's pockets and a bag of groceries that the complainant was holding. The complainant then fled.

The incident was reported to the police. On 1/3/90, police officers of the 60th Precinct spotted the subject who fit the description provided over the radio. In the meantime, a housing police officer transported the complainant and his sister, the 16-year-old girl who was robbed on 12/18/89, and both positively identified the subject.

The subject was then placed under arrest at this time stating, "I was coming from my girlfriend's house." At arrest the subject had about $3.00 and change in his possession.

Prior Record

Arrest Date	Arrest Charges	Place	Disposition
7/31/80	Public Lewdness	Queens Crim.	11/29/80—pled guilty to Disorderly Conduct Sent.: 10 days
11/22/80	Robbery Assault	Kings Supreme	8/22/78—Adjudicated Y. O. for Att. Robbery 1 (C) Sent.: 3 years Paroled 9/9/83 Revoked 5/8/84 Held to M.E. 9/1/84
3/19/81	Public Lewdness	Kings Crim.	9/9/83—dismissed
3/20/81	Public Lewdness	Kings Crim.	7/5/81—dismissed
3/29/81	Public Lewdness	Kings Crim.	7/5/81—dismissed
6/20/81	Crim. Trespass 3 Public Lewdness	Kings Crim.	9/9/83—dismissed
7/11/81	Intent to Fraudulently Obtain Transportation without Pay.	Kings Crim.	9/9/83—dismissed
11/7/83	Public Lewdness	Kings Crim.	8/27/87—pled guilty to Public Lewdness (B Misd.) Sent.: 1 year
5/22/87	Harassment	Kings Crim.	5/23/84—Conditional Discharge
3/31/89	Disorderly Conduct	Kings Crim.	4/1/89—Conditional Discharge

Pending Legal Actions
None.

Parole Interview:
The inmate was interviewed on 9/20/92 at Woodbourne C. F. in regard to the instant offenses. Hughes reluctantly admitted his guilt in all three of the robberies and expressed remorse for his behavior. He attributes his participation to the fact that he was unemployed due to long-term medical problems, and that his unemployment benefits had run out. Hughes felt pressured and needed to feed his children. He also admits to being high on crack at the time.

FIGURE 8.1   (*continued*)

Institutional Adjustment:
Although Hughes initially did not address his drug abuse, he enrolled in drug treatment in 8/91. He has received several certificates for participating in substance abuse programs (Project Aware and Compadre Helper). He received his GED in 1991 and has worked as a teacher's aide at Woodbourne for 8 months, receiving positive evaluations. He also worked in the Barber Shop for 7 months and received satisfactory reports.

Disciplinary:
Inmate's discipline is marginal. The inmate has received disciplinary reports for fighting; however, most disciplinary reports are for being out of place, refusing a direct order, and out of place. The most recent report is dated 7/2/91 for count procedure.

Proposed Residence:
The subject's proposed residence is with his wife, Sylvia Butler Hughes, who resides at 3140 Atlantic Avenue, Apt. 3B, Brooklyn, NY 11212; (718-485-4104). Mrs. Hughes is available after 4:00 P.M.

Proposed Employment:
Needs to be developed. Inmate claims interest in counseling youths. He has no reasonable assurance offers.

Inmate's Plans:
The inmate hopes to pursue a job in the field of youth counseling since he feels that his life experiences qualify him for such a position. He holds a GED and is considering furthering his education. Hughes reports that his wife and three children are extremely supportive, and he plans to reside with them.

Supervision Needs:
Issues of substance abuse and employment are key considerations. Urinalysis is recommended regularly, and outpatient drug treatment is most appropriate. Community based supervision should also be sensitive to Hughes' medical condition, his prior history of public lewdness arrests, and his proclivity for armed robberies of vulnerable victims.

Special Conditions Recommended:
S.O.M.E./Academic Program; periodic urinalysis; outpatient drug counseling.

CONFIDENTIAL INFORMATION

Psychiatric/Psychological Reports:
Hughes was hospitalized at Woodhull Hospital for psychiatric treatment on one occasion prior to his incarceration.
    At this facility, he was interviewed in August of 1981 by a Dr. Goldman who diagnosed: "Unspecified personality disorder with a history of exhibitionism." The inmate's reading level is 9.6; math level is 7.9; Beta I.Q. is 118.

Medical Reports:
A health discharge summary has been requested in this case. Hughes reports that he is on daily medication for hypertension.

Confidential Written Reports:
None.

Evaluation:
The subject has performed fairly well during this period of incarceration by participation in academic programs and substance abuse treatment. This would seem to indicate that Hughes is making efforts to reconcile his lengthy criminal history and significant history of substance abuse. He also has a supportive environment to return to. However, the inmate has demonstrated a long term disregard for the laws of NYS and is currently incarcerated for three robberies of young victims. He expresses some remorse, but seems to feel that he had no other alternative to provide food for his family. Yet, he simultaneously was abusing drugs, a costly habit. Hughes impresses

FIGURE 8.1 *(continued)*

during interview as having a low frustration tolerance. He also has a poor work record in the community and has minimal job skills.

Approved by: _____ *J. Burke* _____   Prepared by: _____ *N. Harrison* _____
                        S.P.O.   P.O.

Date: 9/28/92   *Facility:* Woodbourne C. F.

INVESTIGATION REPORT

COMMUNITY PREPARATION _____   R&E _____ OTHER _____

NAME: Hughes, Sam   NYSID: 4172822M

SENTENCE;   1-6-0/4-6-0   DIN: #87-A-5840
             1-6-0/4-6-0 cs.

DATE OF SENTENCE: 7/8/90   INSTITUTION: Woodbourne C. F.

OFFENSE: Att. Robbery, 1st   LAST BOARD APPEARANCE: 10/91
           Att. Robbery, 1st

MAXIMUM EXPIRATION: 12/27/98   DECISION: Open date 12/27/91

CR DATE: 12/27/95   AREA OFFICE: Brooklyn IV—73rd Precinct

PROSPECTIVE RESIDENCE

ADDRESS: 3140 Atlantic Avenue, Brooklyn   3B   718-485-4104
           NUMBER   STREET   CITY   APT. #   TELEPHONE #

RENT: 230/mo__ PVT. HOUSE _____ APT. _X_ FURNISHED ROOM _____ OTHER _____

ACCOMMODATIONS AVAILABLE TO RELEASE: The subject will share a bedroom with his wife, Sylvia Butler Hughes.

PERSONS IN HOUSEHOLD:

Sylvia Butler Hughes	wife	Turquoise Hughes, Age 6	daughter
NAME	RELATIONSHIP	NAME	RELATIONSHIP
Ronnie Hughes, age 11	son	Saphire Hughes, Age 3	daughter
NAME	RELATIONSHIP	NAME	RELATIONSHIP

Sylvia Butler Hughes	11/30/91	5:00 P.M.	home visit
PERSON CONTACTED	DATE	TIME	METHOD

PROSPECTIVE EMPLOYER/PROGRAM

NAME: Drayton Grocery Store   TYPE OF BUSINESS: Grocery Store

ADDRESS: 395 Livington Street   Brooklyn   718-452-0383
         NUMBER   STREET   CITY   TELEPHONE #

POSITION OFFERED: Grocery Clerk _____ SALARY: 180 HOURS: 5 days Tu-Sat. 12-8 P.M.

SUPERVISOR: George Clark _____ DUTY DESCRIPTION: Check out

PERSON CONTACTED: George Clark _____ DATE: 12/1/91 TIME: 6 P.M. METHOD: visit

COMMENTS

Residence: Subject has a satisfactory residence program in the home of his wife, Sylvia Butler Hughes, at 3140 Atlantic Avenue, Apt. 3B, Brooklyn, NY 11212 (718-485-4104).

FIGURE 8.1   *(continued)*

On 11/90/93, at 5:00 P.M., the writer visited the proposed residence. The residence is located in a high crime area of the 73rd precinct in Brooklyn. The apartment itself is located on the 3rd floor of a N.Y.C.H.A. project development. The building entrance is in disrepair, and access is no problem.

The apartment is at the end of the hallway and is clearly labelled #3B. It contains four rooms (2 bedrooms, kitchen, living room and bathroom). There is only one entrance which opens into the living room and no fire escape. The subject will share the large bedroom with his wife while the three children share the smaller bedroom. The home was neat, clean and well furnished. No pets were reported or seen.

The writer interviewed the subject's wife at the residence. Also present were the subject's three children: Ronnie, Turquoise and Saphire. Mrs. Hughes and the children appear eager for the subject's homecoming. Mrs. Hughes advised that she has had a relationship with the subject since the late 1970s with occasional periods of living together. She attributes Hughes's previous criminal activities to his history of drug abuse. The two were legally married at Woodbourne C. F. in 8/92, and Mrs. Hughes does not anticipate any problems upon her husband's return. She and the children visit Hughes at Woodbourne once a month and letters are exchanged regularly.

During the interview, Mrs. Hughes advised that she maintains the home with her income of approximately $15,000 per year. She has been employed at J & B Retailers at 1433 De Kalb Ave., Brooklyn as a Key Punch Operator from 7:30 A.M. to 3:30 P.M. Monday to Friday for the past 2.5 years. The home rents for $230. month plus utilities. The two older children attend P.S. 101 while the youngest receives day care with Mrs. Hughes's sister, Mildred Butler Fuller, at her home at 732 Livonia Avenue, Brooklyn (718-462-9133). Mrs. Hughes has resided at this residence for the past year. Mrs. Hughes suffers from sickle cell anemia, which requires occasional hospitalization.

According to Mrs. Hughes, she and her husband have relatives in the NYC area, but none maintains contact with the subject other than his brother, Frank Hughes of 732 Lenox Ave., NY, NY (apt. unknown).

The writer advised Mrs. Hughes that our Parole population is at high risk for HIV infection and encouraged her to discuss this with her husband. The Division's educational package, "Healthy New Start" was provided and discussed at this time. The Rules and Regulations of Parole were also discussed during the interview; Mrs. Hughes advised that she understood the conditions.

A check of the parolee residence cross references indicate that parolee Joe Brown NYSID 1473650B, resides at 3140 Atlantic Ave., Apt. 11B, Brooklyn, NY 11212 (P.O. Gilbert).

Employment: Subject has a satisfactory employment offer with Drayton Grocery Store at 395 Livingston Ave., Brooklyn, NY (718-452-0383).

During the home visit, Mrs. Hughes provided the prospective employment program for the subject. On 12/1/89, at 6:00 P.M. the writer interviewed George Clark, the owner of Drayton Grocery at 395 Livingston Avenue, Brooklyn. He advised that he has known the subject for over ten years and is willing to employ him as a grocery clerk upon release. He will provide 40 hours of work per week at $5 to start per hour.

Mr. Clerk presently employs 24 workers and has been in business over 20 years. The store is well known in the area and is suitable considering the subject's limited job skills.

Special Conditions	curfew
	support dependents
	Mental Hygiene referral at discretion
	of P.O.—P.O. to monitor

The subject should make his arrival report within 24 hours of release to the Parole Office at 340 Livingston Street, Brooklyn, NY (5th floor).

FIGURE 8.1   (*continued*)

EXAMINATION BY NELSON HARRIS,
MEMBER OF THE BOARD OF PAROLE

Re: Smith, Louis, No. 092340136

Q: Louis Smith?
A: Yes.
Q: Smith, I am wondering if you got a chance on parole, what do you think would happen? Do you think the time is right?
A: I would go and pick up my life where I left it before.
Q: Do you think there was anything about the way you were living when you came in that needs changing?
A: A little could be altered so I am quite sure I would change them around now.
Q: Can you pinpoint, tell us some of the areas where you think you will change?
A: There is quite a few areas I can see where I am making mistakes. I am making a mistake by coming here, that is one right there.
Q: Anything that you could do to stay out of places like this would definitely be something that would be of good intentions?
A: Yes.
Q: Do you have any plans? How are you going to try and go about making it when you get out of here?
A: First of all, I am starting back to work, which I am doing now and take it on from there.
Q: Staying in the big city area?
A: Yes.
Q: Can you cope with it?
A: I don't understand.
Q: Can you cope with the city, the bigness and all that?
A: Yes, I can.
Q: What is this job that you have?
A: It's the closest thing that they can give me to the job I have in the joint, that was all I have.
Q: Anybody that can get a foothold in that field really has something going for him and can make good money.
A: Yes.
Q: What can you do? How are your skills? What is the most you ever earned from it?
A: Well, the most I earned, brought in in one week was close to $500.
Q: You made that kind of money?
A: Yes.
Q: You noticed I have not referred to the crime?
A: Yes.
Q: You probably talked about it time and again.
A: Not very much, but some.
Q: This is thoroughly reported here. You did not have anything in your past like it and from what I read, it was certainly something you did not intend.
A: You are right, it wasn't intended. It was done through an accident. Mostly I was drinking and that is one problem I think I can handle now.
Q: Do you think you need anything outside yourself with reference to any drinking you did before?
A: I wasn't a regular drinker, I just drank sometimes. Now one thing I learned that if I get a problem, stay away from a bottle, that's what I learned.
Q: As a result of this, you also know that even though you don't drink all the time, it can still be a problem?
A: I found that out.
A: Okay, your recommendations here are reasonably good and folks that have worked with you say they believe that there is no reason why you can't make it.
A: I hope I can.
Q: In the event you get the opportunity-
A: I hope I can make it.
Q: You feel that way?
A: Yes.
Q: Maybe there is something that you want to call to our attention?
A: No.
Q: Thanks for coming in. We will make a decision and let you know what it is.

FIGURE 8.2   Parole examination.

the right to attend a violation hearing to consider revocation of parole.") The South Carolina parole board appoints "an individual on staff to assist victims or witnesses in opposition on any parole or pardon matter." In Alabama, "Victims of violent crimes and families of children who have been abused are notified prior to an inmate's being considered for parole by the Board. The Victim's right to be present at the Parole Hearing and to express their concerns in person and in writing to the Board is provided by law." In New Jersey, at the time of sentencing, the prosecutor notifies any victim injured as a result of a crime in the first or second degree, or the nearest relative of a murder victim, of the opportunity to present a statement to be considered during a parole hearing, or to give in-person testimony before the board concerning the victim's harm. The board notifies victims or relatives who have contacted the board requesting an opportunity to submit a statement or to provide testimony.

MASSACHUSETTS VICTIMS SERVICES UNIT

Established in 1987, the Victims Services Unit provides a wide array of support services to victims who have been certified to receive information regarding offenders by the Criminal History Systems Board. The unit's staff acts as the parole board's representative in addressing and advancing victim/witness issues by collecting victim/witness input for board consideration; providing timely notifications of parole hearing dates and hearing results; providing information about parole and criminal offender record information; assisting citizens in completing impact statements; directing referrals to other criminal justice or social service agencies for collateral assistance; and heightening the community's level of awareness regarding victim/witness issues through both the media and direct contact.

Many states include a victim impact statement (VIS) as part of the documentation considered by the parole board. In New York, state law provides that victims or their representatives may submit a written victim impact statement to the parole board, which must then consider it in reaching a parole decision. "The contents of the statement may set forth information concerning the offense, the extent of the injury or economic loss, the victims's attitude toward the offender's potential parole release, and other information that the victim may consider appropriate." The information is maintained in confidence.

PAROLE BOARD CRITERIA

In states using the indeterminate sentence, the "parole boards exercise some functions that are exactly the same as judicial sentencing—for example, fixing minimum and maximum terms" (Rubin, 1974: 131). What criteria does a parole board use when it sets the minimum and maximum terms of imprisonment (in those states in which this is left to the parole board), or when it is considering the parole release of an inmate? New York statutes provide:

> Discretionary release on parole shall not be granted merely as a reward for good conduct or efficient performance of duties while confined but after considering if there is a reasonable probability that, if such inmate is released, he will live and remain at liberty without violating the law, and that his release is not incompatible with the welfare of society and will not so depreciate the seriousness of his crime as to undermine respect for law. In making the parole release decision . . . the following [must] be considered: (i) the institutional record including program goals and accomplishments, academic achievements, vocational education, training or work assignments, therapy and interpersonal relationships with staff and inmates; (ii) performance, if any, as a participant in a temporary release program; (iii) release plans including community resources, employment, education and training and support services available to the inmate; and (iv) any deportation order issued by the federal government (Figures 8.3 and 8.4).

Parole boards usually consider the crime, the length of time served and the inmate's age, prior criminal history, use of alcohol or drugs, and institutional record. Some parole boards may request a recommendation from the prosecutor. All will certainly consider opposition to an inmate's parole from the police and the news media. In a study of parole decisions in Massachusetts, Betty Luther (1995) found that the election of a "law and order" governor caused the board (whose membership remained almost unchanged) to decrease parole release rates, particularly for high-security inmates for whom they were virtually eliminated. The widespread use of parole guidelines has reduced the importance of general criteria.

PAROLE BOARD COUNTERVAILING PRESSURES

Prison overcrowding   Political (public-media) reaction

--->|<--

PAROLE BOARD GUIDELINES

As criticism of parole and parole boards began to mount in the 1970s, the U.S. Board of Parole engaged a group of researchers to develop a model for improved decision making. In particular, the board was interested in a means of reducing disparity and making the decision-making process intelligible (and defensible) to both inmates and the public. The researchers, headed by Donald

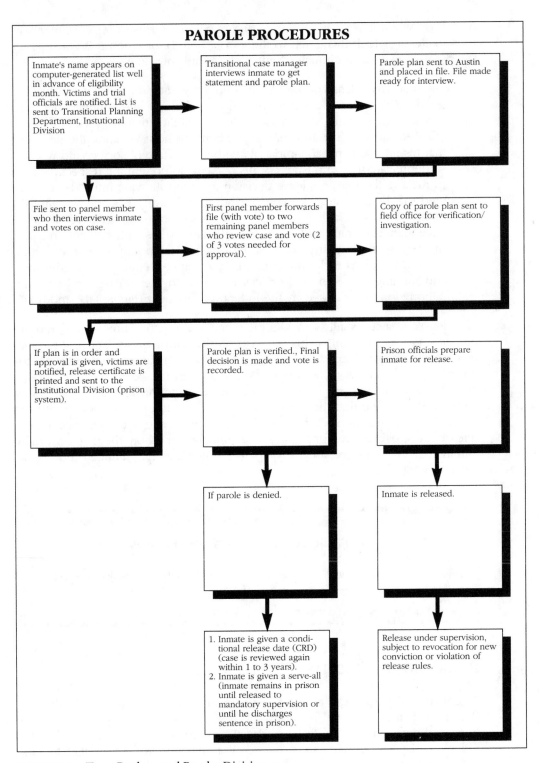

PAROLE PROCEDURES

Inmate's name appears on computer-generated list well in advance of eligibility month. Victims and trial officials are notified. List is sent to Transitional Planning Department, Instutional Division

Transitional case manager interviews inmate to get statement and parole plan.

Parole plan sent to Austin and placed in file. File made ready for interview.

File sent to panel member who then interviews inmate and votes on case.

First panel member forwards file (with vote) to two remaining panel members who review case and vote (2 of 3 votes needed for approval).

Copy of parole plan sent to field office for verification/ investigation.

If plan is in order and approval is given, victims are notified, release certificate is printed and sent to the Institutional Division (prison system).

Parole plan is verified., Final decision is made and vote is recorded.

Prison officials prepare inmate for release.

If parole is denied.

Inmate is released.

1. Inmate is given a conditional release date (CRD) (case is reviewed again within 1 to 3 years).
2. Inmate is given a serve-all (inmate remains in prison until released to mandatory supervision or until he discharges sentence in prison).

Release under supervision, subject to revocation for new conviction or violation of release rules.

FIGURE 8.3   Texas Pardons and Paroles Division.

SELECTING AND SCHEDULING CASES FOR PAROLE

In order to make an informed decision, the Board causes a file to be prepared on all prisoners shortly after they are received in the correctional system. When completed, the file is reviewed and an initial parole consideration date scheduled. . . . By law, the time may be reduced by application of incentive good-time credit. Most other prisoners (except those legally barred from parole and those whose sentence iricludes a mandatory fixed term prior to parole) are scheduled under consideration guidelines.

Under the guidelines, prisoners serving sentences of ten (10) years or more and who have a high potential for violence will not be considered until they have served one-half of their term or fifteen years, whichever is less. Career criminals will be considered after serving from one-third to one-half of their term.

Other guideline cases will be scheduled for initial parole consideration on or before service of one-third of their total term. Factors used in determining the consideration date are past criminal record, pattern and severity of the present offense, community attitude toward the offender.

Each case scheduled for progress review is placed on an automatic calendar. The progress review includes a study of the prisoner's conduct and work record while in prison, his general progress, attitude, and prison officials' reports and recommendations.

Parole is granted

- If the inmate's prison adjustment is good

- If there are no valid protests to parole

- If the inmate's release appears to be compatible with society's welfare

- If the board believes the inmate has served a sufficient portion of his sentence

- If a satisfactory parole plan is available

If Parole is denied

- The inmate may be required to serve the remainder of his sentence if less than three years

- He may be given a new progress review date within a minimum of six months and a maximum of three years

FIGURE 8.4   Alabama Board of Pardons and Paroles.

Gottfredson and Leslie Wilkins, derived a set of variables that they saw as fairly representative of those used by board members in making decisions—the most salient being the seriousness of the offense and parole prognosis. The researchers also conducted a two-year study of 2500 federal parolees and uncovered a variety of "success factors," which they reduced to seven variables. The combined variables for *severity of offense* and *parole prognosis* were arranged in the form of a grid (Figure 8.5) to determine the actual length of imprisonment. For example, an adult offender convicted of forgery under $1000, "Category Two," whose parole prognosis is "good," would normally be released on parole after serving between 8 and 12 months; an offender convicted of multiple robbery, "Category Six," with a parole prognosis of "poor," would normally serve between 78 and 100 months before being paroled (Figure 8.6).

Guidelines typically go well beyond the *rehabilitative/medical model* on which the indeterminate sentence is often presumed to be based. Indeed, satis-

Offense Characteristics:
Offense Severity (Some Crimes Eliminated or Summarized)

OFFENDER CHARACTERISTICS: PAROLE PROGNOSIS

	Very Good	Good	Fair	Poor
Category One *Low:* possession of a small amount of marijuana; simple theft under $1,000.		*Adult Range*		
	6 months	6–9 months	9–12 months	12–16 months
		(Youth Range)		
	( ) 6 months	(6–9) months	(9–12) months	(12–16) months
Category Two *Low/Moderate:* income tax evasion less than $10,000; immigration law violations; embezzlement, fraud, forgery under $1,000		*Adult Range*		
	8 months	8–12 months	12–16 months	16–22 months
		(Youth Range)		
	( ) 8 months	(8–12) months	(12–16) months	(16–20) months
Category Three *Moderate:* bribery; possession of 50 lb. or less of marijuana, with intent to sell; illegal firearms; income tax evasion $10,000 to $50,000; nonviolent propery offenses $1,000 to $19,999; auto theft, not for resale		*Adult Range*		
	10–14 months	14–18 months	18–24 months	24–32 months
		(Youth Range)		
	(8–12) months	(12–16) months	(16–20) months	(20–26) months
Category Four *High:* counterfeiting; marijuana possession with intent to sell, 50 to 1,999 lb.; auto theft, for resale; nonviolent property offenses, $20,000 to $100,000		*Adult Range*		
	14–20 months	20–26 months	26–34 months	34–44 months
		(Youth Range)		
	(12–16) months	(16–20) months	(20–26) months	(26–32) months
Category Five *Very High:* robbery; breaking and entering bank or post office; extortion; marijuana possession with intent to sell, over 2,000 lb.; hard drugs possession with intent to sell, not more than $100,000; nonviolent property offenses over $100,00 but not exceeding $500,000		*Adult Range*		
	24–36 months	36–48 months	48–60 months	60–72 months
		(Youth Range)		
	(20–26) months	(26–32) months	(32–40) months	(40–48) months

FIGURE 8.5 Guidelines for decision making and customary total time to be served before release (including jail time).

Offense Characteristics:
Offense Severity (Some Crimes Eliminated or Summarized)

OFFENDER CHARACTERISTICS: PAROLE PROGNOSIS

	Very Good	Good	Fair	Poor
Category Six		*Adult Range*		
Greatest I : explosive detonation; multiple robbery; aggravated felony (weapon fired—no serious injury); hard drugs, over $100,000; forcible rape	40–52 months	52–64 months	64–78 months	78–100 months
			(Youth Range)	
	(30–40) months	(40–50) months	(50–60) months	(60–76) months
Category Seven		*Adult Range*		
Greatest II : aircraft hijacking; espionage; kidnapping; homicide	52–80 months	64–92 months	78–110 months	100–148 months
			(Youth Range)	
	(40–64) months	(50–74) months	(70–86) months	(76–110) months
Category Eight[a]		*Adult Range*		
	100+ months	120+ months	150+ months	180+ months
			(Youth Range)	
	(80+) months	(100+) months	(120+) months	(150+) months

[a]*Note:* For Category Eight, no upper limits are specified because of the extreme variability of the cases within this category. For decisions exceeding the lower limit of the applicable guideline *by more than 48 months*, the pertinent aggravation case factors considered are to be specified in the reasons given (for example, that a homicide was premeditated or committed during the course of another felony; or that extreme cruelty or brutality was demonstrated).

FIGURE 8.5 *(continued)*

Parole decision guidelines help the Alabama State Board of Pardons and Paroles make a more consistent, soundly based, and understandable decision on an inmate serving a sentence of less than life imprisonment. Guidelines help the board decide on a Tentative Parole Month for the inmate or decide that he will complete his sentence without parole.

A board hearing examiner identifies an inmate's crime severity level from a table of offenses ranked in seven levels from lowest to highest severity. The higher the severity, the longer the inmate is recommended to serve. Then the hearing examiner calculates the inmate's parole success likelihood score by adding weighted factors with proven predictive value from the inmate's criminal and social history. A history of things, such as prior imprisonment, parole or probation failure, heroin use or possession, and joblessness, would increase the risk of paroling the inmate and cause him to be recommended for longer confinement.

The hearing examiner inserts the inmate's crime severity level and parole success likelihood score into a guidelines chart, which, also weighing sentence length and prison capacity, recommends how long the inmate should be confined. This translates into either a recommendation for parole denial or for a tentative parole month in the future.

By majority vote, the parole board members either agree with the guidelines recommendation or, for a stated reason, depart from it and make an independent decision. The inmate is then sent a notice of the board's decision to establish a tentative parole month. The inmate is informed that the decision is provisional upon good conduct and participation in prison education, work, and treatment programs. The decision is subject to change at the discretion of the board. Usually, on the recommendation of the Department of Corrections, misconduct results in parole postponement or cancellation.

Parole guidelines help keep the board on track toward its goal of seeing that inmates serving terms for similar offenses with similar histories are treated the same.

FIGURE 8.6   Board members are assisted by parole decision guidelines.

factory progress in those institutional programs that are "rehabilitative" may not even affect the parole decision. Kevin Krajick (1978) points out that good institutional behavior is *expected*, not rewarded, although poor behavior can be punished with denial of parole. In fact, the institutional adjustment of an offender has never been an accurate guide for predicting postinstitutional behavior (Dolan, Lunden, and Barberet, 1987); some evidence exists that certain offenders (e.g., substance abusers and professional criminals) most often perform well in prison but tend to recidivate.

In effect, the use of guidelines whose primary focus is *just deserts* is a form of deferred sentencing. Some critics claim that no justification exists for deferring sentence (the term of imprisonment) and that it creates problems by adding to the offender's uncertainty. Others argue that the parole board is relatively free of the "heat" that certain crimes and criminals can generate. The board does not typically operate with the same high visibility of a court; unlike a sentencing judge, the parole board is not normally under the gaze of the community and news media. These observers stress that the parole board, using guidelines, is better equipped to make a rational decision commensurate with just deserts than is a sentencing judge.

Guidelines used by state parole boards consider the seriousness of the present offense and prior criminal history; most, as in the federal guidelines, also consider rehabilitative items and parole prognosis. [For a review of the issue of prediction in corrections, see Clear (1988).] For example, the Georgia Board of Pardons and

Paroles, in a mix of the classical and positive theory, states: "Justice demands that punishment should be tailored to fit both the offense and the offender."

A board hearing examiner identifies an inmate's crime severity level from a table of offenses ranked in seven levels from lowest to highest in severity. The higher the severity, the longer the inmate will be recommended to serve. Then the hearing examiner calculates the inmate's parole success likelihood by adding weighted factors with proven predictive value from the inmate's criminal and social history. A history of factors such as prior imprisonment, parole or probation failure, heroin use or possession, and joblessness would increase the risk of paroling the inmate and cause him or her to be recommended for longer confinement (Figure 8.7).

In New York, guidelines consider only offense severity and prior criminal history (Figure 8.8). The parole board determines the actual amount of time to be served within the appropriate range based on

- Institutional adjustment, including but not limited to program goals and accomplishments, academic achievements, vocational education, training or work assignments, therapy, and interpersonal relationships with staff and inmates
- Performance, if any, as a participant in a temporary release program
- Availability of adequate release plans, including community resources, employment, education, training, and support services

The parole board may go beyond the guideline range in the event of mitigating or aggravating circumstances, but the detailed reason for such decisions must be provided to the inmate in writing.

Parole services can be divided into those provided by institutional personnel, field personnel, and the separate category of clemency.

New York State Parole Officers

Parole officers are assigned mainly to area field offices, correctional facilities, or temporary release units. Parole officers in the area offices provide supervision, guidance, and control over an assigned caseload of parolees, which varies depending on the type of offender, and both assist and determine their compliance and conditions of parole; parole officers in the correctional facilities counsel and prepare inmates for release to the community. Parole officers in the temporary release program combine both field and institution functions. A few parole officers are assigned to special programs. Field work requires flexible hours.

A parole officer in the field guides and directs the parolees during their period of adjustment from incarceration to normal community life; investigates and takes appropriate action concerning possible parole violations, new crimes, and other unacceptable behavior; and represents the agency in hearings concerning alleged violations.

Institutional parole officers assigned to correctional facilities guide and direct inmates during their incarceration. They help the inmate develop

PAROLE SUCCESS LIKELIHOOD FACTORS

....
            NAME   NUMBER   INSTITUTION   DATE

These guidelines indicate the customary range of time to be served for various combinations of offense and offender characteristics. It is emphasized that mitigating or aggravating factors may warrant decision outside the guidelines and, in appropriate circumstances, the Board will exercise its discretion as provided by law. The basic guideline presupposes good institutional adjustment and program progress. Deviation from the normal conduct expected of all inmates could result in decisions outside the guidelines.

If the convicted person is servicing sentences for multiple offenses, the most serious offense will determine the crime severity level. "Attempted" offenses will be rated one grade below the principal offense.

Convicted persons will appear for parole consideration when they have met the requirements of Nevada law.

As stated in NRS 213. 10989, the establishment of these standards is not intended to create any right or interest in liberty, nor to create any reasonable expectation of parole, nor to establish any basis for a course of action against the State, its political subdivisions, agencies, boards, commissions, departments, officers or employees. The release or continuation on parole is an act of grace of the State.

Further, the Board's actions are also governed by NRS 213. 1099, which delineates State policy on the granting of parole.

1. Age at first commitment:
   18 or older . . . . = 2
   17 or younger. . . . . = 0 . . . .

2. Prior convictions (F & M):
   None. . . . . = 3
   One . . . . = 2
   Two/three. . . . . = 1
   Four or more . . . . = 0 . . . .

3. Incarcerations since age 17
   prior to instant offense:
   None. . . . . = 2
   One. . . . . = 1
   Two or more . . . . = 0 . . . .

4. Parole/probation failure:
   No failure. = 1
   Otherwise. = 0 . . . .

5. No use, possession or attempt
   to obtain heroin, cocaine, opiates,
   amphetamines . . . . = 2
   History of drug abuse . . . . = 0 . . . .

6. Current offense did not involve
   burglary or forgery, credit card or
   bad checks . . . . = 1
   Otherwise. = 0 . . . .

7. Fully-employed or full-time
   school for 6 months in year
   preceding offense . . . . = 1
   Otherwise . . . . = 0 . . . .

8. Injury to /death of victim:
   Yes . . . . = 0
   Otherwise . . . . = 2 . . . .

9. Use of weapon:
   Yes . . . . = 0
   Otherwise . . . . = 2 . . . .

10. Not previously convicted of
    similar offense . . . . = 1
    Otherwise . . . . = 0 . . . .

11. Prison programming:
    Has addressed educational/voca-
    tional deficiencies . . . . = 1 . . . .
    Has sought and participated in
    counseling on substance abuse,
    alcohol or psychological programs . = 1
    No history of prison problems. . . . = 1
    All . . . . = 3 . . . .

Parole Success Likelihood Score . . .   .

FIGURE 8.7   Parole Success Likelihood Factors, Nevada.

GUIDELINES—RECOMMENDED MONTHS TO SERVE

Read across from your Crime Severity Level and down from your Parole Success Likelihood Score to find your guidelines-recommended months to serve. For Crime Severity Level I through V, the grid reflects a shift in months to serve based on the court-imposed sentence length. If your sentence is less than 25 percent of the statutory maximum penalty, the lesser figure is used. If your sentence exceeds 75 percent of the statutory maximum penalty, the greater figure is used. For all other sentence lengths, the median figure is used. For Crime Severity Levels VI or VII, the guidelines recommendation will be one-third of the court imposed sentence length or the grid recommendation, whichever is greater. The Board, using its descretion in your case, may depart from guidelines recommendation.

PAROLE SUCCESS LIKELIHOOD SCORE

Crime Severity Level	Excellent 15–20	Good 10–14	Average 6–9	Poor 0–5
I	4	6	8	14-16-18
II	12	14	16-18-20	18-20-22
III	20-22-24	22-24-26	24-26-28	26-28-30
IV	28-30-32	30-32-34	32-34-36	34-36-38
V	36-38-40	38-40-42	40-42-44	42-44-46
VI	48	54	60	66
VII	60	66	72	78
VIII	90	102	114	126
IX	138	150	162	174

Crime Severity Level: ....

Parole Success Liklihood Score: ....

Guideline-Recommended Months ....

FIGURE 8.7 (*continued*)

positive attitudes and behaviors, encourage participation in prison programs, and prepare inmates for their parole board appearances. The institutional parole officer prepares the inmates' parole records and makes evaluations and recommendations to the parole board to help it reach the best possible decisions concerning granting and denying of parole release. Decisions by the board are largely dependent on information and analysis provided by the officer.

The activities of both the field and institution parole officers include continuous counseling, direction, and supervision over those offenders assigned to their supervision; providing and obtaining information; solving problems; and influencing positive behavior and compliance with the law. Discussions with relatives, friends, law enforcement and social service agencies, employers, and so on concerning the parolees or inmates are also common. Parole officers receive direct assistance with their cases from their supervisors and are required to prepare detailed reports concerning their case activities. As *peace officers*, parole officers are trained in the use of firearms and deadly physical force, are prepared to apprehend and arrest violators, and must be certified by the Division of Criminal Justice Services. They must pass a mandatory training program approved by the Municipal Police Training Council during the course of their probationary service.

Parole officers conduct individual, group, and family counseling; develop realistic goals with the clients; and assist in developing a comprehensive program of rehabilitation, thereby fostering re-entry into and law-abiding continuance in the community. In general, they engage clients and their families in therapeutic activities designed to reverse criminal attitudes, as well as reverse negative behavior trends that have resulted in dysfunctional behavior. A primary job is to motivate the most difficult and dangerous of clients.

FIGURE 8.8 Guidelines for Parole Board Decision Making, New York.

To derive the guideline time range, the appropriate cell is located on the parole decision-making grid where the offense severity and prior criminal history scores intersect. The offense severity score is located on the vertical axis, the prior criminal history score on the horizontal axis. The cell on the guideline grid where the two scores intersect indicates the suggested time to be served, based on these two major factors. For example, application of the guidelines in the case of an offense score of 5 and a prior criminal history score of 4 yields a range of 20 to 38 months.

GUIDELINES FOR PAROLE BOARD DECISION MAKING

Offense severity score	Prior criminal history score		
	0·1 (Low)	2·5 (Moderate)	6·11 (Serious)
8–9 (most severe)	Specific ranges are not given due to the limited number of cases and the extreme variation possible within the category.		
7	30–60 months	40–72 months	60–96 months
6	22–40 months	30–50 months	46–72 months
4–5	16–30 months	20–38 months	30–54 months
2–3	14–24 months	18–30 months	20–36 months
1 (least severe)	12–18 months	14–24 months	16–28 months

Parole Services

Institutional Services

The basic responsibility of institutional parole staff is to prepare reports on inmates for the parole board. The staff also helps inmates secure furloughs, work release, or halfway house placement, and it may assist with personal problems ranging from matters relating to spouse and children to questions of a technical or legal nature.

Under ideal conditions, when an offender is first received at the institution, he or she is interviewed by a member of the parole staff. The results of the interview, psychiatric and psychological tests, and the information in the presentence report are then used to help plan an institutional program for the inmate. The parole staff periodically updates the material with additional information. Staff members discuss release plans with inmates and request the field staff to visit and interview family members and prospective employers. When an inmate is ready to meet the parole board, the staff provides a report on the inmate that includes an evaluation of changes made since the offender was first received at the prison (Figure 8.9). The report may also contain a completed "parole guidelines" form and a recommendation if requested by the board.

FIGURE 8.9   Pre-parole investigation report.

BOARD OF PAROLE

PRE-PAROLE INVESTIGATION
DATE: January 11, 1995

TO: Carolyn Koslowski, Executive Director

FROM: Karel E. Yedlicka, Jr., Parole Examiner

RE: Robert L. Smith, SP #172362

I. OFFENSE

The subject was involved in a burglary of a home in which merchandise valued at over $1800 was stolen, and damage to the house itself occurred. The presentence report indicates that the victim was in the house at the time of the burglary but thought it was her son and, therefore, did not investigate the subject coming into the home by the back door. The subject also received an enhanced penalty on numerous prior felony convictions with a current parole release date of September 1, 1995.

II. PERSONAL BACKGROUND

Robert Smith will be temporarily staying with his sister who has legal custody of the subject's daughter, Judith Smith, age 14. Judith is currently enrolled in Joseph Mittner Junior High School and has been cared for by the subject's sister, Margaret Smith, since the subject's incarceration in

---

1982. Currently, she is receiving $225 per month in Aid to Dependent Children toward the care of Judith. This sum will be reduced when the subject is able to provide support for his daughter. Ms. Smith indicated that the subject has every intention of living with his daughter, securing his own residence, and raising her. He has not had the benefit of being with her very much during the past 12 years. This examiner recommends that as a special condition of parole, the subject be required to provide adequate support for his daughter, whose mother's whereabouts are unknown at this time.

III. RESIDENCE

The subject will be residing with his sister Margaret Smith, who, along with her brother Raymond Smith, owns a brick and wood frame home with four bedrooms and one bath located at 1526 Cincinnati Street, Madisonville. In 1993, the subject's father moved to Charleston, South Carolina, and turned the house over to Margaret and Raymond. Margaret stated that the subject will probably stay with her without a need to pay for room and board until he can get on his feet.

IV. EMPLOYMENT

The subject is employed on work release at Briarcliff Manor, a 24-hour nursing home at 1001 Briarcliff Boulevard, Madisonville. His employment was verified by Mona Mitchell, the bookkeeper. The day supervisor, Melanie Harris, stated that the subject is an excellent worker and has experienced no problems. He is employed as a dietitian's assistant who helps with meals and other minor duties in the nursing home, earning $6.10 per hour, 30 to 40 hours per week. The subject receives Worker's Compensation but no other benefits at this time. The nursing home also employs more than 30 other individuals on a 24-hour basis.

The subject has been employed at this job, obtained through the work-release center, since 10/13/94. No driver's license is required in that the subject works exclusively in the facility. However, the subject's sister stated that their father left an old car that the subject can use when paroled for transportation back and forth from northside to southside.

V. SPECIAL PROGRAMS OR TREATMENT FEATURES

As previously verified, restitution is owed, and the subject should make restitution accordingly; a recommended rate is $25 per month for a period of four years. In addition to supporting his daughter, a drug-testing clause should reflect his problem with heroin as indicated in the PSI. In view of the seriousness of his criminal history, the subject will need close supervision.

VI. RECOMMENDATIONS

This examiner recommends that the subject be paroled on 3/7/95 for a minimum supervision period of four years because of the severity of the instant offense and the need to pay restitution. The proposed residence appears to be valid, and the subject's employment appears to be an excellent opportunity at this time for him to reintegrate into society. The subject has been out only briefly in the latter part of 1985 before being rearrested in 1986 with the rest of the time spent incarcerated back to 1982. The subject is now 35 years of age, and if he cannot make parole at this time, it is unlikely that he will make one in the future.

Carole Simmons

Parole Examiner

FIGURE **8.9** (*continued*)

Institutional parole staff may also hold group meetings with new inmates to orient them about parole. These group sessions are then followed up with individual interviews. At preparole group sessions, parole staff attempt to lower anxiety about meeting the board or hearing examiners. When an inmate has been granted parole or becomes eligible for conditional release, he or she will meet with a parole staff member for a final discussion of the release program and rules of supervision before leaving the prison.

In some jurisdictions institutional parole staff are responsible for notifying victims and local law enforcement agencies of the impending release of certain offenders. (Some states require that when an offender is released, the police in the area where the parolee is to reside, or where the crime occurred, be notified. In some instances, the parolee must register in person with the local law enforcement agency.) The institutional parole staff must determine the probable disposition of any warrants that have been lodged against an inmate. When appropriate, the staff arranges for an out-of-state program under the Interstate Compact (discussed in Chapter 11). In some states, the nonparole institutional staff performs the same, or similar, functions as institutional parole officers; these persons sometimes have the title of *correctional counselor.*

INSTITUTIONAL PAROLE SERVICES IN NEW JERSEY

Members of the institutional parole staff are housed in 14 major institutions, providing services to all state penal and correctional facilities and training schools. They conduct personal interviews with inmates, provide counseling on specific matters to resolve problems, and help develop suitable pre-parole plans. Staff members afford every inmate prerelease classes. They also assist inmates in obtaining necessary clothing and transportation from institutions to residences. Parole staff members also provide institutional services to county correctional institutions and to various community release/residential centers. The increase in the use of home visits and furloughs and the number of state prisoners in county correctional facilities have added considerably to the workloads of institutional parole office staff.

STREET READINESS PROGRAM IN NEVADA

The Street Readiness Program (SRP) of the Department of Probation and Parole works with inmates about to be released into the community on parole and those committed for 120-day evaluations who are returning to court for sentencing. These inmates become students three hours a day for a period of three weeks, normally just before their release. The curriculum consists of classroom lecture, discussions, activities, and homework. Subjects include parole orientation, goals, decision-making skills, substance abuse, domestic relations, financial responsibility, citizenship, employment skills, sex education, law, insurance, human relations, and driver training. Established in 1981, the program is almost totally dependent on community volunteers.

FIELD SERVICES

The field service staff usually operates out of district offices located throughout the state. The New York State Division of Parole, for example, has field staff assigned to the supervision of parolees and conditional releasees in 20 field area offices throughout New York. Staff members conduct field investigations requested by institutional staff relative to parole release programs and supervise parolees and conditional releasees. Parole field staff may also be involved in a variety of special programs, such as work release and furloughs. In New York, "Some Field Officers are assigned to correctional facilities to supervise Temporary Release participants—inmates permitted by the Department of Correctional Services to work, attend school, provide community service, and reestablish family ties (furloughs)."

FIELD SERVICES IN CALIFORNIA

The California legislature has found and declared that the period immediately following incarceration is critical to successful reintegration of the offender into society and to positive citizenship. In the interest of public safety, the state should provide for the supervision and surveillance of parolees, as well as educational, vocational, family, and personal counseling necessary to assist parolees in the transition between imprisonment and discharge.

The overall objective of the Parole and Community Services Division is to reduce the frequency and severity of criminal behavior and to facilitate the community adjustment of adult offenders, fully recognizing their individual and changing circumstances and actions, through a program structure of appropriate prerelease, supervision, and support management functions.

Supervision, surveillance, and services delivery are the responsibilities of parole field staff throughout the state. The primary means by which a parole agent fulfills these responsibilities is through contacts with parolees and persons involved with the parolee. Parole staff will cooperate and collaborate with criminal justice and human service agencies that may be involved with the parolee. It is the duty and obligation of the parole agent to

- Obtain information about parolee activities and needs.
- Intervene in parolee behavior that violates the conditions of parole or may jeopardize the safety of the public or the parolee.
- Provide supportive services to assist the parolee in the transition between imprisonment and discharge.
- Share information about the parolee with law enforcement personnel and the personnel of other agencies who have a demonstrated or compelling need to know.

FIELD SERVICES IN PENNSYLVANIA

Once the board has made a decision to release an inmate on parole, the board's Bureau of Supervision staff plays a significant role in assisting the parolee in adjusting to life in the community. The parole period is a time of transition from the structured, confined environment of the institution to life as a free citizen. Parole is also a time to test the readiness of the parolee to handle the responsibilities of community life.

The immediate goal of parole supervision is the protection of society, which can best be accomplished by reintegrating the offender into the community as a responsible and productive citizen. Specifically, this goal means helping the parolee obtain and hold a meaningful job; resolving any adjustment problems within the family and the community; meeting education, mental health, or other normative needs, when relevant; and becoming part of the community through participation in activities and organizations that reflect the person's interests and capability. This involves not only working with the person under supervision, but also with the various community agencies and resources that have the capability of assisting in solution of problems of parolees.

One of the tools of the supervision staff is "Conditions Governing Parole/Reparole" established by the board to be used as a structuring force in the life of the parolee. These conditions define what course of behavior is acceptable if the client wishes to complete the period of parole supervision successfully. Although several common conditions are to be adhered to, the board recognizes the needs of the individual offender and has provided for one or more special conditions to be imposed as needed.

CONDITIONS OF PAROLE

Every conditionally released or paroled prisoner is required to sign an agreement to abide by certain regulations. This aspect of parole has its origins in the Ticket of Leave, and as noted in Chapter 7, modern parole conditions resemble Ticket of Leave regulations. Parole conditions are similar throughout most jurisdictions, and they are also similar or identical to probation regulations. Lawrence Travis and Edward Latessa report that since 1969 states have tended to reduce the number of conditions imposed on parolees: "Exceptions to this trend are found when parole . . . conditions relate directly to the control of illegal behavior and the ability of the parole authority to maintain supervision over released offenders. This is seen particularly in conditions relating to the reporting of arrests, compliance with the law, possession of narcotics, and possession of weapons" (1984: 598).

Conditions of parole can generally be grouped into *standard conditions* applicable to all parolees/conditional releasees, which typically involve restrictions on travel, associating with other offenders, drug and alcohol use, employment, and residence; and *special conditions* that are tailored to the individual requirement of a particular offender (Figures 8.10 and 8.11). For example, persons with a history of sex offenses against children will be prohibited from areas where children typically congregate, such as playgrounds; persons with a history of alcohol abuse may be prohibited from using alcohol or being in facilities, such as bars, where alcohol is consumed. In more recent years, some parole agencies have been requiring parolees to pay supervision fees. In Texas, parolees are required to pay a standard monthly fee of $10 plus $5 for the victim's fund; those convicted of certain offenses must pay an additional $8 to the fund.

LENGTH OF SUPERVISION

The length of time an offender must spend on parole/conditional release supervision is governed by the length of the sentence and the laws of the state where convicted. In Oregon, a conditional releasee "is subject to a period of supervision similar to parole, not to exceed six months or the maximum date, whichever comes first." In Indiana, persons are to be discharged no later than one year after conditional release. In Illinois, the length of supervision for conditional releasees varies from one to three years, depending on the class of crime for which the offender was convicted. In California, for persons sentenced under a life sentence, the maximum period, including time under parole supervision and time under revocation status, cannot exceed seven years. For persons sentenced under a nonlife sentence, the maximum period, including time under supervision and time under revocation status, cannot exceed four years.[1]

In most states a parolee/releasee can be discharged before the expiration of sentence or mandated period of supervision. In California, based on satisfactory performance, a nonlife releasee can be discharged from supervision after one year and a lifer after three years. In New York, "If the board of parole is satisfied that an absolute discharge from parole or from conditional release is in the best interests of society, the board may grant such discharge prior to the expiration of the full maximum term to any person who has been on unrevoked parole or conditional release for at least three consecutive years." The Hawaii Paroling Authority can issue a discharge whenever "the parolee has demonstrated for a sustained period of time that the parolee is unlikely to commit another crime and the parolee's discharge is compatible with public safety." In any event, parolees under supervision for at least five years "shall be brought before the Paroling Authority for purposes of consideration for final discharge." In Alabama, however, "early termination in parole cases may be accomplished

---

[1]Three experienced drug researchers recommend that for substance abusers—probably most parolees—the period of supervision should be a lengthy one: "Because most abusers have had several years of dysfunctional drug use before coming to the attention of treatment or criminal justice system authorities, it is not unreasonable to expect that several more years will be necessary to control, reduce, and ultimately eliminate their drug use" (Hser, Longshore, and Anglin, 1994: 33).

Colorado Conditions of Parole

1. RELEASE: (if applicable) Upon arrival from the sending state, Parolee shall report to: _____

2. RESIDENCE: Parolee shall establish a residence of record and shall reside at such residence in fact and on record shall not change this place of residence without the consent of his Parole Officer; and shall not leave the area paroled to nor the State paroled to without the permssion of the Parole Officer.

3. CONDUCT: Parolee shall obey all State and Federal laws and Municipal ordinances at all times. Parolee shall follow the directives of the Parole Officer.

4. REPORT: Parolee shall make written and in person reports as directed by the Parole Officer and shall permit visits to place of residence as required by the Parole Officer.

    a. Parolee further shall submit urinalysis or other tests for narcotics or chemical agents upon the request of the Parole Officer, and is required to pay for all tests.

    b. Parolee further agrees to allow the Parole Officer to search his person, or his residence or any premises under his control or any vehicle under his control upon request.

5. WEAPONS: Parolee shall not own, possess, nor have under his control or in his custody firearms or other deadly weapons.

6. ASSOCIATION: Parolee shall not associate with any person with a criminal record without the permission of the Parole Officer.

7. EMPLOYMENT: Parolee shall seek and obtain employment or shall participate in a full-time education or vocational program, unless waived by the Parole Officer.

8. ALCOHOL/DRUGS: Parolee shall not abuse alcoholic beverages or use illegal drugs.

9. ADDITIONAL CONDITIONS:

I have read the foregoing document or have had it read to me and I have full and intelligent understanding of the contents and the meaning thereof, and I have received a copy of this document.

I hereby affix my signature of my own free will and without reservation or coercion.

_____   _____
Parole Officer   Parolee

                                       _____
                                       Date

FIGURE 8.10   Conditions of parole, Colorado.

FORM 4009

STATE OF NEW YORK
EXECUTIVE DEPARTMENT – DIVISION OF PAROLE
GENERAL RULES GOVERNING PAROLE

When an inmate of a correctional institution is approved for parole or conditional release, he or she must agree to the following conditions of parole which are made a part of the release agreement:

I will voluntarily accept Parole supervision. I fully understand that my person, residence and property are subject to search and inspection. I understand that parole supervision is defined by these Conditions of Release and all other conditions that may be imposed upon me by the Board or its representatives. I understand that my violation of these conditions may result in the revocation of my release.

CONDITIONS OF RELEASE

1. I will proceed directly to the area to which I have been released and, within twenty-four hours of my release, make my arrival report to that Office of the Division of Parole unless other instructions are designated on my release agreement.

2. I will make office and/or written reports as directed.

3. I will not leave the State of New York or any other State to which I am released or transferred, or any area defined in writing by my Parole Officer without permission.

4. I will permit my Parole Officer to visit me at my residence and/or place of employment and I will permit the search and inspection of my person, residence and property. I will discuss any proposed changes in my residence, employment or program status with my Parole Officer. I understand that I have an immediate and continuing duty to notify my Parole Officer of any changes in my residence, employment or program status when circumstances beyond my control make prior discussion impossible.

5. I will reply promptly, fully and truthfully to any inquiry of or communication by my Parole Officer or other representative of the Division of Parole.

6. I will notify my Parole Officer immediately any time I am in contact with or arrested by any law enforcement agency. I understand that I have a continued duty to notify my Parole Officer of such contact or arrest.

7. I will not be in the company of or fraternize with any person I know to have a criminal record or whom I know to have been adjudicated a Youthful Offender except for accidental encounters in public places, work, school or in any other instance with the permission of my Parole Officer.

8. I will not behave in such manner as to violate the provisions of any law to which I am subject which provide for a penalty of imprisonment, nor will my behavior threaten the safety or well-being of myself or others.

9. I will not own, possess, or purchase any shotgun, rifle or firearm of any type without the written permission of my Parole Officer. I will not own, possess or purchase any deadly weapon as defined in the Penal law or any dangerous knife, dirk, razor, stiletto or imitation pistol. In addition, I wIll not own, possess or purchase any instrument readily capable of causing physical injury without a satisfactory explanation for ownership, possession or purchase.

10. In the event that I leave the jurisdiction of the State of New York, I hereby waive my right to resist extradition to the State of New York from any state in the Union and from any territory or country outside the United States. This waiver shall be in full force and effect until I am discharged from Parole or Conditional Release. I fully understand that I have the right under the Constitution of the United States and under law to contest any effort to extradite me from another state and return me to New York, and I freely and knowingly waive this right as a condition of my Parole or Conditional Release.

11. I will not use or possess any drug paraphernalia or use or possess any controlled substance without proper medical authorization.

12. Special Conditions:

13. I will fully comply with the instructions of my Parole Officer and obey such special additional written conditions as he, a Member of the Board of Parole or an authorized representative of the Divison of Parole, may impose.

FIGURE 8.11   General Rules Governing Parole, State of New York.

only by means of a Pardon, which will be considered after a subject has served five years under supervision." The same board that is responsible for parole in Alabama, the Board of Pardons and Paroles, has the power to grant pardons. In Vermont, "although the Board may terminate parole supervision at any time, it will normally consider termination only after successful completion of one half of the maximum parole term." In Virginia, for cases exceeding five years, discharge is considered following the fifth anniversary of release.

WOMEN ON PAROLE IN NEW YORK

Relatively few women are sentenced to prison, and they constitute only 6 percent of the parolee caseload in New York; 76 percent of them reside in the New York City area. Women parolees tend to be older than their male counterparts; their education levels are similar, with their unemployment rate slightly higher. Fewer women than men had a history of alcohol abuse, although they were equal with respect to drug abuse problems.

VIOLATION OF PAROLE/CONDITIONAL RELEASE

Probation violation is linked to the judicial system, whereas parole violation is an administrative function that is typically devoid of court involvement. Although some variation exists with respect to the procedures used, Figure 8.12 presents a general overview of the system and indicates the possibilities available at each stage of the process.

There are two types of parole violation:

1. *Technical violation.* This occurs when any of the conditions of parole have been violated.
2. *New offense violation.* This involves an arrest and prosecution for the commission of a new crime. In practice, new offense violations often involve technical violations. A new offense violation, for example, an arrest for robbery that involves a gun, also constitutes a technical violation of the conditions prohibiting possession of firearms.

In either event, the violation process begins when a parole officer (the title varies: for example, probation and parole officer, parole agent, correctional program officer, probation/parole supervisor) becomes aware of a violation. After discussing the situation with a supervisor, a decision is made relative to the issuance of a warrant. This stage has the greatest amount of variance between agencies. In Pennsylvania, parole agents can use an "order to detain for 48 hours" in lieu of a warrant when circumstances require it. A similar situation obtains in New York, where field parole officers carry a 24-hour detainer-warrant. Thus, in Pennsylvania and New York, a parole agent/officer who

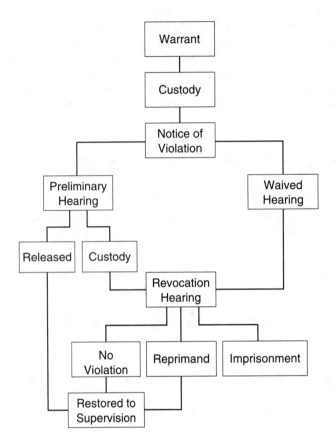

FIGURE 8.12 Probation /conditional release violation flowchart.

becomes aware of a serious violation of parole while in the field can summarily take the violator into custody and receive telephone authorization for the use of the order to detain or 24-hour detainer-warrant. (These temporary detainers must be replaced by a warrant: in Pennsylvania, within 48 hours; in New York, within 24 hours). When I was a parole officer in New York, it was not unusual to encounter parolees, unexpectedly, who were in serious violation of the conditions of their release: for example, those heavily involved in abusing heroin (and engaging in criminal acts to support the habit); those prohibited from the use of alcohol (because of the dangerous nature of their behavior while under the influence) and intoxicated; or child sex offenders found in the company of children. I could take such persons into custody immediately and use the telephone for detainer-warrant authorization. (In the opinion of this writer, agencies that do not provide their officers with this authority endanger public safety. This point is discussed further in Chapter 10.)

In jurisdictions that are rather conservative about issuing violation warrants, the process may be time-consuming and involve a written request to the board of parole. In Oregon, in lieu of a summary arrest, the parole officer may issue a *citation* requiring the parolee/releasee to appear for a violation hearing. This citation is authorized when the person has violated a condition of supervi-

STATE OF COLORADO

DIVISION OF ADULT PAROLE SUPERVISION

REPORT OF INVESTIGATION

To:	Leslee V. Waggener, Supervisor	Name:	BROUWER, Robert
From:	Bill Samudio, Parole Officer	DOC #:	50951
Re:	Parole Search of Residence	Date:	September 23, 1994

On 08/18/94, at approximately 4:00 P.M., at the location of 1450 Reed #2, Lakewood, CO, Supervisor Leslee Waggener and I, Officer Bill Samudio, were on a routine home visit of Robert Brouwer's (DOC 50951) residence.

As we approached the front door of his residence, we saw that it was opened and that no one was in the front room. We walked into the residence, and I called out to see if Mr. Brouwer was in the residence. I heard Brouwer say from the back room, "'I'm in the bathroom."

Supervisor Waggener slowly opened the door of the back room, but we did not see anyone inside. I then walked across the room and positioned myself so I could have a clear view of the bathroom. Mr. Brouwer was sitting on the toilet in the bathroom. I quickly looked around the room and noticed a spoon with white residue on the floor.

We asked Mr. Brouwer to step into the living room and questioned him about his drug use. Mr. Brouwer informed us that he had used methamphetamine and marijuana early that morning, but nothing else that day. I then had Mr. Brouwer sit in a chair in the living room while Supervisor Waggener searched the bedroom. Supervisor Waggener also called the Lakewood Police Department at that time to request assistance.

I placed Mr. Brouwer in custody and informed him that he was under arrest for parole violations. At this time the Lakewood officers arrived. We asked them if they could take custody of Mr. Brouwer while we completed the search of the apartment. We began a thorough search of the apartment and confiscated the following items:

1 check (#95), $100 amount	1 Winchester 30–30 round
1 Remington .44 mag	1 straight-edged razor (container #15551)
2 containers—misc. pills—"Slow K"	2 empty prescription containers: (a) Serax;
1 mirror (12 x 12) w/etched bird	(b) Propoxyphen
48 Insulin syringes (appeared unused)	1 Krazy Glue (container #15557)
1 green leafy substance	1 spoon with residue
1 syringe filled with liquid (container #15491)	2 used syringes (container #5494)
2 syringes (container #15487)	

We then regained custody of Mr. Brouwer, and transported him to the Jefferson County Jail and booked him into the jail. All the evidence was confiscated, placed in evidence bags, properly labeled, and placed in the Denver Parole Safe.

On 8/28/94, I took the evidence collected in this case to the CBI Lab and had it analyzed. On 9/12/94, the CBI Lab provided our office with the results, which indicated the presence of methamphetamine in the clear liquid contained in the syringe and the presence of *cannabis sativa* (marijuana) in the green leafy substance submitted to the lab.

sion, but the nature of the violation does not jeopardize the safety of the general public, and the person, if left undetained, is not likely to flee. In Iowa:

> A parole officer having probable cause to believe that any person released on parole has violated the conditions of parole may arrest such person, or the parole officer may make a complaint before a magistrate, charging such violation, and if it appears from such complaint . . . that there is probable cause to believe that such person has violated the terms of parole, the magistrate shall issue a warrant for the arrest of such person. In either event, the violator must be taken before a magistrate for consideration of

release on bail—"bail is discretionary with the magistrate and is not a matter of right" in Iowa.

Many, if not most, jurisdictions do not permit a parole violator to be released on bail.

In Wisconsin, in lieu of an arrest or warrant issuance, a parole agent's immediate supervisor can order the alleged violator to appear for a *case review*: "The focus of case review is threefold: to determine whether there is probable cause to believe there was a violation of the rules or conditions of probation or parole, to determine whether, if there is probable cause, it makes correctional sense to revoke, and to determine whether the client should remain in custody during revocation proceedings." Although this case review has many of the characteristics of a preliminary hearing, to be discussed shortly, the review is both more broadly focused—can consider issues relating to supervision adjustment—and less formal: "It is hoped by making the proceedings less formal and adversary, the client, the client's attorney, the agent and the agent's supervisor can frankly discuss the issues in an atmosphere that focuses attention on the most important issues."

PRELIMINARY HEARING

If a parolee/conditional releasee has been arrested pursuant to a violation warrant, or if the offender is in custody for a new offense and a violation warrant has been filed as a detainer, the parole officer will provide him or her with a notice of a preliminary hearing and a list of the alleged violations. The purpose of the preliminary hearing is to determine if *probable cause* exists to establish that the offender has committed an act(s) that constitutes a violation of the conditions of release. This hearing is required if the offender is to be detained on a warrant pending a revocation hearing; furthermore, the hearing is required within 15 days of the time the warrant was executed by arrest or filed. If no warrant has been issued—the subject is not being held in custody by parole authorities—but the offender has been summoned to appear for a revocation hearing, a preliminary hearing is not necessary. (About a half-dozen states do not use a preliminary hearing.) The offender may also waive the right to a preliminary hearing (Figure 8.13).

At the preliminary hearing the parolee/conditional releasee will have an opportunity to challenge the alleged violations and (a limited right) to confront and cross-examine adverse witnesses, including the parole officer, and to present evidence on his or her own behalf (Figure 8.14). The offender can be represented by legal counsel, although the state is not constitutionally required to provide an attorney. As opposed to the rules of evidence in the criminal process, hearsay is admissible at preliminary hearings (although hearsay is not used alone to determine probable cause). The hearing officer who presides is usually an attorney regularly employed for this purpose by the agency. However, any agency employee who is not directly involved in the case may fulfill this role. As a senior parole officer in New York, for example, I frequently

DEPARTMENT OF REHABILITATION & CORRECTION
ADULT PAROLE AUTHORITY

WAIVER OF RELEASE VIOLATION PRELIMINARY HEARING

I, _____ Institution Number _____
have been apprised of my right to an On-Site Violation Hearing and the minimum due
process which provides that during this Hearing I have the right to appear and speak in
my own behalf; to bring letters, documents, or other evidence for presentation at the
Hearing; and to have any individuals who can give relevant information to the hearing
officer subpoenaed by the Adult Parole Authority to appear in my behalf; furthermore, I
understand I do have the right to request representation by counsel. Persons who have
provided evidence against me will be made available for questioning in my presence
unless the hearing officer determines that the identity of such persons is not known to
me and that such persons would be subjected to risk of harm if their identities were
disclosed. If the hearing officer determines that there is probable cause to hold me for
return to the institution I am still entitled to a revocation hearing before the Parole
Board upon being returned to the institution. I also understand that I am entitled to a
digest of my On-Site Hearing.
I understand that should I elect to waive said On-Site Hearing, the alleged violations
and evidence against me will be administratively reviewed. Such review may result in
a determination to hold a final revocation hearing by the Parole Board. If I am
returned to the institution for a final revocation hearing, I understand that the hearing
will occur within sixty (60) days of the filing of an Adult Parole Authority detainer
unless I have been unavailable to the Adult Parole Authority, in which case my
revocation hearing will take place within a reasonable time of my availablility to the
Adult Parole Authority.
Being fully advised of these rights and conditions, and having been given notice of my
alleged release violation(s) I do hereby agree to waive my right to such an On-Site
Hearing without promise or threat of any kind having been made.
If releasee is unable to read, the language above was read in his presence and explained
to him.

_____   _____
RELEASEE   DATE   WITNESS   DATE

FIGURE 8.13   Waiver of a preliminary hearing, Ohio.

served as a hearing officer when personnel normally fulfilling this function were
unavailable. Because this hearing is a relatively minimal and informal inquiry,
the hearing officer need not hear all of the allegations for a finding of probable
cause.

If the hearing officer determines that evidence sufficient to make a finding
of probable cause has not been presented, the parolee/conditional releasee will
be restored to supervision. If probable cause is found, the offender will be held
in custody pending a revocation hearing. Before the revocation hearing, the
parole officer will prepare a violation of parole report for use at the hearing
(Figure 8.15).

STATE OF NEVADA BOARD OF PAROLE

SUMMARY OF PRELIMINARY INQUIRY HEARING
RE: Blackstone, John L.
    File No. L82-001
    Criminal Case No. 28001

The above-named subject appeared for a Preliminary Inquiry on July 19, 1994, at the hour of 2:20 P.M. at the Carson City Jail.

RIGHTS VERIFIED

Hearing Officer Sally Gomez inquired of defendant Blackstone if he had received copies of the Violation Report dated July 6, 1988, and the "Notice of Preliminary Inquiry Hearing" form listing his rights per the *Morrissey* and *Scarpelli* decisions. Blackstone replied that he had both documents and had read them. He also indicated that he fully understood the charges and his rights during the violation process as explained in the form. It is noted that Blackstone retained as private counsel for this hearing Michael Smith, Esq., of Carson City. Blackstone says he is satisfied with counsel and the time for preparing the defense case. With the indication that Mr. Blackstone fully understands his rights in this matter, we will proceed with the hearing.

VIOLATION CASE

Parole and Probation Officer James Richards read in part the Violation Report dated July 6, 1994, which indicates that Mr. Blackstone is charged with violation of Rule 9 of the Parole Agreement, WEAPONS. It was read that Blackstone was found in possession of a snub-nose .38 pistol by Police Sergeant John Brown in the After Hours Bar, 111 N. Carson Street, City of Carson, Nevada, at about 11:00 P.M. on July 4, 1994. Blackstone had shown the weapon to another customer of the bar, a Mr. William Mundy, allegedly stating to Mundy: "Sucker, I'm going to blow you apart if you keep bugging me tonight." Mundy left the bar and phoned the police to complain of the threat from Blackstone. Sgt. Brown arrived at the bar with several officers and asked Blackstone about the alleged weapon. Blackstone admitted to having an unloaded revolver in his coat pocket, and Sgt. Brown removed same without incident. Blackstone was then placed under arrest for "assault" and an "ex-felon in possession of a firearm." He was transported to the Carson County Jail and booked. Parole Officer Richards placed a Hold for Parole Violation Investigation on Blackstone the following day, July 5, 1994, at about 10:00 A.M.

Officer Richards called William Mundy as his first witness. Mundy told how Blackstone had come into the bar and sat next to him at the counter. Mundy tried to engage Blackstone in some friendly conversation, but Blackstone told him to "shut up and to quit bugging him" or he'd "blow his body apart," showing Mundy a small pistol taken from his coat pocket. Mundy says that he immediately left the bar and called the police, complaining of the incident and asking that the police arrest Blackstone. Mundy identified John L. Blackstone as the person who threatened him in the After Hours Bar on July 4, 1994. Mundy was dismissed after the defense had no questions of him.

Officer Richards called his second witness, Sgt. John Brown of the Carson City Police Department to testify in this case. Brown related that he was dispatched to the After Hours Bar at about 10:55 p.m. on July 4, 1994, to investigate a citizen's complaint of a man with a gun making threats in the bar to shoot him. On arrival, Brown said he was met by Mr. Mundy at the entrance of the bar and that Mundy pointed Mr. Blackstone out for him in the crowded bar. The officer approached Blackstone and asked him if he was carrying a weapon in his coat pocket; Brown said that Blackstone informed him that he had an unloaded pistol in his righthand coat pocket. Sgt. Brown then removed the weapon from Blackstone's right coat pocket and found that it was empty of shells. Sgt. Brown directed Blackstone to step outside the bar with him. Sgt. Brown

FIGURE 8.14 Summary of a preliminary/probable cause hearing.

advised Blackstone that he was being placed under arrest for "simple assault" on the complaint of Mr. William Mundy and that he would have to come to the jail for booking but could post bail that evening. Blackstone went along to the jail without incident.

On arrival at the jail, the head jailer told Sgt. Brown that Mr. Blackstone was a parolee and should also be booked for the felony charge of "ex-felon with a firearm." Thus, he was so booked. Sgt. Brown was dismissed after the defense offered no cross-examination.

Officer Richards rested his prosecution case, noting that Blackstone has one felony charge of "Felon in Possession of Firearm" pending in Carson Justice Court. A preliminary hearing has been set for July 30, 1994, on the case. The weapon was not present at this hearing but listed as in the evidence locker of the Carson City Police.

DEFENSE CASE

Attorney for the accused Blackstone stated that he would decline to present any evidence or statements at this time regarding the possession of the weapon as the case was a felony charge awaiting disposition in Justice Court. However, attorney Smith did offer a defense witness, Gary Jones, to tell of the alleged threats in the bar. Jones was called into the hearing room and related he was sitting near the counter at a small table next to John Blackstone and Mundy at about 10:30 on July 4, 1994. Mundy, Jones explained, was "pretty drunk" and kept slapping Blackstone on the back, calling him "pal" and "buddy," and so on. Blackstone told Mundy to leave him alone and Mundy got mad and left the bar in a "huff," Jones testified. A short time later, Jones testified, police officers took Blackstone out of the bar and that is the last time he saw Blackstone until today. Attorney Smith suggested that Blackstone did not threaten Mundy in the manner alleged by Mundy. Hearing Officer Gomez asked Jones if he saw Blackstone take anything out of his coat pocket and show it to Mundy. Jones replied, "no." Richards asked Jones if he could have missed seeing Blackstone show Mundy the gun and say he was going to "blow him apart." Jones was hesitant but said, he was pretty sure; because of the back slapping he was watching the incident pretty closely, wondering what Mundy was going to do next.

Attorney Smith closed the defense, advising Blackstone not to make any statements to the hearing officer until the Justice Court case was held.

FINDINGS

Having considered the evidence presented in this case by both the charging officer and the defendant, this hearing officer finds that probable cause exists to continue detention on the charge of violation of parole rule #9, WEAPONS. The hearing officer has determined that probable cause exists to continue detention pending your formal revocation hearing before the Board of Parole. You are duly notified that at the formal revocation hearing the Board of Parole has the discretion to review and act on all charges that were presented at this preliminary inquiry. With no further evidence to be heard, this hearing will be closed at 3:40 p.m., July 19, 1994.

Respectfully submitted,

Sally Gomez

Hearing Officer

FIGURE 8.14 (*continued*)

STATE OF NEW YORK - EXECUTIVE DEPARTMENT - DIVISION OF PAROLE

VIOLATION OF RELEASE REPORT
Warrant issued 3-7-93   *No Warrant Issued*

Name: Hughes, Sam   Date Released: 12-27-92
NYSID NO: 4172822M   Max. Expiration: 12-27-98
Institution: Woodbourne   Date of Warrant: 3-7-93
DIN NO: 87-A-5840   Warrant No.: 1234
Date of Birth: 12-23-62   Date Enforced: 3-20-93
Offense: Att. Robb. 1st°/   Location: Brooklyn House of
    Att. Robb. 1st°   Detention
Sentence:: 1-6-0/4-6-0/1-6-0/4-6-0   PVU No.: 1234

Delinquency Date: 3-4-93

*Since his/her release, the above named individual has violated the Conditions of Release in the
following manner:*

1. The subject, in violation of rule 2, failed to report to Parole Officer Kaplan at 314 West
   40th Street on 3/4/93 as directed on 2/25/93 by P.O. Kaplan.
2. The subject, in violation of rule 4, on or about 3/5/93 admittedly changed his residence of
   3140 Atlantic Avenue, Apt. 3B, Brooklyn, NY, without the knowledge or permission of his
   parole officer.
3. The subject, in violation of rule 13, on 3/5/93 and thereafter admittedly failed to abide by
   a curfew established on 2/10/93 by being out of his approved residence between the
   hours of 11:00 P.M. to 6:00 A.M.
4. The subject, in violation of rule 12, on or about 3/5/93 failed to maintain his employment
   as directed by the Board or Parole by leaving his employment at XYZ Carting and not
   returning to that employment.
5. The subject, in violation of rule 13, on 3/19/93 used alcoholic beverages after having
   been specifically directed by his parole officer on 2/10/93 to abstain from such use. The
   subject was under the influence of alcoholic beverages when apprehended by Sgt. Coors
   at 6:30 P.M. on that date.
6. The subject, on 3/19/93 in violation of rule 9 at 6:30 P.M. on Flatbush Avenue in Brooklyn
   possessed a dangerous knife readily capable of causing physical injury without the
   permission of his parole officer.
7. The subject, in violation of rule 8, on 3/19/93 at 6:30 P.M. on Flatbush Avenue in Brooklyn
   attempted to take a bank bag from a Susan Anthony without her permission while armed
   with a knife. Such behavior is a violation of the provisions of the Penal Law and may
   result in a penalty of imprisonment.

Possible Witnesses:
John Jones
Susan Anthony
Sam Smith
Sgt. Coors, NYPD 84 Precinct

Possible Exhibits:
Arrest Report NYPD
Voluntary Statement
Possible Certificate of Conviction
Special Conditions of Release to Parole Supervision

CRIME OF CONVICTION

The subject is presently serving two consecutive terms of 1–6–0/4–6–0 and 1–6–0/4–6–0 for
attempted robbery 1st and attempted robbery 1st. The first conviction indicates that the

FIGURE 8.15 Violation of Release Report.

subject, while acting in concert, on 8/5/89 followed two 10-year-old male children from a store to the lobby of a building. The subject and his codefendants then displayed a knife, twisted one of the victims' arms and demanded money. During the course of the offense they cut one of the victims on the finger. The second offense indicates that the subject followed a pregnant 16-year-old into an elevator, simulated a weapon and took approximately $105 worth of clothing. An underlying charge also included in the plea on this instant offense occurred at the same location approximately two weeks later when the subject took a bag of groceries and $1.75 from another 10-year-old child. The subject was positively identified by all victims in both charges. The parolee met the Board of Parole at Woodbourne Correctional Facility as an initial applicant and was paroled on 12/27/92. He has a projected maximum expiration date of 12/27/98.

PRIOR VIOLATIONS ON THE INSTANT OFFENSE:
This is the subject's first release from this charge.

CRIMINAL HISTORY:

Arrest Date	Charge	Place	Disposition
7-31-80	Sexual Abuse	Kings Crim. Ct.	Prob. 3 yrs. Plea to Public Lewdness
9-9-80	Harassment	Kings Crim. Ct.	Conditional Discharge
3-10-81	Public Lewdness	Kings Crim. Ct.	Dismissed
7-5-81	Public Lewdness	Man. Crim. Ct.	Dismissed
9-20-82	Assault 1st Robbery 2nd	Kings Sup. Ct.	Adjudicated Youthful Off. 1-4-0/4-0-0 yrs.
10-10-83	Att. Sex. Abu.	Kings Crim Ct.	90 days
7-14-85	Dis. Conduct	Bronx Crim. Ct.	Conditional Dischar.
9-22-86	Public Lewd.	Kings Crim. Ct.	Dismissed
10-17-88	Sex. Abuse	Kings Crim. Ct.	Dismissed

The subject has a prior conviction for robbery and assault for which he received youthful offender consideration. It should also be noted that the subject has amassed a number of arrests for sexually oriented type of behavior.

PRIOR PAROLE HISTORY:

The subject was previously on parole as a youthful offender for the act of assault and robbery. The subject was conditionally released and was cited for a violation within a month. The disposition of the Board of Parole at that time was the subject be ordered returned and held to maximum expiration date.

CURRENT VIOLATION BEHAVIOR:

The subject, following only two months in the community, reverted to prior violative behavior in that he immediately became involved in a similar offense to the crime of conviction. The parolee failed to avail himself of parole services in that he stopped reporting. Additionally, referrals made to a mental hygiene unit at Downstate Medical Center were seldom attended by the subject, and he never reinvolved himself in this program.

FIGURE 8.15 *(continued)*

GENERAL ADJUSTMENT TO PAROLE SUPERVISION:

The subject initially appeared to be making a good adjustment to parole supervision. He reported regularly and appeared to be functioning as a member in the home. The subject was on intensive supervision and had been directed to report weekly; however, he stopped reporting on 3/4/93. Regular home visits had been made and the wife was very interested in the subject's well being and continued rehabilitation. Present in the home beside the subject's wife, Sylvia Butler, were their three children. Despite his initial satisfactory adjustment, his behavior began to relapse; special conditions were placed upon him and then the home situation improved.

The subject suddenly became antagonistic in the home and refused to participate in the family activities. Because of the wife's fear, she and the three children moved out on 2/27/93.

The subject was released to an employment program at a grocery store in Brooklyn. The job, however, never materialized, but he was able to find employment at XYZ Carting Services also located in Brooklyn. The employer reported that he was an excellent employee and that they would not hesitate to rehire him. Employer indicated that he had a short duration of being tardy, but that situation changed; the employer was disappointed when he left work and did not return; he was therefore discharged. The subject's employer John Jones was visited and he appeared very interested in the subject.

The subject was released from the correctional facility with a prescription for hypertension medication. He was referred to Downstate Medical Center, Mental Hygiene Unit to evaluate his mental and physical condition. Additionally, the subject began using and abusing alcohol and was re-referred and directed to attend the program at Downstate Medical Center in an effort to meet all of his needs in one coordinated setting. However, since the subject attended the clinic on an only occasional basis, real change could not occur.

The subject was released from the correctional facility with special conditions of seek, obtain, maintain employment, curfew and support dependents. A Mental Hygiene referral at the discretion of the parole officer was also noted. The subject did abide by the employment condition in that he was employed up until 2/27 with a Carting firm in Brooklyn. He not only complied with this special condition until 2/27, but he appeared to make an excellent adjustment.

A curfew was placed on the subject upon his release; it came to the attention of this writer that he began violating the curfew hours. On 2/10/93 a more strict curfew was established from 11:00 P.M. to 6:00 A.M. A condition of abstention from alcoholic beverages to change his behavior was also mandated. This appeared to work until the end of February when he stopped reporting, quit his job, and his wife left him. The subject had been supporting the home prior thereto. He was referred to Downstate Medical Center for mental hygiene, but his attendance was poor.

PAROLEE STATEMENT:

The parolee was apprehended and a warrant was lodged 3/20/93 at which time he was interviewed at the Brooklyn House of Detention. The subject by his own admission admitted leaving his residence, failing to report, quitting his job and beginning drinking. He stated that everything seemed to be going well and then without notice, everything seemed to start falling apart. He indicated that he couldn't get along at home, people at work didn't like him and people in the community were out to "get him." Subject indicated that he purchased a knife to protect himself. The subject further stated that on 3/19/93 he stopped at the Green Onion Tavern to meet a friend. He indicated that he only had a few drinks, the next thing he knows, he was being booked by NYPD. The subject states that he does not believe he attempted to take anything from anyone, but readily admits that he appears to have blacked out.

PRESENT STATUS:

Time on parole 0 yrs., 2 mos., 7 days
Time owned 5 yrs., 9 mos., 23 days

FIGURE 8.15 (continued)

The subject was afforded a preliminary hearing on 3/30/93 at which time probable cause was found. A final hearing has been scheduled for 5/15/93. The subject was indicted by Kings County Grand Jury on 4/3/93 and is awaiting court action. He is being held at the Brooklyn House of Detention on $30,000 bail and on warrant 1234 is lodged as a detainer; the book and case number is 176-90-14769.

Robert Kaplan

Robert Kaplan
Parole Officer   April 12, 1993

William Haley

William Haley
Senior Parole Officer   April 15, 1993

FIGURE 8.15   *(continued)*

REVOCATION HEARING

A revocation hearing is similar to a preliminary hearing except that it is more comprehensive. The purpose of the revocation hearing is to determine if the violation of parole/conditional release is serious enough to revoke supervision and return the offender to prison or if some less drastic response is sufficient. In Oregon, for example, certain violators are sent to prison for a time-limited term—six months—but under rather austere conditions: They are

> housed in a medium-security facility and for the first 30 days are allowed out of their individual cells (which have no windows) only three times a week for showers, and for one hour three times a week to exercise in a small concrete structure. After 30 days, they are placed in a two-person cell and given slightly more amenities. After the second 30-day period, they spend the next four months in a dormitory with somewhat increased privileges and amenities. (Parent et al., 1994: 20)

In most jurisdictions, the revocation hearing is presided over by one or more members of the parole board; in other states, it is the responsibility of hearing officers who make recommendations to the parole board for or against revocation. If the board votes against revocation, the offender is restored to supervision.

STREET TIME

If parole is revoked, the question arises as to just how much time the parolee must serve in prison. This sentence can vary from jurisdiction to jurisdiction. In California, parolees returned to prison for a technical violation can be confined for only one year. In New York, a parolee receives credit for the time spent under supervision ("street time") before the violation. Thus, in New York, an inmate who is paroled after serving two years of a four-year sentence is required to be on parole for two years, the remainder of the sentence. If, after one year, the parolee violates parole and is returned to prison, he or she will have to serve only the one-year remaining on the sentence. However, in a state that does not give credit for street time, this same parolee would be required to serve two years in prison; the one-year of satisfactory time on parole would not be credited against the four-year sentence in the event of a parole violation that results in being returned to prison.

CLEMENCY

All states and the federal government (Article II of the Constitution) have provisions for clemency. In 31 states and the federal government, the chief executive holds the final clemency power, and in most of these states the parole board or a clemency board appointed by the governor investigates clemency applications at the request of the governor (Krajick, 1978). In some states, clemency authority is vested entirely in a special board, usually a board of pardons and paroles. Some states conduct formal hearings, and the governor generally must report annually to the legislature on all clemencies granted (National Governors' Association, 1988). Clemency consists of the reprieve, the commutation, and the pardon.

REPRIEVE

A reprieve is a *temporary* suspension of the execution of sentence. As noted in Chapter 2, probation developed, in part, out of the judicial reprieve. Its use today is limited and usually concerns cases in which capital punishment has been ordered. In such cases a governor, or the president of the United States, can grant a reprieve—a stay of execution—to provide more time for legal action or other deliberations.

In Georgia, the Board of Pardons and Paroles may grant a reprieve lasting a few hours or a few days to an inmate so that he or she may visit a critically ill member of the family or attend the funeral of an immediate member of the family. A reprieve may also be granted in Georgia when it is shown that an inmate is suffering from a definable illness for which necessary treatment is available only outside the state prison system. An inmate granted a reprieve will have the reprieve period credited to the sentence if he or she does not violate any of the conditions of the reprieve.

COMMUTATION

A commutation is a modification of sentence to the benefit of an offender. Commutation has been used when an inmate provided some assistance to the prison staff, sometimes during prison riots. Commutation may also be granted to inmates with a severe illness, such as cancer. The laws governing commutation differ from state to state. In New York, an inmate sentenced to more than one year who has served at least one-half of the minimum period of imprisonment, and who is not otherwise eligible for release or parole, may have his or her sentence commuted by the governor. In Georgia, the Board of Pardons and Paroles will consider commuting a sentence when it receives substantial evidence that the sentence is either excessive, illegal, unconstitutional, or void; evidence that justice would be served by a commutation; and evidence that commutation would be in the best interests of society and the inmate. The board may also consider commutation of sentences of death after all other legal remedies have been exhausted. A person whose death sentence has been commuted by the board cannot be pardoned or paroled before serving 25 years. In Maryland, correctional personnel identify candidates who meet criteria established by the governor's office for commutation, and their names are submitted to the parole board for a recommendation to the governor. Commutations are traditionally granted at Christmas time.

PARDON

Following the American Revolution, it was necessary to find a new basis for the pardoning power to replace the English theory that it resided in the king as the fountainhead of justice and mercy. This new basis was found in the theory that the power to pardon was a sovereign power, inherent in the state, but not necessarily inherent in the executive or in any given branch of government. Rather, because the people were the ultimate sovereign, the power resided in them, and they could provide for its exercise through any agency of government they deemed proper.

Although historically the executive would seem the most natural agency in which to entrust this power, the attitude of the American people after the Revolution was not such as to lead to this conclusion. The struggle with the mother country had left them suspicious of the executive. This conflict was natural enough, for the royal governor was not usually sympathetic to the colonists. The champion of the people was usually the lower house of the legislature. Not surprisingly, the early constitutions that replaced the colonial charters tended to place restrictions on the governor's power in many respects, including the power to pardon. Only five states left this power with the governor alone. Six, including the newly admitted state of Vermont, provided that the governor could pardon only with consent of the executive council. Georgia deprived the governor of the pardoning power entirely, giving him only power to reprieve until the meeting of the assembly, which could then make such disposition of the matter as it saw fit. Connecticut and Rhode Island continued to function under their colonial charters, by which the pardoning power was exercised by the general assembly.

By the time the federal Constitution was written, however, opinion had begun to swing back toward placing greater power in the hands of the governor. The framers of the Constitution gave the pardoning power to the president without any limitations as to its exercise or supervision by any other official or agency. The executive councils that several states had set up as a means of preventing too much power from being vested in one person began to lose favor about the same time, and several states began abolishing them, giving the power to the governor.

Toward the end of the 19th century, an overwhelming movement occurred to give the governor some assistance in this task by providing an advisory pardon officer or pardon board. Some states set up pardon boards not merely to advise the governor, but actually to exercise pardoning power, although the governor everywhere was a member, if not the controlling member, of the board (U.S. Attorney General, 1939).

As noted in Chapter 7, the pardon has been used historically in the United States as a form of "parole." As the indeterminate sentence came into use, pardon boards, originally established to advise the governor with respect to release, began to act independently, developing into parole boards. Despite widespread use of parole, however, the power of pardon has continued. In Utah, for example, the Board of Pardons, an independent state agency, has rather extraordinary powers. This three-member body serves as a board of parole, deciding when and under what conditions persons convicted and serving sentences should be released from imprisonment. In addition, the board can commute sentences of death, reduce terms of imprisonment, and completely terminate an offender's sentence regardless of whether he or she is an inmate or on parole. The board also has absolute pardoning authority for the state and can forgive the sentence and restore civil rights, although this power is rarely exercised.

The Alabama Board of Pardons and Parole has similar powers (Figure 8.16). Executive clemency is usually limited to deciding on the granting of relief from disabilities, a limited pardon that restores certain civil and political rights, such as the right to apply to vote (the local board of registrars makes final decisions) and hold certain licenses. To be considered for such a pardon, a person discharged from prison without parole must wait two years; parolees after five years under supervision or two years after discharge; and probationers two years after discharge from supervision. The pardon report, which is prepared by state probation and parole officers, is exhaustive and allows the board to determine if the applicant has become a law-abiding person and a useful citizen in the community.

In California, the Board of Prison Terms investigates all pardon petitions from persons who have been free of criminal conduct for nine-and-one-half years since discharge from probation, parole, or custody. In Maryland, a pardon requires at least five years of exemplary crime-free behavior following release from incarceration and after expiration of any parole supervision. Pardon requests are received by the parole board, which investigates and makes a recommendation to the governor. A governor's pardon restores citizenship rights to the person who has demonstrated a high standard of constructive behavior following conviction for an offense. Pardon applications are considered only after an offender has been discharged from probation or parole for at least 10 years and has not engaged in further criminal conduct. The 10-year rule may be waived in truly exceptional circumstances if the applicant can demonstrate an earlier need for the pardon.

The basis for a pardon may vary in different states, but the pardon is not used extensively anywhere. In New York, the only basis for a pardon is new

State Board of Pardons and Paroles
Montgomery, Alabama

CERTIFICATE OF PARDON WITH RESTORATION
OF CIVIL AND POLITICAL RIGHTS

KNOW ALL MEN BY THESE PRESENTS:

It having been made to appear to the Alabama State Board of Pardons and Paroles that

_____

was convicted in _____ County on _____ , 19 ____

of _____ , was sentenced to a term of   years;

And it further appearing to the Board from the official report of the Parole Officer which is a part of the record in this case, and with no further information to the contrary, that the above named has so conducted himself as to demonstrate his reformation and to merit pardon with restoration of civil rights;

NOW, In compliance with the authority vested in the State Board of Pardons and Paroles by the Constitution and the Laws of the State of Alabama to grant pardons and to restore civil and political rights, it is

ORDERED that a pardon be granted to the above named as a result of the above stated conviction, and all prior disqualifying convictions, and it is further ordered that all civil and political rights which were forfeited as a result of the conviction be and they are hereby restored.

GIVEN UNDER THE HAND AND SEAL of the State of Pardons and Paroles,

this the _____ day of _____ ,19 ____ .

STATE BOARD OF PARDONS AND PAROLES

By _____
                   Executive Director

FIGURE 8.16   Certificate of pardon.

evidence indicating that the person did not commit the offense for which he or she was convicted. In Florida, a pardon is a declaration of record that a person is relieved from the legal consequences of a particular conviction. As in New York, a pardon will be granted only to a person who proves his or her innocence of the crime for which convicted. Florida also has a *first-offender pardon*, which carries no implication of innocence and may be granted to an actual first offender. This pardon restores civil and political rights and removes legal disabilities resulting from the conviction. A *ten-year pardon* works the same way and may be granted offenders who have had no further convictions for 10 years after completing his or her sentence.

In Georgia, a pardon is a declaration of record by the board that a person is relieved from the legal consequences of a particular conviction; it restores civil and political rights and removes all legal disabilities resulting from the conviction. A pardon may be granted in two instances. First, a pardon may be granted when a person proves his or her innocence of the crime for which he or she was convicted under Georgia law. Second, a pardon that does not imply innocence may be granted to an applicant who has completed his or her full sentence obligation, including any probated sentence and paying any fine, and who has thereafter completed five years without any criminal involvement. The five-year waiting period may be waived if it is shown to be detrimental to the applicant's livelihood by delaying his or her qualifying for employment in a chosen profession.

The president of the United States typically grants hundreds of pardons: President Gerald R. Ford pardoned former President Richard Nixon in 1974; Jimmy Carter issued 534 pardons during his four years as president; and Ronald Reagan granted 393 during his eight years as president (Moore, 1989). In 1992, as he was leaving office, President George Bush pardoned six persons alleged to have been involved in the Iran-Contra episode; he granted a total of 63 pardons during his four years in office.

LEGAL DECISONS AFFECTING PAROLE

As noted in Part I, legal decisions that affect probation also affect parole. Thus, the decision rendered in *Gagnon v. Scarpelli* (discussed in Chapter 5) relating to probation violation used precedents established in the *Morrissey v. Brewer* decision (discussed later in the section on parole revocation), which relates to parole violation. The three theories of parole violation are also similar, if not identical, to the three theories of probation violation.

PAROLE RELEASE AND PAROLE HEARINGS

In *Menechino v. Oswald* (U.S. Court of Appeals, Second Circuit, 1970), Joseph Menechino was serving a 20-year to life sentence in New York for murder in the second degree. He was paroled in 1963 and returned to prison as a parole violator 16 months later. Subsequently, he appeared before the board of parole and admitted consorting with persons having criminal records and giving misleading information to his parole officer.

Two years later, Menechino appeared before the board for a release hearing and parole was denied. He brought a court action claiming that his rights were violated by the absence of legal counsel at both his revocation and parole release hearings. The case reached the U.S. Court of Appeals, which rendered a decision in 1970. The court held that

- A parole proceeding is nonadversarial in nature because both parties, the board and the inmate, have the same concern—rehabilitation.
- Parole release hearings are not fact-finding determinations because the board makes a determination based on numerous tangible and intangible factors.
- The inmate has "no present private interest" to be protected (*liberty interest*) because he is already imprisoned—has nothing to lose—and this "interest" is required before due process is applicable.

The court further stated that "it is questionable whether a board of parole is even required to hold a hearing on the question of whether a prisoner should be released on parole." Relative to the question of parole revocation, however, the court advised that a minimum of procedural due process should be provided, because at this stage a parolee has a present private interest in the possible loss of conditional freedom.

Although Menechino's case before the federal court was initiated regarding parole release, it set forth important legal arguments relative to parole revocation. The opinions of the three judges who heard the case clearly indicates that if Menechino had initiated an action concerning his parole revocation, he would have won the case on a 2–1 basis. This fact was duly noted by the New York State Court of Appeals in the second *Menechino* case, discussed later.

In 1979, the U.S. Supreme Court reversed a court of appeals decision in a class action brought by inmates of the Nebraska Penal and Correctional Complex [*Greenholtz v. Inmates of Nebraska Penal and Correctional Complex* (442 U.S. 1, 1979)]. The inmates claimed that they had been unconstitutionally denied parole release by the board of parole, but the Court established in its decision that

- A convicted inmate has no constitutional right to be released before the expiration of his or her lawful sentence.
- Although a state may establish a parole release system, it has no constitutional obligation to do so.

According to Nebraska law, at least once a year initial parole hearings must be held for every inmate, regardless of parole eligibility. At the initial hearing, the board examines the inmate's total record and provides an informal hearing during which the inmate can present statements and documents in support of a claim for release.

If the board determines from the record and hearing that the inmate is a likely candidate for release, a final hearing is scheduled. However, the Nebraska law provides that the board "shall order an inmate's release unless in the final hearing, the board concludes that inmate's release should be deferred for at least one of four specified reasons." This procedure is a somewhat unusual, peculiar, perhaps, to the state of Nebraska. Rolando del Carmen (1985: 50) points out that this amounts to a "state-law created liberty interest," an expectation of being granted parole release. As noted earlier, whenever this "interest" exists, some minimum due process is required.

The board then notifies the inmate of the month in which the final hearing will be held. At the final hearing, the inmate may present evidence, call witnesses, and be represented by private counsel of his or her choice. This hearing is not a traditional adversarial one because the inmate is not permitted to hear adverse testimony or to cross-examine witnesses who present such evidence. If parole is denied, the board furnishes a written statement of the reasons for the denial within 30 days.

In upholding the procedure used by the Nebraska parole board, Chief Justice Warren Burger, speaking for the Court, stated:

> When the Board defers parole after the initial review hearing, it does so because examination of the inmate's file and personal interview satisfied it that the inmate is not ready for conditional release. The parole determination, therefore, must include consideration of what the entire record shows up to the time of the sentence, including the gravity of the offense in the particular case. The behavior record of an inmate during confinement is critical in the sense that it reflects the degree to which the inmate is prepared to adjust to parole release. At the Board's initial interview hearing, the inmate is permitted to appear before the Board and present letters and statements on his own behalf. He is thereby provided with an effective opportunity to insure, first, that the records before the Board are in fact the records relating to his case; and second, to present any special considerations demonstrating why he is an appropriate candidate for parole. Since the decision is one that must be made largely on the basis of an inmate's files, this procedure adequately safeguards against serious risks of error and thus satisfies due process.
>
> Next, we find nothing in the due process concepts as they have thus far evolved that requires the Parole Board to specify the particular "evidence" in the inmate's file or at his interview on which it rests the discretionary determination that an inmate is not ready for conditional release. The Board communicates the reason for its denial as a guide to the inmate for his future behavior. To require the parole authority to provide a summary of the evidence would tend to convert the process into an adversary proceeding and to equate the Board's parole release determination with a guilt determination. . . . [T]he parole decision is . . . essentially an experienced prediction based on a host of variables. The Board's decision is much like a sentencing judge's choice—provided by many states—to grant or deny probation following a judgment of guilt, a choice never thought to require more than what Nebraska now provides for parole release determination.

Del Carmen and Paul Louis conclude that "an inmate does not have a constitutional right to be released on parole, nor does he or she enjoy any constitutional right in the parole release process. In more succinct language, the parole board can do just about anything it pleases [with respect to release], and whatever it says and does prevails because it enjoys immense discretion" (1988: 20). Although parole boards are not constitutionally required to provide reasons for denying release, the use of parole guidelines often provides inmates with such documentation.

PAROLE VIOLATION AND THE THREE THEORIES OF PAROLE

Traditionally, a person on parole has not been considered a free person, despite the fact that he or she has been released from imprisonment. The basis for imposing restrictions on a parolee's freedom is contained in three theories:

1. *Grace theory.* Parole is a conditional privilege, a gift from the board of parole. If any of the conditions of this privilege are violated, parole can be revoked.
2. *Contract theory.* Every parolee and (most) conditional releasees are required to agree to certain terms and conditions in return for conditional freedom. A violation of the conditions is a breach of contract, which can result in penalties—a return to prison.
3. *Custody theory.* The parolee is in the legal custody of the prison or parole authorities, and as a result of this quasi-prisoner status, his or her constitutional rights are automatically limited and abridged.

The legal decisions discussed in this chapter often challenge one or more of the foregoing theories.

PAROLE REVOCATION

Until the 1970s, parole agencies operated without any interference from the judiciary. However, this policy changed when the New York Court of Appeals handed down the *Menechino* decision, which, for the first time, granted parolees the right to counsel and the right to call their own witnesses at parole revocation hearings [*Menechino v. Warden* (New York State Court of Appeals, 1971)]. Although the decision applied to New York only, it indicated the direction in which the courts would rule in future decisions.

This 4–3 decision, once again involving Joseph Menechino (a "jailhouse lawyer"), required that an attorney be present at a parole revocation hearing. It also permitted a parolee to call witnesses who would speak in his or her behalf. The New York court recognized that it was entering into an uncharted area of law. The issue the court was called on to resolve was stated succinctly at the beginning of the majority opinion: "whether parolees are constitutionally entitled, under the Federal and State Constitutions, to the assistance of counsel in parole revocation hearings." *Menechino* cited other legal decisions, such as *Mempa v. Rhay* and *In re Gault* (see Chapter 5). Although probationers, juveniles, and welfare recipients had already obtained limited due process protections at hearings that might cause the loss of freedom or financial distress, these protections had not yet been extended to parolees.

The *Morrissey* decision marked the beginning of the U.S. Supreme Court's involvement with parole revocation procedures [*Morrissey v. Brewer* (408 U.S. 471, 1972)]. Up until June 1972, the Court had not ruled in this area. The issue in this case was whether the due process clause of the Fourteenth Amendment required that a state afford a person the opportunity to be heard before revoking parole.

Morrissey was convicted of the false drawing of checks in 1967 in Iowa. After pleading guilty, he was sentenced to seven years in prison. Paroled from the Iowa State Penitentiary in June 1968, seven months later, Morrissey, at the direction of his parole officer, was arrested in his hometown as a parole violator and held in a local jail. One week after review of the parole officer's written report, the Iowa Board of Parole revoked Morrissey's parole, and he was returned to prison. He had received no hearing before the revocation decision.

Morrissey violated the conditions of his parole by buying a car under an assumed name and operating it without the permission of his parole officer. He also gave false information to the police and an insurance company concerning his address after a minor traffic accident. Besides these violations, Morrissey also obtained credit under an assumed name and failed to report his residence to his parole officer. According to the parole report, Morrissey could not explain adequately any of these technical violations of parole regulations.

Also considered in the *Morrissey* case was the petition of Booher, a convicted forger who had been returned to prison in Iowa by the Board of Parole without a hearing. Booher had admitted the technical violations of parole charges to his parole officer when taken into custody.

The Supreme Court considered all arguments that sought to keep the judiciary out of parole matters, and it rejected the "privilege" concept of parole as no longer feasible. The Court pointed out that parole is an established variation of imprisonment of convicted criminals—it occurs with too much regularity to be simply a "privilege": "It is hardly useful any longer to try to deal with this problem in terms of whether the parolee's liberty is a 'right' or a 'privilege.' By whatever name the liberty is valuable and must be seen within the protection of the Fourteenth Amendment. Its termination calls for some orderly process however informal."

The Court pointed out that parole revocation does not occur in just a few isolated cases—it has been estimated that 35 to 40 percent of all parolees are subjected to revocation and return to prison. The Court went on to state that with the numbers involved, protection of parolees' rights was necessary. The Court did note, however, limitations on a parolee's rights:

> We begin with the proposition that the revocation of parole is not part of the criminal prosecution and thus the full panoply of rights due to the

defendant in such a proceeding does not apply to parole revocation. Supervision is not directly by the court but by an administrative agency which sometimes is an arm of the court and sometimes of the executive. Revocation deprives an individual not of absolute liberty to which every citizen is entitled but only the conditional liberty properly dependent on observance of special parole restrictions.

Also found in the decision is the New York State Court of Appeals response to the problem raised by the *Menechino* case. The Supreme Court held: "Society thus has an interest in not having parole revoked because of erroneous information or because of an erroneous evaluation of the need to revoke parole, given the breach of parole regulations. See Parole ex rel *Menechino v. Warden.*"

In *Morrissey* the Supreme Court viewed parole revocation as a two-stage process: (1) arrest of the parolee and preliminary hearing and (2) the revocation hearing. Because a significant time lapse usually occurred between the arrest and revocation hearing, the Court established an interim process for all parole violators, a hearing before the final or revocation hearing: "Such an inquiry should be seen in the nature of a preliminary hearing to determine whether there is probable cause or reasonable grounds to believe that the arrested parolee had committed acts which would constitute a violation of parole conditions."

The Court specified that the hearing officer conducting this preliminary hearing need not be a member of the parole board, only someone who is not involved in the case; that the parolee be given notice of the hearing; and that the purpose be to determine whether there is probable cause to believe that the parolee has violated a condition of parole. On the request of the parolee, persons who have given adverse information on which parole violation is based are to be made available for questioning in the parolee's presence. Based on this information presented before the hearing officer, a determination should be made if a reason exists to warrant the parolee's continued detention (pending a revocation hearing).

The Court stated that "no interest would be served by formalism in this process; informality will not lessen the utility of this inquiry in redressing the risk of error." This writer served as an auxiliary hearing officer, conducting preliminary hearings in New York. These were held at local correctional facilities. All persons were placed under oath, and a legal reporter recorded all testimony verbatim. The parole officer alleging the violation "prosecuted" the case, although in significant cases a legal advocate was provided by the Division of Parole for that purpose. Following all of the testimony, I would write down my decision in summary form: The violation of parole charges considered and sustained were listed and a copy given to the parolee. If none of the charges were sustained, the parole officer would be directed to arrange for the parolee's release from custody.

In reference to the revocation hearing, the Court stated: "The parolee must have an opportunity to be heard and to show if he can that he did not violate the conditions or if he did, that circumstances in mitigation suggest the violation does not warrant revocation. The revocation hearing must be tendered within a reasonable time after the parolee is taken into custody. A lapse of two months as the state suggests occurs in some cases would not appear to be unreasonable."

The Court also suggested minimum requirements of due process for the revocation hearing:

> Our task is limited to deciding the minimum requirements of due process. They include (a) written notice of the claimed violation of parole; (b) disclosures to the parolee of evidence against him; (c) opportunity to be heard in person and to present witnesses and documentary evidence; (d) the right to confront and cross-examine adverse witnesses (unless the hearing officer specifically finds good cause for not allowing confrontation); (e) "neutral and detached" hearing body such as a traditional parole board, members of which need not be judicial officers or lawyers; and (f) a written statement by the fact finders as to the evidence relied on and reasons for revoking parole.

The Supreme Court left open the question of counsel when it stated: "We do not reach or decide the question whether the parolee is entitled to the assistance of retained or to appointed counsel if he is indigent." In practice, parole boards have permitted parolees to be represented by counsel, although they usually do not provide such assistance.

PAROLE BOARD LIABILITY

In a unanimous decision [*Martinez v. California* (444 U.S. 277, 1980)], the Supreme Court affirmed the constitutionality of statutory provisions that provide parole officials with immunity from tort claims. In this instance, Thomas, a parolee convicted of attempted rape, tortured and murdered 15-year-old Mary Martinez 5 months after his parole release from prison. Thomas had been labeled as not amenable to treatment, and the sentencing court recommended that he not be paroled. Nevertheless, after serving 5 years of a 1- to 200-year sentence, Thomas was paroled. The deceased girl's parents argued that in releasing Thomas, parole authorities subjected their daughter to deprivation of her life without due process of law.

Justice Stevens delivered the opinion for the Court:

> Like the California courts, we cannot accept the contention that this statute deprives Thomas' (a paroled offender) victim of her life without due process of law because it condoned a parole decision that led indirectly to her death. The statute neither authorized nor immunized the deliberate killing of any human being. This statute merely provides a defense to potential state tort law liability. At most, the availability of such a defense may have encouraged members of the parole board to take somewhat greater risks of recidivism in exercising their authority to release prisoners

than they otherwise might. But the basic risk that repeat offenses may occur is always present in any parole system.

Although parole boards act in a quasi-judicial capacity, they do not enjoy the total immunity conferred on judges. Justice Stevens pointed out that in this decision, "We need not and do not decide that a parole official could never be deemed to 'deprive' someone of life by action taken in connection with a prisoner on parole."

PAROLE OFFICER LIABILITY

Although no definitive Supreme Court decision exists concerning the liability of parole officers in the supervision process, state and federal cases have established liability for crimes committed by parolees under their supervision within a narrow set of circumstances. The common element in these circumstances, notes del Carmen and Louis, is the rather unclear concept of a "special duty" on the part of the parole officer:

> For this "special duty" to be relevant there must be a *reasonably foreseeable risk* which exists when the circumstances of the relationship between the parolee and a third party suggest that the parolee may engage in criminal or antisocial conduct related to his or her past conduct. This, in turn, results from a combination of three factors: (a) the parolee's job; (b) his or her prior criminal background and conduct; and (c) the type of crime for which he or she was convicted. For example, it is reasonably foreseeable that a parolee convicted of child sexual assault would commit a similar act if employed in a child care center, but not if employed as a janitor on a college campus. (1988: 37, emphasis in original)

Richard Sluder and del Carmen (1990: 11) conclude that the area of law concerning probation/parole officer liability remains unchartered and often confusing, with courts rendering contradictory decisions.

Now that the examination of the historical, administrative, and legal aspects of probation and parole is complete, Chapter 9 turns to treatment theory in probation and parole supervision.

REVIEW QUESTIONS

1. Why is the administration of parole less complex than that of probation?
2. What are the three basic services provided by a parole agency?
3. What are the two basic models for administering parole services? What are the arguments in favor of each?
4. What is conditional release, and how does it differ from parole?
5. Why have parole release hearings been criticized?

6. Why do most parole boards deny inmates the right to legal representation at parole release hearings?

7. What are the two most important factors considered when making a parole release decision?

8. What led to the development of parole release guidelines?

9. How are parole release guidelines used?

10. What is the relationship between institutional rehabilitation and parole release guidelines?

11. Why can the parole board be in a better position than the sentencing judge to render a decision based on just deserts?

12. What is the primary responsibility of institutional parole staff? What other services might they provide?

13. What is the purpose of a preliminary parole violation hearing?

14. What is the difference between a preliminary parole violation hearing and a parole revocation hearing?

15. What are the various forms of clemency?

16. What are the three theories that have traditionally formed the basis for imposing restrictions on parolees?

17. What are the due process requirements mandated by the *Morrissey* decision?

18. What have the courts ruled with respect to the liability of parole boards and parole officers?

TREATMENT THEORY

Some modes of treatment are more easily applied than others to probation and parole (p/p) practice. Some methods require more training than most p/p officers have received, and their use may require an expenditure of time that is not realistic in most p/p agencies. In practice, p/p officers use a variety of treatment techniques, tailoring them to different clients. They often use techniques without understanding the theoretical base or even recognizing it as part of a particular mode of treatment—"flying by the seat of your pants" is sometimes characteristic of p/p. Nevertheless, most p/p officers, even when they do not provide extensive direct treatment, refer clients to programs for such problems as substance abuse and pedophilia. Knowledge of treatment modalities, therefore, is important in p/p. Treatment, however, no matter the discipline, requires a theoretical knowledge and principles applied to specific cases. Being knowledgeable about both theory and treatment enables the p/p officer to make appropriate referrals, understand treatment reports, and relate to treatment professionals.

THEORY

A *theory* is a part of an explanation—a statement about the relationship between two classes of phenomena that permits us to understand our environment better. A theory helps to explain events by organizing events in the world so that they can be placed in perspective; a theory also explains the causes of past events and predicts when, where, and how future events will occur. According to Arnold Binder and Gilbert Geis (1983: 3), "A theory consists of a set of assumptions; concepts regarding events, situations, individuals, and groups; and propositions that describe the interrelationships among the various assumptions and concepts."

Theories are abstract, a necessary dimension if they are to be applied to more than one specific set of circumstances, facts, or observations. We cannot determine the cause of particular criminal behavior based on a satisfactory explanation for a single case. However, if enough individual cases fit into the same explanation, we can develop a theory and test it against future cases of criminal behavior—the ability to predict is a measure of a theory's validity. Validity requires testing, and any theory that cannot be tested—and, therefore, disproved—is not (according to scientific principles) a theory. A purported cause of crime that does not permit testing, therefore, has more in common with theology than criminology—it lacks scientific merit.

There are three basic theoretical models for treatment in p/p:

1. Social casework
2. Reality therapy
3. Behavior/learning theory

To understand these models better, it is necessary to review the theory behind a method of treatment that is not used extensively, if at all, in p/p. The psychologically based methods of treatment discussed in this chapter can be delineated according to the degree to which they accept, use, or reject psychoanalytic theory.

PSYCHOANALYTIC THEORY AND PSYCHOANALYSIS

Psychoanalysis is a method of treatment based on a body of theory fathered by Sigmund Freud (1856–1939). Over the years, both theory and method have undergone change, although Freud's basic contribution, his exposition of the importance of unconscious phenomena in human behavior, remains. [For a discussion of the different models of psychoanalytic theory, see Greenberg and Mitchell (1983).] As Susan Cloninger notes (1993: 25), "simply put, this concept says that people are not aware of the most important determinants of their behavior."

STAGES OF PSYCHOLOGICAL DEVELOPMENT

Freud postulated unconscious processes in the stages of psychological development that, although not directly observable, were inferred from case studies with patients. He divided mental phenomena into three groups:

1. *Conscious*: what a person is thinking at any given time
2. *Preconscious*: thoughts and memories that can easily be called into conscious awareness

3. *Unconscious*: repressed feelings and experiences that can be made conscious only with a great deal of difficulty

"The unconscious is essentially dynamic and capable of profoundly affecting conscious ideational or emotional life without the individual's being aware of this influence" (Healy, Bronner, and Bowers, 1930: 24).

Unconscious feelings and experiences are related to normal stages of psychosexual development through which each person passes on the way to adulthood (psychosexual maturity). These stages of psychosexual development are repressed and, therefore, unconscious—not part of conscious or preconscious memory—yet they serve as a source of anxiety and guilt, the basis for psychoneurosis and psychosis. In brief, they appear as follows:

1. *Oral* (birth to 18 months). The mouth, lips, and tongue are the predominant organs of pleasure for the infant. In the normal infant, the source of pleasure becomes associated with the touch and warmth of the parent, who gratifies oral needs. When this is lacking, deviant behavior, particularly drug and alcohol abuse, is to be expected in the adult. Drugs and alcohol serve as a substitute for maternal attachment, and drug abuse is seen as a regression back to an unfulfilled oral stage. The infant actually enters the world a "criminal," that is, unsocialized and devoid of self-control, guided only by id impulses (discussed later).

2. *Anal* (18 months to 3 years). The anus becomes the most important site of sexual interest and gratification. Pleasure is closely connected to the retention and expulsion of feces, as well as the bodily processes involved and the feces themselves. During this stage, the only partially socialized child acts out rather destructive urges, breaking toys or even injuring living organisms, such as insects or small animals. A great deal of psychopathology in the adult, including violent behavior and sociopathological personality disorders, is traced to disruptions during this stage.

3. *Genital* (3 to 5 years). The main sexual interest begins to be assumed by the genitals and in normal persons is maintained by them thereafter. During this period of life the child experiences *Oedipus* (in boys) and *Electra* (in girls) *wishes* in the form of fantasies of incest with the parent of the opposite sex.[1] The healthy child must relinquish the dependent paternal/maternal attachment and deal with the feelings of sadness that result. Sexual problems and drug and alcohol abuse are traced to failures during this stage of development.

4. *Latent* (5 years to adolescence). A lessening of interest in sexual organs occurs during this period, as well as an expanded relationship with playmates of the same sex and age.

---

[1]Based on his treatment of middle-class women in Vienna, Freud reported that they fantasied sexual activity with their fathers and other male relatives: "Almost all my female patients told me that they had been seduced by their fathers. Eventually I was forced to the conclusion that these stories were false, and thus I came to understand that hysterical symptoms spring from phantasies and not from real events" (Freud, 1933: 164). This "seduction theory" is the most controversial aspect of Freud's psychoanalytic theory. It has recently been revealed that, in fact, many of Freud's female patients had been sexually abused as children by their fathers or male relatives. For an examination of feminism and psychoanalytic theory, see Chodorow (1990) and Appignanesi and Forrester (1993).

5. *Adolescence-adulthood* (13 years to death). A reawakening of genital interest and awareness occurs; the incestuous wish is repressed and emerges in terms of mature (adult) sexuality.

The stages overlap, and transition from one to the other is gradual, the time spans being approximate. Furthermore, each stage is left behind but never completely abandoned. Some amount of psychic energy (*cathexis*) remains attached to earlier objects of psychosexual development. When the strength of the cathexis is particularly strong, it is expressed as a *fixation*. For example, instead of a boy transferring his affection to another woman in the adolescent-adult stage, he may remain fixated on his mother (or a girl on her father—"My Heart Belongs to Daddy"). When a person reverts to a previous mode of gratification, it is referred to as *regression*. This type of behavior can be seen in young children who revert to thumbsucking or have elimination "accidents" when a sibling is born.

When a person is passing through the first three stages of psychosexual development, the mind simultaneously undergoes the development of three psychic phenomena:

1. *Id.* This mass of powerful drives seeks discharge or gratification—it is asocial, devoid of values and logical processes. Constituting wishes, urges, and psychic tensions, according to Freud (1933: 104), the id is "a cauldron of seething excitement," seeking pleasure and avoiding pain. The id is the driving force of the personality, and from birth until about 7 months of age, it is the total psychic apparatus.

2. *Ego.* Through contact with the reality around them and the influence of training, infants modify their expressions of id drives. This ego development permits them to obtain maximum gratification with a minimum of difficulty in the form of restrictions that their environment places on them. For example, an id drive (desire) to harm a sibling rival is controlled by the ego (an awareness of the consequences of one's action—the punishment that may result). Without the ego to act as a restraining influence, the id would destroy the person through its blind striving to gratify instincts in complete disregard for reality. As a result of disturbances in psychosexual development, a person may remain at the ego level of development: "The child remains asocial or behaves as if he had become social without having made actual adjustment to the demands of society" (Aichhorn, 1963: 4). Feelings of rage and aggression associated with the anal stage lurk in the background awaiting an opportunity to break through to satisfaction—unless they are controlled by the superego or the person self-medicates with the use of depressant drugs, such as heroin. At the other end of the spectrum are adults who may use stimulants, such as cocaine, because of a self-directed and intensely competitive personality or to ward off feelings of boredom and depression by artificial stimulation of the ego.

3. *Superego.* Often viewed as a conscience-type mechanism, the superego serves as a counterforce to the id. It exercises a criticizing power, a sense of morality over the ego: "It represents the whole demands of morality, and we see all at once that our moral sense of guilt is the expression of tension between the ego [which strives to discharge id drives] and the super-ego" (Freud, 1933: 88).[2] The superego is tied to incestuous feelings of the genital stage, at which time the development of controls becomes an internal matter and no longer exclusively dependent on external forces (e.g., parents). A healthy superego is the result of an identification with a parent(s) that is accomplished during the genital stage of psychosexual development. In other words, "The role which the super-ego undertakes later in life, is at first played by external power, by parental authority" (Freud, 1933: 89).

The id drives impel a person (via the ego) to activity leading to a cessation of the tension or excitement caused by the drives—the person seeks discharge or gratification. For example, the hunger drive will cause activity through which the person hopes to satisfy (gratify) the hunger experience. These drives are divided into two categories, but elements of each appear whenever either drive is activated:

- *Primary process.* The drive toward immediate and direct gratification of the id impulse.
- *Secondary process.* The tendency to shift from the original object or method of discharge when something blocks it—for example, the superego—or when it is simply inaccessible, to another object or method. For example, a desire to play with feces arising out of an anal cathexis will be transferred to playing with mud or clay as a result of toilet training. This transfer is called *displacement,* and it is one of the many defense mechanisms that the human mind employs to adapt to its environment. Other defense mechanisms include the following:
  - *Repression.* Activity of the ego that prevents unwanted id impulses, memories, emotions, desires, or wish-fulfilling fantasies from entering conscious thought. Repression of charged material (such as incestuous fantasies) requires the expenditure of psychic energy and sets up a permanent opposition between the id and ego. The delicate balance (equilibrium) between the charged material and its opposing expenditure of energy can shift at any time, usually as a result of some stress. When repression is inadequate for dealing with charged material, psychoneurotic symptoms develop.
  - *Reaction formation.* Mechanism whereby a person gives up some form of socially unacceptable behavior in favor of behavior that is social acceptable. This more acceptable behavior usually takes the form of being opposite to the real desire (drive). For example, a child who desires to kill a sibling will become very loving and devoted. In adult behavior, a sadistic impulse toward animals can result in a person becoming involved in the care and treatment of persons or animals.
  - *Projection.* A person's attribution of his or her own wish or impulse to some other person(s). This inclination is pathological in cases of paranoia.

[2]Eli Sagan (1988) points out that a substantial difference exists between the *superego* and the *conscience.* The latter implies an objective sense of morality, whereas the superego, such as in a Nazi society, commands one to live up to genocidal ideals.

- *Sublimation.* When a drive that cannot be experienced in its primary form, such as a desire to play with feces, is accommodated by modeling clay or, perhaps, becoming a proctologist.

A delicate balance is maintained by unconscious forces as a person experiences various sociocultural and biological aspects of existence. When the balance is upset, the psyche passes from the normal to the psychoneurotic or the psychotic (mental illness). The fact that a thin line exists between the normal and the neurotic and between the neurotic and the psychotic is basic to psychoanalytic theory. In fact, only a difference of degree separates the "normal" and the "abnormal." The degree to which there is a malfunctioning in psychic apparatus is the degree to which a person is "abnormal" or "sick," that is, socially dysfunctional.

CRIME AND THE SUPEREGO

The "psychoanalytic theory of crime causation," notes Gerhard Falk (1966: 1), "does not make the usual distinction between behavior as such and criminal action"; the distinction is a legal one—that is, crime is behavior defined by a society as illegal, an issue discussed in Chapter 1. Antisocial behavior is seen as a neurotic manifestation whose origin can be traced back to early stages of development: "There is no fundamental difference between the neurotic criminal and all those socially harmless representatives of the group of neurotic characters; the difference lies merely in the external fact that the neurotic lawbreaker chooses a form of acting out his impulses which is socially harmful or simply illegal" (Alexander and Staub, 1956: 106).

According to August Aichhorn (1963: 221): "[T]he superego takes its form and content from identifications which result from the child's effort to emulate the parent. It is evolved not only because the parent loves the child, but also because the child fears the parent's demands." However, Freud (1933: 92) states that "the superego does not attain to full strength and development if the overcoming of the Oedipus [in males] complex has not been completely successful."

The superego keeps primitive (oral and anal) id impulses from being acted on. Persons with a poorly developed superego—sociopaths—are restrained only by the ego, which alone cannot exercise adequate control over id impulses. Such persons suffer little or no guilt as a result of engaging in socially harmful behavior.

At the other extreme are persons whose superego (internal parental voice) is destructive. Their superego is overwhelming and cannot distinguish between *thinking* about and *doing* bad deeds. Unresolved conflicts of earlier development and id impulses that are normally repressed or dealt with through other secondary processes (such as reaction formation or sublimation; see previous section) create a severe sense of (unconscious) guilt. This guilt is experienced (at the unconscious level) as a compulsive need to be punished. To alleviate this (unconscious) guilt, the actor is impelled toward committing acts for which punishment is virtually certain. Delinquents of this type are the victims of their own morality (Aichhorn, 1963). Persons employed in the criminal justice system often see cases in which the crime committed was so poorly planned and executed that it would appear that the perpetrator *wished* to be caught.

- Richard G. entered the BayBank in Haverhill, Massachusetts, went up to a counter, and wrote on a deposit slip: "This is a holdup. Give me all the money." He left the bank with $5201. With red dye from an explosive device used to mark stolen bills streaming from his bag, Richard G. mounted an old two-speed bicycle. He was caught within minutes, covered with red dye, sneezing, and coughing. The note he had handed the teller was discovered to contain his name and home address (Associated Press, April 18, 1992).
- Lee W. entered a Connecticut bank and presented a withdrawal slip to the teller on which he had written: "The money." He was quickly arrested by police who found $3000 on him—Lee had written his name on the withdrawal slip *twice*.

The FBI catches between 40 and 50 bank robbers a year who write their note demanding money on the back of a deposit slip for their own checking accounts (Martin, 1995).

In sum, criminal behavior is related to the superego function, which is a result of an actor's relationship to parents (or parental figures) during early developmental years. Parental deprivation through absence, lack of affection, or inconsistent discipline stifles the proper development of the superego. Parental influence is thus weakened by deprivation during childhood development, and in adulthood the actor is unable to adequately control aggressive, hostile, or antisocial urges. Overly rigid or punitive parents, conversely, can lead to the creation of a superego that is rigid and punitive, for which the actor seeks punishment as a way of alleviating unconscious "guilt."

A p/p officer must be able to distinguish those offenders with an inadequate superego from those with a punitive one. With the latter, attempts to deter criminal behavior through the application of threats may actually have an opposite effect. With the former, the p/p officer may need to act in a parental role to replace a poorly developed superego. [For a discussion of psychoanalytic theory and drug abuse, see Abadinsky (1993).]

Psychoanalytic Treatment

Psychic disorders are treated by psychoanalysis or one of its variants, such as psychotherapy. Freud stated that psychoanalysis "aims at inducing the patient to give up the repressions belonging to his early life and to replace them by reactions of a sort that would correspond better to a psychically mature condition." To achieve this goal, a psychoanalyst attempts to get the patient "to recollect certain experiences and the emotions called up by them which he has at the moment forgotten" (Reiff, 1963: 274). To the psychoanalyst, present symptoms are tied to repressed material of early life—the primary stages of psychosexual development. The symptoms will disappear when the repressed material is exposed under psychoanalytic treatment.

To enable the patient to relive the early past, the analyst uses *dream interpretation* and *free association*, whereby a patient verbally relates ideas as they come to mind. In addition, psychoanalysis takes advantage of the phenomenon of *transference*. This process involves the development of an emotional attitude, positive or negative, by the patient toward the therapist. Transference is a reflection or imitation of emotional attitudes that were experienced in relationships that had an impact on psychosexual development. Thus, the therapist may (unconsciously) be viewed as a parental figure by the patient. Through the use of transference, the therapist recreates the emotions tied to early psychic development, unlocking repressed material and freeing the patient from his or her burden. As Freud noted, transference "is particularly calculated to favor the reproduction of these (early) emotional conditions" (Reiff, 1963: 274).

Psychoanalysis is not used in p/p treatment because it requires highly trained and thus expensive practitioners, treatment takes many years, and it needs a level of verbal ability in patients beyond that of most persons on p/p. In fact, psychoanalytically oriented therapists may underestimate how difficult it is to verbalize experience, even for otherwise verbal patients (Omer and London, 1988). Instead of psychoanalysis, in probation and parole psychoanalytic theory is applied through the use of *social casework*.[3]

SOCIAL CASEWORK

Social work has its roots in charity work and the supplying of concrete services to persons in need—solving problems rather than changing personalities. Mary Richmond, whose colleagues included many physicians, presented the practice of social work as including (nonpsychoanalytic) psychological and sociological aspects of a person's behavior. She also set the groundwork for what is sometimes referred to as the *medical model* of treatment, dealing with nonphysiological problems through the method of *study, diagnosis*, and *treatment*.

"Following World War I, the social work profession ushered in an era of practice based primarily on the psychoanalytic perspective and the medical model" (Miley, O'Melia, and DuBois, 1995: 65). During the 1930s, some American physicians began to use psychoanalytic treatment and social workers adopted this "talking cure"—one that did not require medical training—to their own practice (Specht, 1990). Psychoanalytic theory was still central to social work education when this writer received his master's of social work degree in 1970.

Social casework is one of the basic specialties of social work. Swithun Bowers (1950: 127) offers the following: "Social casework is an art in which knowledge of the science of human relations and skills in relationship are used to mobilize capacities in the individual and resources in the community appropriate for better adjustment between the client and all or any part of his total

---

[3]Social casework is a primary specialization of social work. Contemporary social work often avoids distinctions between specializations, emphasizing, instead, *generalist practice* (see, for example, Kirst-Ashman and Hull, 1993).

environment." According to Thomas Brennan and his colleagues (1986: 342), casework "can be defined essentially as the development of a relationship between worker and client, within a problem-solving context, and coordinated with the appropriate use of community resources." The purpose of social casework is "the solution of problems that block or minimize the effectiveness of the individual in various roles" (Skidmore, Thackeray, and Farley, 1988: 64).

As Freudian thought had its impact on social work, caseworkers began examining the client's feelings and attitudes to understand and "cope with some of the unreasonable forces that held him in their grip" (Perlman, 1971: 76). The client's behavior was conceived of as purposeful and determined, but some of the determinants are unconscious. Casework was thus expanded to include work with psychological as well as social or environmental stress. Although social casework borrowed much of its theory from psychoanalysis, it avoided the psychoanalytical goal of trying to effect personality changes. Instead, social caseworkers seek to help people "perform in their appropriate social roles by providing information and knowledge, social support, social skills, and opportunity" (Specht, 1990: 354). The caseworker helps clients to maintain constructive reality-based relationships, solve problems, and achieve adequate and satisfying independent social functioning within the client's existing personality structure (Torgerson, 1962). To accomplish this task, social workers use encouragement and moral support, persuasion and suggestion, training and advice, comfort and reassurance, together with re-education and some sort of guidance (Kasius, 1950).

Modern social casework, Margaret Yelloly (1980: 5) points out, has been influenced by neo-Freudians, who stress the impact of social and cultural factors and de-emphasize the instinctual and biological aspects of psychoanalytical theory, and by ego psychologists "who have focussed attention on the psychology of the ego and its development through object-relationships." In contrast to psychoanalytic approaches, ego psychology favored in social casework pays primary attention to those aspects of the ego that derive from its reality orientation on the causal significance of consciousness and affective states. Whereas the medical model searches the past to detect problems in the present, contemporary social work—while not discounting the importance of the developmental past—explores the present for client strengths and resources that can promote effective social functioning (Miley, O'Melia, and DuBois, 1995).

The importance of social casework in p/p practice goes beyond theory and into the skills and training that schools of social work provide. These include "an extension and refinement of information on how to interview, how to obtain facts about the client's background, how to identify and distinguish surface from underlying problems, what community resources exist, and how to refer" (Wilensky and Lebeaux, 1958: 288–89). Harold Wilensky and Charles Lebeaux note that such practice is pragmatic, based on rule-of-thumb experience rather than on theory. (This writer, as a parole officer, was sent to graduate school for a degree in social work and found both the theory and skills relevant and useful for p/p practice.)

There are three basic operations practiced in social casework methodology (Perlman, 1957: 61):

1. *Study/Assessment*: fact-finding activities; gathering relevant information upon which to base a diagnosis, particularly strengths and weaknesses
2. *Diagnosis/Planning*: thinking about and organizing facts into a meaningful goal-oriented explanation
3. *Treatment/Intervention*: implementation of conclusions as to the "what" and the "how" of action upon the problem(s)

Although the following sections review these three operations separately, "study-diagnosis-treatment" have a "close mutual relationship and form one theme." Roland Ostrower also notes that although for teaching purposes these steps are referred to separately, they "are not actually performed in sequence, but are interwoven and in reality comprise a unity" (1962: 86).

STUDY /ASSESSMENT

During the initial phase, the worker must establish a relationship with his or her client. To be able to do this, the worker must be what Gordon Hamilton calls "a person of genuine warmth" (1967: 28). Using face-to-face interviews, the worker conveys acceptance and understanding. Walter Friedlander notes that "caseworkers communicate their respect for and acceptance of the client as a person whose decisions about his own living situation are almost always his own to make" (1958: 22). The p/p officer as caseworker may be bound by statute or agency regulation to make decisions about the client's living situation. Workers know that the way they communicate will have an effect on clients' perception of them and the worker-client relationship. Therefore, workers must be cognizant of the way they greet clients; their tone of voice, facial expressions, and posture; and the way they express themselves verbally. In p/p practice, workers who exude authority, who are curt, and who emphasize the enforcement aspect of their position will encounter difficulties in establishing a sound casework relationship.

Workers engage clients in the helping process, and they make certain judgments about a client's motivation, how much he or she wants to change, and how willing he or she is to contribute to bringing about change. Workers recognize that a client brings attitudes and preconceptions about being on probation or parole. The p/p client is fearful, or at least realistically on guard, because he or she recognizes the power of the p/p worker.

An anxious client will be resistant to a worker's efforts, and in the mandated setting that is probation and parole practice, a worker can easily raise a client's anxiety level, thus increasing *resistance*, including "evasive, angry, and uncooperative behaviors" (Hutchinson, 1987: 591). Psychoanalytic theory also posits resistance that is unconscious. P/p clients frequently have negative impressions of all authority figures. This perception is usually based on experiences with parents, school officials, police officers, court officials, training schools, or prisons. In addition, a client may have a low self-image, a severe superego, or a chronically high anxiety level. The result will be resistance. The worker must not become defensive about client resistance or take negative behavior personally.

To lessen resistance, workers may discuss the client's feelings about being on p/p, allowing him or her to ventilate some feelings and anxiety. This approach will also enable workers to clarify any misconceptions that clients have about p/p supervision. Elizabeth Hutchinson (1987: 592) suggests "letting it all hang out": "It is essential for the social worker to make early acknowledgement of client reluctance toward the mandated transactions and to validate such reluctance as understandable. This makes the issue explicit rather than latent and assures the client of the acceptability of his or her feelings as well as the genuineness of the social worker."

The client's motivation can also be influenced by *transference*. He or she may view the worker as a friendly parent or as an authoritarian and demanding mother or father. The worker can be influenced by *countertransference* because he or she may view the client as a childlike figure; if the worker is a great deal younger than the client, the former may view the latter as a parent or older sibling.

The caseworker prepares a psychosocial study of the client. In nonprobation/parole agencies, workers often stress the importance of early childhood development and experiences with a view toward applying a psychoanalytic explanation to the client's behavior. This practice is not usual in p/p settings, where "the unique constellation of social, psychological, and biological determinants of the client's current stressful situation" (Friedlander, 1958: 47) is more relevant and appropriate to analyze. In p/p practice, the primary focus is on the present or the recent past.

The probation/parole worker seeks information that will provide an indication of the client's view of his or her present situation. The p/p officer is concerned with the client's plans for improving the situation and weighs the sincerity and intensity of the latter's commitment to change. The caseworker reviews the client's relationship with his or her family and evaluates the impact of the client's current situation. While engaged in study, the worker must also be aware of the cultural, racial, and ethnic factors that influence the client.

In p/p, material from the unconscious is not sought. However, with clients who are mentally ill, material that in the better-functioning person is normally repressed may be brought to the fore. In such situations, the worker must direct his or her efforts toward keeping the client in touch with reality and should usually avoid exploring the normally repressed material.

DIAGNOSIS/PLANNING

A diagnosis is a "summation of the symptoms of some underlying causation" (Friedlander, 1958: 146). It determines the nature of the client's difficulty and provides a realistic assessment for individualized treatment. Some of the questions that a diagnosis seeks to answer include

- What are the client's social-role problems?
- What are his or her dominant and alternative modes of adaptation?
- What are the causal factors that can be traced to his or her present situation?
- What are his or her ego strengths and weaknesses? (Friedlander, 1958: 84–85)

The diagnosis focuses particular attention on ego functioning. The client's capacity to deal consciously with difficult inner forces is dependent on his or her ego functioning, a facet of personality that develops its strengths through interaction with other persons (Friedlander, 1958). Ego adequacy will have a direct impact on the client's efforts to deal with his or her difficulties.

Helen Perlman (1957: 168–69) suggests that the diagnosis in casework involves

1. The nature of the problem and the goals sought by the client, in their relationship to
2. The nature of the person who bears the problem, his or her social and psychological situation and functioning, and who needs help with his or her problem, in relation to
3. The nature and purpose of the agency and the kind of help it can offer or make available

For a diagnosis to be complete, psychological testing or a psychiatric evaluation is necessary. The results of a clinical examination will indicate if the client is in need of any special treatment—for example, if he or she is psychotic. In many, if not most, instances in p/p, however, a psychological or psychiatric report will not be available.

In discussing the origin of the client's malfunctioning, Perlman (1957: 176) refers to "this history of his development as a problem-encountering, problem-solving human being"; she notes that this can provide the worker with an understanding of the client's present difficulties and the probable extent of his or her ability to cope with them.

Walter Friedlander notes that "in an on-going relationship, diagnoses are continually reformulated, as the caseworker and the client engage in appropriate corrective action or treatment" (1958: 22).

TREATMENT/INTERVENTION

A basic concept in social work is that the worker has no right to impose his or her goals on the client. The client has a right to *self-determination*. Obviously, the authority inherent in the p/p officer's role limits self-determination. How is this reconciled when social casework is the mode of treatment?

A review of some of the literature on this issue, notes Dale Hardman (1960), is confusing, because it reveals that authority is considered

1. Impossible
2. Possible only in mild cases of delinquency
3. Both detrimental and beneficial
4. Essential but not necessarily harmful

Hardman (1960: 250) states that "authority conflict is a major causative factor in delinquency," a proposition that is widely accepted in correctional treatment. Therefore, helping the offender come to grips with the reality of authority is a basic goal of p/p treatment. The client's relationship with a p/p worker is often the only positive experience he or she has ever had in dealing with an authority figure. Brennan and colleagues (1986: 345) report that "many clients' involvement with the law expresses a need for control they cannot themselves provide. If used with respect and care, the authority of the court can be invoked by the forensic social worker to strengthen the client's weak motive to get treatment and to improve impulse control."

However, social caseworkers in other than correctional settings must also deal with the reality of their authority. They require clients to keep appointments, provide personal information, and pay fees—usually under the threat, implied or expressed, of denying the client the help or service for which the client is asking. Workers in child welfare agencies may even be required to remove children from their parents or guardians in neglect or child abuse cases. In addition, because of the impact of an agency setting, or the phenomenon of transference, the caseworker is always an authority figure. The concept and the use of authority and the limits placed on self-determination by reality are not alien to the practice of social casework. [See Hutchinson (1987) and Hasenfeld (1987) for a discussion of this issue.]

However, we should consider the admonition of Alexander Smith and Louis Berlin (1974: 3), who state that "no matter how evident the need for counseling . . . appears to the probation and/or parole officer, it cannot be forced upon the offender unless it is directly related to his crime." For example, according to Smith and Berlin, a client who has a history of drug usage that has resulted in the need to steal could be required to accept counseling because it is "directly related to his crime." However, I question the usefulness of "counseling" that has to be "forced upon the offender." I would recommend instead that no form of treatment be forced on any offender. This suggestion will preserve the client's right not to be treated, while allowing the worker to use his or her treatment time and skills more productively with clients who both need and want help.

The illusion "that all, or most all, offenders need and will respond to rehabilitative efforts, if such efforts are sufficiently massive and persistent," note Bernard Ross and Charles Shireman, has led to assigning "most offenders to programs of active intervention in their lives. The result is the choking of programs with large numbers of individuals who do not need, do not want, and cannot use the sort of relationship-and-communication-based treatment that is the basis for most probation or parole services" (1972: 24).

In any event, the plan for treatment in social casework will use procedures that, it is hoped, will move the client toward the goal of enhancing the ability to function within the realities placed on him or her by society in general, and the client's present probation/parole status in particular. Three basic techniques are involved.

CHANGING THE ENVIRONMENT

This approach may involve obtaining needed resources if these are available from the agency or locating other agencies that can provide them. In using this technique, the worker may assume a *mediator* or *advocate* role when the client is unable to secure a service that he or she needs and to which he or she is entitled. In p/p practice, this role is common for the worker. The technique is used by the juvenile p/p officer when seeking placement for a youngster in a foster home, group home, or residential treatment center. The aftercare worker who is trying to place a juvenile back in public school after a stay at a juvenile institution is often a *mediator/advocate*. The worker may have to intervene on behalf of clients who require financial assistance from the welfare department. P/p workers may help a client to secure a civil service position or a necessary license/certificate to enter a particular trade or profession.

The p/p worker may help his or her client by talking to an employer or school official, at the same time helping the client to modify behavior relative to problems encountered at work or school. Many p/p clients have had few positive work or school experiences, and their difficulty with authority extends to employers and teachers. By using role playing, reflection, and suggestion, the worker tries to modify the client's behavior, at least to the degree required for continued schooling or employment.

While being of direct assistance when necessary, the p/p worker should promote independence on the part of the client. The worker realizes that he or she is not continually available, and treatment is rarely indefinite. *The worker should not do anything for the client that the client is capable of doing for him- or herself.*

EGO SUPPORT

The use of this technique entails attempts by the worker to sustain the client through expressions of interest, sympathy, and confidence. The worker, through the use of his or her relationship with the client, promotes or discourages behavior according to whether the behavior is consistent with the goals of treatment. The worker encourages the client to ventilate and deals with any anxiety that may inhibit functioning.

Central to the treatment process is the relationship between the client and worker. The worker imparts a feeling of confidence in the client's ability to deal with problems. He or she makes suggestions about the client's contemplated actions and indicates approval or suggests alternatives relative to steps that the client has already taken. The worker may, at the very least, provide a willing and sympathetic ear to a troubled and lonely client. It is not unusual for the p/p worker to be the only person available to an offender to whom he or she can relate and talk. When the relationship is a good one, the client cannot help but view the worker as a friend.

The worker is also supportive of the client's family, parents, or spouse. In p/p practice, home visits are a usual part of the worker's responsibilities. During the home visit, the worker has an opportunity to observe the client's environment directly. This firsthand information adds another dimension to the worker's knowledge of the client.

The knowledge that a client lives in substandard housing or in a high-delinquency area is easy for the worker to incorporate into his or her working methodology, but the concept is an intellectual one. A home visit provides direct information about the smell of urine in the hall, roaches, broken fixtures and bathroom facilities, and housing that is hot in the summer and cold in the winter; a home visit also enables the worker to experience the presence of drug addicts huddling in a hallway, waiting for their connection. The worker is able to see, hear, and smell the environment in which a client is forced to live and to understand the hostility and frustration that fill the life of many p/p clients almost from the time they are born.

By working directly with parents or a spouse, in addition to working with the client, the p/p officer broadens his or her delivery of help to the client. The worker can make referrals for the client's children when special aid is necessary—indeed he or she can intervene on behalf of the client in the role of *mediator/advocate* to get services for any family member. The p/p officer can assist with marital problems. Marital discord is an acute problem in many parole cases when a client has been incarcerated for many years. The worker may try to deal with the problem directly or may provide a referral to a specialized agency for the client and spouse. It is not unusual for a distraught wife to call the p/p officer to complain about her husband. Sometimes she is merely seeking some way of ventilating her feelings; at other times, the situation may be more serious—for example, she may have been subjected to physical abuse.

When a client is living with parents, the worker strives to involve them in the rehabilitation effort, which is often difficult. The client may be the perennial black sheep in a large family. He or she may come from a family that also has other members on probation, in prison, on parole. This may dissipate the family's energy and resources and directly affect their ability to help the client.

CLARIFICATION

Clarification, states Florence Hollis (1950: 418–19), is sometimes called counseling because it usually accompanies other forms of treatment in casework practice. Clarification includes providing information that will help a client to see what steps he or she should take in various situations. The worker, for example, may help the client weigh the issues and alternatives to provide a better picture on which to base a decision. Hollis notes that the client "may also be helped to become more aware of his own feelings, desires and attitudes."

The client is encouraged to explain what is bothering him or her. If the problem is external, verbalizing it may be relatively easy. If the difficulty is internally caused, however, it may go deep and provoke anxiety. This difficulty will cause resistance, and the p/p officer will need great skill to secure enough information about the problem to be able to be of assistance. In response to the information, the worker may provide a direct interpretation to the client; more often, the p/p officer will ask questions and make suggestions designed to help the client to think out the problem more clearly and to deal with it in a realistic manner.

LEARNING THEORY/BEHAVIOR MODIFICATION

To understand learning theory/behavior modification, one may place the various modes of treatment used in p/p practice on a continuum represented by a straight horizontal line. Total acceptance of psychoanalytic theory/treatment is on the extreme left of this line and total rejection on the extreme right; social casework is left of center, and reality therapy (RT) (discussed in a later section in this chapter) is toward the right of center. Learning theory/behavior modification is firmly on the extreme right of this imaginary line.

/ _____ / _____ /

Psychoanalytic theory   Reality therapy   Learning theory
(social casework)   (behaviorism)

Behavior modification, the application of learning theory, which emanated from the science laboratory and experimental psychology, rejects psychoanalytic theory as an unscientific basis for an even more unscientific mode of treatment. Ian Stevenson, a psychiatrist, is critical of the paucity of evidence indicating that the therapeutic procedures that are based on psychoanalytic theory are effective (Wolpe, Salter, and Reyna, 1964: 7). B. F. Skinner, America's foremost behaviorist, argues that analytically oriented therapists "rely too much on inferences they make about what is supposedly going on inside their patients, and too little on direct observation of what they do" (Goleman, 1987: 18). For Skinner, the mind is irrelevant as a basis for understanding human behavior (Anonymous, 1987).

Behaviorists, conversely, take pride in displaying and subjecting their methods and results to rigorous scientific analysis. Indeed, the use of behavior modification requires the maintenance of extensive objective treatment data, including outcomes in quantifiable terms [American Psychiatric Association (APA), 1974]. Psychological dictionaries define *behaviorism* as an approach to psychology that emphasizes the importance of an objective study of actual responses.

Behavior modification proceeds on the theory that all forms of behavior are the result of learning responses to certain stimuli. "Disturbed" behavior, for example, is a matter of learning responses that are inappropriate (London, 1964). The behaviorist contends, and has been able to prove, that animal behavior, human and otherwise, can be modified through the proper application of behaviorist principles. Indeed, such techniques as *conditioned reflex therapy* are "based completely on the work of Pavlov and Bechterev" (Salter, 1964: 21), who demonstrated that such observable and measurable activity as the flow of a dog's saliva could be controlled by the use of laboratory conditioning. [Nobel Prize winner (1904) Ivan Pavlov's dogs were conditioned to salivate at the sound of a bell.] When behavior modification moved out of the laboratory, its use was "confined to specific problems such as children's fears and bedwetting and alcoholism" (Reyna, 1964: 170).

The behaviorist stresses—and has been able to prove—that animal behavior can be modified through the proper application of operant conditioning: positive and negative reinforcement. Behavior is "*strengthened* by its consequences, and for that reason the consequences themselves are called 'reinforcers.' " (Skinner, 1974: 40). When some aspect of (animal or human) behavior is followed by a certain type of consequence—a reward—this action is more likely to be repeated. The reward is called *positive reinforcement*. If the probability of a behavior goes up after the *removal* of a stimulus, then *negative reinforcement* has occurred: "A negative reinforcer strengthens any behavior that reduces or terminates it" (Skinner, 1974: 47). For example, the negative reinforcement that occurs when a heroin addict fails to ingest enough heroin—withdrawal symptoms—strengthens drug-seeking behavior. These terms form the basis for operant conditioning, whereby patterns of behavior are *shaped* incrementally by reinforcement (Skinner, 1972). Antisocial behavior is merely the result of learning directly from others—for example, peers—or the failure to learn how to discriminate between competing norms, lawful and unlawful, because of inappropriate reinforcement. When conforming behavior is not adequately reinforced an actor can more easily be influenced by competing, albeit antisocial, sources of positive reinforcement: "Behavior modification, then, involves altering the nature of the controlling conditions, rather than imposing control where none existed before" (Stolz, Wienckowski, and Brown, 1975: 1037). To be effective for learning, however, reinforcement must follow rather closely the behavior that is to be influenced. When these principles are applied in treatment, therefore, timing is crucial.

The behavioral therapist begins with a functional analysis to develop a treatment program designed to deal with specific target behaviors. The analysis deals with the day-to-day functioning of the subject in order to discern the independent variables causing maladaptive behavior/dependent variables. The therapist attempts to elicit specific descriptions of actual events that constitute a problem so that he or she can evaluate which components of the situation are amenable to change by behavioral techniques (Kanfer and Goldstein, 1975). The specific description, whenever possible, is based on direct observation or interviews with the client and/or significant others (e.g., parents or spouse), and a review of any relevant records. Maladaptive behavior is analyzed in terms of intensity and frequency and is often presented in the form of graphs. Offenders have problematic reinforcement contingencies. They often engage in behavior that provides an immediate payoff but has negative long-term consequences. The therapist, among other techniques, teaches the client to conduct his or her own functional analysis for subsequent self-produced modification of the environmental contingencies that are reinforcing the maladaptive behavior.

The functional analysis can be combined with self-monitoring techniques. Highly motivated clients maintain a daily log of the specific problem—for example, lack of temper control. The client records the number of times that he or she exhibits the specific manifestations of a lack of temper control. Although this technique can be combined with other forms of therapy, alone it seems to have the power to modify behavior because it

> increases awareness and makes the response sequence less automatic. This may provide the opportunity for the person to suppress the response or engage in some incompatible behavior. Additionally, self-monitoring may encourage the person to reward or punish himself depending upon whether appropriate gains have been made. Investigators have shown that self-reinforcing statements such as "I am doing well" are important in maintaining one's own behavior. A recording system which facilitates this process undoubtedly will be effective in helping people to change their own behavior as well. (Bootzin, 1975: 11)

The need for timely reinforcement makes operant conditioning difficult to apply in probation and parole practice. For example, stimulants, such as cocaine, and depressants, such as heroin, are powerful reinforcers—they provide instant gratification to those who find their use pleasant; competing with this reality in many cases is difficult and often impossible. Albert Bandura (1974: 862) points out, however, that in humans, "Outcomes resulting from actions need not necessarily occur instantly." This result may occur because as opposed to lower animals, people "can cognitively bridge delays between behavior and subsequent reinforcers without impairing the efficacy of incentive operations." The cognitive position maintains that it is necessary to look to thoughts, memory, language, and beliefs. The emphasis is on inner rather than environmental determinants of behavior (Hollin, 1990). Bandura (1974) argues that to ignore the influence of covert reinforcement in the regulation of behavior is to deny a uniquely human capacity. Self-reinforcement may also operate in a manner that enhances antisocial behavior. Reinforcement may, however, particularly in humans, take on many tangible or symbolic dimensions. In RT (discussed in a later section in this chapter), praise and encouragement are dispensed by the therapist; in correctional settings, the positive reinforcements are often privileges dispensed through secondary reinforcers or *tokens*.

COGNITIVE SOCIAL LEARNING

According to the cognitive social learning perspective, to describe people's overt behaviors without paying attention to what people are thinking cannot provide an adequate model of personality. Behaviorism that does not involve extended consideration of cognitive variables risks neglecting much that is human. (Cloninger, 1993: 369)

TOKEN ECONOMY

Operant conditioning has been used extensively in prisons (and other "total institutions") where reinforcing variables can be controlled to a degree not possible elsewhere. In the controlled setting of the total institution, the application of behavior modification is often referred to as the *token economy*. Garry Martin and Joseph Pear (1992: 305) point to the advantages of using tokens.

First, they can be given immediately after a desirable behavior occurs and cashed in at a later time for a backup reinforcer. Thus, they can be used to "bridge" long delays between the target response and the backup reinforcer, which is especially important when delivery of the backup reinforcer immediately after the behavior is impractical or impossible. Second, tokens make it easier to administer consistent and effective reinforcers when dealing with a group of individuals.

In some correctional programs, inmates are issued punch cards with numbers every morning. As they move through the various prison activities during the day, points are earned and punched out on the cards by correction officers trained in behavior modification techniques. Points can be earned for a variety of "good" behavior—bed making, vocational and educational performance, and so on. The points accumulated on the punch cards are convertible into access to certain privileges, such as the television room, cigarettes, movies, and snacks. Such programs can often reduce the need for standard forms of coercion typically used in correctional institutions.

A widely heralded token economy was used by Harold Cohen at the National Training School for Boys (NTS) in Washington, DC (Cohen and Filipczak, 1971). The project involved 41 adjudicated juvenile delinquents whose crimes ranged from auto theft to homicide. A point system was tied to educational work and academic achievement. The points that were earned allowed a boy to purchase refreshments, clothing, and even items selected from a mail-order catalog. Cohen reports that by establishing this incentive plan, the program enabled youngsters to increase their academic growth from two to four times the average for American public school students.

Cohen notes that the conventional method used in the public school system and correctional institutions is to assign students on the basis of their IQ score and reading level. Those who score low are assumed to be basically incompetent to perform in such areas as algebra and physics. They are assigned to tasks considered appropriate to their level of ability, and these usually do not require reading and other academic skills. Before Cohen arrived at the NTS, this method was used there.

Cohen began his program by considering every inmate as a potential student capable of upgrading. His goal was to prepare them to return to public school or to pass the high school equivalency test. He set up a planned environment that included choices and perquisites that, although normally available to the average employed person, were not typically available to youths in prison. At the NTS, residents could earn points for academic performance with which they paid for their rooms, clothing, amusements, and gifts. Even showers had to be rented with points. Points could not be gained except through "work"—they could not be given away, loaned, traded, or stolen. Family members were permitted to visit but were not permitted to purchase items for residents—they were completely dependent on the NTS program. In addition, residents were able to earn nonmonetary reinforcements: respect and approval from staff and peers.

The principal objective of the program was the development of appropriate academic behavior. No assumptions were made by the program originators relative to the resident's behavior when he returned to the community. However, a follow-up on recidivism indicated that during the first year after release from the NTS, the rate of recidivism was two-thirds less than the norm, although by the third year the rate was near the norm. Cohen reports that the program evidently delayed a return to delinquent behavior but did not necessarily prevent the problem.

Thomas Stampfl (1970: 105), points out:

> One obvious disadvantage related to TE [token economy] is that rather close control over environmental contingencies is required. The status

of the S [subject] whose behavior is to be modified is that of a "captive." In the absence of environmental control, it is not possible to introduce critical contingencies. If control is present initially, but is then lost for whatever reason, the removal of the contingencies allows the altered behavior to revert in the direction of its original baseline rate. In an effort to maintain behavior when the subject has lost his status as a captive, operant conditioners have attempted to gradually alter the manipulated contingencies in respect to the behavior being modified so that the changed behavior itself would tend to result in natural intrinsic reinforcement.

The difficulty inherent in the latter approach, Stampfl notes, is that delinquents/criminals "tend to be highly resistant to the usual types of natural or intrinsic reinforcement that appear to function so effectively for other 'normal' populations" (1970: 105).

OTHER BEHAVIOR MODIFICATION SYSTEMS

Operant conditioning can also use *aversive therapy*. This approach involves the avoidance of punishment in a controlled situation in which the therapist specifies in advance an unpleasant event that will occur if the subject performs an undesirable behavior. According to a report by the APA (1974: 25), "the most effective way to eliminate inappropriate behavior appears to be to punish it while at the same time reinforcing the desired behavior." This method of treatment is obviously controversial, and many behaviorists disapprove of the use of punishment on both ethical and treatment grounds—its effects do not seem to last as long as results conditioned by positive reinforcement. According to Skinner, "What's wrong with punishments is that they work immediately, but give no long term results. The responses to punishment are either the urge to escape, to counterattack or a stubborn apathy. These are the bad effects you get in prisons or schools, or wherever punishments are used" (Goleman, 1987: 18).

Some have told "horror stories" about the use of aversive therapy, which was portrayed in the Stanley Kubrick movie *A Clockwork Orange*. In real life, California prisoners were injected with Anectine (succinylcholine), a muscle relaxant that causes brief paralysis but leaves the subject conscious. The prisoners were unable to move or breath voluntarily, a sensation that simulates the onset of death. At the same time, the therapist would tell the subjects that they must change their behavior. Some observers state that this program was not an example of aversive conditioning but rather merely punishment.

Drug antagonists can serve a similar function by rendering the use of alcohol or other substances ineffective—lacking positive reinforcement—or extremely unpleasant—negative reinforcement or punishment. Disulfiram (Antabuse), metronidazole, or chlorpropamide can serve this purpose for alcohol abusers. Antabuse—the best known of these substances—disrupts the metabolism of alcohol in the liver producing a severe reaction that includes stomach and head pain, nausea, and vomiting. One substance has the appearance and smell of cocaine and even produces a numbing effect but is not psychoactive. This substance is used in conjunction with an aversive chemical, one that induces vomiting, for example. In voluntary patients, electric shocks may be self-administered whenever a craving for the chemical arises. Alternatively, verbal aversion techniques may be used when a patient is asked to *imagine* strongly aversive stimuli (usually vomiting) in association with imaginal drug-related cues, scenes, or behavior. Similar procedures can be used with sex offenders —for example, pedophiles—by associating erotic feelings toward children with a negative consequence.

Other behavioral therapies use biofeedback and relaxation training, and sometimes assertiveness training, to prepare drug abusers to cope better with stress and anxiety that is believed linked to drug use. Researchers have found that certain environmental cues can serve as triggers to activate drug cravings (Dole, 1980). When desensitization is used "patients are usually first relaxed, then given repeated exposure to a graded hierarchy of anxiety-producing stimuli (real or imaginal)" to provide a form of immunity (Childress, McLennan, and O'Brien, 1985: 957).

In a variant of classical behaviorism, *social learning theory* places the stress on cognitive mediational processes. According to this view, human beings are active participants in their operant conditioning processes—the individual determines what is and what is not reinforcing. For example, to become a drug abuser, one must *learn* that ingesting certain chemicals is desirable. In other words, human behavior is complex and reinforcement often abstract. Thus, notes Albert Bandura (1974: 862), "human beings can cognitively bridge delays between behavior and subsequent reinforcement without impairing the efficacy of incentive operations." Humans have a unique capacity to use abstractions, or symbols, that can serve as important reinforcers, such as the medals and trophies dear to any amateur athlete.

In using operant conditioning with drug abusers, the social learning theorist stresses client analysis to discover the variables that are reinforcing. The therapist attempts to discover the situational demands and their related negative emotions that are related to the patient's drug use. The individual is seen as lacking that level of social competence necessary to cope adequately with a variety of situational demands. The treatment process begins with an assessment of the positive and negative aspects of drug use and a self-report on the type, amount, and frequency of drugs used. The assessment includes a focus on the social, physical, and emotional environments in which the drug use occurs. After the assessment, the role of the therapist is to enable the patient to deal with triggering behavior in a manner that avoids resorting to drugs, with the patient's own report of the negative aspects of drug use serving as a motivator for adopting more positive coping strategies (Donovan, 1988).

CRITICISM OF BEHAVIOR MODIFICATION

Considerable opposition exists to behaviorism in theory and practice. To many cognitive therapists, learning theory lessens the dignity of a human being, reducing people to the level of animals, with techniques used reminiscent of animal training. Ogden Lindsley, a noted behaviorist, for example, humorously reminisces about his early days with behaviorism, stating "that if the bottom fell out of the whole thing, I would drop out of graduate school and try to get a job with Ringling Brothers' circus training gorillas to dance and play the piano" (Hilts, 1974: 7).

Much of what is done in the name of behavior modification is dependent on one's definition of the situation. As a learning tool, behaviorism is amoral and politically neutral and thus easily lends itself to misuse. Some critics maintain that behavior modification is simply a tool for keeping persons with legitimate grievances from expressing or acting on them—behavior modification, as noted, has been successful in helping to maintain prison discipline and order. The point at which legitimate dissent ends and disorder begins is often a matter of obvious subjectivity. "Behavior modification," note Beth Sulzer and G. Roy Mayer (1972: 7), "is an approach that is concerned with how to change behavior, not which behaviors should be changed."

Unlike other forms of treatment, to be successful behavior modification does not require the acquiescence of its subjects. In fact, behavior modification may at times be more successful when used without the knowledge of those whose behaviors are being subjected to it. Because behavior modification serves to modify *undesirable* behavior or attitudes, who is to determine what is undesirable? What one considers *learning*, another views as *brainwashing*. This point was made vivid during the Korean War (1950–53), when some U.S. servicemen who were prisoners of war were subjected (unknowingly) to behavior modification. The success of this practice was not viewed as "learning" by officials in the United States, who coined the term *brainwashing* to describe the behavior modification methods used by the Chinese and North Koreans. [For a discussion of the social, moral, and political implications of behavior modification, see Wheeler (1973).]

"Frequently, the goal of effective behavior modification in a penal institution," note Stephanie Stolz, Louis Wienckowski, and Bertram Brown (1975: 1040), "is the preservation of the institution's authoritarian control." That is, "making the prisoners less troublesome and easier to handle, thus adjusting the inmates to the needs of the institution." A major problem with behavior modification programs in prisons, they argue, "is that positive programs begun with the best intentions may become subverted to punitive ones by the oppressive prison atmosphere" (1975: 1040).

As in psychoanalytic theory, learning theory does not distinguish between behavior as such and criminal behavior; both are seen as based on the same principles of learning. In expounding the behaviorist position on crime, C. Ray Jeffrey (1971: 177) states that "There are no criminals, only environmental circumstances which result in criminal behavior. Given the proper environmental structure, anyone will be a criminal or a noncriminal." In both theories—psychoanalytical and learning—the person defined as a criminal is not in control of his or her behavior—a denial of *free will*—which raises serious legal issues with respect to holding persons accountable for their actions. This concept is known in law as *mens rea*.

Psychoanalytically oriented therapists have been critical of behavior modification over the issue of *symptom substitution*. These therapists do not question the ability of behaviorists to remove or diminish certain undesirable behavior. However, according to traditional psychoanalytic theory, this symptom reduction will merely lead to new symptoms that will replace the old ones with each new emotional difficulty experienced by the subject. Thus Aichhorn argues that "the disappearance of a symptom does not indicate a cure. When a psychic process is denied expression and the psychic energies determining it remain undischarged, a new path of discharge will be found along the line of least resistance, and a new form of delinquency will result" (1963: 39). Psychic disturbances are thus conceived of as producing a lightning-like force, which if manipulated in a way that prevents discharge (i.e., by behavior modification) will merely strike harmfully in another direction. The APA Task Force stated, however, that this result is not necessarily inevitable. Furthermore, it argues, reduction of unwanted behavior provides an opportunity to teach a person more desirable behavior (APA, 1974).

Behaviorists analyze symptoms in terms of observable behavior components. The therapist keeps a record of "frequency counts" on a particular behavioral component. For example, a parent will be asked to record the number of outbursts exhibited by a youngster within a given period. The therapist then makes a functional analysis designed to determine the circumstances under which the undesirable behavior seems to occur, and the elements within the environment that may be supporting (and thus encouraging) the behavior. In this case, the parent may be told to ignore the outbursts, no matter what the intensity, while providing positive reinforcers for positive behavior. The results of this approach will be measured against the original baseline of frequency counts. The empirical nature of the behaviorist approach has significant appeal; however, human behavior is driven by subjective meanings that may be known only to the actor.

Positive reinforcement, the timely application of rewards, is more easily accomplished in an institutional setting, where the environment can be controlled and manipulated to reinforce certain behaviors, than in the community, where most p/p treatment occurs. This accounts for the paucity of articles on the use of behavior modification in p/p in professional journals. In one published report (Thorne, Tharp, and Wetzel, 1967), probation officers were trained in behavior techniques, and they, in turn, gained the cooperation of parents whose youngsters were on probation. The officers explained the behavior techniques to be used and taught the parents how to apply them. Behavior was monitored by the parents, and charts were used to record frequency counts. Positive reinforcers were given for desired behavior, such as attendance at school, scholastic work, and satisfactory behavior, and were withheld when the child misbehaved. The rewards were specific and related directly to the positive behavior. For example, a girl on probation was given telephone privileges and permitted weekend dates, contingent on her attendance at school all day. In this case, the attendance teacher would give a note to the child at the end of the school day attesting to her attendance. When the child gave her mother the note, she earned the privilege of receiving and making calls that day. If she received four notes, she earned a weekend date; five notes earned two weekend dates.

In another case, rewards included both tangible and intangible items. For example, for studying 30 minutes a day, the youngster was both praised and given permission to ride his bicycle. Money, access to television, and other rewards were used as reinforcers for specific behavior on a specified schedule basis. This form of treatment is often referred to as *behavioral contracting*: "an agreement in which the performance of predetermined responsibilities or duties results in receipt of privileges or rewards" (O'Leary and Wilson, 1975: 480). It has been used predominantly with children because (in noninstitutional settings) they can be subjected to greater environmental controls than adults. In another published study on contingency management with adult drug offenders on probation, probation officers used reduction in probation time as a reinforcer (Polakow and Docktor, 1974).

Robert Polakow and Ronald Docktor note that "experimental literature on behavioral approaches to probation work with adults is almost nonexistent" (1974: 63). And the quality of behavioral research in p/p, note Michael Nietzel and Melissa Himelein (1987: 127), "is quite disappointing." Bob and Marina Remington (1987: 170) state that while they have "little doubt as to the promise of behavior modification in probation service contexts," their review of the literature indicates that "the promise has yet to be adequately fulfilled."

REALITY THERAPY

Reality therapy (RT) was developed as a mode of treatment by William Glasser, a psychiatrist. It is probably the easiest of the three modes of treatment to describe, and simplicity has been a major reason for its popularity in probation and parole practice. Glasser's book *Reality Therapy* (originally published in 1965) contains only 166 pages. Glasser describes RT as a method "that leads all patients toward reality, toward grappling successfully with the tangible aspects of the real world" (1975: 6). As opposed to RT, "conventional therapy goals," says Carl Bersani (1989: 177), do not include client responsibility or personal actions as primary."

Although Glasser accepts the developmental theories of psychoanalytic theory, he rejects them as a useful basis for treatment: "It is wishful thinking to believe that a man will give up a phobia once he understands either its origins or the current representation of its origin in the transference relationship" (1975: 53). Glasser (1975: 51) believes that conventional treatment depends far too much on the ability of the patient to change his attitude and ultimately his behavior through gaining insight into his unconscious conflicts and inadequacies. The reality therapist denies the claims of psychoanalytic theorists that cure depends on the recovery of traumatic early memories that have been repressed. The ability of psychoanalysis to cure persons, states Melitta Schmideberg (1975), a psychiatrist whose mother was eminent in the field of psychoanalysis, has never been clinically substantiated.

In a later work, Glasser (1976) reiterates some of his previous positions and elaborates on others. Various mental problems, Glasser argues, are merely symptomatic illnesses that have no presently known medical cause. They act as companions for the lonely people who *choose* them. Glasser states that in cases of so-called mental illness, the behaviors or symptoms are actually chosen by the person from a lifetime of experiences residing in the subconscious. In place of conventional treatment, the reality therapist proposes first substituting the term *irresponsible* for mental health labels (e.g., neurotic, personality disorder, and psychotic). A "healthy" person is called *responsible*, and the task of the therapist is to help an irresponsible person to become responsible. Furthermore, notes Schmideberg, the psychoanalytic approach of "dwelling on the past encourages the patient to forget his present problems, which is a relief at times, but often—undesirably—the patient feels that after having produced so many interesting memories, he is now entitled to rest on his laurels and make no effort to change his attitude or plans for the future" (1975: 29).

This concept diverts attention from the client's current problem(s), which is a reality that should be dealt with directly. Glasser argues that conventional treatment does not deal with whether a client's behavior is right or wrong, in terms of morality or law, but "rather, it contends that once the patient is able to resolve his conflicts and get over his mental illness, he will be able to behave correctly" (1975: 56). Societal realities, however, particularly in probation and parole practice, require direct interventions with a client, with the therapist not accepting "wrong" behavior.

"Reality therapy is based upon the theory that all of us are born with at least two built-in psychological needs: (1) the need to belong and be loved and (2) the need for gaining self-worth and recognition" (Glasser, 1980: 48). According to Glasser, people with serious behavior problems lack the proper involvement with someone; and lacking this involvement, they are unable to satisfy their needs. Therefore, to be a helping person, the therapist must enable the client to gain involvement, first with the worker and then with others. The traditional therapist maintains a professional objectivity or distance, whereas the reality therapist strives for strong feelings between worker and client. This type of relationship is necessary if the worker is to have an impact on the client's behavior. The worker, although always accepting of the client, firmly rejects irresponsible behavior. He or she can then teach the client better ways of behaving.

To accomplish this re-education, the worker must know about the client's reality—the way he or she lives, his or her environment, aspirations, and *total reality*. Reality is always influenced by culture, ethnic and racial group, economic class, and intelligence. The worker must be willing to listen open-mindedly and learn about the client (Schmideberg, 1975). While observing, the worker develops a relationship with the client, a relationship that can lead to responsible behavior. Alluding to the fact that RT does not always work, Glasser states that the fault is with the therapist who is unable to become involved in a meaningful way with the client. However, George Harris and David Watkins (1987: 18) point out that mandated correctional clients may avoid counseling because of their difficulties with intimacy:

> For many people it feels safer to reject someone trying to help them than to risk accepting that help only to be disappointed. Such clients try to create physical and emotional distance in relationships. Paradoxically, a warm and empathetic counselor often is met with barriers to bonding in the therapeutic relationship, and too much pursuit of the client to bring about intimacy only intensifies the client's anxiety.

Glasser expresses a great deal of support for the work of probation and parole officers, although he cautions persons in corrections, as well as other fields, against the use of punishment. "For many delinquents," he notes (1976: 95), "punishment serves as a source of involvement. They receive attention through delinquent behavior, if only that of the police, court, probation counselor, and prison [workers]. . . . A failing person rationalizes the punishment as a reason for the anger that caused him to be hostile."

Like behavior modification, RT is symptom oriented. The p/p client is in treatment because he or she has caused society to take action as a result of his or her behavior. If the worker can remove the symptoms and make the client responsible, that will satisfy society and relieve the client of anxiety caused by fear of being incarcerated. Schmideberg (1975: 24) states that for a delinquent symptom to disappear, it is usually necessary for the person to accomplish three interrelated tasks:

1. Face it full with all of its implications and consequences
2. Decide to stop it and consider the factors that precipitate it
3. Make a definite effort to stop it

She maintains that a general and nondirective method is not likely to change symptoms that the client may find satisfying (e.g., drugs to the addict, excitement and money to the robber, or forced sex to the rapist).

Richard Rachin (1974: 51–53) outlines fourteen steps that the reality therapist follows to attain responsible behavior in his or her client:

1. *Personalizes.* The reality therapist becomes emotionally involved. He is a warm, tough, interested, and sensitive human being who genuinely gives a damn—and demonstrates it.

2. *Reveals self.* He has frailties as well as strengths and does not need to project an image of omniscience or omnipotence. If he is asked personal questions, he sees nothing wrong with responding.

3. *Concentrates on the "here and now."* He is concerned only with behavior that can be tried and tested on a reality basis. He is interested only with the problems of the present, and he does not allow a client to waste time and avoid confronting reality by dwelling on the past. He does not permit a person the luxury of blaming irresponsible behavior on past difficulties.

4. *Emphasizes behavior.* The reality therapist is not interested in uncovering underlying motivations or drives; rather, he concentrates on helping the person act in a manner that will help him meet his needs responsibly.

5. *Rarely asks why.* He is concerned with helping a client understand what he is doing, what he has accomplished, what he is learning from his behavior, and whether he could do better than he is doing now. Asking a person the reasons for his actions implies that they make a difference. To the reality therapist irresponsible behavior is just that—he is not interested in explanations for self-defeating behavior. He conveys to the client that more responsible behavior will be expected.

6. *Helps the person evaluate his behavior.* He is persistent in guiding the client to explore his actions for signs of irresponsible, unrealistic behavior. He does not permit the client to deny the importance of difficult things he would like to do. He repeatedly asks the person what his current behavior is accomplishing and whether it is meeting his needs.

7. *Helps him develop a better plan for future behavior.* By questioning *what* the person is doing now and *what* he can do differently, he conveys his belief in the client's ability to behave responsibly. If the client cannot develop his own plan for future action, the reality therapist will help him develop one. Once the plan is worked out, a contract is drawn up and signed by the person and the reality therapist. It is a minimum plan for behaving differently in matters where the person admits he has acted irresponsibly. If the contract is broken, a new one is designed and agreed upon. If a contract is honored, a new one with tasks more closely attuned to the person's ability is designed.

8. *Rejects excuses.* He does not encourage searching for reasons to justify irresponsible behavior, thus avoiding the implication that the client has acceptable reasons for violating his agreement. Excuses are not accepted—only an honest scrutinizing examination of his behavior.

9. *Offers no tears of sympathy.* Sympathy can indicate that the worker lacks confidence in the client's ability to act responsibly. Sad tales, past and present, are avoided. Sympathizing with a person's misery and self-pity will not lead to more responsible behavior. The worker must convey to his client that he cares enough about him that, if need be, he will try to force him to act more responsibly.

10. *Praises and approves responsible behavior.* The worker makes appropriate indications of recognition for positive accomplishments. However, he does not become unduly excited about the client's success in handling problems that he previously avoided or handled poorly.

11. *Believes people are capable of changing their behavior.* The worker's positive expectations enhance the client's chances of adopting a more productive lifestyle, regardless of what has occurred in the past. The worker is encouraging and optimistic.

12. *Tries to work in groups.* The use of a peer group allows for more influence or pressure on the members. It enables the members to express themselves before people with similar problems. It enables the member to test out "reality" in a controlled environment.

13. *Does not give up.* The worker rejects the idea that anyone is unable to learn how to live a more productive and responsible life. Historical information contained in long case records is not allowed to interfere with the worker's involvement with his client, and his belief that all persons can begin again.

14. *Does not label people.* Avoids the diagnostic rituals, and does not classify people as sick, disturbed, or emotionally disabled—they are either responsible or irresponsible.

Glasser developed RT while he was a psychiatrist at the Ventura School, an institution for the treatment of older adolescent girls who had been unsuccessful on probation. Because this technique evolved within the field of corrections and the realities of dealing with delinquent behavior, many have accepted and applied RT to p/p treatment. RT flows easily from the p/p officer's need to hold the offender accountable for his or her behavior. Some maintain that the value emphasis in RT coincides with the paternalistic and perhaps authoritarian attitudes of some p/p officers. Carl Bersani states that "Glasser's writings do not provide a systematic methodology for clearly separating the moral standards of the counselor from that of the client" (1989: 188). Although Glasser does not deal with theory and RT is practice oriented, the theoretical underpinnings are close to those in behavior modification. Instead of manipulating the environment or using tangible reinforcers, the therapist develops a close relationship with the client and uses praise or concern as positive and negative reinforcers. For this method to be carried out effectively, the worker needs to be a genuinely warm and sympathetic person who can easily relate to persons who have often committed very unpleasant acts and whose personalities may leave a great deal to be desired—no easy task. Thus, although training someone in the use of RT may be relatively easy, success requires qualities of personality that are not part of the basic qualifications for becoming a probation or parole officer.

GROUP WORK

Group work provides a helping milieu wherein individuals agree to help one another; in contrast with the worker in casework the group is the agency of help. The basic operating premise of social group work is that "Groups of people with similar needs can be a source of mutual support, mutual aid and problem solving" (Brown: 10). In the group, notes Allan Brown (1986: 11), "every member is a potential helper." Helen Northern states that "one of the advantages of the use of groups in social work is that stimulation toward improvement arises from a network of interpersonal influences in which all members participate" (1969: 52). The theory underlying the use of the group is that the impact provided by peer interaction is more powerful than worker-client reactions within the one-to-one situation of social casework. Furthermore, groups "help members realize that they are not alone with their problems" (Toseland and Rivas, 1995: 17).

In probation/parole, groups consist of members who share a common status, in this case legally determined. Groups in p/p may also be organized on the basis of age or around a common problem, such as substance abuse. The group is a mutual aid society in which members are given an opportunity to share experiences and assist each other with problems in a safe, controlled environment. The group helps to confirm for each member the fact that others share similar problems—"are in the same boat"—thus reducing the sense of isolation. With the help of the worker, members are able share a sense of purpose and develop a commitment to helping each other through patterns of group interaction: "As members offer solutions to common problems, make supportive comments, and share in the skill development of fellow members by participating in group exercises, they become committed to helping each other" (Shaffer and Galinsky, 1989: 26).

The group can reduce the anxiety of having to report alone to a p/p officer; collaboration tends to offset the more direct authority of the one-to-one situation and to lower the impact of sociocultural differences between client and worker. As Gisela Konopka (1983: 93) points out, "In a group members support each other; they are not alone in the face of authority." In a group, she notes, the offender is surrounded by equals; he or she is not a client, but a *member.* This arrangement permits "feelings of identification that are impossible to achieve on an individual basis with even the most accepting social caseworker" (1983: 97). Group work also requires a level of skill and training that is not widely available in social work in general and p/p practice in particular. In p/p, the groups are typically open-ended, because members enter and leave—complete their sentence or violate supervision—at various intervals.

A variety of approaches to group work may be applied in correctional settings, often depending on the theoretical stance of the agency or worker, including gestalt therapy, transactional analysis, and psychoanalytic group therapy, all of which are rooted in psychoanalytic theory; and guided group interaction, which is based on sociological, small group, theory, and behavior modification. Within the profession of social work several different approaches to group work are available, for example, those espoused by William Schwartz (1976), Robert Vinter (1985), Helen Northern (1969), and Sheldon Rose (1977).

Cognitive Learning Skills Training

A group approach growing in popularity in probation and parole entails the application of cognitive behavior theory and is known as *cognitive learning skills training* (CST) or *problem-solving therapy* (PST). This approach views criminal behavior not as the symptom of some disease but the result of a combination of social and economic situations and behavioral factors. For example, a *low social intelligence* involves offenders who have deficits in the ability to envision the consequences of their behavior and are unable to use means-end reasoning to achieve their goals. Operating at the ego level of development, they are unable to place themselves in someone else's position or understand another's behavior. The CST approach is based on a belief that "individuals can be taught to be better problem-solving thinkers" (Husband and Platt, 1993: 34).

CST/PST "emphasizes the importance of problem-solving skills that can be applied to a variety of problem situations. These include skills such as awareness of interpersonal problems, defining problems, causal thinking, consequential or alternative thinking, means-ends thinking, and perspective-taking" (Husband and Platt, 1993: 33). Training is designed to modify impulsive, egocentric, illogical, and rigid thinking, and to teach offenders to think—consider the consequences—before acting. The sessions can be conducted by p/p officers who receive relevant training. Generally, 40 two-hour sessions with audio visual presentations, role playing, behavior rehearsal, and reasoning exercises are offered. With six to ten offenders, the therapist—called a *coach*—leads the group in problem solving, anger management, negotiation skills, value enhancement, critical reasoning, creative thinking, planning, and decision making. A focus is placed on enabling offenders to think in terms of options/alternatives to gain greater control over their own lives. Exercises ask offenders to respond to dilemmas, target skills, apply the skills and techniques, and then return to the group to discuss the experience.

Some problems in implementing CST/PST include that groups require a specific starting and completion date, which is complicated by offenders being placed on and completing supervision at different times. Also, p/p officers may not feel comfortable in the role of "coach" and may resist training.

Now that this section has examined psychological theories and methods of treatment, the next one looks at some sociological theories that have application to probation and parole practice.

SOCIOLOGICAL THEORY

Psychological theory attempts to identify causes of criminal behavior within the individual actor and to treat the causes accordingly. Although sociological theory does not necessarily offer treatment approaches, sociological theory approaches crime in a social context and can add to understanding individual offenders. The following sections briefly review those sociological theories that are most relevant to p/p practice.

NATURE VERSUS NURTURE

Whenever a theory of crime is offered, two essential elements must be considered. First, theories of crime can be distinguished by how the authors or supporters conceive of the nature of human behavior. Prominent in any discussion of human behavior is the *nature versus nurture* controversy. Both sides address the same question: What is the dominant force shaping human behavior? Supporters of the *nature* position answer that behavior can be explained primarily by genetic, biological, or other properties inherent in the individual. In short, human behavior is inherited. Conversely, proponents of the *nurture* position look to the social environment for the causal factors; that is, human behavior is largely the product of social interaction.

ANOMIE

The concept of *anomie,* derived from the Greek meaning "lack of law," was developed by the French sociologist Emile Durkheim (1858–1917) to explain variations in suicide rates. Durkheim (1951) pointed to periods when abnormal social conditions (e.g., an economic depression) weaken cohesion, causing each individual to pursue his or her own solitary interests. Rapid industrialization and urbanization, for example, can lead to a breakdown of social controls as large numbers of people are suddenly thrown out of adjustment with their typical ways of life (Clinard, 1964). The person is left with a sense of "normlessness"—anomie—leaving him or her adrift without customary guideposts—social constraints on behavior. An accompanying growth of individualism occurs as weakened social controls encourage a breakdown in discipline and allow unbridled human appetite to reign free—a high level of deviance, such as crime and suicide can be expected. In 1938, Robert Merton "Americanized" the concept of anomie, which became part of what are often called *strain theories.*

Merton argued that no other society is as close to the United States in considering economic success as an absolute value. Furthermore, he says, in the United States "the pressure of prestige-bearing success tends to eliminate the effective social constraint over the means employed to this end. The 'end-justifies-the-means' doctrine becomes a guiding tenet for action when the cultural structure unduly exalts the end and the social organization unduly limits possible recourse to approved means" (1938: 681). Ian Taylor, Paul Walton, and Jock Young (1973: 93) state that "the desire to make money without regard to the means in which one sets about doing it, is symptomatic of the malintegration at the heart of American society."

According to Merton, anomie results when people are confronted by the contradiction between goals and means—*strain*—and "become estranged from a society that promises them in principle what they are denied in reality [economic opportunity]." Despite numerous success stories—the poor boy from humble origins who becomes rich and famous—"we know that in this same society that proclaims the right, and even the duty, of lofty aspirations for all, men do not have equal access to the opportunity structure" (1964: 218). This point is particularly true of the most disadvantaged segments of our population who become the clients of our probation, prison, and parole systems.

How do persons respond to the anomic condition? Most simply scale down their aspirations and conform to conventional social norms. Some rebel, rejecting the conventional social structure and seek, instead, to establish a "new social order" through political action or by establishing alternative lifestyles. Two responses, retreatism and innovation, are of particular interest for probation and parole practice.

Retreatism means that all attempts to reach conventional social goals are abandoned in favor of a deviant adaptation—a "retreat" to alcohol and drug abuse. Time and energy are now expended to reach an attainable goal: getting "high." *Innovation* is a term used by Merton to describe the adoption of illegitimate means to gain success. Societal goals of success have been incorporated and accepted, but the person finds access to legitimate means for becoming successful limited—and anomie results. Crime is viewed as a basically utilitarian adaptation to the anomic situation. Thus, with the innovation response, "the ends justify the means," whereas with retreatism, the ends ("getting high") are sufficiently reduced as to make the means readily accessible.

Merton assumes a consensus and commitment to "American values"—that is, an attitude fixated on money making pervades our society. This assumption does not account for nonutilitarian deviance or the class-linked dynamics of criminal behavior. More recent versions of strain theory have expanded the goals of American youth to include such short-term variables as popularity with the opposite sex, good school grades, and athletic achievements. This enlargement would explain conditions of strain experienced by middle-class youth because these goals are not necessarily class linked. For adults, the failure to achieve expected goals causes strain that in some persons leads to anger, resentment, and rage—emotional states that can lead to criminal behavior (Agnew, 1992). Robert Agnew (1992) suggests that social justice or equity might be at the root of strain; in this case, a sense of being dealt with unfairly—adversity is blamed on others—and not simply an inability to reach goals, results in strain.

Does strain really exist among lower-class youth? Does a gap exist between aspirations and expectations, or are the goals of lower-class youth limited and aspirations linked accordingly? Anomie/strain theory has been criticized for:

> (1) being largely culture-bound and restricted to the ethnic and minority situation existing in large urban areas in the United States today; (2) not stating clearly the success-goal aspirations of slum boys, except the economic and educational goals; (3) assuming that such success goals are appreciated in all segments of society; and (4) barely recognizing the extensive violation of ethical and legal norms in the general adult society among all social classes. (Clinard, 1964: 30)

What does the theory of anomie offer the p/p officer and the real problems of his or her practice? One consideration has to do with aspirations. Offenders often have unrealistic goals; their aspirations surpass their ability. In such cases, if anomie is to be avoided, the p/p officer must help the client to make a realistic assessment of the situation, and then to assist him or her with achieving goals that are both constructive and reality based. Each client should be encouraged to achieve to the limits of his or her ability. The officer also has a responsibility to see that the client's goals are not blocked by such barriers as discrimination. In such instances, the PO must make use of the various agencies that are responsible for enforcing equal opportunity laws.

DIFFERENTIAL ASSOCIATION

As proposed by Edwin Sutherland (1883–1950), *differential association* explains how criminal behavior is transmitted (not how it originates). According to Sutherland (1973), criminal behavior is learned, and the principal part of learning criminal behavior occurs within intimate personal groups based on the degree of intensity, frequency, and duration of the association. The person learns, in addition to the techniques of committing crime, the drives, attitudes, and rationalizations that add up to a favorable precondition to criminal behavior. Much criminal and noncriminal behavior has the same goal: securing economic and personal status. Differential association accounts for the difference in selecting criminal or noncriminal methods for achieving the goals.

The basis for this theory is a set of beliefs that

- Criminal behavior is learned (it is not the result of biological or psychological variables).
- Criminal behavior is learned in interaction with other persons in a process of communication.
- The learning of criminal behavior occurs primarily within intimate personal groups (in contrast to the influence of teachers, books, etc.).
- The learning of criminal behavior includes the techniques, motives, and attitudes of a criminal.
- The specific direction of motives and drives is learned from definitions of the legal code as favorable or unfavorable (mixed attitudes to which the person is exposed).
- A person becomes delinquent because of an excess of definitions favorable to violation of law over definitions unfavorable to violation of law (attitudes to which the person is exposed determine behavior).
- Differential associations may vary in frequency, duration, priority, and intensity (the strength of association determines influence).
- The process of learning criminal behavior by association with criminal and anticriminal patterns involves all of the mechanisms that are involved in any other learning (Boy Scouts and gangsters learn behavior in the same manner).
- Although criminal behavior is an expression of general needs and values, this type of action is not explained by those general needs and values because noncriminal behavior is an expression of the same needs and values (both criminals and the law-abiding citizens have the same drives and motivations).

In sum, criminal behavior results from the strength or intensity of criminal associations and is the result of an accumulative learning process. A pictorial portrayal of differential association can easily be conceived of in terms of a balanced scale that starts out level. On each side is accumulated the varying weights of criminal and noncriminal associations. At some theoretical point, criminal activity will result from an excess of criminal associations over the noncriminal or prosocial ones.

What import does this theory have for p/p practice? As noted earlier in the discussion of p/p regulations (see Chapters 3, 5, and 8), they usually contain prohibitions against certain associations. A person on p/p is usually cautioned against associating with others similarly situated. This recommendation can easily be seen as a practical attempt to respond to the theory of differential association. In addition, the p/p officer can provide exposure to prosocial associations, an exposure and influence that conceivably can help to balance out our theoretical scale. The officer can assist the client with securing and encouraging association with community, charitable, religious, athletic, fraternal, and other such organizations.

The emphasis on crime as a *learning* process is similar to behaviorist (*learning theory*) views of criminal behavior. This point led Robert Burgess and

Ronald Akers (1969: 315) to reformulate Sutherland's central premise into a "differential association *reinforcement* theory" of criminal behavior:

> A person will become delinquent if the official norms or laws do not perform a discriminate function and thereby control "normative" or conforming behavior. We know from the law of differential reinforcement that the operant which produces the most reinforcement will become dominant. Thus, if lawful behavior did not result in reinforcement, the strength of the behavior would be weakened, and a state of deprivation would result. This, in turn, would increase the probability that other behaviors would be emitted which are reinforced and hence would be strengthened and, of course, these behaviors, though common to one or more groups, may be labeled deviant by the larger society. Also such behavior patterns themselves may acquire conditioned reinforcing value and subsequently be reinforced by the members of a group by making various forms of social reinforcement, such as social approval, esteem, and status, contingent upon that behavior.

DELINQUENT SUBCULTURES

According to James Short (1968: 11), "subcultures are patterns of values, norms, and behavior which have become traditional among certain groups. These groups may be of many types, including occupational and ethnic groups, social classes, occupants of 'closed institutions' [e.g., prisons, mental hospitals] and various age grades." They are "important frames of reference through which individuals and groups see the world and interpret it."

Albert Cohen (1965: 86) argues that certain lower-class subcultures negate middle-class values, and this negation is a severe handicap. Cohen says that certain cultural characteristics are necessary to achieve success in our society, and the upbringing of a middle-class child is more likely to develop these characteristics:

- Ambition
- Sense of individual responsibility
- Skills for achievement
- Ability to postpone gratification
- Industry and thrift
- Rational planning (e.g., budgeting time and money)
- Cultivation of manners/politeness
- Control of physical aggression
- Respect for property
- Sense of "wholesome" recreation

Certainly, most probation and parole clients lack many or sometimes all of these requisites for adjustment to the wider society.

Cohen (1965: 86) states that class-linked differences "relegate to the bottom of the status pyramid those children belonging to the most disadvantaged classes, not by virtue of their class position as such but by virtue of their lack of requisite personal qualifications resulting from their class-linked handicaps." These youngsters simply lack the attributes listed previously and react in a manner that some (e.g., Cloward and Ohlin, 1960) have referred to as the conflict subculture.

According to Cohen (1965: 80), the delinquent ("conflict") subculture "takes its norms from the larger culture but turns them upside down." Thus, the subcultural delinquent's conduct is correct "by the standards of his subculture, precisely *because* it is wrong by the norms of the larger culture." His delinquent activities are totally nonutilitarian; they are "malicious, negativistic—'stealing for the hell of it'—and apart from considerations of gain and profit." The goal is status, not financial profit. According to Cohen, rules (those of the wider society) are not something merely to be evaded, they are to be *flouted*: An element of active spite, malice, contempt, ridicule, challenge, and defiance is present.

Short (1968: 16) disagrees with Cohen. He concludes that the subcultural delinquent gang merely discourages expression of conventional values, and "values which are given active support within the context of gang interaction, for example, toughness and sexual prowess, are not conducive to conventional types of achievement." Walter Miller (1958) states that law-violating acts committed by members of adolescent street corner groups in lower-class communities are not geared toward flouting conventional middle-class norms. Instead, the delinquent is merely adhering to forms of behavior as they are defined within his community. The delinquent subculture, according to Miller, did not rise in conflict with the larger, middle-class culture, nor is it geared to the deliberate violation of middle-class norms. Instead, lower-class culture is simply *different*, the focal concerns being

1. *Trouble*: law-violating behavior
2. *Toughness*: physical prowess and daring
3. *Smartness*: ability to "con" and shrewdness
4. *Excitement*: thrills, risk, and danger
5. *Fate*: luckiness
6. *Autonomy*: independence from external restraint

Trouble often involves fighting or sexual adventures while drinking; troublesome behavior for women frequently means sexual involvement with disadvantageous consequences. Miller contends that any desire to avoid troublesome behavior is based less on a commitment to legal or larger social order norms than on a desire to avoid the possible legal and other undesirable consequences of the action. This position would justify the threat of a probation/parole violation as a valuable tool for p/p officers. Although trouble-producing behavior is a source of status, non-trouble-producing behavior is required to avoid legal and other complications. This source of conflict for the lower-class youngster may be resolved in a legitimate manner by becoming part of an organization with high levels of discipline, such as the military or the police.

The emphasis on *toughness* is traced by Miller (1958: 9) to the significant proportion of lower-class boys reared in female-dominated households and the resulting concern over homosexuality, which "runs like a persistent thread through lower-class culture." Gambling, which is also prevalent in lower-class culture, has its roots in the belief that "their lives are subject to a set of forces over which they have relatively little control" (1958: 11). Miller refers to some of the sentiments commonly expressed in lower-class culture: "No one's going to push me around," and "I'm gonna tell him to take the job and shove it." He states that expressions of autonomy often contrast with actual patterns of behavior and that many lower-class persons actually desire a highly restrictive social environment (ranging from prison to the armed forces) with strong external controls over their behavior. Miller contends that for the lower-class person "being controlled is equated with being cared for" (1958: 13). Thus, the p/p officer will find clients resentful of controls, yet acting in such a manner as to ensure recommitment after a short period of relative freedom. The p/p officer must strive to moderate these extremes for the benefit of the client.

Albert Cohen believes that the delinquent subcultural rejection of middle-class standards is more apparent than real. He contends that the standards of the wider society actually linger on, requiring, for example, a reaction formation in the form of acts that are grossly antisocial. Walter Miller, conversely, asserts that the lower-class culture is distinct, significantly different from the larger middle-class culture. *Trouble* results because of culture conflict: The standards of the middle-class emerge as legal codes, thus entangling the lower-class person, who is acting according to his or her cultural standards, in a web of officialdom. Gresham Sykes and David Matza (1957) disagree with Cohen and Miller; they refer to a social psychological mechanism—*neutralization*—which permits a delinquent to accept the social norms of the wider society and, at the same time, violate these norms.

THE NEW CULTURE CONFLICT

Elijah Anderson (1994: 82) describes a "street [sub]culture" in African American communities with a "set of informal rules governing interpersonal public behavior, including violence. The rules prescribe both a proper comportment and a proper way to respond if challenged." At the center of this subcultural arrangement is preoccupation with the need for respect, being treated "right," with proper deference. The participant in this street subculture is obsessed with the possibility of being "dissed"—sensitive to slights middle-class persons would regard as petty. Status is associated with showing "nerve," a willingness to "mess" with others' property coupled with a cavalier attitude toward death. "Generally people outside the ghetto have other ways of gaining status and regard, and thus do not feel so dependent on such physical displays" (1994: 89).

The code of the streets is actually a cultural adaptation to a lack of faith in criminal justice and the frustrations of chronic poverty. "The police are most often seen as representing the dominant white society and not caring to protect inner-city residents"—the subcultural adaptation to this dilemma requires "taking care of yourself" (1994: 82). Frustrations associated with chronic poverty create the short-fuse phenomenon; verbal and physical abuse become routine. Children "learn that to solve any kind of interpersonal problem one must quickly resort to hitting or other violent behavior" (1994: 83). Furthermore, inner-city children, who are frequently subjected to neglect, must learn to fend for themselves, further hardening the street code adaptations.

NEUTRALIZATION

Gresham Sykes and David Matza (1957: 664) maintain that the delinquent actually retains his belief in the legitimacy of official, middle-class norms: "The juvenile delinquent frequently recognizes both the legitimacy of the dominant social order and its moral rightness." They argue that "if there existed in fact a delinquent sub-culture such that the delinquent viewed his illegal behavior as morally correct, we could reasonably suppose that he would exhibit no feelings of guilt or shame at detection or confinement. Instead, the major reaction would tend in the direction of indignation or a sense of martyrdom." However, the authors note, many delinquents do, indeed, experience a sense of guilt, "and its outward expression is not to be dismissed as a purely manipulative gesture to appease those in authority" (1957: 664–65).

Sykes and Matza postulate that

- The delinquent does not necessarily regard those who abide by the legal rules as wrong or immoral.
- Many delinquents probably are not totally immune from the demands for conformity made by the dominant social order.

Therefore, "the juvenile delinquent would appear to be at least partially committed to the dominant social order in that he frequently exhibits guilt or shame when he violates its proscriptions, accords approval to certain conforming figures, and distinguishes between appropriate and inappropriate targets for his deviance" (1957: 666). They conclude that "the delinquent represents not a radical opposition to law-abiding society but something like an apologetic failure, often more sinned against than sinning in his own eyes" (1957: 667).

By using various *techniques of neutralization,* delinquents are able to avoid guilt feelings for their actions. They contend that rules are merely qualified guidelines limited to time, place, and person conditions. This line of reasoning is in accord with the legal code that requires *mens rea,* criminal intent, to be present for penal sanctions to be imposed. Delinquents justify their actions in a form that, although not valid to the larger society, is valid for them. Sykes and Matza present five types of neutralization:

1. *Denial of responsibility:* rationalizing that deliquency was not their fault (e.g., they were simply a victim of circumstances)
2. *Denial of injury:* thinking that nobody got hurt (e.g., just a prank was involved, or the insurance company will cover the damage)

3. *Denial of the victim:* believing that the victim deserved to be hurt.
4. *Condemnation of the condemners:* dwelling on the weakness and motives of those in authority or judgment (e.g., police, school officials, and judges are corrupt, hate kids, etc.)
5. *Appeal to higher loyalties:* convincing themselves about necessity of action for friends, family, neighborhood, and so on

These sentiments, or variants of them, are often encountered by p/p officers in the course of presentence investigations or p/p supervision. Sykes and Matza (1957) caution against dismissing them as merely post-act rationalizations because they indicate a genuine commitment to societal norms and a basis for rehabilitation.

DIFFERENTIAL/LIMITED OPPORTUNITY

Richard Cloward and Lloyd Ohlin (1960) attempt to integrate anomie with differential association to explain how delinquent subcultures arise, develop various law-violating ways of life, and persist or change over time. They distinguish among three types of delinquent subculture that are a result of anomie and differential association:

1. *Criminal subculture:* gang activities devoted to utilitarian criminal pursuits (e.g., racketeering)
2. *Conflict subculture:* gang activities devoted to violence and destructive acting out as a way of gaining status
3. *Retreatist subculture:* activities in which drug abuse is the primary focus

Each of these subcultural adaptations arises out of a different set of social circumstances, or *opportunity.* Cloward and Ohlin state that the dilemma of many lower-class people is that they are unable to locate alternative avenues to success or goals (1960: 107): "Delinquent subcultures, we believe, represent specialized modes of adaptation to this problem of adjustment." The criminal and conflict subcultures provide illegal avenues, and the retreatist "anticipates defeat and now seeks to escape from the burden of the future." Criminal behavior is not viewed as an individual endeavor but as part of a collective adaptation.

Cloward and Ohlin note (1960: 106–107) that

> many lower-class adolescents experience desperation born of the certainty that their position in the economic structure is relatively fixed and immutable—a desperation made all the more poignant by their exposure to a cultural ideology in which failure to orient oneself upward is regarded as a moral defect and failure to become mobile as proof of it.

The turn toward alternative means of success is to be understood in terms of this social-psychological phenomena. However, Cloward and Ohlin also point out that illegitimate means of success, like legitimate means, are not equally distributed throughout society (1960: 145): "Having decided that he 'can't make it legitimately,' he cannot simply choose among an array of illegitimate means, all equally available to him." Thus, for the average lower-class adolescent, a career in professional or organized crime (Abadinsky, 1994; Sutherland, 1972); can be as difficult to attain as any lucrative career in the legitimate sphere of society.

This difficulty warns the p/p officer of the need to be able to differentiate persons involved in "professional" and "organized" criminality from the more frequent offender who has only limited skills and contacts. Professional and organized criminals are usually not good candidates for the rehabilitative efforts of probation and parole agencies. Such persons are not likely to give up criminal skills and status, which were achieved only after a considerable expenditure of time and effort, for a more conventional and law-abiding lifestyle. In these cases, the investigative and control—not the therapeutic—skills of the p/p officer must be used.

SOCIAL CONTROL THEORY

If as control theorists generally assume, most persons are sufficiently motivated by the potential rewards to commit criminal acts, why do only a few engage in criminal behavior? According to control theorists, "delinquent acts result when an individual's bond to society is weak or broken" (Hirschi, 1969: 16). The strength of this bond is determined by internal and external restraints. In other words, internal and external restraints determine if we move in the direction of crime or law-abiding behavior.

Internal restraints include what psychoanalytic theory refers to as the *superego;* they provide a sense of *guilt.* As noted earlier, dysfunction during early stages of childhood development, or parental influences that are not normative, can result in an adult who is devoid of prosocial internal constraints; some refer to this as psychopathology or sociopathology. (Some evidence also ties psychopathology to a brain defect.) Criminal behavior, devoid of any genuine remorse, can be explained according to this dimension. Whether they are conceived of in terms of psychology or sociology, internal constraints are linked to the influence of the family (Hirschi, 1969)—an influence that can be supported or weakened by the presence or absence of significant external restraints, such as the p/p officer.

External restraints include social disapproval linked to public shame or social ostracism and fear of punishment. In other words, people are typically deterred from criminal behavior by the possibility of being caught and the punishment that can result, ranging from public shame to imprisonment (and in extreme cases capital punishment). The strength of official deterrence—force of law—however, is measured according to two dimensions: risk versus reward. Risk involves the ability of the criminal justice system to detect, apprehend, and convict the offender. The amount of risk is weighed against the potential rewards. Both risk and reward, however, are relative to one's socioeconomic situation. In other words, the less one has to lose, the greater is the willingness to engage in risk. The greater the reward, the greater is the willingness to engage in risk. This theory explains why persons in deprived economic circumstances would be more willing to engage in certain criminal behavior. However, the potential rewards and a perception of relatively low risk may also explain why persons in more advantaged economic circumstances would engage in remunerative criminal behavior, such as corporate crime.

Instead of conforming to conventional norms, through differential association some persons organize their behavior according to the norms of a delinquent or criminal group with which they identify or to which they belong. This affiliation is most likely to occur in environments characterized by relative social disorganization, where familial and communal controls are ineffective in exerting a conforming influence. The increasing number of children living below the poverty level intertwined with a collapse of many inner-city families is creating "America's new orphans" (Gross, 1992). Conforming, prosocial behavior may be dependent on the ability of the p/p officer to monitor the client carefully combined with a realistic threat of punishment. From the casework dimension, the p/p officer may offer the client an opportunity to repair weak or broken bonds and thereby move the client in the direction of conventional behavior.

As the p/p officer seeks to promote and reinforce prosocial associations; opens opportunities for education, training, and employment; and monitors client behavior, an integration of differential association reinforcement, strain, and social control theories may occur.

DRIFT

Does the juvenile delinquent move on to become an adult criminal, or does the youngster mature—and *drift*—into becoming a law-abiding member of society? David Matza (1964: 59) views the delinquent's lifestyle as not fully committed: "He drifts between criminal and conventional action." Matza denies the portrayal of a juvenile delinquent as a person committed to an oppositional culture; instead, the delinquent reveals a basic ambivalence toward his behavior. Matza believes that juveniles are less alienated than others in society, and that most of the time the delinquent behaves in a noncriminal manner (1964: 28):

> The image of the delinquent I wish to convey is one of drift; an actor neither compelled nor committed to deeds nor freely choosing them; neither different in any single fundamental sense from the law abiding, nor the same; conforming to certain traditions in American life while partially unreceptive to other more conventional traditions.

Although Matza (1964: 158) does not contradict the idea of a delinquent subculture, he finds that the subculture is not a binding force on its members: "Loyalty is a basic issue in the subculture of delinquency partially because its adherents are so regularly disloyal. They regularly abandon the company at the age of remission for more conventional pursuits." The "age of remission" is a time when adolescent antisocial behavior is abandoned in favor of adult prosocial or conventional behavior. The crime-prone years for young men are roughly ages 15 to 25, with remission occurring after age 25. Matza's theory has important policy implications: Justice system intervention can stigmatize—

label—a juvenile, thereby blocking entry into a conventional lifestyle as he or she matures into adulthood.

LABELING

A stigma, sometimes referred to in terms of labeling or *societal reaction theory*, is the concern of a sociological perspective known as *symbolic interactionism*:

> Symbolic interactionists suggest that categories which individuals use to render the world meaningful, and even the experience of self, are structured by socially acquired definitions. They argue that individuals, in reaction to group rewards and sanctions, gradually internalize group expectations. These internalized social definitions allow people to evaluate their own behavior from the standpoint of the group and in doing so provide a lens through which to view oneself as a social object. (Quadagno and Antonio, 1975: 33)

The focus is not the behavior of any social actor (person), but on how that behavior or actor is viewed by others—society.

The societal reaction labels—stigmatizes—the actor, which results in a damaged self-image, deviant identity, and a host of negative social expectations. Think about the societal reaction to the terms *mentally ill, ex-convict,* and *parolee*. Furthermore, some argue, the damaged self-image and its ramifications can result in a "self-fulfilling prophesy." Edwin Schur (1973: 124) notes that "once an individual has been branded as a wrongdoer, it becomes extremely difficult for him to shed that new identity." The ex-convict finds it difficult to secure employment, increasing the attraction of further criminal activity. Furthermore, according to Edwin Lemert, the labeled deviant reorganizes his or her behavior in accordance with the societal reaction and "begins to employ his deviant behavior, or role based upon it, as a means of defense, attack, or adjustment to the overt and covert problems created by the consequent societal reaction to him" (1951: 76). Lemert has termed this process *secondary deviation*, which is evidenced by deviants seeking to associate with others like themselves. The negative influence of the delinquent label is viewed as so detrimental to future conduct, that Edwin Schur (1973) argues for *radical nonintervention*: The focus should be on avoiding the movement of adolescents into the official agencies of social control.

The p/p officer is constantly faced with the dynamics of labeling as clients encounter difficulty in returning to school, securing employment, obtaining housing, and making friends because of the stigma (label) inherent in the terms *delinquent, criminal, probationer,* and *parolee*. The label results in a negative self-image whereby the offender's view of him- or herself is that of an inferior and unworthy person. In such a condition, he or she may seek the companionship of others similarly situated and may engage in further antisocial activities in an effort to strike back at the society that is responsible for the labeling.

CONFLICT THEORY

Conflict theory takes its fundamental philosophy primarily from the work of Max Weber and Karl Marx. Conflict theorists are concerned with differences in power relationships. More recent conflict theorists, usually of a Marxist bent, are an outgrowth of the sociopolitical—civil rights, anti–Vietnam War, counterculture—movements of the 1960s and early 1970s. They conceive of society as better characterized by conflict than by consensus; what passes for crime and criminal justice actually represents the interests of powerful classes. Otherwise, they argue, how could a burglary netting a few dollars be classified as a felony, whereas corporate officials who pad defense contracts with millions of dollars in overcharges, or who flagrantly violate safety and restraint of trade laws, avoid incarceration or even the labeling that accompanies the processing of conventional (i.e., poor) delinquents/criminals? As noted in Chapter 6, a specific class of persons always inhabits our prisons—the poor.

The conflict approach eschews theory that treats criminal behavior as a manifestation of individual pathology. Instead, crime is seen as a phenomenon generated by a capitalist system. Capitalism leads to a class system of severely differentiated wealth and power; inequities in wealth and power—in life chances—causes alienation; an alienated segment of the underclass, those whose interests are not furthered by capitalism, reacts in ways defined as criminal. The legal apparatus, including a monopoly over sanctions and the use of force, serves to control the alienated population and helps to perpetuate domination by the ruling class. The criminal justice system is simply a mechanism through which the self-interests of the ruling classes are protected by functionaries in their employ. Their rule is given legitimacy by an ideology of democracy, free enterprise, and property rights whose benefits accrue primarily to those who already have wealth and power. As Karl Marx pointed out, the ideas of the ruling class are always the ruling ideas.

Within this approach, criminal behavior is sometimes romanticized as "rebellion," and criminals as some type of "primitive rebel," although most conventional crime is committed by the underclass against the underclass. During the 1960s and early 1970s, some offenders on probation or parole or prison inmates espoused conflict theory—a reflection of a politically active era. Conflict theory sensitizes the p/p officer to some of the basic inequities in our society, certainly as they are reflected in criminal justice. Although dealing with system inequities is beyond the role of the p/p officer, he or she does have an advocate role, which is discussed in Chapter 10.

GETTING TOUGH ON CRIME?

A 1994 report for the Carnegie Foundation by a panel of prominent Americans provides some insight into the intractable problem of crime. The study revealed millions of children deprived of medical care, loving supervision, and intellectual stimulation, the result of parents overwhelmed by poverty. Many are subjected to child abuse and frequently witness random acts of violence (Chira, 1994).

REVIEW QUESTIONS

1. How is psychoanalytic theory applied in probation and parole practice?
2. According to psychoanalytic theory, what is the importance of unconscious feelings and experiences?
3. According to psychoanalytic theory, what are the causes of behavior defined as criminal?
4. How can the superego cause criminal behavior?
5. What is the relationship between social casework and the medical model?
6. What is the basis of changing behavior in reality therapy?
7. Why has RT been attractive to probation and parole agencies?
8. According to behavior modification/learning theory, what is the cause of criminal behavior?
9. What are the techniques for changing behavior according to learning theory?
10. Why is it difficult to apply behavior modification techniques to probation and parole practice?
11. What are the advantages of social group work over the more traditional one-to-one approach to counseling in probation and parole?
12. What is CST?
13. What is the difference between psychological and sociological explanations of criminal behavior?
14. How does Robert Merton use the concept of anomie to explain certain types of criminal behavior in the United States?
15. According to the theory of differential association, what determines if a person becomes a criminal?
16. According to Richard Cloward and Lloyd Ohlin (differential opportunity), what are the three types of delinquent subcultures that are the result of anomie and differential association?
17. According to control theory, what determines if persons engage in criminal behavior?
18. What are the characteristics that Albert Cohen states are necessary to achieve success in our society—characteristics that lower-class youth do not possess?
19. What are "techniques of neutralization"?
20. What are the negative results of labeling?
21. What is the conflict view of criminal behavior?

PROBATION
AND
PAROLE OFFICERS

This chapter examines probation/parole officer roles and qualifications, as well as the use of paraprofessionals and volunteers. The first section lists the varied work roles of p/p officers.

WORK ROLES OF PROBATION/PAROLE OFFICERS

Ann Strong (1981) provides 11 work roles for the p/p officer:

1. *Detection.* Detection can involve identifying when a client is at risk or when the community is at risk (from the client). The first objective for the officer is to identify the individuals who are experiencing difficulty (at crisis) or who are in danger of becoming a risk to the community. A second objective is to identify conditions in the community itself that may be contributing to personal problems of the client and that might raise his or her assigned risk level (such as lack of jobs or job training or the influx of easily available controlled substances). A third objective is to determine when the community is at risk from the probationer and steps are needed to protect the community.

2. *Broker.* The primary objective is to steer (refer) clients to existing services that can be of benefit to them. The focus is on enabling or helping people to use the system and to negotiate its pathways. A further objective is to link elements of the service system with one another. The essential benefit of this objective is the physical hookup of the person with the source of help and the physical connection of elements of the service system with one another.

3. *Advocate.* The primary objective is to fight for the rights and dignity of people in need of help. The key assumption is that there will be instances when practices, regulations, and general conditions will prevent individuals from receiving services, using resources, or obtaining help. This position includes the notion of advocating changes in laws, rules, and regulations on behalf of a whole class of persons or segment of society. Advocacy aims at removing the obstacles or barriers that prevent people from exercising their rights or receiving the benefits and using the resources they need. When I was a parole officer in New York, because of Department of Motor Vehicles regulations, parolees with legitimate employment needs had a difficult time obtaining a motor vehicle license. Advocacy on the part of the Parole Officers Association was effective in changing these regulations and removing the unnecessary obstacles.

4. *Evaluator.* This role involves gathering information, assessing personal or community problems, weighing alternatives and priorities, and making decisions for action.

5. *Mobilizer.* The foremost objective is to assemble and energize existing groups, resources, organizations, and structures; or to create new groups, organizations, or resources and to bring them to bear on problems that exist; or to prevent problems from developing. The principal focus is on available or existing institutions, organizations, and resources within the community.

6. *Enabler.* The primary objective is to provide support and to facilitate change in the behavior patterns, habits, and perceptions of individual clients. The key assumption is that problems may be alleviated or crises may be prevented by modifying, adding, or extinguishing discrete bits of behavior; increasing insights; or changing values and perceptions.

7. *Information manager.* The primary focus is the collection, classification, and analysis of data generated within the community. Contents would include data about the individual case and the community.

8. *Mediator.* The primary objective is to mediate between people and resource systems and among resource systems. The key assumption is that problems do not exist within people or within resource systems, but rather in the interactions between people and resource systems and between systems. As opposed to the advocate, the mediator stance is one of neutrality.

9. *Educator.* Instruction is used in the sense of an objective rather than a method. The primary objectives are to convey and impart information and knowledge and to develop various kinds of skills. A great deal of what has been called social casework or therapy is simple instruction.

10. *Community planner.* This role involves participating in and assisting neighborhood planning groups, agencies, community agents, or governments in the development of community programs to assure that client needs are represented and met to the greatest extent feasible.

11. *Enforcer.* This role requires the officer to use the authority of his or her office to revoke the probationer/parolee's standing because of changes in the status quo, which involves heightened community or individual risk outside the control of the officer.

The degree to which one work role will be favored over another is dependent on the particular model of agency that employs the p/p officer.

SOUTH CAROLINA PROBATION/PAROLE AGENT

Agents with the South Carolina Department of Probation, Parole and Pardon Services conduct various investigations that are ordered by the court or parole board and monitor the activity and behavior of those on their caseload to ensure that offenders are complying with the conditions of supervision. They guide offenders to various community agencies and resources for direct assistance in meeting needs that the agents have identified or assessed. Agents enforce the conditions of supervision and, should an offender violate any of these conditions, the agents take appropriate action, up to and including issuing a citation or arrest warrant, which could result in the revocation of the offender's supervision by the proper authority. Agents must successfully complete an intensive basic training course at the South Carolina Criminal Justice Academy, which includes training in offender supervision skills, legal issues, and agent safety issues, including arrest procedures and firearms certification.

PROBATION/PAROLE OFFICER ROLES AND AGENCY MODELS

What role will the p/p officer assume toward the client? Harry Allen, Eric Carlson, and Evalyn Parks (1979: 58) report that a review of the literature reveals four basic role typologies:

1. The *punitive/law enforcement officer,* whose primary concern is the protection of the community through control of the p/p client
2. The *welfare/therapeutic officer,* whose primary concern is the improved welfare of the p/p client
3. The *protective/synthetic officer,* who attempts to effect a blend of treatment and law enforcement

4. The *passive/time server officer,* who has little concern for the welfare of the community or the client but sees the work merely as a sinecure, requiring minimum effort

Role 4 is meaningless because this position is not particular to p/p or even criminal justice settings in general. The first three roles are deficient when discussed outside one of the three agency contexts or models:

1. *Control model.* Control of the p/p client's activities is the primary focus. Unannounced home and employment visits, checks for drug use, and a close working relationship with law enforcement agencies are the standard practice.
2. *Social service model.* The focus is on the client's needs, including employment, housing, and counseling that provides social and psychological support. These agencies often have contracts with private service providers.
3. *Combined model.* This model requires p/p officers to provide social services, while attending to control functions.

/ _____ / _____ /

Control model   Combined model   Social service model

Most p/p agencies would fall somewhere between the *combined* and *social service* models, with parole agencies tending toward the *combined* model and probation agencies tending toward the *social service* model. The *control* model would not be found in its pure form, although specific programs—such as electronic monitoring, intensive supervision, or community control (discussed in Chapter 12)—may be based on a control model. P/p role typologies indicate that the punitive/law enforcement officer is more likely to be found in—indeed, would be appropriate for—the control model agency. The welfare/therapeutic officer would be most likely found in the social service model agency. The issue, then, is not what role the p/p officer will assume with respect to clients but rather whether the role is compatible with the agency model. In the combined model, some use can be made of p/p officer role variation (I prefer the term *style*). Supervisors can assign cases on the basis of matching the officer's style with the salient characteristics of the offender. For example, an officer with a more authoritarian style would be matched with "heavy" (i.e., professional or career) criminals. An officer with a gentler style would be appropriate for certain situational offenders or perhaps youthful clients.

In a combined model agency, officers should integrate their control or community protection role with their social service role, while maintaining flexibility to stress one over the other in an individualized response to each case. For example, a young offender under supervision for joyriding in a stolen car will receive a different response than an experienced offender who is associated with organized criminal activity. In p/p treatment, officers adapt those methods that are useful to their practice, while sacrificing the rest (sometimes cynically) on the altar of reality. Support for combining the social service with control function comes from Elizabeth Hutchinson (1987), who argues that social workers should avoid sending out other people to carry out coercive actions.

THE PROBATION/PAROLE OFFICER AS TREATMENT AGENT

Chapter 9 reviewed a variety of treatment approaches—the implication being that p/p officers could operationalize these approaches with their clients. However, requirements for p/p officer positions (discussed later in this chapter) are usually a bachelor's degree, hardly adequate to provide the background, let alone the skill, for carrying out a sophisticated treatment role. Shelle Dietrich (1979: 15) points out that "the probation officer usually has not received extensive specialized training for the function of change agent; that is, the function of being competent to facilitate another person's changing his behavior, attitude, affect, or personality style." Generally, the p/p officer is not educated or trained to be a treatment agent: "It is an unrealistic expectation of probation [and parole] officers to expect themselves to be competent in an area for which they have not received adequate training" (1979: 15).

In a review of the literature purporting to advise p/p officers whose background is otherwise deficient how to become effective change agents, Dietrich (1979: 16–19) found it simplistic and at times potentially harmful to the client. Thus, she argues, professional intrusion is often advocated in areas for which the p/p officer lacks training. Cynically, she (1979: 17) proposes, "Why not go ahead and prescribe medications, prepare legal documents, or write an insurance plan for the probationer?" Dietrich (1979: 18) cautions: "And what about the probationer? Certainly, his position in relation to the probation officer is a vulnerable one. Shouldn't the probationer be protected from being the involuntary patient of an unlicensed and untrained person, even if the person's intentions are the most purely humanistic?"

Dietrich raises two other related issues:

1. Is the therapeutic enterprise possible in a p/p setting? Given a positive response to this question, another one is raised.
2. Is it realistic to expect the delivery of treatment in p/p, where caseloads usually average between 80 and 100? (Although 80 to 100 cases may have been standard when Dietrich was writing, 100 to 200 is more today's norm.)

She argues that even if the p/p officer "were optimally skillful in such therapeutic endeavors," without the full promise of confidentiality (impossible in a p/p setting), full and open discussion, the basis for a therapeutic relationship, is not possible (1979: 18). Dietrich is using a rather narrow definition of *therapy*, however, and within that definition she is correct—therapy is not possible in a p/p setting. I believe that therapy is more usefully defined here as the purposeful use of self to improve the social and psychological functioning of a client, and thus therapy is possible within the confidentiality limitations of a p/p agency.

Therapy, however, is *not* possible given the lack of adequate education and training and the usual excessive caseloads encountered in p/p practice. Accordingly, some propose that treatment should take the form of the p/p officer acting as broker or advocate.

THE PROBATION/PAROLE OFFICER AS BROKER OR ADVOCATE

The provision of necessary services in p/p practice often requires an advocacy stance on the part of the p/p officer. Private and public agencies may view the p/p client as undesirable or even undeserving. Welfare, mental health, and educational agencies may see the client as threatening. Their responses to a client's needs may lead to frustration and a frustrated client who reacts in a manner that does, indeed, appear threatening—frustration control is often a problem with p/p clientele—a self-fulfilling prophecy.

Eric Carlson and Evalyn Parks (1979: 120) see the *brokerage* approach in p/p as almost diametrically opposed to the treatment approach because the p/p officer "is not concerned primarily with understanding or changing the behavior of the probationer, but rather with assessing the concrete needs of the individual and arranging for the probationers to receive services that directly address these needs" (1979: 120). They point out that:

> There is significantly less emphasis placed on the development of a close, one-to-one relationship between the probation officer and the probationer. The probation officer functions primarily as a manager or broker of resources and social services which are already available from other agencies. It is the task of the probation officer to assess the service needs of the probationer, locate the social service agency which addresses those needs as its primary function, to refer the probationer to the appropriate agency, and to follow up referrals to make sure that the probationer actually received the services. Under the brokerage approach, it can be said that the probation officer's relationship with community service agencies is more important than his relationship with an individual probationer. The brokerage approach does share with the casework approach the importance of the probationer's participation in developing his own probation plan. (1979: 120–21)

Carlson and Parks (1979: 123) note that "the essential tasks of the brokerage orientation to probation are the management of available community resources and the use of those services to meet the needs of probation clients."

Little emphasis is placed on the quality of the relationship that is developed between probation officers and the probationer; rather, more emphasis is placed on the close working relationship between the probation officer and the staff members of community social service agencies. Counseling and guidance are considered inappropriate activities for the probation officer; no attempt is made to change the behavior of the probationer. The primary function of the probation officer is to assess the concrete needs of each probationer and make appropriate referrals to existing community services. Should the needed service not be available in the community, the probation officer is responsible for encouraging the development of that service.

THE PROBATION/PAROLE OFFICER AS LAW ENFORCEMENT AGENT

The p/p officer as law enforcement agent is related to the *control model* of supervision in much the same way as the treatment or broker-advocate role is related to the *social service model.* For a discussion of the law enforcement role of the p/p officers to be meaningful, one must consider this position within the context of agency model. However, many critics of a law enforcement role for p/p officers render unequivocal statements without any discussion of the model. Thus, without any attention to agency model, the American Correctional Association (1981: 36), in its *Standards for Adult Probation and Parole Field Services,* states: "Probation/parole officers do not routinely carry weapons in the performance of their duties."

A more productive approach is to identify the agency model and then decide if it is compatible with a law enforcement role. Paul Keve (1979: 432) states that agencies "suffer sharp internal problems when agency policy seems to require surveillance and arrest activities while at the same time the agency prohibits use of firearms." For example, community corrections (parole) officers in the state of Washington are required to complete arrest, search, and seizure training. They are not, however, permitted to carry firearms while performing these peace officer functions. A more rational approach was taken by the Texas Adult Probation Commission, which voiced its opposition to *both* arrest powers and the carrying of firearms by probation officers (now called community supervision officers). A similar policy is in force in Virginia where probation and parole officers do not carry firearms and "the functions of apprehension and arrest of clients shall be delegated to police officers." This policy is also followed by Texas Youth Commission parole officers: They are not authorized to carry firearms or to make arrests.

In 1975, I surveyed 53 adult parole agencies in the United States (the 50 states, the District of Columbia, Puerto Rico, and the U. S. Division of Probation, which also supervised parolees). The survey indicated that parole agencies differ greatly with respect to officers carrying firearms and arresting violators. Several years later, Keve (1979) conducted a similar survey of top administrators in probation and parole in the United States and found that a little more than half of the jurisdictions prohibited the carrying of a firearm. In 1986, the Oklahoma Department of Corrections surveyed all 50 states with respect to the carrying of firearms by probation and parole officers: "The study indicated that about 48 percent of all p/p agencies allowed their officers to carry a gun on the job. Only

24 percent of the jurisdictions polled said their officers routinely carried a weapon" (Jones and Robinson, 1989: 90).

In recent years, as more and more p/p agencies move toward a control model of supervision, arrest powers and the carrying of firearms by p/p officers have become increasingly common—for several compelling reasons. Many agencies are confronted by p/p personnel who feel endangered by having to enter high-crime areas, particularly during evening hours, to visit serious offenders at home. In Illinois, for example, while probation officers are usually prohibited from carrying firearms, the Administrative Office of the Illinois Courts mandates home visits. In Winnebago County, "the concern of officer safety became apparent because of escalating violence in the community which brought in discretion and common sense in terms of when and when not to accomplish certain field contacts. This also resulted in the development of specific home visit procedural guidelines and availability of pepper spray and a radio." In many agencies, officers are demanding protective training and the right to carry firearms, and William Parsonage (1990: 35) reports that "during the past few years, an increasing number of agencies have authorized the carrying of firearms under various circumstances."

In many jurisdictions, particularly in high-crime urban areas, the police/sheriff are either unwilling or unable to provide sufficient warrant-enforcement services. If the agency does not enforce its own warrants, they go unattended; the potential danger to the public is obvious as hundreds or, in larger jurisdictions, thousands of p/p warrants go unenforced. (For example, Cook County, Illinois, whose county seat is Chicago, has more than 100,000 outstanding warrants.) Warrants turned over to outside agencies may also be used to force p/p violators into becoming informants (or in some cases the warrants are used for corrupt purposes, such as extortion).

HAZARDS OF PAROLE SUPERVISION

The very nature of parole work subjects parole officers to potentially hazardous events on a routine basis. Fortunately, not every parole officer has had a bad or harrowing experience, but many have. On one occasion, New York State parole officer Tom Brancato was strangled almost to the point of unconsciousness in a remote wooded area where he stopped to see his parolee at work. This attack occurred by surprise after Officer Brancato had asked the parolee to have a seat in his car. As soon as they were seated the parolee reached over, grabbed Officer Brancato by the throat, and wedged him between the bucket seats of his Volkswagen. His right arm and gun were pinned beneath him. After considerable effort he managed to get his gun with his left hand and stick the barrel in the parolee's ear.

In practice, probation and parole agency policy with respect to firearms falls into one of three categories:

1. *Officers are not permitted to carry firearms at any time based either on state law or agency policy.* For example:
   - In Maryland, p/p agents are social workers and have no peace officer responsibilities or powers.
   - In South Dakota, parole agents are not by statute considered law enforcement officers and do not carry weapons.
   - In New Jersey, the state supreme court has determined that probation work is guidance and assistance, not law enforcement, and has directed that probation officers not be permitted to carry firearms.
   - In Virginia, p/p officers are prohibited from carrying firearms while on duty.
   - In Kansas, although they are authorized to make arrests, probation officers (judicial branch) and parole officers (executive branch) are not permitted to carry firearms while on duty.
   - Hawaii parole officers do not have arrest powers or carry firearms.
   - Winnebago County (Illinois) probation officers are not authorized to carry firearms; although state law authorizes POs to make arrests, according to agency policy, "probation officers are not to effect a forcible custodial arrest."
   - Oregon juvenile parole officers do not have arrest powers and do not carry firearms.

2. *Officers are by statute peace/law enforcement officers, but the agency either restricts or discourages the carrying of weapons.* For example:
   - The Montgomery County (Ohio) Adult Probation Department allows officers to carry firearms *only* on special assignments, such as transportation of a probation violator; or in emergency situations, such as the escape of a dangerous offender, or a "highly threatening office disturbance."
   - The Adult Probation Department of Allen County (Indiana) states that, although its personnel are allowed by statute to carry firearms and arrest probationers, the court discourages the carrying of a firearm.
   - The San Francisco Adult Probation Department prohibits the routine carrying of firearms but permits certain officers to carry weapons, for example, those assigned to the gang violence suppression program.
   - The New York City Probation Department and Cook County, Illinois, Adult Probation Department prohibit the carrying of firearms by probation officers except those assigned to special units, such as intensive supervision.
   - Minnesota corrections (parole) agents are peace officers, but agency policy prohibits the carrying of firearms.
   - The state of Washington permits Community Corrections Officers to carry firearms only as a result of a threat while on duty and then only for a maximum of 90 days.

3. *Officers are by statute peace/law enforcement officers and the agency permits or requires all qualified personnel to carry firearms.* For example:

- Employment as a probation and parole officer in Alabama and Nevada requires firearms qualification and carrying of weapons while on duty. New York State parole officers are required to carry a Glock 9-mm semi-automatic while on duty.
- Firearms training is mandatory for all California (adult and youth) parole agents and all Oklahoma p/p officers.
- Illinois, Massachusetts, New Jersey,[1] Ohio, and Pennsylvania parole officers/agents are permitted to carry firearms provided that they have met applicable training and proficiency standards.
- All training-certified probation and parole officers in Kentucky and Michigan are authorized to carry firearms.
- Probation officers for the Georgia Department of Corrections who complete firearms training and receive permission from the deputy commissioner may carry firearms on duty.
- In Dauphin County, Pennsylvania; Bibb County, Georgia; Suffolk County, Nassau County, and Onondaga County, New York, probation officers who have qualified in the handling of weapons may carry a firearm.
- All Colorado parole officers must qualify with firearms and are authorized to carry weapons.
- Florida correctional probation officers who complete firearms training may carry firearms.
- Connecticut correctional rehabilitation services (parole) officers must qualify with firearms and are authorized to carry department-issued weapons.

A gray area on this issue may exist, exemplified by the policy of the Federal Probation and Pretrial Services Division. Although federal probation and pretrial services officers are not permitted to carry firearms routinely, an officer who has presented sufficient reasons why carrying a firearm is necessary in general or for a specific assignment can be granted authority. The actual degree to which firearms authority is granted varies considerably from district to district. In Idaho, although p/p officers are weapons-trained peace officers, they do not routinely carry weapons; however, the district manager can give permission to carry a weapon. In Iowa, each of the state's eight judicial districts is free to decide if its p/p officers shall carry firearms.

Should probation/parole officers make arrests and carry firearms? In 1975, while still a parole officer, I answered with a resounding "yes." Two decades later, I find myself still in agreement with the legendary parole chief in New York, David Dressler (1951: 152), who wrote: "I am convinced a parole system worth its salt *has* to make its own arrests." Departments that fail to provide the maximum amount of community protection possible within a p/p setting are in danger of

---

[1]This policy is new. Pursuant to legislation signed August 9, 1993, New Jersey began training and arming its parole officers.

having their services shifted or contracted out to public or private social service agencies. The privatization of prisons and, in certain instances, presentence investigation reports, should serve as a warning to the self-interests of p/p personnel.

Although many (typically nonpractitioner) observers bemoan the existence of a role conflict in p/p, or an incompatibility between control and treatment, this writer never experienced such conflicts in practice—nor did any of his colleagues in New York. Indeed, given the nature of p/p clientele, sound treatment demands the use of appropriate methods of control—offenders under supervision often engage in behavior that is self-destructive and dangerous to the community. As a trained social worker, I found that the application of casework principles was enhanced by the legal powers inherent in p/p settings. Indeed, if role conflict is inherent in p/p practice, as Todd Clear and Edward Latessa (1989: 2) note, such is the nature of many professional positions. However, "among other professions, role conflict is seldom seen as a justification for eviscerating the profession of a few less salient tasks; rather, it is felt that the 'true' professional finds a way of integrating various role expectations, balancing them and weighing the appropriateness of various expressions of the roles."

Misunderstanding of the control/enforcement role vis-à-vis the social service role, is highlighted by Norval Morris and Michael Tonry—typical of many nonpractitioners who delve into the p/p field. They argue, for example, that "there is no way in which effective, regular, but unpredictable urine testing to ensure that the convicted offender is drug free can be made other than as a police-type function" (1990: 185). As a social worker, I beg to disagree: Preventing drug abuse—the purpose of drug testing—is to the client's advantage; testing enhances the ego function of the offender, strengthening resolve to avoid harmful substances. This approach is sound social work.

As a private citizen with a working knowledge of p/p, I have certain concerns about personal safety—that of my family, friends, and neighbors. From this (I believe typical) layperson's perspective, I evaluate a p/p agency. Let me provide some examples. During the course of an office or home visit, a p/p officer may discover that a client is using heroin or cocaine. If the offender is unemployed, the drug habit is probably financed by criminal activities—the client is a clear and present danger to him- or herself and to the community. A p/p agency whose officers cannot immediately (and safely) arrest such a person is not providing an adequate level of client service or community protection. P/p agencies also supervise offenders who have been involved in (1) sex offenses against children, (2) vehicular homicide as a result of intoxication, (3) burglary, and (4) armed robbery. A p/p agency whose officers have no responsibility to enforce prohibitions, through investigation and arrest, against (1) frequenting play areas, (2) drinking and driving, and (3) carrying tools for forced entry or who cannot (4) investigate money or a lifestyle that cannot be supported by the offender's employment status is not providing the minimum acceptable level of community safety.

Furthermore, the adult (and, frequently, the juvenile) p/p client is often a serious law violator who has proved to be a potential danger to the community. Many have been involved in crimes of violence, and the public and elected officials expect that probationers and parolees, if they are to remain in the community, will be under the scrutiny of p/p authorities. This scrutiny is why the law of most jurisdictions empowers p/p agencies with law enforcement responsibilities. However, the question is often raised whether the p/p officer should be the law enforcer or merely the treatment agent.

P/p agencies may employ warrant officers or use outside law enforcement officers to do their enforcement work—the "dirty work." Do arrest powers and the carrying of a firearm interfere with the p/p officer's ability to form a casework relationship with which to provide treatment? I am of the opinion that they do not. Indeed, because of p/p officers' relationships with their clients, in delinquency situations, they are able to effect an arrest without the tension and hostility that often accompanies arrests made by other law enforcement officers (who have no relationship with the client). In fact, whether the p/p officer actually makes the arrest, the client knows that the p/p officer initiated the warrant action.

P/p clients are potentially dangerous and usually reside in high-crime neighborhoods, which is reason enough to be armed. (In Massachusetts, when it was decided in 1993 that unarmed probation officers from the Dorchester Division of the District Court Department would make unannounced home visits at night, they required police escorts—poor social work practice.) This facet of parole work was revealed dramatically while I was a parole officer in New York. My colleague, 32-year-old Donald Sutherland, attempted to arrest a parole violator and was shot to death. The parolee was subdued at the scene by other parole officers. After being convicted of murder, the parolee escaped from prison and eluded law officers for several weeks (on one occasion after an exchange of gunfire). He was finally killed after refusing to surrender to a combined force of city and state police and parole officers.

IN THE FIELD

Georgia parole officer Joje Wilson-Gibbs turns into East Lake Meadows, a housing project just inside Atlanta city limits and notes that the surroundings are particularly lively for so early an hour. Throughout the warren of circling streets sprawl barracklike apartments, several tattooed with graffiti and one encircled by a flower garden. A gray-bearded old man crouches in the corner of his stoop; two carloads of young men pass while slowly inspecting the sedate blue sedan driven by the parole officer.

Wilson-Gibbs is checking on her parolee, but it's not him she fears. Like most parole officers, the unpredictability of the environment most concerns her. Next to her on the seat is a bulky purse, on which is perched a can of pepper gas spray and in which is concealed a .38-caliber revolver.

"I don't want to use my gun in a real-life situation," she says. "I don't want to use pepper gas, either, but I feel better knowing I'm trained and can react with these weapons if I'm in a life-threatening situation. All sorts of things add up to a sense of security for me—including having good tires on a reliable car that won't leave you stranded."

Source: Georgia Community Corrections Division.

A study by William Parsonage and Comway Bushey (1989: 24) in Pennsylvania highlights the danger of probation/parole work: They found that the "victimization of Pennsylvania probation and parole workers is extensive and pervasive." Parsonage (1990) expresses concern over similar findings in other states. Although carrying a firearm does not guarantee safety, a person with a firearm may discourage attacks by carrying him- or herself more confidently than others who might be selected for victimization. Knowing that p/p officers are routinely carrying firearms has a deterrent value for criminals. Indeed, many *unarmed* p/p officers (unknowingly) gain a degree of safety because they are perceived as police officers or otherwise believed to be armed.

Related to this issue is a peculiar prohibition: Some agencies that permit the carrying of firearms on duty forbid p/p officers from carrying a firearm while off duty. This policy appears to be based on a lack of trust and a fear that weapons would be used off duty in an inappropriate manner by the very officers employed and trained by the agency. The policy is bad for morale and public safety, and unsound p/p practice. If a p/p officer is trained in law enforcement and firearms, he or she should have the same privilege of carrying a weapon off duty as do almost all other law enforcement personnel. Officers may encounter their clients during off-duty hours, and a hostile (perhaps ex-) client can be dangerous under such circumstances. P/p personnel must not be intimidated, or their effectiveness will be undermined. Yet the nature of their clientele and the powers of p/p officers make them vulnerable to intimidation. The ability to carry a weapon at all times reduces feelings of vulnerability and, therefore, the potential for intimidation. Furthermore, a community that provides for the salaries of p/p officers is that much safer by having in its midst trained and armed personnel sworn to enforce the law.

ABSCONDERS

In most states, p/p agencies expend few, if any, resources on the problem of absconders, and overburdened police departments and sheriffs are generally not interested in enforcing p/p warrants. Although absconders represent a serious risk to the public, p/p warrants usually remain unenforced until the violator is arrested for a new crime. In New York, the Division of Parole has always made the apprehension of absconders a priority and, in 1986, created a special unit to intensify its efforts. The Absconder Apprehension Task Force (AATF) comprised twelve investigative teams and four supervisors, each team comprised of one parole officer and one New York City Police Department (NYPD) investigator. The task force targeted career criminals and persons wanted on outstanding police warrants, significantly increasing the apprehension of dangerous parole violators. In 1992, the AATF was disbanded after the NYPD pulled its officers and equipment because of "conflicting staffing needs"—budgetary considerations. The Division of Parole participated in the U.S. Marshals Service "Operation Gunsmoke," which targeted violent absconders—two parole officers were deputized as federal marshals. The ten-week operation succeeded in apprehending 26 violent offenders.

Several other jurisdictions have developed absconder units. Some examples include the Fugitive Apprehension Project of the Hennepin County (Minneapolis) Bureau of Community Corrections, the Massachusetts Parole Board Special Operations Unit and the Apprehension Unit of the California Youth Authority.

SELECTION OF PROBATION AND PAROLE OFFICERS

The selection of probation and parole officers is typically done by a process similar to that used to select most public employees. One of three systems is generally employed: the merit system, the appointment system, or a combined system.

1. *Merit system.* Under the merit system, applicants who meet the minimum qualifications for the position are required to pass a competitive written examination. Persons who score at or above the minimum passing grade are placed on a ranked list. From this list, candidates are selected, generally in the order of their rank. In some systems applicants are graded on the basis of their education and employment background. The merit system was developed to remove public employment from political patronage. Critics argue, however, that a written examination cannot determine who will be a good p/p officer.

2. *Appointment system.* Under the appointment system, applicants who meet minimum requirements are hired on the basis of an evaluation by the agency. Applicants do not take a written examination, although they are usually interviewed by an agency representative(s). This system provides agency officials with the greatest amount of flexibility; it also has a history of being used for political purposes.

3. *Combined system.* Some jurisdictions use elements of both the merit and appointment systems. Applicants are first screened through a qualifying examination. Those who receive a passing grade are placed on a list from which candidates are selected, usually after an interview with an agency representative(s).

GEORGIA'S PAROLE OFFICERS

Georgia's parole officers are among the most highly qualified, best-trained community supervision professionals in the country. All are required to have an undergraduate degree and must pass through a complete background check that includes a psychological test to determine their job competency. Some come to the board directly from college, whereas others come from backgrounds as diverse as law enforcement, social work, education, and private enterprise.

SIX WEEKS OF BASIC TRAINING

Soon after they are hired, all parole officers attend the agency's Basic Training Program, a six-week package of instruction at the Georgia Public Training Center in Forsyth. The course of instruction prepares them for the many roles that they will fill as they go about their daily duties. Included are classes and hands-on training in report writing, interpersonal communications, cultural diversity, arrest procedures, lifesaving techniques, and firearms training and certification. On graduation, the new parole officers have the critical knowledge to return to their respective offices and begin their work. Every year parole officers return for more training in the form of 40 hours of agency-mandated in-service training.

Parole officers perform many roles. Charged with the task of protecting Georgia's citizens by assisting the reintegration of the inmate back into the community and returning to prison those who fail, they are, on the one hand, a counselor and mentor and, on the other hand, a law enforcement officer and a prosecutor. In the course of one day a parole officer may participate in the arrest of a parole violator, help another get a job, counsel a family dispute, interview an inmate or his family, assist in obtaining treatment for a substance abuser, testify at a parole revocation hearing, and make an assortment of contacts with parolees, their families, and their employers.

ALWAYS ON CALL

Every day, parole officers travel Georgia's city streets and rural backroads, including many areas that are potentially dangerous, to monitor parolee compliance with the conditions of parole and to help them break with their criminal past. Being a parole officer means being accessible around the clock, with after-hours calls from parolees, anxious families, and law enforcement always a possibility. As certified peace officers, they are frequently called on to assist in emergency situations, such as floods and tornadoes. Still, many parole officers find the time to volunteer for community projects, school programs, church activities, and an assortment of other ways that they know will positively impact the quality of their hometown life.

Georgia's parole officers work every day quietly and without fanfare to intervene with and to successfully bring about change in others who had until that point been unable to abide by the rules of society. In doing so, they assure that Georgia will be a safer place to live.

PERSONAL QUALITIES

The characteristics generally considered desirable for probation and parole officers can be classified into four categories:

1. *Basic knowledge.* A p/p officer should have a working understanding of psychology, sociology, the criminal statutes, police operations, and the court and correctional systems.

2. *Individual characteristics.* A p/p officer needs the ability to relate to all offenders and to deal with their sometimes subtle or overt hostility, to exercise authority in an appropriate manner, to work well with other staff members, and to be able to organize work properly and prepare written reports in a coherent and timely manner.

3. *The agency.* The p/p officer must be willing to accept the responsibilities engendered by working for a public agency that handles offenders, and to enforce rules and adhere to regulations.

4. *Other agencies.* The p/p officer has to be able to deal effectively with many kinds of agencies and persons, usually divided into criminal justice (police, prosecutors, judges, and correctional officials) and social service (treatment, welfare, employment, and educational). These agencies often have varying attitudes toward offenders that must be handled appropriately.

QUALIFICATIONS FOR PROBATION/PAROLE OFFICERS

The American Correctional Association sets the following standard for entry-level probation and parole field positions: "An entry-level probation or parole officer possesses a minimum of a bachelor's degree or has completed a career development program that includes work-related experience, training, or college credits providing a level of achievement equivalent to a bachelor's degree."

These are standards set by various jurisdictions throughout the United States:

- *Alabama.* Probation and Parole Officer I: Bachelor's degree.
- *California.* Santa Clara County Deputy Probation Officer I: Bachelor's degree with specialization in sociology, criminology, penology, or a related major, preferably with an emphasis in the correctional field. Youth Authority Parole Agent I: Education equivalent to graduation from college and one year of social casework, group guidance work, or community organization experience, or one year of graduate education in social work, guidance, psychology, sociology, or criminology. San Francisco County Adult Probation Officer: Bachelor's degree with a social science or related major, and one year of experience in counseling. Parole Agent, Adult: Education equivalent to graduation from a college and one year of social work or related experience, one year of graduate education in a relevant discipline, or two years' experience as a correction officer, or two years' experience investigating crimes for a law enforcement agency where interviewing and writing reports were key components of the position.
- *Colorado.* Parole Officer: Bachelor's degree with a major in corrections, criminal justice, behavioral science, or counseling. Must possess a Peace Officer's Standards Training certificate.

- *Connecticut.* Correctional Rehabilitation Services Officer: Bachelor's degree.
- *Florida.* Correctional Probation Officer: Bachelor's degree.
- *Georgia.* Probation Supervisor: Bachelor's degree or completion of two years of college and one year of professional or paraprofessional experience in law enforcement, social work, counseling, or related human service delivery areas.
- *Hawaii.* Corrections/Parole Officer: Bachelor's degree plus six months of social work experience, a bachelor's degree in social work, or one year of graduate social work education.
- *Idaho.* Probation/Parole Officer: Some knowledge of criminal investigation and related areas and social counseling techniques.
- *Illinois.* Probation Officer: Bachelor's degree. Corrections Parole Agent I: Knowledge, skill, and mental development equivalent to the completion of four years of college with a bachelor's degree in the behavioral or social sciences or law enforcement.
- *Indiana.* Probation Officer: Bachelor's degree. Parole Officer: Fifteen hours of relevant college education and four years of experience in social work or related experience; college education may be substituted on a year-for-year basis for a maximum of three years; relevant graduate education may be substituted for the one year of necessary experience.
- *Kansas.* Parole Officer I: Bachelor's degree that includes 24 credits of course work in criminology/criminal justice, law, guidance, counseling, or social work. Two years of relevant work experience may be substituted for two years of education. Court Services (Probation) Officer: Bachelor's degree with a major in criminal justice, psychology or sociology, social work, or related fields.
- *Kentucky.* Probation and Parole Officer: Bachelor's degree; professional experience in p/p work can be substituted for the required education on a year-for-year basis.
- *Maine.* Probation/Parole Officer, Juvenile Caseworker: Bachelor's degree and six months of experience in probation/parole work, youth/adult counseling, law enforcement, or directly related experience/training.
- *Maryland.* Parole and Probation Field Supervisor: Bachelor's degree with 30 hours in social, behavioral, or correctional sciences and one year of counseling or other relevant experience.
- *Massachusetts.* Probation Officer: Bachelor's degree and one-year experience in human or allied services or a graduate degree in the behavioral sciences, education, administration, management, law, or criminal justice. Junior Parole Officer: Two years of experience in probation or parole work, social work, vocational counseling, employment counseling, rehabilitation counseling. College education may be substituted for the required experience on the basis of one year of such education for six months of the required experience.
- *Michigan.* Parole/Probation Officer: Bachelor's degree in criminal justice, psychology, sociology, social work, or related fields.
- *Mississippi.* Corrections Field Officer I: Bachelor's degree in criminal justice, counseling, guidance, psychology, sociology, social work, or related majors; or, graduation from high school and four years of relevant experience.

- *Missouri.* Probation and Parole Officer: Bachelor's degree in the field of criminal justice, social work, psychology, or sociology. Jackson County Deputy Juvenile Officer and Kansas City Probation Officer: Bachelor's degree in behavioral science or related field. Prefer graduate counseling education or social work experience.

- *Nevada.* Adult Probation and Parole Officer I: Graduation from high school and four years' experience in p/p supervision or duties above the journey level in the correctional system (sergeant or above), four years in the area of social work or similar activities, or a bachelor's degree in the behavioral sciences or law enforcement.

- *New Jersey.* Probation Officer: Bachelor's or master's degree in psychology, sociology, corrections, criminology, criminal justice, penology, or social work. Parole Officer: Bachelor's degree and one year of relevant experience or a relevant master's degree; experience may be substituted for education on a year-for-year basis.

- *New Mexico.* Probation/Parole Officer: Bachelor's degree, including fifteen credits in sociology, psychology, corrections, guidance, counseling, social work, or police science.

- *New York.* Parole Officer: Bachelor's degree and three years of relevant experience in social work or counseling. A graduate degree in social work or law will qualify for two years of experience; master's degrees in sociology, psychology, or criminal justice may be substituted for one year of experience. Nassau County and Onondaga County Probation Officer: Bachelor's degree and two years of counseling or casework experience or a master's degree in social work, education, public administration, sociology, psychology, criminology, law, or a related field. Suffolk County Probation Officer Trainee: Bachelor's degree including at least 30 credits in the social or behavioral sciences.

- *Ohio.* Adult Probation Officer Trainee: Any combination of training and work experience that indicates possession of the skills, knowledge, and abilities required for a probation officer. A bachelor's degree in psychology, sociology, social work, corrections, or a related field qualifies for this position. Parole Officer I: Completion of an undergraduate major program with core coursework in behavioral or social science, or criminal justice; or two years of training or experience in probation and parole field services.

- *Oklahoma.* Probation and Parole Officer: A bachelor's degree with 24 credits in the behavioral/social sciences, education, or police science.

- *Oregon.* Juvenile Parole Officer: A bachelor's degree in a behavioral science or three years of counseling experience.

- *Pennsylvania.* Juvenile Probation Officer: A bachelor's degree with at least 18 credits in a social science. Parole Agent I: Bachelor's degree or any equivalent experience or training. Philadelphia Probation Officer Trainee: Bachelor's degree in social work, psychology, criminal justice, sociology, law enforcement, corrections, criminology, counseling, or guidance.

- *Texas.* Adult Probation Officer: Bachelor's degree and one year of graduate study in sociology, social work, counseling, criminology, psychology, or law; or one year of full-time casework or counseling experience with offenders or disadvantaged persons. Candidates must pass a certifying examination promulgated by the Texas Adult Probation Commission. Youth Commission Parole Officer: Bachelor's degree in a relevant discipline (not law enforcement or police science) and two years of social work experience. Parole Caseworker: Bachelor's degree in criminal justice or a related discipline.

- *Virginia.* Probation and Parole Officer: Bachelor's degree with a preference for sociology, psychology, criminology, or counseling majors; preference for those with counseling experience.
- *Wisconsin.* Probation and Parole Agent: Graduation from a four-year college in a human services field is preferred.

PARAPROFESSIONALS

Many jurisdictions also employ workers (sometimes referred to as *paraprofessionals*) who assist in the p/p supervision process but do not have the full responsibilities or qualifications of a p/p officer. For example, Georgia employs p/p aides, Nevada employs probation aides, and Santa Clara County, California, employs probation community workers. Typically, experience in such a position can qualify the person for employment as a p/p officer.

Paraprofessionals are frequently recruited from among persons sharing the same social, economic, racial, or ethnic background as many p/p clients. In some states, this approach has opened p/p employment to ex-offenders. The basic motives for employing paraprofessionals emerged during the years of President Lyndon Johnson's "war on poverty" (Anonymous, 1974: 44):

1. To compensate for the shortage of skilled personnel, particularly workers trained at the graduate level
2. To increase employment opportunities among disadvantaged workers and the unemployed poor
3. To develop an efficient division of labor so that personnel with different levels of skill could be assigned appropriate duties
4. To modify organizations so that the resulting service delivery system could be more directly related to the problem of clients and more efficient in meeting their needs
5. To provide work experience in which workers, by helping clients with problems similar to their own, improve social functioning and become better prepared for work

Paraprofessionals are likely to come from the same environment as the largest segment of the p/p population. Indeed, this reason is a basic one for employing ("indigenous") paraprofessionals in p/p; they are seen as better able to relate to persons alienated from middle-class society. In his essay "Changing Criminals," Donald Cressey (1955) argues that the reduction of alienation is a first step in rehabilitating criminals. This rehabilitation is effected by "positive association" with prosocial persons who are "just like me." According to Carlson and Parks (1979: 192):

It is very difficult for the professional to serve as an effective role model. The indigenous worker, conversely, has often experienced situations and problems similar to those that confront certain clients. The indigenous worker has the advantage of proximity in time and space, while typically the professional is limited to a nine to five, Monday to Friday schedule, living some distance from those served. The indigenous worker, living closer to his clients, has much greater familiarity with their environments, and has greater freedom to move about at times other than business hours. Interracial tensions in certain areas point out the need for nonprofessionals recruited from groups having an ethnic or racial affinity with certain offender populations. A communications gap resulting from social and cultural differences between middle-class professionals of any race and lower class minority group members is a growing problem in rehabilitation services.

In p/p, the use of paraprofessionals has included hiring ex-offenders—this procedure is sometimes the basis of a paraprofessional program. The use of ex-offenders can be seen as a logical extension of Cressey's (1955) stress on correctional workers who are "just like me." Toborg and her colleagues (1978: 13) review some of the advantages of using ex-offenders as counselors:

> Ex-offenders are often considered to make good counselors, because they can more easily identify with the client. This may result both in greater understanding of the client's needs and in a lesser likelihood of being manipulated (or "conned") by the client. Additionally, some staff members think that certain clients may be more at ease with ex-offender counselors and this will lead to greater honesty and openness, resulting in early identification of problems and high levels of client success.

Disadvantages also exist, as Toborg and her colleagues (1978: 13) point out:

> Ex-offender counselors may pose problems, however. One problem which may occur from selecting an insufficiently mature ex-offender of the same background as the client is that the two may become stuck on the point of their fight against the "establishment" [which] becomes the scapegoat; no behavior change is demanded, and no responsibility is accepted, though the staff member may teach the participant how to beat the system.
>   Another problem arises when ex-offender staff think that their status as ex-offenders automatically makes them good counselors. Such staff members may resist efforts to train them in counseling techniques. In addition, ex-offenders may experience a number of role conflicts, caused by having "establishment" jobs where they deal with clients experiencing a community readjustment which the ex-offender counselors may themselves have undergone quite recently. Also, in some cases ex-offender staff may be so assertive about rejecting their criminal past that they antagonize clients,

rather than creating the rapport with them which is often considered an advantage of ex-offender counselors.

Paraprofessionals receive a lower salary than professionals employed by the same agency. Some professionals in p/p agencies believe that the presence of lower-paid personnel doing essentially the same work may undermine their efforts at securing greater salary and employment benefits. Some contend that the willingness of paraprofessionals to accept lower rates of pay than professionals is often the *real* reason that they are employed.

Some probation and parole officers maintain that paraprofessionals over-identify with clients, sometimes in opposition to the agency and its policies. However, others maintain the opposite: that paraprofessionals tend to over-identify with the agency (and middle-class values) and are less flexible than their professional colleagues. Still other observers have found neither criticism valid.

VOLUNTEERS

Probation in the United States originated as a volunteer service; in probation, the tradition was reactivated in 1959 by Keith J. Leenhouts, judge of the Royal Oak, Michigan, municipal court. In that city, the municipal (misdemeanor) court probation department was staffed entirely by volunteers. Through the efforts of Judge Leenhouts a national organization, Volunteers in Prevention, Probation, and Prisons, Inc. (VIP) was formed. (VIP merged with the National Council on Crime and Delinquency in 1972; in 1983, it reverted to independent status. For more information write to VIP, 163 Madison Avenue, Suite 120, Detroit, MI 48226; 313-964-1110).

VOLUNTEERS IN PAROLE PROGRAM, NEW JERSEY

As a component of the Bureau of Parole, the Volunteers in Parole Program is designed to provide help through a pool of individuals from the community. These individuals are qualified and willing to assist the Bureau personnel in serving the varied needs of its many diverse clients.

The following volunteer categories reflect the service needs of the Bureau of Parole while showing the scope of ways in which volunteers can provide valuable assistance.

Parole Officer Aide: helps the parole officer with various investigations and assists as officer of the day for routine office interviews; however, involvement with law enforcement activities is prohibited

Professional Aide: a member of a profession offering specific services on an as needed basis

Administrative Aide: works in a district office in an administrative or clerical capacity

Student Intern: assumes the same role as parole officer aide. Students from various colleges and universities serve internships within the Bureau as part of a cooperative arrangement

Carlson and Parks (1979: 237) report four volunteer service models:

1. *One-to-one model.* On a one-to-one basis, volunteers seek to obtain the trust and confidence of p/p clients and help them to maintain their existence, clarify their role in society, and plan for the future.
2. *Supervision model.* Working as a case aide to a p/p officer, the volunteer provides services to several clients at the direction of the PO.
3. *Professional model.* The volunteer is a professional or semiprofessional in his or her field—teacher or mechanic, for example—who provides specialized services to several clients, for example, help with literacy or skills training. In Florida, the Department of Corrections has volunteer financial planning specialists available to assist probationers with help in maintaining a realistic family budget.
4. *Administrative model.* The volunteer assists with project administrative functions and interacts only indirectly with clients.

VOLUNTEER PROBATION OFFICER PROGRAM

For 20 years, the Brockton, Massachusetts, district court has operated the state's largest continuing volunteer program. With its own director and board of directors—probation officers, past volunteers, and community representatives—the program uses about 600 volunteer probation officers (VPOs) who have completed formal training. The program focuses on repeat offenders aged 17 to 25. Each VPO is matched with three clients to whom they provide a mentoring relationship. The VPO does not substitute for the probation officer, who maintains overall responsibility for supervision, but functions more in the role of older sibling, friend, or even parent surrogate. Several volunteers have been recruited from the ranks of successful probationers. The VPO is in contact with each client at least an hour a week for a year (or less if the client has completed the court's sentence). VPOs report on their activity through weekly contact sheets and attend monthly VPO meetings.

Some p/p agencies and staff members are critical of the use of volunteers. They may view the efforts of volunteers as interference with their prerogatives, and they may be concerned about sharing information with volunteers because of the confidential aspect of p/p practice.

Chris Eskridge and Eric Carlson (1979) report that in some agencies the regular probation/parole workers see volunteers as a threat to their jobs. Some probation/parole officers resent the fact that volunteers are able to play the "good guy" while they have control and enforcement functions. Some complain of volunteers acting as advocates for the offender in opposition to the regular worker.

VICTIM WITNESS SERVICES—JUVENILE COURT OF JACKSON COUNTY

In Kansas City, Missouri, the juvenile court of Jackson County has a victim assistance program staffed by volunteers. The program assists victims by empowering them with knowledge of the juvenile court process and being with them at the court hearing. The services provided by the volunteers include:

1. Visiting victims in cases of delinquency and preparing an impact statement that informs the court of the victim's losses and attitude toward the offense and the offender
2. Providing referrals for those requiring crisis counseling, repair of property, emergency funding, and other vital services
3. Informing the victim of the ability to file a civil action to recover losses
4. Assisting in the filling out of victim compensation claims
5. Assisting victims in recovering their property from police departments where it is being held as evidence
6. When necessary, providing transportation to court
7. Preparing letters for victims/witnesses for employers relative to any loss of work time
8. Meeting with victims/witnesses before their court appearance and staying with them until the hearing is complete
9. Providing for mediation of restitution payments if the court decides that the victim should meet with the offender, and the victim agrees
10. Providing information to the public on the juvenile court process

Volunteers are used by the Missouri Board of Probation and Parole and the Delaware Department of Correction on a one-to-one basis. Both agencies use volunteers to increase the services available to p/p clients. In Missouri they are provided with training in reality therapy (discussed in Chapter 9) and are expected to influence behavior by setting an example while being patient listeners. The volunteer helps the client to develop and carry out realistic plans, provides advice and encouragement, and may offer concrete assistance by helping the client secure employment. The South Carolina Department of Probation, Parole, and Pardon Services uses volunteers as job developers who help offenders find employment and learn job search skills. They also make referrals to employment assistance agencies and develop a job bank for offenders (Macgargle, 1994).

YOUR SKILLS ARE NEEDED IN ONE OF SEVERAL VOLUNTEER JOB ROLES

OFFENDER SERVICES

Job Developer

As a VSP Job Developer, you'll help offenders find employment and learn new job skills. You'll lend a hand in the offender's job search, and give him pointers on interviewing, demeanor, and handling job conflicts. You'll also make referrals to employment agencies and develop a job bank for offenders.

Community Sponsor

As a VSP Sponsor, you'll be matched with an offender, to develop a relationship of guidance, support and motivation for him. You'll assist the offender with obtaining the support and rehabilitative services he needs. Through recreation, conversation, and other activities, you'll provide a positive role model for him.

SYSTEM SERVICES

Court Assistant

As a Court Assistant, your job will be to assist with Department tasks within the Courthouse. You'll help with the processing of offenders placed on probation, the investigation and collection of information from the Clerk of Court, the review of information with the offender, and the monitoring of other court activity.

Agent/Team Assistant

When you volunteer as an Agent/Team Assistant, you'll provide Probation/Parole agents with assistance in monitoring and meeting the needs of offenders. Your job will involve maintaining contacts with service and referral agencies, law enforcement agencies, court offices, family members, and employers, so information can be monitored for better supervision and treatment of offenders.

Office Assistant

As an Office Assistant you'll be involved with many of the daily operations of the Probation/Parole Office. You'll assist with the duties of support staff and help compile and update informational materials for Probation/Parole Agents.

Special Services Assistant

When you volunteer as a Special Services Assistant, you'll help with the implementation and operation of one of the Department's many specialized programs. Volunteer functions in this role are adapted to the specific activities of the program.

Source: South Carolina Department of Probation, Parole, and Pardon Services

Because volunteers are not paid, they need to derive some satisfaction from their efforts. Satisfaction results when a level of success exists, and to be successful, volunteers require adequate training and supervision. In other words, the successful use of volunteers is not "cost free"; staff is required for the training, coordination, and supervision of volunteers. If additional staff is not to be employed for these tasks, the agency has to take away from the working time of regular p/p personnel. Eskridge and Carlson (1979) report that lack of success in volunteer programs is a function of management operations rather than the volunteer concept. Faulty management includes the inability to assign volunteers expeditiously, inadequate volunteer training, poor supervision or support for volunteers, and a lack of communication between volunteers and officers.

REVIEW QUESTIONS

1. What are the various work roles of the p/p officer?
2. What are the three basic p/p agency models?
3. What are the four basic role typologies that may be assumed by p/p officers?
4. What are the three basic categories with respect to agency policy regarding p/p officers making arrests and carrying firearms?
5. What are the arguments for and against p/p officers making arrests and carrying firearms?
6. What are the systems used to select p/p officers?
7. What are paraprofessionals, and what are the reasons they used in p/p?
8. What are the advantages and disadvantages of using volunteers in p/p?

CLASSIFICATION
AND
SUPERVISION

Prisons have traditionally classified inmates on the basis of the security needs of the institution and the physical limitations—handicaps—if any, of the prisoner. As noted in Chapter 7, with the advent of the corrections model, the classification process was expanded to include items relevant to treatment programs offered by the correctional department in its various facilities. According to the National Advisory Commission on Criminal Justice Standards and Goals (1973), classification is a process for determining the needs and requirements of offenders and thereby assigning them to programs according to their needs and existing resources. This categorization can be done by officials at the institution where the offender will serve his or her sentence, or at a reception center that receives all inmates for the purpose of classification and assignment to the appropriate institution.

The de-emphasis of the corrections model has, correspondingly, lessened the importance of institutional classification (at least for treatment). However, a noticeable upsurge has occurred in the use of classification in probation and parole/conditional release supervision. (Hereafter, p/p will stand for probation, parole, and conditional release.)

CLASSIFICATION IN PROBATION AND PAROLE

During the 1970s, p/p administrators increasingly realized that their resources would never be sufficient even to approach the service needs of their clientele.

They also realized that the typical p/p officer approximated agency objectives (protection of the community and rehabilitation of the offender) through the use of an unofficial and unarticulated classification system. S. Christopher Baird, Richard Heinz, and Brian Bemus (1982: 36) note that

> because not all offenders require the same level of supervision or exhibit the same problems, most experienced probation and parole agents utilize an intuitive system of classifying offenders into differential treatment or surveillance modes, usually based on their judgments of client needs and their perception of the client's potential for continued unlawful behavior. It seems reasonable to assume that without this type of case load management, successes would diminish and failures increase.

However, as Baird, Heinz, and Bemus (1982: 36) point out, "this untested, highly individualized approach does not provide information necessary to rationally deploy staff and other resources." To explore this point, the next subsection discusses risk/needs assessment.

RISK/NEEDS ASSESSMENT

During the late 1970s and early 1980s, the use of formal classification in probation and parole supervision expanded greatly. This movement was led by the state of Wisconsin, which in 1975 received funding from the Law Enforcement Assistance Administration for a Case Classification/Staff Deployment Project. After four years, the risk/needs assessment system was designed, implemented, and evaluated statewide. The basic strength of the risk/needs assessment system is in its completeness and simplicity and its utility to management.

The risks/needs concept developed in Wisconsin was adopted by the National Institute of Corrections and, subsequently, many other probation and parole jurisdictions. Although variations exist between jurisdictions, all risks/needs classification schemes quantify variables along two dimensions:

1. The degree to which the offender presents a *risk* of recidivating (committing new offenses)
2. The degree to which the offender requires assistance, *needs,* from the probation/parole agency

Taken together, these two dimensions allow for a prognostication that has implications for the level of supervision required and thus for caseload management and deployment of personnel.

The system tested in Wisconsin demonstrated its effectiveness in predicting success or failure in completing probation/parole terms. In a sample of 8250 clients, the percentage of individuals rated low risk and later revoked was 3 percent; of the cases rated high risk 37 percent were revoked. Other jurisdictions have also tested the system. The Los Angeles Probation Department found that the risk scale compared with intuitive judgments by probation officers did well in predicting which cases would be successful and which would not; the needs scale, however, was found to have almost no predictive value (Program Services Office, 1983). In Massachusetts, Marjorie Brown (1984) found that with a variation of the Wisconsin instrument half the clients classified as "maximum" risk were subsequently recidivists compared with 36 percent of those classified as "moderate" and 17 percent of those classified as "minimum." The predictive ability of the assessment could be improved by utilizing four levels of supervision/risk: intensive, maximum, moderate, and minimum. A test of the Wisconsin Juvenile Probation and Aftercare Risk instrument by José Ashford and Craig LeCroy (1988) revealed that this was not suitable for predicting recidivism.

SUPERVISION LEVELS IN GEORGIA

ADMINISTRATIVE CLASSIFICATION

Although no standard of supervision is required for this classification, probationers who have absconded, who are serving a prison sentence on a new offense and have not been revoked on the present offense, and probationers receiving no direct supervision per court approval, should be classified as administrative.

MINIMUM (NONDIRECT SUPERVISION)

1. Division minimum requirement. Mail in change of address or employment, monthly payment of fine, restitution, court cost, etc.
2. Monthly mail-in report.
3. Monthly telephone contact with probationer.

MINIMUM (DIRECT SUPERVISION)

1. Division minimum requirement. Monthly telephone contact with probation officer.
2. Quarterly face-to-face contact with probation officer.
3. Monthly telephone contact with probation officer *and* quarterly face-to-face contact with probation officer.

MEDIUM

1. Division minimum requirement. Monthly telephone contact with probation officer *and* quarterly face-to-face contact with probation officer.
2. Monthly face-to-face contact with probation officer and one field contact or collateral contact quarterly.

HIGH

1. Division minimum requirement. Monthly face-to-face contact with probation officer *and* one field contact or collateral contact quarterly.

2. Monthly face-to-face contact with probation officer *and* monthly field contact or collateral contact (two contacts per month).
3. Two monthly face-to-face contacts with probation officer, monthly field contact, *and* monthly collateral contact (four contacts per month).

MAXIMUM

1. Division minimum requirement. Two monthly face-to-face contacts with probation officer, monthly field contact, *and* collateral contact (four contacts per month).
2. Two monthly face-to-face contacts with probation officer and two monthly field contacts (four contacts per month).
3. Four monthly face-to-face contacts with probation officer, two monthly field contacts, *and* two monthly collateral contacts (eight contacts per month).

The p/p officer interviews a new client and with the help of the presentence report, institutional reports (for parolees), and other relevant documents, fills out a risk/needs instrument (Figure 11.1a, b). From the scoring of information on the instrument a total is derived, which is plugged into a particular level of supervision; typically, a reassessment is performed every six months. Because clients with a higher level of supervision require a greater expenditure of p/p officer time, equity is determined, not simply on the total number of clients supervised (*caseload*), but on the basis of the anticipated amount of time each case will demand (*workload*). This quantification allows for the easy use of computers, which can determine the need for more p/p officers in a particular jurisdiction (or, if additional officers are not economically feasible, a corresponding reduction in the amount of supervisory time devoted to each case). The Probation Division of the Georgia Department of Offender Rehabilitation sets out the purpose for probation classification: "The purpose of case classification is (1) to improve the effectiveness of service delivery to the probationer; (2) to develop a uniform standard for classification on a statewide basis; and (3) to provide a data base for budgeting and staff deployment on a workload rather than on a caseload model."

The instrument used by the Pennsylvania Board of Probation and Parole is typical of most jurisdictions (Figure 11.2). The PO places a number in a box that corresponds with the case record or the officer's assessment for each of the 11 *risk* assessment variables. Then the officer adds up the score and records that in a box labeled "Total." He or she then proceeds to do the same for the 13 *needs* assessment variables. Afterward, the two final scores are compared; whichever is higher (risk or needs) determines the level of supervision—reduced, regular, close, and intensive. (In some jurisdictions, only three levels of supervision exist: minimum, medium, and maximum.) Some flexibility is possible because the procedures provide for an override: "If, after completing the Initial Client Assessment or Client Reassessment, there is a compelling reason to raise or lower the client's grade of supervision, the agent may recommend such a change to his/her supervisor for review and approval/disapproval."

CLASSIFICATION FOR PROBATION SUPERVISION IN NEW YORK

An increase in arrests and convictions—particularly for drug offenses, while jail and prison overcrowding continues and budget reductions are made to close city budget gaps, has sent caseloads skyrocketing. In response, the New York City Department of Probation devised the Violent Probationers Program (VPP) to screen out for intensive supervision probationers with a history of violent crime. VPP clients are further divided into Enforcement and Treatment Tracks. Newly sentenced probationers who meet the VPP criteria are assessed by a 45-minute interview and the completion of a questionnaire. Those routed to Treatment Services receive standardized group treatment for violent behavior and specialized group treatment to deal with particular types of violence, such as domestic violence and crimes of a sexual nature. Those assigned to the Enforcement Services receive close supervision—high levels of contacts and, if appropriate, drug testing and electronic monitoring.

To free up staff to provide the intensive services of the VPP, probationers who do not meet the program criteria are placed on "paper caseloads"—that is, they do not report in person or receive regular visits by probation officers. Tracking is in the form of reports submitted by each probationer on a regular basis. A third classification, probationers who do not meet VPP criteria but are not candidates for nonreport status, receive a modicum of supervision, including in-person reporting.

Cases classified on the basis of risk/needs are assigned to probation/parole officers according to a predetermined workload distribution. For example, in Texas, Department of Criminal Justice probation guidelines require assignment of cases to POs in "such a manner as to promote public protection through offender supervision and the attainment of a 100 point workload," using the following weights:

Level I	=	4.0
Level II	=	2.5
Level III	=	1.33
Level IV	=	1.00

TEXAS CLASSIFICATION LEVELS

LEVEL I

This classification is calculated as 4 workload points and extends the most restrictive nonresidential supervision to offenders who:

1. Have a documented pattern of serious noncompliance while supervised at a less restrictive level

Client Name	Last	First	Middle	OID Number
Date of Review (Month, Day, Year)	Agent Last Name	Agent Number	Convicted Offense(s)	

Select the appropriate answer and enter the associated weight in the score column. Total all scores to arrive at the risk assessment score.

SCORE

Number of address changes during last 12 months client was in community
- 0 None
- 2 One
- 3 Two or more _____

Age of first conviction (or juvenile adjudication)
- 0 24 or older
- 2 20–23
- 4 19 or younger _____

Number of prior probation/parole/supervised release adjudicated violations (adult or juvenile)
- 0 None
- 4 One or more _____

Number of prior felony convictions (or juvenile adjudications
- 0 None
- 2 One
- 4 Two or more _____

Convictions or juvenile adjudications for:
(select applicable and add for score—do not exceed a total of 5—include current offense)
- Burglary, theft, auto theft or robbery 2
- Worthless checks or forgery 3
- 0 N/A _____

Percentage of time employed during last 12 months client was in community
- 0 60%
- 1 40%–59%
- 2 Under 40%
- 0 N/A _____

Alcohol usage problems (last 12 months in community):
- No interference with functioning 0
- Some interference with functioning 2
- Serious interference with functioning 4 _____

Other drug usage problems (last 12 months in community):
- No interference with functioning 0
- Some interference with functioning 1
- Serious interference with functioning 2 _____

Attitude:
- Motivated to change; receptive to assistance 0
- Dependent or unwilling to accept responsibility 3
- Negative; rationalizes/justifies behavior or not motivated to change 5 _____

Number of prior supervised periods of probation/ parole/supervised release (adult or juvenile)
- 0 None
- 4 One or more _____

Conviction or juvenile adjudication of any crime against a person (felony, gross misdemeanor or misdemeanor) within the last five years
- 15 Yes
- 0 No _____

TOTAL _____

FIGURE 11.1a   Assessment of client risk. (*Source:* Minnesota Department of Corrections)

Clients are assigned to the highest level of supervision that is indicated on the following scale:

Risk	**Level of Supervision**
15 and above	Maximum
8 to 14	Medium
7 and below	Minimum

Risk Scale SCORE _____

LEVEL OF
SUPERVISION _____

_____

If the agent feels that the level of supervision should be higher, supervisory approval is required. State the reasons for higher classification:

_____

_____

_____

_____

In light of the above, the client shall be classified:

_____

Approved: _____

_____

If the agent feels that the classification should be lower, supervisory approval is required. State the reasons for changing the classification:

_____

_____

_____

_____

In light of the above, the client shall be classified:

_____

Approved: _____

TOTAL _____

FIGURE 11.1b   Assessment of client risk (*continued*).

COMMONWEALTH OF PENNSYLVANIA
BOARD OF PROBATION AND PAROLE
PBPP-20 (1/85)   **INITIAL CLIENT ASSESSMENT**

CLIENT NAME (Last, First, Middle Initial)	PAROLE NO.	AGENT NAME	OFFICE	DATE

RISK ASSESSMENT

1. Age at First Conviction: (or juvenile adjudication)
- 24 or older 0
- 20-23 2
- 19 or Younger 4

2. Number of Prior Probation/Parole Revocations: (adult or juvenile)
- None 0
- One or more 4

3. Number of Prior Felony Convictions: (or juvenile adjudications)
- None 0
- One 2
- Two or more 4

4. Convictions or Juvenile Adjudications for:
(Select applicable and add for score. Do not exceed a total of 5. Include current offense.)
- Burglary, theft, auto theft, or robbery 2
- Worthless checks or forgery 3

5. Number of Prior Periods of Probation/Parole Supervision:
(Adult or Juvenile)
- None 0
- One or more 4

6. Conviction or Juvenile Adjudication for Assaultive Offense within Last Five Years: (An offense which involves the use of a weapon, physical force or the threat of force.)
- Yes 15
- No 0

7. Number of Address Changes in Last 12 Months:
(Prior to incarceration for parolees)
- None 0
- One 2
- Two or more 3

8. Percentage of Time Employed in Last 12 Months:
(Prior to incarceration for parolees)
- 60% or more 0
- 40%- 50% 1
- Under 40% 2
- Not applicable 0

9. Alcohol Usage Problems: (Prior to incarceration for parolees)
- No interference with functioning 0
- Occasional abuse: some disruption of functioning 2
- Frequent abuse; serious disruption; needs treatment 4

10. Other Drug Usage Problems: (Prior to incarceration for parolees)
- No interference with functioning 0
- Occasional abuse: some disruption of functioning 1
- Frequent abuse; serious disruption; needs treatment 2

11. Attitude:
- Motivated to change; receptive to assistance 0
- Dependent or unwilling to accept responsibility 3
- Rationalizes behavior; negative; not motivated to change 5

TOTAL

INITIAL ASSESSMENT SCALES

Risk Scale		Needs Scale
0-5	Reduced Supervision	-8-10
6-18	Regular Supervision	1-10
19-30	Close Supervision	11-25
31 & above	Intensive Supervision	26 & above

SCORING AND OVERRIDE

Score Based/ .... Intensive ....☐   Regular ....☐
Supervision Level
                        Close ....☐   Reduced ....☐

Score Override .... No ....☐   Yes ....☐

FINAL GRADE .... Intensive ....☐   Regular ....☐
OF SUPERVISION

Override Explanation: Close ....☐   Reduced ....☐

NEEDS ASSESSMENT

1. Academic/Vocation Skills
- High school or above skill level .... -1
- Adequate skills; able to handle everyday requirements ... 0
- Low skill level causing minor adjustment problems .... +2
- Minimal skill level causing serious adjustment problems .... +4

2. Employment
- Satisfactory employment for one year or longer .... -1
- Secure employment; no difficulties reported; or homemaker, student or retired 0
- Unsatisfactory employment; or unemployed but has adequate job skills .... +3
- Unemployed and virtually unemployable; needs training .... +6

3. Financial Management
- Long-standing pattern of self-sufficiency; e.g., good credit rating .... -1
- No current difficulties 0
- Situational or minor difficulties .... +3
- Severe difficulties; may include garnishment, bad checks or bankruptcy .... +5

4. Marital/Family Relationships:
- Relationships and support exceptionally strong .... -1
- Relatively stable relationships 0
- Some disorganization or stress but potential for improvement .... +3
- Major disorganization or stress .... +5

5. Companions
- Good support and influence .... -1
- No adverse relationships 0
- Associations with occasionally negative results .... +2
- Associations almost completly negative .... +4

6. Emotional Stability
- Exceptionally well adjusted; accepts responsibility for actions .... -2
- No symptoms of emotional instability; appropriate emotional responses 0
- Symptoms limit but do not prohibit adequate functioning e.g., excessive anxiety .... +4
- Symptoms prohibit adequate functioning; e.g., lashes out or retreats into self .... +7

7. Alcohol Usage
- No interference with functioning 0
- Occcasional abuse; some disruption of functioning ...... +3
- Frequent abuse; serious disruption; needs treatment .... +6

8. Other Drug Usage
- No interference with functioning 0
- Occasional substance abuse; some disruption of functioning .... +3
- Frequent substance abuse; serious disruption; needs treatment .... +5

9. Mental Ability
- Able to function independently 0
- Some need for assistance; potential for adequate adjustment; mild retardation .... +3
- Deficiencies severely limit independent functioning; moderate retardaton .... +6

10. Health
- Sound physical health; seldom ill 0
- Handicap or illness interferes with functioning on a recurring basis .... +1
- Serious handicap or chronic illness; needs frequent medical care. .... +2

11. Sexual Behavior
- No apparent dysfunction 0
- Real or perceived situational or minor problems .... +3
- Real or perceived chronic or severe problems .... +5

12. Recreation/Hobby
- Constructive 0
- Some constructive activities .... +1
- No constructive leisure-time activities or hobbies .... +2

13. Agent's Impression of Client's Needs
- Minimum .... -1
- Low 0
- Medium .... +3
- Maximum .... +5

TOTAL

FIGURE 11.2 Initial Client Assessment, Pennsylvania.

    2. Have a motion to revoke filed for a law violation

    3. Match the jurisdiction's profile of offenders historically committed to prison/jail

    4. Have regressed from a less restrictive level of supervision

LEVEL II

This classification is calculated as 2.5 workload points and extends a heightened level of supervision to offenders who:

    1. Are a demonstrable risk based on:
       a. Shock community supervision
       b. In lieu of revocation
       c. Direct sentence

    2. Have progressed from a more restrictive level of supervision, including residential supervision

    3. Have regressed from a less restrictive level of supervision

    4. Have documented special risk or needs which are included in the CSCD's profile of offenders historically committed to prison/jail

LEVEL III

This classification is calculated as 1.33 workload points and extends a moderate level of supervision to offenders who:

    1. Regressed from a less restrictive level of supervision

    2. Progressed from a more restrictive level of supervision, including residential supervision

    3. Demonstrate a documentable necessity for a moderate level of supervision

LEVEL IV

This classification is calculated as 1 workload point and extends a minimum level of supervision to offenders who:

    1. Progressed from a more restrictive level of supervision

    2. Present the least risk to the community

    3. Are considered to be initial or interim community supervision placements but have not been classified

PROBATION/PAROLE SUPERVISION

The supervision process in both probation and parole is similar, if not identical. In fact, probation and parole are handled by the same agency in some states. However, parolees, by definition, have been imprisoned, and imprisonment generally reflects the severity of the offense and the criminal history of the offender. Therefore, parolees are generally considered a greater danger to the community than are probationers. Furthermore, given the lack of adequate educational and training resources in prison, most parolees leave the institution without the literacy and job skills necessary for employment.

Parolees differ from probationers as a result of their prison experiences. Elliot Studt (in Law Enforcement Assistance Administration, 1973) reports that certain highlights of the reintegration process stand out in most parole cases. She notes that the changeover from prison life to community living requires a major readjustment. In prison, the offenders' lives are rigidly controlled: They are told when to sleep, when to eat, when to work, and when to have recreation. When they are released into the community, they must adjust to managing their own lives. This may be compounded by police harassment, particularly in smaller communities. Social agencies often do not recognize parolees' needs and somehow believe that they should be receiving assistance from the parole agency. Unfortunately, most parole (and probation) agencies are extremely limited in their ability to deliver tangible services. This fact, coupled with the usual lack of employable skills, often makes parolees a burden on their families, worsening what may have been an already difficult family situation.

Parolees have told this author that even so minor an experience as taking a bus ride can be traumatic to a newly released offender. Several stated they were not aware of the required fare, and they had a feeling that everyone on the bus, especially the driver, recognized that they had just been released from prison. Being in prison also isolated them from normal social contacts with members of the opposite sex. They were self-conscious and often felt that because of the way they looked at women, everyone would realize that they had been in prison.

Studt points out that parolees must "unlearn" prison habits and acquire new patterns of behavior if readjustment is to be accomplished quickly. Parolees are often subjected to social rejection because of their status, and they usually lack the necessary connections and economic resources that are effective in dealing with crisis situations.

CASE ASSIGNMENT

The supervision process begins when the offender is placed on the caseload/workload of a p/p officer. This aspect of supervision, case assignment, can be accomplished in a variety of ways, depending on the practice used by the particular agency and the scope of its jurisdiction. In agencies that have statewide jurisdiction (such as all parole agencies), district/area offices are located throughout the state and each office covers a specific geographic area. County probation agencies, depending on the size of the county, may also have (sub)offices scattered throughout the jurisdiction. Offenders on p/p are directed to report to the office responsible for the area in which they (intend to) reside. At the p/p office, they will be assigned to a caseload either on a totally random basis or according to the specific area in which they plan to reside. Caseloads incorporating geographic considerations are advantageous insofar as they limit the travel time involved in supervising the offender. Each officer also gains greater familiarity with his or her territory, the social and law enforcement agencies therein (not to mention places to eat and clean washrooms) that can enhance the supervision process. In more rural areas, where travel will be extensive, the caseloads will be smaller than in urban areas, where offenders are usually clustered in certain areas of the city. In the caseload assignment process, the agency typically attempts to achieve parity by keeping the size of caseloads roughly equal.

Offenders are assigned to *specialized caseloads* by virtue of a salient characteristic, such as a history of drug abuse or mental retardation. (Specialized caseloads are discussed later in this chapter.) A final model uses classification schemes; quantitative weights are assigned to each case based on the level of supervision prognosticated by case (e.g., risk/needs) classification, and workloads are balanced by maintaining ongoing comparative statistics for p/p officers assigned to field supervision. Although this approach is the most rational one to achieving parity in supervision, it is also the most difficult to operationalize, particularly for an agency that has statewide responsibilities.

INITIAL INTERVIEW

The first meeting between the client and the p/p officer usually occurs in the probation or parole office—it is a time of apprehension and anxiety. José Arcaya (1973: 58–59) states that the officer "represents a power that can, and does, limit his freedom." The offender is in the office *involuntarily* in a situation "where two individuals are joined by legal force in a counseling . . . relationship." The offender encounters the p/p officer for the first time with a mixture of fear, weariness, and defiance. Ann Strong (1981: 12) notes: "Particularly difficult is the nonvoluntary nature of the probationer; this individual places a premium on the skills of the probation officer who must counter resistance with patience, persistence, and good will."

The "sizing up" process at the time of the initial interview works both ways. The p/p officer is meeting a stranger who is usually known only through information in the case record and/or presentence investigation report. Although the record may say a great deal about the offender's background, it may not accurately reflect his or her current attitude toward p/p supervision. How will the client deal with current problems? Will the probationer/parolee follow regulations? Will he or she abscond from supervision if pressured or frustrated? Will the officer be responsible for having a warrant issued and having the offender sent to prison? Will this be, instead, an easy case with a minimum of problems?

The client is asking similar questions. Will the p/p officer give me a difficult time? Will my PO be rigid about every minor rule? Is he or she quick to seek delinquency action? Does the officer have the knowledge and ability to help me secure employment, training, education, a place to live?

During an initial interview, the officer explains the p/p rules, answering questions while attempting to set realistic standards for a client (see Figure 11.2). Several items are usually emphasized:

- The need to make in-person, telephone, or mail reports
- The need to keep the p/p officer informed of his or her place of residence
- The need to seek and maintain lawful employment
- The need to avoid unlawful behavior and report contacts with law enforcement officers

When a particular problem exists, the officer may set special conditions. An offender with a history of sex offenses against children will be required to keep out of areas where children normally congregate, such as playgrounds. An offender with a history of alcoholism may be directed to refrain from using any intoxicating beverages. A young offender may be required to keep a curfew. Offenders with chemical abuse problems may be required to attend treatment programs.

The p/p officer explains that he or she will be visiting the offender's residence periodically. Officers offer clients assistance with employment or other problems. Some clients need financial assistance—one of the immediate problems encountered by a newly released parolee is financial. The money that an inmate receives on release, *gate money*, is usually inadequate for even immediate housing and food needs: This problem continues, despite research (Berk, Lenihan, and Rossi, 1980) indicating that support payments to just-released prisoners in Georgia and Texas reduced recidivism. A parolee may have some funds as a result of prison work, but wages are well below that received on the outside. The p/p officer may refer the client to the department of welfare (some states, for example, Illinois, will not provide assistance to able-bodied persons without dependent children) or to private agencies such as the Salvation Army or a halfway house.

An additional issue in placing parolees are statutes that require notification of local officials and sometimes neighbors when certain offenders plan to live in their community—more than 35 states have such legislation. In some highly publicized cases, officials have been unable to provide housing for sex offenders, particularly when their crimes involved children or violence.

The initial interview in p/p practice is considered a crucial time in the supervision process. An accompanying box lists the guidelines with which a New York State parole officer is provided for the initial interview.

INITIAL INTERVIEW

As the name implies, this is the first major interview between the parole officer responsible for the supervision of the case and the newly released parolee. If the arrival report is taken by the parole officer who will supervise the case, it may be combined with the initial interview. It is at this time that the parole officer initiates a counseling or casework relationship with the parolee.

Since the parole officer is endeavoring to establish this relationship with individuals whose knowledge of and acceptance of parole varies to a great degree, the interview must be planned and handled with best casework skills. There are those whose attitudes toward parole are based on prejudices, doubt, and fears brought about by rumors. With this group, only patience and skill will overcome the hostility and resistance to a working relationship.

This is the interview on which the planning for future supervision of the parolee will be based. Therefore, it is important that the parole officer prepare for it by studying all the pertinent information contained in the case folder. It is also important that this interview be well planned, unhurried, and without interference, if possible. It is the key to the future of the case.

The parole officer undertakes the initial interview with four major objectives in mind:

1. Establish a casework relationship with the parolee.
2. Secure the parolee's participation in an analysis of his or her problems.
3. Make constructive suggestions that will give the parolee "something to do" toward beginning the overall parole program.
4. Leave the parolee with some positive assurance of what there is to look forward to as the parole period progresses.

SUGGESTED CONTENT OF INITIAL INTERVIEW

The initial interview will vary with the needs and problems, both immediate and long-range, of the individual case. However, the following items are presented as a general guide to areas that the parole officer might wish to cover in conducting his or her initial interview with the parolee. Several of these areas would have been addressed during the parolee's arrival report, if it was conducted at an earlier time. In that case, these items should now be discussed further to ascertain if there are any continuing or additional problems, and to learn whether the parolee's situation has altered.

1. Description of the Parolee.

At this time, the parolee's physical appearance should be updated from the time of his arrival report, with any particular changes, such as his mode of dress and attitude, noted. It should be borne in mind that an individual's habit of dress and mannerisms often offer nonverbal communication that can tell us much about how a person regards himself and those about him. (From time to time during the parolee's period of supervision, the parole officer should note whether there are any significant changes in the parolee's mode of dress and mannerisms, as these may signal changes in how the parolee regards himself or in his adjustment pattern.)

2. Analysis of Problems and Initiating
the Casework Process.

In conducting an initial interview, the parole officer is expected to encourage the parolee's participation in discussion of his problems and goals. This discussion should be based upon information contained in the parolee's folder, other knowledge that the parole officer might have, and the parolee's input.

There should be a discussion of the parole program. Both the residence and employment aspects of the program should be carefully reviewed to ascertain that it is as approved, and the parole officer should take pains to fill in any information regarding the residence and employment that may otherwise be missing in the reports. Care should be exercised to make sure that any questions or concerns the parolee has regarding his program are addressed.

The parole officer should ensure that the parolee understands his employment program, and, if necessary, arrangements should be made for the parolee to report to his employer. The parolee's prompt reporting to his prospective employer or employment program, is, of course, a necessity. The parolee's actual employment or participation in employment program should be verified as soon as possible by the parole officer.

If the parolee has no specific employment or alternative program, he should report promptly to any party or agency that may have offered him approved assistance in securing employment. If no such program has been previously established, the parole officer must assist the parolee during the initial interview to devise a plan for seeking employment. If possible, the parole officer may provide the parolee with referrals to potential employers or parties who might assist the parolee in securing employment.

Information should be provided to the parolee concerning the provisions for discharge after three years of successful parole supervision as well as possible eligibility for a Certificate of Relief from Disabilities or a Certificate of Good Conduct.

Before conducting the initial interview, the parole officer should make every attempt to determine whether or not the parolee has any questions, reservations, or misconceptions concerning his relationship with parole and the conditions of parole to which he is subject. This should be done in such a manner as to ensure him that the parole officer is ready and willing to assist him in any constructive manner with the problems which might arise during his time on parole.

3. Reporting Instructions.

Before concluding the initial interview, the parolee should be clearly told why office reports are necessary and helpful. He should also understand when, where, and with what frequency he is to report to his parole officer. If he is to report to his parole officer at a different location, he should be given the address of that location and the time to report. The parole officer should give the parolee one of his official business cards, writing the parolee's name on the front and reporting instructions on the back.

Further, the parolee is to be clearly informed that, should he be unable to make a scheduled report, he must contact his parole officer in advance, for permission to miss a scheduled report and to obtain an alternative appointment.

4. His Attitude toward the Parole Officer
and the Interview.

In noting the parolee's attitude toward the parole officer and the interview, the parole officer should include a description of the parolee's attitudes, interpretation of these attitudes, and his basis for such interpretation.

RECORDING THE INTERVIEW

The initial interview is the foundation on which the relationship between the parolee, the parole officer, and the parole system is established. The way it is conducted and its content are highly important to that relationship. It is also important, from both a casework and a legal perspective, that what transpired during the initial interview be clearly and promptly recorded in the parole case folder. Since much of the information discussed during the initial interview is already recorded in the case folder, it is not necessary to repeat that information except where it relates directly to the problems that were discussed during the initial interview.

In recording the initial interview, the parole officer should bear in mind any immediate problems the parolee has and any long range problems that the parole officer anticipates. In making this assessment, the parole officer should also indicate what immediate intervention on the parolee's behalf has been undertaken or is contemplated, what immediate and obtainable goals have been established for, or preferably with, the parolee, and what long-range plans for the parolee are being considered.

THE SUPERVISION PLANNING PROCESS—UNITED STATES PROBATION

The supervision planning process is designed to create a strategy-based plan of action to address specific issues. This process requires that all supervision activities, including personal contacts, be structured to ensure compliance with the conditions of supervision, protect the community, and provide for correctional treatment. The linking of supervision activities to what is necessary to fulfill relevant statutory responsibilities in each case is intended to provide for efficient and effective use of the officer's time.

This process does not de-emphasize the importance of personal contact with the offender but recognizes that the quality of supervision depends on what is accomplished by a particular activity rather than its frequency. The measure of success of the supervision program is the degree to which the offender conforms to the conditions of supervision, identified supervision issues are resolved, and officer intervention is timely and appropriate.

Supervision planning begins with an initial assessment period during which the officer will obtain and evaluate information regarding the conditions of release, the degree and the kind of risk the offender poses to the community, and the characteristics and conditions of the offender that indicate the need for correctional treatment. Based on the information gathered, the officer will identify as supervision issues those specific conditions of supervision and case problems that require direct action by the officer during the period and then select the supervision strategies necessary to address those issues.

The plan will be reviewed by a supervisor and, when approved, implemented. The officer is responsible for accomplishing those supervision activities selected as being necessary to enforce the conditions, control risk, and provide for correctional treatment for as long as the supervision issue is relevant.

HIV/AIDS

A relatively new issue in probation and parole supervision involves cases in which the client has HIV. Although some officers have personal concerns, the manner in which the disease is transmitted places them at low risk. Difficult questions concern enforcement of rules and confidentiality. Offenders who are sexually active place their partners in jeopardy. Can the client be required to refrain from unprotected sexual activity? How would this rule be enforced? Should the spouse or sexual partner(s) be informed of the client's condition? If so, how is this to be accomplished? These are serious public safety and liability issues that probation and parole agencies are struggling with (Hunt, Moini, and McWhan, 1989; Kleinig and Lindner, 1989; Takas and Hammett, 1989). In response to this problem, the New York State Division of Parole has formed special AIDS caseloads (discussed later in this chapter), and each parolee in New York is provided with a specially prepared booklet on AIDS.

MONTGOMERY COUNTY, OHIO
ADULT PROBATION DEPARTMENT
PROBATION ORIENTATION PROGRAM

Each probationer will be expected to attend one probation orientation program within the first thirty days of his placement under probation supervision. At least two orientation programs will be presented each month—that is, the first and third Mondays.

PURPOSE

Probationers often have a personal view of what probation is all about as influenced by their own assigned probation officer or fellow probationer. There is often a thought that there is a difference between probation officers—the way officers handle their cases in terms of service to the client, police tactics, use of special conditions of probation, and so on. The orientation programs are meant to give each client a clearer understanding of the official probation process and, more important, to introduce them to the services that are available to them through the Community Resource Division of the Adult Probation Department. It is further hoped that the orientation program schedule will allow each client to participate in an orientation session before the formulation of case plans. With the background of the orientation program, the probationer should have more of an opportunity to discuss with the probation officer the types of needs and concerns that he or she personally has that can be addressed by programs within the department, or directly or indirectly supported by it. It is also an opportunity to convey to the new probationers that they can have an active part in the development of programming within the department.

ONGOING SUPERVISION

Offenders are usually relieved to be out of the office after their first visit. They generally leave with mixed feelings. If the officer has been warm, concerned, and helpful, positive feelings will predominate. If the officer was not sensitive to the attitude conveyed and did not evince a feeling of acceptance, negative feelings will predominate. Claude Mangrum (1972: 48) notes that "there is nothing necessarily incompatible between warmth and acceptance and firm enforcement of the laws of the land. We must take whatever corrective measures are necessary, but these must not permit us to demean the dignity of the individual."

During the periodic visits to the client's residence, the p/p officer should try to spend enough time to be able to relate to the client and the client's family. The home visit provides an opportunity to meet family members and interpret the role of the p/p agency to them. The worker should leave a business card and invite inquiries for information or help. The home visit also provides an opportunity to ensure that spouse or child abuse is not a problem. When visiting the home, it is incumbent on the officer to try to protect the confidentiality inherent in each case. Officers do not advertise their business or draw unnecessary attention to the visit to a client's home. Florida advises its correctional probation officers:

> In order to help maintain the confidentiality of the probation and parole status of offenders under supervision, unmarked vehicles shall be used by officers. Correspondence shall be sent in envelopes which do not contain references to the Department of Corrections or Probation and Parole Services. Notes left at an offender's residence should be done with discretion to avoid broadcasting the status of the offender to others who may have access to the note.

In many cases, the client's p/p status is known to neighbors, and the officer may be a familiar figure in the neighborhood. A client or the client's family may escort the officer back to his or her automobile or public transportation as a gesture of concern in high-delinquency areas.

HOME VISITS BY COLORADO PAROLE OFFICERS

Home visits are conducted to

- Confirm parolees' residence locations
- Identify conditions in which parolees live and potential problems that may exist
- Acquaint parole officers with parolees' household relationships
- Provide parole officers with opportunities to enforce conditions of supervision, issue lawful directives, advise, and counsel parolees

- Provide parole officers with opportunities to scrutinize parolees' residence for contraband
- Provide parole officers with opportunities to collect urine specimens from parolees
- Address any other purpose deemed appropriate for case supervision

---

The accompanying excerpt from a case record shows how increased understanding of an offender caused a change in the direction of treatment. It also reveals the value of home visits as a means of gaining new insights into an offender's situation. The second excerpt describes an interview with an offender in jail to indicate how the probation officer approached a hostile and uncooperative offender. The officer guides the interview to avoid futile and repetitious rationalizations and also explores to find some area in which he and the offender can work constructively together.

QUARTERLY SUMMARY, MARCH

3/9	Office report.
3/23	Failed to report.
3/30	Home visit. Mother and aunt seen.
4/6	Failed to report. Notice sent, giving 48 hours to report.
4/8	Reported
4/13	Failed to report.
4/20	Home visit. Offender and aunt seen.
4/27	Reported.
5/1	Contact made with Community Settlement.
5/11	Reported.
5/25	Reported.

During March and April attempts were made to get the offender to look for work. Early in March, he reported that he had a temporary job as a truck driver, and thought that because of this he did not have to report. I corrected this idea and emphasized the importance of keeping his appointments. He had little to say but seemed amenable to conforming. The failure to report in April was excused because of illness.

During home visits, the mother reported that the offender is keeping reasonable hours. She informed me that he spends most of his spare time at the Community Settlement and recently won a trophy for basketball. The aunt, a single woman who lives in the home, takes an active interest in him. She said that the offender is really very shy and needs special attention, which she tries to give him because the mother has little time to spare from the younger children. She has accompanied him to the State Employment Office, where he has been trying to obtain work, but as he is unskilled, he has few opportunities. Such protectiveness seems inappropriate for a 19-year-old youth.

I called at the Community Settlement and talked with the director, Mr. Apt. He is very much interested in the offender, but told me confidentially that he is afraid the subject might be getting into a neighborhood gang that is beginning to form. He has noticed that when the offender leaves the settlement, he often joins other young men, some of whom have been in trouble. The settlement has an employment service for members and will try to help the offender obtain employment. When the offender reported, I suggested that he apply at the settlement employment service. The next day, Mr. Apt telephoned. The offender had been referred to a job in a downtown warehouse. He returned to the settlement in tears. He was so frightened that he had been unable to apply. He doesn't think he could do such work, although it is simple unskilled labor. Mr. Apt thinks that the offender needs psychiatric attention, but this may be the first time the offender has tried to seek work by himself.

At the time of the last report, the offender discussed some of his fears about work. He speaks warmly of the personnel at the settlement, but somewhat resentfully of his mother and aunt, who "keep nagging" him about work.

It is planned to try to encourage this offender by building up his self-esteem, giving recognition to his success in settlement activities and, by planning visits when he is at home, dealing with him directly rather than with relatives. The possibility of psychiatric referral will be explored.

PETER

Peter, aged eighteen, has been on probation for two months. He was accorded youthful offender treatment following indictment for an assault during which he threatened to, but did not use a knife. During the course of our contact, he has been on a weekly reporting schedule. I have concentrated on trying to help him get work. He has conformed in rather surly fashion, and never has volunteered to discuss any of his problems. He lives at home with his mother, a divorcee, and an older brother, who is a conforming person who did well in school, has regular employment, and generally does everything he should, thereby winning the mother's approval.

Recently, Peter was arrested for drunk and disorderly conduct. He pleaded guilty and received a 30-day jail sentence, which he is just beginning to serve. The arresting officer's report indicated that he was assaultive and that it required three policemen to get him to the station. I visited him at the jail to obtain information for a violation report to be submitted to the court for action regarding his probation status. When I explained this, Peter went into what threatened to be a long harangue against the police and everyone connected with the current offense. He was in jail, he said, only because his girlfriend's father objected to him and was trying to keep him from dating her. I stated briefly and flatly what I knew about his present situation and noted that his own conduct was the reason for his being here. I asked him to tell me something about his girl, but he cut this off by saying that she and her family had moved to get the girl away from him, and he would not be seeing her any more. I asked what he had been assigned to do in jail. He was just washing dishes and it was a bore and everyone here was a jerk. Had his family visited him? His mother had, but not his brother. I wondered how he got along with his brother. As if I had turned on a faucet, the story of his resentment toward his brother gushed out. He recalled things that had happened when he was only about 6 years old, and revealed that he is conscious of his jealousy over the mother's favoritism.

OFFENDER EMPLOYMENT

The securing and maintaining of employment or training for employment are crucial aspects of p/p supervision: "Perhaps the greatest single factor influencing the quality of life of parolees in their communities is the ability to secure and maintain employment" (Davidoff-Kroop, 1983: 1). Many believe that a relationship exists between successful employment and avoidance of further legal difficulties. A study in California revealed that unemployment and underemployment are closely associated with recidivism (Grogger, 1989). Joy Davidoff-Kroop (1983: 1) states: "Two parolee follow-up studies in New York showed a high rate of unemployment amongst parolees returned to prison". Mary Toborg and her colleagues (1978: 2) state:

> The observed relationship between criminality and unemployment has been explained in different ways. Some researchers have proposed that there is a *causal relationship* between unemployment and crime, while analysts have agreed that unemployment and recidivism are highly correlated only because each is associated with another factor (e.g., the influence of family members or a decision to "go straight"), which induced widespread behavioral change. Whatever the explanation, unemployment and recidivism are often closely related. (Emphasis in original)

Thus, the variable *employment* may not be the cause of the variable *go straight*, but both variables may actually be dependent on the (independent) variable *motivation*. In other words, whatever it is that motivates an offender to seek and maintain gainful employment also tends to motivate that offender to avoid criminal behavior.

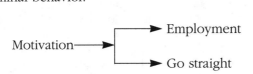

In addition to providing economic rewards, employment also enhances the self-worth and image of the client. When economic conditions are poor and unemployment is high, these factors have a direct effect on p/p supervision.

Davidoff-Kroop (1983: 1) notes: "Given the present day realities of high unemployment, parolees [and probationers] who are often undereducated and with few skills learn that finding work is problematical and frustrating." The employment problem for parolees is often a great deal more difficult than for probationers. The parolee has been separated from employment and community contacts, usually for at least 18 months, often longer. The prison environment offers little help. The Comptroller General of the United States (1979: 46) has reported that federal and state prison systems have been deficient in their approach to training and educating inmates for employment. In view of the shift toward "just deserts" and the scarcity of tax dollars, no reason exists to believe that the situation has gotten better since that report was published.

In assisting clients with employment, officers make direct referrals to particular employers if they have the necessary contacts, or they may refer clients to other agencies, such as state employment services. Officers may have to provide guidance and counseling concerning some of the basic aspects of securing employment, items that for middle-class persons are taken for granted. For example, officers will emphasize the need to be on time for interviews, in fact, the need to arrive a few minutes early. They will help to fill out applications or help the client to prepare for this aspect of the job search. Some officers may use role playing to accustom clients to job interview situations. Officers should discuss the importance of good grooming and what type of clothes to wear to an interview. The accompanying checklist is an example of interview instructions that might be given to a client.

CHECKLIST FOR OFFENDER EMPLOYMENT

Greet Receptionist

1. Give your name and reason for visit. Example: "Good morning, my name is John Smith and I have a 10:00 A.M. employment interview with Mr. Jones."
2. Be punctual. Example: For a 10:00 A.M. interview, try being there by 9:30 or 9:45 A.M.
3. Be prepared to fill out an application. Example: (refer to point 2): By arriving at 9:30 or 9:45 A.M., you can fill out an application and go in at 10:00 A.M. to see Mr. Jones.
4. Have a copy of your social security number, names of past jobs with addresses and dates, names of references with addresses, etc., written on a card to aid you in filling out the application.
5. Be prepared to take a test for the job you are applying for if required. Example: Electronic, clerical or industrial machines, etc.
6. Have a list of questions you wish to ask prepared. Example:
   a. How old is the company?
   b. How many employees are with the company?
   c. What is the potential for promotion and growth?
   d. What are the duties that the job entails?

e. What is the starting salary?

f. What is the top salary potential?

g. What are the working hours?

h. Is there paid overtime?

i. What benefits are offered by the company?

j. Does the company offer tuition for night school?

k. Does the company promote from within?

Procedure for the Interview

1. Walk slowly and quietly, stand correctly, hold your head up.
2. Greet the interviewer.

   a. Shake hands firmly if interviewer offers his hand.

   b. Look interviewer in the eye and say, "How do you do, Mr. Jones?"

   c. Stand until the interviewer asks you to be seated.

   d. Wait for the interviewer to start the interview and lead it.

   e. Be prepared to answer questions. Examples:

   - Why do you want to work for this company?
   - Where do you see yourself in five years?
   - Are you planning to further your education?
   - What do you know about this company?
   - Do you have any particular skills or interests that you feel qualify you for a position with this company?
   - What makes you feel you are qualified for this particular job?

Now is when you present your questions.

Attitudes and Behavior During the Interview

1. Sit up straight, feet on the floor, hands in lap.
2. Sit quietly (do not keep moving around or fidget).
3. Use your best manners.

   a. Be attentive and polite.

   b. Speak slowly and clearly.

   c. Look interviewer in the eye (do not wear sunglasses)

   d. Use correct English, avoid slang.

   e. Emphasize your good points.

4. Speak of yourself in a positive manner.
5. Talk about what you can do.
6. Do not apologize for your shortcomings.
7. Do not talk to excess about your personal problems.

What an Interviewer Sees Immediately During an Interview

1. Hygiene

   a. Bathe just before an interview.

   b. Clean and clip nails if necessary.

    c. Brush teeth.

    d. Use a good deodorant.

    e. Wear an outfit that is clean and conservative regardless of the fashion trend or style.

Interviewer Closes the Interview

1. Do not linger when he indicates it is time to stop.
2. Be sure to thank the interviewer as you leave.

Staying on the Job

1. With great shortage of available jobs, employers can afford to be highly selective in choosing an employee.
2. Accept positions in related fields so when positions are reopened, you will have first choice at these positions.

In Conclusion

Remember the four *A*s:

1. Attendance
2. Attitude
3. Appearance
4. Ability

Source: Adapted from Phyllis Groom McCreary and John M. McCreary, *Job Training and Placement for Offenders and Ex-offenders* (Washington, DC: Government Printing Office, 1975), pp. 79–80.

One critical aspect of employment for ex-offenders is the question of revealing their record. I allowed my clients to decide for themselves. However, I did provide guidance by discussing the experiences of other clients relative to this issue. Many clients reported that their candor resulted in not securing employment. Others reported that some employers were interested in providing them with an opportunity "to make it." Unfortunately, many, if not most, employers will not hire an ex-offender if any alternative exists.

Some offenders are required by law or p/p agency policy to reveal their records when applying for certain jobs. For example, most positions with the government require people having a criminal conviction to reveal this fact; they are frequently fingerprinted for this purpose. Banks, hospitals, and other sensitive areas of employment may also require disclosure. Certainly, allowing an offender with a history of drug abuse to work in a hospital or similar situation would not be advisable, especially if the employer did not know of the person's record. Some states, for example, Illinois, are now making most criminal conviction records available to the public.

An expert in the field of ex-offender employment, Sol Tropp, recommends that "the employer should be made aware of an offender's status only when the pattern of the offender's behavior may result in antisocial behavior," such as a former drug addict working in a medical setting (New York State Employment Services Vocational Rehabilitation Service, 1965: 8). The vocational director of the Osborne Association, a prison reform group, states: "We do not lie about the individual's record but, because of the prejudice that employers may have, we try to postpone complete revelation until the employer has had a chance to try out the offender on the job" (New York State Employment Services Vocational Rehabilitation Service, 1965: 8).

THE STIGMA OF CONVICTION

John Reed and Dale Nance (1972: 27) have stated what is all too often obvious in p/p practice: "A record of conviction produces a loss of status which has lasting consequences." They note that although probation and parole, in terms of rehabilitation, are thought of as more desirable than prison, "both visibly display the offender in the community under a disability—his conditions of probation or parole. In some jurisdictions, he must register as a criminal, supposedly for the protection of the community. The unintended effects of registration are to broadcast his conviction and preserve his criminal stigma." Reed and Nance refer to this result as a form of value conflict, whereby the protective concerns of society run counter to the rehabilitative philosophy that is espoused.

One of the few studies on the impact of a criminal conviction was conducted by Richard Schwartz and Jerome Skolnick (1962). They studied the effects of a criminal record on the employment opportunities of unskilled workers. Four employment folders were prepared, which were the same in all respects except for the criminal record of the applicant, as follows:

1. The first folder indicated that the applicant had been convicted and sentenced for assault.
2. The second noted that he had been tried for assault and acquitted.
3. The third again showed that he was tried for assault and acquitted, but with a letter from the judge certifying the finding of not guilty.
4. The fourth made no mention of any criminal record.

The study involved 100 employers who were divided into units of 25, with each group being shown one of the four folders on the mistaken belief that they were actually considering a real job applicant:

- Of the employers shown the "no record" folder, 36 percent gave positive responses.
- Of the employers shown the "acquitted" folder with the judge's letter, 24 percent expressed an interest in the application.
- Of the employers shown the "acquitted" folder, 12 percent expressed an interest in the applicant.

- Of the employers shown the "convict" folder, only 4 percent expressed interest in the applicant.

Because most persons on p/p are unskilled, the ramifications of these findings are obvious.

In an effort to minimize the legal harm caused by a criminal record, some states have removed various statutory restrictions on gaining licenses necessary for employment, and a few have even enacted "fair employment" laws for ex-offenders. New York, for example, prohibits the denial of employment or license because of a conviction unless there is a *direct relationship* between the conviction and the specific employment or license, or unless it involves an "unreasonable risk" to persons or property. A direct relationship requires a showing that the nature of the criminal conduct for which the person was convicted has a direct bearing on the fitness or ability to carry out duties or responsibilities related to the employment or license. The statute requires that a public or private employer provide, on request, a written statement setting forth the reasons for a denial of license or employment and provides for enforcement by the New York State Commission on Human Rights. The U.S. Department of Labor has a long-standing program that provides bonding for probationers and parolees without any cost to either employee or employer.

States vary in the method and extent to which they provide relief from disabilities incurred by probationers and parolees. Some states have adopted automatic restoration procedures on satisfactory completion of p/p supervision, and many states have statutes designed to restore forfeited rights, although they may be subjected to restrictive interpretation in licensing and occupational areas. Pardon is another method, although its use is generally limited; some states (e.g., Alabama, Florida, and Georgia), however, have limited forms of pardon that restore certain rights (discussed in Chapter 8). In New York, the judiciary and parole board have the power to restore certain rights through the granting of a "relief from disabilities."

New York State Relief from Civil Disabilities

I. Certificates of Relief from Disabilities

A. Effect of a Certificate of Relief

A Certificate of Relief removes any legal bar of disability imposed as a result of conviction of the crime or crimes specified in the certificate, although specific disabilities (such as those relating to weapon possession) may be excepted by the Board of Parole. In addition, by law, the Certificate of Relief may not enable an individual to retain or be eligible for public office. Although removing legal bars does restore to the certificate holder the right to apply, it does compel the granting of employment or license or prevent the potential employer or licensing agency from taking the criminal record into consideration. *Possession of a certificate does not authorize an individual to deny that he or she has ever been convicted of a crime.*

B. Eligibility

A Certificate of Relief may issued by the Board of Parole to any eligible offender who has been committed to an institution under the jurisdiction of the New York State Department of Correctional Services. The Board of Parole may also issue a Certificate of Relief to an eligible offender who has been convicted in any other jurisdiction and who now resides in New York State. By law an eligible offender is defined as one who has *not been convicted more than once of a felony*. (Two or more felony convictions stemming from the same indictment count as one conviction. Two or more convictions stemming from two or more separate indictments filed in the same court prior to conviction under any of them count as one conviction.) A plea or a verdict of guilty upon which sentence or the execution of sentence has been suspended or upon which a sentence of probation, conditional discharge, or unconditional discharge has been imposed *shall be deemed to be a conviction*. (It should be noted that Juvenile Offenders are eligible for Certificates of Relief.)

A Certificate of Relief may be issued upon an eligible individual's release from a correctional facility or at any time thereafter.

II. CERTIFICATES OF GOOD CONDUCT

A. Effect of a Certificate of Good Conduct

A Certificate of Good Conduct has the same effect as the Certificate of Relief. In addition, the Certificate of Good Conduct may restore the right of an individual to apply for public office. The certificate may be issued to remove all legal bars or disabilities or to remove only specific bars or disabilities. The Board may subsequently issue a supplementary certificate removing those disabilities or bars not previously removed.

B. Eligibility

The Certificate of Good Conduct is available to those individuals convicted of more than one felony. Such individuals, however, do not become eligible for a Certificate of Good Conduct until a minimum period of time has elapsed from the date of conviction, or, if incarcerated, from the date of unrevoked release from custody by parole or termination of sentence. In those cases where the most serious conviction is a misdemeanor, the minimum period of good conduct required is one year. In those cases where the most serious conviction is a C, D, or E Felony, the minimum period of good conduct is three years. In those cases where the most serious conviction is an A or B Felony, the minimum period is five years.

A NEW MODEL OF SUPERVISION: RESTORATIVE JUSTICE

At present, the criminal justice system views the state as victim, with the actual individual victim placed in a passive and secondary (at best) role (Carlson, 1993); "restorative justice views crime as a violation of one person by another, rather than against the state" (Maloney and Umbreit, 1995: 43). Emerging during the 1970s as part of the victim's movement, *restorative justice* (RJ) is the guiding philosophical framework for a new paradigm that seeks to promote maximum involvement of the victim, the offender, and the community (Bazemore and Maloney, 1994). Instead of simply punishing those who commit crimes—*retributive* justice—the focus is on allowing the offender an opportunity to make amends to his or her victim (Wright, 1991).

> Crime is a violation of people and relationships. It creates obligations to make things right. Restorative Justice involves the victim, the offender, and the community in a search for solutions which promote repair, reconciliation, and reassurance. (Zehr 1990: 181)
> [Restorative justice] views crime as a violation of one person by another, rather than a violation against the state. (Umbreit and Carey, 1995: 47)

As Jim Sinclair (1994: 16) points out:

> the depersonalized mechanisms of corrections fail to deliver the message to the offender that by his/her actions s/he has harmed another human being; and that part of the offender's habilitation or rehabilitation should be geared toward making the victim whole again. The evolution of the criminal justice system in this country has resulted in a deemphasis on the responsibility of the offender toward the victim(s) of his/her wrongful acts.

Punishment—retributive justice—"may have several counterdeterrent effects on offenders, including stigmatization, humiliation, and isolation, that may minimize prospects for regaining self-respect and the respect of the community" (Bazemore and Umbreit, 1995: 300). And the treatment response provides little in the way of a message that the offender has harmed someone and should take action to repair damages to the victim.

RJ offers a new way to look at the response to crime and criminal behavior beyond the traditional debate over treatment and punishment. Instead of advocating more/better treatment or greater punishment, the new model seeks systemwide change, a new philosophical framework in which the victim is at the center: "While probation and parole place a plethora of educational, counseling and social services at the disposal of the offender, little is done to reach out to crime victims with services they may desperately need" (Sinclair, 1994: 15). RJ argues for not only bringing the victim back into the criminal justice system, but that all parties—victim, offender, and community—should be included in the response to crime. Probation and parole agencies are in a unique position to implement RJ because of their long-term relationships with offenders (Sinclair, 1994).

RJ is accomplished by means of victim-offender mediation through which the parties are given a human face:

> Facing the person they violated is not easy for most offenders. While it is often an uncomfortable position for offenders, they are given the equally unusual opportunity to display a more human dimension to their character. For many, the opportunity to express remorse in a very direct and personal fashion is important. The mediation process allows victims and offenders to deal with each other as people, oftentimes from the same neighborhood, rather than as stereotypes and objects. (Umbreit, 1994: 9)

Although this approach appears appropriate for less serious crimes and offenders, particularly when a prior relationship exists between victim and offender, with more serious crimes and more hardened criminals, restorative justice appears more complex. When either victim or offender is unwilling to participate, or when the offense is too heinous or the suffering too severe, the offender meets with other victims, often through victim advocate organizations rather than his or her own victim(s) as a step toward assuming responsibility (Zehr, 1990).

In targeting only offenders for intervention, notes Gordon Bazemore (1994: 19), both the surveillance and individual treatment models ignore two primary "clients" or constituents of community corrections—victims and the community—and offer weak choices to criminal justice decision makers. Victim and offender are placed in passive roles: "Holding the offender accountable and responsible—RJ does not simply seek to punish and reintegrate the offender back into the community." Some offenders need incarceration—RJ does not substitute for that need. The offender must take responsibility and perform to restore that which he or she destroyed—damage to the victim and loss of a sense of security to the community. Instead of rehabilitation, RJ seeks competency development—beyond simply trying to get the offender to give up crime—providing life skills so that he or she can give back to the victim and community. Risk management during the time when an offender is under supervision does not enhance community safety in the long range; only offender competence can do this. Providing skills, however, is not enough. The offender must develop empathy for the victim along with skills, or else there will be an offender with skills who continues committing crimes (Bazemore and Umbreit, 1994).

RESTORATIVE JUSTICE FOR JUVENILES

A restorative sanctioning model could provide clear alternatives to punishment-centered sanctioning approaches now dominant in juvenile justice and could ultimately redefine the sanctioning function. Specifically, by shifting the focus of offender accountability or "debt" from the state to the victim, restorative justice sanctions could meet the need of communities to provide meaningful consequences for crime, confront offenders, denounce delinquent behavior, and relay the message that such behavior is unacceptable—without primary reliance on punishment and incarceration. (Bazemore and Umbreit, 1995: 302)

Instead of punishment, accountability is the goal. Instead of taking "their punishment," RJ seeks to get offenders to take responsibility for the victim and help repair the loss suffered by the community. According to RJ, the most important aspect of crime is the harm caused the victim, the community, and the offender. RJ says that criminal justice should be about repairing the damage caused by crime—helping communities get offenders to undo the damage their crimes caused. Instead of the needs of the offender, the focus is on the needs of the victim. Under RJ, the three clients are the victim, the community (needs to feel safe/secure), and the offender. RJ seeks to make the victim whole by providing for social, psychological, and financial needs (Carlson, 1993).

Now that we have examined the details of probation and parole supervision, we look at special programming in probation and parole.

SPECIALIZED PROBATION/PAROLE UNITS

It has long been recognized that offenders with certain salient characteristics could benefit from the services of a specialist—a p/p officer who, as a result of education, training, and experience, is in a better position to provide social services and control functions. As a result, many p/p agencies have specialized units for particular offenders. Traditionally, these have included:

- Drug-abusing offenders
- Alcohol-abusing offenders
- Dangerous felony offenders
- Gifted offenders
- Mentally ill offenders
- Retarded offenders
- Young offenders

New York, for example, has specialized units for all of these categories. More recently, some probation agencies have expressed concern for the problem of DWI (driving while intoxicated) by establishing special units to deal with such offenders. The New York State Division of Parole has established special AIDS caseloads.

NEW YORK STATE AIDS UNIT

As noted in Chapter 6, AIDS is the single leading cause of death in the New York State prison system. As a result, the Division of Parole established two specialized AIDS caseloads in Brooklyn to develop a working model for providing special assistance to HIV/AIDS parolees; the parole officers are volunteers. The need for specialized assistance was increased by a law passed in 1992 that permits the parole board to release certain terminally ill inmates before their release eligibility date—many of these candidates have AIDS. Parolees often experience difficulties with the community reintegration process and AIDS is an additional complicating factor. The parole officers participate in ongoing training regarding the illness and its management, and each supervises no more than 20 clients, permitting time to visit clients and arrange contracts with service providers or negotiate with service agencies. About 20 percent of the clients are hospitalized during some point each month, and many others are on nonreport status because of their physical condition; caseload attrition through death is extraordinarily high, which can have an serious impact on officer morale.

Parole officer activities resemble those typically provided by medical social workers, including aid with securing Social Security, public assistance, and Medicaid. The PO works with the client's family providing support and information under trying circumstances. In many cases, the PO must arrange for housing for clients who lack family resources. Parolees are not required to disclose their condition. With respect to disclosure of the client's HIV/AIDS:

> From a legal perspective, disclosure of anyone's HIV-status without consent is against the law. In keeping with this, the Division of Parole's policy is that education, rather than disclosure, is key. While the Division may have knowledge that certain parolees are HIV-positive, there are others that the Division is not aware of. Therefore, even if disclosure were permitted, it would only be marginally effective at reducing transmission. The most effective course of action for the Division to take in response to the risk of transmission is to educate all parolee's families regarding HIV, and appropriate measures to take to reduce potential risks.

Home visits are often accomplished in teams that facilitate working with families as well as parolees. The visits are considerably longer than those with routine caseloads. Some parole officers utilize group methods (discussed in chapter 9) with their clients. Despite their medical condition, some HIV clients manage to get involved with serious criminal activity and are returned to prison. Because of the problem of HIV-infected clients who also suffer from tuberculosis, parole officers take special precautions to reduce the possibility of infection.

TEXAS SEX OFFENDER CASELOAD

Although child sexual abuse is a serious and widespread problem in the United States, probation and parole agencies have been slow to respond adequately to this type of offender when he (they are overwhelmingly male) is on a supervision caseload. Indeed, Arthur Lurigio, Marylouise Jones, and Barbara Smith (1995) note that child sexual offenders often end up on probation because of the extreme level of prison overcrowding. And relatively few probation agencies have specialized units to monitor these offenders—units with intensively trained officers and reduced caseloads.

In Texas, each district office of the Pardons and Paroles Division has at least one designated sex offender officer. Such officers receive specialized training and attend ongoing seminars to stay current with treatment and supervision issues concerning this special category of client. Offenders classified as exhibitionists, pedophiles, and rapists are referred to a Sex Offender Caseload that provides specialized treatment through contractual arrangement with public and private resources. Sex offender caseloads do not exceed 45. Place of residence is closely monitored and a sex offender is not permitted to reside with a past victim or potential victims. Pedophiles are prohibited from any contact with children under the age of 17 unless specific arrangements have been made and permission has been granted by the parole officer after consultation with the therapist. An adult must be present during such contacts. POs also ensure compliance with the state's Sex Offender Registration Program. With the endorsement of his or her therapist, a parolee may be transferred from the Sex Offender Caseload to regular supervision.

NASSAU COUNTY DWI UNIT

Increasing public concern, if not outrage, over the fatalities resulting from driving while intoxicated, has led to increased penalties for those convicted of DWI. However, this response has impacted on correctional officials attempting to deal with jail and prison overcrowding, hence, the logic for community-based responses that protect the public while not contributing to the jail/prison crisis. In response, many states have established diversion programs for DWI cases.

In Nassau County (Long Island), New York, the DWI unit is provided with a list of DWI defendants for whom PSI reports have been requested by the court. Each case is computer checked for prior criminal record, outstanding warrants, and motor vehicle record. Cases with multiple DWI arrests are flagged, and their names entered into a prescreening log. This log is used by the unit supervisor to monitor DWI court activity in anticipation of future screening and assignment to probation supervision. This information is then sent to the PO assigned to conduct the PSI.

When the case is flagged by the DWI unit, the PSI officer sends it to the mental health unit, where a consultant determines if the defendant is a candidate for the county's drug and alcohol abuse agency. The consultant also makes a recommendation regarding therapy that will accompany the final PSI report sent to the sentencing judge. The judge revokes the defendant's motor vehicle license at this time (six months for misdemeanors and one year for felonies), and the case is submitted for DWI unit screening. Eligible defendants are those

- With a blood/alcohol level of 0.15 or above at the time of arrest or who refuse to submit to a chemical test
- With two or more DWI arrests (including the instant offense)
- Who are county residents

- Who are not on parole or a defendant in another case
- For whom alcohol is the primary drug of abuse
- Without an extensive psychiatric history
- Whose evaluation indicates they are suitable for therapy
- Who are available for evening therapy sessions
- Who are required to participate because of a concerned family member

Each unit PO maintains a caseload of no more than 30 DWI probationers in a designated area of the county (which is updated periodically in order to conform better to the distribution of DWI clientele). The PO is responsible for the program objectives:

- To hold DWI offenders accountable for their behavior through individual and group treatment
- To hold the probationer accountable for observing all the laws of the state of New York, including those involving vehicular traffic
- To interrupt the cycle of the disease of alcoholism within the family unit
- To provide vocational services as needed
- To provide alcohol support services to other family members

DWI supervision requires the offender to report weekly to a designated agency where he or she completes a 10-week alcohol education program and a 24-week closed group therapy session program. The group sessions are co-led by a probation officer and alcohol counselor. Individual counseling is made available on an as-needed basis. Clients are subjected to random alcohol testing, and a positive reading can result in a variety of sanctions. On completion of the agency program, the client is encouraged to participate in an Alcoholics Anonymous program. The client is required to report in person to the PO, and the officer makes periodic home visits. On successful completion of the program, a letter is sent to the Department of Motor Vehicles indicating that the subject is no longer prohibited from obtaining a driver's license.

PHILADELPHIA DRUG UNIT

The Pennsylvania Board of Probation and Parole operates a drug unit in Philadelphia that utilizes extensive urinalysis. Caseloads are limited to 50 and all offenders referred for supervision must have been actively involved in drug use for at least three years. Parole agents assigned to the unit have undergone specialized training and are rotated every two to three years to regular units to avoid burnout. All clients are tested for drug use upon being assigned to the unit and they are tested every 90 days thereafter, unless circumstances demand more frequent testing. Offenders who remain drug free for nine months are reviewed for transfer to general supervision units. Immediately prior to such a transfer, however, a final urinalysis is performed.

Clients whose test results are positive are tested weekly; two positive opiate urinalyses within a four-month period require placement in a withdrawal treatment program. If the parole agent believes that a client's pattern of drug abuse is disruptive to the reintegration and treatment process, or if the client's behavior constitutes a threat to the community or the client, the agent may place the offender in "protective custody" for 48 hours. If the agent believes that the client should be subjected to violation of parole procedures, the detention continues until the preliminary hearing.

CUYAHOGA COUNTY (CLEVELAND), OHIO, MENTALLY RETARDED OFFENDER UNIT

Compared with the size of regular caseloads, usually more than 200, the mentally retarded offender (MRO) unit averages between 55 and 65 probationers. Clients have a tested IQ of 75 or less, and the level of supervision for each offender is determined by a risk/needs classification: extended (mail contact only), low, medium, high, and superhigh. The unit has a clinical director who is a licensed psychologist. Each case is evaluated by the PO and clinical director; probationers are then referred for appropriate services. An interdisciplinary team—representatives from public and private service and advocacy groups specializing in retardation, and public welfare agencies—aids in case planning for each probationer.

The rules and regulations of probation have been drafted in a form more easily understood by this population, and probation violation hearings are conducted in a manner more likely to be understood by the retarded offender. For purposes of evaluation, the unit receives cases the court believes are mentally retarded. Probation officers spend a great deal of time securing services for their clients: Many social service agencies are reluctant to aid retarded offenders, both out of fear and the difficulties such clients present due to their handicap.

HIGH CONTROL SUPERVISION

In California, the High Control Project was the last of several new programs implemented as part of a three-year evaluation effort undertaken by the Department of Corrections to determine more effective ways of running the parole system in the future (*Investigation and Surveillance in Parole Supervision,* 1981). The project tested control-oriented models of parole supervision, in which specially trained parole agents conducted intensified investigative and surveillance activities on selected high-risk parolees. The objectives of the project were to

1. Identify those parolees who presented the most serious threat to public safety
2. Deter those parolees who had not returned to criminal activity but had a high potential for doing so
3. Increase the frequency and severity of sanctions applied to those parolees verified as having returned to criminal activity

The high-control model of parole supervision differed from traditional approaches to parole supervision on several dimensions. First, this model represented an exclusively control-oriented, as opposed to a service-oriented or mixed, approach to supervision. Second, it placed primary emphasis on monitoring parolee activity indirectly through a variety of means (as opposed to direct agent-parolee contact). Third, it targeted a group of parolees selected by agents as being higher-risk cases. Fourth, by using specialist (as opposed to generalist) agents working within a small team of agents (rather than independently), it used a different organizational and management structure.

IDAHO MAXIMUM SUPERVISION FOR DRUG OFFENDERS

The Idaho Department of Corrections Field and Community Services uses drug offender caseloads that do not exceed 25 supervised by specially trained probation/parole officers. Supervision is intensive: a minimum of six face-to-face contacts per month, including four home visits during day and evening hours, weekdays, and weekends; close monitoring of employment or efforts to secure employment; periodic urinalysis; and curfew. Participants must present a daily activity schedule for which they are held accountable, and some are subjected to electronic monitoring (discussed in Chapter 12).

RESTITUTION, COMMUNITY SERVICE, AND SUPERVISION FEES

RESTITUTION

Restitution—an act of restoring, or a condition of being restored, or a making good or giving an equivalent for some injury—has become a popular condition of p/p. In addition to being required to pay for court costs, fines, and fees, a probationer may be required to make restitution; paying a percentage of his or her income, as determined by the court or parole board, to the victim of the offense for any property damage or medical expenses sustained as a direct result of the commission of the offense. This concept has an ancient history: The Bible (*Exodus* 21, 22; *Leviticus* 5) orders restitution for theft, burglary, or robbery, and a form of "community service"—indentured servitude—in the event the criminal has no means of providing restitution. Restitution fell out of favor when monarchs, seeking to centralize power, made crime a public (state) matter and directed payments (fines) away from the victim or his or her kin, in favor of the crown. (Personal claims had to be brought in civil court.) Community service emerged as a modern sentencing option in Alameda County, California, in 1966, and the Minnesota Restitution Program was established in 1972. Persons convicted of property offenses were given the opportunity to reduce their jail sentence or avoid incarceration altogether if they secured employment and provided restitution to their victims. The idea soon spread to other states.

Douglas McDonald (1988: 2) notes one impulse animating restitution:

> The hope and belief [is] that both may contribute to the rehabilitation of offenders. Disciplined work has long been considered reformative. In addition, offenders performing community service may acquire some employable skills, improved work habits, and a record of quasi-employment that may be longer than any job they've held before. Victim restitution, when it brings offenders and victims face to face, also forces offenders to see firsthand the consequences of their deeds and thus may encourage the development of greater social responsibility and maturity.

Texas is so committed to the concept of restitution that since 1983, based on models established in Georgia and Mississippi, it has operated "restitution centers" throughout the state. As a condition of probation, nonviolent, employable felony offenders who would have otherwise been imprisoned can be sent to a restitution center for between 6 and 12 months, during which time the restitution center director attempts to secure employment for each resident. The director also attempts to place each probationer as a worker in a community service project either during off-work hours if the probationer is employed, or full-time if the probationer is unable to find employment. The restitution facility, which is operated by probation staff, accommodates between 30 to 60 persons and is usually located in light industrial areas for access to employment.

The probationer's salary is submitted by the employer directly to the director of the restitution center. The director deducts the cost of food, housing, and supervision, support for the probationer's dependents, and restitution to the victim(s)—the remainder, if any, going to the probationer upon release from the center. However,

> if a restitution center director determines that the probationer is knowingly or intentionally failing to seek employment, the director shall request the court having jurisdiction of the case to revoke the probationer's probation and transfer the probationer to the custody of the Texas Department of Corrections. If the judge determines that a resident has demonstrated an acceptance of responsibility, the court may order the resident released from the center. The first two months following release, the former resident will be intensely supervised before being transferred to a regular probation caseload.

COMMUNITY SERVICE

Because relatively few offenders coming into the criminal justice system are in a position to provide meaningful financial restitution, the alternative of community service has gained in popularity. The state of New Jersey (Administrative Office of the Court, n.d.: 11) points out:

Community service by offenders is being utilized as a sentencing alternative with ever increasing frequency. Offenders are sentenced to community service work without monetary compensation at public or private nonprofit agencies in the community. These offenders usually perform their community service during the evenings and on weekends to complete their sentences. The punitive aspect of a community service order is reflected in the imposition upon the time and freedom of offenders. While functioning in the traditional role as punishment, a community service order also directly benefits the public through the performance of services that may otherwise not be available.

Community service in Georgia is seen as "an alternative sentencing option which is definitely punitive, yet is not perceived as being as harsh as incarceration, nor as lenient as regular probation." In the state of Washington, compulsory service without compensation performed for the benefit of the community is available as an alternative to incarceration for certain nonviolent crimes. The Department of Corrections Division of Community Services solicits requests for personnel services from nonprofit or governmental agencies. Community service has included chore service, work in food banks, park and street cleanup, industrial oil removal, and recycling. The requesting agency is expected to:

1. Refrain from displacing a paid worker with an offender
2. Supply a description of the work site and tasks
3. Assign a supervisor for training and supervision of the offender
4. Provide working conditions for the offender equal to that of paid staff (Figure 11.3)
5. To provide written verification of offender performance (Figure 11.4)

Similar programs exist in several states, including Georgia, Indiana, Kansas, Louisiana, Maryland, Minnesota, Ohio, Oregon, and Virginia. In Illinois and New Jersey, community service is used as an alternative for persons convicted of driving while intoxicated. In New Jersey, the community service program is the responsibility of the county probation department. Although no offender is automatically disqualified for the community service alternative in New Jersey, the Administrative Office of the Courts recommends that persons suffering from chronic alcohol or drug abuse problems, persons convicted of arson or assaultive offenses, and those with previous convictions for certain sex offenses, be excluded. In Georgia, community service is recommended for, but not limited to, persons convicted of traffic and ordinance violations, and nonviolent, nondestructive misdemeanors and felonies. In other cases: "The judge may confer with the prosecutor, defense attorney, probation supervisor, community service officer, or other interested persons to determine if the community service program is appropriate for an offender." Typical placements in Georgia have included hospitals, Red Cross, parks and recreation systems, senior citizen centers, associations for the blind and deaf, and humane societies.

```
                    _____  COUNTY PROBATION DEPARTMENT
                         COMMUNITY SERVICE PROGRAM
```

Community Service Conditions and Release of Information

I, _____ , having been (convicted of) (charged with)
_____ in _____ Court, understand that
I am required to perform _____ days, or _____ hours, of Community Service work.

I understand that as a participant in the Community Service Program, I am not an
employee of the County and, therefore, am not entitled to employee benefits
including Workmen's Compensation Coverage. I am covered by an
accident/medical expense insurance policy. Notice of injury must be given to
Community Service staff within 24 hours of the accident. I must provide verification
that the injury was related to the performance of Community Service.

I agree to give the Community Service staff permission to release information
about me to participating agencies. Community Service staff employees have
the authority to assign me to a work site and to supervise the work performed.
Community Service staff will be notified immediately of any change of job,
residence, telephone number, or health conditions. Inquiries from Community
Service staff will be answered promptly and truthfully.

I am expected to perform a minimum of _____ hours of Community Service
per week. I must report at the time assigned and notify the agency in advance
whenever I am unable to appear for work. Any extended absence for illness
will be documented by a physcian's note.

While at the work site, I will be cooperative, courteous and reliable, and obey all rules
and directions. I understand that I am not to report to a work site having consumed
alcohol or used illegal drugs. I am responsible for ensuring that a record of Community
Service hours is accurately maintained. Agencies will report my work progress to the
Community Service Program and this information will be made available to the court.

I understand that failure to comply with the rules and procedures of the program
and participating agencies may be cause for returning my case to court for another
disposition that may include sentence to a period of incarceration.

The above has been explained to me and I have been provided with a copy of
this document.

                                        _____
                                                DEFENDANT

                                        _____
                                            PROBATION OFFICER

                                        _____
                                                  DATE

FIGURE 11.3   Community Sservice Conditions and Release of Information.

COMMUNITY SERVICE REPORT

TO: _____

FROM: _____ County Community Service Program

DATE: _____

RE: _____

Docket No.: _____

Charge: _____

Court Date: _____

PLEASE BE INFORMED THAT: (Check appropriate lines and fill in the blanks.)

_____Client has completed the community service requirement of _____ hours
at: _____

Client's performance was rated:

_____Client's performance in community service has been unsatisfactory because

_____Client is inappropriate for community service because:

THEREFORE WE:

_____Are closing our interest in this case.

_____Recommend returning the client for court.

_____Recommend the following action:_____
_____

_____Other _____

PLEASE ADVISE THIS OFFICE OF COURT ACTION.

Respectfully submitted,

FIGURE 11.4   Community Service Report.

The Dauphin County (Pennsylvania) Adult Probation/Parole Department has a Community Resource Program in conjunction with the Harrisburg chapter of the American Red Cross. Clients placed at the Red Cross are regarded as volunteers (even though participation is a mandatory condition of the sentence of probation or county parole) and are provided with the same training, expectations, and benefits that any Red Cross volunteer receives. The Red Cross provides monthly evaluation reports. If work is satisfactory, a completion letter is given to the client and a copy to the p/p officer; unsatisfactory work results in a termination letter. Clients have served as first-aid providers and assistants to an instructor of first aid courses and have conducted their own courses in first aid using multimedia systems; others serve in clerical, public relations, custodial, and research positions. Although no restrictions are placed on who may enter the program, clients have been nonviolent offenders.

SUPERVISION FEES

The imposition of "user" fees has grown in popularity: About two-thirds of probation agencies impose them as a condition of supervision, and 21 states were collecting parole supervision fees by 1991. These fees frequently account for a significant portion of the probation budget, 20 percent for county departments and 10 percent for state p/p agencies (Wheeler et al., 1989; Mills, 1992); in Texas they provide more than one-half the cost of basic probation services. Dale Parent (1989a) reports that in Texas there is considerable pressure on probation officers for successful collection of fees, some departments reporting monthly the percentage of fees each officer has actually collected (Finn and Parent, 1992). Although Texas has had a great deal of success in imposing and collecting fees, Jim Mills (1992) states that a few states scrapped their collection programs because they did not generate enough money to make the effort worthwhile. Instead of collecting monthly fees, Kansas imposes a one-time probation fee: $50 for felonies and $25 for misdemeanors. New York state law permits a 5 to 10 percent fee on restitution cases, the higher amount when actual collection costs exceed 5 percent. The Onondaga (Syracuse), New York, Probation Department imposes a variety of fees for different services (e.g., $200 for a custody/visitation investigation and $150 to $500 for an adoption investigation), depending on adjusted gross income. The department charges $50 for alcohol/drug testing, whereas probationers under supervision for driving while intoxicated pay $30 a month.

The use of probation violation as a fee-compliance mechanism has been rare; in fact, states Parent (1989), prison overcrowding has made judges reluctant to revoke probation even for willful failure to pay. Instead, intermediate punishments, such as a short jail stay or several weeks of community service, are imposed. In 1992, New York enacted legislation requiring parolees to pay a supervision fee of $30 per month. Failure to comply does not result in a violation of parole; instead, interest and late payment fees are assessed through (civil) court action that can lead to garnishment of wages or attachment of income tax refunds. Parolees falling below economic standards set by the Division of Parole can be given a temporary waiver. Those who are disabled or suffering from a terminal medical condition can be given a permanent waiver.

VICTIM SERVICES

In South Carolina, the Department of Probation, Parole, and Pardon Services created an Office for Victim Services. Coordinators are experienced p/p agents who manage a caseload of victims, providing information, education, protection, and support services to crime victims. In particular:

1. Initial victim notification of conviction and sentence within 30 days of court date
2. Monitoring restitution payments
3. Collection and distribution of victim impact statements to supervising agents
4. Community-resource referrals for victims in need of services
5. Victim notification of any violation hearings and their dispositions

DISCUSSION

Steven L. Chesney (n.d.: 158) studied the use of restitution in Minnesota and reports that

> It is clear that the most important determinant of whether an otherwise eligible defendant was to be ordered to make restitution was his supposed "ability to pay." As evident from both interviews with judges and from the cases themselves, this criterion was generally operationalized by choosing offenders who were white, well-educated, and from the working and middle classes. This contrasted markedly with what is known about the criminal justice system in general. Those caught up in the system are overwhelmingly the poor, the lower class, and members of minority groups.

Chesney raises some issues with respect to the use of restitution:

- Perhaps the relatively well-educated and well-employed group of offenders that is able to pay restitution is the group of offenders for whom restitution has the least meaning.
- Restitution may be one way that members of the more affluent social classes can avoid incarceration.

Chesney (n.d.: 169) concludes:

Restitution is not addressed to a rehabilitative or a victim compensatory need; instead, it answers a moral need. It reflects the way we feel that people should treat other people. As such, the evaluations of the effects of restitution may need to show only that it is no worse than other rehabilitative alternatives and that it does compensate some victims. Any effects beyond these are serendipitous because the primary goal of restitution is the elimination of the contradictions between our systems of morality and our criminal justice system.

Although restitution would appear to be a win-win practice, the use of supervision fees raises serious questions:

- Will persons who can pay fees be more likely to be granted p/p?
- Will the need to collect fees change the focus of p/p supervision away from providing services?
- Will the failure to pay fees result in p/p revocation?
- Will persons be kept under supervision longer because of their ability to pay fees or a need to collect unpaid fees? Will a person who can pay fees be less likely to be cited for a p/p violation?
- Will the imposition of fees cause an increase in absconding from supervision?
- Will fee collection responsibilities detract from the work of already overburdened p/p officers?

Answers to these questions are part of the continuing debate over supervision fees.

In 1983, the Supreme Court (*Beardon v. Georgia*, 461 U.S. 660) ruled that probation cannot be revoked because of an inability to pay a fine and restitution as a condition of probation, that is, as a result of indigence and not a refusal to pay. This point would appear to apply to supervision fees.

Fahy Mullaney found that failure to pay restitution or fees often results in an extension of time an offender is under supervision: "In fact, some offenders are kept on intensive supervision although they completed all their probation conditions except final payment on a fee" (1988: 15). Furthermore, collection-related tasks require 10 percent additional staff time, whereas extending supervision further increases the demands on staff. Thee also are "subtle value shifts in community corrections agencies, raising the priority of fiscal matters rather than of community safety, community justice, or human restoration" (1988: 15). She cautions: "In the early history of incarceration, offenders were required to pay for admission to jail, to pay the jailer for food and bedding while there, and finally to pay upon release. Today we are aghast that such counterproductive, unjust practices could ever exist."

"Across this country, we are swiftly adopting new sanctions, especially fees and special assessments, that have a dramatic financial impact on those who go through our criminal justice system. Without thoughtful development of policy and practice to guide and limit this movement, we may well repeat history rather than learn from it (Mullaney, 1988: 21)."

Defenders of the system used in Texas, where about three-fourths of the state's counties collect fees equal to one-half or more of their total expenses, state that

> rather than detracting from casework, aggressive fee collection actually furthers the goal of helping probationers avoid relapsing into criminal behavior. They argue that the regularity of fee payments is a good barometer of a probationer's overall adjustment to supervision. . . . Some probation staff believe that the emphasis on fee collections provides an opportunity to help teach offenders how to budget and meet ongoing financial obligations on time. (Finn and Parent, 1992: 11–12)

WORK RELEASE

Many states have prison work-release programs, and in some instances these programs involve p/p staff. Work release allows people serving sentences to work in the community, returning each evening to the institution. They are still subject to institutional controls (and absconding is considered an escape from confinement), and additional regulations apply to their extrainstitutional status. Under this system, inmates are able to earn a salary and pay taxes, contribute to their families' income, repay debts, make restitution, and even contribute to their keep at the institution. In addition, work release enhances an inmate's self-image.

Legislation authorizing work-release programs was enacted in Wisconsin in 1913, but it took more than 40 years before it spread to other states: California and North Carolina enacted work-release legislation in 1957. By 1965, 24 states had such legislation, and by 1975 all 50 states and the federal government had legislation authorizing some form of community work and educational release (Rosenblum and Whitcomb, 1978).

States vary with respect to the criteria used in selecting inmates for work-release programs; some automatically excuse those serving life sentences or inmates who have detainers filed against them. In some states the court must authorize work release; in others the parole board has this responsibility. The final responsibility for selecting candidates, however, is usually under the aegis of the correctional authorities who administer the program. Most states do not have specific restrictions governing who may participate in work release, but they often use such general expressions as "not a high-security risk" or "not likely to commit a crime of violence" (Root, 1972). States vary in the number of inmates involved in work release, and in some the program is combined with furloughs enabling eligible inmates to leave the institution for specific periods of time to seek employment or educational opportunities.

Unfortunately, many, if not most, correctional institutions are isolated from urban areas where employment opportunities are more readily available. Responding to this deficiency, some states operate a variety of facilities for housing work-release participants in proximity to areas of employment. These facilities include minimum security prisons or work-release centers, halfway houses, or rented quarters in hotels or Young Men's Christian Associations. Idaho, for example, operates community work-release centers that provide four- to six-month prerelease programming for inmates within ten months of their release date. Violent and sex offenders are ineligible.

Basic restrictions are typically placed on the employment situation available to inmates:

- Inmates cannot work in a skilled area where a surplus labor force already exists.
- Conditions of employment must be commensurate with nonoffenders.
- If a union is involved, it must be consulted, and no work releasee can work while a labor dispute is in progress.

HALFWAY HOUSES

"The concept of halfway houses was introduced in 1817 by the Massachusetts Prison Commission. This group recommended the establishment of temporary homes for destitute released offenders as a measure to reduce recidivism" (Rosenblum and Whitcomb, 1978: 9):

It is intended to afford a temporary shelter in this building, if they choose to accept it, to such discharged convicts as may have conducted themselves well in prison at a cheap rate, and have a chance to occupy themselves in their trade, until some opportunity offers a placing of themselves where they can gain an honest livelihood in society. A refuge of this kind, to this destitute class, would be found perhaps humane and politic. (Commonwealth of Massachusetts Legislative Document, Senate No. 2, 1830)

According to Donald Thalheimer (1975: 1):

The very name halfway house suggests its position in the corrections world: halfway-in, a more structured environment than probation and parole; halfway-out, a less structured environment than institutions. As halfway-in houses they represent a last step before incarceration for probationers and parolees facing or having faced revocation; as halfway-out houses, they provide services to prereleasees and parolees leaving institutions. Halfway houses also provide a residential alternative to jail or outright release for accused offenders awaiting trial or convicted offenders awaiting sentencing.

Victor Goetting notes that "it is accepted that these facilities are based on sound correctional theory; in order to ultimately place a person in society successfully that person should not be any further removed from that society than is necessary" (1974: 27). When used in conjunction with prison or training school release programs, the halfway house provides (1) assistance with obtaining employment, (2) an increased ability to use community resources, and (3) needed support during the difficult initial release period (Griggs and McCune, 1972).

The various types of halfway houses operated by public and private agencies and groups can be divided basically into those that provide bed, board, and some help with employment and those that provide a full range of services, including treatment. The latter includes a variety of methods, from guided group interaction, to psychotherapy, reality therapy, or behavior modification. A halfway house may be primarily for released inmates, for parolees, or for probationers as an alternative to imprisonment. Halfway houses may also be used for probationers or parolees who violate their conditions of supervision but not seriously enough to cause them to be imprisoned.

The Texas Adult Probation Commission has funded a series of halfway houses (called residential treatment facilities) throughout the state. These facilities house felony offenders in need of a brief residency in a structured environment that offers treatment services, rather than placing them in prison or on regular probation. These offenders often need treatment for drug or alcohol abuse, job skills training, and basic education. The facilities offer a homelike atmosphere with a minimum of security measures. Residents are classified according to their individual needs and assigned to a treatment regimen that usually includes counseling, educational classes, and vocational training; they also share in the housekeeping responsibilities. As residents advance in the program, they are allowed to check in and out of the facility to go to work or training in the community. If unemployed, they may be assigned to do community service work. When residents have advanced to an acceptable level in their treatment plan, they are released from the center and placed under regular probation supervision.

The Georgia Department of Offender Rehabilitation has established more than a dozen halfway houses (called residential diversion centers) to provide judges with an option for sentencing "marginal cases"—an alternative between imprisonment and regular probation. Two centers for female offenders are available. The program requires residents to work, pay for their room and board, and provide restitution to their victims. To qualify for the program a defendant must:

1. Be one who would otherwise be incarcerated
2. Be a nonviolent property offender
3. Not be regarded as a habitual criminal
4. Be capable of maintaining employment

Each center has the capacity for between 40 and 50 residents who serve an average of four to five months before being released to regular probation supervision. The centers provide counseling, basic education, high school equivalency examination preparation, and recreation. Release is based on a satisfactory completion of the treatment contract that the offender needs to qualify for the program. The centers serve three daily meals, and take-out lunches are furnished to residents who are out to work. Residents are responsible for maintaining the facility and are allowed visitors on the weekends during specified hours. After the fourth week, residents may earn weekend passes. Failure to comply with rules and regulations, or absconding from the facility, means imprisonment.

MASSACHUSETTS HALFWAY HOUSES, INC. (MHHI)

MHHI is a private nonprofit corporation that began its operations in 1965 serving 31 parolees in a fifteen-bed facility. The corporation now operates halfway house programs in eight locations providing residential services to more than 1300 juvenile and adult offenders each year. In addition to its extensive residential program, MHHI also offers nonresidential vocational and employment placement services. Most clients are from the greater Boston area, although MHHI now has contracts with the sheriffs of Suffolk and Norfolk Counties to provide services to prerelease residents as a result of overcrowding at county jails. A preparole residential program also exists for state prison inmates who have been granted parole and a residential program for parole violators "whose parole adjustment might be enhanced by a structured community environment as an alternative to reimprisonment in an overcrowded and costly state or county institution."

The basic residential program lasts from 60 to 90 days and each resident is assigned a counselor. The program uses a mutual agreement contract to set specific goals to be achieved within that time frame. These include full-time vocational activity; money management; steps to overcome any specialized problem, such as substance abuse or family difficulties; and the development of a network of community resources, for example, new peer associates and new recreational activities. Once developed, reintegration plans are formalized into a written mutual agreement program contract. This document spells out the mutual responsibilities of residents and staff in each of the primary areas as well as time frames for achievement of specific objectives. The counseling process follows the tenets of reality therapy, a behavior-focused approach that recognizes that people are responsible for their own actions, concentrates on the here and now, and maintains that the option to succeed is open to those willing to apply themselves to that end. The counselor initially acts as the resident's advocate in dealing with community agencies.

ST. LEONARD'S HOUSE

St. Leonard's House, on Chicago's West Side, was established in 1956 by, and continues to be operated under the auspices of, the Episcopal Church. The facility provides residential and rehabilitative services for 23 men recently released from prison who are under parole supervision; a close working relationship exists between parole agents and house staff. Each resident stays between 30 and 90 days, and they are many more requests for services than the facility can handle. St. Leonard's enforces a curfew and residents are permitted to have visitors as well as weekend passes. Drugs, alcohol, sex, threats, violence, stealing, gambling, or lending money results in immediate expulsion.

Staff members include job counselors, addiction counselors, mental health counselors, former residents, as well as numerous volunteers. The program is staffed 24 hours a day; from 6:30 A.M. to 9 P.M. the counseling staff staggers hours to be available to clients, especially in the early hours before school and job training and before the search for employment begins. They are on duty again late in the day when the men return for supper and evening meetings at the house. Education leading to a GED is available at the house,

No fees are charged, although residents are expected to complete various housekeeping chores. A personal program for each resident begins at intake, during which he spends several hours a day, over a period of three to five days, being interviewed. While his needs are assessed, he begins to feel his way into the program and with the help of counselors sets personal goals. There follows a program of personal and group counseling, peer meetings, opportunities to meet with the chaplain and the employment counselor—all designed to assure that each resident gets as much help as possible in reestablishing and reordering his life.

The major difficulty with opening and maintaining a halfway house is community reaction. A Lou Harris poll, for example, found that 77 percent of the representative U.S. sample favored the halfway-house concept, whereas 50 percent would not want one in *their* neighborhood, and only 22 percent believed that people in *their* neighborhood would favor a halfway house being located there. Experts stress the importance of getting community support for the project before opening a halfway house. Among some of the strategies used in gaining support is the formation of an advisory board made up of influential community people. Community residents may be placed on the board of directors and hired as staff for the facility. Victor Goetting (Bakal, 1974) notes that local citizenry often fear that unwanted criminal elements will come into the area, and he suggests two ways of dealing with such fears; first, the facility can be restricted to serve people who would ordinarily reside in the community; second, if outside persons are to be brought in, a screening panel can be formed to alleviate some of the fear. The committee can be made up of community persons who work for the police, sheriff, courts or p/p agencies.

INTERSTATE ADULT AND JUVENILE COMPACTS

In the Crime Control Consent Act of 1934, Congress authorized two or more states to enter into agreements or compacts for cooperative efforts and mutual assistance in the prevention of crime. Pursuant to this legislation, in 1937 a group of states signed the *Interstate Compact for the Supervision of Probationers and Parolees*, which enabled them to serve as each other's agents in the supervision of persons on probation and parole. By 1951, all 48 states (and now all 50 states and the District of Columbia), Puerto Rico, and the Virgin Islands were signatories of the compact. The compact provides a system whereby a person under supervision can leave the state of conviction and proceed to another state for employment, family, or health reasons, and at the same time guarantees that the receiving state will provide supervision of the offender. The state of original jurisdiction (where the offender was convicted) retains authority over the probationer/parolee and is kept advised of his or her whereabouts and activities by the receiving state. The compact also provides for p/p violators to be returned without the need to resort to time-consuming extradition procedures. Because it is based on a federal statute and governed by the substantive law of contracts, the Interstate Compact supersedes state law. (The U.S. Supreme Court has never ruled on the constitutionality of the compact, having denied certiorari whenever the issue has been raised.)

Before the establishment of the compact, thousands of convicted felons were permitted to leave the state of conviction with no verified or approved plan of residence and employment in the receiving state. On occasion, dangerous criminals were released by states and permitted (sometimes forced into "internal exile" or "sundown probation/parole") to enter other states without any provision for supervision or even the knowledge of any official body in the receiving state. The compact provides a systematic method for supervision purposes for the receiving state to verify and approve a plan of residence and employment or education before a probationer or parolee is permitted to enter the state.

The compact also regulates interstate travel by probationers and parolees; each state issues a travel pass, a copy of which is sent to the interstate administrator, who notifies the receiving state of the impending visit (Figure 11.5). A probationer or parolee requests an interstate transfer (Figure 11.6). After a probationer or parolee is accepted for supervision by the receiving state (Figure 11.7), the latter sends quarterly "progress and conduct" reports to the sending state (Figure 11.8).

The Association of Administrators of the Interstate Compact (now called the Parole and Probation Compact Administrators' Association), formed in 1946 and to which each state has designated an administrator, meets at least once per year, prepares uniform reports and procedures, and attempts to reconcile any difficulties that have arisen with respect to the compact. The Council on State Governments serves as a secretariat for the association and publishes the *Interstate Movement of Probationers and Parolees Under the Probation and Parole Compact.*

Some problems remain. One is the difference in probation and parole administration. In all states parole is an executive function with statewide procedures; interstate activities are centralized through a compact administrator in each state. Probation, however, is often administered on a county basis, and it may lack statewide coordination. The local autonomy that often exists in the

STATE OF ARIZONA
DEPARTMENT OF CORRECTIONS

<u>TRAVEL PERMIT</u>
(Out-of-State)

Date Issued_____

TO WHOM IT MAY CONCERN:

_____   _____   _____
(Parolee's Name)   (Number)   (Age)

Address in Arizona _____

By order of the Director or his authorized representative, and under the provisions of the appropriate Interstate Compact, permission is hereby granted for the above-named parolee to go to the following destination:_____
(Street Number)

_____   _____   _____
(City)   (State)   (Name of person to be visited & relationship)

Reason for trip: _____

Parolee will leave _____ and will travel by _____
(Date)

_____ Companions on this trip will
(If by auto, give license number and name of owner)

be: _____
(Name and relationship, if any, to parolee)

If permission is for emergency visit only (fill in the following): Parolee is to return to Arizona address shown above by _____

SPECIAL INSTRUCTIONS TO PAROLEE:

I have been given this permission with the understanding I am to continue to follow the rules and regulations of my parole, that I am to cooperate with my supervising officer, or any authorized officer of the Arizona Department of Corrections while on this trip. If I should be arrested in any other state, I will waive extradition and will not resist being returned to the State of Arizona. I fully understand that I am to return to Arizona under the terms of this permit within 30 days hereof or be in violation of my parole.

ISSUING OFFICER:

_____   _____
                                       Parolee's signature

By: _____   Date: _____

Prepared in quadruplicate
Distribution as follows:

        Original – Parolee
        Copy 2 – Parolee's file in appropriate Parole Field Office
        Copy 3 – For mailing to Receiving State
        Copy 4 – Parolee's Master File – Central Office

FIGURE 11.5 Out-of-state travel permit.

STATE OF FLORIDA
DEPARTMENT OF CORRECTIONS
APPLICATION FOR COMPACT SERVICES AND AGREEMENT TO RETURN.

Sending State—Florida   Receiving State_____

I, _____ hereby apply for supervision as a
probationer/parolee/community controlee pursuant to the Interstate Compact for the Supervision
of Probationers/Parolees/Community Controlees. I understand that the very fact that supervision
will be in another state makes it likely that there will be certain differences between the
supervision I would receive in Florida and the supervision I will receive in any state to
which I am asking to go. However, I urge the authorities to whom this application is made, and
all other judicial and administrative authorities, to recognize that supervision in another state, if
granted as requested in this application, will be a benefit to me and will improve my
opportunities to make a good adjustment. In order to get the advantages of supervision under
the Interstate Compact for the Supervision of Probationers/Parolees/Community Controlees, I do
hereby accept such differences in the course and character of supervision as may be provided,
and I do state that I consider the benefits of supervision under the Compact to be worth any
adjustments in my situation which may be occasioned.

In as much as I agree to the above, I do hereby apply for permission to be supervised on
probation/parole/community control in _____, for the following reaaons:

1. That I will make my home with _____
                                          (Name)

    _____, until a change of

    residence is duly authorized by the proper authorities of _____
                                                              (Receiving State)

2. That I will comply with the conditions of probation/parole/community control as fixed by
    both the State of Florida and _____

3. That I will, when duly instructed by the Florida authorities, return at any time to the said
    state.

4. That I hereby do waive extradition to the State of Florida from any jurisdiction in or outside
    the United States where I may be found and also agree that I will not contest any effort by
    any jurisdiction to return me to the State of Florida.

5. Failure to comply with the above will be deemed to be a violation of the terms and
    conditions of probation/ parole/community control for which I may be returned to the State
    of Florida.

        I (have read the above) (have had the above read and explained to me), and
        I understand its meaning and agree thereto.

Date _____   Signed _____

Witnessed by _____

Witnessed by _____

    On the _____ day of _____, 19__, permission was granted to the
above probationer/parolee/community controlee to reside in the State of _____ and be
supervised by _____.

                                          _____
                                                        Officer

FIGURE 11.6   Florida application for compact services.

COLORADO DEPARTMENT OF CORRECTIONS
DIVISION OF ADULT PAROLE SUPERVISION
COOPERATIVE CASE REPORT.

To: Texas Interstate   Date: 12-5-94
     P. O. Box 13401
     Capitol Station   Name: Smith, Robert
     Austin, TX 78711   TX # 574,566
                                                             D0C#   CO # X94-1294

SUBJECT MATTER: REPORT OF INVESTIGATION/ACCEPTANCE

The proposed residence at 433 Briar Drive, Woodland Park, Colorado, 80863, is verified.
This is the residence of Mr. Richard Smith, the parolee's father. The father is a willing sponsor,
and the residence is certainly adequate to house the addition of the parolee in the home. The
Woodland Park Police Department was also contacted on December 1, 1994 and they are aware
of Mr. Richard Smith's hunting business called the Ace Sports Club and note that the parolee's
father has a good reputation in the community.

Regarding employment the plaement request from the State of Texas notes that the father has
offered employment with his business known as the Ace Sports Club, 1400 W. Hwy 24,
Woodland Park, Colorado 80866. However, it should be noted that this is a seasonal business
and that Richard Smith would not be able to offer his son employment until the hunting season
started next year. Therefore, the parolee would, in effect, have to secure his own employment
for approximately the next six months until the Colorado hunting season started for the 1995
calendar year. Of primary concern to Colorado authorities is the offense for which the parolee
was most recently incarcerated, that being Aggravated Robbery With A Deadly Weapon. For this
reason, the Texas Department of Criminal Justice has listed the parolee's supervision level as
"L"—highest level. For this reason, Colorado will accept the parolee's supervision with the
understanding that he will be on ISP supervision with electronic monitoring for 180 days. The
potential sponsors have already agreed to this type of supervision in their home. Also, the
parolee will be expected to submit to drug and other substance abuse counseling through our
TASC Office and will be held financially responsible for any treatment expenses.

If the parolee is willing to agree to these conditions, please have him report to Parole Officer
Tom Peterson immediately upon arrival in the Colorado Springs area at the address listed below.

TOP/js

Direct Correspondence to: _Tom Peterson_
                                                       Tom Peterson
                                                       Parole Officer

Office: Colorado Springs Parole Office   _Larry C Stuart_
         25 N. Spruce Street, Suite 300   Larry C. Stuart
         Colorado Springs, CO 80905   Reviewing Officer
         (719) 635-0800 Fax (719) 473-5152

FIGURE 11.7   Colorado case report.

O.S. PROBATION & PAROLE FORM IV
PROGRESS AND CONDUCT REPORT

INTERSTATE COMPACT UNIT
ALABAMA BOARD OF PARDONS AND PAROLES
750 Washington Avenue
Suite 312
Montogmery, Alabama 36130
(205) 261-5533

To: ____State of Georgia_____ Date of Report __1-14-94__

_____ Date Forwarded _____

Re: ____John C. Rivers_____ No. __OS 24,115__ State ____Georgia____

Address of Parolee or Probationer:
  Route 1, Box 14
  Montgomery, Alabama 36114

Name and Relationship of Others in Home
  Jane Doe—Wife
  3 children

Contact Dates:
  8/5/94, 9/3/94, 10/4/94 and 12/6/94

Marital Status:
  Married

Employer—Address:
  Dana Corporation
  Route 2
  Montgomery, Alabama 36104

Is Subject's Record Known to Employer:
  No

Type of Work—Hours—Wages:
  Laboror
  40 hr/wk $7.85 hr.

Conduct, Progress and Attitude
  Subject's conduct has been good. He received two traffic
  citations in November, 1989, but has had no other contact with Law
  Enforcement Officials. Attitude remains good.

_____*Jack. C. Smith*_____   _____*Michael Jones*_____
Alabama Probation & Parole Officer   Interstate Compact Administrator

_____Montgomery_____
Field Office

FIGURE 11.8   Progress and Conduct Report.

judicial branch can cause difficulties in using and administering the pact in probation cases. In such cases, the probation officer of the sending state may need to make direct contact and arrangements with the court of the receiving jurisdiction.

Another problem results from different approaches to supervision in various states. One state may exercise close control and require strict enforcement of the conditions of probation or parole. Another state may be more flexible, or it may simply be incapable of close supervision and control because of the size of caseloads. When a "strict" state notifies a "permissive" sending state that one of its probationers or parolees is in violation, the sending state may not consider it serious and may leave the offender in the receiving state with a request that it continue supervision. In some cases, the sending state may not wish to incur the expense of transporting the violator back to one of its state prisons, which are probably overcrowded anyway. The receiving state has two options: continue to supervise an offender it considers in violation, or discontinue supervision and leave the offender without any controls at all. Problems are also associated with the collection of restitution and supervision fees. These types of situations may make a receiving state reluctant to accept future cases from a particular sending state, a situation that needs to be reconciled at the compact administrator's meeting (Figure 11.9).

FIGURE 11.9   Interstate compact violation report.

OKLAHOMA DEPARTMENT OF CORRECTIONS

DIVISION OF COMMUNITY SERVICES

CASE REPORT

TO: Interstate Compact Administrator
     State of Florida Probation
NAME: Mitchell Barton, W/M, DOB 11/30/58
NUMBER: 93-1134-CFA DOC #456095
CRIME: False Imprisonment/Aggravated Assault
CONVICTED: 1/14/94; Seminole County; Fifteen (15) years
RECEIVED FOR SUPERVISION: 3/12/94 DISCHARGE DATE: 1/03/2009

VIOLATION REPORT

Subject has violated the following rules of his probation:

RULE 1: Not later than the fifth of each month, you will make a full and truthful report to your probation officer on the form provided for that purpose.

RULE 3: You will not change your residence or employment or leave the county of your residence without first securing the consent of your probation officer.

RULE 17: To immediately leave the State of Florida and reside with your uncle, Jason Barton, until placement in a Veteran's Administration (VA) hospital.

RULE 18: Enter the VA Hospital in Oklahoma City, Oklahoma within 15 days. and actively participate in and successfully complete such programs as are reasonably related to your past and future criminality or to the rehabilitative purpose of probation

---

On 4/26/94, subject was transported to and admitted by the VA Hospital in Oklahoma City. On his admittance to the hospital he was diagnosed as having Post Traumatic Stress Syndrome. On 5/27/94, subject's counselor called and advised that he was being released from their hospital due to his refusal to take medication, fighting, disruptive nature, and belligerence. This officer talked to the subject and advised him of the consequences of this behavior. He was released that same fay. Subject claimed he would re-enter the VA Hospital on 6/9/94 when he returned for evaluation. On 7/10/94, this officer contacted the VA Hospital and was advised that the subject reported to the hospital on 6/9/94, but was denied admittance due to his attitude. This officer then contacted Mrs. Barton, his aunt, who claims that the last time she heard from the subject was 6/8/94. She claims no knowledge of his whereabouts.

Subject's last contact with this officer was 6/01/94 by telephone. This officer has no knowledge of the subject's whereabouts.

SUMMARY/RECOMMENDATION

Subject's last known address was Rt. 8, Box 1214, Ponca City, Oklahoma. Subject's employment consisted of sporadic farm work around Perry, Oklahoma. His reporting habits until 5/29/94 were satisfactory. His attitude toward community supervision was ambivalent; one meeting would be positive and the next extremely belligerent. When he would become belligerent he would complain about the rules that are depriving him of his freedom and that he has no reason to want to continue living. The latter is apparently related to his mother's suicide.

This officer respectfully recommends that subject's suspended sentence be revoked due to the above violations. It is this officer's opinion that Mitchell Barton is extremely dangerous.

On issuance of a warrant, the subject should be submitted to the NCIC. Please forward a copy of the warrant and application to revoke.

Harrison McDonnell

Harrison McDonnell
Team Supervisor, District V

FIGURE 11.9   (*continued*)

States sometimes allow probationers or parolees to go to a receiving state under the guise of a visit, when the offender's intentions are to stay permanently. The receiving state is then contacted by the sending state to investigate "with a view toward accepting supervision." The receiving state is faced with a *fait accompli.*

INTERSTATE COMPACT FOR THE SUPERVISION OF PAROLEES AND PROBATIONERS

*Consented to by the Congress of the United States
of America, 1934 The Uniform Enabling Act*
An act providing that the state of . . . may enter into a compact with any of the united states for mutual helpfulness in relation to persons convicted of crime or offenses who may be on probation or parole

BE IT ENACTED, ETC.:

Section 1.

The governor of this state is hereby authorized and directed to execute a compact on behalf of the state of_____with any of the United States legally joining therein in the form substantially as follows:

A Compact

Entered into by and among the contracting states, signatories hereto, with the consent of the Congress of the United States of America, granted by an act entitled "An act granting the consent of Congress to any two or more states to enter into agreements or compacts for cooperative effort and mutual assistance in the prevention of crime and for other purposes."

The contracting states solemnly agree:

(1) That it shall be competent for the duly constituted judicial and administrative authorities of a state party to this compact (herein called "sending state"), to permit any person convicted of an offense within such state and placed on probation or released on parole to reside in any other state party to this compact (herein called "receiving state"), while on probation or parole, if

(a) Such person is in fact a resident of or has his family residing within the receiving state and can obtain employment there;

(b) Though not a resident of the receiving state and not having his family residing there, the receiving state consents to such person being sent there.

Before granting such permission, opportunity shall be granted to the receiving state to investigate the home and prospective employment of such person.

A resident of the receiving state, within the meaning of this section, is one who has been an actual inhabitant of such state continuously for more than one year prior to his coming to the sending state and has not resided within the sending state more than six continuous months immediately preceding the commission of the offense for which he has been convicted.

(2) That each receiving state will assume the duties of visitation of and supervision over probationers or parolees of any sending state and in the exercise of those duties will be governed by the same standards that prevail for its own probationers and parolees.

(3) That duly accredited officers of a sending state may at all times enter a receiving state and there apprehend and retake any person on probation or parole. For that purpose no formalities will be required other than establishing the authority of the officer and the identity of the person to be retaken. All legal requirements to obtain extradition of fugitives from justice are hereby expressly waived on the part of states party hereto, as to such persons. The decision of the sending state to retake a person on probation or parole shall be conclusive upon and not reviewable within the receiving state, *Provided, however,* that if at the time when a state seeks to retake a probationer or parolee there should be pending against him within the

receiving state any criminal charge, or he should be suspected of having committed within such state a criminal offense, he shall not be retaken without the consent of the receiving state until discharged from prosecution or from imprisonment for such offense.

(4) That the duly accredited officers of the sending state will be permitted to transport prisoners being retaken through any and all state parties to this compact, without interference.

(5) That the governor of each state may designate an officer who, acting jointly with like officers of other contracting states, if and when appointed, shall promulgate such rules and regulations as may be deemed necessary to more effectively carry out the terms of this compact.

The *Interstate Compact on Juveniles* governs the movement of juvenile cases interstate. In the early 1950s, legal and financial problems involving the supervision, transportation, and control of juvenile cases among states reached the point where most of those involved acknowledged the need for some form of interstate compact patterned on the one used for adult cases. In 1954, the National Council on Juvenile Court Judges drafted a preliminary compact on juveniles. Later that year, several groups, under the coordination of the Council on State Governments, drafted the Interstate Compact on Juveniles. In 1955, ten states adopted the compact and currently all states and the District of Columbia are signatories. In addition to providing for cooperative supervision, the compact provides for the return of juvenile probation and parole absconders and escapees and the return of nondelinquent runaways (Figure 11.10).

In contrast to the compact for adults, the juvenile compact has mandatory and discretionary cases (Figure 11.11). Thus, the receiving state must accept supervision whenever a juvenile will be returning to or has already been placed in the home of his or her legal parents or guardians, and each state must accept its own residents. Other cases are discretionary. When supervision has been arranged, the sending state retains jurisdiction and the receiving state becomes the agent of the sending state. Because of variations in state laws regarding juveniles, a person who is a juvenile in one state may be considered an adult in another. The compact overcomes this problem by applying the law of the state from which the juvenile has run away or from which he or she was sent for supervision: If a person is a juvenile under law in his or her home state, he or she is a juvenile to all member states. Although the compact does not deal with child custody cases, it can provide for the return of a child to wherever a court has determined legal custody is maintained.

Now that the details of probation and parole supervision have been examined, Chapter 12 explores the concept and programs of intermediate punishments.

STATE OF MISSOURI
INTERSTATE COMPACT ON JUVENILES
REQUISITION FOR RUNAWAY JUVENILE

TO: _____ DATE: _____

FROM: _____

RE: _____

This court requisitions the return of _____

in accordance to the Interstate Compact on Juveniles, Article IV, Return of Runaway.

Said juvenile is believed to be in your jurisdiction. (Additional information attached, if

available).

On the basis of the evidence before it, this court finds said juvenile was born on _____

Juvenile's physical description: Height _____, Weight _____, Eyes _____,

Hair _____. Identifying marks or scars: _____

_____

This court further finds that said juvenile should rightfully be in the custody of _____

_____ who is the _____ and who is located at
                                       (Relationship to Juvenile)

_____, within the territorial jurisdiction of this court; that said juvenile
      (address)

has run away without permission and that said juvenile's continued absence from rightful

custody and control is detrimental to the best interest of said juvenile and the public.

If requisition is honored, please notify _____
                                      (Name, title, address and telephone)

_____ by collect telephone call or wire when _____

minor will be available for release to our agent.

Attached are: Petition for Requisition to Return a Runaway Juvenile verified by Affidavit,

and certified documents verifying petitioner's entitlement to the juvenile's custody.

Signed _____
                                      Judge

FIGURE 11.10   Requisition for Runaway Juvenile.

MISSOURI INTERSTATE COMPACT ON JUVENILES

Application for Compact Services

To: _____

I, _____, hereby apply for supervision as a parolee or probationer pursuant to the Interstate Compact on Juveniles. I understand that the very fact that supervision will be in another state makes it likely that there will be certain differences between the supervision I would receive in this state and supervision which I will receive in any state to which I am asking to go. However, I urge the authorities to whom this application is made, and all other judicial and administrative authorities, to recognize that supervision in another state, if granted as requested in this application, will be a benefit to me and will improve my opportunities to make a good adjustment. In order to get the advantages of supervision under the Interstate Compact on Juveniles, I do hereby accept such differences in the course and character of supervision as may be provided, and I do state that I consider the benefits of supervision under the Compact to be worth any adjustments in my situation which may by occasioned.

In view of the above, I do hereby apply for permission to be supervised on (parole/probation) in _____, for the following reasons:
                                    (state)

I have read the above or have had the above read and explained to me, and I understand its meaning and agree thereto.

                                        Signed _____
                                                        (Juvenile)

Witnessed by_____
Date _____

                                        Signed _____
                                        (Guardian Ad Litem or person or
                                        agency having legal custody)

FIGURE 11.11   Application for Compact Services.

Review Questions

1. How did the advent of the corrections model alter the prison classification process?
2. What led to the widespread use of classification in probation/parole?
3. What are the two dimensions weighed by a risk/needs assessment instrument?
4. What are the purposes of classifying offenders in p/p?
5. What is the difference between a *caseload* and a *workload* in p/p?
6. Why do parolees often encounter difficulties not experienced by probationers?
7. What are the various methods for assigning cases to p/p officers?
8. Why can the first meeting between p/p officer and client be characterized as a time of apprehension and anxiety?
9. What are the factors that hamper treatment in p/p settings?
10. What are the various problems in p/p supervision generated by clients with AIDS?
11. How can there be a relationship between employment and "going straight" that is not causal?
12. What are the goals of the RJ model of supervision?
13. Why are the advantages and disadvantages of specialized units in p/p?
14. How do the two types of halfway houses differ?
15. Why is a work-release program difficult to implement?
16. What are the problems associated with restitution and fees for supervision?
17. What is the purpose of the Interstate Compact in p/p?

INTERMEDIATE PUNISHMENTS

The stated explanation for intermediate punishments is a classical emphasis matching the sanction to the offense; the real goal is to reduce incarceration, particularly that in excess of six months. The trend in favor of the classical school, just deserts, and determinate sentencing has been intertwined with jail and prison overcrowding. Widespread support for punishment and deterrence through greater use of incarceration has encountered serious financial limitations. Judges have been unwilling to permit conditions of incarceration that violate the Eighth Amendment's prohibition against cruel and unusual punishment, thereby increasing the cost of a punishment-by-way-of-incarceration policy. In response, a scramble has occurred to create alternative systems that satisfy a public appetite for punishment, while limiting the financial costs involved (Figure 12.1).

This concern has led to the development of intermediate punishments that are community-based, although Belinda McCarthy (1987: 3) argues that cost-effectiveness is not the only reason:

> The vast majority of "correcting" has always been done in the community, because this is the best place to deal with offenders. While it *can* be the most economical site for dispositions, the community *is* invariably the most humane setting and the richest environment in which to meet offender needs. If community corrections today is suffering from a lack of credibility, it is because we have used many community programs, espe-

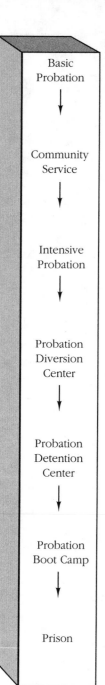

Basic Probation

Probationers are assessed as to risk and need. The level of supervision afforded the offender is based on the resulting score. Additional special conditions such as fines, restitution, community service, etc., may be included.

Community Service

As a special condition of probation, the offender may be ordered to perform uncompensated work for the community under the supervision of the Community Service Program. Primary consideration should be given to traffic or ordinance violations and noninjurious, nondestructive, nonviolent misdemeanors and felonies.

Intensive Probation Supervision

The IPS program provides more structured supervision than can be afforded under basic probation supervision for felony offenders who pose a manageable risk to the community. Requirements include one to four contacts per week, as well as home, employment, night, and weekend checks.

Diversion Center

As a condition of probation, a judge may require that a probationer be assigned to a Diversion Center. The probationer lives at the center, works at a regular job in the community, performs community service, and may participate in a variety of educational and counseling programs. The probationer's paycheck is turned in to the Center, and room, board, fines, restitution and family support are deducted.

Detention Center

The Detention Center is a community-based, residential facility housing nonviolent offenders in a secure, restrictive environment. Offenders work on unpaid community work details supervised by correctional officers. No age restrictions apply, but the probationer must be physically able to comply with program requirements.

Probation Boot Camp

The 90-day Probation Boot Camp offers felony offenders ages 17 to 30 an alternative to long-term incarceration. The program combines military-style basic training and programs to address substance abuse and other offender problems. A supervised period of community adjustment on probation follows release.

State Prison

Imprisonment is a last resort—either for a clearly dangerous violent offender who can be housed nowhere else, or for a nonviolent offender who has exhausted all alternative forms of punishment.

FIGURE 12.1 Continuum of sentencing options for Georgia's judiciary.

cially our richest option—probation—unwisely. Too many offenders have been poorly supervised by overworked and undertrained staff with a confused sense of purpose.

Malcolm Feeley and Jonathan Simon (1992: 461) argue that this approach constitutes a "new penology" that "can be understood in terms of risk management rather than rehabilitative or correctional aspirations. Rather than instruments of reintegrating offenders into the community, they function as mechanisms to maintain control, often through frequent drug testing, over low-risk offenders for whom the more secure form of custody are judged too expensive or unnecessary." Intermediate punishments are also being used to expand the response to probation and parole violators: "In the past, officials had two sanctions for violators—either to continue supervision (perhaps with modest changes in conditions) or to revoke and imprison the violator. Often the choice of options was either too lenient or too harsh for the circumstances of the violation" (Parent et al., 1994: 13).

IOWA VIOLATION PROGRAM

The Iowa Violation Program (IVP) provides an intermediate sanction for individuals who would otherwise be admitted to the prison system. Offenders who successfully complete the program are returned to community supervision to complete their probation or parole. The 60-day residential program has sites at the Women's Reformatory and the Release Center; the former has 60 beds and the latter 100, dedicated to the program. At each facility, participants are segregated from the general population and have treatment staff assigned solely to the program. Residents are assigned at p/p revocation hearings on the recommendation of the p/p officer.

The IVP employs a cognitive approach aimed at changing thinking styles. The major underlying assumption is that offenders typically exhibit cognitive deficiencies such as lack of self-control and lack of problem-solving skills. On admission to the program, participants have a one- to five-day orientation period, during which administrative paperwork and some diagnostic procedures are completed. Participants are acquainted with general rules of the program and the institution. Orientation time varies because inmates are assigned to a group of three to twelve who go through the program together—the administration will wait for all members of a new group to arrive and be oriented together. Following orientation, participants settle into a routine of attending classes from 7:30 A.M. to approximately 4:30 P.M. Classes are organized into different modules representing various facets of the program: drug abuse, reasoning, problem-solving, values, and group therapy. Each class lasts about two hours and employs a variety of techniques including various exercises and role playing. Physical fitness activities and homework also must be completed during free hours.

Intensive Probation/Parole Supervision

If one can judge by the amount of agency literature and research efforts, intensive supervision (IPS) has become the most popular program in probation and parole. Early versions of intensive supervision were based on the premise that increased client contact would enhance rehabilitation while affording greater client control. Current programs are simply a means of easing the burden of prison overcrowding. Thus, the Colorado Department of Corrections notes that its intensive supervision program "expands prison capacity by requiring participation of selected offenders who would otherwise be incarcerated in departmental facilities." In any event, by 1990, jurisdictions in all 50 states had instituted a community-based sanction called *intensive supervision probation* (ISP) (Petersilia and Turner, 1991).

In probation, intensive supervision is usually viewed as an alternative to incarceration. In other words, persons who are placed on intensive probation supervision are supposed to be those offenders who, in the absence of intensive supervision, would have been sentenced to imprisonment. In parole, intensive supervision is viewed as risk management—allowing for a high-risk inmate to be paroled but under the most restrictive of circumstances. In either case, intensive supervision is a response to prison overcrowding. Thus, although intensive supervision is invariably more costly than regular supervision, the costs "are compared not with the costs of normal supervision but rather with the costs of incarceration" (Bennett, 1988: 298).

Types of IPS

The types of intensive p/p supervision can be classified into those that stress diversion and those that stress enhancement:

> *Diversion* is commonly referred to as a "front door" program because its goal is to limit the number of offenders entering prison. Prison diversion programs generally identify lower-risk, incoming inmates to participate in IPS as a substitute for a prison term.

> *Enhancement* programs generally select already sentenced probationers and parolees and subject them to closer supervision in the community than regular probation or parole. People placed on IPS-enhanced p/p show evidence of failure under routine supervision or have committed offenses deemed to be too serious for supervision on routine caseloads.

Source: Petersilia and Turner (1993).

Intensive supervision takes many shapes. In Texas, for example, intensive probation supervision simply involves an experienced probation officer whose maximum caseload does not exceed 40. In Suffolk County, New York, ISP clients are required to attend a day reporting center where they pass through four program phases until placed on regular supervision. The following sections review representative ISP programs in several jurisdictions.

TEXAS INTENSIVE SUPERVISION PROGRAM

Created in 1981 to deal with a prison crisis, the Texas ISP attempts to divert selected felony offenders by offering an alternative to incarceration. For these offenders, intensive supervision is a condition of probation. In most Texas probation departments, ISP caseloads do not exceed 40, and the probation officers are specially selected and trained for the assignment. In some Texas jurisdictions, however, probation officers supervise a mixed ISP and regular caseload. Whenever this occurs, the mixed caseloads may comprise no more than 125 regular probationers before officers receive the first ISP case, and then they must be reduced by five regular cases each time a new ISP case is assigned to the caseload. Either cases are received directly from the court after sentencing or they involve persons facing probation revocation and shock probationers (discussed later in this chapter). To qualify, offenders must meet one or more of the program's criteria:

- One or more prior jail or prison commitments
- One or more convictions

Documentable

- Chronic unemployment
- Alcohol dependency
- Drug dependency
- Mental retardation or psychological problem
- Seriousness of current offense

Using a risk/needs assessment classification, the ISP officer develops a supervision plan that outlines behavioral objectives to be met by the offender within specific time frames. By contracting with various community resources, the ISP officer negotiates for the exact type of services needed for each client. A formal reassessment occurs every 90 days. Typically, an ISP client remains under intensive supervision for one year or less and is then transferred to regular supervision. However, the court may amend the terms of probation to continue the offender under intensive supervision for an additional year. In rare and exceptional cases, the period may last beyond two years.

Texas also has a *superintensive supervision* program called "surveillance probation." It is reserved for cases whose regular probation has been revoked, those sentenced to shock probation, or as a special judicially imposed condition pursuant to a grant of probation. Each offender remains in the program for 90 days, although an extension can be granted, during which time two probation officers (who supervise no more than 20 cases) maintain a minimum of five contacts a week, three of which are in person. A mandatory curfew exists, and frequent drug and alcohol testing is performed.

GEORGIA INTENSIVE PROBATION SUPERVISION

In 1982, faced with the reality of prison overcrowding, the Department of Offender Rehabilitation inaugurated IPS. Although this plan began as a pilot program, IPS has now become a routine method of keeping down prison commitments. In addition to seeking to divert offenders from prison, the program attempts to accomplish the goal of punishment. IPS provides close community supervision to selected offenders who normally would have entered prison if it were not for the existence of the program: "The IPS team, composed of an experienced Probation Officer and a Surveillance Officer, supervise a maximum caseload of twenty-five (25) offenders who present no unacceptable risk to the community in which they are supervised. The caseload consists primarily of non-violent felony offenders who have been convicted of property offenses."

Program standards include:

- Five face-to-face contacts per week
- A total of 132 hours of mandatory community service
- Mandatory curfew
- Mandatory employment
- Weekly check of local arrest records
- Automatic notification of arrest elsewhere via the state crime information system
- Routine and unannounced alcohol and drug testing

Supervision is provided by a team consisting of a probation officer and one (25 cases) or two (40 cases) surveillance officers. Georgia IPS skims off low-risk offenders for the program—persons who are nonviolent property offenders and drug- and alcohol-related offenders—although most have been sentenced to imprisonment. An analysis of the program revealed that as a result of IPS, the percentage of offenders sentenced to prison has decreased and the number of probationers has increased. Furthermore, the "kinds of offenders diverted were more similar to prison inmates than to regular probationers, suggesting that the program selected the most suitable offenders" (Erwin and Bennett, 1987: 2). However, Michael Sullivan (1987) points out that about 85 percent of the prisoners released by the Georgia parole board have been confined for nonviolent offenses, including driving with a suspended driver's license, punishable in Georgia by up to five years in prison. In other words, the program is indeed diverting offenders from prison, but there is a serious question of why such persons are being subjected to imprisonment in the first place. As noted in Chapter 6, Georgia is in the "top ten" when it comes to rates of incarceration.

FLORIDA COMMUNITY CONTROL

According to the Florida Department of Corrections, their program of community control "is not intensive probation. It is a distinctively different type of program that is punishment oriented and allows selected offenders to serve their sentences confined to their homes under 'house arrest' instead of prison." That is, they must remain home when not at, or traveling to and from, their place of employment or mandated public service job. They are supervised by special (community control) correctional probation officers who have a maximum caseload of 20. In addition to being armed, the officers are equipped with portable radios for quick access to law-enforcement assistance: "Florida's community control initiative represents the single largest intensive supervision prison diversion program in the Nation" (Wagner and Baird, 1993: 1).

Persons may be placed on community control by the sentencing judge if found guilty of a noncapital felony but are considered unsuitable for regular probation, or they may be probation or parole violators. The target population, however, is offenders who have committed nonviolent crimes and would not otherwise be placed on regular probation because of the seriousness of their criminal history (Baird and Wagner, 1990). A correctional probation officer conducting a presentence investigation, who plans to recommend that a particular offender be sent to prison because of his or her criminal background or the seriousness of the crime, may recommend community control as an alternative. Officers are required to make a minimum of seven contacts per week with the offender and others in the community, for example, employers and law enforcement agencies. Two of these visits must be in person, including at least one in the field. The offender is required to make weekly office visits during which he or she can be subjected to urinalysis. The officer also makes at least 16 personal telephone contacts to ensure that the offender is at home as required by curfew restrictions.

DAUPHIN COUNTY (PENNSYLVANIA) INTENSIVE JUVENILE PROBATION

The Dauphin County Probation Department has a juvenile intensive probation supervision program geared to reduce the level of institutional commitments. Each youngster is placed on a suspended commitment to an appropriate juvenile institution with the understanding that he or she would have been committed to this institution if intensive supervision did not exist. Each case is screened to ensure that the youngster is not a distinct serious threat to either him- or herself or the community. In addition, sufficient family stability must exist so that the probation officer can work with the family as a unit. And the family has to be willing to cooperate with the program. If the screening PO determines that the case is appropriate for intensive supervision, the youngster is scheduled for a juvenile court hearing and the PO recommends that the respondent be sentenced to a suspended commitment to an appropriate institution and placed in the intensive supervision program.

Each caseload with a maximum of 18 cases is supervised by one probation officer and one part-time PO; the term of IPS supervision is six to nine months. Each juvenile must follow regulations that include a curfew and mandatory school or work attendance. A treatment plan is based on the needs and interests of each client. Each youngster is seen three to five times weekly, which includes counseling sessions in the office and at home, in both individual and family sessions. The IPS officer maintains a high level of visibility with both the client and the community.

Lucas County (Toledo), Ohio, Juvenile Intensive Probation Supervision

To reduce institutional commitments, the Lucas County Juvenile IPS selection is limited to those juveniles already sentenced to incarceration. For youngsters meeting program requirements, the judge is petitioned for a change in the commitment order. And supervision is indeed intensive: IPS probation counselor caseloads are no more than 15; they see the youth a minimum of twice per week during the first four to five months; surveillance staff see the youth at least twice each day seven days per week for the first several months. Individual and group counseling is mandatory and clients may be subjected to urinalysis, house arrest, or hourly monitoring of school attendance and behavior. On Saturdays, youngsters spend six to eight hours for about two months engaged in work activities. There are also bimonthly family conferences and the use of tokens for positive reinforcement, in this case, coupons that can be redeemed for prizes and privileges, such as concert tickets and relaxed curfew (Wiebush and Hamparian, 1991).

New York and Colorado

Demonstrating through empirical evidence that 80 percent of the parolees who violate their parole conditions do so during their first 15 months under supervision, the critical determinant of *differential supervision* is time under supervision. In both New York and Colorado, those parolees within their first 15 months on the street are designated "intensives." After 15 months, the offender is placed on a "regular" supervision with less stringent contact standards. Although regular caseloads average 97 parolees, parole officers with intensive cases supervise 38 parolees. In areas where density of parolees is sparse and traveling time between clients poses an obstacle to efficient supervision, parole officers have mixed—intensive and regular—caseloads on a weighted formula of 2.55—each intensive case is counted as 2.55 regular cases.

Colorado also has a time-limited intensive supervision program for parolees, but the time ranges from a minimum of 90 days to a maximum of 180 days at which time the parolee is transferred to regular supervision. ISP caseloads do not exceed 20 and the focus is clearly on control: weekly face-to-face meetings, daily telephone contact, electronically monitored curfew, and weekly alcohol and drug testing.

RESEARCH FINDINGS

Before we begin our examination of the effectiveness of intensive supervision, we should note that the establishment of IPS programming was not based on careful research and evaluation but is simply a response—perhaps ill conceived—to jail and prison overcrowding (Clear, Flynn, and Shapiro, 1987). Policy implications of evaluative research into IPS may be irrelevant: "If the results are negative . . . then these findings will be viewed as support for both the continued use of incapacitation and the development of even more intrusive, surveillance-oriented community control programs" (Byrne, 1990: 8). In fact, although evidence of the effectiveness of IPS is wanting, the program has been a public relations success (Clear and Hardyman, 1990).

Intensive supervision is usually accomplished by severely reducing caseload size per p/p officer, based on the assumption that it will lead to increased contact between the officer and the client or their significant others (such as spouse or parents), and that this increased contact will improve service delivery and control and, thus reduce recidivism. Some programs, however, have had difficulty achieving *intensity*: "While it may be inconceivable for intensive supervision to occur in caseloads that exceed some finite number, such as fifty persons, it is certainly conceivable that much smaller caseloads might not result in significant levels of intensity" (Clear and Hardyman, 1990: 44). Eric Carlson and Evalyn Parks claim that intensive supervision does indeed increase case contacts, often by 50 percent or more, and the amount of time spent in contact also increases significantly: "The difference between spending one-half hour per month with a client and spending an hour per month," however, "is, relatively speaking, an extremely small difference considering the magnitude of the treatment and service provision task which the probation officer is trying to accomplish" (1979: 72).

Intensive supervision for drug offenders on probation in seven cities (Seattle, Washington; Des Moines, Iowa; Santa Fe, New Mexico; Atlanta, Georgia; Macon, Georgia; Waycross, Georgia; Winchester, Virginia) did not appear to impact on recidivism: Research revealed that there were no significant differences between the arrest rates for ISP participants and a control group receiving regular supervision during a 12-month period (Petersilia, Turner, and Deschenes, 1992). Similar findings were reported in a study of IPS programs in 14 cities (Petersilia and Turner, 1993). As noted by the researchers, however, drawing conclusions from recidivism statistics can be misleading because recidivism could be a feature of the intensity of the supervision; IPS could increase the probability of new criminal activity being *discovered.*

Research into the effectiveness of intensive supervision dates back to 1953, when California conducted "probably the most extensively controlled experiment in American correctional history" (Glaser, 1969: 311).

CALIFORNIA

The Special Intensive Parole Unit (SIPU) experiment ran from 1953 until 1964, during which time caseload sizes were varied from 15 to 35. In addition, research was conducted into the impact of increased supervision on particular risk classes of offender. A positive outcome occurred only with those parolees classified as "lower-middle risk"—they had significantly fewer violations. In a review of this research, however, Robert Martinson (1974: 47) found that the successful cases were concentrated in northern California, where agents were more apt than agents in southern California to cite both the experimentals and the controls for violating parole. The limited success, Martinson argues, was not due to the intensive nature of supervision, but was the result of a realistic threat of reimprisonment. A problem also exists with using parole violation as a criterion for success because of what researchers refer to as the "halo effect," a tendency on the part of p/p officers to tolerate greater levels of misbehavior than is usual to prove the experiment successful.

More recent research into California IPS was conducted in three counties. Cases were randomly assigned from a pool of high-risk offenders on probation to IPS caseloads of 40 (Contra Costa), 19 (Ventura), and 33 (Los Angeles), or control caseloads that averaged 150 to 300 offenders. After six months, IPS clients received more intensive supervision: two to three times the usual number of contacts. About 30 percent of the IPS cases had a technical violation, a much higher rate than the control caseloads; however, no statistically significant difference existed between new arrest rates for IPS or control cases. The research revealed that intensive supervision in these counties did not affect the rate of new arrests: IPS failed to enhance the rehabilitative or control function of supervision (Petersilia and Turner, 1990). The researchers conclude: "When compared with routine probationers, the ISP participants, with few exceptions, had similar rates of technical violations and new arrests" (Petersilia and Turner, 1991: 9).

Research by Michael Agopian (1990) on a Los Angeles Probation Department ISP program involving gang-member drug offenders also had disappointing results. However, as he reports, although caseloads were intensive—33 as opposed to 300—the supervision that resulted was hardly intensive—home visits were infrequent. Reducing caseload size and calling a program *intensive* is not the same as providing intensive supervision.

GEORGIA

Research in Georgia has produced mixed results for the concept of intensive supervision. Probationers in the intensive supervision program are under the joint supervision of a probation officer and a surveillance officer in caseloads that do not exceed 25. One comparison of outcomes (Erwin, 1984) for IPS probationers (N = 542) and a matched sample (n = 752) of regular probationers, revealed that 13.7 percent of the IPS group had their probation revoked for new crimes (none for violent crimes), whereas 10.2 percent was the figure for the control sample. The IPS group had a higher rate of technical violations (11.8 percent) than the control sample (6.5 percent)—which the researchers argue is to be expected considering the intensive supervision—and there was little difference in the absconder rate: 2.2 for the IPS, 2.4 for the control sample. A second study of the program (Erwin and Bennett, 1987) revealed that 18.5 percent of the IPS probationers and 24.0 percent of the regular probationers were convicted of new crimes. However, 42.3 percent of prison releasees during the same period were convicted of new offenses, and "59.4 percent of the IPS cases were more similar to those incarcerated than to those placed on probation" (1987: 4).

According to Joan Petersilia (1988a), any number of states have adopted IPS programming based on the apparent success of the Georgia program. However, she cautions, judges in Georgia, like those in many southern states, tend toward the punitive, imposing more sentences of imprisonment and for longer terms than elsewhere. Thus, there is a greater pool of IPS prospects—nonviolent offenders—than would be expected outside of the South in general, and Georgia in particular. In fact, when it comes to the risk of new criminal behavior, IPS clients are not markedly different from the regular probation population in Georgia. The basic claims of IPS in Georgia with respect to cost-effectiveness, diversion of offenders, and improved public safety "are not supported by the available research evidence" (Clear, Flynn, and Shapiro, 1987: 35). In fact, "a convincing argument can be presented that the Georgia evaluation actually demonstrates the opposite" (Byrne, Lurigio, and Baird, 1989: 27).

PER DAY COST COMPARISONS IN GEORGIA

Basic probation	$ 1.01*
Intensive probation	4.07*
Diversion centers	35.54
Detention centers	35.41
Probation boot camps	35.41
Prison	45.33

*In Illinois, basic probation costs about $2.75; intensive about $10.95.

According to the plan, the IPS probation officer is supposed to provide typical professional casework services, while the probation surveillance officer (with less education, training, and salary) provides "24 hour surveillance capability through day, night, and weekend visits and telephone contacts." Surveillance officers, however, developed greater rapport with clients and their families than did probation officers. The surveillance officer had more direct contact with, and was more easily accessible to, the client and his or her family. Billie Erwin and Lawrence Bennett (1987: 6) report:

> One of the most interesting findings of the IPS evaluation is the near impossibility of separating treatment from enforcement. The Georgia design places the Probation Officer in charge of case management, treatment and counseling services, and court-related activities. Surveillance Officers, who usually have law enforcement or correctional backgrounds, have primary responsibility for frequently visiting the home unannounced, checking curfews, performing drug and alcohol tests using portable equipment, and checking arrest records weekly. The Surveillance Officer becomes well acquainted with the family and is often present in critical situations. Both the Probation and Surveillance Officers report a great deal of overlap of functions and even a reversal of their roles.

In practice, the surveillance officer was doing the work of a professional PO, while the latter's role was either redundant or was often reduced to that of a paper-pushing case analyst.

LOUISIANA

In a study of shock incarceration, Doris MacKenzie, James Shaw, and Claire Souryal (1992: 450) found that positive results were a function of the intensive supervision offenders received after being paroled: "the more intense the supervision, the better these offenders adjusted during community supervision." In addition, "parolees' performance declined over 6 months of community supervision as the intensity of supervision was reduced." They conclude: "In general, the more intense the supervision the better the offenders performed, probably because this was required of them. There was a threat of revocation if they did not comply." In another study of shock incarceration in Louisiana, MacKenzie and Shaw (1993) found that boot camp graduates were subjected to more technical violations than regular supervisees; regular p/p supervisees, however, were convicted at higher rates for new crimes. They ascribe the differences to the impact of the intensive supervision given to boot camp graduates.

MINNESOTA

Intensive supervision has centered mostly on probation: "Relatively few jurisdictions have implemented prison-diversion ISP programs—programs that divert offenders from prison sentences to terms of supervision in the community" (Deschenes, Turner, and Petersilia, 1995: 331). Intensive supervision was tested in Minnesota as a cost-saving device using 300 cases. Experimental and control groups were randomly assigned from a cohort of recently convicted inmates with sentences of 27 months or less and probation violators committed to prison. None had a record of victim harm or weapons use, and they were employable with a suitable residence. A second set of experimental and control groups consisted of good-time releasees who had served two-thirds of their sentence.

Parole agents in the intensive units supervised caseloads of 12 to 15 offenders (size of control units not indicated). Intensive cases spent the first six months on home confinement during which time they could leave their residence only for employment or with specific permission. Results: There were no statistically significant outcome differences between the experimental and control caseloads, but savings were realized—$5,000 per offender per year—from the early release of inmates.

NEW JERSEY

IPS in New Jersey is limited to 500 highly select offenders who are diverted from prison after several months of incarceration. IPS cases were compared with a sample of offenders who were eligible for the program but were, instead, incarcerated and released on parole. Frank Pearson (1988) reports that the IPS participants' new conviction rate averaged roughly 10 percentage points lower than that of the comparison group. He concludes that in New Jersey IPS

> works fairly well with felons who are neither dangerous nor habitual criminals. The program does save a modest amount of prison space without increasing recidivism; it has been cost-effective compared to ordinary terms of imprisonment and parole; it has been monetarily beneficial (in terms of earnings, taxes, payments to a fund for victims, and so on); and it does provide a level of punishment between probation on the one hand and ordinary imprisonment on the other. (1988: 447)

The "New Jersey program evaluation—by design—should make the IPS program look quite good because it compares IPS cases with a group of class 3 and class 4 felons who represent the poorest risks and who receive the harshest treatment by the New Jersey corrections system" (Byrne, Lurigio, and Baird, 1989: 30). Other researchers find it ironic that the relatively low-risk offenders in the New Jersey program are receiving intensive supervision, whereas the far higher-risk parolee joins a caseload in excess of 100 (Clear, Flynn, and Shapiro, 1987).

NEW YORK

Research conducted by the New York State Division of Parole (Collier, 1980) indicates that intensive supervision can have a modest effect on violent felony offenders. In 1978, the legislature provided funding for the supervision of violent felony offenders. In 1979, all released inmates who had been convicted of a violent felony (crimes ranging from robbery to arson—most were imprisoned for robbery) were placed in intensive units whose parole officers supervised no more than 35 cases: 97 percent were male; the median age was 27.3; blacks constituted 57.5 percent, whites 23 percent, and Hispanics 19.5 percent; 62 percent completed less than the twelfth grade, and 80 percent were unskilled laborers. Interestingly, two-thirds of this group had little or no prior criminal history.

After one year, the violent felony offenders released in 1979 and placed under intensive supervision (N = 1905) were compared with the same population released in 1978 to regular supervision (N = 1732), with the following results:

- 12.6 percent of the (1978) controls and 1.8 percent of the (1979) intensives were returned to prison for a new offense.
- 3.3 percent of the controls and 4.0 percent of the intensives were returned to prison for technical violations of parole.
- 5.0 percent of the controls and 3.4 percent of the intensives absconded from supervision.
- As of the end of the one-year research period (3/31/80), 6.5 percent of the controls, and 3.9 percent of the intensives had parole violation or court hearings pending.

Even regular parole supervision in New York, as contrasted with that typically operating in other states, is relatively "intensive." During this writer's almost 15 years as a parole officer and senior parole officer (supervisor), the average caseload size rarely exceeded 60, and was usually closer to 50, and a high number of in-person client contacts between officers and offenders occurred, particularly unannounced visits to the client's residence.

OHIO

Edward Latessa and Gennaro Vito (1988) conducted research into the intensive probation supervision of shock probationers in Lucas County (Toledo), Ohio. Funded by a state probation subsidy program, the Incarceration Diversion Unit (IDU) consists of four probation officers, each with a caseload maximum of 25, with the exception of the supervisor, who is assigned 15. The IDU probationers were compared with a group of shock probationers under regular supervision. (The study did not indicate the size of regular shock probation caseloads.) The researchers found that the IDU officers recorded almost four times as many client contacts, and more social services were provided to their clients. However, no statistically significant differences with respect to recidivism occurred; the IDU group did have significantly fewer technical violations, which the researchers conclude was the result of a realistic fear of being sent to prison because of the nature of IDU supervision and strict violation practices. (An alternative hypothesis would raise questions about the quality of the supervision.) Latessa and Vito (1988: 327) conclude that their study "should provide a word of caution to officials seeking ways to limit incarceration rates" by using intensive supervision.

The Lucas County Intensive Supervision Unit (ISU) was designed to divert nonviolent felony offenders who had already been committed to a Department of Youth Services (DYS) facility; DYS facilities were under pressure from overcrowding. The program excluded youth whose instant offense involved drugs, use of a weapon, or victim injury. Research compared ISU youngsters to similar youth committed to a DYS facility and paroled. The supervision provided by ISU was indeed intensive, both with respect to control and rehabilitative services, but no significant difference in recidivism occurred: It was rather high for both—almost 50 percent of both groups were reinstitutionalized within the 18-month period of the research. However, there was a potential savings: The annual per client cost of ISU was a little over $6000, as contrasted with more than $32,000 for incarceration (Wiebush, 1993).

A study conducted by Susan Noonan and Edward Latessa (1987) in Montgomery County (Dayton), Ohio, compared matched samples from IPS units, with 25 cases per officer, and regular units. The research revealed that 11.7 percent of the intensive supervision cases ended with a felony conviction, against 3.8 percent for regular supervision; 1.2 percent of the intensive cases were incarcerated for misdemeanors as opposed to 6.2 percent of the regular cases. Interestingly, the IPS officers, on average, made fewer than one face-to-face contact per month with their clients in the client's home—hardly an *intensive* level of supervision.

Stephen Haas and Latessa (1995) conducted a study of IPS in the rural Ohio county of Clermont. They note that implementing a special supervision program in rural areas is difficult because of long travel times to reach clients, making unannounced visits problematic. The researchers found that persons assigned to IPS were clearly higher risk than those on regular caseloads, but they were not able to determine if these were prison-bound cases. As might be expected if supervision is indeed intensive, the IPS clients had a higher rate of technical violations: 39 percent IPS; 24 percent regular; however, "there were no significant differences in the number of felony arrests, convictions, or completion rates of probation. A high percentage of both groups was classified as successful" (1995: 168).

WASHINGTON STATE

The objective of the Washington State Adult Corrections Division was to save tax dollars by removing *low-risk offenders* from the state's prisons. Persons released into the program had on average served less than three months in prison. They ($N = 289$) were placed under the intensive supervision of a parole officer whose caseload did not exceed 20. At the end of one year, it was determined whether the individual's behavior warranted a conditional discharge from supervision or whether further supervision by a regular parole officer was indicated.

To evaluate the program a matched historical sample ($n = 102$) was selected as the control group. Random assignment was ruled out because of "equal treatment under the law considerations." The control group was made up of inmates who were paroled at the same time as those selected for early release and intensive supervision. However, the control group subjects were released after having served normal sentences to a parole officer who supervised an average caseload of 73. A person in the control group was selected on basis of the same criteria as for those in the test group. David Fallen and his colleagues (1981) report the following outcomes:

- After one year of supervision, 19 percent of the test (IPS) group had been arrested or convicted for new (nontraffic) offenses, while the figure for control cases was 40 percent.
- However, the IPS parole officers showed a strong tendency to invoke delinquency action: After one year 42 percent of the test group had been cited for technical parole violations as opposed to 24 percent for the control group.
- The one-year revocation rate for the IPS group was 17 percent; for the control group it was 6.1 percent (the average for general supervision in Washington is 15 percent).

The researchers speculate on explanations for their findings:

- Intensive parolees were less likely to commit new offenses because of a fear of detection produced by increased supervision.
- By brief incarceration, intensive parolees received the initial "shock value" of prison but were not in long enough to learn the "skills" or adopt the values of the incarcerated criminal population.
- Because many intensive parolees received formal technical violations, these served as effective warnings that undesirable behavior would not be tolerated.
- Because many intensive parolees were revoked for technical violations only, this occurrence may have screened out those disposed to commit new offenses.

WISCONSIN

In 1984, the Wisconsin Division of Corrections established an experimental IPS program for high-risk offenders. Thirty offenders (later increased to 40) were supervised by two-agent teams in two locations. The research did not indicate the caseload for non-IPS parole agents. The experienced agents screened all new cases in their areas and selected only high-risk offenders (HRO) as clients. To qualify as an HRO, the client must have a history of assaultive behavior; other distinguishing characteristics include a lengthy criminal record, poor prison adjustment record, and poor attitude toward community supervision, as well as an unwillingness to participate in drug, alcohol abuse, or mental health programs.

As part of intensive supervision, specialized rules were tailored for each offender; these restricted certain associations, use of motor vehicles, and evening hours: "The general tactic is to establish rules which restrict behavior(s) associated with a past criminal pattern" (Wagner, 1989: 23). Offenders were required to provide a weekly schedule indicating where they will be at any given time. Each client registered with the local police, submitting a photograph, fingerprints, handwriting sample, past offense history, and current address. The police were expected to assist in the offender-monitoring process. Parole agents made at least four in-person contacts each month, including two visits, scheduled and unscheduled, to the offender's residence. Frequent collateral visits with police, employers, landlords, and associates occurred. In at least one case, school officials and parent association members were informed of the release of a child sex offender so that they could aid in the surveillance process.

The HRO group under IPS was compared to a matched sample that received regular supervision. The results were dramatic; after one year, only 3 percent of the IPS parolees had been convicted of a felony; it was 27 percent for the control group. The statistics for parole violation provide at least a partial explanation for these differences: Only 12 percent of the control group were returned to prison for parole violations, whereas the number was 40 percent for the IPS group. Dennis Wagner, a researcher for the state of Wisconsin, concludes that "the IPS program suppresses criminal behavior by preempting it" (1989: 26). The research does not indicate how many of the remaining IPS clients successfully completed their entire supervision period.

DISCUSSION

To evaluate IPS, we need to examine the two premises on which it is based.

PREMISE ONE *Intensive probation supervision will divert offenders who would otherwise be incarcerated.* In any number of jurisdictions this goal is not being accomplished. A study in Tennessee, for example, revealed that even though some offenders were being diverted away from prison, many more IPS clients would have normally been sentenced to regular probation (Whitehead, Miller, and Myers, 1995). Judges continue to send probation-eligible offenders to prison, while using IPS for those who would be sentenced to probation in any event. A study of IPS in Colorado found no significant differences between cases recommended for IPS and those not recommended, leading the researchers to conclude that this program "may not be one of prison-diversion as the state guidelines proclaim" (Reichel and Sudbrack, 1994: 57). Needless to say, this will affect the results of any research on an IPS program. For the diversion goal to be accomplished, cases need to be assigned to IPS *after* a sentence of imprisonment. Only after conviction, sentence, and remand to jail pending transportation to prison should the IPS screening officer review the case and, if appropriate, submit a recommendation for resentencing. Cases not intercepted should proceed to state prison. With respect to parole, parole boards often assign cases to intensive supervision that would have been granted parole even in the absence of an IPS program. If intensive supervision is to serve the goal of reducing the prison population, it should be reserved for cases that have been denied parole. An IPS screening officer (institutional parole officer) should review the case *after* parole has been denied and, if appropriate, submit a recommendation for reconsideration of parole with IPS.

In sum, many, if not most, intensive supervision programs are not actually diverting offenders—they are simply providing judges and parole boards with an additional supervision option that is not being used in lieu of prison. Although this may not have the effect of lowering prison commitments, it certainly has merits of its own. For example, the Florida IPS (Community Control)

Program received offenders who were often more serious offenders than those on probation or in jail, but less serious than those sentenced to prison. An undetermined number of these borderline cases, perhaps more than one-half, would have been sent to prison in the absence of IPS (Baird and Wagner, 1990). Many IPS programs, however, appear to be accepting those offenders who are not at high risk, who probably should have been on regular probation in the first instance. In some counties, the probation department routinely recommends inappropriate cases for IPS. This serves two intertwined purposes: First, it ensures that the IPS program will deliver "good stats"; second, it helps to keep down regular caseloads by shifting some cases to probation officers funded by special allocations (and the continuation of these allocations is dependent on "good stats").

However, intensive supervision for inappropriate cases unnecessarily increases the cost of probation and it may be harmful to the client: "Behavioral scientists have long speculated that the addition of strains and controls to a human system can, at some time, result in a reaction that is contrary to the direction of the controls" (Clear and Hardyman, 1990: 55). According to the labeling perspective (discussed in Chapter 9), an offender inappropriately identified as "high risk" by virtue of IPS status may indeed assume that role and organize his or her behavior accordingly.

An additional problem involves offenders who feel that intensive supervision is as punitive as imprisonment: "In many states, given the option of serving prison terms or participating in IPS, many offenders have chosen prison" (Petersilia, 1990: 23; emphasis deleted). Joan Petersilia points out that for many/most serious offenders, imprisonment and the stigma that can result are not the frightening phenomena that they are for the community at large: "For many offenders, it may seem preferable to get that short stay in prison over rather than spend five times as long in an IPS" (1990: 25; see also 1994). Under these conditions, in order for intensive supervision to work, it may be necessary to offer it as an option for much more serious offenders than are now being subjected to IPS.

In sum, large amounts of scarce resources are being allocated to the less serious offenders, while more dangerous offenders are released to the community under parole supervision that is often inadequate because of lack of funding (Clear, Flynn, and Shapiro, 1987) or is simply nonexistent in those states that have discontinued postprison community supervision. It is the worst "Alice-in-Wonderland" situation when armed robbers and other dangerous offenders are released from prison with inadequate or no supervision, and property offenders are placed on intensive probation supervision. In Florida, for example, lesser offenders are placed on intensive community control, whereas the more serious offenders released from prison are not supervised (Wagner and Baird, 1993).

This irrational approach to crime and justice is exemplified by a Texas study (Texas Adult Probation Commission, 1988). IPS cases were compared with cases eligible for probation but sentenced to imprisonment, and cases not eligible for probation and sentenced to imprisonment, using the "risk" part of the Texas Risk/Needs Assessment form. The mean scores were

Intensive probation supervision	20.10
Eligible for probation but incarcerated	18.93
Ineligible for a sentence of probation	26.26

In other words, although the IPS program was apparently diverting offenders from prison (a risk mean of 20.10), there were less serious risks (risk mean of 18.93) who were, nevertheless, imprisoned; and the high-risk offenders (risk mean 26.26) who were imprisoned will be released to parole supervision that is not intensive. A similar situation existed in Illinois, where the state has been funding extensive IPS programs; in 1987, 60 percent of the state's parole agents were laid off, causing caseloads to approach the 400 mark. (The positions were restored in 1989, and caseloads went to 110.)

Alan Schuman (1989: 29) argues that "the new IPS concept actually depicts local communities' original image of how probation services should operate. IPS provides the type of comprehensive surveillance services, restitution payments, drug testing and treatment, employment verification, and networking with other community services that should be expected of all probation agencies that are adequately funded." Gerald Buck (1989: 66) argues that intensive supervision "*is* probation practiced as it was originally intended to be. Other probation programs are a sham that ought not be called probation supervision" (emphasis in original).

PREMISE TWO   *More of whatever it is that the p/p agency does with routine cases will have a salutary effect on cases at greater risk.* Although several research studies have challenged this premise, a strong, if unproven, belief in p/p is that *more is better.* I want to dwell on the question *more of what.* The implication of intensive supervision—the bait that hooks funding from elected officials—is that offenders will be closely monitored, under surveillance, and made to fear detection for any violations they might be inclined to commit. Thus note Arthur Lurigio and Joan Petersilia (1992: 9):

> An important assumption of IPS programs is that close supervision should increase the probability of detecting and arresting offenders who are not deterred by the program and who continue to commit crimes. Speedy revocation to custody results in incapacitation, and, because IPS participants are encouraged to be employed and to attend counseling sessions, rehabilitation *may* occur. However, newer IPS programs are designed to boost offenders' perceptions of the effectiveness of the system in detecting and punishing their criminal behavior.

Probation and parole officers are portrayed as making unannounced contacts with offenders, whom they are monitoring around the clock, ready to take immediate action to prevent any danger to the community. For agencies whose officers are armed and trained in law enforcement, this approach is a natural extension of the services they are already providing.

Agencies in which officers do not have adequate law enforcement training or authority, however, cannot live up to the image of *intensive.* Indeed, agencies that adopt a meaningful form of intensive supervision—one that does indeed increase unannounced face-to-face in-field contacts—but fail to equip and train their officers accordingly, place these officers in danger. In Vermont, for example, officers expressed a great deal of concern for their safety because intensive supervision meant frequent unannounced visits by unarmed officers. When I worked as a parole officer in New York, unannounced visits found parolees with firearms left on the dresser, large amounts of heroin and drug paraphernalia on the kitchen table, and other potentially dangerous situations. Minnesota parole agents providing intensive supervision "are required to make visits to clientele at all hours in a variety of situations and neighborhoods." But they carry no firearms, although they are authorized to carry chemical substances to aid in a "safe retreat."

IPS programs are typically set up outside the traditional supervision structure: Clients and officers are hand picked; the latter receive special training, sometimes salary increases, and report to their own supervisory chain of command. This hierarchy can affect general agency morale, because the IPS unit receives a disproportionate share of resources and attention. These "special" units experience strong pressure to demonstrate results:

> This is one reason why these programs often seem to be encased in an atmosphere of caution—they are very vulnerable to errors. Based on a rationale of effective offender control, and in contrast to seemingly more lenient traditional probation methods, the idea of intensive probation can be seriously damaged by even one publicized incident of serious client failure, such as a violent crime. Therefore, despite the control rhetoric, program officials seem to bend over backward to avoid the riskiest clients and to resist giving accepted clients many chances to violate probation. (Clear, Flynn, and Shapiro, 1987: 42)

This point accounts for the relatively high rate of probation violations in most IPS programs.

In New York, when I was a parole officer, each caseload had some (usually two or three out of about 45) cases that were designated "intensive" by the parole board. These cases required at least one face-to-face home visit and at least four in-person office visits each month. Cases were subjected to more supervisory review, and there was less latitude—in the event of a technical violation of the rules, such offenders were more likely to be taken into custody and returned to prison. This system avoided the "elitism" that has apparently reared its head in other probation/parole agencies with IPS programs.

There is also a problem inherent in evaluating IPS effectiveness. Random assignment of high-risk cases between the IPS and routine caseloads fails to account for the classification and unofficial intensive supervision typically carried out by probation and parole officers. When confronted with unmanageable caseloads, POs identify those cases with greatest risk/needs and devote most of their quality working time with these clients (at the expense of most other cases that receive little but "paper" attention). Thus, experimental model research is often comparing IPS with quasi-IPS. Recidivism rates may vary according to the ability of the police, the skill of perpetrators, and cooperation between p/p agencies and law enforcement agencies (General Accounting Office, 1990).

ELECTRONIC MONITORING

Electronic monitoring (EM) is used in conjunction with a variety of programs, in particular, home detention instead of jail for defendants awaiting trial (Cooprider and Kerby, 1990) and intensive community supervision. New York has initiated a pilot EM program that provides an alternative to incarceration for parole violators, who must remain confined to their homes for not less than 60 or more than 120 days. Home confinement with electronic monitoring has proven appealing because it has the potential to satisfy the goals of imprisonment without the social and financial costs normally associated with imprisonment:

- To satisfy the demand for punishment
- To provide a deterrent effect
- To provide for community protection

In 1988, electronic monitoring was being used in 33 states for 2277 offenders: "most of those monitored were sentenced offenders on probation or parole, participating in a program of intensive supervision in the community" (Schmidt, 1989: 2). EM can serve to enforce curfews, usually restricting the offender from leaving home at night; for detention—a stricter curfew—requiring the offender to remain at home at all times except for employment, education, or other specified activities; or incarceration, whereby the offender is required to be at home at all times except for very limited activities, such as medical treatment (U.S. Bureau of Justice Assistance, 1989).

The first system of electronic monitoring was apparently inspired by Ralph Schwitzgebel (1968, 1969a,b) who proposed "electronic parole" as an alternative to imprisonment. The Switzgebel-inspired research program monitored the location of parolees, mental patients, and volunteers in Massachusetts from 1964 through 1970. Roger Przybylski suggests that even though interest in electronic monitoring of offenders always existed, until the crisis in prison overcrowding "market conditions were never attractive enough to make the technology commercially available" (1988: 1). Reputedly inspired by a "Spiderman" comic strip, Albuquerque District Court Judge Jack Love asked Michael Goss to develop a device suitable to monitor probation curfews. The "Gosslink" was first attached to the ankle of a 30-year-old probation violator for a one-month period starting in 1983. Judge Love subsequently sentenced four other offenders to monitored home confinement.

Meanwhile, a Monroe County, Florida, judge tried a new (Moody) EM system with twelve offenders over a six-month period; they served house-confinement sentences ranging from two days to four months. As a result, the state of Florida incorporated electronic home confinement in the Correctional Reform Act of 1983, and the following year a pilot program was initiated in Palm Beach County for misdemeanants, mostly drunken drivers. By the beginning of 1986, more than 5000 offenders were on EM home confinement in Florida. By the beginning of 1987, more than 50 programs existed in 21 states using some form of monitored home confinement; according to the National Institute of Justice, more than a dozen firms are marketing systems designed to verify that an offender is in a specified location at a given time (Ford and Schmidt, 1985; Petersilia, 1988b; Przybylski, 1988).

EM has been associated primarily with probation, and there is little literature on its use in a parole setting. Parole officers in Utah have used continuously signaling EM on a limited scale to supplement curfew restrictions:

> A parole officer assisted by a correctional technician operates the program according to policies and procedures established for IPS. Staff of a community correctional center in Salt Lake currently monitor the host unit for alarms and play a role in the primary response to an alarm. If the center is unable to verify that an offender is at his/her residence, a parole agent is paged. Parole officers have vehicles and other necessary equipment with which to respond to alarms. Backup is provided by other parole officers in the field or law enforcement. (U.S. Bureau of Justice Assistance, 1989: 17)

Several different types of systems are used for electronic monitoring, but they can be divided into two basic categories (Przybylski, 1988):

1. Active/continuously signaling
2. Passive/programmed contact

CONTINUOUSLY SIGNALING SYSTEMS

Two primary types of continuously signaling systems are available: those that use telephone lines and those that use a radiolike transmitter and receiver. One system that uses the telephone lines involves the offender wearing a battery-powered moisture-, water-, and shock-proof transmitter that is about the size of a pack of cigarettes and weighs about six ounces. (Figures 12.2 and 12.3). The device is securely fastened by riveted plastic straps just above the ankle or on the wrist. Once strapped on it can only be removed by stretching or cutting the straps in a manner easily detected by visual inspection. More modern versions provide an immediate electronic alert if the band is subjected to tampering. A circuit board contained in the transmitter has an individually calibrated and unique identification code. The transmitter emits a signal at regular intervals with a range of about 100 to 150 feet. The signal is monitored by a receiver connected to a 110-volt alternating current (ac) outlet and a standard telephone jack installed in the residence. The receiver automatically dials a central computer describing the time the person goes beyond the range of the signal or returns within range and automatically dials the computer when it has been subjected to tampering. If the dialer is disconnected or loses its source of power (by a power outage, for example), the message is stored until such time as the unit is

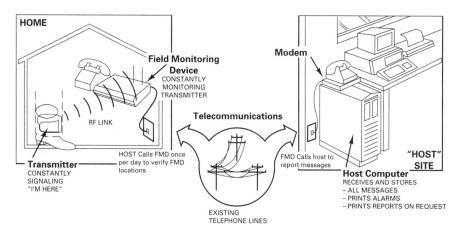

FIGURE 12.2   Continuously signaling system. (BI Home Escort, Boulder, CO)

reconnected to the ac power and telephone; at that time, a delayed message describing the time of each activity is sent to the computer.

Simpler continuously signaling systems that do not use a telephone consist of only two basic components: a transmitter and a portable receiver. The transmitter, which is strapped to the offender's ankle or wrist or worn around the neck, emits a radio signal that travels about one city block. By driving past the offender's residence, place of employment, or treatment center, with the hand

FIGURE 12.3   Field monitoring device and ankle transmitter. (BI Home Escort, Boulder, CO)

held portable receiver (Figure 12.4) the officer can verify his or her presence. This system was used in a pilot program by the New York State Division of Parole to provide enhanced monitoring of parolees whose behavior indicated they were reverting to criminal behavior or otherwise in violation of parole rules. Few hardware failures occurred, and the parole officer was able to repair them on site. The agency concluded that electronic monitoring offered a feasible community supervision alternative to incarceration, allowing certain parolees the opportunity to seek treatment while remaining in the community.

A consent form for participation in a home confinement program appears in Figure 12.5.

PROGRAMMED CONTACT SYSTEMS

One of the programmed contact systems relies on the telephone and computerized voice identification. The computer records the offender's voice and is then programmed to call him or her at random times and request that a series of words or phrases be repeated. They are then matched with the earlier recording to verify presence. In the event of a failure to answer the telephone or a voice verification failure, the computer reports a monitoring infraction. Another pro-

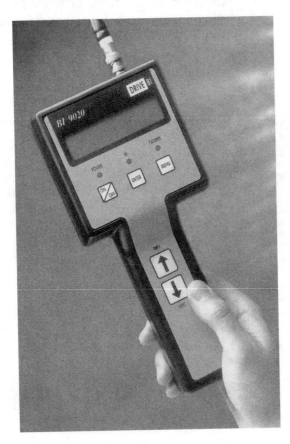

FIGURE 12.4 Drive-by portable monitor. (BI Home Escort, Boulder, CO)

grammed contact system uses visual verification through telephone units that transmit black-and-white still pictures of the callers on a three-inch screen. Still another program uses an encoder device attached to a wrist band; the band cannot be removed without breaking it. The encoder must be inserted into a verifier box attached to the telephone whenever a computer-generated call is received.

HOME DETENTION PROJECT

In an effort to address the problem of the repeat drunk driving offender, Kent County and the Maryland Division of Parole and Probation began a home detention project alternative to incarceration for second- and third-time offenders. These persons, who would have normally been sent to jail, are allowed to remain in the community under probation supervision but are restricted to their homes during the evening hours. This latter aspect of supervision is accomplished via a computer that dials the client's home telephone number on random days and times during evening hours. The client answers and, by placing an electronic bracelet attached to his or her wrist to the telephone, sends a code to the computer. The computer then asks several questions of the client. After the call has been processed, a report is sent to the office that confirms that the client's phone number was dialed and verified and gives the date and time. The report is reviewed by the parole and probation agent the following morning.

DISCUSSION

The appeal of this method of responding to offenders is easy to understand when we consider that the cost of imprisonment is $10,000 to $20,000 per year, and the cost of building a new prison is $50,000 to $100,000 per bed. [Unfortunately, as noted by Douglas McDonald (1989), accurate estimates of the cost of imprisonment and the cost of community supervision, intensive or otherwise, do not exist.] However, startup costs for electronic monitoring are high—Albuquerque paid $100,000 for its first 25 devices. To offset these costs, offenders can be required to pay supervision fees or pay for the cost of installing the monitoring telephone, a practice that raises important ethical and legal issues. Should an offender who is otherwise qualified for home confinement be denied access to the program—and thereby face imprisonment—because he or she lacks the ability to pay fees or does not have a residence? If the answer is "no," how far should the county or state go in providing a residence and, in some systems, a telephone? The answers will impact the cost-effectiveness of any electronic home-confinement program. Some firms rent and monitor the equipment, but this can be costly, about $15 dollars a day per offender, which does not include personnel costs involved in responding to signal disruptions or checking to see that the equipment has not been tampered with.

HOME CONFINEMENT PROGRAM
PARTICIPANT AGREEMENT

1. I _____ have been placed in the Home Confinement Program. I agree to comply with all program rules set forth in this Agreement, and the instructions of my probation or pretrial services officer. Failure to comply with this Agreement or any instructions of my officer will be considered a violation of my supervision and may result in an adverse action. I agree to call my officer immediately if I have any questions about these rules or if I experience any problems with the monitoring equipment.

2. I will remain at my approved residence at all times, except for employment and other activities approved in advance by my probation or pretrial services officer. Regularly occurring activities are provided for in my written weekly schedule which remains in effect until modified by my officer. I must obtain my officer's advance permission for any special activities (such as doctor's appointments) that are not included in my written schedule.

3. I shall not deviate from my approved schedule except in an emergency. I shall first try to get the permission of my officer. If this is not possible, I must call my officer as soon as I am able to do so. If I call during non-business hours, I will leave a message on my officer's answering machine, including my name, the date, the time, a brief description of the emergency, and my location or destination. I agree to provide proof of the emergency as requested by my officer.

4. While under home confinement supervision I agree to wear a non-removable ankle bracelet which will be attached by my officer.

5. I agree to provide and maintain a telephone, with modular telephone connectors, at my residence and maintain telephone and electrical service there at my own expense.

6. On the line to which the monitoring equipment is connected, I agree to not have party lines, telephone answering machines, cordless telephones, "call forwarding", "Caller ID", "call waiting", and other devices and services that may interfere with the proper functioning of the electronic monitoring equipment.

7. I agree to allow a monitoring device (receiver/dialer) to be connected to the telephone and the telephone outlet at my residence.

8. I acknowledge receipt of receiver/dialer number_____, and transmitter number_____. I understand that I will be held responsible for damage, other than normal wear, to the equipment. I also understand that if I do not return the equipment, or do not return it in good condition, I may be charged for replacement or the repair of the equipment and I agree to pay these costs. I understand that I may be subject to felony prosecution if I fail to return my monitoring equipment.

9. I agree to not move, disconnect or tamper with the monitoring device (receiver/dialer).

10. I agree to not remove or tamper with the ankle bracelet (transmitter) except in a life threatening emergency or with the prior permission of my officer.

11. I agree to allow authorized personnel to inspect and maintain the ankle transmitter and receiver/dialer.

12. I agree to return the receiver/dialer and transmitter to my officer upon demand.

13. I agree that I will not make any changes in the telephone equipment or services at my residence without prior approval of my officer.

14. I agree to provide copies of my monthly telephone bill when requested by my officer.

15. I agree to notify my officer immediately if I lose electrical power at my residence, if I have to remove the ankle bracelet because of an emergency, or if I experience any

FIGURE 12.5 Participant agreement form for a home confinement program

problems with the monitoring equipment. During non-business hours, I agree to call my officer and leave a message on his/her answering machine including my name, the date, the time, and the nature of my problem. If there is a power problem, I agree that I will call and leave another message when the power is restored. I also agree to notify my officer of any problems with my telephone service as soon as I am able to do so.

16. I agree that I will not attempt to use my telephone when the Receiver/Dialer's "Phone Busy" or "Phone Indicator" light is on.

17. I understand that my officer will also use telephone calls and personal visits to monitor my compliance with my approved schedule. When I am at home, I agree to promptly answer my telephone or door. If I fail to answer my telephone or door when I am supposed to be at home, my officer will conclude that I am absent, and in violation of my curfew restrictions.

18. I understand that my officer must be able to contact me at work at any time. If I do not have a job with a fixed location (as in construction work) my officer must be able to locate me by calling my employer and promptly obtaining my work location. I also understand that jobs that do not meet these requirements are not permitted while I am under home confinement supervision. I understand that all job changes must be approved in advance by my officer.

19. I agree to refrain from the excessive use of alcohol or any use of controlled substances unless the controlled substance is prescribed by a licenced medical practitioner.

20. I understand that I will be required to undergo periodic, unscheduled urine collection and testing.

21. I agree to comply with all other conditions of my release and supervision as imposed by the court or parole board.

22. I understand and agree that all telephone calls from the monitoring contractor to my residence will be tape recorded by the monitoring contractor.

23. I understand that I may be ordered to pay all or part of the daily cost of my electronic monitoring. If so ordered, I agree, as directed by my officer, to pay _____ per day directly to the monitoring service.

24. Additional Rules (As needed)

I acknowledge that I have received a copy of these rules and that they have been explained to me. I understand that I must comply with these rules until _____, or until otherwise notified by my probation/parole officer. I further understand that any violations of these rules will also constitute a violation of supervision and may cause immediate adverse action.

_____   _____
(PARTICIPANT)   (DATE)

_____   _____
(WITNESS)   (DATE)

FIGURE 12.5   (*continued*)

Candidates for electronic home confinement are typically low-risk offenders who, in most jurisdictions, would be candidates for probation. Thus, the program may actually be adding to the cost of supervision without affecting the problem of jail/prison overcrowding. Conversely, the system is typically used for drunk drivers, and some object that home confinement does not serve as a significant deterrent for a crime that is potentially life threatening, while leaving the offender in a position to repeat his or her criminal act. Home confinement is devoid of any rehabilitative dimension: It provides no services to persons who often have extensive social service needs.

Richard Ball, Ronald Huff, and Robert Lilly (1988) found that the electronic surveillance programs they examined have not affected jail or prison commitments in any noticeable manner. They found that the persons selected for EM are typically from social and economic circumstances that, in any event, would predict a positive outcome. The researchers (1988: 97) also expressed concern over the impact of such programming on probation/parole officers: "Are these professionals going to see their relationships to offenders change from helping agents to surveillance agents?" EM has the potential to downgrade the role of p/p officers. Furthermore, there has been no research on the impact of home confinement on the offender's family.

During 1992, as the popularity of EM grew, news stories began to appear with some frequency detailing the inadequacies of controlling offender behavior through electronic means. The articles highlighted three problems:

1. Offenders committing crimes after taking off the device—some while still wearing them
2. Failure to replace older devices with more advanced technology, resulting in a failure to monitor offenders adequately
3. Lack of personnel available to respond quickly to tampering or other violations of the conditions of EM

Many agencies using EM fail to recognize that EM does not prevent crime; it is designed simply to assist in curfew enforcement. Curfew enforcement is dependent on having sufficient personnel monitoring the equipment and personnel to dispatch to check into reported violations.

In addition to community-based intermediate punishments are those using short-term incarceration that "shock" the miscreant while saving prison space.

SHOCK PROBATION/PAROLE

Shock probation/parole was pioneered by the state of Ohio, which enacted legislation in 1965 permitting the early release from prison of convicted felons either on probation (within 30 to 120 days of imprisonment) or parole (within six months of imprisonment). Since that time, other states (such as Idaho, Indiana, Kentucky, Maine, North Carolina, and Texas) have adopted similar statutes. To be eligible for shock probation in Ohio, the offender must be otherwise eligible for a sentence of probation and must file a petition with the court. Those not eligible for probation may file a request with the parole board for shock parole (which excludes those convicted of such crimes as rape, armed robbery, kidnaping, major drug violations, and some burglaries).

Shock probation was authorized by the Texas legislature in 1977 as a rehabilitation technique in which an offender is given a sample of prison or jail and is then placed on probation for the remainder of the sentence. Data from Texas indicate that the typical shock probationer is a white, single male in his early twenties, a laborer with a tenth- or eleventh-grade education. He was convicted of burglary as a first offense, and the crime is usually drug or alcohol related.

The state of New Jersey uses a form of shock probation that includes intensive supervision as an intermediate form of punishment (Figure 12.6), that is, punishment that is less costly than prison but much more onerous than traditional probation, to achieve the criminal justice objective of deterrence—general and specific—as well as rehabilitation. The program is highly restrictive: Only persons serving a sentence for a nonviolent felony are eligible, and no more than 500 persons can be in the program at any one time.

Offenders typically serve four months before entry into the New Jersey program (Pearson, 1988); to be eligible, the inmate must develop a personal plan that will govern activities on release. The plan must include provisions for such diverse activities as finding living accommodations and meeting financial obligations. If appropriate, the inmate must develop a plan for drug or alcohol treatment, education, vocational training, or restitution. The plan must include a series of realistic and relevant goals against which the feasibility of the applicant's admission is assessed by a three-judge resentencing panel.

Each applicant must obtain a community sponsor who will be responsible for the applicant's actions while in the community. The sponsor serves as an adjunct to and a resource for the probation officer. Specific activities can include:

- Providing transportation to work
- Checking on compliance with curfew or other restrictions
- Assisting with emergent problems with respect to housing and employment
- Maintaining contact with the probation officer

The offender is required to perform community service, usually physical labor, "which contributes to the goal of intermediate punishment in the program" (Pearson, 1988: 440). Probation supervision is "intensive": The PO is responsible for a minimum of five contacts per week per participant.

In the first six months of supervision, the frequency of contact per case averages 31 per month, including 12 face-to-face, 7 curfew (10 P.M. to 6 A.M.) checks, and 4 urinalyses. In addition,

a program requirement is that participants who fail to abide by the program rules will be immediately returned to prison. IPS officers go out in

New Jersey Conditions for Placement of Adults on Intensive Supervision

I have applied for, and been granted, an opportunity to be placed on intensive supervision by the Resentencing Panel for a period of _____

Based on the plan I submitted, the Resentencing Panel believes that I am capable of living a useful and law-abiding life in the community and has suspended my sentence with the condition that I comply with the provisions of the intensive supervision program. My being granted the opportunity of intensive supervision is subject to my compliance with the plan I submitted as part of my application along with the conditions listed below. If there is probable cause to believe that I have committed another offense or if I have been held to answer thereto, the Resentencing Panel will commit me to the institution to which I have been sentenced, without bail, to await trial on the new charges. I am required to notify promptly my ISP officer if I am arrested at any time during my sentence to the intensive supervision program.

1. I will obey the laws of the United States, and the laws and ordinances of any jurisdiction in which I may be.
2. I will report as directed by the court or my ISP officer.
3. I will permit the ISP officer to visit my home.
4. I will answer promptly, truthfully, and completely all inquiries made by my ISP officer and report any address or residence change to that officer. If the change of address or residence is outside the region in which I am under supervision, I will request approval of my ISP officer at least thirty days in advance of such change.
5. I will cooperate in any medical and/or psychological examination, tests and/or counselling my ISP officer recommends.
6. I will support my dependents, meet my family responsibilities, continue gainful employment, and/ or pursue such alternatives as may be part of the program and promptly notify my ISP officer prior to any change in my place of employment or if I find myself out of work.
7. I will participate in a counseling program as scheduled by my ISP officer.
8. I will not leave the state of New Jersey without permission of my ISP officer.
9. I will not have in my possession any firearm or other dangerous weapon.
10. I will perform community service in accordance with the ISP officer
11. I will partcipate in group activities scheduled by my ISP officer.
12. I will maintain a diary of my activities while under supervision.
13. I will maintain weekly contact with my community sponsor and network team.

I will comply with the following conditions of intensive supervision imposed in accordance with N.J.S.A. 2C:45-1 et. seq., as communciated to me by my ISP officer:

_____ I will pay a fine of $ _____ in strict accord with the terms described.
_____ I will make restitution of $ _____ in strict accord with the terms described.
_____ I will pursue the course of study or vocational training described.
_____ I will attend/reside in the facility described for the required period of time.
_____ I will refrain from frequenting the unlawful or disreputable places or consorting with the disreputable persons described.
_____ I am required to satisfy the following additional conditions as outlined in my plan:

_____

_____

_____

FIGURE 12.6 Conditions for Placement of Adults on Intensive supervision, New Jersey.

the field actively looking for violations. They conduct curfew checks; they test for drug use; they do not tolerate nonperformance of community service [16 hours per month] or nonpayment of fines, restitution, and so on, and in various ways run a tight program. (Pearson, 1988: 439)

SHOCK INCARCERATION/BOOT CAMP

In 1983, the states of Georgia and Oklahoma, in an effort to deal with their problems of prison overcrowding, devised *boot camp shock incarceration* (SI). In Georgia, there are community-based probation boot camps (Figure 12.7) that receive offenders directly from the sentencing court, as well as inmate boot camps whose candidates are selected by the Board of Pardons and Paroles. By the end of 1988, 11 states had initiated similar programs; except for New York and Michigan they are all in the South. By 1992, SI state-operated programs for adult offenders were availible in 25 states (MacKenzie and Souryal, 1994). The boot camp resembles its military counterpart—a spartan regimen of rigorous discipline and exercise. (It is of historical interest to note that the use of military discipline was standard in New York's Elmira Reformatory well into the 20th century—"reinventing the wheel" is symptomatic of American penology.)

BOOT CAMP FOR YOUNG OFFENDERS—HISTORICAL ANTECEDENT

As part of the institutional regime, they [inmates] *are advisedly ordered for supreme military test as to all-around steadiness, which embraces everything a soldier should do, or leave undone; everything from the strictest of undivided attention under command, to execution that exemplifies the highest order of muscular reaction to command, of which constantly improving stature is a component exaction.* [Col. Vincent M. Masten, Military Instructor, Elmira Reformatory, 1896–1924 (in Allen 1926: 378)]

The SI program requires short stays of imprisonment—three to six months—combined with shaved heads, marching, close order drills, exercise, and harassment by correction officer/drill instructors during 12-hour days. No television, radio, or telephone privileges are available. According to MacKenzie et al., 1995: 327, "Most are designed for young offenders convicted of nonviolent crimes who do not have a prior history of imprisonment." Doris MacKenzie and her colleagues point out that although "all boot camp prisons use military basic training as a model, they differ considerably in other aspects. For example, some programs select participants from a pool of prisoners sentenced to a

Hours	Activity
0500	Count
0530	Wake up
0530–0600	Building and quarters cleanup, standby inspection, outside-of-quarters cleanup, sick call, count
0600–0700	Physical training
0700–0800	Breakfast, quarters inspection, laundry turn-in, mail pick-up
0800	Work call
1130	Return to quarters, prepare for lunch
1200	Count
1215–1300	Lunch
1300–1640	Work call/program call
(1400–1500)	Commissary call (Friday only)
1640–1700	Return to quarters, police grounds, mail call, building and quarters cleanup
1700	Count
1715–1800	Dinner, police grounds
1820–2130	Program call, privileged telephone use, religious services, counseling, life skills groups, programs
2130–2200	Return to quarters
2200	Lights out
2400	Count

FIGURE 12.7   Typical weekday schedule of activities for a boot camp in Georgia.

traditional sentence of incarceration. Other programs receive inmates directly from the sentencing court" (1995: 328).

Women in Shock Incarceration

Rita finishes 50 sit-ups and springs to her feet. At 6 A.M. her platoon begins a 5-mile run, the last portion of the morning's physical training. After 5 months in New York's Lakeview Shock Incarceration Correctional Facility, the morning workout is easy. Rita even enjoys it, taking pride in her physical conditioning.

When Rita graduates and returns to New York City, she will face 6 months of intensive supervision before moving to regular parole. More than two-fifths of Rita's platoon did not make it this far; some withdrew voluntarily, and the rest were removed for misconduct or failure to participate satisfactorily. By completing shock incarceration, she will enter parole 11 months before her minimum release date.

The requirements for completing shock incarceration are the same for male and female inmates. The women live in a separate housing area of Lakeview. Otherwise, men and women participate in the same education, physical training, drill and ceremony, drug education, and counseling programs. Men and women are assigned to separate work details and attend Network group meetings held in inmates' living units.

Source: Clark, Aziz, and MacKenzie, 1994.

One program operates in the medium-security prison near Baton Rouge, Louisiana: At dawn there is reveille, and inmates quickly dress in fatigue uniforms, make tight beds, and one-hour later have formed into four platoons marching to breakfast in step and cadence (Spencer, 1987):

> *Warden, warden can't you see*
> *What this program's done for me.*
> *Sat me down in a barber chair*
> *Turned around and had no hair.*
> *Took away my faded jeans*
> *Now I'm wearing army greens*

They also spend a considerable portion of their day in counseling and treatment before release to intensive supervision (MacKenzie, Shaw, and Souryal, 1992). At a prison facility in Beaver Dams (in Schuyler County) New York: A bugle blares at precisely 5:30 A.M., and 32 inmates leap from their bunks:

"Good morning, Sir!" they scream to the scowling corrections officer/drill instructor.

"Are you motivated?" he barks.

"Motivated! Motivated! Motivated! Sir," the young inmates shout.

In a fury they are dressed, beds made tight, and roaring in unison they are out the door single file. The last man out, a drug dealer from the Bronx, grabs the platoon flag as he runs by (Martin, 1988: 15). This regimen lasts six months, and on successful completion the inmates are released to parole supervision. The program is limited to persons under 26 who have been convicted of nonviolent crimes and are serving their first prison sentence (Bohlen, 1989).

The New York program (Figure 12.8) was authorized by the legislature in 1987 as a way of easing overcrowding—it is the only way inmates (male and female) can be released before reaching their parole eligibility date. Successful SI graduates are typically released nine months before their eligibility date. By 1991, New York had the largest SI program in the country and estimated that for every 100 SI inmates released, the state saved $1.94 million that would other-

FIGURE 12.8   Daily schedule for offenders in New York Shock incarceration facilities.

A.M.	
5:30	Wake up and standing count
5:45–6:30	Calisthenics and drill
6:30–7:00	Run
7:00–8:00	Mandatory breakfast/cleanup
8:15	Standing count and company formation
8:30–11:55	Work/school schedules
P.M.	
12:00–12:30	Mandatory lunch and standing count
12:30–3:30	Afternoon work/school schedule
3:30–4:00	Shower
4:00–4:45	Network community meeting
4:45–5:45	Mandatory dinner, prepare for evening
6:00–9:00	School, group counseling, drug counseling, prerelease counseling, decision-making classes
8:00	Count while in programs
9:15–9:30	Squad bay, prepare for bed
9:30	Standing count, lights out

wise be expended for care and custody, plus capital costs associated with the need for greater institutional space. The daily per-inmate expense for SI, however, exceeds that of medium-security facilities or camps. The relatively high cost may be linked to the services provided at the New York SI camps—the state rejects the "boot camp" label because that term belies the therapeutic environment that the program strives to achieve.

To be eligible for SI, inmates must be nonviolent offenders between ages 16 and 29—most have been convicted for drug offenses. Although the sentencing judge cannot send a defendant to SI, for older offenders (26 to 29) he or she must approve of program participation and early release. SI inmates serve six months in the program and are then placed on special caseloads of no more than 38 parolees supervised by a team of two parole officers, and they receive enriched services from contracted agencies. Although the New York program is considered one of the best, it has a dropout rate of about 25 percent.

The idea behind shock incarceration "is to break the prisoners down, strip them of their street identity, and then systematically build them up by providing discipline and self-control" (Spencer, 1987: Sec. 3: 1). Offenders must be young, usually 17 to 25 years old, and in good health; they must volunteer for the program—dropouts return to complete their sentences of imprisonment, and many drop out (Parent, 1988). New York SI uses a recycling program for inmates removed for disciplinary reasons and for those who are in danger of being removed for unsatisfactory adjustment. It consists of being sent back for refresher training during which behavior is closely monitored. Success in recycling leads to being integrated into an existing platoon that will graduate at a date closest to the time owed by the inmate. Inmates who do not perform well after two weeks in recycling are removed from the program and returned to prison.

New York, which runs the nation's largest shock incarceration program, has a focus on treatment that is absent from most boot camp programs.[1] More than 40 percent of inmate time is spent on treatment and education: 12 hours of academic education, drug and alcohol treatment, prerelease counseling, and decision-making classes (Clark, Aziz, and MacKenzie 1994; Seventh Annual Shock Legislative Report, 1995).

BOOT CAMP, ILLINOIS STYLE

In Greene County, the Illinois Department of Corrections operates a 200-bed facility where inmates rise at 5:30 A.M. and retire at 9:30 P.M. During that time they perform six hours of manual labor, two 1.5-mile jogs, and end the day with about two hours of basic education and drug treatment. The shaven-

---

[1]A national study of shock incarceration programs revealed that although many of the inmates have drug histories, few programs provide meaningful drug abuse treatment (Cowles, Castellano, and Gransky, 1995).

headed inmates move double-time everywhere, while correction officers shout orders and refer to them as "knotheads," "vermin," and "maggots." They are constantly quizzed on the camp's general rules that include always asking for permission to speak; not "gaping" at visitors; and taking one step back, turning, and waiting for permission to leave after receiving an order. The boot camp term lasts four months.

Source: Marx (1994).

DISCUSSION

Critics of the "shock" approach argue that it has not proven to have any salutary effect on the offender, and (even) short-term imprisonment exposes the offender to the destructive effects of institutionalization, disrupts his or her life in the community, and further stigmatizes the offender for having been imprisoned (National Advisory Commission on Criminal Justice Standards and Goals, 1975). Furthermore, the SI inmate is released without having received any additional education or having developed any additional employment skills, although some observers report more treatment being incorporated into boot camp programs (Gransky, Castellano, and Cowles, 1993). No doubt exists that these programs do release strong, healthy, unemployed young men into the community after only a brief term of incarceration. However, in an Oklahoma study, SI graduates returned to prison at a higher rate than did other inmates; in Alabama, boot camp residents, who were first-time, nonviolent offenders, had a recidivism rate slightly worse than that of a comparative group of regular inmates (Burns and Vito, 1995). A Georgia study found no difference in return rates between SI and regular inmates (Parent, 1989a).

In Louisiana, Doris MacKenzie, James W. Shaw, and Claire Souryal (1992) found no evidence that shock incarceration reduces recidivism. They report no significant differences in recidivism between SI inmates and either parolees from traditional prisons or probationers: All had recidivism rates of approximately 30 percent during their first year of community supervision. A New York in-house research effort revealed that 23 percent of shock parolees were returned to prison within one year of their release compared with 28 percent of a comparison group (New York State Office of Policy Analysis and Information, 1989). In a later effort (1992), SI graduates in New York were compared with parolees who matched the SI criteria but who were committed to prison before the establishment of the program (pre-SI); as well as to parolees who had been removed from the program (removals); and, finally, to a group who met the SI criteria but did not enter the program (considered). SI graduates were more likely than the comparison groups to be drug offenders with longer maximum sentences. (Those with shorter sentences were less likely to volunteer for SI and more likely to drop out.) After all subjects were out at least one year, the following rates of return to prison for violations were recorded:

	Total	Percentage Violation	Percentage Technical-Criminal
SI	1641	7	7
Pre-SI	1418	11	8
Removals	1662	11	9
Considered	366	11	11

After 24 months, SI parolees continued to have lower rates of return to prison for technical and new arrest violations than those of any of the comparison groups (although many of the comparison group members had already been discharged from parole supervision). The New York researchers conclude that SI parolees are more likely to be successful than are comparison group parolees after the completion of 12, 18, and 24 months' time, despite having spent considerably less time in a state prison. A subsequent in-house study (Seventh Annual Shock Legislative Report, 1995) revealed that shock parolees are generally more likely, or just as likely, to be successful than a similar comparison group. Shock incarceration was found particularly effective for young drug offenders.

The boot camp programs are in place to save prison resources; an offender sent to a shock program avoids long-term incarceration. This point assumes that in the absence of such programming, the offender would have been sent to prison and not placed on probation. In Florida, for example, candidates for SI are selected from among those sentenced to traditional imprisonment, although one study found that they tended to be those who were less serious offenders (Sechcrest, 1989). In Georgia, however, SI is used by judges as part of probation sentences. In Alabama, boot camp is part of the discretionary sentencing power of a judge and is sometimes the result of a plea bargain agreement (Burns, 1993). In Arizona, which established its program in 1988, research found that only some of the inmates in boot camp were diverted from prison—"the rest would have been placed on regular probation or intensive probation" (Palumbo and Peterson, 1994: 8).

Although SI might not meet the needs of rehabilitation and community safety, it appears to meet the short-term needs of political officials who can boast of "doing something" about crime and criminals. Dale Parent found that SI was given to "the very offenders who would likely have been given nonconfinement sentences if SI were not available—thus using more, not less, prison space"—referred to as "net widening" (1989: 12). This is not the case in New York, where Department of Corrections (DOC) personnel, not judges, have charge of the program:

New York law defines SI eligibility criteria. The New York DOC screens prison admissions to identify cases that meet these criteria. If inmates pass their physical examinations, they may volunteer to participate. Judges have no veto power. When inmates complete the program, they are released by the parole board, not by judges. By consulting New York's parole guidelines, the DOC estimates that the average inmate who completes SI will shorten his or her prison term by 12 to 18 months. (Parent, 1989a: 15)

An element of absurdity exists in the prison–as–boot camp approach, particularly in light of the fact that the military has drastically changed the way it trains recruits, away from abusive or degrading methods: "While the military has reduced the harshness of its training, boot-camp prisons have embraced an outdated version of military basic training" (Jacoby et al., 1994: 32). "The very idea of using physically and verbally aggressive tactics in an effort to 'train' people to act in a prosocial manner is fraught with contradiction" (Morash and Rucker, 1990: 214). Such programs run the risk of turning out young men who are more aggressive and hostile than they would have been under routine imprisonment: "The irony in emphasizing an aggressive model of masculinity in a correctional setting is that these very characteristics may explain criminality" (1990: 216). A cynic might argue that the boot camp approach is simply a scam for gaining public acquiescence to the (otherwise politically unacceptable) early discharge of inmates. Feeley and Simon (1992: 464) posit a grim possibility—that "the effect of boot camp is that it will be effective for those who will subsequently put their lessons of discipline and organization to use in street gangs and drug distribution networks." Rudolf Mathias and James Mathews (1991: 322) note that after boot camp military personnel "enter a structured, stable environment which provides for the basic needs, food, shelter, clothing, employment and health care," very different from the environment to which most shock incarceration subjects return. MacKenzie (1994: 65) concludes: "If the core components of boot camps (military atmosphere, drill, hard labor, physical training) reduced recidivism, we would have expected that the boot camp releasees in all states would do better than the offenders in the comparison groups. This did not happen; therefore, the military atmosphere does not appear to reduce recidivism." The military atmosphere, she notes, also did not increase recidivism among boot camp graduates; also, intensive supervision—as measured by increased contacts—was associated with better adjustment for both boot camp and comparison groups, suggesting that offenders could be coerced to participate in positive activities while they are in the community without the need for boot camp (Cronin with Han, 1994; MacKenzie and Souryal, 1994). In 1994, Connecticut closed the nation's first boot camp for juveniles run by the National Guard, after an investigation revealed gang activity, drug use, and violence (K. Johnson, 1994).

Now that this chapter has examined intermediate punishments, we will review research and issues related to the effectiveness of probation and parole.

REVIEW QUESTIONS

1. What is the purpose of an intensive supervision program in p/p?
2. What has research into intensive supervision revealed?
3. What led to the use of EM in p/p?

4. How is EM accomplished?
5. What are the advantages of shock p/p?
6. What are the shortcomings of shock p/p?
7. What are the advantages of SI?
8. What are the shortcomings of SI/boot camp?
9. What has research into the effectiveness of SI found?

In Conclusion . . .

This concluding chapter examines the question of "success" and the interrelated issue of recidivism. The following sections explore the direction probation and parole appear to be headed in the 21st century.

Probation and Parole: Success or Failure?

In examining the degree to which probation and parole are "successful," the results are often contradictory. The methodology of some research efforts is simply unsound; however, even methodologically sound research has not allowed us to answer the question: *probation and parole: success or failure?* For example, Mark Jay Lerner (1977) found that parole supervision in New York reduced the postrelease criminal activity of a group of (conditional) releasees compared to a group of dischargees released from the same institution without supervision. A similar study by Howard Sachs and Charles Logan (1979) found that in Connecticut parole supervision resulted in only a modest reduction in recidivism. In California, however, Deborah Star (1979) and Patrick Jackson (1983) found no significant difference in the recidivism rates of persons released with or without parole supervision.

Michael Geerken and Hennessey Hayes (1993) found that 8 percent of adult arrests in New Orleans from 1974 to 1986 for burglary or armed robbery involved offenders who were on probation; the figure for parolees was less than 2 percent. A study in New York of 22,941 conditional releasees (15 percent) and parolees (85 percent) released in 1991 and tracked for two years found that fewer than 13 percent were returned to prison for new felony convictions (New York State Division of Parole, 1994).

A major part of the problem is the word "success." For example, Mark Wiederanders (1983: 4), a researcher for the California Youth Authority, candidly portrays his own findings:

> Depending on which statistics one decides to use, parole behavior in the sample of wards can be made to look quite good, especially considering the high levels of pre–Youth Authority crime, or quite bad. For example, only 13 percent were sent to state prison for parole-period offenses during the 24 months of followup, resulting in an 87 percent "success rate" by this criterion. Some correctional jurisdictions who report spectacularly high success rates, in fact use such a restricted measure. Alternatively, regarding the same sample we could accurately report that 77 percent of the sample had been arrested or temporarily detained during the 24 months leaving a "success rate" by this criterion of only 23 percent.

The effectiveness of a probation or parole system is usually conceived of in terms of *recidivism* (Maltz, 1984: 54):

> When recidivism is discussed in a correctional context, its meaning seems fairly clear. The word is derived from the Latin *recidere*, to fall back. A recidivist is one who, after release from custody for having committed a crime, is not rehabilitated. Instead, he or she falls back, relapses, into former behavior patterns and commits more crimes. This conceptual definition of recidivism may seem quite straightforward; however, an operational definition, one that permits measurement, is not so simple.

The 1976 edition of the *Dictionary of Criminal Justice Data Terminology* defines recidivism as "the repetition of criminal behavior; habitual criminality." However, the 1981 edition avoids providing a definition and, instead, notes:

> Efforts to arrive at a single standard statistical definition of recidivism have been hampered by the fact that the correct referent of the term is the actual repeated criminal or delinquent behavior of a given person or group, yet the only available statistical indicators of that behavior are records of such system events as rearrests, reconvictions, and probation or parole violations or revocations. It is recognized that these data reflect agency decisions about events and do not closely correspond with actual criminal behavior.

Jay Albanese and his colleagues (1981: 51) point out:

- A wide disparity exists in the definition of revocation and recidivism.
- Revocation/recidivism rates without a standardized definition have little comparative value.
- A criterion (or criteria) of "effectiveness" is not well defined.

Gordon Waldo and David Griswold (1979: 230) note that being arrested and convicted for any crime is not sufficient as an operational definition of recidivism. They quote Charles Tittle: "Being arrested for gambling cannot be accepted as evidence of recidivism for a burglar." In addition, the extensive use of plea bargaining means that merely looking at the crime for which a person is convicted does not allow for a determination of whether the person has committed the same crime again, or a less serious or more serious crime. Then there is the problem of technical violations—do we rate them as "recidivism"? No consistent definition of recidivism exists, and "one cannot state with any degree of assurance whether a given recidivism rate is high or low; there is no 'normal' recidivism rate as there is a normal body temperature" (Maltz, 1984: 23).

FELONY PROBATION

Joan Petersilia and her colleagues (1985: v), researchers for the Rand Corporation, note that "over one-third of California's probation population consists of felons convicted in Superior Court—persons who are often quite different from the less serious offenders probation was originally conceived and structured to handle." They found that 51 percent of a sample of California felony probationers who were sentenced in 1980 and tracked for 40 months were reconvicted, 18 percent for violent crime. They conclude (1985: vi) that "felons granted probation present a serious threat to public safety" and this threat is not being adequately managed by probation agencies in California and probably elsewhere. (In Massachusetts, for example, the number of persons sentenced to probation for crimes against persons increased between 1982 and 1993 by more than 250 percent.)

Research into felony probation in Missouri and Kentucky revealed a different outcome. Both studies were designed to replicate that of Petersilia and her colleagues in California, to determine whether felony offenders placed on probation in Missouri and Kentucky presented risks similar to those in California; significant differences were found (McGaha, Fichter, and Hirschburg, 1987):

	CALIFORNIA (%)	MISSOURI (%)	KENTUCKY (%)
Rearrests	65.0	22.3	22.1
Reconvictions	51.0	12.0	17.7
Violent felony	18.0	7.1	4.1

The results of research into felony probation in New Jersey fell about midway between the findings in California and those in Kentucky and Missouri: four years after they were sentenced to probation, 40 percent had been rearrested, and 35 percent were reconvicted (Whitehead, 1989).

Petersilia et al. (1985: 64) argue that "routine probation, by definition, is *inappropriate for most felons.*" What, other than imprisonment, *is appropriate* for most felons?

We believe that the criminal justice system needs an alternative, indeterminate form of punishment for those offenders who are too antisocial for the relative freedom that probation now offers, but not so seriously criminal as to require imprisonment. A sanction is needed that would impose intensive surveillance, coupled with substantial community service and restitution. It should be structured to satisfy public demands that the punishment fit the crime, to show criminals that crime really does not pay, and to control potential recidivists. (1985: ix)

The Rand Corporation researchers (Petersilia et al., 1985: xiii) recommend a different form of probation supervision:

In response to changes in the probation population, the system should redefine the role and powers of probation officers. Probation officers cannot deal with felony probationers in the same ways they have dealt with misdemeanants. We certainly do not recommend that they abandon their counseling or rehabilitative roles; however, because the probation population includes a large number of active criminals, we support the growing legal and policy trend toward quasi-policing roles for probation officers, whenever the situation warrants it. Attention should be paid to the recruitment and training of probation officers. Different skills may be required of officers whose primary responsibility is surveillance rather than rehabilitation.

GOALS OF PROBATION AND PAROLE

What are the goals of probation and parole? Success can only be measured against anticipated outcome. If a p/p agency is based on a *service model*, success is measured by the delivery of, or by referral to, services, such as education, training, employment, and counseling, and client-consumer satisfaction with the level of service. This type of agency will often be affected by variables beyond its control, for example, variations in the unemployment rate particularly for low-skilled workers. A jurisdiction with a relatively low unemployment rate will presumably do better at job placement than the same agency in a jurisdiction that has a relatively high rate of unemployment. Similarly, an agency located in a community with a variety of available social services will be more likely to show a greater level of success than will one in a community with a paucity of such agencies. The interrelated problems of poverty and the collapse of inner-city families complicate matters: In 1992, 35.7 million Americans were living in poverty—the highest number in more than a quarter century, with more than 10 percent of the nation's children living in households not headed by a parent (Gross, 1992; Pear, 1992). These are important problems with which p/p agencies have to contend but are helpless to affect.

If a p/p agency is based on a *control model*, success is measured according to the agency's ability to hold the offender accountable for his or her behavior—which could increase recidivism rates—or to limit recidivism. However, recidivism may also be related to unemployment—and to the extent that it is, the success of this type of agency will depend in part on the state of the economy. Recidivism is also related to other practical issues. First, one cannot account for undetected criminality; second, arrest and prosecution are often a measure of the law enforcement activity in a given community. Thus, different levels of law enforcement will produce different levels of official (statistical) recidivism, regardless of p/p agency effectiveness. Indeed, a more effective *control model* agency may enhance the law enforcement function (e.g., through close cooperation with the police) and will thus help to *produce* more recidivism—arrests and convictions of agency clientele. David Stanley points out that if we use recidivism as a measure, "An offender can be unemployed, ignorant, promiscuous, and drunk but still a success as far as the criminal justice system is concerned if he commits no crime" (1976: 173). Indeed, a cynic (realist?) might suggest encouraging drug abusers to become alcoholics instead.

Two related issues need to be considered. How are technical violations of p/p rules to be treated (statistically) with respect to agency goals? More vigorous (i.e., intensive) supervision may *produce* more technical violations (although the research is still not clear on this issue), whereas an agency that provides little or no supervision will have few (detected) technical violations—hence, fewer revocations of p/p. The level of individual and agency tolerance for technical violations will also affect the revocation rate, and a higher revocation rate of technical violations may result in a lower number of convictions—higher-risk offenders screened out of supervision before they can be arrested for new crimes. A second issue concerns the screening of agency clients by judges and parole boards. A conservative judge/parole board, or perhaps one fearful of an adverse public reaction, will release fewer offenders to probation or parole. Those who are placed on probation or parole will tend to be the "boy scouts"— lower-risk offenders who will probably *produce* impressive (statistical) measurements of success for the agency. The reverse of this situation is also true.

For example, research has identified a number of variables that correlate well with success or failure on probation: age (younger offenders have greater difficulty adhering to probation conditions); employment (those who are employed and financially stable do better); marital status (those who are married are less likely to violate probation); and offense (those on probation for theft-related crimes have higher recidivism rates) (Liberton, Silverman, and Blount, 1990).

We promised far too much, and created unrealistic expectations among politicians and public. [Barry J. Nidorf, Chief Probation Officer, Los Angeles County.]

Because neither the *social service* nor the *control model* agency need make any claim about rehabilitation, the question of postsupervision arrests and convictions need not be raised. In agencies that include rehabilitation as a (or perhaps *the*) goal, this issue needs to be considered. How long does the agency retain (statistical) responsibility for success or failure of a client who has completed supervision—six months, a year, or life? The implication is that such an agency will succeed in producing a lasting change in client behavior. An added question is how to weigh recidivism when the instant offense is a great deal less serious than the original crime: For example, is an armed robber convicted of shoplifting considered a success or failure?

Perhaps the most difficult agency to evaluate in terms success or failure is one based on a *combined model.* Most p/p agencies in the United States fall into this category. In this type of agency, an explicit or implicit claim is usually related to service, rehabilitation, *and* control. An agency with such broad purposes—a plethora of complicated goals—cannot *fail,* nor can it *succeed*—it presents no clear-cut basis for measuring anticipated outcome. The claims are too broad, too many, and too dependent on variables beyond agency control (such as the economy, level of law enforcement in the community, screening of offenders by judges/parole boards, availability of resources in the community, and so on) for a research effort to analyze in any relevant manner. As a result, this type of agency has been subjected to criticism on the basis of research that "microscopes" one goal and finds it wanting. The goals are literally picked apart, leaving the agency vulnerable to those who would discredit probation or parole.

Joan Petersilia (1993: 69) argues that p/p agencies need to "customize their mission statement, methods, and performance indicators so that they reflect local resources and priorities." The mission should be one that can reasonably be expected to be fulfilled, clearly related to the unique services provided by the agency, and performance indicators should be specified. "When public agencies fail to define their mission internally, political influences are more apt to define it for them. And when they fail to articulate how they should be evaluated, outcome measurements such as recidivism rates will likely be imposed upon them" (1993: 76).

One should consider the very reason that p/p exist. As penological history in the United States indicates, p/p (devoid of the humanistic dynamic) exist for *economic reasons.* If p/p were as costly (in terms of budgetary considerations) as, or even equal in cost to, imprisonment, it would be so severely restricted as no longer to constitute an important issue in criminal justice. The following discussion examines the various options available.

Most serious crimes do not result in an arrest. Of those arrested for felonies, well in excess of 50 percent are not prosecuted for felony crimes. Most of those prosecuted for felonies plead guilty, usually the result of negotiations—plea bargaining. Thus, when discussing issues of punishment, *residuals* are involved—but these are sufficiently large so that common sense indicates that they all cannot be incarcerated. Even if that were a proper response, enough prison space could not be created expeditiously, nor would taxpayers be willing to pay the required taxes. We have already reached the 1 million mark with respect to the inmate population. What are the remaining options?

Probation offers the first line of defense against prison overcrowding. If no parole system is in operation, probation becomes *the* method by which prison populations are controlled. As a result, serious felony offenders, for whom probation has historically not been intended, become probation clients. At the other end, mandatory prison releasees typically receive inadequate, if any, supervision, because little incentive exists for politicians to expend tax dollars on programs for nondiscretionary-released offenders—absence of a public official on whom to lay blame. In any event, relatively few offenders will remain in prison their entire lives. Who will make the release decision: judges, prison officials, or parole boards? Will these decisions involve a careful analysis of the case, comparing it to similar cases—issues of equity—and reasonable predictions of future behavior, or risk control?

The Alabama Board of Pardons and Paroles believes that its primary business is community protection. With or without parole, approximately 95 percent of incarcerated offenders will walk the streets again. The real question then is not whether offenders should be released, but rather when should offenders be released and what are the best circumstances for their release?

WHERE HAVE WE BEEN, WHERE ARE WE NOW, AND WHERE ARE WE GOING?

When the first edition of this book was published in 1977, the indeterminate sentence and parole were under great scrutiny and pressure, the result of Robert Martinson's "What Works?" (1974) and publication of the full study (Lipton, Martinson, and Wilks, 1975) the following year. In the years that followed, about a dozen states adopted determinate sentencing and abolished parole release. Although failing to accomplish equal punishment for crimes of equal severity, as per classicalism, determinate sentencing removed one vehicle for responding to prison overcrowding. Policy makers and public officials failed to learn the lessons of penal history: The establishment of parole with the onset of the Great Depression was a means of alleviating prison overcrowding—rehabilitation was not a motivating factor.

The rightward movement of politics in the United States swept the criminal justice system into overdrive; "law and order" rhetoric beget a policy that led to more arrests and more convictions, particularly for drug offenses. This policy was the driving force behind corrections overload—prison populations reached record levels and the courts began to intervene. Overcrowding and court intervention led to forced releases and some states passed "one-in/one-out" legislation. This law proved insufficient; as pressure built, criminal justice systems increased their use of probation, particularly in those states without parole release. Offenders who would otherwise have been incarcerated, serious felons who were not candidates for traditional probation, burdened ill-equipped probation agencies.

A hurried scramble for ways to deal with opposing pressures—arrest and incarcerate/decrease prison populations—ensued. New terminology resulted: *Corrections* was displaced by the buzzwords of a new era—*intermediate sanctions*. Under this rubric were regurgitated models from the late 19th century—boot camps—the old Elmira System reinvented for the 1990s; the California Special Intensive Parole Unit of the early 1950s was reinvented as IPS, intensive p/p supervision; fondness for technology led penology to adopt electronic surveillance. New "What Works?" research was critical of these schemes because they failed to control recidivism while having little impact on the central problem of prison overcrowding. Prison overcrowding continues to increase with the enactment of more "get tough" legislation. For example, Arizona, in 1994, when the state ranked sixth in rates of incarceration, enacted a "Truth-in-Sentencing" law eliminating parole and reducing good time to no more than 15 percent of the sentence. "Three strikes and you're out" became a popular metaphor—life without parole on the third felony conviction. As a crime policy, it raises important questions, not the least of which is cost: prisons may turn into high-security (and thus expensive) nursing homes for elderly offenders. California went on a prison-building binge, and for the first time in its history, the state is spending more money on prisons than on universities; other states are following California's lead (Butterfield, 1995).

Traditional probation and parole still bear the major burden, and some states that had gone over to determinate sentencing, such as Connecticut, grew tired of the constant need for new schemes, and reintroduced parole release. At the same time, the law enforcement role and training of p/p officers increased dramatically as the control model became predominant.

The relevant question remains: Do we entrust the role of reducing prison populations and the risk management of criminal offenders to judges, prison officials, or parole boards? A review of the history that led to the establishment of parole in the first instance argues for this discretion to be the responsibility of a professional parole board.

Review Questions

1. Why is it difficult to provide a definition of recidivism for statistical purposes?
2. What are the variables over which a p/p agency has no control and that can affect case outcome?
3. What were the findings of the "felony probation" research in California?
4. Why is it so difficult to determine whether p/p are a success or failure?

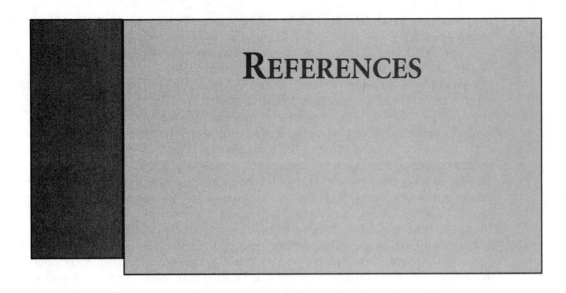

REFERENCES

Note: Much of the material in this book has been derived from agency sources—see the acknowledgments in the front matter.

Abadinsky, Howard

    1976   "The Status Offense Dilemma: Coercion and Treatment." *Crime and Delinquency* 22 (October): 456–60.

    1993   *Drug Abuse: An Introduction*, 2nd ed. Chicago: Nelson-Hall.

    1994   *Organized Crime*, 4th ed. Chicago: Nelson-Hall.

    1995   *Law and Justice*, 3rd ed. Chicago: Nelson-Hall.

Adair, David N., and Toby D. Slawsky

    1991   "Looking at the Law: Fact-Finding in Sentencing." *Federal Probation* 55 (December): 58–72.

Agnew, Robert

    1992   "Foundation for a General Strain Theory of Crime and Delinquency." *Criminology* 30 (February): 47–87.

Agopian, Michael W.

    1990   "The Impact of Intensive Supervision Probation on Gang-Drug Offenders." *Criminal Justice Policy* 4 (3): 214–22.

Aichhorn, August

    1963   *Wayward Youth*. New York: Viking Press.

Albanese, Jay S., Bernadette A. Fiore, Jerie H. Powell, and Janet R. Storti
  1981   *Is Probation Working?* Washington, DC: University Press of America.

Alexander, Franz, and Hugo Staub
  1956   *The Criminal, the Judge, and the Public.* Glencoe, IL: Free Press.

Allen, Fred C., ed.
  1926   *Extracts from Penological Reports and Lectures Written by Members of the Managment and Staff of the New York State Reformatory, Elmira, N.Y.* Elmira, NY: Summary Press.

Allen, Harry, Eric Carlson, and Evalyn Parks
  1979   *Critical Issues in Probation.* Washington, DC: U.S. Government Printing Office.

Altman, Lawrence K.
  1995   "Inquiry Finds Man with TB Infected 45 at Bar in 1992." *New York Times* (July 27): 9.

American Bar Association
  1970   *Standards Relating to Probation.* Chicago: American Bar Association.

American Correctional Association (ACA)
  1981   *Standards for Adult Probation and Parole Field Services.* Rockville, MD: ACA.

American Friends Service Committee
  1971   *Struggle for Justice.* New York: Hill and Wang.

American Justice Institute
  1981   *Presentence Investigation Report Program.* Sacramento, CA: American Justice Institute.

American Probation and Parole Association
  1995   *Abolishing Parole: Why the Emporor Has No Clothes.* Lexington, KY: American Probation and Parole Association.

American Psychiatric Association
  1974   *Behavior Therapy in Psychiatry.* New York: Jason Aronson.

American Response to Crime
  1983   Washington, DC: U.S. Government Printing Office.

Anderson, Elijah
  1994   "The Code of the Streets." *Atlantic Monthly* (May): 81–94.

Andrews, D.A., Ivan Zinger, Robert D. Hoge, James Bonta, Paul Gendreau, and Francis T. Cullen
  1990   "Does Correctional Treatment Work? Clinically Relevant and Psychologically Informed Meta-Analysis." *Criminology* 28 (August): 369–404.

Annual Report of the San Francisco Adult Probation Department
  1991   San Francisco, CA.

Anonymous
  1974   *Overview Study of Employment of Paraprofessionals.* Washington, DC: U.S. Government Printing Office.

1985a   "Role of the Probation Pre-sentence Investigation." *Perspectives* 9 (spring).

1985b   "Tennessee Inmates Riot over Uniforms." *New York Times* (July 3): 11.

1985c   "Washington Talk." *New York Times* (August 15): 12.

1987   "B. F. Skinner Insists It's Just Matter over Mind." *New York Times* (September 13): E6.

1989   "Drug Offenders Push Population Estimates Higher." *Illinois Department of Corrections Perspectives* 12 (August): 5.

Anspach, Donald F., and S. Henry Monsen

1989   "Indeterminate Sentencing, Formal Rationality, and Khadi Justice in Maine: An Application of Weber's Typology." *Journal of Criminal Justice* 17: 471–85.

Appignanesi, Lisa, and John Forrester

1993   *Freud's Women.* New York: Basic Books.

Arcaya, Jose

1973   "The Multiple Realities Inherent in Probation Counseling." *Federal Probation* 37 (December).

Ashford, José B., and Craig Winston LeCroy

1988   "Predicting Recidivism: An Evaluation of the Wisconsin Juvenile Probation and Aftercare Risk Instrument." *Criminal Justice and Behavior* 15 (June): 141–49.

Associated Press

1995   "Sweep of State Prison for Drugs Termed Largest Such Raid Ever." *New York Times* (October 24): 12.

Atherton, Alexine L.

1987   "Journal Retrospective, 1845–1986: 200 Years of Prison Society History as Reflected in the *Prison Journal*." *Prison Journal* (spring-summer): 1–37.

Attica Commission. *See* New York State Special Commission on Attica.

Auerbach, Barbara J., George E. Sexton, Franklin C. Farrow, and Robert H. Lawson

1988   *Work in American Prisons: The Private Sector Gets Involved.* Washington, DC: U.S. Government Printing Office.

Augustus, John

1972   *John Augustus, First Probation Officer.* Montclair, NJ: Patterson Smith.

Baird, S. Christopher, and Dennis Wagner

1990   "Measuring Diversion: The Florida Community Control Program." *Crime and Delinquency* 36 (January): 112–25.

Baird, S. Christopher, Richard C. Heinz, and Brian J. Bemus

1982   "The Wisconsin Case Classification/Staff Development Project: A Two-Year Follow-Up Report," in *Classification: American Correctional Association Monographs.* College Park, MD: American Correctional Association.

Bales, William D., and Linda G. Dees

1992   "Mandatory Minimum Sentences in Florida: Past Trends and Future Implications." *Crime and Delinquency* 38 (July): 309–29.

Ball, Richard A., C. Ronald Huff, and J. Robert Lilly

    1988   *House Arrest and Correctional Policy: Doing Time at Home.* Beverly Hills, CA: Sage.

Bandura, Albert

    1974   "Behavior Theory and the Models of Man." *American Psychologist* 29 (December): 859–69.

Barnes, Carole Wolff, and Randal S. Franz

    1989   "Questionably Adult: Determinants and Effects of the Juvenile Waiver Decision." *Justice Quarterly* 6 (March): 117–35.

Bazemore, Gordon

    1994   "Developing a Victim Orientation for Community Corrections: A Restorative Justice Paradigm and a Balanced Mission." *Perspectives* (special issue): 19–24.

Bazemore, Gordon, and Dennis Maloney

    1994   "Rehabilitating Community Service: Toward Restorative Service Sanctions in a Balanced Justice System." *Federal Probation* 58 (March): 24–35.

Bazemore, Gordon, and Mark S. Umbreit

    1994   *Balanced and Restorative Justice: Program Summary.* Washington, DC: Office of Juvenile Justice and Delinquency Prevention.

    1995   "Rethinking the Sanctioning Function in Juvenile Court: Retributive or Restorative Responses to Youth Crime." *Crime and Delinquency* 41 (July): 296–316.

Beaumont, Gustave de, and Alexis de Tocqueville

    1964   *On the Penitentiary System in the United States and Its Application in France.* Carbondale, IL: Southern Illinois University Press. (Originally published in 1833.)

Becker, Gary S.

    1968   *The Economic Approach to Human Behavior.* Chicago: University of Chicago Press.

Benekos, Peter J.

    1992   "Public Policy and Sentencing Reform: The Politics of Corrections." *Federal Probation* 56 (March): 4–10.

Bennett, Lawrence A.

    1988   "Practice in Search of a Theory: The Case of Intensive Supervision—An Extension of an Old Practice." *American Journal of Criminal Justice* 12: 293–310.

Berk, Richard A., Kenneth J. Lenihan, and Peter Rossi

    1980   "Crime and Poverty: Some Experimental Evidence from Ex-offenders." *American Sociological Review* 45 (October).

Bersani, Carl A.

    1989   "Reality Therapy: Issues and a Review of Research." In *Correctional Counseling and Treatment*, edited by Peter C. Kratcoski, 2: 177–95. Prospect Heights, IL: Waveland Press.

Binder, Arnold, and Gilbert Geis

    1983   *Methods of Research in Criminology and Criminal Justice.* New York: McGraw-Hill.

Bishop, Donna M., Charles F. Frazier, and John C. Henretta

    1989   "Prosecutorial Waiver: Case Study of a Questionable Reform." *Crime and Delinquency* 35 (April): 179–201.

Blumberg, Abraham

    1970   *Criminal Justice.* Chicago: Quadrangle Books.

Blumenstein, Alfred

    1984   "Sentencing Reforms: Impacts and Implications." *Judicature* 68 (October–November).

Bodapati, Madhava R., James W. Marquart, and Steven J. Cuvelier

    1993   "Influence of Race and Gender in Parole Decision Making in Texas: 1980–1991." Paper presented at the annual meeting of the Academy of Criminal Justice Sciences, Kansas City, MO, March 16–20.

Bohlen, Celestine

    1989   "Expansion Sought for 'Shock' Prison." *New York Times* (June 8): 14.

Bootzin, Richard R.

    1975   *Behavior Modification and Therapy: An Introduction.* Cambridge, MA: Winthrop.

Boswell, John

    1989   *The Kindness of Strangers: The Abandonment of Children in Western Europe from Antiquity to the Renaissance.* New York: Pantheon.

Bowers, Swithun

    1950   "The Nature and Definition of Social Casework." In *Principles and Techniques in Social Casework: Selected Articles, 1940–1950,* edited by Cora Kasius, 97–127. New York: Family Service Association of America.

Bowker, Arthur L., and Robert E. Schweid

    1992   "Habilitation of the Retarded Offender in Cuyahoga County." *Federal Probation* 56 (December): 48–52.

Bradsher, Keith

    1995a   "Gap in Wealth in U.S. Called Widest in West." *New York Times* (April 17): 1, C4.

    1995b   "Low Ranking for Poor American Children." *New York Times* (August 14): 7.

    1995c   "Widest Gap in Incomes? Research Points to U.S." *New York Times* (October 27): C2.

Brennan, Thomas P., Amy E. Gedrich, Susan E. Jacoby, Michael J. Tardy, and Katherine B. Tyson

    1986   "Forensic Social Work: Practice and Vision." *Social Casework* 67: 340–50.

Brockway, Z. R.

    1926   "Character of Reformatory Prisoners." In *Extracts from Penological Reports and Lectures Written by Members of the Management and Staff of the New York State Reformatory, Elmira, N.Y.,* edited by Fred C. Allen, 110–18. Elmira, NY: Summary Press.

Brown, Allan G.

    1986   *Group Work*, 2nd ed. Brookfield, VT: Gower.

Brown, Marjorie

    1984   *Executive Summary of Research Findings from the Massachusetts Risk/Need Classification System, Report 5*. Boston: Office of the Commissioner of Probation.

Brown, Waln K., Timothy Miller, Richard L. Jenkins, and Warren A. Rhodes

    1991   "The Human Costs of 'Giving the Kid Another Chance.'" *International Journal of Offender Therapy and Comparative Criminology* 35: 296–302.

Buck, Gerald S.

    1989   "Effectiveness of the New Intensive Supervision Programs." *Research in Corrections* 2 (September): 64–75.

Bureau of Justice Statistics

    1995   *Prisoners in 1994*. Washington, DC: U.S. Department of Justice.

Burgess, Robert L., and Ronald L. Akers

    1969   "Differential Association-Reinforcement Theory of Criminal Behavior." In *Behavioral Sociology*, edited by Robert L. Burgess and Don Bushell, Jr., 291–320. New York: Columbia University Press.

Burke, Peggy B.

    1988   *Current Issues in Parole Decisionmaking: Understanding the Past; Shaping the Future*. Washington, DC: National Institute of Corrections.

Burns, Jerald C.

    1993   "Rediscovering That Rehabilitation Works: The Alabama Boot Camp Experience." Paper presented at the Annual Meeting of the Academy of Criminal Justice Sciences, Kansas City, MO, March 16–20.

Burns, Jerald C., and Gennaro F. Vito

    1995   "An Impact Analysis of the Alabama Boot Camp Program." *Federal Probation* 59 (March): 63–67.

Butterfield, Fox

    1995a   "Prison-Building Binge in California Casts Shadow on Higher Education." *New York Times* (April 12): 11.

    1995b   "Private Tennessee Prison Is Praised in State Studies." *New York Times* (August 19): 6.

Byrne, James M.

    1990   "The Future of Intensive Probation Supervision and the New Intermediate Sanction." *Crime and Delinquency* 36 (January): 6–41.

Byrne, James M., Arthur J. Lurigio, and S. Christopher Baird

    1989   "The Effectiveness of New Intensive Probation Supervision Programs." *Research in Corrections* 2 (September): 1–48.

Cahalan, Margaret Werner

    1986   *Historical Corrections Statistics in the United States, 1850–1984*. Washington, DC: U.S. Government Printing Office.

California Department of Corrections

    1981   *Investigation and Surveillance in Parole Supervision: An Evaluation of the High Control Project*, Research Report No. 63. Sacramento: California Department of Corrections.

Campbell, Curtis, Candace McCoy, and Chimezie A. B. Osigweh

    1990   "The Influence of Probation Recommendations on Sentencing Decisions and Their Predictive Accuracy." *Federal Probation* 54 (December): 13–21.

Carlson, Eric, and Evalyn Parks

    1979   *Critical Issues in Adult Probation: Issues in Probation Management.* Washington, DC: U.S. Government Printing Office.

Carlson, Jill M.

    1993   "Restorative Justice: Beyond Crime and Punishment." Master of science thesis, Mankato State University, Minnesota.

Carter, Robert M.

    1966   "It Is Respectfully Recommended . . ." *Federal Probation* (June).

    1978   *Presentence Report Handbook.* Washington, DC: U.S. Government Printing Office.

Carter, Stephen A., and Ann Chadwell Humphries

    1987   *Inmates Build Prisons in South Carolina.* Washington, DC: National Institute of Justice.

Champion, Dean J.

    1988a   "Felony Plea Bargaining and Probation: A Growing Judicial and Prosecutorial Dilemma." *Journal of Criminal Justice* 16: 291–301.

    1988b   *Felony Probation: Problems and Prospects.* New York: Praeger.

Chapin, Bradley

    1983   *Criminal Justice in Colonial America: 1600–1660.* Athens, GA: University of Georgia Press.

Chesney, Steven L.

    n.d.   "The Assessment of Restitution in the Minnesota Probation Services." In *Restitution in Criminal Justice*, edited by Joe Hudson. St. Paul, MN: Minnesota Department of Corrections.

Chesney-Lind, Meda

    1988   "Girls in Jail." *Crime and Delinquency* 34 (April): 150–68.

Childress, Anna Rose, A. Thomas McLellan, and Charles P. O'Brien

    1985   "Behavioral Therapies for Substance Abuse." *International Journal of the Addictions* 20: 947–69.

Chira, Susan

    1994   "Study Confirms Worst Fears on U.S. Children." *New York Times* (April 12): 1, 11.

Chodorow, Nancy J.

    1990   *Feminism and Psychoanalytic Theory.* New Haven, CT: Yale University Press.

Clark, Cherie L., David W. Aziz, and Doris L. MacKenzie

    1994   *Shock Incarceration in New York: Focus on Treatment.* Washington, DC: National Institute of Justice.

Clark County Juvenile Court

    1984   *Information for Victims and Witnesses of Juvenile Crime.* Las Vegas, NV: Clark County Juvenile Court.

Clarke, Stevens H., Yuan-Huei W. Lin, and W. LeAnn Wallace

    1988   *Probationer Recidivism in North Carolina: Measurement and Classification of Risk.* Chapel Hill, NC: University of North Carolina Institute of Government.

Clear, Todd R.

    1988   "Statistical Prediction in Corrections." *Research in Corrections* 1 (March): 1–39.

Clear, Todd R., Suzanne Flynn, and Carol Shapiro

    1987   "Intensive Supervision in Probation: A Comparison of Three Projects." In *Intermediate Punishments: Intensive Supervision, Home Confinement and Electronic Surveillance*, edited by Belinda R. McCarthy, 31–50. Monsey, NY: Criminal Justice Press.

Clear, Todd R., and Patricia R. Hardyman

    1990   "The New Intensive Supervision Movement." *Crime and Delinquency* 36 (January): 42–60.

Clear, Todd R., and Edward J. Latessa

    1989   "Intensive Supervision: Surveillance vs. Treatment." Paper presented at the annual meeting of the Academy of Criminal Justice Sciences, Washington, DC, March 30.

Clemmer, Donald

    1958   *The Prison Community.* New York: Holt, Rinehart and Winston.

Clinard, Marshall B., ed.

    1964   *Anomie and Deviant Behavior.* New York: Free Press.

Clinard, Marshall B., Peter C. Yeager, Jeanne Brissette, David Petrashek, and Elizabeth Harries

    1979   *Illegal Corporate Behavior.* Washington, DC: U.S. Government Printing Office.

Clines, Francis X.

    1993   "Inmates with AIDS Long for Death at Home." *New York Times* (January 5): 1, 8.

Cloninger, Susan C.

    1993   *Theories of Personality: Understanding Persons.* Upper Saddle River, NJ: Prentice Hall.

Cloward, Richard A., and Lloyd E. Ohlin

    1960   *Delinquency and Opportunity.* New York: Free Press.

Cohen, Albert K.

    1965   *Delinquent Boys.* New York: Free Press.

Cohen, Harold L., and James Filipczak

    1971   *A New Learning Environment*. San Francisco: Jossey-Bass.

Cohen, Noam S.

    1992   "20 Years After Siege Ended in Blood, Attica Is New Prison but Wary Town." *New York Times* (September 1): 15.

Collier, Walter V.

    1980   *Summary of First Year Evaluation of the Special Parole Supervision for Violent Felony Offenders*. Albany, NY: New York State Division of Parole.

Comptroller General of the United States

    1979   *Correctional Institutions Can Do More to Improve the Employability of Offenders*. Washington, DC: U.S. Government Printing Office.

Conrad, John P.

    1985   *The Dangerous and the Endangered*. Lexington, MA: D. C. Heath.

Cooper, Irving Ben

    1977   "*United States v. Unterman*: The Role of Counsel at Sentencing." *Criminal Law Bulletin* 13.

Cooprider, Keith W., and Judith Kerby

    1990   "A Practical Application of Electronic Monitoring at the Pretrial Stage." *Federal Probation* 54 (March): 28–35.

Covey, Herbert C., and Mary Mande

    1985   "Determinate Sentencing in Colorado." *Justice Quarterly* 2 (June).

Cowles, Ernest L., Thomas C. Castellano, and Laura A. Gransky

    1995   *"Boot Camp" Drug Treatment and Aftercare Interventions: An Evaluation Review*. Washington, DC: National Institute of Justice.

Crawford, Cheryl A.

    1994   "Health Care Needs in Corrections: NIJ Responds." *National Institute of Justice Journal* (November): 31–38.

Crawford, William B., Jr.

    1988   "Inmates Suing Over Gangs Lose Case." *Chicago Tribune* (March 8): Sec. 2: 3.

Cressey, Donald R.

    1955   "Changing Criminals: The Application of the Theory of Differential Association." *American Journal of Sociology* 61 (September): 116–20.

Cripe, Claire A.

    1977   "Religious Freedom in Prisons." *Federal Probation* 41 (March).

Cromwell, Paul F., Jr.

    1978   "The Halfway House and Offender Reintegration." In *Corrections in the Community*, 2nd ed., edited by George C. Killinger, and Paul F. Cromwell, Jr. St. Paul, MN: West.

Cromwell, Paul F., Jr., George C. Killinger, Hazel B. Kerper, and Charles Walker

    1985   *Probation and Parole in the Criminal Justice System*, 2nd ed. St. Paul, MN: West.

Cronin, Roberta C., with Mei Han

1994   *Boot Camp for Adult and Juvenile Offenders: Overview and Update.* Washington, DC: National Institute of Justice.

Cullen, Francis T., and Karen E. Gilbert

1982   *Reaffirming Rehabilitation.* Cincinnati: Anderson.

Curran, Daniel J.

1988   "Destructuring Privatization and the Promise of Juvenile Diversion: Compromising Community-Based Corrections." *Crime and Delinquency* 34 (October): 363–78.

Czajkoski, Eugene H.

1973   "Exposing the Quasi-Judicial Role of the Probation Officer." *Federal Probation* 37 (September).

Darrow, Clarence

1975   *Address to the Prisoners in the Cook County Jail, 1902.* Chicago: Charles H. Kerr.

Davidoff-Kroop, Joy

1983   *An Initial Assessment of the Division of Parole's Employment Services.* Albany, NY: New York State Division of Parole.

Dawson, Robert O.

1969   *Sentencing.* Boston: Little, Brown.

1983   *Texas Adult Probation Law Manual and Supplement.* Austin: Texas Adult Probation Commission.

Degler, Carl N.

1991   *In Search of Human Nature: The Decline and Revival of Darwinism in American Social Thought.* New York: Oxford University Press.

del Carmen, Rolando V.

1985   "Legal Issues and Liabilities in Community Corrections." In *Probation, Parole, and Community Corrections: A Reader,* edited by Lawrence F. Travis III, 47–70. Prospect Heights, IL: Waveland Press.

del Carmen, Rolando V., and Paul T. Louis

1988   *Civil Liabilities of Parole Personnel for Release, Non-Release, Supervision, and Revocation.* Washington, DC: National Institute of Corrections.

Denzlinger, Jerry D., and David E. Miller

1991   "The Federal Probation Officer: Life Before and After Guideline Sentencing." *Federal Probation* 55 (December): 49–63.

Deschenes, Elizabeth Piper, Susan Turner, and Joan Petersilia

1995   "A Dual Experiment in Intensive Community Supervision: Minnesota's Prison Diversion and Enhanced Supervised Release Programs." *The Prison Journal* 75 (September): 330–56.

Dickey, Walter

1979   "The Lawyer and the Accuracy of the Presentence Report." *Federal Probation* 43 (June).

Dietrich, Shelle

  1979   "The Probation Officer as Therapist: Examination of Three Major Problem Areas." *Federal Probation* 43 (June).

Dilulio, Jr., John J.

  1993   "Rethinking the Criminal Justice System: Toward a New Paradigm." In *Performance Measures for the Criminal Justice System,* 1–16. Washington, DC: Bureau of Justice Statistics.

Division of Probation

  1974   "The Selective Presentence Investigation." *Federal Probation* 38 (December).

Dolan, Edward J., Richard Lunden, and Rosemary Barberet

  1987   "Prison Behavior and Parole Outcome in Massachusetts." Paper presented at the annual meeting of the American Society of Criminology, Montreal, November 11–14.

Dole, Vincent P.

  1980   "Addictive Behavior." *Scientific American* 243: 138–54.

Donovan, Dennis M.

  1988   "Assessment of Addictive Behaviors: Implications for an Emerging Biopsychosocial Model." Pages 3–48 in *Assessment of Addictive Behaviors,* edited by Dennis M. Donovan and G. Alan Marrlatt. New York: Guilford.

Doom, Andrew E., Connie M. Roerich, and Thomas H. Zoey

  1988   "Sentencing Guidelines in Minnesota: The View from the Trenches." *Federal Probation* 52 (December): 34–38.

Dressler, David

  1951   *Parole Chief.* New York: Viking.

Dumm, Thomas L.

  1987   *Democracy and Punishment: Disciplinary Origins of the United States.* Madison, WI: University of Wisconsin Press.

Dunn, Ashley

  1995   "U.S. Inquiry Finds Detention Center Was Poorly Run." *New York Times* (July 22): 1, 8.

Durham, Alexis M., III

  1989a   "Origins of Interest in the Privatization of Punishment: The Nineteenth and Twentieth Century American Experience." *Criminology* 27 (February): 107–39.

  1989b   "Rehabilitation and Correctional Privatization: Observations on the 19th Century Experience and Implications for Modern Corrections." *Federal Probation* 53 (March): 43–52.

  1989c   "Newgate of Connecticut: Origins and Early Days of an Early American Prison." *Justice Quarterly* 6 (March): 89–116.

Durkheim, Emile

  1951   *Suicide.* New York: Free Press.

Empey, LaMar T., ed.

    1979   *Juvenile Justice: The Progressive Legacy and Current Reforms.* Charlottesville: University Press of Virginia.

Erez, Edna

    1990   "Victim Participation in Sentencing: Rhetoric and Reality." *Journal of Criminal Justice* 18: 19–31.

Erikkson, Torsten

    1976   *The Reformers: An Historical Survey of Pioneer Experiments in the Treatment of Criminals.* New York: Elsevier.

Erwin, Billie S.

    1984   *Evaluation of Intensive Supervision in Georgia.* Atlanta, GA: Georgia Department of Offender Rehabilitation.

Erwin, Billie S., and Lawrence A. Bennett

    1987   *New Dimensions in Probation: Georgia's Experience with Intensive Probation Supervision.* Washington, DC: National Institute of Justice.

Eskridge, Chris W., and Eric W. Carlson

    1979   "The Use of Volunteers in Probation: A National Synthesis." *Journal of Offender Counseling Services and Rehabilitation* 4 (winter).

Fabricant, Michael

    1983   *Juveniles in the Family Courts.* Lexington, MA: D. C. Heath.

Falk, Gerhard

    1966   "The Psychoanalytic Theories of Crime Causation." *Criminologica* 4 (May).

Fallen, David L., Craig D. Apperson, Joan Hall-Milligan, and Steven Aos

    1981   *Intensive Parole Supervision.* Olympia: Washington Department of Social and Health Services.

Feeley, Malcolm M.

    1979   *The Process Is Punishment: Handling Cases in a Lower Court.* New York: Russell Sage Foundation.

Feeley, Malcolm M., and Jonathan Simon

    1992   "The New Penology: Note on the Emerging Strategy of Corrections and Its Implications." *Criminology* 30 (November): 449–74.

Feld, Barry C.

    1988   "In Re Gault Revisited: A Cross-State Comparison of the Right to Counsel in Juvenile Court." *Crime and Delinquency* 34 (October): 393–424.

    1992   "Criminalizing the Juvenile Court: A Research Agenda for the 1990s." In *Juvenile Justice and Public Policy: Toward a National Agenda*, edited by Ira M. Schwartz, 59–88. Lexington, MA: Lexington Books.

Female Offender Resource Center

    1979   *Little Sisters and the Law.* Washington, DC: U.S. Government Printing Office.

Finckenauer, James O.

    1984   *Juvenile Delinquency and Corrections: The Gap Between Theory and Practice.* New York: Academic Press.

Finn, Peter, and Dale Parent

    1992   *Making the Offender Foot the Bill: A Texas Program.* Washington, DC: National Institute of Justice.

Fogel, David

    1975   *We Are the Living Proof.* Cincinnati, OH: Anderson.

    1984   "The Emergence of Probation as a Profession in the Service of Public Safety: The Next Ten Years." In *Probation and Justice: Reconsideration of Mission,* edited by Patrick D. McAnany, Doug Thompson, and David Fogel. Cambridge, MA: Oelgeschlager, Gunn and Hain.

Ford, Daniel, and Annesley K. Schmidt

    1985   *Electronically Monitored Home Confinement.* Washington, DC: National Institute of Justice.

Fox, Vernon

    1977   *Community-Based Corrections.* Upper Saddle River, NJ: Prentice Hall.

France, Anatole

    1927   *The Red Lily,* translated by Winifred Stephens. New York: Dodd, Mead

Freud, Sigmund

    1933   *New Introductory Lectures on Psychoanalysis.* New York: W. W. Norton.

Friedlander, Kate

    1947   *The Psychoanalytic Approach to Juvenile Delinquency.* New York: International Universities Press.

Friedlander, Walter A.

    1958   *Concepts and Methods of Social Work.* Upper Saddle River, NJ: Prentice Hall.

Friedman, Lawrence M.

    1973   *A History of American Law.* New York: Simon and Schuster.

Gaylin, Willard

    1974   *Partial Justice: A Study of Bias in Sentencing.* New York: Alfred A. Knopf.

Geerken, Michgael R., and Hennessey D. Hayes

    1993   "Probation and Parole: Public Risk and the Future of Incarceration Alternatives." *Criminology* 31 (November): 549–64.

Gendreau, Paul, and Robert R. Ross

    1987   "Revivification of Rehabilitation: Evidence from the 1980s." *Justice Quarterly* 4 (September): 350–407.

Gillin, John T.

    1931   *Taming the Criminal.* New York: Macmillan.

Glaser, Daniel

    1969   *The Effectiveness of a Prison and Parole System.* Indianapolis, IN: Bobbs-Merrill.

Glasser, William

    1975   *Reality Therapy.* New York: Harper and Row. (Originally published in 1965.)

    1976   *The Identity Society.* New York: Harper and Row.

1980   "Reality Therapy: An Explanation of the Steps of Reality Therapy." In *What Are You Doing? How People Are Helped Through Reality Therapy*, edited by Naomi Glasser. New York: Harper and Row.

Glueck, Sheldon, ed.

1933   *Probation and Criminal Justice*. New York: Macmillan.

Goetting, Victor L.

1974   "Some Pragmatic Aspects of Opening a Halfway House." *Federal Probation* 38 (December).

Goffman, Erving

1961   *Asylums: Essays on the Social Situation of Mental Patients and Other Inmates*. Garden City, NY: Doubleday.

Goleman, Daniel

1987   "Embattled Giant of Psychology Speaks His Mind." *New York Times* (August 25): 17, 18.

Goodstein, Lynne, and John Hepburn

1985   *Determinate Sentencing and Imprisonment: A Failure of Reform*. Cincinnati, OH: Anderson.

Gransky, Laura A., Thomas C. Castellano, and Ernest L. Cowles

1993   "Is There a 'Next Generation' of Shock Incarceration Facilities?: The Evolving Nature of Goals, Program Components, and Drug Treatment Services." Paper presented at the annual meeting of the Academy of Criminal Justice Sciences, Kansas City, MO, March 16–20.

Greenberg, David F.

1975   "Problems in Community Corrections." *Issues in Criminology* 10 (spring): 1–33.

Greenberg, David F., and Drew Humphries

1980   "The Cooptation of Fixed Sentencing Reform." *Crime and Delinquency* 26 (April).

Greenberg, Jay R., and Stephen A. Mitchell

1983   *Object Relations in Psychoanalytic Theory*. Cambridge, MA: Harvard University Press.

Griggs, Bertram S., and Gary R. McCune

1972   "Community-Based Correctional Programs: A Survey and Analysis." *Federal Probation* 36 (June).

Grissom, Grant R., and William L. Dubnov

1989   *Without Locks and Bars: Reforming Our Reform Schools*. New York: Praeger.

Griswold, David B.

1989   "Florida's Sentencing Guidelines: Six Years Later." *Federal Probation* 53 (December): 46–50.

Grogger, Jeffrey

1989   *Employment and Crime*. Sacramento: Bureau of Criminal Statistics and Special Services.

Gross, Jane

    1992   "Collapse of Inner-City Families Creates America's New Orphans." *New York Times* (March 29): 1, 15.

Haas, Stephen, and Edward J. Latessa

    1995   "Intensive Supervision in a Rural County: Diversion and Outcome." In *Intermediate Sanctions: Sentencing in the 1990s*, edited by John Ortiz Smykla and William Selke, 153–69. Cincinnati: Anderson.

Hagerty, J. E.

    1934   *Twentieth Century Crime, Eighteenth Century Methods of Control.* Boston: Stratford.

Hahn, Paul H.

    1976   *Community Based Corrections and the Criminal Justice System.* Santa Cruz, CA: Davis.

Hall, Jerome

    1952   *Theft, Law and Society.* Indianapolis, IN: Bobbs-Merrill.

Hamilton, Gordon

    1967   *Theory and Practice of Social Casework.* New York: Columbia University Press.

Hammett, Theodore M.

    1989   *1988 Update: AIDS in Correctional Facilities.* Washington, DC: U.S. Government Printing Office.

Hammett, Theodore M., Lynne Harrold, and Joel Epstein

    1994   *Tuberculosis in Correctional Facilities.* Washington, DC: U.S. Government Printing Office.

Hammett, Theodore M., Lynne Harrold, Michael Gross, and Joel Epstein

    1994   *1992 Update: HIV/AIDS in Correctional Facilities.* Washington, DC: U.S. Government Printing Office.

Hammett, Theodore M., and Saira Moini

    1990   "Update on AIDS in Prisons and Jails." *AIDS Bulletin.* Washington, DC: National Institute of Justice.

Hamparian, Donna M., Linda K. Estep, Susan M. Muntean, Ramon R. Prestino, Robert G. Swisher, Paul L. Wallace, and Joseph L. White

    1982   *Youth in Adult Courts: Between Two Worlds.* Columbus, OH: Academy for Contemporary Problems.

Hardman, Dale G.

    1960   "Constructive Use of Authority." *Crime and Delinquency* 6 (July).

Harper, Robert Francis

    1904   *The Code of Hammurabi.* Chicago: University of Chicago Press.

Harris, George A., and David Watkins

    1987   *Counseling the Involuntary and Resistant Client.* College Park, MD: American Correctional Association.

Harris, Patricia M., and Lisa Graff

    1988   "A Critique of Juvenile Sentence Reform." *Federal Probation* 52 (September): 66–71.

Hartman, Todd

    1994   "Suit Targets Neighbors Who Oppose Group Home." *Miami Herald* (November 11): B1, 3.

Hasenfield, Yeheskel

    1987   "Power in Social Work Practice." *Social Service Review* 61 (September): 469–83.

Hawaii Paroling Authority

    1987   *Annual Report.* Honolulu: Hawaii Paroling Authority.

Healy, William, Augusta F. Bronner, and Anna Mae Bowers

    1930   *The Structure and Meaning of Psychoanalysis.* New York: Alfred P. Knopf.

Herman, Ellen

    1995   *The Romance of American Psychology: Political Culture in the Age of Experts, 1940–1970.* Berkeley, University of California Press.

Hibbert, Christopher

    1968   *The Roots of Evil: A Social History of Crime and Punishment.* Boston: Little, Brown.

Hilts, Philip J.

    1974   *Behavior Mod.* New York: Harpers Magazine Press.

Hinds, Michael deCourcy

    1993   "But Does Punishment Fit the Budget?" *New York Times* (January 22): B16.

Hirsch, Adam Jay

    1992   *The Rise of the Penitentiary: Prisons and Punishment in Early America.* New Haven, CT: Yale University Press.

Hirschi, Travis

    1969   *Causes of Delinquency.* Berkeley: University of California Press.

Hobbs, Leo, and J. Kevin Kennedy

    1992   "Community Based Day Treatment for Troubled Youth." *Perspectives* 16 (Summer): 14–17.

Hollin, Clive R.

    1990   *Cognitive-Behavioral Interventions with Young Offenders.* New York: Pergamon Press.

Hollis, Florence

    1950   "The Techniques of Casework." In *Principles and Techniques of Social Casework: Selected Articles, 1940–1950,* edited by Cora Kasius, 412–26. New York: Family Service Association of America.

Holloway, Lynette

    1995   "Home for Handicapped Stilll Faces Rough Path." *New York Times* (July 18): 13.

Holt, Norman

    1995   "California's Determinate Sentencing: What Went Wrong?" *Perspectives* (summer): 19–22.

Hser, Yih-Ing, Dounglas Longshore, and M. Douglas Anglin

    1994   "Prevalence of Drug Use Among Criminal Offender Populations: Implications for Control, Treatment, and Policy." In *Drugs and Crime: Evaluating Public Policy Initiatives*, edited by Doris Layton MacKenzie and Craig D. Uchida, 18–41. Thousand Oaks, CA: Sage.

Hughes, Robert

    1987   *The Fatal Shore: The Epic of Australia's Founding*. New York: Alfred A. Knopf.

Hunt, Dana Eser, with Saira Moini, and Susan McWhan

    1989   *AIDS in Probation and Parole*. Washington, DC: U.S. Government Printing Office.

Hurst, Hunter IV, and Patricia McFall Torbet

    1993   *Organization and Administration of Juvenile Services: Probation, Aftercare, and State Institutions for Delinquent Youth*. Pittsburgh, PA: National Center for Juvenile Justice.

Hurst, James W.

    1950   *The Growth of American Law: The Law Makers*. Boston: Little, Brown.

Husband, Stephen D., and Jerome J. Platt

    1993   "The Cognitive Skills Component in Substance Abuse Treatment in Correctional Settings: A Brief Review." *Journal of Drug Issues* 23 (winter): 31–42.

Hutchinson, Elizabeth D.

    1987   "Use of Authority in Direct Social Work Practice with Mandated Clients." *Social Service Review* 61 (December): 581–98.

Ignatieff, Michael

    1978   *A Just Measure of Pain: The Penitentiary in the Industrial Revolution*. New York: Pantheon.

Illinois Department of Corrections

    1992   *Human Services Plan*. Springfield, IL: Department of Corrections.

Irwin, John

    1980   *Prisons in Turmoil*. Boston: Little, Brown.

Irwin, John, and James Austin

    1994   *It's About Time: America's Imprisonment Binge*. Belmont, CA: Wadsworth.

Jackson, Patrick G.

    1983   "Some Effects of Parole Supervision on Recidivism." *British Journal of Criminology* 23 (January): 17–34.

Jacobs, James B.

    1980   "The Prisoners' Rights Movement and Its Impacts, 1960–80." In *Crime and Justice*, edited by Norval Morris and Michael Tonry, 2: 429–70. Chicago: University of Chicago Press.

Jacoby, Joseph E., Scott A. Desmond, Edna Green, Lori I. Kepford, Jacinto F. Mendoza, and Monte D. Staton

    1994   "Why Bootcamps Fail: Historical and Theoretical Analysis." Paper presented at the annual meeting of the American Society of Criminology, Miami, Florida, November.

Jeffrey, C. Ray

    1971   *Crime Prevention Through Environmental Design*. Beverly Hills, CA: Sage.

Johnson, Kirk

    1989a   "U.S. Sues Town over Rights of Retarded." *New York Times* (June 27): 7.

    1989b   "Long Terms Hit Barrier in Connecticut: Early Releases by Crowded Jails." *New York Times* (July 25): 24.

    1994   "Connecticut Closes Boot Camp Built to Assist Troubled Youths." *New York Times* (June 11): 8.

Johnson, Louise C.

    1995   *Social Work Practice: A Generalist Approach*. Boston: Allyn and Bacon.

Jones, Justin, and Carol Robinson

    1989   "Keeping the Piece: Probation and Parole Officers' Right to Bear Arms." *Corrections Today* (February): 88, 90.

Kanfer, Frederick H.

    1975   "Self-Management Methods." In *Helping People Change: A Textbook of Methods*, edited by Frederick H. Kanfer and Arnold P. Goldstein, 309–56. New York: Pergamon Press.

Kanfer, Frederick H., and Arnold P. Goldstein

    1975   "Introduction." In *Helping People Change: A Textbook of Methods,* edited by Frederick H. Kanfer and Arnold P. Goldstein, 1–14. New York: Pergamon Press.

Kasius, Cora, ed.

    1950   *Principles and Techniques in Social Casework*. New York: Family Service Association of America.

Kelly, William R., and Sheldon Ekland-Olson

    1991   "The Response of the Criminal Justice System to Prison Overcrowding: Recidivism Patterns Among Four Successive Parolee Cohorts." *Law and Society Review* 25 (3): 601–20.

Kelman, Mark

    1987   *A Guide to Critical Legal Studies*. Cambridge, MA: Harvard University Press.

Kennedy, Thomas D.

    1988   "Determinate Sentencing: Real or Symbolic Effects?" *Crime and Justice* 11: 1–42.

Keve, Paul

    1979   "No Farewell to Arms." *Crime and Delinquency* 25 (October).

Kingsnorth, Rodney, and Louis Rizzo

    1979   "Decision-Making in the Criminal Court: Continuities and Discontinuities." *Criminology* 17 (May).

Kirst-Ashman, Karen K., and Grafton H. Hull Jr.

    1993   *Understanding Generalist Practice*. Chicago: Nelson-Hall.

Kleinig, John, and Charles Lindner

    1989   "AIDS on Parole: Dilemmas in Decision Making." *Criminal Justice Policy Review* 3 (March): 1–27.

Kolbert, Elizabeth

    1989   "Court Awards $1.3 Million to Inmates Injured at Attica." *New York Times* (October 26): 14.

Konopka, Gisela

    1983   *Social Group Work: A Helping Process*, 3rd ed. Upper Saddle River, NJ: Prentice Hall.

Krajick, Kevin

    1978   "Parole: Discretion is Out, Guidelines Are In." *Corrections Magazine* 4 (December).

Krauth, Barbara

    1987   "Parole: Controversial Component of the Criminal Justice System." In *Observations on Parole: A Collection of Readings from Western Europe, Canada and the United States*, edited by Edward E. Rhine and Ronald W. Jackson, 51–57. Washington, DC: U.S. Government Printing Office.

Krisberg, Barry

    1988   *The Juvenile Court: Reclaiming the Vision*. San Francisco: National Council on Crime and Delinquency.

Krisberg, Barry, Orlando Rodriquez, Audrey Bakke, Deborah Newenfeldt, and Patricia Steel

    1994   *Juvenile Intensive Supervison: An Assessment*. Washington, DC: Office of Juvenile Justice and Delinquency Prevention.

Lab, Steven P., and John T. Cullen

    1990   "From 'Nothing Works' to 'The Appropriate Works': The Latest Stop on the Search for the Secular Grail." *Criminology* 28 (August): 405–17.

Larkins, Norm

    1972   "Presentence Investigation Report Disclosure in Alberta." *Federal Probation* 36 (December).

Latessa, Edward J., and Gennaro F. Vito

    1988   "The Effects of Intensive Supervision on Shock Probationers." *Journal of Criminal Justice* 16: 319–30.

Law Enforcement Assistance Administration

    1973   *Reintegration of the Offender into the Community*. Washington, DC: U.S. Government Printing Office.

Lefcourt, Robert, ed.

    1971   *Law Against the People*. New York: Random House.

Leland, John, with Vern E. Smith

    1995   "Back on the Chain Gang." *Newsweek* (May 15): 58.

Lemert, Edwin M.

1951   *Social Pathology*. New York: McGraw-Hill.

Lenroot, Katherine F., and Emma O. Lundberg

1925   *Juvenile Courts at Work*. Washington, DC: U.S. Government Printing Office.

Lerner, Mark Jay

1977   "The Effectiveness of a Definite Sentence Parole Program." *Criminology* 15 (August).

Lewis, W. David

1965   *From Newgate to Dannemora*. Ithaca, NY: Cornell University Press.

Liberton, Michael, Mitchell Silverman, and William R. Blount

1990   "An Analysis Used to Predict Success of First-Time Offenders While Under Probation Supervision." Paper presented at the annual meeting of the Academy of Criminal Justice Sciences, April, Denver, CO. Published in 1992 in the *International Journal of Offender Therapy and Comparative Criminology* 36 (4): 335–47.

Lilly, J. Robert, and Richard A. Ball

1987   "A Brief History of House Arrest and Electronic Monitoring." *Northern Kentucky Law Review* 13: 343–74.

Lipton, Douglas, Robert Martinson, and Judith Wilks

1975   *The Effectiveness of Correctional Treatment: A Survey of Treatment Evaluation Studies*. New York: Praeger.

Logan, Charles H.

1990   *Private Prisons: Cons and Pros*. New York: Oxford University Press.

Lombroso, Cesare

1968   *Crime: Its Causes and Remedies*. Montclair, NJ: Patterson Smith. (Originally published in 1911.)

London, Perry

1964   *The Modes and Morals of Psychotherapy*. New York: Holt, Rinehart and Winston.

Lou, Herbert H.

1972   *Juvenile Courts in the United States*. New York: Arno Press. (Originally published in 1925.)

Lurigio, Arthur J., Marylouise Jones, and Barbara E. Smith

1995   "Child Sexual Abuse: Its Causes, Consequences, and Implications for Probation Practice." *Federal Probation* 69 (September): 69–76.

Lurigio, Arthur J., and Joan Petersilia

1992   "The Emergence of Intensive Probation Supervision Programs in the United States." In *Smart Sentencing: The Emergence of Intermediate Sanctions*, edited by James M. Byrne, Arthur J. Lurigio, and Joan Petersilia, 3–17. Newbury Park, CA: Sage.

Luther, Betty

1995   "The Politics of Criminal Justice: A Study of the Impact of Executive Influence on Massachusetts Parole Decisions Between 1985 and 1992." Paper presented at the annual meeting of the Academy of Criminal Justice Sciences, Boston, March 7–11.

Macgargle, Brett M.

1994   "South Carolina Volunteers in Probation and Parole Assist Crime Victims." *Perspectives* (special issue): 48–49.

MacKenzie, Doris Layton

1989   "The Parole Performance of Offenders Released from Shock Incarceration (Boot Camp Prisons): A Survival Time Analysis." Paper presented at the Annual Training Institute of the American Probation and Parole Association, Milwaukee, WI, August.

1994   "Results of a Multistate Study of Boot Camp Prisons." *Federal Probation* 58 (June): 60–66.

MacKenzie, Doris Layton, Robert Brame, David McDowall, and Claire Souryal

1995   "Boot Camp Prisons in Eight States." *Criminology* 33 (August): 327–57.

MacKenzie, Doris Layton, and James W. Shaw

1993   "The Impact of Shock Incarceration on Technical Vioations and New Criminal Activities." *Justice Quarterly* 10 (September): 463–87.

MacKenzie, Doris Layton, James W. Shaw, and Claire Souryal

1992   "Characteristics Associated with Successful Adjustment to Supervision: A Comparison of Parolees, Probationers, Shock Participants, and Shock Dropouts." *Criminal Justice and Behavior* 19 (December): 437–54.

MacKenzie, Doris Layton, and Claire Souryal

1994   *Multisite Evaluation of Shock Incarceration.* Washington, DC: National Institute of Justice.

1995   "Inmates' Attitude Change During Incarceration: A Comparison of Boot Camp With Traditional Prisons." *Justice Quarterly* 12 (June): 325–53.

MacNamara, Donal E. J.

1977   "The Medical Model in Corrections: Requiescat in Pace." *Criminology* 14 (February).

Maestro, Marcello

1973   *Cesare Beccaria and the Origins of Penal Reform.* Philadelphia: Temple University Press.

Malcolm, Andrew H.

1989a   "Florida's Jammed Prisons: More in Means More Out." *New York Times* (July 3): 1, 7.

1989b   "More and More, Prison Is America's Answer to Crime." *New York Times* (November 26): E1, 4.

1989c   "Explosive Drug Use in Prisons Is Creating a New Underworld." *New York Times* (December 30): 1, 10.

Maloney, Dennis M., and Mark S. Umbreit

1995   "Managing Change: Toward a Balanced and Restorative Justice Model." *Perspectives* 19 (spring): 43–46.

Maltz, Michael D.

1984   *Recidivism.* Orlando, FL: Academic Press.

Mande, Mary

    1987   *Getting Tough on Crime in Colorado.* Denver, CO: Colorado Division of Criminal Justice.

Mangrum, Claude

    1972   "The Humanity of Probation Officers." *Federal Probation* 36 (June).

Mann, Dale

    1976   *Intervening with Convicted Serious Juvenile Offenders.* Washington, DC: U.S. Government Printing Office.

Margolick, David

    1992   "Chorus of Judicial Critics Assail Sentencing Guides." *New York Times* (April 12): 1, 20.

Marshall, Franklin H.

    1989   "Diversion and Probation Under the New Sentencing Guidelines: One Officer's Observations." Paper presented at the annual meeting of the Academy of Criminal Justice Sciences, Washington, DC, March 30.

Martin, Andrew

    1995   "Few Brains Behind Bank Heists." *Chicago Tribune* (June 28): Sec. 2: 1, 4.

Martin, Douglas

    1988   "New York Tests Inmates' Boot Camp." *New York Times* (March 4): 15.

Martin, Garry, and Joseph Pear

    1992   *Behavior Modification: What It Is and How to Do It,* 4th ed. Upper Saddle River, NJ: Prentice Hall.

Martinson, Robert

    1974   "What Works?: Questions and Answers about Prison Reform." *The Public Interest* 35 (spring): 22–54.

Martinson, Robert, and Judith Wilks

    1975   "A Static-Descriptive Model of Field Supervision." *Criminology* 13 (May).

Marx, Gary

    1994a   "Hard Time." *Chicago Tribune* (October 24): Sec. 5: 1, 6.

    1994b   "Industrious Prisoners Make Money Doing Time." *Chicago Tribune* (August 7): 1, 14.

    1995a   "Lonely Mission." *Chicago Tribune* (June 23): Sec. 5: 1, 2

    1995b   "No Country Club for Reynolds." *Chicago Tribune* (August 24): Sec 2: 3.

Mathias, Rudolf E. S., and James W. Mathews

    1991   "The Boot Camp Program for Offenders: Does the Shoe Fit." *International Journal of Offender Therapy and Comparative Criminology* 35: 322–27.

Matza, David

    1964   *Delinquency and Drift.* New York: Wiley.

McAnany, Patrick D., Doug Thompson, and David Fogel, eds.

    1984   *Probation and Justice: Reconsideration of a Mission.* Cambridge, MA: Oelgeschlager, Gunn and Hain.

McCarthy, Belinda R.

1987   "Introduction." In *Intermediate Punishments: Intensive Supervision, Home Confinement and Electronic Surveillance*, edited by Belinda R. McCarthy, 1–12. Monsey, NY: Criminal Justice Press.

McCarthy, Belinda Rogers, and Bernard J. McCarthy

1984   *Community-Based Corrections*. Monterey, CA: Brooks/Cole.

McCorkle, Richard C.

1995   "Correctional Boot Camps and Change in Attitudes: Is All This Shouting Necessary?" *Justice Quarterly* 12 (June): 365–75.

McDonald, Douglas C.

1988   *Restitution and Community Service*. Washington, DC: National Institute of Justice.

1989   "The Cost of Corrections: In Search of the Bottom Line." *Research in Corrections* 2 (February): 1–25.

McDowell, Edwin

1991   "Inmates Fill the Front Lines for Tourism." *New York Times* (November 24): 1, 15.

McGaha, Johnny, Michael Fichter, and Peter Hirschburg

1987   "Felony Probation: A Re-Examination of Public Risk." *American Journal of Criminal Justice* 11: 1–9.

McKelvey, Blake

1972   *American Prisons: A Study in American Social History Prior to 1815*. Montclair, NJ: Patterson Smith.

1977   *American Prisons: A History of Good Intentions*. Montclair, NJ: Patterson Smith.

McShane, Marilyn D., and Frank P. Williams III

1989   "The Prison Adjustment of Juvenile Offenders." *Crime and Delinquency* 35 (April): 254–69.

Melossi, Dario, and Massimo Pavarini

1981   *The Prison and the Factory: Origins of the Penitentiary System*. Totowa, NJ: Barnes and Noble.

Mennel, Robert M.

1973   *Thorns and Thistles: Juvenile Delinquents in the United States, 1825–1940*. Hanover, NH: University Press of New England.

Merton, Robert K.

1938   "Social Structure and Anomie." *American Sociological Review* 3: 672–82.

1964   "Anomie, Anomia, and Social Interaction." In *Anomie and Deviant Behavior*, edited by Marshall B. Clinard, 213–42. New York: Free Press.

Miley, Karla Krogsrud, Michael O'Melia, and Brenda L. DuBois

1995   *Generalist Social Work Practice: An Empowering Approach*. Boston: Allyn and Bacon.

Miller, Jerome
  1992   *Last One over the Wall: The Massachusetts Experiment in Closing Reform Schools*. Columbus: Ohio State University.

Miller, Walter B.
  1958   "Lower Class Culture as a Generating Milieu of Gang Delinquency." *Journal of Social Issues* 14: 5–19.

Mills, Jim
  1992   "Supervision Fees." *Perspectives* (Fall): 10–12.

Mohler, Henry Calvin
  1925   "Convict Labor Policies." *Journal of Criminal Law, Criminology and Police Science* 15: 530–97.

Moore, Kathleen Dean
  1989   *Pardons: Justice, Mercy, and the Public Interest*. New York: Oxford University Press.

Morash, Merry, and Lila Rucker
  1990   "A Critical Look at the Idea of Boot Camp as a Correctional Reform." *Crime and Delinquency* 36 (April): 204–22.

Morris, Norval, and Michael Tonry
  1990   *Between Prison and Probation: Intermediate Punishments in a Rational Sentencing System*. New York: Oxford University Press.

Mullaney, Fahy G.
  1988   *Economic Sanctions in Community Corrections*. Washington, DC: National Institute of Corrections.

Mullen, Joan
  1985   "Corrections and the Private Sector." *NIJ Reports* (May).

Mydans, Seth
  1995   "Racial Tensions on the Rise in Los Angeles Jail System," *New York Times* (February 6): 8.

Myers, Linnet
  1995   "Cultural Divide over Crime and Punishment." *Chicago Tribune* (October 13): 1, 8.

Nader, Ralph
  1985   "America's Crime Without Criminals." *New York Times* (May 19): F3.

National Advisory Commission on Criminal Justice Standards and Goals
  1973   *Corrections*. Washington, DC: U.S. Government Printing Office.
  1975   *A National Strategy to Reduce Crime*. New York: Avon.

National Commission on Law Observance and Law Enforcement
  1931   *Report on Penal Institutions*. Washington, DC: U.S. Government Printing Office.

National Governors' Association

    1988   *Guide to Executive Clemency Among the American States.* Washington, DC: National Institute of Corrections.

Navarro, Mireya

    1994   "Perils of Inmates' Work Release Mount." *New York Times* (April 25): B10.

Nelson, E. Kim, Howard Ohmart, and Nora Harlow

    1978   *Promising Strategies in Probation and Parole.* Washington, DC: U.S. Government Printing Office.

New Jersey Administrative Office of the Courts

    n.d.   *Standards for Community Service Programs in New Jersey.* Trenton: Office of the Courts.

New York State Department of Correctional Services

    1970   *Corrections in New York State.* Albany: New York Department of Correctional Services.

New York State Division of Parole

    1953   *Parole Officer's Manual.* Albany: Division of Parole.

    1984   *1982–1983 Annual Report.* Albany: Division of Parole.

    1994   *1993–1994 Annual Report.* Albany: Division of Parole.

New York State Employment Services Vocational Rehabilitation Service

    1965   "Vocational Counseling with the Offender" (mimeo). Albany, Vocational Rehabilitation Service.

New York State Office of Policy Analysis and Information

    1989   *Shock Incarceration: One Year Out.* Albany: New York State Division of Parole.

New York State Special Commission on Attica

    1972   *Attica.* New York: Praeger.

Nietzel, Michael T., and Melissa J. Himelein

    1987   "Probation and Parole." In *Behavioral Approaches to Crime and Delinquency: A Handbook of Application, Research, and Concepts,* edited by Edward K. Morris and Curtis J. Braukmann, 109–33. New York: Plenum.

Noonan, Susan B., and Edward J. Latessa

    1987   "Intensive Probation: An Examination of Recidivism and Social Adjustment." *American Journal of Criminal Justice* 11: 45–61.

Northern, Helen

    1969   *Social Work with Groups.* New York: Columbia University Press.

    1988   *Social Work with Groups,* 2nd ed. New York: Columbia University Press.

O'Leary, K. Daniel, and G. Terrance Wilson

    1975   *Behavior Therapy: Application and Outcome.* Upper Saddle River, NJ: Prentice Hall.

Omer, Haim, and Perry London

    1988   "Metamorphosis in Psychotherapy: End of the Systems Era." *Psychotherapy* 25 (Summer): 171–80.

Ostrower, Roland

    1962   "Study, Diagnosis, and Treatment: A Conceptual Structure." *Social Work* 7 (October).

Palumbo, Dennis J., and Rebecca D. Peterson

    1994   "Shock Incarceration and Intermediate Punishments: Reform or Recycled 'Get Tough' Policy?" Paper presented at the annual meeting of the American Society of Criminology, Miami, Florida, November.

Parent, Dale G.

    1988   "Overview: Shock-Incarceration Programs." *Perspectives* 12 (July): 9–15.

    1989a   "Probation Supervision Fee Collection in Texas." *Perspectives* 13 (Winter): 9–12.

    1989b   *Shock Incarceration: An Overview of Existing Programs.* Washington, DC: U.S. Government Printing Office.

Parent, Dale G., Dan Wentworth, Peggy Burke, and Becky Ney

    1994   *Responding to Probation and Parole Violations.* Washington, DC: National Institute of Justice.

Parker, William

    1975   *Parole.* College Park, MD: American Correctional Association.

Parsonage, William H.

    1990   *Worker Safety in Probation and Parole.* Longmont, CO: National Institute of Corrections.

Parsonage, William H., and W. Conway Bushey

    1989   "The Victimization of Probation and Parole Workers in the Line of Duty: An Exploratory Study." Paper presented at the annual meeting of the Academy of Criminal Justice Sciences, Washington, DC, March.

Pear, Robert

    1992   "Ranks of U.S. Poor Reach 35.7 Million, the Most since '64." *New York Times* (September 4): 1, 12.

Pearson, Frank S.

    1988   "Evaluation of New Jersey's Intensive Supervision Program." *Crime and Delinquency* 34 (October): 437–48.

Perlman, Helen Harris

    1957   *Perspectives on Social Casework.* Philadelphia: Temple University Press.

    1971   *Perspectives on Social Casework: A Problem Solving Process.* Chicago: University of Chicago Press.

Petersilia, Joan M.

    1987   *Expanding Options for Criminal Sentencing.* Santa Monica, CA: Rand Corporation.

    1988a   "Georgia's Intensive Probation: Will the Model Work Elsewhere?" In *Intermediate Punishments: Intensive Supervision, Home Confinement and Electronic Surveillance*, edited by Belinda R. McCarthy, 15–30. Monsey, NY: Criminal Justice Press.

    1988b   *House Arrest.* Washington, DC: National Institute of Justice.

1990   "When Probation Becomes More Dreaded Than Prison." *Federal Probation* 54 (March): 23–27.

1993   "Measuring the Performance of Community Corrections." In *Performance Measures for the Criminal Justice System*, 61–85. Washington DC: Bureau of Justice Statistics.

Petersilia, Joan, and Elizabeth Piper Deschenes

1994   "What Punishes? Inmates Rank the Severity of Prison vs. Intermediate Sanctions." *Federal Probation* 68 (March): 3–8.

Petersilia, Joan and Susan Turner

1990   "Comparing Intensive and Regular Supervision for High-Risk Probationers: Early Results from an Experiment in California." *Crime and Delinquency* 36 (January): 87–111.

1991   "Is ISP a Viable Sanction for High Risk Probationers?" *Perspectives* 15 (summer): 8–11.

1993   *Evaluating Intensive Supervision Probation/Parole: Results of a Nationwide Experiment.* Washington, DC: National Institute of Justice.

Petersilia, Joan, Susan Turner, and Elizabeth Piper Deschenes

1992   "Intensive Supervision Programs for Drug Offenders." In *Smart Sentencing: The Emergence of Intermediate Sanctions*, edited by James M. Byrne, Arthur J. Lurigio, and Joan Petersilia, 18–37. Newbury Park, CA: Sage.

Petersilia, Joan, Susan Turner, James Kahan, and Joyce Peterson

1985   *Granting Felons Probation: Public Risks and Alternatives.* Santa Monica, CA: Rand Corporation.

Pisciotta, Alexander W.

1992   "Doing Parole: The Promise and Practice of the Minnesota and Illinois Reformatories, 1889–1920." Paper presented at the annual meeting of the American Society of Criminology, New Orleans, LA, November.

1994   *Benevolent Repression: Social Control and the American Reformatory -Prison Movement.* New York: New York University Press.

Platt, Anthony M.

1974   *The Childsavers: The Invention of Delinquency.* Chicago: University of Chicago Press.

Polakow, Robert L., and Ronald M. Docktor

1974   "A Behavioral Modification Program for Adult Drug Offenders." *Journal of Research in Crime and Delinquency* 11 (January) 63–69.

Pollock-Byrne, Joycelyn M.

1990   *Women, Prison, and Crime.* Pacific Grove, CA: Brooks/Cole.

Porter, Bruce

1995   "Terror on an Eight-Hour Shift." *New York Times Magazine* (November 26): 42–47, 56, 59, 72, 76, 80, 82.

President's Commission on Law Enforcement and Administration of Justice

1972   *The Challenge of Crime in a Free Society.* New York: Avon.

President's Commission on Organized Crime

1986   *The Impact: Organized Crime Today.* Washington, DC: U.S. Government Printing Office.

Prison Association of New York

    1936   *The Ninety-First Annual Report.* Albany, NY: J. B. Lyon.

Program Services Office

    1983   *Probation Classification and Service Delivery Approach.* Los Angeles: County Probation Department.

Przybylski, Roger

    1988   *Electronically Monitored Home Confinement in Illinois.* Chicago: Illinois Criminal Justice Information Authority.

Purdy, Matthew

    1995   "Bars Don't Stop Flow of Drugs Into the Prisons." *New York Times* (July 2): 1, 12, 13.

Quadagno, Jill S., and Robert J. Antonio

    1975   "Labeling Theory as an Oversocialized Conception of Man: The Case of Mental Illness." *Sociology and Social Research* 60 (October).

Rachin, Richard

    1974   "Reality Therapy: Helping People Help Themselves." *Crime and Delinquency* 20 (January).

Reed, John, and Dale Nance

    1972   "Society Perpetuates the Stigma of a Conviction." *Federal Probation* 36 (June).

Reichel, Phillip L., and Billie D. Sudbrack

    1994   "Differences Among Eligibles: Who Gets an ISP Sentence?" *Federal Probation* (58): 51–62.

Reiff, Phillip, ed.

    1963   *Freud, Therapy and Techniques.* New York: Crowell-Collier.

Reiman, Jeffrey

    1995   *The Rich Get Richer and the Poor Get Prison,* 3rd ed. New York: Macmillan.

Remington, Bob, and Marina Remington

    1987   "Behavior Modification in Probation Work." *Criminal Justice and Behavior* 14 (June): 156–74.

Reyna, L. J.

    1964   "Conditioning Therapies, Learning Theory, and Research." In *The Conditioning Therapies,* edited by Joseph Wolpe, Andrew Salter and L. J. Reyna, 169–79. New York: Holt, Rinehart and Winston.

Robbins, Ira P.

    1988   *The Legal Dimensions of Private Incarceration.* Washington, DC: American Bar Association.

Robbins, William

    1989   "Seeing a Prison Project as Economic Freedom." *New York Times* (May 25): 11.

Robertson, John A.

    1974   *Rough Justice: Perspectives on Lower Courts.* Boston: Little, Brown.

Robitscher, Jonas
    1980   *The Power of Psychiatry*. Boston: Houghton Mifflin.

Root, Lawrence P.
    1972   "Work Release Legislation." *Federal Probation* 36 (March).

Rose, Sheldon D.
    1977   *Group Therapy: A Behavioral Approach*. Upper Saddle River, NJ: Prentice Hall.

Roshier, Bob
    1989   *Controlling Crime: The Classical Perspective in Criminology*. Chicago: Lyceum.

Ross, Bernard, and Charles Shireman
    1972   *Social Work and Social Justice*. Washington, DC: National Association of Social Workers.

Ross, Robert R., Elizabeth A. Fabiano, and Crystal D. Ewles
    1988   "Reasoning and Rehabilitation." *International Journal of Offender Therapy and Comparative Criminology* 32: 29–35.

Rothman, David
    1971   *The Discovery of the Asylum*. Boston: Little, Brown.

Rousseau, Jean Jacques
    1954   *The Social Contract*. Chicago: Henry Regnery.

Rubin, H. Ted
    1980   "The Emerging Prosecutor Dominance of the Juvenile Court Intake Process." *Crime and Delinquency* 26 (July).

Rubin, Sol
    1974   "The Impact of Court Decisions on the Correctional Process." *Crime and Delinquency* 20 (April).

Runda, John C., Edward E. Rhine, and Robert E. Wetter
    1994   *The Practice of Parole Boards*. Lexington KY: Association of Paroling Authorities, International.

Rush, George E.
    1988   "Electronic Surveillance: An Alternative to Incarceration (An Overview of the San Diego County Program)." *American Journal of Criminal Justice* 12: 219–42.

Sachs, Howard, and Charles Logan
    1979   *Does Parole Make a Difference?* West Hartford, CT: University of Connecticut Law School.

Sagan, Eli
    1988   *Freud, Women, and Morality*. New York: Basic Books.

Sagatun, Inger, Loretta McCollum, and Michael Edwards
    1985   "The Effect of Transfers from Juvenile to Criminal Court: A Loglinear Analysis." *Journal of Crime and Justice* 8: 65–92.

Salter, Andrew

    1964   "The Theory and Practice of Conditioned Reflex Therapy." In *The Conditioning Therapies*, edited by Joseph Wolpe, Andrew Salter, and L. J. Reyna, 21–37. New York: Holt, Rinehart and Winston.

Sanborn, Joseph B., Jr.

    1992   "Pleading Guilty in Juvenile Court: Minimal Ado about Something Very Important to Young Defendants." *Justice Quarterly* 9 (March): 127–50.

Schlossman, Steven L.

    1977   *Love and the American Delinquent: The Theory and Practice of "Progressive" Juvenile Justice, 1825–1920.* Chicago: University of Chicago Press.

Schmideberg, Melitta

    1975   "Some Basic Principles of Offender Therapy: Part II" *International Journal of Offender Therapy and Comparative Criminology* 1.

Schmidt, Annesley K.

    1989   "Electronic Monitoring of Offenders Increases." *NIJ Reports* (January-February): 2–5.

Schneider, Keith

    1993   "Hollow Note Heard in a Trumpeted Pollution Fine." *New York Times* (June 3): 12.

Schram, Donna D., Jill G. McKelvy, Anne L. Schneider, and David B. Griswold

    1981   *Preliminary Findings: Assessment of the Juvenile Code* (mimeo). State of Washington.

Schultz, J. Lawrence

    1973   "The Cycle of Juvenile Court History." *Crime and Delinquency* 19 (October).

Schuman, Alan M.

    1989   "The Cost of Correctional Services: Exploring a Poorly Charted Terrain." *Research in Corrections* 2 (February): 27–33.

Schur, Edwin M.

    1973   *Radical Non-Intervention: Rethinking the Delinquency Problem.* Englewood Cliffs, NJ: Prentice Hall.

Schwartz, Ira M., Linda Harris, and Laurie Levi

    1988   "The Jailing of Juveniles in Minnesota: A Case Study." *Crime and Delinquency* 34 (April): 133–49.

Schwartz, Richard, and Jerome H. Skolnick

    1962   "Two Studies in Legal Stigma." *Social Problems* 10: 133–42.

Schwartz, William

    1966   "Some Notes on the Use of Groups in Social Work Practice." Address delivered to the Annual Workshop for Field Instructors and Faculty of the Columbia School of Social Work (mimeo).

    1976   "Between Client and System: The Mediating Function." In *Theories of Social Work with Groups*, edited by Robert W. Roberts and Helen Northern, 171–97. New York: Columbia University Press.

Schwitzgebel, Ralph K.

    1968   "Electronic Alternatives to Imprisonment." *Lex et Scientia* 5 (3): 99–104.

    1969a   "Issues in the Use of an Electronic Rehabilitation System with Chronic Recidivists." *Law and Society Review* 3: 597–611.

    1969b   "Development of an Electronic Rehabilitation System for Parolees." *Law and Computer Technology* 2: 9–12.

Sechcrest, Dale K.

    1989   "Prison 'Boot Camps' Do Not Measure Up." *Federal Probation* 53 (September): 15–20.

Sechrest, Lee, Susan O. White, and Elizabeth D. Brown

    1979   *The Rehabilitation of Criminal Offenders: Problems and Prospects.* Washington, DC: National Academy of Sciences.

Sellin, Thorston

    1967   "A Look at Prison History." *Federal Probation* 31 (September).

Seventh Annual Shock Legislative Report

    1995   Albany, NY: State of New York Department of Correctional Services and Division of Parole.

Shaffer, John, and M. David Galinsky

    1989   *Models of Group Therapy*, 2nd ed. Englewood Cliffs, NJ: Prentice Hall.

Sheldon, Randall G., John A. Horvath, and Sharon Tracy

    1989   "Do Status Offenders Get Worse? Some Clarifications on the Question of Escalation." *Crime and Delinquency* 35 (April): 202–16.

Shenon, Philip

    1985a   "Data Sought on SmithKline Inquiry." *New York Times* (September 14): 8.

    1985b   "Drug Case Divided Officials at F.D.A. and Justice Department." *New York Times* (September 19): 1, 14.

Shichor, David, and Clemens Bartollas

    1990   "Private and Public Juvenile Placements: Is There a Difference?" *Crime and Delinquency* 36 (April): 286–99.

Short, James R., Jr.

    1968   *Gang Delinquency and Delinquent Subcultures.* New York: Harper and Row.

Sickmund, Melissa

    1994   *How Juveniles Get to Criminal Court.* Washington, DC: Office of Juvenile Justice and Delinquency Prevention.

Silverman, Mitchell

    1994   "Ethical Issues in the Field of Probation." *International Journal of Offender Therapy and Comparative Criminology* 37 (1): 85–94.

Simon, Jonathan

    1993   *Poor Discipline: Parole and Social Control of the Underclass, 1890–1990.* Chicago: University of Chicago Press.

Sinclair, Jim

 1994 "APPA's Public Hearings Explore Probation and Parole's Response to Victim's of Crime: Speakers Call for a New Approach to Victim Issues." *Perspectives* (special issue): 15–17.

Skidmore, Rex A., Milton G. Thackeray, and O. William Farley

 1988 *Introduction to Social Work*, 4th ed. Englewood Cliffs, NJ: Prentice Hall.

Skinner, B. F.

 1972 *Beyond Freedom and Dignity*. New York: Alfred A. Knopf.

Sluder, Richard D., and Rolando del Carmen

 1990 "Are Probation and Parole Officers Liable for Injuries Caused by Probationers and Parolees?" *Federal Probation* 54 (December): 3–12.

Smith, Alexander, and Louis Berlin

 1974 "Self-Determination in Welfare and Corrections: Is There a Limit?" *Federal Probation* 38 (December).

Smith, Carolyn, and Terence C. Thornberry

 1995 "The Relationship Between Childhood Maltreatment and Adolescent Involvement in Delinquency." *Criminology* 33 (November): 451–77.

Smith, Richard Austin

 1961a "The Incredible Electrical Conspiracy." *Fortune* (April): 161–64, 210, 212, 217–18, 221–24.

 1961b "The Incredible Electrical Conspiracy." *Fortune* (May): 132–37, 170, 175–76, 179–80.

Snyder, Howard N. and Melissa Sickmund

 1995 *Juvenile Offenders and Victims: A Focus on Violence. Statistics Summary.* Washington, DC: Office of Juvenile Justice and Delinquency Prevention.

Specht, Harry

 1990 "Social Work and the Popular Psychotherapies." *Social Service Review* 64 (September): 345–57.

Spencer, Herbert

 1961 *The Study of Sociology.* Ann Arbor, MI: University of Michigan Press. (Originally published in 1871.)

Spencer, Jim

 1987 "'Knock 'em Out, Trainee.'" *Chicago Tribune* (July 26): Sec. 3: 1, 2.

Stampfl, Thomas G.

 1970 "Comment" [on token economies]. In *Learning Approaches to Therapeutic Behavior Change*, edited by Donald H. Levis. Chicago: Aldine.

Stanley, David T.

 1976 *Prisoners among Us: The Problem of Parole.* Washington, DC: Brookings Institution.

Star, Deborah

 1979 *Summary Parole: A Six and Twelve Month Follow-Up Evaluation.* Sacramento, CA: California Department of Corrections.

Stolz, Stephanie B., Louis A. Wienckowski, and Bertram S. Brown

1975 "Behavior Modification: A Perspective on Critical Issues." *American Psychologist* 30 (November).

Strong, Ann

1981 *Case Classification Manual, Module One: Technical Aspects of Interviewing.* Austin: Texas Adult Probation Commission.

Sullivan, John, and Matthew Purdy

1995 "In Corrections Business, Shrewdness Pays." *New York Times* (July 23): 1, 13.

Sullivan, Michael P.

1987 "Parole Guidelines: An Effective Prison Population Management Tool." In *Observations on Parole: A Collection of Readings from Western Europe, Canada and the United States,* edited by Edward E. Rhine and Ronald W. Jackson, 83–85. Washington, DC: U.S. Government Printing Office.

Sulzer, Beth, and G. Roy Mayer

1972 *Behavior Modification Procedures for School Personnel.* Hinsdale, IL: Dryden.

Sutherland, Edwin H.

1972 *The Professional Thief.* Chicago: University of Chicago Press.

1973 *Edwin Sutherland: On Analyzing Crime,* edited by Karl Schuessler. Chicago: University of Chicago Press.

Sutherland, Edwin H., and Donald R. Cressey

1966 *Principles of Criminology.* Philadelphia: J. B. Lippincott.

Sutton, John R.

1988 *Stubborn Children: Controlling Delinquency in the United States, 1649–1981.* Berkeley: University of California Press.

Swanger, Harry F.

1988 "Hendrickson v. Griggs: A Review of the Legal and Policy Implications for Juvenile Justice Policymakers." *Crime and Delinquency* 34 (April): 209–27.

Sykes, Gresham M., and David Matza

1957 "Techniques of Neutralization: A Theory of Delinquency." *American Sociological Review* 22 (December): 664–70.

Takagi, Paul

1975 "The Walnut Street Jail: A Penal Reform to Centralize the Powers of the State." *Federal Probation* 39 (December): 18–26.

Takas, Marianne, and Theodore M. Hammett

1989 *Legal Issues Affecting Offenders and Staff.* Washington, DC: U.S. Government Printing Office.

Task Force on Corrections

1966 *Task Force Report: Corrections.* Washington, DC: U.S. Government Printing Office.

Taylor, Ian, Paul Walton, and Jock Young

1973 *The New Criminology.* New York: Harper and Row.

Teeters, Negley K.

  1970   "The Passing of Cherry Hill: Most Famous Prison in the World." *Prison Journal* 50 (Spring–Summer): 1–12.

Terry, Don

  1993   "Town Builds a Prison and Stores Its Hopes There." *New York Times* (January 3): 9.

Texas Adult Probation Commission

  1988   *A Comparison of Special Program Probationers and Prison Inmates.* Austin: Texas Adult Probation Commission.

Thalheimer, Donald J.

  1975   *Halfway Houses*, Vol. 2. Washington, DC: U.S. Government Printing Office.

Thompson, James W., Michelle Sviridoff, Jerome E. McElroy, Richard McGahey, and Orlando Rodriguez

  1981   *Employment and Crime: A Review of Theories and Research.* Washington, DC: U.S. Government Printing Office.

Thorne, Gaylord L., Roland G. Tharp, and Ralph J. Wetzel

  1967   "Behavior Modification Techniques: New Tools for Probation Officers." *Federal Probation* 31 (June): 21–27.

Toborg, Mary A., Lawrence J. Carter, Raymond H. Milkman, and Dennis W. Davis

  1978   *The Transition from Prison to Employment: An Assessment of Community-Based Programs.* Washington, DC: U.S. Government Printing Office.

Tolchin, Martin

  1985   "As Privately-Owned Prisons Increase, So Do Their Critics." *New York Times* (February 11): 1, 12.

Tonry, Michael, and Richard Will

  1988   "Intermediate Sanctions." Preliminary report to the National Institute of Justice.

Torgerson, Ferndando G.

  1962   "Differentiating and Defining Casework and Psychotherapy." *Social Casework* 43 (April).

Toseland, Robert W., and Robert F. Rivas

  1995   *An Introduction to Group Work Practice*, 2nd ed. Boston: Allyn and Bacon.

Travis III, Lawrence F., and Edward J. Latessa

  1984   "'A Summary of Parole Rules—Thirteen Years Later': Revisited Thirteen Years Later." *Journal of Criminal Justice* 12.

Treaster, Joseph B.

  1994a   "Hard Time for Hard Youths: A Battle Yields Few Winners." *New York Times* (December 28): 1, 8.

  1994b   "Beyond Probation: Breaking the Cycle of Juvenile Arrests." *New York Times* (December 29): 1, 11.

Twentieth Century Fund Task Force on Sentencing

  1976   *Fair and Certain Punishment.* New York: McGraw-Hill.

Umbreit, Mark S.

  1994   *Victim Meets Offender: The Impact of Restorative Justice and Mediation.* Monsey, NY: Willow Tree Press.

Umbreit, Mark S., and Mark Carey

  1995   "Restorative Justice: Implications for Organizational Change." *Federal Probation* 59 (March): 47–54.

U.S. Attorney General

  1939   *Attorney General's Survey of Release Procedures: Pardon.* Washington, DC: U.S. Government Printing Office.

U.S. Bureau of Justice Assistance

  1989   *Electronic Monitoring in Intensive Probation and Parole Programs.* Washington, DC: U.S. Government Printing Office.

U.S. Bureau of Justice Statistics

  1983   *The American Response to Crime.* Washington, DC:

U.S. Department of Justice

  1987   *White Collar Crime.* Washington, DC: U.S. Government Printing Office.

U.S. General Accounting Office

  1990   *Intermediate Sanctions: Their Impacts on Prison Overcrowding, Costs, and Recidivism Are Still Unclear.* Washington, DC: U.S. General Accounting Office.

Velie, Lester, and Jerome G. Miller

  1985   "More Prisons Aren't the Answer." *New York Times* (July 30): 31.

Vinter, Robert D.

  1985   "The Essential Components of Group Work Practice." In *Individual Change through Small Groups*, edited by Martin Sundel, Paul Glasser, Rosemary Sarri, and Robert Vinter, 11–34. New York: Free Press.

Vito, Gennaro F.

  1986   "Felony Probation and Recidivism: Replication and Response." *Federal Probation* 50 (December): 17–25.

Vold, George B., and Thomas J. Bernard

  1986   *Theoretical Criminology*, 3rd ed. New York: Oxford University Press.

Von Hirsch, Andrew

  1976   *Doing Justice: The Choice of Punishments.* New York: Hill and Wang.

Von Hirsch, Andrew, and Kathleen J. Hanrahan

  1978   *Abolish Parole?* Washington, DC: U.S. Government Printing Office.

Wagner, Dennis

  1989   "An Evaluation of the High Risk Offender Intensive Supervision Project." *Perspectives* 13 (Summer): 22–27.

Wagner, Dennis, and Christopher Baird

  1993   *Evaluation of the Florida Community Control Program.* Washington, DC: National Institute of Justice.

Waldo, Gordon, and David Griswold

1979   "Issues in the Measurement of Recidivism." In *The Rehabilitation of Criminal Offenders: Problems and Prospects*, edited by Lee Sechrest, Susan O. White, and Elizabeth D. Brown. Washington, DC: National Academy of Sciences.

Walker, Samuel

1980   *Popular Justice: A History of American Criminal Justice.* New York: Oxford University Press.

Weber, Max

1958   *Protestant Ethic and the Spirit of Capitalism.* New York: Scribner's.

Weisheit, Ralph H., and Diane M. Alexander

1988   "Juvenile Justice and the Demise of Parens Patriae." *Federal Probation* 52 (December): 56–63.

Wellisch, Jean, M. Douglas Anglin, and Michael L. Prendergast

1993   "Numbers and Characteristics of Drug-Using Women in the Criminal Justice System: Implications for Treatment." *Journal of Drug Issues* 23 (winter): 7–30.

Wheeler, Gerald R., Rodney V. Hissong, Therese M. Macan, and Morgan P. Slusher

1989   "The Effects of Probation Service Fees on Case Management Strategy and Sanctions." *Journal of Criminal Justice* 17: 15–24.

Wheeler, Harvey, ed.

1973   *Beyond the Punitive Society.* San Francisco: W. H. Freeman.

White, Joseph L.

1987   "The Waiver Decision: A Judicial, Prosecutorial or Legislative Responsibility?" *Justice for Children* 2 (1–2): 28–30.

Whitehead, John T.

1989   "The Effectiveness of Felony Probation: A Replication and Extension of Three Studies." Paper presented at the annual meeting of the American Society of Criminology, Reno, NV, November; *Justice Quarterly* 4 (December 1991): 525–43.

Whitehead, John T., Larry T. Miler, and Laura B. Myers

1995   "The Diversionary Effectiveness of Intensive Supervison and Community Corrections Programs." In *Intermediate Sanctions: Sentencing in the 1990s,*" edited by John Ortiz Smykla and William Selke, 135–51. Cincinnati: Anderson.

Wicker, Tom

1975   *A Time to Die.* New York: Quadrangle.

Wiebush, Richard G.

1993   "Juvenile Intensive Supervision: The Impact on Felony Offenders Diverted From Institutional Placement." *Crime and Delinquency* 39 (January): 68–89.

Wiebush, Richard G., and Donna M. Hamparian

1991   "Variations in 'Doing' Juvenile Intensive Supervision: Programmatic Issues in Four Ohio Jurisdictions." In *Intensive Interventions with High-Risk Youths in*

Juvenile Probation and Parole, edited by Troy L. Armstrong,. 153–88. Monsey, NY: Criminal Justice Press.

Wiederanders, Mark R.

1983   *Success on Parole*. Sacramento, CA: California Department of Corrections.

Wilensky, Harold L., and Charles N. Lebeaux

1958   *Industrial Society and Social Welfare*. New York: Russell Sage Foundation.

Wines, Frederick Howard

1975   *Punishment and Reformation: A Study of the Penitentiary System*. New York: Thomas Y. Crowell.

Wolpe, Joseph, Andrew Salter, and L. H. Reyna, eds.

1964   *The Conditioning Therapies*. New York: Holt, Rinehart and Winston.

Wright, Martin

1991   *Justice for Victims and Offenders: A Restorative Response to Crime*. Philadelphia: Open University.

Yelloly, Margaret

1980   *Social Work Theory and Psychoanalysis*. New York: Van Nostrand Reinhold.

Zawitz, Marianne W., ed.

1988   *Report to the Nation on Crime and Justice*. Washington, DC: U.S. Government Printing Office.

Zehr, Howard

1990   *Changing Lenses: A New Focus for Crime and Justice*. Scottdale, PA: Herald Press.

Zevitz, Richard G., and Susan R. Takata

1988   "Paroling Prisoners Sentenced to County Jail: An Analysis of 75 Years of Misdemeanor Parole Legislation." *Journal of Criminal Justice* 11: 61–86.

Zimring, Franklin E., and Gordon Hawkins

1995   *Incapacitation: Penal Confinement and the Restraint of Crime*. New York: Oxford University Press.

Zingraff, Matthew T., and Michael J. Belyea

1986   "Child Abuse and Violent Crime." In *The Dilemmas of Punishment*, edited by Kenneth C. Haas and Geoffrey P. Alpert, 49–63. Prospect Heights, IL: Waveland Press.

AUTHOR INDEX

Bersani, Carl A., 308, 312
Binder, Arnold, 286
Bishop, Donna M., 72
Blount, William R., 454
Blumberg, Abraham, 141
Blumenstein, Alfred, 217, 225
Bohlen, Celestine, 444
Bootzin, Richard R., 301
Boswell, John, 43
Bowers, Anna Mae, 287
Bowers, Swithun, 287, 292
Bradsher, Keith, 3, 176
Brennan, Thomas P., 293, 297
Brockway, Z. R., 212, 213
Bronner, Augusta F., 287
Brown, Allan G., 312
Brown, Bertram S., 301, 306
Brown, Elizabeth D., 216
Brown, Marjorie, 355
Brown, Waln K., 67
Buck, Gerald S., 429
Burgess, Robert L., 317
Burke, Peggy, 226
Burns, Jerald C., 446, 447
Bushey, W. Conway, 340
Butterfield, Fox, 205, 457
Byrne, James M., 419, 421, 423

C

Cahalan, Margaret Werner, 213, 214
Campbell, Curtis, 142
Carey, Mark, 379
Carlson, Eric, 330, 333, 346, 349, 350, 352, 419
Carlson, Jill M., 378, 381
Carter, Robert M., 112, 113
Carter, Stephen A., 187
Castellano, Thomas C., 445, 446
Champion, Dean J., 149
Chapin, Bradley, 178
Chesney, Steven L., 392
Chesney-Lind, Meda, 56,
Childress, Anna Rose, 305
Chira, Susan, 327
Chodorow, Nancy J., 287
Clark, Cherie L., 443, 445
Clear, Todd R., 248, 338, 419, 421, 423, 428, 430
Clemmer, Donald, 188
Clinard, Marshall B., 1, 315, 316
Clines, Francis X., 196
Cloninger, Susan C., 302
Cloward, Richard A., 319, 322
Cohen, Albert K., 318, 319, 320
Cohen, Lawrence E., 65
Cohen, Noam S., 195

Cohen, Harold L., 303
Collier, Walter V., 423
Cooper, Irving Ben, 142
Cooprider, Keith W., 431
Covey, Herbert C., 222
Cowles, Ernest L., 445, 446
Crawford, Cheryl A., 197
Crawford, William B., Jr., 201
Cressey, Donald R., 150, 346, 347
Cripe, Claire A., 199
Cromwell, Paul F., Jr., 31, 202
Cronin, Roberta C., 448
Cullen, Francis T., 194, 217, 226
Curran, Daniel J., 86
Czajkoski, Eugene H., 142, 156

D

Darrow, Clarence, 5
Davidoff-Kroop, Joy, 372, 373
Dawson, Robert O., 142
de Beaumont, Gustave, 180, 184
Deschenes, Elizabeth Piper, 419, 422
Dees, Linda G., 221
Degler, Carl N., 10
del Carmen, Rolando V., 278, 279, 283
Denzlinger, Jerry D., 139, 140
de Tocqueville, Alexis, 180, 182, 184
Dickey, Walter, 141, 144, 145
Dietrich, Shelle, 332
DiIulio, John J., Jr., 12
Docktor, Ronald M., 308
Dolan, Edward J., 248
Dole, Vincent, 305
Donovan, Dennis M., 305
Doom, Andrew E., 124
Dressler, David, 214, 337
Dubnov, William L., 86, 88
DuBois, Brenda L., 292, 293
Dumm, Thomas L., 181
Dunn, Ashley, 205
Durham, Alexis M., III, 79, 186
Durkheim, Emile, 314

E

Edwards, Michael, 72
Ekland-Olson, Sheldon, 226
Empey, LaMar T., 44
Epstein, Joel, 197
Erez, Edna, 106
Erikkson, Torsten, 184
Erwin, Billie S., 416, 421, 422
Eskridge, Chris W., 350, 352

F

Fabricant, Michael, 52
Falk, Gerhard, 290
Fallen, David L., 425
Farley, O. William, 293
Feeley, Malcolm M., 29, 413, 448
Feld, Barry C., 52, 66, 70
Fichter, Michael, 452
Filipczak, James, 303
Finckenauer, James O., 87
Finn, Peter, 389, 394
Flynn, Suzanne, 419, 421, 423, 428, 430
Fogel, David, 217, 223
Ford, Daniel, 432
Forrester, John, 287
Fox, Vernon, 203
France, Anatole, 8
Franz, Randal S., 73
Frazier, Charles F., 72
Freud, Sigmund, 287, 288, 289, 290
Friedlander, Walter A., 294, 295, 296
Friedman, Lawrence M., 27, 29, 30

G

Galinsky, M. David, 312
Gaylin, Willard, 142
Geerken, Michael R., 450
Geis, Gilbert, 286
Gendreau, Paul, 216, 217
Gilbert, Karen E., 194, 226
Gillin, John T., 185
Glaser, Daniel, 420
Glasser, William, 308, 309, 311, 312
Glueck, Sheldon, 32, 33
Goetting, Victor L., 395, 398
Goffman, Erving, 202
Goldstein, Arnold P., 301
Goleman, Daniel, 300
Goodstein, Lynne, 219
Graff, Lisa, 66
Gransky, Laura A., 445, 446
Greenberg, David F., 204, 226
Greenberg, Jay R., 278
Griggs, Bertram S., 396
Grissom, Grant R., 86, 88
Griswold, David B., 222, 452
Grogger, Jeffrey, 372
Gross, Jane, 324, 453

H

Haas, Stephen, 435
Hagerty, J. E., 185

Hahn, Paul H., 202
Hall, Jerome, 178
Hamilton, Gordon, 294
Hammett, Theodore M., 196, 197, 368
Hamparian, Donna M., 73, 418
Han, Mei, 448
Hanrahan, Kathleen J., 217
Hardman, Dale G., 296
Hardyman, Patricia R, 419, 428
Harlow, Nora, 34
Harold, Lynne, 197
Harper, Robert Francis, 5
Harris, George A., 309
Harris, Linda, 56
Harris, Patricia M., 66
Hartman, Todd, 85
Hasenfield, Yeheskel, 297
Hayes, Hennessey D., 450
Hawkins, Gordon, 218
Healy, William, 287
Heinz, Richard C., 354
Henretta, Charles F., 72
Hepburn, John, 219
Herman, Ellen, 214
Hibbert, Christopher, 225
Hilts, Philip J., 306
Himelein, Melissa J., 308
Hinds, Michael deCourcy, 178
Hirsch, Adam Jay, 178, 179, 182
Hirschburg, Peter, 452
Hirschi, Travis, 323
Hobbs, Leo, 84
Hogarth, John, 113
Hollin, Clive R., 302
Hollis, Florence, 299
Holloway, Lynette, 85
Holt, Norman, 225
Horvath, John A., 67
Howard, John, 179
Huff, C. Ronald, 57, 438
Hughes, Robert, 210
Hull, Grafton H., Jr., 292
Humphries, Ann Chadwell, 187
Humphries, Drew, 226
Hunt, Dana Eser, 368
Hurst, Hunter IV, 75
Hurst, James W., 29
Husband, Stephen D., 313
Hutchinson, Elizabeth D., 294, 295, 297, 331

I

Ignatieff, Michael, 180
Irwin, John, 187, 188, 195

Morris, Norval, 338
Mullaney, Fahy G., 393
Mullen, Joan, 205
Mydans, Seth, 201
Myers, Laura B., 176, 427

N

Nader, Ralph, 2
Nance, John, 376
Navarro, Mireya, 226
Nelson, E. Kim, 34, 35
Nietzel, Michael T., 308
Noonan, Susan B., 345
Northern, Helen, 312, 313

O

O'Brien, Charles P., 305
Ohlin, Lloyd E., 319, 322
Ohmart, Howard, 34
O'Leary, K. Daniel, 308
O'Melia, Michael, 292, 293
Omer, Haim, 292
Osigweh, Chimezie A. B., 142
Ostrower, Roland, 294

P

Palumbo, Dennis J., 447
Parent, Dale G., 40, 271, 391, 394, 413, 445, 446, 447, 448
Parker, William, 216, 233
Parks, Evalyn, 330, 333, 346, 349, 419
Parsonage, William H., 335, 340
Pavarini, Massimo, 178, 182
Pear, Robert, 302, 453
Pearson, Frank S., 423, 439, 443
Perlman, Helen Harris, 293, 296
Petersilia, Joan M., 414, 420, 431, 422, 428, 429, 432, 452, 453, 455
Peterson, Marina, 447
Pisciotta, Alexander W., 212, 213
Platt, Anthony M., 45, 48
Platt, Jerome J., 313
Polakow, Robert L., 308
Porter, Bruce, 198
Prendergast, Michael L., 196
Przybylski, Roger, 431, 432
Purdy, Matthew, 205

Q

Quadagno, Jill S., 325

R

Rachin, Richard, 310
Reed, John , 376
Reichel, Phillip L., 437
Reiff, Phillip, 291, 292
Reiman, Jeffrey, 2
Remington, Bob, 308
Remington, Marina, 308
Reyna, L. J., 300
Rhine, Edward E., 229
Rivas, Robert F. 312
Rizzo, Louis, 142, 144
Robbins, Ira P., 206
Robbins, William, 205
Robertson, John A., 29
Robinson, Carol, 335
Robitscher, Jonas, 142, 215
Roerich, Connie M., 124
Root, Lawrence P., 394
Rose, Sheldon D., 313
Rosenblum, Robert, 394, 395
Roshier, Bob, 7, 9
Ross, Bernard, 297
Ross, Robert R., 216, 217
Rossi, Peter, 364
Rothman, David, 45, 178, 182
Rousseau, Jean Jacques, 6, 7
Rubin, H. Ted, 52
Rucker, Lila, 448
Runda, John C., 229

S

Sachs, Howard, 450
Sagan, Eli, 289
Sagatun, Inger, 72
Salter, Andrew, 300
Sanborn, Joseph B., Jr., 58
Schlossman, Steven L., 44
Schmideberg, Melitta, 308, 309, 310
Schmidt, Annesley K., 431, 432
Schneider, Keith, 2
Schram, Donna D., 66
Schultz, J. Lawrence, 33
Schuman, Alan M., 429
Schur, Edwin M., 67, 325
Schmidt, Annesley K., 431
Schwartz, Ira M., 56
Schwartz, Richard, 375
Schwartz, William, 313
Schwitzgebel, Ralph K., 431
Sechcrest, Dale K., 448
Sechrest, Lee, 216, 447
Sellin, Thorston, 179, 185, 186

Shapiro, Carol, 419, 421, 423, 428, 430
Shaffer, John, 312
Shaw, James W., 433, 443, 446
Sheldon, Randall G., 67
Shenon, Philip, 2
Shichor, David, 85
Shireman, Charles, 297
Short, James R., Jr., 318, 319
Sickmund, Melissa, 71
Silverman, Mitchell, 35, 454
Simon, Jonathan, 214, 413, 448
Sinclair, Jim, 379
Skidmore, Rex A., 293
Skinner, B. F., 300, 301, 304
Skolnick, Jerome H., 376
Slawsky, Toby D., 125, 140
Sluder, Richard D., 283
Smith, Alexander, 297
Smith, Barbara E., 382
Smith, Carolyn, 176
Smith, Richard Austin, 1
Smith, Vern E., 227
Snyder, Howard N., 71
Souryal, Claire, 422, 442, 443, 446, 448
Specht, Harry, 293
Spencer, Herbert, 10
Spencer, Jim, 443, 445
Stampfl. Thomas G., 303, 304
Stanley, David T., 239, 241, 454
Star, Deborah, 450
Staub, Hugo, 290
Stevenson, Ian, 300
Stolz, Stephanie B., 301, 306
Strong, Ann, 328, 363
Sudbrack, Billie D., 427
Sullivan, Michael P., 205, 416
Sulzer, Beth, 306
Sutherland, Edwin H., 150, 316, 323
Sutton, John R., 44
Swanger, Harry F., 67
Sykes, Gresham M., 320, 321, 322

T

Takagi, Paul, 180
Takas, Marrianne, 368
Takata, Susan R., 213
Taylor, Ian, 7, 8, 9, 315
Teeters, Negley K., 179, 182
Terry, Don, 205
Thackeray, Milton G., 293
Thalheimer, Donald J., 395
Tharp, Roland G., 307
Thornberry, Terence C., 176

Thorne, Gaylord L., 307
Tittle, Charles, 452
Toborg, Mary A., 347, 372
Tonry, Michael, 338
Torbet, Patricia McFall, 75
Torgerson, Ferndando G., 293
Toseland, Robert W., 312
Tracy, Sharon, 67
Travis, Lawrence F., III, 257
Treaster, Joseph B., 73, 96
Tropp, Sol, 376
Turner, Susan, 414, 420, 422

U

Umbreit, Mark S, 379, 380, 381

V

Velie, Lester, 195
Vinter, Robert D., 313
Vito, Gennaro F., 424, 446
Vold, George B., 6
Von Hirsch, Andrew, 217, 223

W

Wagner, Dennis, 417, 426, 427, 428
Waldo, Gordon, 452
Walker, Samuel, 44
Walton, Paul, 7, 8, 9, 315
Watkins, David, 309
Weber, Max, 178
Weisheit, Ralph, 47
Wellisch, Jean, 196
Wetter, Robert E., 229
Wetzel, Ralph J., 307
Wheeler, Gerald R., 306, 389
Whitcomb, Debra, 394, 395
White, Susan O., 216
Whitehead, John T., 427, 452
Wicker, Tom, 194
Wiebush, Richard G., 418, 425
Wiederanders, Mark R., 451
Wienckowski, Louis A., 301, 306
Wilensky, Harold L., 293
Wilks, Judith, 216, 456
Williams, Frank P. III, 72
Wilson, G. Terrance, 308
Wines, Frederick Howard, 180, 183, 212, 213
Wolpe, Joseph, 300
Wright, Martin, 379

Y

Yelloly, Margaret, 293
Young, Jock, 7, 8, 9, 315

Z

Zawitz, Marianne W., 21, 52, 169, 207
Zehr, Howard, 370, 380

Zevitz, Richard G., 213
Zimring, Frank, 218
Zoey, Connie M., 124

SUBJECT INDEX

Learning theory, *see* Behavior modification
Lee v. Washington, 199
Locke, John, 6, 7

M

Maconocie, Alexander, 210
Mapp v. Ohio, 170
Martinez v. State of California, 282–83
Marx, Karl, 326
McKeiver v. Pennsylvania, 169
Medical model, 215–16, 292, 293
Medina v. O'Neil, 206
Mempa v. Rhay, 166, 167, 172, 280
Menechino v. Oswald, 276–77, 281
Menechino v. Warden, 279–80
Mens rea, 9, 20, 321; *see also* Free will
Mexican Mafia, 201–202
Minnesota v. Murphy, 171
Miranda v. Arizona, 167
Mistretta v. United States, 124
Morrissey v. Brewer, 173, 276, 280–82

N

National Crime Survey, 4
Neoclassicalism, 9
Neutralization, 320, 321–22

O

Oswald, Russell G., 194
Owens v. Kelly, 171

P

Paraprofessionals, 346–48
Pardons, *see* Executive clemency
Paranoia, 289
Parens patriae, 44, 47, 170
Parole
   administration of, 229–32
   boards, 217, 225, 226, 232–56
   classification, *see* Classification
   conditional release, 231–32
   conditions/rules, 257–60
   county, 230
   cost of, 22
   criticism of, 216–18, 221–22
   executive clemency, role in, *see* Executive
      clemency
   fees, *see* Fees
   field services, 256–57

   guidelines, 243–52
   history, 30–33, 209–15, 274
   institutional services, 253–55
   juvenile, 97–104
   law enforcement in, *see* Law enforcement role
      in probation/parole
   offender employment, *see* Employment of
      offenders
   officers, 249, 251–52
      appointment, 341–42
      personal qualities, 342–43
      qualifications, 343–46
      work roles, 328–30, 330–41
   paraprofessionals in, *see* Paraprofessionals
   research, *see* Research
   special units, *see* Special units
   shock, *see* Shock probation/parole
   street time, 271
   supervision, *see* Supervision in
      probation/parole
      intensive, see Supervision, intensive
      length, 258
      violation of, 251–72
   victim participation, 241–42
   volunteers in, *see* Volunteers
Pavlov, Ivan, 300
Pennsylvania Prison Society, 180
Plea bargaining, 19, 122
Positive theory/positivism, 9–11
Predisposition report, juvenile, 58–64
Presentence investigation, 105–46
   confidentiality, 139–41
   criticism of, 141–45
   parole, use for, 253
   plea bargaining and, 20, 122–24
   purposes, 105–106
Pretrial court appearances, 17
Pretrial services, 17, 18–19, 203
Prisonization, 188
Prisons
   Auburn system, *see* Auburn system
   boot camp, *see* Shock incarceration
   classification, *see* Classification, prison
   courts and, 199–200
   drugs in, 197–98
   gangs, 198, 200–202
   history, 178–95
   labor, 185–87
   overcrowding, 22–23, 176–78, 214, 221
   Pennsylvania system, 179–82
   private, 204–207
   Quakers and, 178–79, 180
   riots, 191–92; 214; *see also* Attica riot
   violence in, 198
   women in, 196
Probation
   administration of, 33–41

Winship, In Re, 169
Wolff v. McDonnell, 199
Work release, 204, 226, 394–95

Y

Younger v. Gilmore, 199